Prehistoric Europe

BLACKWELL STUDIES IN GLOBAL ARCHAEOLOGY

Series Editors: Lynn Meskell and Rosemary A. Joyce

Blackwell Studies in Global Archaeology is a series of contemporary texts, each carefully designed to meet the needs of archaeology instructors and students seeking volumes that treat key regional and thematic areas of archaeological study. Each volume in the series, compiled by its own editor, includes 12–15 newly commissioned articles by top scholars within the volume's thematic, regional, or temporal area of focus.

What sets the *Blackwell Studies in Global Archaeology* apart from other available texts is that their approach is accessible, yet does not sacrifice theoretical sophistication. The series editors are committed to the idea that useable teaching texts need not lack ambition. To the contrary, the *Blackwell Studies in Global Archaeology* aim to immerse readers in fundamental archaeological ideas and concepts, but also to illuminate more advanced concepts, thereby exposing readers to some of the most exciting contemporary developments in the field. Inasmuch, these volumes are designed not only as classic texts, but as guides to the vital and exciting nature of archaeology as a discipline.

Prehistoric Europe
Theory and Practice

Edited by

Andrew Jones

WILEY-BLACKWELL

A John Wiley & Sons Ltd., Publication

This edition first published 2008

© 2008 Blackwell Publishing Ltd except for editorial material and organization © 2008 Andrew Jones

Blackwell Publishing was acquired by John Wiley & Sons in February 2007. Blackwell's publishing program has been merged with Wiley's global Scientific, Technical, and Medical business to form Wiley-Blackwell.

Registered Office
John Wiley & Sons Ltd, The Atrium, Southern Gate, Chichester, West Sussex, PO19 8SQ, United Kingdom

Editorial Offices
350 Main Street, Malden, MA 02148-5020, USA
9600 Garsington Road, Oxford, OX4 2DQ, UK
The Atrium, Southern Gate, Chichester, West Sussex, PO19 8SQ, UK

For details of our global editorial offices, for customer services, and for information about how to apply for permission to reuse the copyright material in this book please see our website at www.wiley.com/wiley-blackwell.

The right of Andrew Jones to be identified as the author of the editorial material in this work has been asserted in accordance with the Copyright, Designs and Patents Act 1988.

Library of Congress Cataloging-in-Publication Data

Prehistoric Europe : theory and practice / edited by Andrew Jones.
    p. cm. – (Blackwell studies in global archaeology ; 12)
  Includes bibliographical references and index.
  ISBN 978-1-4051-2597-0 (hardcover : alk. paper) – ISBN 978-1-4051-2596-3 (pbk. : alk. paper)
1. Prehistoric peoples–Europe. 2. Archaeology–Europe. 3. Europe–Antiquities. I. Jones, Andrew, 1967–

  GN803.P73   2008
  936–dc22

                                                                                    2007050955

A catalogue record for this book is available from the British Library.

Set in 10 on 12 pt Plantin by SNP Best-set Typesetter Ltd., Hong Kong

Contents

Figures and Tables

FIGURES

TABLES

Notes on Contributors

Dusan Boric is a research associate at the Department of Archaeology, University of Cambridge, UK with specific research interests in European and Near Eastern Prehistory and archaeological theory. At present he is researching the nature of changes in beliefs on the basis of mortuary data and iconographic representations of the human body in early Prehistory. He has (co-)edited two volumes that are forthcoming: *Archaeology and Memory* (Owbow) and *Past Bodies* (with John Robb, Berghahn Books). His current archaeological field project is based in the region of the Danube Gorges, Serbia.

Ing-Marie Back Danielsson received her PhD in archaeology from Stockholm University, Sweden. She has particular interests in archaeologies of bodies, the contemporary political significance of archaeological creations of identities and the Scandinavian Iron Age. Although specializing in issues of identity, her research interests also include cultural heritage management and museum studies. Ing-Marie's previous publications have focused on archaeological approaches to sex, gender and corporealities in the past. She currently works within the research project 'Bones and births' at the Department of Archaeology and Classical Studies at Stockholm University.

John Chapman is a reader in archaeology in Durham University, UK. He is Britain's leading expert in Balkan prehistory, with over 30 years research and field-work experience in all of the major countries. His principal projects are the 'Neo-thermal Dalmatia Project' in Croatia, the 'Upper Tisza Project' in Hungary, the 'Prehistoric Exploitation of Salt' in Bulgaria and Romania and current research into material culture in Bulgaria. His recent publications include the landmark volume *Fragmentation in Archaeology* (2000, Routledge), and, with B. Gaydarska, *Parts and Wholes: Fragmentation in Prehistoric Context* (2006, Oxbow).

John Collis is Professor Emeritus in the Department of Archaeology, Sheffield University, UK where he taught for over 30 years. He is a specialist on the European Iron Age, field methodologies, especially excavation, and on the university and professional training of archaeologists. He has mainly excavated in southern England and central France. His books include *The European Iron Age* (Batsford, 1984); *Oppida: Earliest Towns North of the Alps* (1984); *Digging up the Past* (2001) and *The Celts: Origins, Myths and Inventions* (Tempus, 2003/2006).

David Fontijn is Assistant Professor in European Prehistory at Leiden University, the Netherlands. His research focuses on the long-term histories of prehistoric landscapes from the Neolithic up until the Roman Period, with a special interest in deliberate deposition of objects in 'natural' places on the one hand and the histories of 'barrow landscapes' on the other. He is the author of *Sacrificial Landscapes* (2003), a book about the remarkable phenomenon of selective deposition of valuables during the Bronze Age of the southern Netherlands and North Belgium. It was awarded the Dutch archaeology Prize for PhD theses (*W.A. van Es-prijs*) and the *Praemium Erasmianum* award for PhD theses in social, literary and philosophical sciences. His current research project (the Barrow landscapes project) focuses on Neolithic and Bronze Age burial mounds in the Netherlands, and involves the first sizeable fieldwork to be carried out on this type of site.

Fokke Gerritsen is Lecturer in Archaeology at the Vrije Universiteit Amsterdam, the Netherlands and Director of the Netherlands Institute in Turkey, Istanbul. His research focuses on human–landscape interactions and the social construction of time, place and community. He is currently writing a landscape biography of the Southern Netherlands, which will cover the period from the Bronze Age to the end of the Middle Ages, while also conducting excavations at a prehistoric settlement in Anatolia. His dissertation was published as *Local Identities. Landscape and Community in the Late Prehistoric Meuse-Demer-Scheldt Region* (Amsterdam University Press, 2003).

Joakim Goldhahn is an associate professor at the University of Umea, Sweden and lecturer at the University of Kalmar, Sweden. His research interests span archaeological theory, research history, rock art, north European Bronze Age and the archaeology of death. He has published a handful of monographs and edited several anthologies on Scandinavian rock art and the Bronze Age, including *Rock Art as Social Representation* (1999) and *Bilder av Bronsalder* (2002). His PhD dealt with the Sagaholm barrow, the largest find of rock art from a burial context in northern Europe which was published as an individual monograph *Sagaholm: Hällristningar och Gravritual* (1999). He has just completed a monograph on the relationship between the bronze smith and the rock smith during the Bronze Age, stressing the importance of studying ritual specialists in prehistoric contexts, and he is currently working on a monograph on the famous Kivik cairn in Scania, southern Sweden.

Bryan Hanks is an assistant professor in the Department of Anthropology at the University of Pittsburgh, USA. He graduated with a PhD in archaeology from the University of Cambridge in 2003. His theoretical interests include trajectories of development connected with early complex societies and anthropological perspectives on death and burial traditions and prehistoric warfare and violence. He has been actively engaged in collaborative archaeological field work with the Russian Academy of Sciences in north-central Eurasia since 1998 and has published a number of articles focusing on the Bronze and Iron Ages of the Eurasian steppe region.

Daniela Hofmann is a research associate in the Cardiff School of History and Archaeology, Cardiff University, UK. Her main focus of study is the European Neolithic, and she has so far concentrated on the Lower Bavarian sequence. She is especially interested in the development of architecture and village layout, the creation and representation of personal identity in death and Neolithic figurines. She has published papers in *Journal of Iberian Archaeology* (2006) and *Mesolithic Studies in the 21ˢᵗ Century* (2006, eds. N. Milner and P. Woodman), and co-edited (with J. Mills and A. Cochrane) *Elements of Being: Identities, Mentalities and Movements* (2005).

Andrew Jones is a lecturer in archaeology at the University of Southampton, UK. He has previously held a fellowship at the McDonald Institute for Archaeological Research, Cambridge (1999–2001) and a lectureship at University College Dublin, Ireland (1998–1999). He is the author of *Archaeological Theory and Scientific Practice* (CUP, 2002) and editor (with G. Macgregor) of *Colouring the Past* (Berg, 2002). He has recently completed a book on memory and material culture entitled *Memory and Material Culture* (CUP, 2007).

Katina T. Lillios is Associate Professor of Anthropology at the University of Iowa, USA. She received her PhD in anthropology at Yale University (1991). Her research and fieldwork have been directed at understanding the nature and evolution of inequality in late prehistoric Iberia, the political uses of archaeology and the relationship between material mnemonics and power. Her publications appear in the journals *American Antiquity*, *Journal of Archaeological Method and Theory*, and the *European Journal of Archaeology*. She is the author of *Heraldry for the Dead: Memory, Identity, and the Engraved Stone Plaques of Neolithic Iberia* (2008) and the editor of *The Origins of Complex Societies in Late Prehistoric Iberia* (1995).

Barbara S. Ottaway is Emeritus Professor of Archaeological Sciences at the University of Sheffield, UK where she taught until 2003. She is now Visiting Professor at the Department of Archaeology at the University of Exeter, UK. Her research and publications have spanned many aspects of central and east European archaeometallurgy, concentrating on the procurement, production and use of prehistoric copper and early bronze. She has excavated and published several late Neolithic settlement sites, such as the Galgenberg near Kopfham, in Bavaria. Her interest in experimental archaeology has led to the publication (with Quanyu Wang) on casting experiments and microstructure of bronzes.

Mark Pluciennik is Senior Lecturer in archaeology at the University of Leicester, UK. He was educated at the University of Sheffield, UK. His major fieldwork focus has been in the central Mediterranean and especially Sicily, where he currently co-directs a multi-period project. Although his major period focus has been the Mesolithic and Neolithic, and particularly the transition to farming in Europe, he has also published on archaeological theory and philosophy, the historiography of archaeology and hunter-gatherer studies, the European dimension in contemporary archaeology and archaeological ethics. Publications include the edited volumes *The Responsibilities of Archaeologists: Archaeology and Ethics* (2001) and *Thinking Through the Body: Archaeologies of Corporeality* (2002) (with Yannis Hamilakis and Sarah Tarlow); papers on 'The invention of hunter-gatherers in seventeenth-century Europe' (*Archaeological Dialogues* 9.2: 98–151, 2002) and 'A regional biological approach to the spread of agriculture to Europe' (*Current Anthropology* S45: 59–82); and the book *Social Evolution* (Duckworth, 2005).

Ben Roberts is currently Curator of the European Bronze Age at the British Museum. He recently completed his PhD at Cambridge University UK, looking into the origins and early development of metal objects and metal production in Western Europe (c.3500–2000 BC). His previous research includes publications on ornamentation in Britain during the Middle Bronze Age (c.1600–1200 BC) and (with Barbara S. Ottaway) developing a method for identifying use-wear on prehistoric bronze objects.

Peter S. Wells is Professor in the Department of Anthropology at the University of Minnesota, USA. Among his principal interests are Iron Age, Roman Period, and early medieval Europe, trade and other kinds of interactions between communities, visual representation and meanings of material culture. He has directed excavations at Bronze Age and Iron Age settlements in Bavaria, Germany. Publications include *The Barbarians Speak: How the Conquered Peoples Shaped Roman Europe* (Princeton University Press, 1999), *Beyond Celts, Germans and Scythians: Archaeology and Identity in Iron Age Europe* (Duckworth, 2001), and *The Battle that Stopped Rome: Emperor Augustus, Arminius, and the Slaughter of the Legions in the Teutoburg Forest* (W.W. Norton, 2003).

Alasdair Whittle is Distinguished Research Professor in the Cardiff School of History and Archaeology, Cardiff University, UK. He has researched Neolithic societies in Britain and Europe for many years. His publications include *Europe in the Neolithic: The Creation of New Worlds* (CUP, 1996), *The Harmony of Symbols* (Oxbow, 1999, with Joshua Pollard and Caroline Grigson), *The Archaeology of People* (Routledge, 2003) and *Building Memories* (Oxbow, 2006, edited with Don Benson).

Preface

Edited volumes can be difficult to put together; they involve endless cajoling from the editor, numerous changes back and forth between editor and contributors, and an attention to mundane and dull typographic details. Nevertheless they have inestimable academic value and are particularly useful as 'state of the art' statements which draw together all practitioners on a given subject.

The process of editing this volume has encompassed both the positive and negative aspects of editing. Negatively, as the contributors will be aware, the volume has required cajoling and threats from the editor. Positively, it has enabled the editor to put together a first class roster of contributors. It has given me the opportunity to elicit contributions from some of the very best scholars working in European Prehistory today. I am particularly pleased to present a diverse mixture of younger scholars alongside well-established names. The intention is to provide a flavour of the diversity of research in European Prehistory.

Finally, the rocky process of editing has been smoothed by a number of individuals, in particular Joshua Pollard, the editor of the companion volume on British Prehistory, who helped keep the volume moving during periods of crisis. In addition, the series editors Lynn Meskell and Rosemary Joyce have been on hand with carefully considered advice. I would like to thank them all for their continued encouragement.

Introduction

Andrew Jones

Introduction

The study of prehistoric Europe has been of critical importance to the development of the discipline of archaeology. By studying prehistoric Europe scholars developed the 'three ages' framework of technological development, providing them with a sense of chronology and with a set of methodologies – typology and stratigraphic analysis – whose utility persists to this day. There are therefore good reasons for arguing that Europe is one of the most important regions for the study of prehistory. The chapters in this volume provide an insight into the range of theoretical issues and areas of urgent debate in the contemporary study of European prehistory. What do we mean by the term 'prehistory', and why do we group together the discussion of very different societies, from different regions under the umbrella term 'prehistoric Europe'?

Despite the elegance of the 'three age' scheme the prehistory of Europe is both diverse and complex. The designation 'European prehistory' not only covers an enormous time period – from the emergence and development of agriculture in the Neolithic (c.7000 BC) to the development of urban living and interaction with early states during the Iron Age (between 140 BC and 300 AD) – it also covers an immense geographical range from Ireland in the west to the Ural mountains in the east, from Scandinavia in the north to the Iberian peninsula in the south. Traditionally the immense geographic and temporal scope of prehistoric Europe has prompted scholars to rely upon culture-historical or social evolutionary accounts of prehistoric society. Although social evolutionary and culture-historical schemes prevail, accounts of European prehistory have undergone huge changes in terms of their theoretical treatment in recent years and the veracity of traditional schemes have begun to be questioned; much research is now motivated by broader thematic, topical and theoretical interests. At the same time, political changes since 1989 have fostered new levels of communication and co-operation amongst archaeologists across Europe, culminating in the creation of the European Association of Archaeologists (EAA) in 1994. In this introduction I will explore the meaning of the term 'prehistory' and the history and utility of the 'three age' system. I will also address contemporary theoretical developments in Europe to examine where the study of prehistoric Europe stands today.

About this Book

By discussing these fresh theoretical frameworks this book differs from many similar titles. The aim of this book is to offer an up-to-date understanding of the range of contemporary approaches to prehistoric Europe. The chapters cover the period from the emergence of agriculture at the transition between the Late Mesolithic to Neolithic periods to the development of urban living and the interaction with early states during the Iron Age. The aim is to provide the reader with a comprehensive understanding of the key theoretical issues and themes that motivate the study of European prehistory, accompanied by a series of in-depth analyses of sites and regions.

Essays are arranged in a series of paired chapters that examine the key themes of:

- key frameworks for prehistory (Chapter 1);
- place and landscape (Chapter 2);
- the lifecycle of the house (Chapter 3);
- the emergence of novel technologies (Chapter 4);
- the archaeology of death and the significance of remembrance (Chapter 5);
- the shaping of the body and the person (Chapter 6);
- and the role of exchange and communication (Chapter 7).

Necessarily many of these themes cross-cut each other. For example, you will see discussions of memory in chapters on settlement and the body, while settlement will be discussed in chapters on landscape etc.

Each chapter is comprised of two sections and offers a discussion of the theme from the perspective of earlier prehistory (Late Mesolithic to Early Bronze Age) and later prehistory (Late Bronze Age to Late Iron Age). Some of these chapters represent traditional themes, such as exchange and settlement, while others reflect recent changes in perspective, such as those focusing on the body and memory.

This book is complimented by other volumes in the *Global Archaeologies* series. Detailed coverage of earlier prehistory (the Palaeolithic and Early Mesolithic) will be covered in a companion volume. Geographic regions that border on the area covered by this volume are discussed in two companion volumes *Mediterranean Prehistory* (Blake and Knapp 2005) and *British Prehistory* (Pollard forthcoming).

The 'Three Age' System and the Idea of Prehistory

How were people to account for the remains of the prehistoric past that littered every corner of the continent of Europe? Two major avenues of enquiry were open to scholars: investigation of the remains themselves or investigation of historical texts that might shed light on the nature and purpose of the remains, and the peoples associated with them.

Mid-19th-century scholars, in opposition to the perceived authority of texts, constructed an empirical, scientific methodology for archaeology. Prior to this, historical texts of one sort or another had been enormously useful to those interested in the reconstruction of the past – whether classical accounts of European societies, such as those of Tacitus or Julius Caesar, or biblical accounts pertaining to the age of the earth.

The idea that the history of humankind went back perhaps dozens of millennia was common to the Greeks, and before them to the Egyptians and to the Assyrians and Babylonians; though this long view of history was hotly disputed as heretical by St. Augustine in the 5th century AD (Schnapp 1996:224). Scholarly study of the problem crystallized in the 17th century and is perhaps exemplified by the work of a figure like Isaac Lapeyrère whose 1656 book which translates as *The Pre-Adamites, or an Essay on Verses Twelve, Thirteen and Fourteen of the Letters of Paul to the Romans* was seen by its many detractors as undermining the foundations of the Holy Scripture. In fact, as Schnapp (1996:223) points out, its aim was both more modest and more dangerous – Lapeyrère aimed to distinguish in biblical texts between what was owed to humans and what to things divine. Although there had been much doubt about the antiquity of man, and the age of the earth, prior to Lapeyrère's publication few had subjected the matter to as much detailed forensic analysis. One of the key elements of his critique was the denial of the Adamite origins of humanity. In this, Lapeyrère echoed a debate that had persisted in heresy trials throughout the 14th and 15th centuries.

The discovery of America placed this critique at centre stage since it posed serious questions about the origin of American peoples (we shall see that the existence of America also posed interesting questions for a later generation of scholars); it was problematic because it was well known that these people used a much longer chronology than that set out in the Bible. In the 1584 *Spaccio della bestia trionfante* of Giordano Bruno it was argued that if the Americans were accepted as humans, then the long chronology demonstrated by the Aztec stone calendars discovered in 1551 (and buried by the Spanish church seven years later) equally demonstrated the antiquity of humans. Today, a perfectly reasonable supposition, but this form of biblical criticism earned Giordano Bruno a route to the stake, where he was burnt to death.

The struggle between a philological (text based) account of the past and an empirical account of the past (based on the observation of objects) has a long, and sometimes bloody, history. The historian of archaeology Alain Schnapp (1996:235–7) argues that the Benedictine philologist Bernard de Montfaucon was a pioneer in this debate, in his 1722 work *L'Antiquité Expliqueé et Representée en Figures* in which an early systematic study of ancient objects was complimented with, and accompanied by, explanatory historical texts. Montfaucon's philologically-based method was to establish a strict relationship between text and object. Here texts were not so much rejected or criticized, as used as an adjunct to the study of objects from the past. Montfaucon's method was reinforced by the Comte de Caylus, working in the middle of the 18th century, who radically proposed to replace the philological model with an experimental model, transforming the antiquary into a kind of 'physicist of the past'. For Caylus the graphic representation of artefacts was key to their empirical study (Schnapp 1996:238–41). In this Caylus differed from his contemporaries in that he laid less emphasis on the collection of artefacts, and more on their record and description. He helped lay the foundations of a descriptive typology which became central to the development of prehistoric archaeology.

The collection of past artefacts had grown apace over the 17th and 18th centuries, culminating in the creation of cabinets of curiosities, or *Wunderkammer* (cabinet of rarities or wonders), intended both for empirical study and as a medium for display-ing the ingenuity and prestige of the collector. One of the most famous of these collections was that of Ole Worm in Denmark. Worm, born in 1588 in Aarhus, Denmark travelled extensively throughout Europe and eventually became Professor of Latin in Copenhagen in 1613. On his travels he had visited the collections of noted antiquaries, such as that of Ferrante Imperato in Naples, and on his return to Denmark began to compile a collection of his own. Unlike the cabinets of his predecessors Worm arranged his collection in a novel way. The scheme was pub-lished in his *Musei Wormiani Historia* in 1655; like his contemporaries he arranged *naturalia* and *artificiosa*, or natural and cultural objects, alongside each other cheek by jowl. Like earlier collectors he also arranged natural objects according to the scheme – animal, vegetable and mineral; but his real innovation came in arranging culturally derived objects into classes based on their material. He divided the col-lection into 12 classes: clay objects, amber objects, stone objects, gold and silver objects, bronze and iron objects, coins, glass and similar materials, objects made from plantstuffs, wooden objects, *fructibus* (fruits), objects made from animal prod-ucts and finally unclassifiable objects (Schnapp 1996:174).

Worm did not confine his zeal for classification to his collection; he also produced one of the first field studies of archaeological monuments, producing a six-volume catalogue of Danish sites and monuments, the *Danicorum Monumentorum Libri Sex*, in 1643 in which he classified sites by composition and function. This work drew on earlier Scandinavian traditions of landscape archaeology, but its innovation (like that of his collection) was the systematic observation and classification of antiquities.

The true importance of Ole Worm, alongside other Scandinavian scholars, was his desire to write histories of the northern nations which broke from established interest in the Graeco-Roman past of the south of Europe. The motivation of these Scandinavian scholars was both patriotic and principled. They felt the need to write histories based on the empirical study of antiquities, both of collections of artefacts and sites and monuments in the landscape. The patriotic bent of Scandinavian archaeology lent the study of antiquities state support, and Sweden and Denmark were among the first European states to legislate for monument protection and to form an archaeological service for the study and regulation of archaeological sites. The close association between the work of antiquaries and the state is exemplified by the fact that on his death Ole Worm's collection of antiquities was incorporated into the museum of King Frederick III in Copenhagen. The collection eventually provided the foundation for the National Museum of Denmark in 1819.

We will take up the story of the development of prehistoric archaeology at this momentous juncture. The curator of the collection in the National Museum of Denmark was Christian Jürgensen Thomsen. Thomsen drew on the earlier typologi-cal principles of scholars like the 18th-century antiquarian Comte de Caylus and the late-17th-century British antiquarian John Aubrey, as well as earlier Danish scholars like P. F. Suhm, L. S. V. Simonsen and R. Nyerup to re-organize the col-lection according to a developmental scheme of stone–bronze–iron (Daniel 1967:91). Thomsen's scheme was not a theoretical model based upon speculation and intuition, rather it was the product of detailed descriptions of assemblages sys-tematically compared with each other (Schnapp 1996:300); it was published in 1836 as *A Guide to Northern Antiquities*.

The typological or evolutionary development of artefacts was not unique to Thomsen; in fact in the mid-18th century the German art historian and archaeologist Johann Joachim Winckelmann had proposed a similar scheme of stylistic analysis for Graeco-Roman sculpture that encompassed both the aesthetic and the typological (Preziosi 1998:21–30).

Likewise, the notion of defining units of time as specific technological ages has a deep antiquity. As Moser (1998:22–4) shows the successive stages of humankind were described by the Greek writer Hesiod in the 8th century BC. Hesiod presented the legend of the Five Races or generations of the world, in which the successive races of humankind are described: the Golden race came first; they were succeeded by the Silver race, then the Bronze race, then the race of Heroes who were followed by the Iron race. This scheme views the races as slowly deteriorating from an earlier ideal, so the Golden race are peaceful, happy and harmonious, as are the race of Heroes; the Bronze race and Iron race on the other hand represent periods of flesh-eating savagery and barbarism. The Greek author Lucretius, writing in the 1st century BC adopted this idea of succession but developed an alternative view of gradual progress rather than decline.

In Thomsen's 'three age' system such schemes of progression were married with a knowledge of stratigraphy, developed from geologists such as the Frenchman George Cuvier and the Englishman William Buckland, whose work on the stratigraphic succession of fossils provided geology with knowledge of the deep antiquity of the earth. Cuvier established a link between the types of fossils and the strata which contained them, as each type of fossil was then assigned to a definable geological period or formation; this offered geologists the chance to understand the earth's chronology (Daniel 1967:57–89).

Critically Cuvier not only categorized fossil types, but, by integrating them with geological strata, placed them in chronological succession. In a similar fashion Thomsen's analyses were not solely based on categorizing collections of artefacts, but were based upon detailed fieldwork and excavation, placing the artefacts in a chronological scheme. Thomsen's scheme was confirmed by excavation, conducted in collaboration with his talented successor at the museum, Jens Jacob Worsaae, who in 1843 produced a synthesis of this research and excavation as *Danemarks Oldtid oplyst ved Oldsager og Gravhoje* (published in Oxford in 1849 as *The Primeval Antiquities of Denmark*).

The principles of the 'three age' system were extended beyond continental Europe when in 1846, under the auspices of the Scottish antiquarian Robert Chambers, Worsaae advised the Society of Antiquaries of Scotland on the categorization of their collections (Kehoe 1998:16). With the transferral of the Society of Antiquaries of Scotland's collections to the National Museum of Scotland in 1851 the 'three age' scheme was adopted by the museum's curator, Daniel Wilson.

Like Thomsen before him, Daniel Wilson published the 'three age' scheme for Scotland in *The Archaeology and Prehistoric Annals of Scotland* in 1851. The key word in the title of this publication is 'prehistoric', since this marks its earliest usage. The adoption of the 'three age' system and the idea of prehistory went hand in hand as the 'three age' scheme opened the way for constructing a history without reliance on historical texts: a pre-history. After taking up a professorship in the University of Toronto, Canada, Wilson followed his earlier volume with another titled *Prehistoric Man*, published in 1862, which expanded his analysis to include data from the New World, including material from his encounter with native Indian societies near Lake Superior, and his visits to Moundville, Mississippi. His was an approach that combined the emerging fields of ethnology and archaeology, Native American societies being treated as analogs for prehistoric Europe. Like an earlier generation of scholars Wilson again used America as a framework for understanding the prehistory of the Old World (Kehoe 1998).

Such was the popularity and significance of his work (the first edition of *Prehistoric Man* sold out only a few months after publication) that it attracted a rival in the shape of John Lubbock's *Pre-historic Times*, published in 1865. Paradoxically, it is often Lubbock's work that is cited as the originator of the term 'prehistory', possibly due to his London contacts and connections, amongst whom were the evolutionists Herbert Spencer and Thomas Huxley as well as Charles Darwin.

With the development of the 'three age' system and its link to the method of stratigraphic analysis scholars studying the history of humankind had now adopted the paradigm of natural science rather than the centuries-old approach of philology. As Wilson noted C. J. Thomsens' Stone, Bronze and Iron periods laid 'the foundations of Archaeology as a science' (Wilson 1851:18; quoted in Kehoe 1998:17). This was a decisive shift in both theory and method which presaged, but was eventually confirmed by, the publication of Darwin's *Origin of Species* in 1859.

The extension of the 'three age' system

Glyn Daniel argues that prehistoric archaeology really came of age in the years between the 1851 Great Exhibition in London and the 1867 Paris Exhibition (Daniel 1967:144). While the Great Exhibition contained no archaeological exhibits, the Paris Exhibition contained archaeological exhibits with an accompanying text written by Gabriel de Mortillet entitled *Promenade Préhistoriques à l'Exposition Universelle*. In this he described some important archaeological facts and principles: the progress of humanity, the deep antiquity of man and the principle of comparative typology. De Mortillet's later work published in 1881, *Musée Préhistoriques*, written with Adrien de Mortillet, takes the principle of division and subdivision initiated by Thomsen and Worsaae as its starting point. De Mortillet saw archaeology as an exercise in classification. His task was to create further subdivisions and to place artefacts correctly in place within these subdivisions.

While the principle of chronological ordering was begun by Thomsen and Worsaae, it by no means ended with them and over the later years of the 19th century and the early years of the 20th century the scheme was further sub-divided and extended, so that by the 20th century prehistoric archaeology was better structured according to a 'five age' system. The 'three age' system had become a 'four age' system when in 1865 John Lubbock proposed dividing the Stone Age into a Palaeolithic (Old Stone Age) and Neolithic (New Stone Age). In 1866 the scheme was further refined as H. M Westropp proposed to distinguish prehistoric stone artefacts as Palaeolithic, Mesolithic (Middle Stone Age) and Neolithic in his lecture to the Anthropological Society in London. By 1872, with the publication of Westropp's *Prehistoric Phases, or Introductory Essays on Prehistoric Archaeology* the term 'Mesolithic' was fully established. In the early years of the 20th century the 'five age' scheme was further supplemented by the division of the Iron Age into an earlier pre-Roman Iron Age, and a later Historic Iron Age. While relative chronology provided an important principle of archaeological classification, in the absence of stratigraphical evidence, typology was also used as a classificatory tool. Typology depends upon the assumption that types (of archaeological artefact) evolve regularly.

The typological principles established by Thomsen and Worsaae were extended through detailed analysis by the Swedish archaeologist Oscar Montelius. In 1885 Montelius published the results of 15 years research on Bronze Age chronology utilizing museum collections across Europe. His scheme was mainly developed to understand the phasing of the Scandinavian Bronze Age, but his unparalleled knowledge of Bronze Age chronology could be extended across Europe. His chrono-typological approach, refined by his dialogue with the Danish archaeologist Sophus Müller, has stood the test of time. In addition to Montelius the work of the German archaeologist Paul Reinecke in the early years of the 20th century developed a chronological scheme for the Central European Bronze Age.

The schemes developed by Montelius and Reinecke established the chronology and typological succession of the European Bronze Age and Iron Age, and the Montelius/Reinecke schemes still form the chronological framework for research in these periods.

Problems with the 'three age' system

Despite its advantages as a tool for the organization of archaeological data the 'three age' system is not without its problems. One obvious problem is simply that it is not applicable universally. For example, the prehistory of Africa shifts from a Stone Age to an Iron Age, while the scheme is also not applicable in the Americas. The technologically based scheme assumes comparable social and economic changes, whereas modern research indicates that the transition between technological stages is of less importance. If we are to divide European prehistory we are better recognizing a social and economic split that divides the Late Mesolithic, Neolithic and Early Bronze Age from the Late Bronze Age and Early Iron Age. The observant reader will notice that this division has been used as a means of organizing this volume.

As I have noted above the 'three age' system is not universally applicable, it is a crude tool of typological and chronological subdivision and it cannot be assumed to work in the same way, at the same time, across Europe. For example the changes that are heralded by the Neolithic occur at different times across Europe. The same can be said of the Bronze Age and Iron Age. As we see in this volume the 'Late Iron Age' discussed by different authors occurs at different time periods. For example, in Chapter 7 (b), Wells discusses the interactions between Iron Age peoples and the Roman Empire in the last centuries BC/early centuries AD, while Back-Danielsson's account of the treatment of the body in the Late Iron Age of Scandinavia in Chapter 6 (b) discusses material between 400–1050 AD (a period often designated as 'early historic', or 'early Medieval' in other regions of Europe). These two case studies are presented here in part to demonstrate to the reader the mutable definition of different periods of prehistory, and the variability of the archaeological record across Europe. Definitional problems of this kind occur when we apply the basic technological divisions of the 'three age' system across large regions, and when we simply designate a period as 'prehistoric' by the absence of written texts. It is for this reason that the 'three age' system has been further subdivided and, by the later 20th century, carefully calibrated against the available radiocarbon chronology. It is also due to the fuzzy distinctions between prehistory and early history that the term 'Protohistory' is often adopted to define the period during the Late Bronze

Age and Iron Age when prehistoric societies interacted with those with written texts.

A more recent problem lies in the fact that, once created, the three ages have tended to serve as a means of academic specialization and demarcation. Academic departments of archaeology often have specialists in each period of later prehistory: the Neolithic, Bronze Age and Iron Age. Such is the volume of data now produced for each period of prehistory that an overview which takes in social and economic changes over the span of later prehistory is becoming well nigh impossible and it is now increasingly rare to see communication between the practitioners of each period specialism (see Kristiansen 1998:24–7 for an expansion of this theme). It is the intent of this volume to provide an overview of common themes, which cross the traditional chronological divisions.

The Study of Archaeology in the 20th Century: New Frameworks, New Paradigms

We have left the account of the development of prehistoric archaeology with the extension and development of the 'three age' system at the end of the 19th century. We also noted that an important development was the further sub-division of the various elements of the 'three age' system based on typological distinctions in material culture. While this approach had its place, as Glyn Daniel notes, archaeologists working in different regions of the world realized that some of the epochs into which prehistoric time had been divided were contemporary with each other (Daniel 1967:264). These did not represent different periods of time, but different patterns of material culture. It soon began to be realized that archaeologists were not collecting sub-divisions of a 'three age' or even a 'five age' system, but were collecting cultures which could be grouped together technologically into the five main divisions.

In many ways the sub-divisions created by Thomsen and Worsaae were now performing a new task; they were no longer being used as a simple technological model of development, but were at the start of the 20th century used as a means of providing names for artefacts and cultures and even stood in for chronology.

The analysis of assemblages or groups of objects in terms of cultural groupings emerged in the late 19th century and early 20th century. Two important figures emerge: the Australian philologist and archaeologist Vere Gordon Childe and the German philologist Gustav Kossinna. Kossinna was interested in tracing the tribal names of ancient peoples known from classical texts including Celts and Germans. He was particularly interested in defining the Indo-Europeans as they had been defined linguistically. With the rise in the analysis of groupings of material cultures in terms of the distribution of archaeological cultures Kossinna combined the study of linguistics with the analysis of cultures in a series of works which saw him propose that continuity in archaeological cultures could imply ethnic continuity. His most famous lecture was published in 1885 as *The Prehistoric Distribution of the Germans*. Much effort was expended in the period between the end of the 19th century and the Second World War in defining the distribution of ancient material culture in a programme of 'settlement archaeology' whose intention was to map the extent and continuity of ancient peoples. The racial overtones of this kind of work are not hard to discern, and after the Second World War and their infamous abuse by the Nazi regime such ideas fell out of favour (Arnold 1996).

Although the racist aspects of these ideas had always been subject to critique in Scandinavian and Anglo-American archaeology, in fact the notion of cultures and cultural groupings, divested of its ethnic baggage, was in use for much of the early 20th century in the guise of culture-history. Gordon Childe, one of the great archaeological theorists of the early 20th century, did much to refine the notion of culture. In one of his earliest works, *The Danube in Prehistory* (Childe 1929), he has this to say about culture:

> We find certain types of remains – pots, implements, ornaments, burial rites, house forms – constantly recurring together. Such a complex of regularly associated traits we shall term a 'cultural grouping' or just a 'culture'.

The mapping of these 'cultures' and their movements and migrations across geographical space formed the backbone of the culture-historical method. The broad brush, synthetic approach championed by Gordon Childe in works such as *The Dawn of European Civilization* and *The Danube in Prehistory*, exemplifies the culture-historical approach. Alongside the classification of cultural groups culture-historians were also interested in the social development of prehistoric societies. Gordon Childe, a lifelong Marxist, adopted the framework used by Marx and Engels in *The Origin of the Family, Private Property and the State* (published in German in 1884 and in English in 1902). Marx and Engels in turn adopted the scheme set out by the American scholar Lewis Henry Morgan in his *Ancient Society or Researches in the Lines of Human Progress from Savagery through Barbarism to Civilization* of 1877. Morgan had researched the social organization and origins of the American Indians, and as the title suggests he produced a scheme based on his research which divided human societies into three progressive stages: savagery, barbarism and civilization. It is easy to see the antecedents to Morgan's work in the works of Worsaae, Wilson, Lubbock and De Mortillet (Daniel 1967:141). In many ways the progressivist model of Morgan bore many resemblances to the progressivist scheme of the 'three age' system, and indeed Gordon Childe attempted to combine the model devised by Morgan with the 'three age' system.

While mapping of the mosaic of ancient cultures across the face of Europe proved a useful way of synthesizing large bodies of archaeological data the notion of culture itself began to be questioned. During the late 1950s and early 60s it gradually began to be felt that the archaeology of the early 20th century was simply gathering more and more data with little increase in knowledge about the past; essentially archaeologists were simply adding material to pre-existing categories with little increased understanding in past cultural dynamics. It was felt that traditional archaeology spent much time charting the movement and distribution of artefacts without thinking about the people and cultural processes that lay behind the artefacts. The critique of culture-historical archaeology was largely an Anglo-American affair. In Britain the chief protagonists of this New Archaeology included David Clarke and Colin Renfrew, while in America Lewis Binford was the key figure. The concept of culture utilized by culture-historians was held to be to 'normative'; it treated culture as a set of norms or values held rigidly in common by all members of that culture. Instead culture was viewed as possessing an internal dynamic. Traits were not simply randomly configured as culture-historians had supposed, but rather culture was a system of interacting elements whose primary role was adaptational (Binford 1962). New Archaeology laid emphasis upon cultural evolution, and – a little like Lewis Henry Morgan a century before – classified societies in a trajectory from simple to complex. Cultures were thought to evolve from one state of complexity to another; from band, to tribe, to chiefdom, to state. The key point here is that if culture was conceived as a system, then the task was to analyse its internal dynamics and the trajectory these different elements were taking in order to determine its evolutionary status. The analysis of the *processes* of cultural adaptation and change were paramount, as well as the processes by which the archaeological record was formed. It is the analysis of the relationship between these two things: the formation processes of the archaeological record and the processes of cultural change which forms a focus for the developed form of New Archaeology, often described as 'Processual Archaeology'.

The advantage here is that with this dynamic view of culture as a system New Archaeology could claim to be a generalizing science. New Archaeology was *scientific* in that it emphasized the rigorous analysis of past cultural systems; *anthropological* in that the analysis of past cultural dynamics was comparative in emphasis; *generalizing* and *explanatory* in its aims in comparing past societies with one another and explaining its cultural dynamics and trajectory. This new paradigm in archaeology developed over the 1960s and 70s, and its influence is still felt today in many European countries, as well as the USA. It is also during this period that science-based archaeology matured. With the application of a host of instrumental techniques developed in chemistry and physics archaeologists were beginning to answer fundamental questions about European prehistory. It is worth observing that in some senses the development of a rigorous scientific discipline under the banner of 'New Archaeology' was the logical outcome of the scientific framework adopted for prehistoric archaeology in the last decades of the 19th century.

In a European context it is worth considering the work of Colin Renfrew in some detail, in particular his development of 'social archaeology' and his analysis of trade and exchange. Renfrew was especially interested in examining social organization. Many of his classic studies focus on the distribution of megalithic monuments during the Neolithic as a means of determining the level of social organization. Two of his studies examine the distribution of monuments in relation to agricultural land-use to determine the scale of territories in the Scottish Isles of Arran and Rousay (Renfrew 1976; Renfrew 1979). Two important studies examine changes in social organization over time in Orkney (Renfrew 1979) and on the Wessex chalklands, Southern England (Renfrew 1973a). Renfrew applies the same *modus operandi* to both studies, examining three key elements: the distribution of monuments, the scale of labour required to build them (as an index of the level of social organization) and the chronology of the monuments (using the available radiocarbon dates). In Orkney he proposes a segmented tribal society during the Early Neolithic shifting to a centralizing chiefdom in the Late Neolithic. In a series of regions in Wessex he argues from the increasing scale of monuments over time, and the change from dispersed to centralized distribution, for an evolving hierarchy from tribal to emergent chiefdoms during the Late Neolithic and Early Bronze Age.

Renfrew's work was not confined to the study of 'social archaeology'. He was also instrumental in the development and application of a series of scientific techniques for the study of European prehistory. He was an early advocate of the importance of radiocarbon dates, and in a classic study showed how the systematic analysis of radiocarbon dates questioned the hitherto simple schemes of cultural diffusion of culture-historical archaeology (Renfrew 1973b).

Furthermore he also applied scientific techniques to the study of trade and exchange (see Chapter 7 (a) for more details). A clear example of the application of such techniques is the analysis of *Spondylus* shells in Neolithic Europe. Marine *Spondylus* shells had been discovered in a number of contexts throughout Neolithic Europe, but since the source of the shells was indeterminate it was difficult to know if this was the due to trade or local procurement. Characterization studies using oxygen isotope analysis of the shells indicated a source in the Aegean (Shackleton and Renfrew 1970). Comparison between the oxygen isotopes of shells found in this region and those from Central Europe and the Black Sea region confirmed that exchange or trade had taken place in the past. The analysis of traded artefacts was a component of a wider project which sought to categorize different systems of exchange and correlate them with particular levels of social organization, and thereby examine the series of interactions between societies. Renfrew supposed that different patterns of trade left different traces in the archaeological record. Not only could these traces be described by archaeologists in the present, but each trace represented a form of trade or exchange specific to different levels of social organization. Understanding interactions between groups was a powerful tool for understanding socio-political change (Renfrew 1996).

By the end of the 1970s there was a growing dissatisfaction with the claims and approaches of New Archaeology. Part of this dissatisfaction came from the spatial analysis of the archaeological record and in particular the analysis of patterns of trade and exchange. It was realized that quite different spatial processes could lead to the same patterns in the archaeological record. This lead to criticism of Renfrew's strong claims for the analysis of patterns of trade and exchange (Hodder and Lane 1982). In turn, this lead to a critique of the notion of culture as a system. It was not sufficient to simply view artefacts as the products of adaptive behaviour, the central tenet of the systemic view of culture. Instead it began to be argued that artefacts were better treated as being actively used by people, rather than being the passive products of adaptive behaviour (Hodder 1982). Given this, culture was better seen as a set of ideas and practices and the task of archaeologists should be to investigate past people's thoughts and symbolism.

This fresh approach to archaeology is often designated in opposition to previous approaches as 'Post-Processual Archaeology', although a preferable term might be 'Contextual Archaeology', based on the fact that archaeological context was seen as an important factor in framing the meaning of past material culture (Hodder 1986). Past material culture was instead – following the approaches of structuralism and semiotics – treated as a code or text to be deciphered or interpreted by archaeologists in the present (Hodder 1989, Hodder 1995). Equally the term 'Interpretative Archaeology' is often used to describe a developed form of this approach, which encompasses the realization that archaeologists always take up a theoretical and political position on the past. The task is to acknowledge this interpretative relationship and to interpret past activities represented by the material traces left by past peoples using a variety of theoretical tools from Marxism to semiotics and hermeneutics (Tilley 1993).

Although an earlier generation of archaeologists claimed that the adoption of scientific principles constituted a loss of innocence or naivety for archaeology (Clarke 1972), the same claim could be made for these fresh contextual or interpretative approaches. Positivist scientific approaches had long been out of favour in cognate disciplines such as geography and anthropology, and archaeology had been criticized for its adherence to archaic methods and approaches (Leach 1973). 'Interpretative Archaeology' constituted archaeology's adoption of a series of approaches derived from continental philosophy, which had animated a host of disciplines from anthropology to literary theory from at least the 1960s onwards. In many senses this new paradigm clearly situated archaeology amongst the humanities and social sciences. The common theoretical framework adopted by a series of disciplines allowed for increased dialogue across disciplinary boundaries.

Ian Hodder is a major figure in the development of contextual and interpretative archaeology. It is worth reviewing his work on European prehistory. Hodder's major interest is Neolithic Europe and his most coherent analysis of the period, *The Domestication of Europe* (Hodder 1990), offers a persuasive and intriguing narrative for the emergence of agriculture throughout Europe during the Neolithic. Hodder treats the European Neolithic as an extended text. His work traces the development of symbolism from the origins of the first agricultural societies in the Near East, to the Balkans, Central Europe and Western Europe. He contends that agriculture is a far from economic phenomenon, rather the symbolism of domestication instead entrains the development of agriculture. The formation of settled villages, the adoption of agriculture and the construction of monuments are components of a single coherent concept: domestication. Domestication therefore acts as both a metaphor and mechanism for social and economic transformation. His work is a clear articulation of contextual archaeology, as it treats artefacts as symbols, and as components of symbolic structures. Hodder analyses the archaeological contexts in which certain artefacts and architectures occur across Europe to argue for the expression and development of long-term symbolic structures.

Conclusion

I now want to conclude this lengthy overview of the development of prehistoric archaeology. It is worth pointing out that the relationship between material culture and text has had a long and varied history throughout the development of prehistoric archaeology. Above, I have described a narrative for the formation of the discipline of prehistoric archaeology over the past four centuries from early attempts to divest past material culture from philological accounts, to the emergence of the principles of typology and stratigraphy and the chronological classification of past artefacts according to the 'three age' system. The system evolved under culture-historical archaeology as a refined method of cultural classification, and with the emergence of 'New Archaeology' the scientific principles laid down for the discipline in the 19th century were finally fully realized. In some senses, with the emergence of interpretative archaeology at the end of the 20th century, the relationship between artefacts and texts was re-awakened. Artefacts were no longer explained by texts as they had been in the 16th and 17th centuries, but in a theoretical twist artefacts were now to be treated *as texts*. This should in no way be seen as a regressive shift on the part of interpretative archaeology, rather it is simply part of the long conversation between material culture and language.

REFERENCES

Arnold, B. 1996 The Past as Propaganda: Totalitarian Archaeology in Nazi Germany. *In* Contemporary Archaeology in Theory: A Reader. R. W. Preucel and I. Hodder, ed. Pp. 549–69. Oxford: Blackwell.

Binford, L. R. 1962 Archaeology as Anthropology. American Antiquity 28:217–25.

Childe, V. G. 1929 The Danube in Prehistory. Oxford: Clarendon.

Clarke, D. L. 1972 Models in Archaeology. London: Methuen.

Daniel, G. 1967 The Origins and Growth of Archaeology. Harmondsworth: Penguin.

Hodder, I. 1986 Reading the Past. Cambridge: Cambridge University Press.

Hodder, I. 1989 The Meaning of Things. London: Unwin Hyman.

Hodder, I. 1990 The Domestication of Europe. Oxford: Blackwell.

Hodder, I. 1995 Theory and Practice in Archaeology. London: Routledge.

Hodder, I., and P. Lane 1982 A Contextual Examination of Neolithic Axe Distribution in Britain. *In* Contexts for Prehistoric Exchange. J. E. Ericson and T. K. Earle, eds. Pp. 213–35. New York: Academic Press.

Kehoe, A. B. 1998 The Land of Prehistory: A Critical History of American Archaeology. London: Routledge.

Kristiansen, K. 1998 Europe Before History. Cambridge: Cambridge University Press.

Leach, E. 1973 Concluding Address. *In* The Explanation of Culture Change: Models in Prehistory. C. Renfrew, ed. Pp. 761–71. London: Duckworth.

Moser, S. 1998 Ancestral Images. Stroud: Sutton.

Preziosi, D. 1998 Art as History. *In* The Art of Art History: A Critical Anthology. D. Preziosi, ed. Pp. 21–30. Oxford: Oxford University Press.

Renfrew, C. 1973a Monuments, Mobilisation and Social Organisation in Neolithic Wessex. *In* The Explanation of Culture Change: Models in Prehistory. C. Renfrew ed. Pp. 539–58. London: Duckworth.

Renfrew, C. 1973b Before Civilization. Harmondsworth: Penguin.

Renfrew, C. 1976 Megaliths, Territories and Populations. *In* Acculturation and Continuity in Atlantic Europe. S. J. De Laet ed. Pp. 198–220. Bruges: De Tempel.

Renfrew, C. 1979 Investigations in Orkney. London Society of Antiquaries Monograph Series. London: HMSO.

Renfrew, C. 1996 Peer Polity Interaction and Socio-Political Change. *In* Contemporary Archaeology in Theory: A Reader. R. W. Preucel and I. Hodder, eds. Pp. 114–42. Oxford: Blackwell.

Schnapp, A. 1996 The Discovery of the Past. I. Kinnes and G. Varndell, trans. London: British Museum Press.

Shackleton, N. and C. Renfrew 1970 Neolithic Trade Routes Re-Aligned by Oxygen Isotope Analysis, Nature 228:1062–4.

Tilley, C. 1993 Interpretative Archaeology. Oxford: Berg.

I

Frameworks for the Analysis of European Prehistory

Introduction

Key Frameworks for Prehistory

In the introduction we discussed the emergence of archaeology as a scientific discipline, and its subsequent theoretical development from culture-history to New or Processual archaeology and Interpretative or Contextual archaeology. These are general frameworks for understanding past behaviour which have been generated by continuous disciplinary argument and debate. In this section we will focus upon theoretical frameworks related to specific periods of prehistory.

Sometimes these frameworks appear to be so much part of common sense that they have not been questioned. This is often because they are bound up with contemporary beliefs and prejudices. For example, as *Mark Pluciennik* shows in **Chapter 1 (a)**, the belief that hunter-gatherers live in a state which is 'closer to nature' and that the act of hunting and gathering places them alongside animals is the result of the adoption of economy and technology as structuring frameworks of analysis during the emergence of Capitalism in the 17th and 18th centuries. Indeed these perceptions of hunter-gatherer populations are still in operation today as they are often used as a means of justifying the extermination of supposedly 'backward' indigenous populations by nation states. The denigration of hunter-gatherers and the promotion of agriculture over foraging are therefore bound up with the analysis and justification of capitalism, and with the territorialist and expansionist policies of nation states. These assumptions have influenced the debate concerning the transition between the Mesolithic to the Neolithic for at least a century.

For later prehistory the subject of the Celts, discussed by *John Collis* in **Chapter 1 (b)**, is equally bound up with contemporary and historically recent concerns. In this case the belief in the Celts intersects with the emergence of the nation state and the romantic belief in the origins of certain nationalities and populations. The assumption of the historical reality of 'the Celts' has influenced scholars of later prehistory – the Late Bronze Age and Iron Age – for centuries. Witness the number of books and university courses with the prefix 'Celt' or 'Celtic'. Nor is the critique of the concept of the Celts without its detractors. So powerful is the notion, and so bound up with national ideologies that there are many vested interests in the retention of a belief in the Celts.

So we observe that for Earlier and Later European Prehistory the analysis of the past is bound up with politically strong narratives, of nation building and of the emergence of capitalist economics. It is little wonder then that these narratives have remained unquestioned for so long since they are so closely tied up with contemporary economics and the formation and maintenance of the nation state. It is only with the critical awareness fostered by interpretative or contextual approaches over the last few decades that the political position of archaeologists has been acknowledged, and with this many long-cherished frameworks are now open to challenge.

I (a)
Hunter-Gatherers to Farmers?

Mark Pluciennik

We all 'know' that historical and archaeological periodizations are present-day constructions, which is not to say that they do not have a basis in empirical fact. Such periodizations, however, can often become reified and form barriers to thinking afresh. Even substantial and sustained critique about the meaning of the 'labels' can serve to reinforce rather than challenge the original framework. Nowhere has this been more apparent than for the span of prehistory traditionally covered by the Mesolithic and Neolithic, and for most archaeologists today relating not to lithic technology – the 'polished stone' of the neo-lithic – but rather to a much longer-standing division between foragers and farmers. The longevity of this distinction – one can plausibly argue that it goes back to classical times, though subsequently restated and elaborated in the seventeenth and eighteenth centuries in western Europe in particular – itself should serve as a warning that we may like to stand back and try to consider afresh what it is that we are trying to do when we study these periods of prehistory, primarily the earlier Holocene for most of Europe.

History

The recognition of difference between human collectivities is no doubt one with its roots deep in the prehistory of evolution. Here the issue is how and why the *subsistence* categories of 'hunter-gatherer' and 'farmer' became incorporated within anthropology and archaeology in the particular ways that they did, and eventually and uniquely substituted for the *technological* category represented by the 'Stone Age' part of the Three Age system which still forms the basis of European archaeological periodizations today. In general we might describe all these schemes as social evolutionary, though one must be careful not to fall prey to the anachronistic fallacy. From a historiographic perspective, though, it is legitimate to ask: how old is a meaningful contrast between hunter-gatherers and farmers?

There are perhaps two major strands in the genealogy of these types of socio-economic categories. The first, geographical or 'ethnographic' strand, relates to the ways in which others – those not like the particular 'us' in question – were described and valorised. Given that the earliest known ideas and texts derive from settled

farming societies or 'civilizations', part of the descriptions of others often referred
to the real or apparent lack of these attributes in the society concerned. Thus from
the Greek point of view 'barbarians', beyond speaking a non-Greek language, might
also be pejoratively characterized as being unsettled and without agriculture, as well
as possessing unsavoury customs. Sometimes these views were undoubtedly based
on experience or 'knowledge', of peoples such as the Scythians, whether hearsay or
otherwise; at other times they pass seamlessly into myth with reports of cannibals,
races without heads, and so forth (e.g. the Blemmyes with their eyes and mouths
in their chests, said to inhabit Africa south of Egypt found in Pliny the Elder's *Historia naturalis* [V.8.46]). The second strand also relates to myth but in the form of
general or universal 'histories', which can be recognized from many parts of the
world. These represent forms of explanation of how current customs and conditions
arose. Again, they typically describe the writer's society as the norm, whether judged
as morally good, bad or indifferent, and the preceding peoples or stages as those
lacking some or all of those 'normal' attributes. Thus one can find classical or earlier
writers presenting historical schemes of either progressive development or degen-
eration, in which the lack of farming is seen as a vice or virtue. Hesiod's *Works and
Days* from perhaps the eighth century BCE; and later Thucydides (*History of the
Peloponnesian War*) Dicaearchus, Lucretius (*De Rerum Natura, Book V*) and poetic
reworkings by Virgil, Strabo, Tacitus others have all been cited as early examples of
forms of social evolution and the use of the categories of hunter-gatherers and
farmers (Lovejoy and Boas 1965; Nisbet 1980; Rudebeck 2000; Zvelebil 2002; but
cf. Pluciennik 2002). However, one can equally argue that a (mythical) distinction
between non-agricultural and agricultural times and hence people is found much
earlier, in Babylonian and biblical myth, for example, and also find parallel examples
in south Asian, Chinese and Arabic texts and thinkers (Pluciennik 2004). In my
reading, however, the content and salience of these particular categorical descriptions was refined, and politically as well as intellectually operationalized, during the
mercantile capitalist and colonialist era of the seventeenth and eighteenth centuries,
initially in northwestern Europe and within European colonies. I have argued that
it is during this period that we see the ascription of particular positive values to
agriculture (and the associated ideas of technical, economic, rational and moral
'improvement'), and consequent negative values to especially 'hunting' (with connotations of nomadism, lack of property, laziness and general immorality). It was
in the mid-eighteenth century that we see the typical three or four stage schemes
in which 'savage' Hunters, 'barbarian' Herders, and 'civilized' Farmers and Traders
(contemporary early capitalist societies: Adam Smith's 'Age of Commerce') are
distinguished and ranked in ascending order. Barnard has made a related argument,
in suggesting that earlier European writers and thinkers were primarily concerned
with abstract or *a priori* contrasts between asocial and social beings, and hence that
the notion that there could be such a thing as a characteristic hunter-gatherer form
of *society* only arose in the eighteenth century (Barnard 2004). The nuances are
many and complex, but it is clear that particular and modern notions of hunter-
gatherers, especially, arose in the context of a radical change in ideas about what
constituted properly rational and moral social and economic behaviour. From the
middle of the eighteenth century the concept of such a division between hunter-
gatherers and farmers became widespread and even formulaic.

Nevertheless, it would be wrong to suggest that this schema simply survived
and became transferred to the much later introduced archaeological labels of the

Mesolithic and Neolithic. Ethnology and archaeology had other traditions to draw upon. The most important of these was the suggestion of Lucretius, that technologically one could expect successive Ages of Stone, Bronze or Copper, and Iron. This had been reinforced by 'ethnographic' descriptions, especially from North America, of peoples without knowledge of the latter. The third was the early and rapid development of Scandinavian archaeology proper, which was to have a huge and lasting influence. By 1813 Vedel-Simonsen, in his *Aperçu sur les periodes le plus anciennes et les plus remarquables de l'histoire nationale*, had 'already argued for 3 periods of Scandinavian antiquity – a Stone, a Copper or Bronze, and an Iron Age' (Lowie 1938). More famously Thomsen, who had experimented with different ways to classify his museum collections, wrote in 1825:

> I find it essential, in placing archaeological specimens accurately in context, to keep a chronological sequence in mind, and I believe that the validity of the old [Lucretian] notion of first stone, then copper, and finally iron is constantly gaining new support in Scandinavia. (Cited in Klindt-Jensen 1975:52)

Although there were exceptions in Europe, specifically Sven Nilsson, who attempted directly to correlate a four-stage theory with the archaeological record through his regional survey (1838–43), by and large these nineteenth-century ethnologists and archaeologists did not draw on their immediate predecessors. E. B. Tylor, the first professor of anthropology in Britain, was absolutely explicit why this should be the case:

> Criticizing an 18th-century ethnologist is like criticizing an 18th-century geologist. The older writer may have been far abler than his modern critic, but he had not the same materials. Especially he wanted the guidance of Prehistoric Archaeology, a department of research only established on a scientific footing within the last few years. (Tylor 1871, I:48)

Part of the reason for this was the shift of emphasis in the intellectual climate from materialism to idealism, and the associated interest in matters other than subsistence. Earlier Tylor had noted the 'most important problems' to be addressed in writing an 'Early History of Man' were 'the relation of the bodily characters of the various races, the question of their origin and descent, the development of morals, religion, law, and many others' (Tylor 1865:2–3). As Voget (1967:133) commented, at that time the aim of comparative anthropology was rather the 'total study of mankind's progressive cultivation of mind, morality, refinement in tastes, and advances in technical skills. . . . Above all, the new science of man would focus on a history of the human mind'. Much of such a programme was not obviously conducive to direct empirical archaeological exploration and materialist explanation. However the importance of subsistence as a category, and its eventual mapping onto archaeological periods, arose from two routes (Pluciennik 2001, 2006).

The first can be seen as a direct response to archaeological discoveries. Even before the influential British scholar Lubbock was persisting with his purely technological definition of the Neolithic – he would maintain this stance for 50 years and through 13 editions of his *Pre-historic Times* (1865) – others had noted important distinctions within the archaeological record. In 1862 Worsaae contrasted the 'hunting and fishing tribes' of the middens of southern Scandinavia with 'a higher civilisation with domestic animals, with agriculture, and with better formed implements (Daniel 1975:88). In France, de Mortillet's 1872 definition of the 'Robenhausian' (from a Swiss village site) included farming and pottery, as well as polished stone tools. In Britain Dawkins (1894:248) contrasted nomadic Palaeolithic man with 'Neolithic Man', whose skills and attributes included herding and tilling, pottery, textiles and mining, sedentism and burial in tombs: 'There is obviously a great gulf fixed between the rude hunter civilisation of the one, and the agricultural and pastoral civilisation of the other'. Many had also noted that 'polished stone' did not necessarily correlate with these other 'Neolithic' characteristics. By the earlier twentieth century such views were commonplace across Europe (e.g. Burkitt 1921; Peake 1927; Vayson de Pradenne 1935). By the same time, the idea of a Mesolithic or middle stone age, first proposed in 1872, was finally beginning to be accepted as a useful archaeological and chronological period, if not social evolutionary stage (Zvelebil 1986a:5–6). Almost defined by default against the Neolithic, as non-farmers, social evolutionary history repeated itself and the term Mesolithic became reserved for the last hunter-gatherers of Europe. One of those reluctant to use 'Mesolithic' was Gordon Childe, who preferred the Palaeolithic to remain as a baseline against which to measure the subsequent Neolithic (considered as 'food production') Revolution.

The second route at least in part arose via a transatlantic detour. The extremely influential American ethnologist Lewis Henry Morgan, as Kehoe (1998:175) has noted, was in a circle who were intellectually much closer to the eighteenth-century conjectural historians of the Scottish Enlightenment. His famous seven 'ethnical stages' (1877:9) were closely related to changes in technology and subsistence. Indeed, the whole of the second chapter of *Ancient Society* is dedicated to the 'Arts of Subsistence' and in it he argues that since

> Mankind are the only beings who may be said to have gained an absolute control over the production of food. . . . It is accordingly probable that the great epochs of human progress have been identified, more or less directly, with the enlargement of the sources of subsistence. (Morgan 1877:19)

Morgan's views were generally more clearly materialist and indeed open to empirical verification than those of many of his European contemporaries, which explains one of the attractions of his framework. In addition, the particular importance of Morgan for European prehistory is that his work was well-known and received there (by Tylor, for example, whose 1881 *Anthropology* was clearly influenced by what he had read, and later by Childe); but even more importantly, by Karl Marx and Friedrich Engels, whose 1884 *The Origin of the Family, Private Property and the State* was subtitled 'in the Light of the Researches of Lewis H. Morgan'. This and other Marxist writings often influenced the terminologies and categories used in Eastern Europe, such as Para-neolithic or Forest Neolithic (hunter-gatherer societies with pottery) (Zvelebil 1986a:7, Table 2). There was also however a concentration on issues such as ethnogenesis (Trigger 1989:218–43), which tended to support investigations of indigenous development and process, in contrast to the prevailing tradition of a much more descriptive 'culture history' typical of much western European prehistory in which migration was the most common explanation of change. Most people are familiar with the culture group approach of this period (and see Collis, this volume). But the basic figures for the change from hunter-gatherers to farmers

were invasion, colonization and migration. Even though there was occasional reference to the fact that 'Mesolithic' populations could have interacted with farmers
and even adopted farming, the primary model was one of diffusion through migration and colonization, itself marked by the spread of the material culture (primarily
pottery) whose typologies formed the units of the maps and chronological charts.
As an example I shall simply offer two quotes from one of Childe's last publications,
Prehistoric Migrations in Europe, and so well after his important *The Dawn of European Civilisation* (1925). In 1950 he acknowledged that 'the spread of Neolithic
cultures in our continent depended, therefore, not merely on colonisation by immigrant farmers but also on the multiplication of established populations that had
adapted [*sic*] the new productive economy' (Childe 1950:36). But in his subsequent
text it is difficult to find any reference to the latter process. Greece, the Balkans
and the north Mediterranean coast are discussed almost exclusively in terms of
migrations from the east. Elsewhere, 'early Neolithic farmers colonised the whole
area from the Atlantic coasts to the Alpine foothills, the Jura, Vosges and Ardennes,
crossed to the British Isles and subsequently spread from Switzerland into Upper
Italy and across the Rhine to central Europe, invading territories already colonised
by other peasantries' (Childe 1950:84) – the equally exogenous Danubian cultures.
The only exception Childe was prepared to make was in northern France and
Switzerland, where he suggested that 'groups of gatherers were gradually admitted
into the food producer's societies' (ibid:88). Similar approaches characterized
Mesolithic researchers, with ever more elaborate schemes or rather maps and charts
based on sometimes minute differences in lithic typologies or assemblages, and
often equated explicitly or implicitly with ethnic or quasi-ethnic 'peoples'. In this
scenario, the *doyens* of Mesolithic (and Palaeolithic) studies tended to be the lithic
specialists who often erected grand chronotypological schemes: This would include
those such as Escalon de Fonton and de Lumley (e.g. 1955) and Laplace (1954,
1966) in France, or J. Koslowski in Poland, and Barandiaran in Spain, all of whose
influence spread far beyond their native countries; later on one might point to the
monumental works and incredibly detailed knowledge represented by those such
as Rozoy (1978), or the contents of the edited pan-European volumes such as S.
Koslowski (1973) or Gramsch (1981).

The Mesolithic Neolithic Transition

One of the outcomes of the migrationist/colonist model was that in effect there was
little to be explained about the change from hunter-gatherer to farmer. For various
reasons including the legacy of the stadial social evolutionary schemes discussed
above, farmers were perceived as essentially and radically different from foragers.
They were also closer to 'us' not only in terms of practical subsistence, but also in
their lifestyle (sedentary villages), the richness of their material culture, relationships
with the land (the old trope of 'property'), social organization and more generally
conceptually and culturally (Pluciennik 1998). It was often felt that, for example,
evidence for practices such as fertility cults and associated cult objects, ancestral
tombs and the like were self-evident – understandable – in a way that Mesolithic
hunter-gatherers were not (see Zvelebil 1996 for an exploration of how this played
out within nationalist histories). Interest in a social or societal archaeology was often
reserved for the Neolithic and later, while the typically less rich material culture for

earlier periods reinforced ecological and functional approaches to the Mesolithic. Nowhere is this better shown than by the great British archaeologist Graham Clark, who did so much to raise awareness of the value of the Mesolithic as an archaeological period (e.g. 1936). His last brief book was entitled *Mesolithic Prelude*. In the introduction he felt he had to restate the case for the term:

> it is now perceived to be of crucial significance for understanding the course of prehistory, and not least for explaining the rise and spread of the Neolithic societies that laid the foundations of the diverse civilisations of mankind. (Clark 1980:5)

The Mesolithic was thus 'an essential *prelude* to fundamental advances in the development of culture' (ibid:7) – a curiously apologetic tone for one who had done so much to advance study of the period. But for many the Mesolithic remained a chronological and geographical backwater: interesting perhaps because it represented the final European hunter-gatherers – the last or even degenerate descendants of the virile, art-making, hunters of the Upper Palaeolithic – but in social evolutionary terms irrelevant to the broader picture. History at this time was being written elsewhere, especially in southwest Asia where the first integrated agricultural societies were forming and spreading, and where hunter-gatherers were part of the origins, rather than spread, of agriculture. It was thus essential, if the change from hunter-gatherer to farmer in Europe was to be investigated and discussed as a process – as an archaeological topic – for Mesolithic communities to be considered as interesting in their own right, as well as relevant to consideration of the spread, or even indigenous origins, of farming in Europe.

There are perhaps three major factors to be considered here. First, there was inevitably more and better data, not only in a cumulative but also qualitative sense (the discovery of hunter-gatherer cemeteries, for example, in the Balkans and in southern Scandinavia; the excavation of the famous Iron Gates sites in the 1960s [e.g. Srejovic 1972]). The still-increasing trend towards geomorphologically and/or period-focused field surveys (e.g. Chapman et al. 2003; Jochim 1976, 1998; Runnels et al. 2005) has vastly increased our knowledge of Mesolithic occupation especially in those areas (central Europe, Greece) once thought to be only sparsely or even un-populated. There were also improved or more widely and systematically applied techniques such as those within palynology and archaeozoology, often once again pioneered in Scandinavia. But perhaps most important of all was the introduction and increasing availability of radiocarbon dates, the impact of which will be discussed further below. The second factor related to the more imaginative use of ethnography and anthropology generally as a source of analogies or models for interpretation; the third factor was the academic (and wider) re-evaluation of hunter-gatherers generally, in ways which inverted or at least challenged the social evolutionary hierarchy. Gradually, during the post-war period, but more particularly from the 1980s onwards, there were a series of projects and publications which made it clear that hunter-gatherers – and perhaps particularly those pertaining to the post-glacial period – were worthy of extended discussion; their demise, or transformations into other types of (farming) societies were complex and sometimes long-lasting. Grahame Clark's own works, and in particular his excavation and publication of the famous British site of Star Carr (1954) can be seen as an early example and promulgations of this shift; following his own travels through northern Europe and especially Scandinavia he applied many of the techniques he had observed to this site with far-reaching consequences (Lane and Schadla-Hall 2004). This Scandinavian influence and interchange on post-glacial archaeology continued in Britain: see e.g. Clarke (1976) and Mellars (1978). Southern Scandinavia (and also the Netherlands) became 'hot spots' for debate about the transition during the 1980s especially (see e.g. de Roever 1979; Fischer 1982; Jennbert 1985; Larsson 1986; Louwe Koiijmans 1993; Madsen 1986; Rowley-Conwy 1983, 1985; Zvelebil & Rowly-Conwy 1984). In other parts of Europe too ecological approaches became more common. Feeding into these debates were changes in approaches towards hunter-gatherers more generally: a key moment is often seen as the 1966 *Man the Hunter* conference in Chicago (Lee and DeVore 1968), at which Sahlins' (1968) paper suggesting that hunter-gatherers were the 'original affluent society' was a sign of a return in some ways to a vision of pre-agricultural times as a Golden Age (for wider discussion of this change in perception of hunter-gatherers see Bender & Morris 1988; Pluciennik 2001:751-3). It was at this time that some proposed that at least some aspects of agricultural subsistence could have been independently invented in Europe (e.g. Barker 1985; Dennell 1983). Another outcome of these wider trends was a new interest in the possibility of Mesolithic 'complex' hunter-gatherers (Price and Brown 1985), for example. All this served to complicate what had once been the simple issue of the colonization of central and western Europe at least by farmers from the Near East; as well as conventional culture historical wisdom that once farming arrived, there was little else to be said. A new set of ethnographically-derived 'frontier models' (Dennell 1985; Zvelebil 1986a; Zvelebil and Rowley-Conwy 1984) was suggested for the investigation of potentially highly-variable relations and interactions between forager and farmer communities. The conceptual divide between foragers and farmers was so much lessened that, by 1986, in what has been perhaps the most influential expression (in Europe and beyond) of this revised attitude towards the transition, Zvelebil asked:

> If the postglacial hunters of the temperate zone can really be characterised by logistic, rather than residential mobility, storage, intensive resource-use strategies, non-egalitarian social organisation and the use of pottery, polished stone and other technological innovations traditionally associated with the Neolithic, what is left of the difference between the Mesolithic and the Neolithic? (Zvelebil 1986b:168)

Dating, Genetics, Linguistics

At the same time, however, there has been a counter-current to these social anthropologically informed approaches. In 1965 Grahame Clark made use of the existing radiocarbon dates to investigate whether one could plot the spread of 'the Neolithic' across Europe. Soon after the archaeologist Albert Ammerman and geneticist Luigi-Luca Cavalli-Sforza (1971; 1973; 1984) presented a demographic model for the spread of farming in Europe. Discussing the apparent rate of spread, they explained this through contemporary studies which suggested that small-scale farming societies in general have a higher rate of population growth than those of hunter-gatherer societies (for a recent re-examination of the large-scale radiocarbon dates, see Pinhasi et al. 2005). Over the long term, one did not therefore have to think in terms of migrations and directed colonizations; rather, population increase among farming groups and consequent fissioning around the margins would produce a 'wave of advance'. One could visualize this as the move of kin-groups over a range of around 25 kilometres perhaps once a generation, thus producing the apparent average rate of spread of around 1 kilometre a year. In fact this also fitted in with then current ideas about the nature of, say, LBK 'slash-and-burn' agriculture and settlement in central Europe, with the timber longhouses also argued to last for a relatively short period before being abandoned. Together with survey, as radiocarbon dating became cheaper, more prolific and more accurate, better resolution has enabled one to talk in detail about process on the regional scale – 'fringe' effects around the LBK and the delayed spread into the North European Plain for example (Bogucki 2000; Gronenborn 1999; Jeunesse 2003; Verhart 2000); the Balkans (Biagi et al. 2005) and the Adriatic (Biagi and Spataro 2002); central Italy (Skeates 1999), or northern Spain (Ruiz 2005). Nonetheless it should be noted that here too it has been argued that biased sampling and the way we excavate has sometimes served to maintain the division between hunter-gatherers and farmers (Pluciennik 1997; Skeates 2003).

Even more influentially, though, Ammerman and Cavalli-Sforza noted that, assuming that early farming in Europe was initially associated with an exogenous and biologically distinct population from the Near East, there were 'possible genetic implications of the model'.

> The population wave of advance accompanying the spread of early farming should be reflected, if this [demic diffusion] explanation is the correct one, in the genetic compositions of the resulting populations. (Ammerman and Cavalli-Sforza 1971:687)

Since that date there have been hundreds of articles exploring precisely what one can learn from genetic studies of contemporary populations and occasionally from ancient DNA too. This latter would appear to offer much more specific information from individuals and groups of individuals who can be culturally-situated, contextualized and dated archaeologically, but so far has made little impact, primarily because of problems of contamination (though see e.g. Chandler et al. 2005; Haak et al. 2005). It should be noted that this problem of contamination of ancient DNA is not an issue for animal and plant material, and there have been many interesting – though often still inconclusive – studies using ancient and modern material for materials including wheat (see e.g. Jones and Brown 2000) and cattle (Beja-Pereira et al. 2006; Bollongino et al. 2006).

Technically, there are now many direct studies of geographic variation in different parts of the human genome including mitochondrial DNA and the Y-chromosome, which in principle should even allow us to distinguish between female and male 'contributions' from differing population groups. The investigation of haplogroups and phylogenetics – the history of genetic lineages – allows much more regionally nuanced studies than the original work in 'classical markers' such as blood proteins. Dating remains a key problem (rates of change are often uncertain, and hence the range of possible dates from genetic information alone is usually much too wide for archaeological purposes), although mtDNA (mitochondrial DNA) studies in particular have suggested that many of the existing patterns of distribution of genetic variation should be ascribed to the Upper Palaeolithic and post Last Glacial Maximum movements of resettlement. (For an excellent recent review see Richards 2003, though 'archaeogenetics' is an especially fast-moving field). For some, who in effect ignored the problem of the inherent lack of resolution, the apparent large-scale patterns produced by this genetic data suggested a need for equally large-scale explanations. Key figures in this field have been Cavalli-Sforza (Cavalli-Sforza et al. 1994), Colin Renfrew (e.g. 1987; 1992; 1997; Renfrew and Boyle 2000) and Peter Bellwood (Bellwood 2001; 2004; Bellwood and Renfrew 2002). Both have been active in promoting explanations, which rely primarily on the demographic growth of early agriculturalists 'swamping' indigenous hunter-gatherers biologically and culturally, and thus providing mutually supporting evidence from archaeology, genetics and language. Indeed, Bellwood and Sanchez-Mazas (2005:483) recently concluded that the complexity of the data meant that 'We need to propose overarching hypotheses that can account for the comparative data from linguistics, genetics, and archaeology with as little stress as possible'. However others have remained unconvinced by such cavalier use of Ockham's Razor, helped by the persistent conflation of genetic, linguistic and cultural 'entities' including those derived from archaeology, and a particular problem with work stemming from geneticists: the major work by Cavalli-Sforza et al. (1994) came in for particular criticism for this reason (see e.g. Bandelt et al. 2002; Gamble et al. 2005; MacEachern 2000; Moore 1994; Pluciennik 1996; Terrell and Stewart 1996; Zvelebil 2000). The assumption that these forms of biology, culture and identity almost inevitably go together bears an uncanny resemblance to earlier versions of culture history equating material culture and ethnicity.

The contribution of the study of the human genome to archaeology, or rather to our understanding of human (pre)history is so far unclear. The data is often ambiguous, and many would see attempts (by archaeologists such as Renfrew and Bellwood) to link genetic data to those of archaeology, and then to linguistic 'historical evidence' as well, as misguided or at best grossly over-simplified. One could also argue that a disproportionate amount of time and money has been spent on pursuing genetic data of dubious value: molecular biology is currently a fashionable (and exciting) discipline which attracts research funds in a way that a proposal, say, to carry out yet another archaeological field survey is not. On the other hand some of the excesses, as well as genuine new evidence deriving from 'archaeogenetics' have forced archaeologists to confront new questions or consider them again: what kinds of demographic (and associated cultural) processes should we be thinking about in the past? How varied were they? Are there patterns to this variation? What kinds of spatial and chronological scales should we be looking at? What might be the relationships between language and other forms of identity? What are the processes involved in such changes? How far can we distinguish between migration of various kinds, and diffusion? In this way archaeogenetics has certainly reinvigorated or influenced the parameters for debates about many periods, places and processes in the past. The immediate value of the study of non-human genetic material seems more clear. Although many of the same doubts about rates of change in the genome may remain, it is often much easier to extract and work with ancient (that is, archaeologically-derived) material with a much fuller context and generally much better dates. Demonstrating that some species appear to have undergone multiple domestications, for example, while others seem to have been domesticated uniquely and then diffused, tells us something of much interest about the history of human–animal or human–plant relations, and subsequent cultural processes, as well as those of the plant and animal species themselves.

The Shock of the New

As is suggested by the above, archaeology is very much a mixture of disciplines, methods, techniques and approaches; though even apparently convergent data rarely offers unambiguous historical or archaeological answers. Pinhasi and Pluciennik (2004) recently examined the Mesolithic Neolithic transition in southern Europe using relatively 'hard' data (skeletal morphometrics – in this case measurements of human skulls), which are indeed partly related to genotypes, as well as other factors such as environment and diet. However they suggested that such data are rather another point of triangulation in the complex debate about *some* aspects of the demographic and cultural processes in this period of prehistory. It is a necessarily woolly picture. In that paper they wrote:

> Neither skeletal nor genetic nor archaeological [nor linguistic] data alone will provide 'solutions' to questions about the nature of the Mesolithic-Neolithic transition. Different data sets address a variety of processes at different scales and chronological and geographical resolutions. (Pinhasi & Pluciennik 2004:74)

Nevertheless, as is often the case, carrying out one or more types of analysis on the same samples helps either to confirm interpretations, or suggests anomalies, which need to be investigated. For example, a series of papers by Alex Bentley, Douglas Price and collaborators, primarily using strontium isotope analysis of skeletal material from Germany, has shown that it is possible to distinguish between those originating or spending substantial parts of their lives in the geologically older uplands – and perhaps associated with either foraging or herding – and those associated with the perhaps more agricultural lowlands (e.g. Bentley et al. 2002; 2003; Bentley & Knipper 2005). Interestingly, these differences sometimes map onto other biological or cultural differences including sex and burial goods, perhaps giving a tantalizing glimpse into marriage and residence patterns in parts of early Neolithic Europe.

Similarly, the use of carbon and nitrogen isotope ratios has been illuminating and provocative. The first European archaeological carbon isotope analysis of human skeletons was by Tauber (1981: see Richards et al. 2003a for an updated review). Tauber examined Mesolithic and Neolithic specimens from Denmark, and found a marked difference between the former (associated with marine and aquatic resource remains) and the latter (presumed to be much more dependent on agriculture). In a related way, the nitrogen isotope ratio $N^{15}:N^{14}$ is enhanced as it passes up the food chain: low values suggest a predominantly plant food diet, high values a marine/aquatic diet. Because relatively dense populations of hunter-gatherers are often associated with coastal or aquatic zones, with tendencies towards sedentism and associated cemeteries, both carbon and nitrogen isotope values have thus often been used to explore the nature of any dietary shifts associated with the transition to agriculture (e.g. Bonsall et al. 2004; Boric et al. 2004 for the Iron Gates). Although the Mesolithic individuals generally cluster towards the 'aquatic' end of the spectrum, there are some interesting anomalies – in some cases possibly 'Neolithic' incomers who had until very recently been eating mainly plant foods. These debates over interpretation continue. In a recent series of papers Schulting and Richards have analyzed skeletal remains from northern and western Europe – primarily the British Isles, Brittany and southern Scandinavia, again focusing on the Mesolithic to Neolithic transition. What they have found is a very marked and rapid shift in isotope values between the two periods – far greater than might have been expected – which suggests that 'Neolithic' populations, even those living near the coast, virtually shunned marine foods which had been so important to

Mesolithic people. (See e.g. Richards et al. 2003b). This radical shift, at least as seen through the isotope data, is so pronounced that it has led to questioning of the methodology (see Milner et al. 2004; Milner et al. 2006; Richards and Schulting 2006), although until recently isotope analysis has been seen as a relatively robust technique. Others have accepted the results implied by the analyses, but suggested that perhaps for some reason sea foods became the subject of a strict taboo in Neolithic times, with water and the sea in particular associated with the dead (Thomas 2003). But this too would seem a surprising homogeneity of belief.

Recent Models for Transition

As noted above, in the 1980s many of the most influential ideas and models came from non-Balkan and non-Mediterranean areas, principally northern and north-eastern Europe, where there were very different historical and theoretical, as well as archaeological, conditions. It is interesting that many of the 'social' models and more complex ideas came from this pan-Baltic area from the 1980s onwards. One of the key areas is Poland, where, despite problems of palimpsests and difficult-to-date sites on sandy soils, it is now very clear (Nowak 2001; 2006) that there was a huge chronological 'overlap' of several millennia, and interaction and co-existence between 'Mesolithic', 'Neolithic' and indeed 'Bronze Age' societies and communities. The emergence of the Neolithic TRB tradition is strongly or largely related to 'hunter-gatherer' communities; there are long-term and varying interactions between foragers, farmers, forager-herders, forager-farmers, pastoralist-foragers which raise fascinating issues of cultural hybridization and historical change, and not only how people became farmers. It is thus here and in Scandinavia that the categories of Mesolithic and Neolithic, and hunter-gatherer and farmer have come under the greatest tension. Another key area has been that of the Iron Gates area of the Danube, where the extraordinary material of late Mesolithic and Neolithic date has provoked many re-examinations and interpretations (e.g. Boric et al. 2004; Rado-vanovic 2006; Radanovic & Voytek 1997; Tringham 2000). Survey, excavation and dating in the Balkans and the Adriatic too has forced a rethink of the pace, nature and meaning of the changes from hunter-gatherer to farmer (e.g. Banffy 2004; 2006; Biagi et al. 2005; Budja 2001; Forenbaher and Miracle 2005). The link between Neolithic occupation and sedentism has been challenged, especially in northwestern Europe (Bailey et al. 2005; Whittle 1996), but contrasting work in Ireland, for example, suggests that regional trajectories and variation are one of the keys to understanding the transition and 'the Neolithic' too (Cooney 1997; Woodman 2000). This blurring of categories has been further reinforced by archaeological (as well as ethnographic) evidence that plant (e.g. water chestnut) and animal management, and domestication of some animals such as pig was certainly not confined to the Neolithic and the Near East (Larson et al. 2005).

The result is that while there is a spectrum of contemporary understandings of the change from hunter-gatherer to farmer, the majority view among archaeologists is that it is the local and regional scales which are currently driving the arguments and demonstrating the complexities of these historical and primarily socio-cultural (rather than ecological or social evolutionary) processes. Zvelebil (2004:44–5) terms this rather broad consensus the integrationist paradigm, that is, those who are willing to accept that indigenous adoption, diffusion and various forms of 'colonization' are differentially influential, and geographically and chronologically variable. In short, 'the direction and pace of the adoption of farming reflected as much the existing Mesolithic social context . . . [as the] conditions of the Neolithic communities and the regional ecological circumstances' (Zvelebil 2004:45). That this paradigm is generally accepted across Europe can be seen in recent publications such as Price (2000); but see Ammerman and Biagi (2003). The shift in hunter-gatherer studies is also well represented in Larsson et al. (2003), though this has a marked northern European bias.

Discussion

> Do you wish to understand the true history of a Neolithic Ligurian or Sicilian? Try, if you can, to become a Neolithic Ligurian or Sicilian in your mind. If you cannot do that, or do not care to, content yourself with describing and arranging in series the skulls, implements, and drawings which have been found belonging to these Neolithic peoples. (Croce 1921:134)

What might constitute 'true history'? Croce's intellectual context was the lengthy debates about the differences between varying types of knowledge (theological, philosophical, scientific, humanist), which originally blossomed in mid-nineteenth-century Germany. The original conflict has remained a particularly important one for archaeology, though, often seen as straddling the latter two boundaries. This has been even more so for the periods under discussions here, where generalized ecological explanations of hunter-gatherers have often contrasted with more localized, materially and culturally richer and intuitively closer – more understandable? – descriptions of farmers. In modern terms Croce's 'true history' might perhaps be glossed as 'social archaeology' or one informed by (past) cultural meanings. But what is it that we are trying to understand and explain? If we are wishing to examine the period encompassing – and defined by – the various shifts from hunter-gatherers to farmers in Europe, then we are talking about a timespan covering 5,000 and arguably 8,000 years. Should we then confine ourselves to only examining the change to agriculture, however that is defined, assuming that it is a single process or outcome – what Zvelebil (2004:45) called 'the overarching coherence of the historical process of agricultural transition' (cf. Zvelebil 1989)? Or at least a set of processes that will show relatively little variation – arguing that the underlying generalizations about demography, language shift or risk-avoidance work at a regional, continental or even global scale (e.g. Bellwood 2004; Renfrew 1987; 1992; 1997; Smith 1995)? Clearly, the nature of the transition to agriculture is an important, interesting and legitimate question to ask: partial or total reliance on domesticated resources has many implications beyond diet, though the ways in which that is practiced and expressed is also highly variable. When 'the Neolithic' was understood to represent such a radically different and indeed superior state of society to those of hunter-gatherers, it was necessary to explain the coherent and simultaneous shift in socio-economic attributes from one evolutionary stage to the next. Since both 'stages' were defined by subsistence, it was indeed the obvious place to start. However, focusing on this single subsistence transition could also lead to a conceptually homogenous Neolithic, in the same way that hunter-gatherers were often characterized in ecological terms. There is also the effect of hindsight. If Zvelebil

(1998:26) argues that 'the Neolithic is the process of agricultural transition', Rowley-Conwy (2001:129) looks to the Jomon period of Japan to suggest other ways of approaching the Mesolithic, pointing out that 'Eight thousand years of complexity did not lead to an indigenous Jomon agriculture. Jomon studies have freed themselves from this predestination, so groups can be examined for their own sake – not for what they might become'. There are methodological and epistemological issues here too, of course. Different data sets (including contemporary distributions of genetic traits, skeletal morphometrics, material culture attributes, radiocarbon dates, settlement patterns, comparative linguistics, palaeoecological information etc.) do not refer to the same entities, or even where they do (or might) they are unlikely to possess the same spatial, chronological or social resolutions.

Studies of the earlier Holocene in Europe have changed markedly over the last few decades. The variation within hunter-gatherer societies including especially the potential for social and economic complexity is much better recognized qualitatively and quantitatively, with the middens and cemeteries of Portugal and southern Spain, evidence of sea voyages from Sicily and north Africa to Pantelleria to acquire obsidian, and from mainland Italy and France to Corsica. To the Iron Gates sites in the Balkans, and the astonishingly rich and varied record from southern Scandinavia, the Baltic and northeast Europe must be added the expansion in the number of hunter-gatherer sites provided by more sensitive and focused survey. The variability of 'the Neolithic' too is better described and understood across a series of axes – cosmological, ecological, subsistence practices, the economy, social structure and of course material culture, all varying across space and time. We have at the European scale a mosaic of variably connected and variably-bounded 'cultures' which characterize both the Mesolithic and the Neolithic: a continuously varying landscape of sociocultural and economic processes and traditions. We are reaching the point at which for many regions at least it is clear that to treat 'the transition to agriculture' as the only or most important lens through which to view the archaeological record runs the danger of downplaying other trajectories – other histories. Other themes, other axes of variation which cut across the traditional period boundaries – mobility in things, people and genes; long-term histories of societal interactions (as in Poland); changes in cosmology; cultural hybridization; the ebb and flow of directionality of relations within regions; new cross-period ecological or landscape histories; shifting social structures – all these and more are now possible in many parts of Europe, especially as our ability and willingness to ascribe agency and history to hunter-gatherers has improved. The conceptual shadow cast by a morally evaluative social evolution is beginning to dissipate, in large part brought about by persistent exploration of stadial difference engendered by that very same scheme. 'Only history can free us from history', suggests Bourdieu (1982:9), and so itself produce a framework for change. It does not mean that 'the transition to agriculture' will disappear as a topic; it might mean that different questions and perspectives will present themselves – and help us see Others.

REFERENCES

Ammerman, A., and P. Biagi, eds. 2003 The Widening Harvest. The Neolithic Transition in Europe: Looking Back, Looking Forward. Boston: Archaeological Institute of America.

Ammerman, A., and L.-L. Cavalli-Sforza 1971 Measuring the Rate of Spread of Early Farming in Europe. Man (NS)6:673–88.

Ammerman, A., and L.-L. Cavalli-Sforza 1973 A Population Model for the Diffusion of Early Farming in Europe. *In* The Explanation of Culture Change: Models in Prehistory. C. Renfrew, ed. Pp. 343–57. London: Duckworth.

Ammerman, A., and L.-L. Cavalli-Sforza 1984 The Neolithic Transition and the Genetics of Populations in Europe. New Jersey: Princeton University Press.

Bailey, D., A. Whittle, and V. Cummings, eds. 2005 (Un)settling the Neolithic. Oxford: Oxbow Books.

Bandelt, H.-J., V. Macaulay, and M. Richards 2002 What Molecules Can't Tell Us About the Spread of Languages and the Neolithic. *In* Examining the Farming/Language Dispersal Hypothesis. P. Bellwood and C. Renfrew, eds. Pp. 99–107. Cambridge: McDonald Institute Monographs.

Banffy, E. 2004 The 6th Millennium BC Boundary in Western Transdanubia and its Role in the Central European Neolithic Transition. Varia Archaeologica Hungarica 15. Budapest: Archaeological Institute of the HAS.

Banffy, E. 2006 Eastern, Central and Western Hungary – Variations of Neolithisation Models. Documenta Praehistorica 33:125–42.

Barker, G. 1985 Prehistoric Farming in Europe. Cambridge: Cambridge University Press.

Barker, G. 2006 The Agricultural Revolution in Prehistory: Why Did Foragers Become Farmers? Oxford: Oxford University Press.

Barnard, A. 2004 Hunting-and-Gathering Society: An Eighteenth-Century Scottish Invention. *In* Hunter-Gatherers in History, Archaeology and Anthropology. A. Barnard, ed. Pp. 31–43. Oxford: Berg.

Beja-Pereira, A., and 26 other authors 2006 The Origin of European Cattle: Evidence from Modern and Ancient DNA. Proceedings of the National Academy of Sciences of the United States of America (PNAS published online May 11, 2006). http://www.pnas.org/cgi/reprint/0509210103v1.

Bellwood, P. 2001 Early Agriculturalist Population Diasporas? Farming, Languages, and Genes. Annual Review of Anthropology 30:181–207.

Bellwood, P. 2004 First Farmers: The Origins of Agricultural Societies. Oxford: Blackwell.

Bellwood, P., and C. Renfrew, eds. 2002 Examining the Farming/Language Dispersal Hypothesis. Cambridge: McDonald Institute Monographs.

Bellwood, P., and A. Sanchez-Mazas 2005 Human Migrations in Continental East Asia and Taiwan: Genetic, Linguistic, and Archaeological Evidence. Current Anthropology 46:480–4.

Bender, B., and B. Morris 1988 Twenty Years of History, Evolution and Social Change in Hunter-Gatherer Studies. *In* Hunters and Gatherers Volume 1: History, Evolution and Social Change. T. Ingold, D. Riches, and J. Woodburn, eds. Pp. 4–14. Oxford: Berg.

Bentley, R. A., and C. Knipper 2005 Transhumance at the Early Neolithic Settlement at Vaihingen, Germany. Antiquity 79:306.

Bentley, R. A., R. Krause, T. D. Price, and B. Kaufmann 2003 Human Mobility at the Early Neolithic Settlement of Vaihingen, Germany: Evidence from Strontium Isotope Analysis. Archaeometry 45:471–86.

Bentley, R. A., T. D. Price, J. Lüning, D. Gronenborn, J. Wahl, and P. D. Fullagar 2002 Human Migration in Early Neolithic Europe. Current Anthropology 43:799–804.

Biagi, P., S. Shennan, and M. Spataro 2005 Rapid Rivers and Slow Seas? New Data for the Radiocarbon Chronology of the Balkan Peninsula. *In* Prehistoric Archaeology and Anthropological Theory and Education. L. Nikolova and J. Higgins, eds. Pp. 41–50. Reports of Prehistoric Research Projects 6–7.

Biagi, P., and M. Spataro 2002 The Mesolithic/Neolithic Transition in North Eastern Italy and in the Adriatic Basin. *In* El Paisaje en el Neolítico Mediterráneo. E. Badall, J. Bernabeu, and B. Martí, eds. Pp. 167–78. Saguntum. Supp. 5.

Bogucki, P. 2000 How Agriculture Came to North-Central Europe. *In* Europe's First Farmers. D. Price, ed. Pp. 197–218. Cambridge: Cambridge University Press.

Bollongino, R., C. Edwards, K. Alt, J. Burger, and D. Bradley 2006 Early History of European Domestic Cattle as Revealed by Ancient DNA. Biology Letters 2(1):155–9.

Bonsall, C., G. Cook, R. Hedges, T. Higham, C. Pickard, and I. Radovanovic 2004 Radiocarbon and Stable Isotope Evidence of Dietary Change from the Mesolithic to the Middle Ages in the Iron Gates: New results from Lepenski Vir. Radiocarbon 46(1):293–300. Available from Glasgow ePrints: http://eprints.gla.ac.uk/2029.

Boric, D., G. Grupe, J. Peters, and Z. Mikic 2004 Is the Mesolithic-Neolithic Subsistence Dichotomy Real? New Stable Isotope Evidence from the Danube Gorges. European Journal of Archaeology 7(3):221–48.

Bourdieu, P. 1982 Leçon sur la Leçon. Paris: Editions de Minuit.

Budja, M. 2001 Neolithization in the Caput Adriae Region. *In* From the Mesolithic to the Neolithic. R. Kertesz and J. Makkay, eds. Pp. 125–36. Budapest: Archeolingua.

Burkitt, M. 1921 Prehistory. Cambridge: Cambridge University Press.

Cavalli-Sforza, L.-L., P. Menozzi, and A. Pizza 1994 The History and Geography of Human Genes. Princeton: Princeton University Press.

Chandler, H., B. Sykes, and J. Zilhão 2005 Using Ancient DNA to Examine Genetic Continuity at the Mesolithic-Neolithic Transition in Portugal. *In* Actas del III Congreso del Neolítico en la Península Ibérica. P. Arias, R. Ontañon, and C. García-Moncó, eds. Pp. 781–6. Santander: Monografías del Istituto Internacional de Investigaciones Prehistóricas de Cantabria 1.

Chapman, J., R. S. Shiel, D. G. Passmore, E. Magyari, and M. Gillings 2003 The Upper Tisza Project: Studies in Hungarian Landscape Archaeology. E-book 1: Introduction and Archaeological Field Survey in the Polgár Block. York: AHDS Archaeology. http://ads.ahds.ac.uk/catalogue/projArch/uppertisza_ba_2003.

Childe, V. G. 1925 The Dawn of European Civilization. London: Kegan Paul, Trench, Trubner & Co.

Childe, V. G. 1950 Prehistoric Migrations in Europe. Oslo: H.Aschebourg & Co.

Clark, G. 1936 The Mesolithic Settlement of Northern Europe. Cambridge: Cambridge University Press.

Clark, G. 1954 Excavations at Star Carr. Cambridge: Cambridge University Press.

Clark, G. 1965 Radiocarbon Dating and the Expansion of Farming Culture from the Near East over Europe. Proceedings of the Prehistoric Society 31:58–73.

Clark, G. 1980 Mesolithic Prelude. Edinburgh: Edinburgh University Press.

Clarke, D. 1976 Mesolithic Europe: The Economic Basis. *In* Problems in Economic and Social Archaeology. G. Sieveking, I. Longworth, and K. Wilson, eds. Pp. 449–81. London: Duckworth.

Cooney, G. 1997 Images of Settlement and the Landscape in the Neolithic. *In* Neolithic Landscapes. P. Topping, ed. Pp. 23–31. Neolithic Studies Group Seminar Papers 2. Oxford: Oxbow.

Croce, B. 1921 Theory and History of Historiography. D. Ainslie, trans. London: G.G. Harrap and Co.

Daniel, G. 1975 150 Years of Archaeology (second edition). London: Duckworth.

Dawkins, B. 1894 On the Relation of the Palaeolithic to the Neolithic Period. Journal of the Royal Anthropological Institute (O.S.) 23:242–57.

Dennell, R. 1983 European Economic Prehistory. London: Academic Press.

Dennell, R. 1985 The Hunter-Gatherer/Agricultural Frontier in Prehistoric Temperate Europe. *In* The Archaeology of Frontiers and Boundaries. S. Green and S. Perlman, eds. Pp. 113–40. New York: Academic Press.

de Roever, J. 1979 The Pottery from Swifterbant – Dutch Ertebolle? Helinium 19: 13–36.

Escalon de Fonton, M., and H. de Lumley 1955 Quelques civilisations de la Mediterranée Septentrionale et leur intercurrence (Epipaléolithique, Leptolithique, Epileptolithique). Bulletin de la Societé Préhistorique Française 52:379–94.

Fischer, A. 1982 Trade in Danubian Shaft-Hole Axes and the Introduction of Neolithic Economy in Denmark. Journal of Danish Archaeology 1:m7–12.

Forenbaher, S., and P. Miracle 2005 The Spread of Farming in the Eastern Adriatic. Antiquity 7979:514–28.

Gamble, C., W. Davies, P. Pettitt, L. Hazelwood, and M. Richards 2005 The Archaeological and Genetic Foundations of the European Population During the Late Glacial: Implications for 'Agricultural Thinking'. Cambridge Archaeological Journal 15:193–223.

Gramsch, B., ed. 1981 Mesolithikum in Europa. Veröffentlichungen des Museums für Ur- und Frühgeschichte, Potsdam, 14/15. Berlin: Deutscher Verlag.

Gronenborn, D. 1999 A Variation on a Basic Theme: The Transition to Farming in Southern Central Europe. Journal of World Prehistory 13(2):123–210.

Haak, W., P. Forster, B. Bramanti, S. Matsumara, G. Brandt, M. Tänzer, R. Villems, C. Renfrew, D. Gronenborn, K. W. Alt, and J. Burger 2005 Ancient DNA from the First European Farmers in 7500-Year-Old Neolithic Sites. Science 310:1016–18.

Jennbert, K. 1985 Neolithisation – A Scanian Perspective. Journal of Danish Archaeology 4:196–7.

Jeunesse, C. 2003 Néolithique 'initial', néolithique ancien et néolithisation dans l'espace centre-européen: une vision rénovée. Revue d'Alsace 129:97–112.

Jochim, M. 1976 Hunter-Gatherer Subsistence and Settlement: A Predictive Model. New York: Academic Press.

Jochim, M. 1998 A Hunter-Gatherer Landscape: Southwest Germany in the Late Paleolithic and Mesolithic. New York: Plenum Press.

Jones, M., and T. Brown 2000 Agricultural Origins: The Evidence of Modern and Ancient DNA. The Holocene 10(6):769–76.

Kehoe, A. 1998 The Land of Prehistory: A Critical History of American Archaeology. New York: Routledge.

Klindt-Jensen, O. 1975 A History of Scandinavian Archaeology. London: Thames & Hudson.

Koslowski, S., ed. 1973 The Mesolithic in Europe. Warsaw: Warsaw University Press.

Lane, P., and T. Schadla-Hall 2004 The Many Ages of Star Carr: Do 'Cites' Make the 'Site'? In Hunter-Gatherers in History, Archaeology and Anthropology. A. Barnard, ed. Pp. 145–61. Oxford: Berg.

Laplace, G. 1954 Application des méthodes statistiques à l'étude du Mésolithique. Bulletin de la Societé Préhistorique Française 51:127–39.

Laplaces, G. 1966 Recherches sur l'Origine et l'Évolution des Complexes Leptolithiques. Mélanges d'Archéologie et d'Histoire, Supp. 4. Paris: Ecole Française de Rome.

Larson G., K. Dobney, U. Albarella, M. Fang, E. Matisoo-Smith, J. Robins, S. Lowden, H. Finlayson, T. Brand, E. Willerslev, P. Rowley-Conwy, L. Andersson, and A. Cooper 2005 Worldwide Phylogeography of Wild Boar Reveals Multiple Centres of Pig Domestication. Science 307:1618–21.

Larsson, L., H. Kindgren, K. Knutsson, D. Loeffler, and A. Akerlund, eds. 2003 Mesolithic on the Move. Oxford: Oxbow.

Larsson, M. 1986 Neolithization in Scania – A Funnel Beaker Perspective. Journal of Danish Archaeology 5:244–7.

Lee, R., and I. DeVore, eds. 1968 Man the Hunter. Chicago: Aldine Press.

Louwe Koijmans, L. 1993 The Mesolithic/Neolithic Transformation in the Lower Rhine Basin. In Case Studies in European Prehistory. P. Bogucki, ed. Pp. 95–145. Boca Raton: CRC Press.

Lovejoy, A., and G. Boas 1965 Primitivism and Related Ideas in Antiquity. New York: Octagon Books.

Lowie, R. 1938 The History of Ethnological Theory. New York: Rinehart & Co.

Lubbock, J. 1865 Pre-Historic Times, as Illustrated by Ancient Remains, and the Manners and Customs of Modern Savages. London: Williams & Norgate.

MacEachern, S. 2000 Genes, Tribes, and African History. Current Anthropology 41:357–84.

Madsen, T. 1986 Where Did All the Hunters Go? Journal of Danish Archaeology 5:229–39.

Mellars, Paul, ed. 1978 The Early Post-Glacial Settlement of Northern Europe. An Ecological Perspective. London: Duckworth.

Milner, N., O. Craig, G. Bailey, and S. Andersen 2006 A Response to Richards and Schulting. Antiquity 80:456–8.

Milner, N., O. Craig, G. Bailey, K. Pedersen, and S. Andersen 2004 Something Fishy in the Neolithic? A Re-Evaluation of Stable Isotope Analysis of Mesolithic and Neolithic Coastal Populations. Antiquity 78:9–22.

Moore, J. 1994 Putting Anthropology Back Together Again: The Ethnogenetic Critique of Cladistic Theory. American Anthropologist 96:925–48.

Morgan, Lewis H. 1877 Ancient Society, or Researches in the Lines of Human Progress from Savagery through Barbarism to Civilization. New York: Henry Holt.

Nisbet, R. 1980 History of the Idea of Progress. New York: Basic Books.

Nowak, M. 2001 The Second Phase of Neolithisation in East-Central Europe. Antiquity 75:582–92.

Nowak, M. 2006 Transformations in East-Central Europe from 6000 to 3000 BC: Local vs. Foreign Patterns. Documenta Praehistorica 33:143–58.

Peake, Harold 1927 The Beginning of Civilization. Journal of the Royal Anthropological Institute (O.S.)57:19–38.

Pinhasi, R., J. Fort, and A. Ammerman 2005 Tracing the Origin and Spread of Agriculture in Europe. Public Library of Science Biology 3(12):e410.

Pinhasi, R., and M. Pluciennik 2004 A Regional Biological Approach to the Spread of Farming in Europe: Anatolia, the Levant, South-Eastern Europe, and the Mediterranean. Current Anthropology 45 (Supplement):S59–S82.

Pluciennik, M. 1996 A Perilous But Necessary Search: Archaeology and European Identities. In Nationalism and Archaeology. J. Atkinson, I. Banks, and J. O'Sullivan, eds. Pp. 35–58. Glasgow: Cruithne Press.

Pluciennik, M. 1997 Radiocarbon Determinations and the Mesolithic-Neolithic Transition in Southern Italy. Journal of Mediterranean Archaeology 10.2:115–50.

Pluciennik, M. 1998 Deconstructing 'the Neolithic' in the Mesolithic-Neolithic Transition. In Understanding the Neolithic of North-Western Europe. M. Edmonds and C. Richards, eds. Pp. 61–83. Glasgow: Cruithne Press.

Pluciennik, M. 2001 Archaeology, Anthropology and Subsistence. Journal of the Royal Anthropological Institute (N.S.) 7:741–58.

Pluciennik, M. 2002 The Invention of Hunter-Gatherers in Seventeenth-Century Europe. Archaeological Dialogues 9.2:98–151.

Pluciennik, M. 2004 The Meaning of 'Hunter-Gatherers' and Modes of Subsistence: A Comparative Historical Perspective. In Hunter-Gatherers in History, Archaeology and Anthropology. A. Barnard, ed. Pp. 17–29. Oxford: Berg.

Pluciennik, M. 2006 From Primitive to Civilised: Social Evolution in Victorian Anthropology and Archaeology. In The Victorians and the Ancient World: Archaeology and Classicism in Nineteenth-Century Culture. R. Pearson, ed. Pp. 1–24. Newcastle: Cambridge Scholars Press.

Price, D., ed. 2000 Europe's First Farmers. Cambridge: Cambridge University Press.

Price, T. D., and J. A. Brown, eds. 1985 Prehistoric Hunter-Gatherers: The Emergence of Cultural Complexity. Orlando: Academic Press.

Radovanovic, I. 2006 Further Notes on Mesolithic-Neolithic Contacts in the Iron Gates Region and the Central Balkans. Documenta Praehistorica 33:107–24.

Radovanovic, I., and B. Voytek 1997 Hunters, Fishers or Farmers: Sedentism, Subsistence and Social Complexity in the Djerdap Mesolithic. Analecta Praehistorica Leidensia 29:17–29.

Renfrew, C. 1987 Archaeology and Language. The Puzzle of Indo-European Origins. London: Jonathan Cape.

Renfrew, C. 1992 Archaeology, Genetics and Linguistic Diversity. Man 27:445–78.

Renfrew, C. 1997 World Linguistic Diversity and Farming Dispersals. *In Archaeology and Language. I.* R. Blench and M. Spriggs, eds. Pp. 82–90. London: Routledge.

Renfrew, C., and K. Boyle, eds. 2000 Archaeogenetics: DNA and the Population Prehistory of Europe. Cambridge: McDonald Institute Monographs.

Richards, M. 2003 The Neolithic Invasion of Europe. Annual Review of Anthropology 32:135–62.

Richards, M., T. D. Price, and E. Koch 2003a Mesolithic and Neolithic Subsistence in Denmark: New Stable Isotope Data. Current Anthropology 44:288–95.

Richards, M., R. J. Schulting, and R. Hedges 2003b Sharp Shift in Diet at Onset of Neolithic. Nature 425:366.

Richards, M., and R. Schulting 2006 Touch Not the Fish: The Mesolithic-Neolithic Change of Diet and its Significance. Antiquity 80:444–56.

Rowley-Conwy, P. 1983 Sedentary Hunters: The Ertebolle Example. *In* Hunter-Gatherer Economy in Prehistory: A European Perspective. G. Bailey, ed. Pp. 111–26. Cambridge: Cambridge University Press.

Rowley-Conwy, P. 1985 The Origins of Agriculture in Denmark: A Review of Some Theories. Journal of Danish Archaeology 4:188–95.

Rowley-Conwy, P. 2001 Time, Change and the Archaeology of Hunter-Gatherers: How Original is the 'Original Affluent Society'? *In* Hunter-Gatherers: An Interdisciplinary Perspective. C. Panter-Brick, R. Layton, and P. Rowley-Conwy, eds. Pp. 39–72. Cambridge: Cambridge University Press.

Rozoy, J.-G. 1978 Les Derniers Chasseurs, L'Epipaléolithique en France et en Belgique: Essai du Synthèse (3 vols.). Société Archéologique Champenoise, Numéro Spécial. Charleville: J.-G. Rozoy.

Rudebeck, E. 2000 Tilling Nature, Harvesting Culture: Exploring Images of the Human Being in the Transition to Agriculture (Acta Archaeologica Lundensia [8th Series] 32). Stockholm: Almqvist & Wiksell International.

Ruiz, A. A. 2005 The Transition Between the Last Hunter-Gatherers and the First Farmers in Southwestern Europe: The Basque Perspective. Journal of Anthropological Research 61:469–94.

Runnels, C., E. Panagopolou, P. Murray, G. Tsartsidou, S. Allen, K. Mullen, and E. Tourloukis 2005 A Mesolithic Landscape in Greece: Testing a Site-Location Model in the Argolid at Kandia. Journal of Mediterranean Archaeology 18:259–85.

Sahlins, M. 1968 Notes on the Original Affluent Society. *In* Man the Hunter. R. Lee and I. DeVore, eds. Pp. 85–9. Chicago: Aldine Press.

Skeates, R. 1999 Unveiling Inequality: Social Life and Social Change in the Mesolithic and Early Neolithic of East-Central Italy. *In* Social Dynamics of the Prehistoric Central Mediterranean. R. Tykot, J. Morter, and J. Robb, eds. Pp. 15–45. Specialist Studies on the Mediterranean 3. London: Accordia/UCL.

Skeates, R. 2003 Radiocarbon Dating the Mesolithic-Neolithic Transition in Italy. *In* The Widening Harvest. The Neolithic Transition in Europe: Looking Back, Looking Forward. A. Ammerman and P. Biagi, eds. Pp. 157–87. Boston: Archaeological Institute of America.

Smith, B. 1995 The Emergence of Agriculture. New York: Scientific American Library.

Srejovic, D. 1972 Europe's First Monumental Sculpture: New Discoveries at Lepenski Vir. London: Thames & Hudson.

Tauber, H. 1981 ^{13}C Evidence for Dietary Habits of Prehistoric Man in Denmark. Nature 292:332–3.

Terrell, J., and P. Stewart 1996 The Paradox of Human Population Genetics at the End of the Twentieth Century. Reviews in Anthropology 26:13–33.

Thomas, J. 2003 Thoughts on the 'Repacked' Neolithic Revolution. Antiquity 77:67–74.

Trigger, B. 1989 A History of Archaeological Thought. Cambridge: Cambridge University Press.

Tringham, Ruth 2000 Southeastern Europe in the Transition to Agriculture in Europe: Bridge, Buffer or Mosaic. In Europe's First Farmers. D. Price, ed. Pp. 19–56. Cambridge: Cambridge University Press.

Tylor, E. B. 1865 Researches into the Early History of Mankind and the Development of Civilization. London: John Murray.

Tylor, E. B. 1871 Primitive Culture: Researches into the Development of Mythology, Philosophy, Religion, Art, and Custom (2 vols.). London: John Murray.

Vayson de Pradenne, A. 1935 The World-Wide Expansion of Neolithic Culture. Antiquity 9:305–10.

Verhart, L. 2000 Times Fade Away: The Neolithicization of the Southern Netherlands in an Anthropological and Geographical Perspective (Archaeological Studies, Leiden University 6). Leiden: Faculty of Archaeology, Leiden University.

Voget, F. 1967 Progress, Science, History and Evolution in Eighteenth- and Nineteenth-Century Anthropology. Journal of the History of the Behavioural Sciences 3:132–55.

Whittle, A. 1996 Europe in the Neolithic. Cambridge: Cambridge University Press.

Woodman, P. 2000 Getting Back to Basics: Transitions to Farming in Ireland and Britain. In Europe's First Farmers. D. Price, ed. Pp. 219–59. Cambridge: Cambridge University Press.

Zvelebil, M. 1986a Mesolithic Prelude and Neolithic Revolution. In Hunters in Transition. M. Zvelebil, ed. Pp. 5–15. Cambridge: Cambridge University Press.

Zvelebil, M., ed. 1986b Hunters in Transition. Cambridge: Cambridge University Press.

Zvelebil, M. 1989 On the Transition to Farming in Europe, or What Was Spreading with the Neolithic: A Reply to Ammerman (1989). Antiquity 63:379–83.

Zvelebil, M. 1996 Farmers, Our Ancestors and the Identity of Europe. In Cultural Identity and Archaeology: The Construction of European Communities. P. Graves-Brown, S. Jones, and C. Gamble, eds. Pp. 145–66. London: Routledge.

Zvelebil, M. 1998 What's in a Name: The Mesolithic, the Neolithic, and Social Change and the Mesolithic-Neolithic Transition. In Understanding the Neolithic of North-Western Europe. M. Edmonds and C. Richards, eds. Pp. 1–36. Glasgow: Cruithne Press.

Zvelebil, M. 2000 The Social Context of the Agricultural Transition in Europe. In Archaeo-genetics: DNA and the Population Prehistory of Europe. C. Renfrew and K. Boyle, eds. Pp. 57–79. Cambridge: McDonald Institute Monographs.

Zvelebil, M. 2002 The Invention of Hunter-Gatherers in Seventeenth-Century Europe? A Comment on Mark Pluciennik. Archaeological Dialogues 9.2:123–9.

Zvelebil, M. 2004 Who Were We 6000 Years Ago? In Search of Prehistoric Identities. In Traces of Ancestry: Studies in Honour of Colin Renfrew. M. Jones, ed. Pp. 41–60. Cambridge: McDonald Institute for Archaeological Research.

Zvelebil, M., R. Dennell, and L. Domanska, eds. 1998 Harvesting the Sea, Farming the Forest: The Emergence of Neolithic Societies in the Baltic Region. Sheffield: Sheffield Academic Press.

Zvelebil, M., and P. Rowley-Conwy 1984 Transition to Farming in Northern Europe: A Hunter-Gatherer Perspective. Norwegian Archaeological Review 17(2):104–28.

I (b)
The Celts as 'Grand Narrative'

John Collis

Introduction

The trend in the last decade or two of the twentieth century has been away from the 'big picture' to detailed local studies, the world 'as lived' by individuals and small groups, an approach often labelled 'Post-Processual' or 'Post-Modernist'. This has led to detailed analysis of the structure and layout of settlements and the processes of deposition, especially where these can be related to belief systems or the way in which ancient peoples may have perceived themselves and their environment. Though these matters are clearly vitally important not only in themselves, but also in terms of how they fundamentally affect our understanding of the nature of the archaeological record (what is, or is not, buried in such a way that much later we archaeologists can find and interpret it), nonetheless there were wider processes going on which affected these often very different societies and linked them into wider networks – local, regional even pan-European – and it is essential to attempt to document and understand these processes as well. Why, at certain periods of time, do we get similar types of monument such as hill-forts and oppida occurring over wide areas of central and western Europe? Why at certain periods are there fashions in burial rite, in decoration of ornaments or ceramic styles which are widely distributed, or, conversely, why at other periods is there considerable regional variation (e.g. pottery styles in southern Britain during the Middle Iron Age)? Why is there similarity of languages (Celtic, Germanic, Iberian), and what dictated their boundaries?

Several explanations have been put forward over the last couple of centuries. The linguistic similarities were recognized earliest, starting in the 16th century, and from the 19th century there was the recognition of a large related group of languages found from central Asia and northern India to the western limits of Europe – the Indo-Germanic or Indo-European languages, encompassing several big families: Romance, Germanic, Sanskrit, Celtic, Slav, etc. The relationship between them was likened to a tree, the trunk being the original 'Indo-European' language from which all the others derived by a process of expansion and splitting, the so-called Stammbaum theory. It also gave a relative chronology: Latin was clearly older than the Romance languages such as French, Italian and Spanish which were derived from it.

In the 19th century languages were assumed to correlate with 'Races', and these races were in turn assumed by many scholars also to be physically distinctive, distinguishable especially from the shapes of their skulls (craniology). From the mid-19th century archaeological criteria were added in the form of art styles, burial rites, ceramic and metal types, culminating in the concept of the 'Culture Group' as defined by Gustaf Kossinna and Gordon Childe, and it is to this category of explanation that the archaeological 'Celts' belong. For the pioneers of prehistory, Culture History (i.e. the History of 'Cultures') was the primary aim of the subject; as Hans-Jürgen Eggers, the major critic of Kossinna wrote: 'Prehistory would cease to be an historical science if it were to stop its continuous attempt to solve the problems of ethnic meaning' (1959:200; translation: author). For Childe one of the major themes of prehistory was the study of the interplay between these 'Culture Groups' or 'Cultures' as he more commonly called them, their expansion and contraction, and these 'Cultures' he equated with 'peoples'. But there was also 'progress', the adoption of new technologies or economic and social forms (e.g. metalworking, urbanization) which generally emanated out from areas of higher civilization in the Near East (*ex oriente lux*), under the all-embracing term of 'diffusion'.

In the 1960s this concept of diffusion was often rejected, and new models developed to explain the exchange of ideas, such as 'peer polity' interaction or trade and exchange. This was especially invoked for the Neolithic and Bronze Age (e.g. the appearance of megalithic tombs or of copper working). For the Iron Age, though such models were useful and were adopted, the traditional models continued to be employed, in part because there was plentiful historical evidence for migration (Celts) and colonization (Greeks and Phoenicians), or of military expansion (Persians, Romans), and also, because of the tighter historically based chronologies, diffusion could be clearly demonstrated, for instance in the adoption of iron working or coinage, or the process of 'orientalizing' in art styles, all genuinely *ex oriente lux*. But what does 'diffusion' actually mean? It is in fact merely a descriptive term, and offers no explanation. A number of different mechanisms can be invoked for the spread of orientalizing: movement of craftsmen (Greece); colonization (Phoenicians and Greeks); trade (central Italy, central Europe, Iberia); local emulation of prestige goods (Situla and La Tène Art). But even this does not explain what traits may be accepted, or rejected, or whether we are looking merely at surface change or more fundamental changes within society. The composite animals such as the sphinx, the winged horse or the chimera introduced by orientalizing played important roles in Greek foundation myths. But especially for the Iron Age we also cannot assume a unidirectional flow of ideas, nor a single locus of innovation, indeed cultural manifestations may have multiple origins, very much like the Wellen (wave) theory for linguistic innovations (Mallory 1989).

The Celts

All these models are applicable to the Celts. The historical migrations of the Celts into northern Italy and Asia Minor are well documented, and this migration model has been used to explain the presence of Celtici and Celtiberians in Iberia, and Celtic languages in central Europe, Iberia, Britain and Ireland. The orientalizing of art styles in the 5th century, producing 'Celtic' or 'La Tène' art, is seen as a local imitation of classical Greek and Etruscan prototypes which arrived via trade into eastern France and southern Germany, and this art was then 'diffused' to Ireland and Bulgaria, to northern Italy and Denmark. Many local versions of weapons, ornaments and ceramic styles were developed, some of which remained highly localized in their distribution, but others of which achieved wide distributions across Europe. For instance, the development from the Early to the Middle La Tène brooch is typified by the foot being bound on to the bow, and in the Late La Tène it was cast on. These features were recognized by Tischler as early as 1885, and ever since have formed the basic chronology for the La Tène period from Britain to Romania, simply because they were so widespread.

The picture of the Celts that has been disseminated in a large number of books in the 20th century consists of a number of elements. Ultimately the existence of the Celts is derived from a number of mentions and descriptions by ancient authors between the 6th century BC and the 5th century AD, but with a continuity along the Atlantic coast in Brittany, Wales, Ireland and western Scotland into modern times. The Celts are primarily defined by their languages, a part of the wider group of Indo-European languages which derive from eastern Europe or Asia Minor. When the language group was disseminated and when the Celtic languages became differentiated from neighbouring languages such as Germanic and Italic is still a matter of debate; Colin Renfrew (1991) links it with the spread of agriculture in the 6th–5th millennia; linguists generally date it to the Chalcolithic starting in the 3rd millennium BC with the Celts arriving in their present location during the Iron Age (Mallory 1989). Since then the Celts have gradually been 'pushed' westwards by later invaders, by Romans and peoples of Germanic stock. The post-Roman Irish, Scots Gaelic, Welsh and Bretons and their descendants are seen as preserving the culture of their continental ancestors wiped out by the Roman and Germanic expansions, in the form of the language, social structure, 'spirit', art and literature (e.g. the heroic poetry of Ireland).

Archaeologists assign a particular culture group to the Ancient Celts, the La Tène Culture, with a distinctive material culture and art. The origin of both is considered to lie in the Champagne area of northern France, the hill ranges of the Eifel and the Hunsrück on either side of the Mosel and the central Rhine, and the upper Danube, a river whose source, according to Herodotus, lay in the territory of the Celts. In these areas, and in parts of Bavaria, Bohemia and Austria there is considerable continuity from the late Hallstatt Culture of the 6th century. This core area is depicted on most maps as the origin of the Celts from which they expanded by migration, taking with them their La Tène Culture to Spain, Italy, Asia Minor, western France, Britain and Ireland (Figures 1.1 and 1.2).

This is the now generally accepted view of the Celts, but in almost every aspect it can be questioned if not demolished on theoretical, methodological and factual grounds, and I shall try to describe these new arguments in the rest of this chapter, summarizing the views I have argued in greater detail in my recent book and elsewhere (Collis 2003; 2004; forthcoming).

The Modern, or 'Secondary' Celts

One problem in studying the Ancient Celts is that they are interpreted through the lens of the Modern Celts, and modern concepts are imposed on the ancient population, for instance in the definition of the Celts as a people who speak, or whose

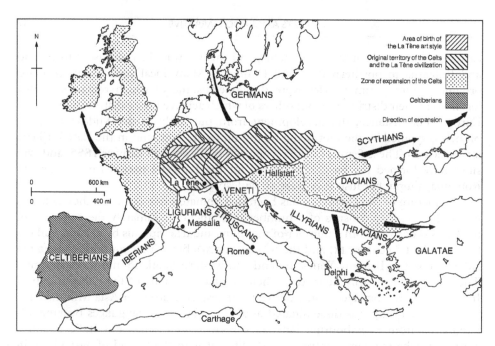

Figure 1.1 The origin and expansion of the Celts. This is the most widely produced map, and has appeared in various forms in the last half century, with variations especially in the way in which Britain and Ireland are treated. See also Figure 1.7 (Source: Megaw and Megaw 1989)

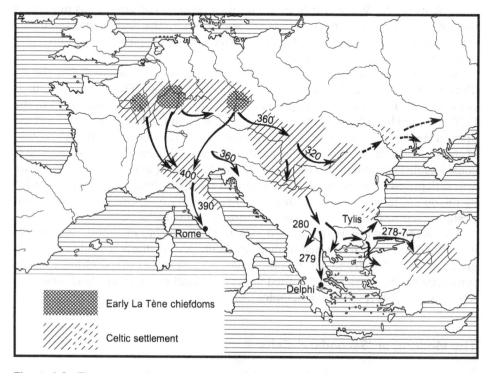

Figure 1.2 This version of the origin and expansion of the Celts first appeared in James 1993, and later in Cunliffe 1997. It is based on archaeological evidence, and largely ignores the historical sources such as Livy (Source: Cunliffe 1997)

recent ancestors spoke, a Celtic language. In fact we are dealing with two very different groups of Celts, whose links with one another are fairly tenuous. Firstly they are divided by a gulf of over 1,000 years. Between the last mention in the 5th–early 6th centuries AD in authors such as Sidonius Apollinaris and Isidore of Seville and their rediscovery in the Renaissance in the 16th century, the name 'Celt' virtually disappears, with authors either referring to specific tribal names (e.g. Bede refers to the Morini, and Geoffrey of Monmouth to the Allobroges), or using the cognate term of the Galli both for the ancient inhabitants of Gaul and their descendants who became the French nation. They are also divided geographically, with almost no overlap except in Brittany and perhaps Galicia (Figure 1.3), and there the populations are usually interpreted as descended from Late or Post-Roman immigrants from the British Isles.

The 16th century saw the dissemination of Greek and Latin texts, many recently rediscovered, and made widely available through the adoption of the printing press. But at the same time the feudal basis of medieval Europe had started crumbling, with the rise of a new class of small landowners and merchants, and the emphasis of historical interest started shifting from the genealogy of the noble families to the origins of peoples and the constitutional basis of the developing nation states. Though sociologists argue that the rise of the nation state is primarily a feature of the 18th century, many elements already existed in the 16th century, for instance

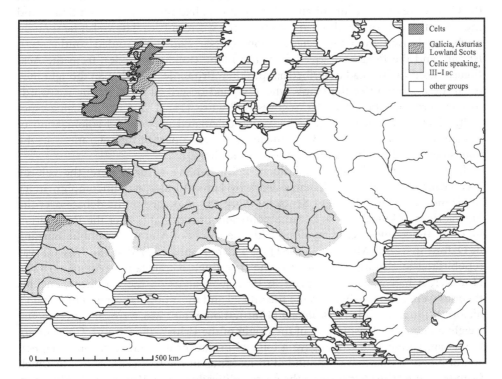

Figure 1.3 Areas occupied by the Modern or 'Secondary' Celts, compared with the earlier distribution of Celtic languages. The distribution of the Modern Celts is based on the location and post-Roman colonization of the Celtic-speaking peoples of the British Isles, though the status of the Lowland Scots and the Galicians of northern Spain is ambiguous. Note the contrast with Figure 1.8 (Source: the author)

Shakespeare's evocation of the English (and Welsh) in his play Henry V, and Ferguson (1998) has similarly argued for a sense of Scottishness perhaps as early as the 15th century, amalgamating different ethnic groups and kingdoms: the Picts; the Scots from Ireland; the Norse in the western and northern isles; and English and British speakers in the south.

It is precisely in Scotland that we find the first evocation of the Celts as ancestral to the modern nations, specifically the Irish and Scots. The Scottish scholar, playwright and politician George Buchanan, in his book *De Rerum Scoticarum Historia* (1582), in true Renaissance tradition rejected the medieval myths which derived the Britons from the Trojan Brutus, and the Irish from the Greek Gaythelos and the Egyptian princess Scota, and he looked for a more logical origin for the inhabitants of the British Isles and Ireland using the historical evidence of the Latin and Greek sources (Collis 1999; MacNeill 1913–14). He argued for an origin of the pre-Roman British in France, Iberia and the Baltic, mainly on the evidence of shared place names: the Roman town names ending in -dunum, -durum, -briga and -magus which he recognized as being cognate to words found in Scots Gaelic. He was also the first to claim in print that there was a group of related languages which included Irish, Welsh and Scots Gaelic which derived from the languages spoken by the Ancient Britons and the Gauls. He termed these languages 'Gallic', with Celtic, Belgic and Britannic dialects, and contrasted them with the Germanic- and Latin-based groups of languages, the first such distinction ever made. For him the Celts were only the inhabitants of Ireland who had immigrated from Spain, and their Scottish off-spring who had colonized the Western Isles. The Welsh he thought might be derived from the Belgae whom Caesar said had invaded southeastern Britain, and the Picts he derived from the Baltic (following Bede), from the Aestiones whom Tacitus had described as speaking 'Britannice'; Buchanan thought they might be a remnant of the Gauls who Livy had described as migrating eastwards to the Hercynian Forest under Segovesus (Figure 1.4). Using the evidence especially of Irish and Scottish genealogies, he calculated the original colonization of Britain to be around the 4th–3rd centuries BC, and so part of the migrations of the Gauls described by Livy and other ancient authors.

It is a matter of debate how influential Buchanan's writings were; the volume was recalled soon after Buchanan's death by James VI as it was uncomplimentary to his mother, Mary Queen of Scots; his work was also used in the debate over the 'divine right of kings' and so became politically unacceptable after the Restoration in 1660. Indeed were chosen, along with the works of Milton, for public burning in Oxford in 1683 (McFarlane 1981). It was not until 1827 that the *Historia* was republished in Britain, and this was the first English translation (Aikman 1827). However, it had remained in print in Protestant areas on the continent, and his theories were cited in what became the official and most popular version of Britain's history, William Camden's *Britannia* (1586), though his ideas were only given equal weight alongside other theories of the origin of the British: the Cimbri, Cimmerian, Gomerian connection which gave a biblical origin through Gomer, son of Japhet, son of Noah (a link first propounded in Josephus in the first century AD, to which Camden added the Cymry); and the more politically correct Brutus myth. However, the well-known reference to the Celtic origin of the Scots mentioned by the Reverend Donald Macqueen, a priest on Skye, and recorded in James Boswell's description of Samuel Johnson's visit to the Hebrides in 1782, comes in a context where Buchanan's work was being discussed, indeed venerated (Pottle and Bennett

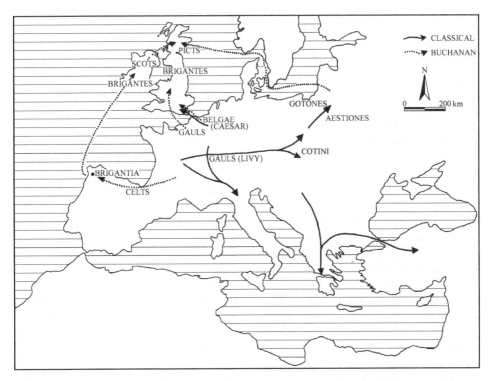

Figure 1.4 A reconstruction of the migrations recorded by Livy and of the original settlement of the British Isles, based on the writing of George Buchanan (1582) (Source: Collis 1999)

1936). But Camden himself never used the world 'Celt'; he always wrote of the 'Ancient Britons'.

In Britain the Celts did not reappear in the literature until the beginning of the 18th century. It derived from two disparate sources. The first was a discussion of the Druids and the interpretation of the prehistoric monuments such as Stonehenge and Avebury; the second was linguistic. In 1703 the Abbé Paul-Yves Pezron published a book on the origins of the Breton language (he was himself a Breton), which he considered to be the last remnant of the language of the Celtae described by Julius Caesar (Brittany fell into the area defined by Caesar as Celtic Gaul). He believed that the language of the Celts was one of the original languages from the Tower of Babel, and, like Camden, he associated it with the original colonization of Europe by Japhet and his descendants, and specifically correlated the Gomerians with the Celts. He noted similarities of certain words between the Celtic, Germanic, Latin and Greek languages, and suggested that these were due to periods when these other nations had been dominated by the Celts during their gradual migration towards the west. Pezron's book caused considerable interest in Britain, as he recognized that Welsh was closely linked with Breton, so he considered them as Celts as well, though he makes no mention of Irish or Scots Gaelic. His work was quickly translated into English, and so became widely available (Jones 1705). He is really the first author to consider that the Celts were people who spoke a Celtic language, though most linguists would now consider his basic premise was wrong, and that Breton, rather than being a survival of the language of the Celts, was rather a British language introduced in the Late or Post-Roman period from Cornwall and Wales (Giot et al. 2003; Snyder 2003).

One person who was profoundly influenced by Pezron's writing was Edward Lhuyd, though they never met, and Lhuyd complains that Pezron had failed to respond to his letters (Gunther 1945). He had worked on the 1695 'Gibson' version of Camden's *Britannia*, and so one assumes he knew something of Buchanan's work as well, though he never cites it. As a result of his efforts to update Camden he decided to carry out a survey of the archaeological monuments and the early languages of Britain though, due to his early death, only the survey of the languages was published, in 1707. In it he compared the vocabulary of Irish, Scots Gaelic, Welsh, Cornish and Breton, and recognized their common source and their similarity with other languages such as Latin and Greek, a comparative study which was not to be superseded for over a century. His introduction is not entirely clear, but he cites Pezron's work, and decided to follow him and to call the language group 'Celtic' even though he recognized that this should properly only be applied to the continent. He also made the division between 'C' ('Q')-Celtic which encompassed Irish and Sots Gaelic, and which he suggested had been introduced by 'Goidels', and a 'Brythonic' 'P-Celtic' which included Welsh, Cornish and Breton. Lhuyd is thus the first person to use the term 'Celtic' to encompass all the early languages and peoples of Britain, and this was to have a profound effect on later developments.

Interest in the Druids had been rekindled during the Renaissance (Owen 1962), but it was also not until the end of the 17th and the beginning of the 18th century that they were linked with the megalithic monuments of western Europe. In 1689 John Aubrey had written a work assigning the construction of Stonehenge to the Druids, and though this was not published, his ideas were incorporated into the 1695 version of Camden's *Britannia*. In 1723 we find the first two authors who put together the Druids, the megalithic monuments and the Celts: Henry Rowlands in his *Mona Insula Restaurata*; and William Stukeley in his unpublished work *The Antient Temples of the Druids* (Piggott 1985). Interest in the Druids had also been stimulated in the religious debate generated by the Deists, and John Toland had planned to write a book attacking the Druids from a Deist perspective (Huddleston 1814). Stukeley explicitly states that one of his aims in studying Avebury and Stonehenge was 'to attack the Deists from an unexpected quarter'. In his later works (1740; 1743) Stukeley drops references to the Celts, and usually uses the term 'Druidic' to describe the monuments. Thus, by the mid-18th century there was a general acceptance in academic circles that the early inhabitants of Britain were 'Celts' though it had not yet been popularized.

Celtomania in the Late 18th and Early 19th Centuries

Though the Anglo-Saxon scholar Bede had made a clear distinction between the Germanic and the native British populations in the 6th and 7th centuries in Britain, and the early language classifications by Buchanan and by Scaliger (1610) had distinguished between Gallic and Germanic languages, the actual relationship between the Celts and the Germans was confused, based largely on conjecture on the vague biblical references. Thus, in his *Histoire des Celtes* (1740) Simon Pelloutier suggested that the Germani were descended from the Celtae, and this is also found in Mallet's *Northern Antiquities* (Blackwell 1898), translated and published in English by Bishop Thomas Percy in 1770 (Kidd 1999). It was in his Preface to the volume that Percy elaborated on what for him and Evan Evans (Lewis 1957) were the clear contrasts between the languages and the customs of the Celts and of the Goths, a distinction which was generally taken up in Britain.

The second half of the 18th century also saw the rise of Romanticism and Primitivism, and the Celts formed an important component of these fashions. In Britain it was in part triggered by Thomas Gray's poem 'The Bard' published in 1757, lamenting the loss of the Welsh bardic tradition under the English onslaught under Edward III. This proved a popular theme in art, with pictures of a lone bard playing his harp against a backdrop of stone circles or megalithic tombs, with the advancing English army in the background (Smiles 1994). More specifically 'Celtic' were the poems of the Ossian cycle ('Fingal', 'Temora') published by James Macpherson in 1760–3, which, whatever their status (collations, fabrications), achieved European-wide fame for the literature of the Irish and Gaelic world, and even to the development of a tourist industry encompassing the Hebrides, of which Felix Mendelssohn's Hebrides Overture ('Fingal's Cave', 1832) is a lasting reminder. In the early 19th century this sense of Scottish Celticity was further developed in the novels of Sir Walter Scott such as *Rob Roy* (1817) in which the eponymous hero is specifically referred to as a Celt. Scott is often credited with the invention and popularization of the outward trappings of Scottish culture – the tartan, the kilt and its associated ornaments, (sporrans, penannular brooches, etc.), and the bagpipes – ideas which were finally given the seal of approval by the British royal family under George IV and Victoria (Trevor-Roper 1983). The Scottish tradition represents an interesting mixture of features taken over from the politically dominant Lowlands (the church, legal system and especially the English language), and from the 'suppressed' Highland tradition such as poetry, and dress, the romantic aura, and the name of the country (the Scoti were, according to Bede, settlers from Ireland).

A parallel development occurred in Wales, with the increasing concept of 'Welshness', epitomized for instance in the foundation of the Honourable Society of Cymmrodorion in London by Welsh émigrés in 1751, and the promotion of early Welsh literature by collectors of manuscripts such as Evan Evans. But as in Scotland, many of the Welsh traditions were fabrications of the late 18th and early 19th centuries, or at best a revival in a new guise of medieval traditions which had been allowed to lapse. Thus, in 1791 Edward Williams (Iolo Morgannwg) founded the druidical Gorsedd, based on the romantic concept of the bards who had provided the historical record and the poetry in aristocratic courts, but using antiquarian ideas such as stone circles; he too specifically used the term 'Celtic' to describe these developments. In 1819 the Eisteddfod was re-established, and the two traditions were soon linked, proving a strong incentive to the survival of the Welsh language (Morgan 1983).

The reasons for the popularity of a Celtic identity in the late 18th century are not clear (Collis forthcoming). It was a time when the idea of the nation state was developing, and Linda Colley (1992) has claimed that 'Britishness' was based on a combination of anti-French and anti-Catholic sentiment. However, Celticity cuts across this. Not only does it unite a predominantly Catholic Ireland and a French Brittany with strongly Protestant areas, but even among the Protestants there were divisions, between a Presbyterian Scotland and a Methodist Wales. James (1999) has argued that it was a political response by the Scots against the Act of Union in

1707; I have suggested its roots lay in the rise of Romanticism (Collis 2003), not only in Britain, but also in France (e.g. de La Tour d'Auvergne-Corret 1796). Hechter (1975) for more recent times has documented the peripheral nature of these societies and their shared reaction to the centralization of power within the British and French nation states. However, in France the Celts were also seen as a source of unity, with the origin of the state being sought in 'nos ancêtres les Gaulois' as portrayed in Amédée Thierry's influential Histoire des Gaulois (1828). The idea of a Celtic unity was based purely on a scholastic, academic construction, that of a language group, yet within a century this had been translated into a widely held feeling of common empathy between very disparate groups.

Celtic Art and Archaeology

All authors up to the mid-19th century were working on a biblical timescale, so the Celts, Gauls and Britons were seen as the first inhabitants of western Europe with dates for their arrival varying between about 1500 BC (Thierry) and the late first millennium (Buchanan). However, this chronology was under attack from two quarters. Firstly there were developments in Geology, with an increasing recognition of the great antiquity of the world, the occurrence of extinct animals in the deposits and the occasional association of human-made tools with them, culminating in the events of 1859 when not only was the concept of evolution published by Darwin, but the great antiquity of mankind was formally recognized by the scientific world. The second driving force for new ideas was in linguistics, with the identification of the 'Indo-Germanic' languages by Franz Bopp, Jakob Grimm and others. In Europe Basque and Finnish were recognized as non-Indo-European, raising questions about earlier populations and the date of the arrival of the Indo-European languages, of which Celtic formed a major group.

From the 18th century language had been linked with the idea of 'race', so initially it was hoped that the speakers of these different languages might be identifiable from their physical remains, especially the skull, and various attempts were made in Scandinavia and Britain to characterize 'racial groups' during the 19th century (Morse 1999; 2005), though some anthropologists were sceptical about whether this was possible; James Cowles Prichard, for instance, suggested language might be a better indicator as human populations might change their physical characteristics to adapt to changing environments (e.g. develop dark skins as protection against the sun), and he wrote the first book on the Celtic languages, their origin and relationship to other Indo-European languages (Prichard 1831). However, some relative dating was needed for the graves from which the skulls were derived, and this was provided by the Three Age System of Christian Thomsen, first published in 1836, and translated into English in 1848, though writers such as Prichard were using it before this date (discussed in Morse 2005; Prichard 1973). On the evidence of skull shape, craniologists suggested that there was a change from long-headed 'dolichocephalic' to a round-headed 'brachycephalic' population at the beginning of the Bronze Age, and that this marked the arrival of the Celts.

From the 1840s onwards, led by the staff of the British Museum (Samuel Birch, Augustus Wollaston Franks), an alternative way of recognizing racial groups was attempted, through distinctive art styles. Thus, newly discovered objects such as the 'Tara' brooch and the Battersea shield were termed 'Celtic', but it was not until 1856, in a lecture in Dublin, that the characteristics of this art style were first defined by John Kemble. His death soon after prevented him publishing his work, but it was used by William Wilde in his description of the objects in the collections of the Royal Irish Academy (1861), and was finally published by Franks in 1863 (Kemble et al. 1863), and named by him 'Late Keltic Art'. Franks was able to parallel the British finds with objects on the continent, notably with the newly discovered finds from La Tène, and the concept was further developed by British authors, especially in the first book on Celtic art by J. Romilly Allen, published in 1904.

It is important to note that the nomenclature and definition of the art style as 'Celtic' was based on the presumption that the early inhabitants of Britain were Celts. No continental author used the term in this way, or applied it to the ancient historical Celts, until Joseph Déchelette in 1914, and he used Allen and Franks as his major sources. However he was able to draw on other developments on the continent to produce the first recognizably modern definition of the Celts incorporating historical, linguistic, art historical and archaeological sources, as well as concepts such as the archaeological 'Culture Group' ('les civilisations d'Hallstatt et La Tène'), and a firm chronology. The chronology for the Iron Age had been developed rapidly in the last quarter of the 19th century, from the first realization that the two stylistic groups identified by Hans Hildebrand in 1874, of Hallstatt and La Tène, in fact represented a chronological succession. This was followed in 1885 by Otto Tischler's division of the La Tène period into Early, Middle and Late on the basis of the typological development of brooches and scabbards, and later refined and extended by Paul Reinecke's papers in the first decade of the 20th century on both Hallstatt and La Tène chronology in southern Germany, using nomenclature still in use today (Reinecke 1963). Déchelette developed his own chronology, giving it some absolute dates on the basis of the presence of Greek and Etruscan imported vessels in some of the Early La Tène graves. On this evidence he suggested an origin for 'Celtic Art' in the 5th century BC in the zone extending from northern France through the central Rhine and Mosel to Bohemia (Figure 1.5).

For his linguistic and historical interpretation Déchelette relied heavily on the work of Henri d'Arbois de Jubainville, first director of Celtic Studies in the Sorbonne (Collis 2004). He had envisaged a series of 'Empires' in the history of human settlement of Europe (he ignored archaeological data which he claimed was outside his competence): a period of cave dwellers, epitomized by the Cyclops Polyphemus; an Iberian empire of hunters and gathers perhaps originating from Atlantis in 6000 BC; Indo-European Ligurians who introduced agriculture around 2000 BC; and the Celts or Gauls who arrived in the later 1st millennium BC. On the evidence of place names he suggested the arrival of Celtic languages in France was relatively late, and that their origin should be sought on the central Rhine–Main area (Figure 1.6); the Germans arrived in historical times. Déchelette translated this into archaeological terms mainly using the evidence of burial rites: crouched inhumation (e.g. beaker burials) for Ligurians; extended inhumation for Celts; and cremation for Germani and Belgae. For the Celts he envisaged an expansion into France in the Iron Age, with the early Celts epitomized by the distribution of Hallstatt inhumation burials from central France to Bohemia (Figure 1.5). The two areas thus defined by Déchelette for the origin of the Celts and for the origin of La Tène art reappear on most of the modern maps of the origin and of expansion the Celts (e.g. Figure

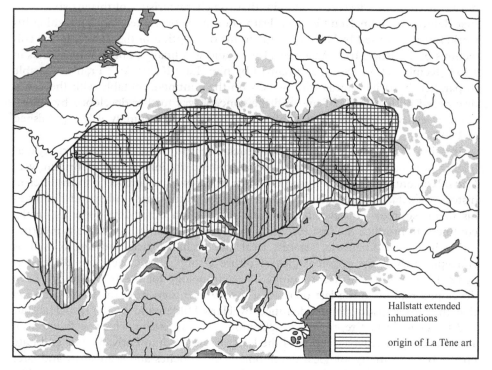

Legend:
- IIIIII Hallstatt extended inhumations
- ≡ origin of La Tène art

Figure 1.5 The homeland of the Celts (areas of Hallstatt inhumation burials) and the origin area of La Tène art, a reconstruction based on the writings of Joseph Déchelette (1914). Note how this reappears in Figure 1.1 (Source: the author)

1.1), a map which appeared in its earliest version in Aymard 1954 (Figure 1.7). In recent years it has been reproduced in various forms (with numerous variations on how to deal with Britain and Ireland), even though on methodological grounds we would no longer accept the simplistic interpretations of d'Arbois de Jubainville and Déchelette, indeed they can be shown to be factually incorrect – the recently discovered cemetery at Mont Beuvray, excavated by Jon Dunkley and Jean-Loup Flouest, in the heart of Celtic territory consists entirely of cremations!

The Celtic Migrations

A major aspect of the 'grand narrative' of the Celts are the historical migrations: the Celtic settlement in Spain; the invasion of northern Italy culminating in the attack on Rome around 390 BC; the attacks on Delphi and Olbia; the settlement of the Galatians in central Asia around Ankara in 287 BC; and the invasions of the Belgae into northern Gaul and southern Britain. Early authors such as Thierry who believed the Celts or Gauls were the original inhabitants of western Europe assumed the homeland of the Celts to be in Gaul, and that the tribes mentioned by Livy as taking part in the invasion of Italy were already in position (i.e. in central Gaul) in the 5th century BC, and that the more precise information from the 1st century, in Caesar, Strabo, and later Ptolemy, allows us to locate these tribes more precisely. However, this view came under attack in the late 19th century mainly from d'Arbois

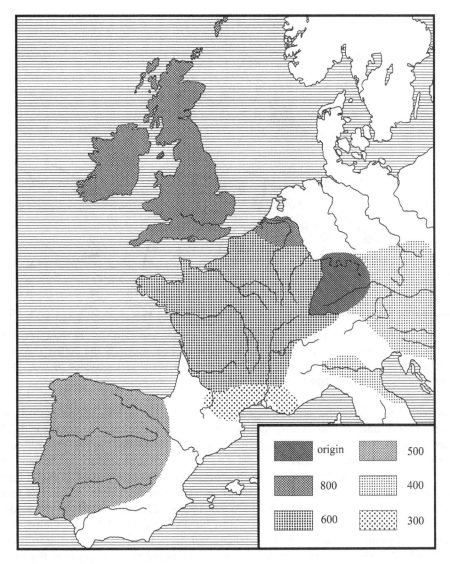

Figure 1.6 The origin and expansion of the Celts in western Europe, reconstructed from the theories of Henri d'Arbois de Jubainville (1903, 1904) (Source: Collis 2004)

de Jubainville and Alexandre Bertrand (1889, the first systematic attempt to link archaeology with the historical sources), both of whom argued for an origin of the Celts (or in the case of Bertrand, the Gauls) east of the Rhine, a view which has largely survived to the modern day.

In 1870–1 Gabriel de Mortillet and Emile Désor argued that the objects in the burials from the Etruscan town of Marzabotto were most closely paralleled in the burials from northern France and from the finds from La Tène, and so were evidence of the Gauls, and specifically the Senones, who had invaded Italy in the early 4th century BC. The date of the invasion is ambiguous; the text of Livy implies an early date, around 600 BC, while Polybius suggests a date around 400. Bertrand linked the arrival of the Celts with the Hallstatt period burials in northern Italy,

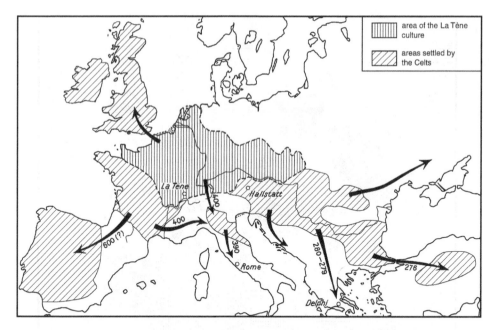

Figure 1.7 This is the earliest map to appear of the origin and expansion of the Celts, and is the source for many later maps such as that in Figure 1.1; note especially the outline area of the Celtiberians in Spain, though this has little to do with the actual area occupied by them, but it appears in all subsequent maps (Source: Aymard 1954)

but with Déchelette the emphasis was placed back on the La Tène period, and Livy's earlier date has since largely been ignored in the archaeological world. The view that Hallstatt and La Tène could be viewed not merely as chronological periods, but also as 'Culture Groups' had been developing during the late 19th century, and in 1911 the idea that such groups could be interpreted in racial terms was firmly advocated by Gustaf Kossinna in respect of the Germans (a view taken up more generally by Gordon Childe in the 1920s). Déchelette was never so dogmatic with his *Civilisation de La Tène*, and he distinguished between Celtic, Germanic and Insular versions of the La Tène culture. However, under the influence of Childe and his contemporaries, during the course of the 20th century the racial/ethnic interpretation of La Tène became much stronger, and in central Europe and elsewhere the appearance of a 'La Tène Culture' and 'flat inhumation cemeteries' was directly correlated with the 'arrival' of the Celts and the Celtic language (e.g. Filip 1960; Kruta 2000; Szabó 1992). This 'Culture-Historical' interpretation is fundamental to most of the recent surveys of the Celts (e.g. Cunliffe 1997; Haywood 2004; James 1993; Kruta et al. 1991; Powell 1958), though from the 1960s in other areas of prehistoric studies it has been generally abandoned as methodologically unsound.

The Ancient or 'Primary' Celts

When reviewing the evidence for the Ancient Celts, we must remove our preconceptions derived from more recent developments, especially a definition of the Celts which relies on linguistic and archaeological data. As we have seen much of this is based on presumptions which have proved false; that Breton is a survival of the ancient language of the historical Celts (making the term 'Celtic' for the language group a misnomer). 'Celtic' art is also a misnomer, based on the false assumption that the ancient inhabitants of Britain were Celts, indeed we can demonstrate that it was not employed by all peoples who spoke a Celtic language or may have considered themselves to be Celtic (e.g. in the Iberian peninsula), nor was it confined to Celtic speakers – it was employed by Iberian speakers in southern France (e.g. Ensérune), and probable Germanic speakers in Denmark (Kaul 1991). There was also no continuity between the ancient and the modern Celts – there is a thousand year gap when the term disappeared, and there is virtually no geographical overlap between the two groups. The simple problem is that we do not know how the Ancient Celts were defined (linguistically, geographically, culturally), and it is also clear that different authors in the ancient world employed the term 'Celt' in different ways, either as something very general for all the people who lived in western Europe, or for very specific groups who lived within well-defined boundaries. There are also differences in the way authors used the cognate words Galli and Galatai; usually they are simply equated with Celts, but in some authors they are used to contrast two different groups.

We must also not be misled by the bias of deposition in the archaeological record. The areas defined by Caesar as the territory of the Celts in Gaul do not have rich burials at any period during the Iron Age (e.g. the territories of the Arverni, the Aedui, the Sequani in the modern Auvergne, Burgandy and Franche Comte), and the areas with rich burials especially in the 5th century and the 2nd–1st century are in the Belgic, not the Celtic areas, even though the ancient sources tell us the latter were much richer. The area of the Mosel which is often claimed as the origin of 'Celtic Art' and of the Celts is in fact nowhere stated to be Celtic in the ancient sources; Caesar is ambiguous, and Tacitus says the Treveri thought of themselves as Germani, though they spoke a Celtic language. The only reason that it may be claimed as the origin of the art style is because we have evidence from the rich burials, whereas Celtic central France is not considered simply because there are no rich burials, and so no art objects. In fact the richest settlement in terms of the Mediterranean imports in the 5th century BC outside the Mediterranean area is Bourges, though the burial evidence is not especially rich; it reminds us of the importance assigned to the Bituriges, after whom Bourges is named, in the version of the Celtic migrations given by Livy.

We only know of the Celts and their migrations because we have the written sources, and if we are to locate the Celts, we need to go back to these, but be aware of their bias and ambiguity. Some authors were better informed than others, either because they themselves were Celtic (Martial, Pompeius Trogus, Sidonius Apollinaris), came from or near Celtic areas (Pliny, Livy and perhaps Tacitus), or travelled extensively in Celtic areas (Poseidonius, Caesar). The early sources are vague or partial in their evidence; much has been made, for instance, of the periplous or coastal voyaging manuals which do, or do not, mention, Celts (Himilco, Scylax, etc.), but they do not tell us what was happening inland (the lack of mention of the Volcae in southern Gaul, for instance, was perhaps because they did not inhabit the coastal areas). Geographical knowledge could be limited – when Herodotus talks about the Danube rising in the territory of the Celts, did he mean north of the Alps, or, as seems likely because of his mention of

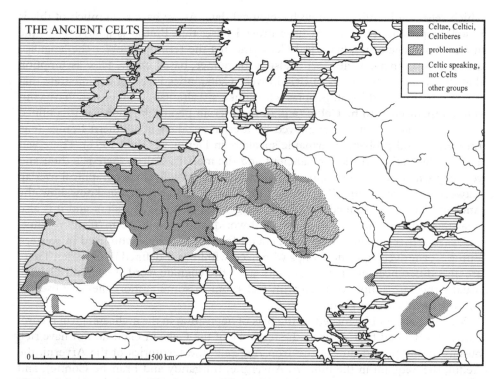

THE ANCIENT CELTS

	Celtae, Celtici, Celtiberes
	problematic
	Celtic speaking, not Celts
	other groups

0 |_____| 500 km

Figure 1.8 Areas occupied by the Ancient Celts, Celtici and Celtiberians, based on an interpretation of the classical written sources, and compared with areas where Celtic languages are likely to have been spoken. Note especially the category of ancient peoples who spoke Celtic languages but were not considered to be Celts (Vettones, Lusitanians, Ligurians, Belgae, Britanni) (Source: the author)

Pyrene, did he, like Aristotle, believe the source of the Danube lay in the Pyrenees? In fact, the evidence we have from these early sources is just as consistent with the Celts being where they were five centuries later, that is in central France and parts of Spain, than in southern Germany and northern France as argued by d'Arbois de Jubainville and others, and a view which appears in all the 'grand narratives' of the Celts.

I have shown the location of the Celts and related groups based on the written sources (Figure 1.8), though it inevitably contains many value judgements on what weight can be placed on specific sources, or how to deal with vague statements. However, it does change the emphasis from northern France and Germany as the territory of the Celts back to central and western France and central Spain. It also breaks the links between historical Celts and the so-called West Hallstatt and La Tène cultures (not that these are concepts which I find particularly useful). In some cases, as in Asia Minor, we can still reasonably make the link between the arrival of people from western Europe (the Galatians) with the appearance in that area of a Celtic language and La Tène artefact types (brooches, weapons, etc.) which are foreign to the local societies. In other areas such as the Hungarian Plain the evidence is more ambiguous, but perhaps new techniques such as isotope analysis may be able to tell us more about the movements of groups and individuals during the Iron Age. We should also start posing different questions, for instance, to what extent did new ideas flow between areas which already had linguistic similarities?

In summary, the popular stories of the origins and the spread of the Celts are in fundamental need of revision; we need to shed ourselves of stereotypic preconceptions such as 'Celtic Society', 'warrior societies', etc., and study the historical, linguistic and archaeological sources in a much more critical way. However, it will also be interesting to see how this new critique of the Celts will affect those who nowadays consider themselves to be Celts, or descendants of the Ancient Celts. Is the link with the distant past really important for present ethnic sentiment? The Modern Celts were originally fashioned on academic constructs; will modern academic deconstruction have a comparable effect?

REFERENCES

Aikman, J. 1827 The History of Scotland, translated from the Latin of George Buchanan, with Notes and a Continuation to the Union in the Reign of Queen Anne. Glasgow: Blackie, Fullerton & Co., and Edinburgh: Archibald Fullerton & Co.

Allen, J. R. 1904 Celtic Art in Pagan and Christian Times. London: Methuen and Co. First edition (reprinted by Bracken Books, Studio Editions, London 1993).

Aymard, A. 1954 Les Gaulois. In Histoire Générale des Civilisations, Vol. II, Rome et son Empire. A. Aymard and J. Auboyer, eds. Pp. 51–75. Paris: Presses Universitaires de France.

Bertrand, A. 1889 Archéologie Celtique et Gauloise: mémoires et documents relatifs au premiers temps de notre histoire nationale. Paris: Ernest Leroux.

Blackwell, I. A. 1898 Northern Antiquities translated from the French of M. Mallet by Bishop Percy. London: George Bell and Sons.

Buchanan, G. 1582 Rerum Scoticarum Historia. Edinburgh: Alexander Arbuthnet.

Camden, W. 1586 Britannia. Sive florentissimorum regnorum Angliae, Scotiae, Hiberniae, et Insularum adiacentium ex intima antiquitate Chorographica descriptio, etc. London: Radulphus Newbery.

Camden, W. 1695 Camden's Britannia, newly translated into English; with large additions and improvements. Publish'd by Edmund Gibson. London: A. & J. Churchil.

Colley, L. 1992 Britons: Forging the Nation 1707–1837. Newhaven and London: Yale University Press.

Collis, J. 1999 George Buchanan and the Celts of Britain. In Celtic Connections, Vol. 1. R. Black, W. Gillies, and R. Ó Maolalaigh, eds. Pp. 91–107. Proceedings of the Tenth International Congress of Celtic Studies. East Linton: Tuckwell Press.

Collis, J. 2003 The Celts: Origins, Myths and Inventions. Stroud: Tempus Publishing.

Collis J. 2004 D'Amédée Thierry à Joseph Déchelette: hypothèses du XIXᵉ siècle sur l'arrivée des Celtes en Gaule. In Les Marges de l'Armorique à l'âge du Fer: archéologie et histoire: culture matérielle et sources écrites. B. Mandy and A. de Saulce, eds. Pp. 363–8. XXIIIᵉ Colloque de l'Association française pour l'étude de l'âge du fer, Nantes, Musée Dobrée, 1999. Rennes: Revue archéologique de l'Ouest. Supplément 10.

Collis, J. forthcoming Die Entwicklung des Kelten-Konzepts in Britannien während des 18. Jahrhunderts. Symposium Deutschsprachicher Keltologinnen und Keltologen, Linz 2005.

Cunliffe, B. 1997 The Ancient Celts. Oxford: Oxford University Press.

d'Arbois de Jubainville, H. 1903 Conquéte par les Gaulois de la région située entre le Rhin et l'Atlantique. Revue Celtique 1903:162.

d'Arbois de Jubainville, H. 1904 Les Celtes depuis le Temps les plus anciens jusqu'au l'An 100 avant notre Ère. Paris.

Déchelette, J. 1914 Manuel d'Archéologie Préhistorique, Celtique et Gallo-Romaine. II–3: Deuxième Age du Fer ou Époque de La Tène. Paris: Librairie Alphonse Picard et fils.

de La Tour d'Auvergne-Corret, T. M. 1796 Origines Gauloises, celles de plus anciens peuples de l'Europe.

de Mortillet, G. 1870–1. Les Gaulois de Marzabotto dans l'Apennin. Revue Archéologique 22:288–90.

Eggers, H.-J. 1959 Einführung in die Vorgeschichte. Munich: Piper Verlag.

Ferguson, W. 1998 The Identity of the Scottish Nation. Edinburgh: Edinburgh University Press.

Filip, J. 1960 Keltská Civilizace a její Dědictví (rev. edn. 1963). English translation Celtic Civilisation and its Heritage (1962). Prague: Akademia.

Giot, P.-R., G. Philippe, and B. Merdrignac 2003 The British Settlement of Brittany: The First Bretons in Armorica. Stroud: Tempus Publishing.

Gunther, R. T. 1945 Early Science in Oxford. Vol. XIV. Life and Letters of Edward Lhwyd, Second Keeper of the Musæum Ashmoleanum. Oxford: privately printed.

Haywood, J. 2004 The Celts: Bronze Age to New Age. Harlow: Pearson Education.

Hechter, M. 1975 Internal Colonialism: The Celtic Fringe in British Nation Development 1536–1966. London: Routledge and Kegan Paul.

Hildebrand, H. 1874 Sur les commencements de l'Âge du fer en Europe. Congrés Internationale d'Anthropologie et d'Archéologie Préhistorique, Stockholm, pp. 592–601.

Huddleston, R., ed. 1814 A New Edition of Toland's History of the Druids with an Abstract of his Life and Writings. Montrose.

James, S. 1993 Exploring the World of the Celts. London: Thames and Hudson.

James, S. 1999 The Atlantic Celts. London: British Museum Press.

Jones, D. 1705 The Antiquities of Nations; more particularly of the Celtae or Gauls, taken to be originally the same people as our Ancient Britains, by Monsieur Pezron, englished by Mr. Jones. London: S. Ballard.

Kaul, F. 1991 The Ball Torcs. In The Celts V. Kruta, O.-H. Frey, B. Raftery, and M. Szabó, eds. Pp. 540. London: Thames and Hudson.

Kemble, J., A. Wollaston Franks, and R. G. Latham 1863 Horae Ferales. Studies in the Archaeology of the Northern Nations. London: Lovell Read and Co.

Kidd, C. 1999 British Identities Before Nationalism: Ethnicity and Nationhood in the Atlantic World 1600–1800. Cambridge: Cambridge University Press.

Kossinna, G. 1911 Zur Herkunft der Germanen. Zur Methode der Siedlungsarchäologie. Mannus–Bibliothek 6.

Kruta, V. 2000 Les Celtes: histoire et dictionnaire. Manchecourt: Robert Laffont.

Kruta, V., O.-H. Frey, B. Raftery, and M. Szabó, eds. 1991 The Celts. London: Thames and Hudson.

Lewis A. 1957 The Percy Letters: The Correspondence of Thomas Percy and Evan Evans. Louisiana State University Press.

Lhuyd, E. 1707 Archaeologia Britannica, giving some account additional to what has been hitherto publish'd of the Languages, Histories and Customs of the Original Inhabitants of Great Britain, from Collections and Observations in Travels through Wales, Cornwal, Bas-Bretagne, Ireland and Scotland. Oxford: Oxford Theatre.

McFarlane, I. 1981 Buchanan. London: Duckworth.

MacNeill, E. 1913–14 The Re-Discovery of the Celts. The Irish Review: 522–32.

Mallory, J. 1989 In Search of the Indo-Europeans: Language, Archaeology and Myth. London: Thames and Hudson.

Megaw, R., and V. Megaw 1989 Celtic Art, from its Beginnings to the Book of Kells. London: Thames and Hudson.

Morgan, P. 1983 From a Death to a View: The Hunt for the Welsh Past in the Romantic Period. In The Invention of Tradition. E. Hobsbawm and T. Ranger, eds. Pp. 43–100. Cambridge: Cambridge University Press.

Morse, M. 1999 Craniology and the Adoption of the Three-Age System in Britain. Proceedings of the Prehistoric Society 65:1–17.

Morse, M. 2005 How the Celts Came to Britain: Druids, Ancient Skulls and the Birth of Archaeology. Stroud: Tempus Publishing.

Owen, A. L. 1962 The Famous Druids; A Survey of Three Centuries of English Literature on the Druids. Oxford: Oxford University Press (republished by Sandpiper Press, 1997).

Pelloutier, S. 1740 Histoire des Celts et particulièrement des Gaulois et des Germains depuis les Temps fabuleux jusqu'à la Prise de Rome par les Gaulois. La Haye: Isaac Beauregard.

Percy, T. 1770 Preface. In Northern Antiquities, translated from the French of M. Mallet by Bishop Percy. I. A. Blackwell, ed. 1898. Pp. 1–21. London: George Bell and Sons.

Pezron P.-Y. 1703 Antiquité de la Nation et de la Langue de Celtes autrement appellez Gaulois. Paris.

Piggott, S. 1985 William Stukeley: An Eighteenth-Century Antiquarian. London: Thames and Hudson.

Pottle, F., and C. Bennett 1936 Boswell's Journal of a Tour to the Hebrides with Samuel Johnson LL.D., now first published from the Original Manuscript. London: William Heinemann.

Powell, T. 1958 The Celts. London: Thames and Hudson.

Prichard, J. C. 1831 The Eastern Origin of the Celtic Nations. London: Houlston and Wright, and Bernard Quaritch.

Prichard, J. C. 1973 Researches into the Physical History of Man, edited and with an introductory essay by George Stocking Jnr. Chicago and London: University of Chicago Press.

Reinecke, P. 1963 Mainzer Aufsätze zur Chronologie der Bronze- und Eisenzeit. Bonn: Habelt (reprint of papers 1903–9).

Renfrew, C. 1991 Archaeology and Language: The Puzzle of Indo-European Origins. Harmondsworth: Penguin Books (first published by Jonathan Cape in 1987).

Rowlands, H. 1723 Mona Antiqua Restaurata: an archaeological discourse on the antiquities, natural and historical, of the Isle of Anglesey, the antient seat of the British Druids. Dublin: Robert Owen.

Scaliger, J. 1610 Diatriba de Europaeorum linguis. In Opuscula Varia antehac non edita. Pp. 119–22. Paris.

Snyder, C. 2003 The Britons. Oxford: Blackwell.

Smiles, S. 1994 The Image of Antiquity: Ancient Britain and the Romantic Imagination. New Haven: Yale University Press.

Stukeley, W. 1723 The History of the Temples of the Antient Celts. Unpublished manuscript.

Stukeley, W. 1740 Stonehenge: A Temple Restored to the British Druids. London.

Stukeley, W. 1743 Abury: A Temple of the British Druids. London.

Szabó, M. 1992 Les Celtes de l'Est: le Second Age du fer dans la cuvette des Karpates. Paris: Editions Errance.

Thierry, A. 1828/1857 Histoire des Gaulois. Paris.

Tischler, O. 1885 Ueber Gliederung der La-Tène-Periode und über der Dekorierung der Eisenwaffen in dieser Zeit. Correspondenz-Blatt der Deutschen Gesellschaft für Anthropologie, Ethnologie und Urgeschichte 14:157–61, 172.

Trevor-Roper, H. 1983 The Invention of Tradition: The Highland Tradition of Scotland. In The Invention of Tradition. E. Hobsbawm and T. Ranger, eds. Pp 15–41. Cambridge: Cambridge University Press.

Wilde, W. 1861 A Descriptive Catalogue of the Antiquities of Animal Materials and Bronze in the Museum of the Royal Irish Academy. Dublin: Hodges, Smith and Co.

2

Landscape and Place

Introduction

Landscape archaeology has significantly developed over the past 15 years. We can observe two emerging strands in landscape archaeology, the first the computer-based analysis of site location, the second the analysis of the experiential dimension of sites and monuments in their landscape. The first involves GIS (Geographical Information Systems), in which the landscape location and aspect of sites and monuments can be investigated by the manipulation of digital maps and images. This strand of research perpetuates the kinds of frameworks prominent in the early days of 'New Archaeology' (see for example Renfrew's territorial analyses of megaliths discussed in the introduction). This spatial framework treats space as homogenous and uniform and the analytical focus is upon the investigation of the location and distribution of sites positioned around units of space.

Another significant strand of research has also emerged. This second strand, which we might call experiential landscape archaeology, takes its cue from the philosophical tenets of phenomenology. The major theoretical premise here is that space is never neutral and homogenous, but is instead always meaningful. Rather than thinking of landscapes as territories or units of space, filled with sites located according to the vagaries of topography and economy this strand of research instead treats landscape as made up of a series of meaningfully constituted *places*. Place are made up of the memories and emotions of the people who inhabit them. Rather than sites simply being located in neutral space, places are intimately and meaningfully bound up with the landscape of which they are a part. Landscapes are then experienced bodily, rather than being manipulated on the computer screen. The task of this strand of research is to investigate the dynamic relationship between sites and monuments and their landscape. The two strands of research I have described are often treated as being theoretically opposed, and there is much debate between the proponents of both approaches, though in truth the best landscape archaeology often combines aspects of both. The experiential landscape approach is highlighted in the chapters in this section.

There has been much discussion of the role of monuments in the emergence of the Neolithic (Bradley 1993; Hodder 1990; Tilley 1994), and experiential studies of monument location have emphasized how monuments are built as part of a way of making the landscape meaningful (Cummings and Whittle 2004; Tilley 1994).

Chapter two examines two approaches to place and landscape in Bronze Age Europe, in **Chapter 2 (a)** *Joakim Goldhahn* focuses on the relationship between place and landscape in the construction of Early Bronze Age burial monuments in Scandinavia. In a wide-ranging contribution he discusses the way in which analyses of burial monuments have focused on the dead at the expense of the living, by discussing the materials employed in barrow or cairn construction he argues we can reconsider the role of the living in prehistoric burial rituals. Such an approach allows us to focus on the dynamic interrelationship between monument and landscape.

Goldhahn's contribution is part of a broader tradition of landscape research that has focused upon examining the relationship between sites and monuments and their landscape. One aspect missing from such accounts are the ephemeral activities that take place in the landscape, how do ephemeral activities draw on ideas of place or landscape? In **Chapter 2 (b)** *David Fontijn* redresses that imbalance. He takes a holistic approach to the Later Bronze Age landscapes of the southern Netherlands as he argues that metalwork deposition is related to a coherent organization of the landscape. Here artefact deposition is not so much part of landscape acculturation as a meaningful activity conducted in a highly ritualized and organized cultural landscape. The chapters in this section examine two differing aspects of past landscapes – monuments and artefact deposition – however both emphasize the importance of treating landscapes as meaningfully constituted. The discussion of place and landscape presented here provides an excellent indication of the power of the contextual or interpretative approaches to provide a coherent and satisfying account of past belief systems and behaviour.

REFERENCES

Bradley, R. 1993 Altering the Earth. Edinburgh: Scottish Society of Antiquaries Monograph Series.

Cummings, V., and A. Whittle 2004 Places of Special Virtue: Megaliths in the Neolithic Landscapes of Wales. Oxford: Oxbow.

Hodder, I. 1990 The Domestication of Europe. Oxford: Blackwell.

Tilley, C. 1994 The Phenomenology of Landscape: Places, Paths and Monuments. Oxford: Berg.

2 (a)

From Monuments in Landscape to Landscapes in Monuments: Monuments, Death and Landscape in Early Bronze Age Scandinavia

Joakim Goldhahn

From the Dead to the Living

It is an ontological truism to state that dead people do not build monuments. Despite this fact, most Scandinavian archaeologists have traditionally been preoccupied with the study of dead individuals, their status, rank and gender. This chapter attempts to move beyond this traditional archaeological perspective and argues for the need to broaden our views, by incorporating the living in our studies of mortuary rituals and mortuary monuments. One way of doing this is to place more emphasis on the materiality of mortuary monuments. This chapter will consider these issues in relation to a series of well-known Early Bronze Age mortuary sites from Scandinavia, including Bredarör on Kivik, Sweden; Skelhøj, Denmark; Sagaholm, Sweden and Mjeltehaugen, Norway.

Death may not have been the most important occasion in the life of a person during the Bronze Age, but it is the event that has left the most impression on the archaeologist. Throughout Scandinavia, there are thousands of monuments dating from the Bronze Age. In the south, barrows are most commonly constructed, while further north stone-built cairns are more common (Kristiansen 1987). These monuments have been a continual subject of curiosity; who built these monuments? How was it done? When were they built?

This chapter will not answer these or any related questions, instead I will extend the traditional archaeological discussion and interpretation of monuments in the landscape, to consider questions about how and why different components of landscapes are manifested in the 'mindscape' of the builders of the monument. The need for these perspectives are several and related.

First and foremost, death, as we know it, is less of a problem for the deceased than for the living. Just as Marcel Mauss (1990) describes exchange as a 'total social phenomenon' which encompasses all aspects of social relations, so death may also be described as a 'total social phenomenon', with economic, social, juridical, political, moral, religious, aesthetical and ontological implications (e.g. Bloch and Parry 1987; Cederroth et al. 1988; Humphrey and King 1981; Metcalf and Huntington 1991). These implications rarely consider the deceased person *per se*, but generally focus upon the living.

Even if a person spends all her life preparing herself for the unavoidable end (such as by living a righteous life), the fate of her soul rests on the goodwill of others, to conduct the proper ceremonies and rituals so that the soul can begin its (last) journey in the proper manner (e.g. Oestigaard and Goldhahn 2006). The proper treatment of the dead is exemplified by the erection of the burial monuments of the Scandinavian Early Bronze (1500 to 1100 cal. BC).

Although there are exceptions to the rule, it seems unconvincing to argue that the deceased created the burial monuments of the Early Bronze Age (Fleming 1975; Hyenstrand 1980). Despite this, many archaeologists remain focused on the deceased individual; her gender and status (e.g. Fernståls 2005; Runcis 2002); her grave goods (e.g. Rundkvist 2003); the meaning of different burial traditions (e.g. Andersson 2005; Feldt 2005; Svanberg 2003; Theliander 2005), or the placing of different kinds of monuments in the landscape (e.g. Strömberg 2005; Thedéen 2004; Widholm 1998). Even when burial rituals are discussed more explicitly (e.g. Artelius 2000; Artelius and Svanberg 2005; Gansum 2004; Goldhahn 1999; Kyvik 2005; Nilsson Stutz 2003; Stensköld 2004), interpretations about *if* and *how* the living were manifested in the monuments are not discussed. In this chapter I want to propose that an appreciation of the materiality of monuments is one means by which we may gain an insight into the role of the living in the construction of mortuary monuments (Figure 2.2).

Archaeologists have become increasingly aware that monuments help to shape the perception of landscape (Figure 2.1). Monuments may alter both the form and content of a landscape (e.g. Bergh 1995; Gansum et al. 1996; Tilley 1994). Monuments help to promote and create senses of time, place and notions of identity and belonging (Bradley 1993; 1998). In this chapter I will discuss the converse, the role of landscape in monument building, and the role of place and identity in monument construction.

I will begin by considering the internal time-depth of monument construction and use. It has been suggested that the temporal sequence of construction is equivalent to the temporal rhythm of different burial ceremonies (Gansum 2004; Gansum and Oestigaard 2004; Goldhahn 1999; 2000), which reflects the way that the monument was planned, through the different phases of the burial ceremony and the building of the monument, to the afterlife of the monument; how it ages, decays, expires and passes away. Archaeological analyses have shown that burial ceremonies can have considerable time-depth, and can also extend over considerable distances spatially (Oestigaard 1999). The famous Viking Age ship burial at Oseberg in Vestfold, Norway, extended over several months, the ship was pulled up and deposited over well-preserved spring flowers, and autumn apples were found on board the ship (Gansum 2002:271–82). The well-known 'princely-burial' from Hochdorf, Baden Württemberg, Germany, has also been interpreted as having a long burial ceremony, and the use of the monument is believed to have extended over five years (Olivier 1999).

Hochdorf is a complex monument with a lengthy life-history. However, less prominent monuments sometimes also display a complex morphology with a

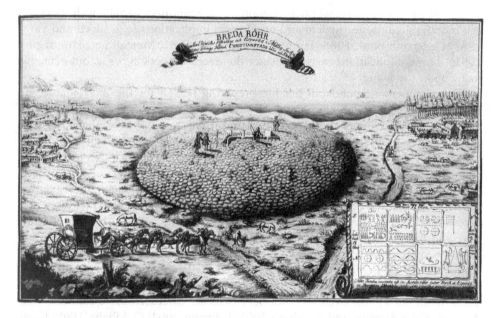

Figure 2.1   Bredarör on Kivik around 1760 (Drawing by Beckanstedt, ATA/Stockholm)

Figure 2.2   Katty Wahlgren at the burial monument of Oscar Montelius (Photo: Joakim Gold-hahn). Montelius, one of the founders of the typological method, died in 1921 after a lifelong dedi-cation to the science he helped to create. This monument was not raised until the late 1920s, after the initiative of some of his 'disciples'. Whose purpose did the erection of this monument serve, Montelius or his disciples?

pronounced architectural layout. In his analysis of coastal Bronze Age cairns from Ångermanland in central Sweden, Evert Baudou has emphasized the temporal processes and labour evident in the construction of different monuments. According to his analysis, every cubic metre of a finished burial monument is equivalent to around a full working day for an adult (Baudou 1968:156). To build a monument like the famous Lusehøj barrow from the Danish island of Funen, which was around 36 metres in diameter and 6 metres high, would take about 3,200 working days (cf. Thrane 1984:152; for similar logistic analysis see also Berntsson 2005; Nordenborg Myhre 1998; Goldhahn 1999; Ragnesten 2005; Ringstad 1987; Skre 1997).

It is important to stress that while the perception and cognition of landscape is altered by the construction of a monument, the actual physical landscape is also altered. At the same time as the monument is materialized in the landscape, the landscape is materialized in the monument. This dialectic process is essential; the materials used in monument construction – wood, earth, turf, stone, sand, fire cracked stones, ash, charcoal, seaweed, beach sand, snails, etc. – are gathered from specific places in the landscape and are incorporated into a new composite construction in the form of the monument.

Occasionally the social and ritual performance of monument construction has altered entire landscapes (e.g. Gansum and Oestigaard 2004; Skre 1997). For example, the turf used in the Lusehøj barrow, mentioned above, incorporated more than 7 hectares of fertile land (Thrane 1984:151–2). Gad Rausing (1993) has therefore suggested that the incorporation of land should be interpreted as a burial gift to the deceased, possibly as land for ploughing or pasture in the afterlife; or as Terje Gansum (2002:252) suggests, this land may be interpreted as a ritual offering to honour the deceased.

While the building of earthen barrows had an immense impact through the incorporation of fertile soils, the construction of stone-built cairns had a more productive impact on the landscape through the clearance of stones from the fields. An 'average' cairn, in this case 16 metres across and two metres high, has a volume about 200 metres^3 (Figure 2.3). It would contain 13,768 stones and rocks of various size, with a total weight of around 225 tons (Ragnesten 2005:353–5). Ulf Ragnesten has

Figure 2.3 This average-sized cairn from Arendal on Hisingen, situated in the suburban parts of Göteborg on the Swedish west coast, which measures 16 × 2 metres, contained 13,768 stone with a total weight of 225 tons! (Photo: Ulf Ragnesten/Göteborg Stadsmuseum)

calculated that a cairn of this size could be built by five people in two months (Rag-nesten 2005:365), or around 200 working days if we follow Baudou's analysis above.

Larger cairns demand more work. It has been suggested that Bredarör on Kivik, one of the most impressive monuments of the Scandinavian Bronze Age, measured about 75 metres across with a height of around 7 metres (Larsson 1993; Randsborg 1993). Based on Ragnesten's analysis of the size of an average cairn, this would mean that Bredarör once contained about 1,077,346 stones with a total weight of 17,600 tons. It would then demand about 15,650 working days/metres[3] to build, which equals 43 years of work for a single person, or 43 persons working an entire year. Even if these abstract numbers are vast and may be inaccurate, it is telling that the reconstruction of this cairn to a height of 3.5 metres back in 1932 and 1933 demanded more than 10,000 tons of stones, or 80,000 cartloads (Randsborg 1993:7–8). In this regard Lars Larsson has calculated that the building of Bredarör would have cleared around 20 hectares of land of stones in the vicinity of this gigantic monument (Larsson 1993:141). To create fertile land through the clearing of stones must have been a prestigious and honourable act, whether the land comprised viable settlement areas, arable fields, pasture, or some other purposes. Whatever the use of the land its clearance was an arduous activity, which again may have honoured the dead. Building monuments of this scale must have been as important for the living as they were for the dead (Goldhahn 2000:29; Skoglund 2005:96–103). The building of barrows and the ritual *incorporation* of fertile soils, as well as the *creation* of fertile soils by building cairns, had an impact on the land-scape. However the monuments also had further consequences for the living.

While I stress that the mathematical equations relating to monument construc-tion are abstractions, I believe that they illustrate some of the driving forces for the vast monumental building projects that took place during the Scandinavian Bronze Age. One paradox worth considering here is the fact that the only individuals who were unable to take part in the cognitive representation of landscape were the same ones these monuments were built to commemorate. It would seem that these monu-ments were built for much more than the commemoration of the dead.

In this chapter I argue that as well as interpreting the meaning of monuments in the landscape, we also should try to consider how different landscapes were manifested in the monument (see Rowlands and Tilley 2006:507 for similar approaches). The aim here is to broaden our knowledge of the meaning of death in the past. To this end it is important to extend the framework of the archaeological analysis to include both the dead and the living (e.g. Oestigaard and Goldhahn 2006). By doing this, we will begin to explore the meaning of different burial monu-ments and will broaden the scope of traditional interpretations of mortuary prac-tices (cf. Arnold and Wicker 2001; Binford 1971; Chapman et al. 1981; Kjeld Jensen and Høilund Nielsen 1997; Parker Pearson 1999; Tainter 1978; Wason 1994).

The broadened scope of interpretation discussed above will be exemplified by analyzing four different monumental burials dating to the Early Bronze Age, approximately Montelius period II and III (1500 to 1100 cal. BC). These monuments include: 1) Bredarör on Kivik in southeastern Scania, Sweden; 2) Skelhøj, central Jutland, Denmark; 3) the Sagaholm barrow, northern Småland, southern Sweden; and 4) Mjeltehaugen on the island of Giske, Sunnmøre, Norway (Figure 2.4).

Each of these monuments is different, and the precondition for an archaeological analysis differs for each monument. They were all excavated at different times,

Figure 2.4 South Scandinavia with the discussed monuments in this chapter marked out; 1) Bredarör on Kivik in Scania; 2) Skelhøj from Jutland; 3) Sagaholm from the northern parts of Småland; and, 4) Mjeltehaugen from Giske in Sunnmøre on the Norwegian west coast

with different methods, aims and standards. The documentation of the dig from Mjeltehaugen and Bredarör can best be described as poor (Linge 2004; Randsborg 1993), while the situation for the Sagaholm barrow is much better (Goldhahn 1999). Only Skelhøj has been excavated in modern times with a detailed scientific analysis and documentation in line with contemporary standards (Holst et al. 2004). Further; Skelhøj, Sagaholm and Mjeltehaugen are earthen barrows, the latter with a large central cairn, while Bredarör is best described as a 'broad cairn' (which is actually what the etymology of *Bredarör* means in Swedish).

Bredarör, Sagaholm and Mjeltehaugen are known for being some of the largest finds of rock art found in stratified archaeological contexts in Scandinavia (Glob 1969; Goldhahn 1999; Mandt 1983; Randsborg 1993; Syvertsen 2003), while Skelhøj lacks any such finds. As I hope to show, all monuments have one thing in common: these monuments to the dead were also constructed to commemorate the living (Figure 2.2).

Bredarör on Kivik

There are few burial monuments in Scandinavia that have been so well studied as Bredarör on Kivik (Figures 2.1 and 2.5). Ever since this 75 metre-diameter cairn was robbed and plundered in 1748, it has been one of the most cited prehistoric monuments in Scandinavian Bronze Age and rock art research (Goldhahn 2006:27–8). Most of the studies of Bredarör have either discussed: 1) the fascinating rock art and its dating (e.g. Kristiansen 2004; Randsborg 1993; Verlaeckt 1993); 2) the social status, age and gender of the individual buried in the cairn (see Goldhahn 2005), and/or; 3) the rock art and its continental influences (e.g. Kristiansen and Larsson 2005; Randsborg 1993; Sjögren 2005; Thrane 1990). More recently the eschatological and cosmological significance of the rock art from Bredarör has also been discussed (Goldhahn 2005:101–8; Kaul 2004a:173–90).

Most researchers agree that the rock art from Bredarör embodied social and religious components, and that they depict parts of the burial ritual that surrounded the construction of this impressive monument (Figure 2.5, see especially slab nos. 7 and 8). Most researchers have also interpreted the deceased individual as a male chief – a Nordic counterpart to the famous Odysseus.

Figure 2.5 Bredarör on Kivik as the monument was presented to thousands of school children from the 1930s to the 1960s. The poster was created in 1936 by Arvid Fougstedt (1888–1949) (Photo: Joakim Goldhahn)

SÖDER   NORR

Figure 2.6 The rock engravings from Bredarör documented by Harald Faith-Ell in 1942 (After Goldhahn 1999)

If this is the case it is curious that the 'travelling chief' (see Kristiansen 2004; Kristiansen and Larsson 2005; Randsborg 1993), is not depicted on any of the decorated slabs incorporated in the cairn (Figure 2.6), while the participants in these ceremonies and rituals seems to have 'seized the moment' and depicted their performance on the decorated slabs (Figure 2.5). We see different gendered processions; musicians, rituals performed around a bowl, possibly the bronze bowl that was found in the cist itself (Randsborg 1993), we also observe a wagon drawn by horses (Figure 2.6, slab nos. 7–8). The presumed focus of these elaborate ceremonies and rituals, the dead individual in the grave, whether a chief or not (Goldhahn 2005:246–50), does not seem to be depicted. Instead the participants in the mortuary ritual are represented on the slabs (see Figure 2.2).

The symbolic representations of the participants of this mortuary ceremony, who face the deceased for eternity, underline the fact that death implies a greater change for the living than for the dead. The social, economic and political bonds that are dissolved when there is a death in the community had to be renegotiated among the living, and one way to do this was to pay respect to the deceased by honouring her at her funeral (Figure 2.7). Sometimes death may be a powerful political medium for the living (e.g. Oestigaard and Goldhahn 2006).

At this juncture it is important to underline the point that while the ceremonies and rituals conducted at the Bredarör cairn acted to materialize the monument in the landscape (Figure 2.1), the surrounding landscape was simultaneously materialized in the monument.

Figure 2.7 Photo from the funeral ceremony of King Hussein, Jordan's monarch for 46 years who died on February 27 in 1999 (After Oestigaard and Goldhahn 2006). The 63-year-old monarch was given a state burial the next day. It was estimated that more than 800,000 Jordanians were grieving in the streets of Amman. Kings, presidents and delegates from almost 70 countries participated in the funeral. It was the largest gathering of royal and political leaders since the funeral of the Israeli Prime Minister Yitzhak Rabin in 1995, and sworn enemies were standing next to each other. The world's leaders hailed the deceased monarch as one of the greatest statesmen of the 20th century and as one of the crucial architects in the peace process in the Middle East. Hussein's charisma and skills were central to breaking many impasses in the Arab-Israeli conflict. President Bill Clinton and the former US presidents Bush, Carter and Ford represented the United States. Iraq was represented by vice-president Taha Marouf, and former US president George Bush, whose forces had previously attacked Iraq, was at the same funeral. Hamas was present with several representatives. The Czech president Vaclav Havel and the Russian President Boris Yeltsin, both of them seriously ill, came to the funeral, Yeltsin against the advice of his doctors. UN Secretary General Kofi Annan and his wife participated as well as the president of the European Union, Jacques Santer. Prime Minister Benjamin Netanyahu led the Israeli delegation. From Israel there was also a delegation led by Chief Rabbi Yisrael Lau and a representative of families of seven teenage girls slain by a deranged Jordanian soldier in 1997, and the king-to-be personally consoled the families. King Hussein's funeral brought together enemies, including the leader of the Democratic Front for the Liberation of Palestine, Nayef Hawatmeh, who approached the Israeli President Ezer Weizman, praised him as a man of peace and shook his hand. However, Syrian President Hafez Al Assad and Israeli Prime Minister Benjamin Netanyahu, harsh enemies, did not meet personally during the funeral, but it was the very first time that they came together in same place. Death has it own terms

As mentioned above, the construction of a monument such as Bredarör on Kivik, taking more than 15,000 working days to create, must been an astonishing event. When the monument was finished (the completion of the monument is likely to have taken several years), more than 20 hectares of previously infertile land had been cleared of stone. At the same time the monument became a prominent part of the landscape, the landscape became a prominent part of the monument. While the monument in the landscape expressed fundamental beliefs and desires and materialized a history, the materiality of the different landscapes incorporated in the monument also told their own story. How these histories and memories were gathered in the final monument must be considered as a form of explicit action, in which a variety of economic, social, political, aesthetic, eschatological and cosmological issues were manifested and materialized.

During the excavation of Bronze Age monuments in Scandinavia, it is not unusual to find that different materials have been deliberately chosen for specific architectural features; sometimes cairns are built of stones of different kinds, which seem to be deliberately chosen and used for different parts of the monuments, such as kerbs and cists, etc., which imply that their original position in the landscape was vital to their position in different monuments. In Scandinavia, it is well documented that different coloured stones, with specific shape, size and even sound, seem to be deliberately chosen for different purposes (see Artelius 2000; Burström 1992; Carlie 1999; Carlsson 2000:16–18; Elfstrand 1980; 1983; Gansum 2004; Gerdin 1994; Simonsen and Vogt 2005; Sköldebrand 1997; Stjernquist 1990; Thedéen 2004:102; Westergaard 1987; Wihlborg 1978; Victor 2002), but it is seldom that this phenomenon is taken as a starting point for any explicit interpretations. An exception to this rule is the Skelhøj project in Denmark.

Skelhøj

Jørgen Jensen has shown that around 85,000 barrows were built within the present borders of Denmark during prehistory (Jensen 2002:144). Most of them were built over a short time-span of the Early Bronze Age, stretching from Montelius period II to III, approximately 1500 to 1100 cal. BC (Jensen 1998). Some of them, such as the famous oak cist burials from Egtved, Muldebjerg and Skrydsrup, are extremely well preserved. Their preservation depends on the fact that the anaerobic qualities of the turf have preserved the oak coffins. Traditionally it is the deceased and their burial gifts in these monuments that have attracted most attention from archaeologists (Aner and Kersten 1973–; Boye 1896; Jensen 1998; 2002; Kyvik 2005; Randsborg 1974). The people who built these barrows are seldom considered. We will turn to consider them below.

An ordinary barrow has at least a volume of 200 metres³, which implies that it took at least 17,000,000 working days to build the 85,000 barrows known in Denmark. About 80 per cent of these barrows were probably built during period's II and III of the Scandinavian Bronze Age, which means that about 34,000 working days were required for building barrows throughout the Early Bronze Age. This vast building project implies that around 100 people per day were building monuments – within Denmark alone. Many of these barrows have a greater volume (e.g. Aner and Kersten 1973–; Bech 2003; Jensen 1998; Larsson 2005; Thrane 1984), and we must consider the above estimates as an absolutely minimum.

The Skelhøj barrow is situated near the Konge river in central Jutland (Figure 2.4). This barrow is around 30 metres in diameter and was originally around 7.5 metres high (Figure 2.8). The landscape around the Konge river is well known for barrows with wealthy burials with well preserved oak coffins, such as Trindhøj, Guldhøj, Store Kongehøj and Storehøj at Tobøl (Boye 1896; Jensen 1998; Johansen et al. 2004; Laursen et al. 2003; Thrane 1963).

Figure 2.8 Skelhøj during the excavation (Photo: Per Poulsen)

One of the major aims of the Skelhøj project was to study the mechanism that allowed the preservation of the oak coffin and its contents. By experimentation the Skelhøj project reached the conclusion that preservation was caused by a chemical 'iron capsule' that formed around the oak coffins. This capsule developed through a rapid reduction process occurring when the oak coffin in the middle of the barrow was deliberately 'drowned' in large amounts of water. This initiated a process which transformed the natural occurrence of Fe^{3+} and Mn^{4+} in the soil to Fe^{2+} and Mn^{2+} (Breuning-Madsen et al. 2001). The Skelhøj project interpreted this reduction process as the result of an explicit and standardized burial tradition that was both localized and occurred for only a short period of time (Breuning-Madsen et al. 2001:696; Holst et al. 2001:132–5); most of the well preserved oak coffins originate from central Jutland, and they where all built within a time-span of around 125 years, from about 1425 to 1300 cal. BC (Holst et al. 2001:131–2; Jensen 2002).

Prior to the excavation of Skelhøj, soil samples taken from the barrow suggested that it was built of a variety of different turfs from the surrounding landscape; some originated from grassland, others from heathland (Holst and Rasmussen 2002; Holst et al. 2004:12). The ensuing excavation had a threefold aim: 1) to study the mechanism behind the preserved oak coffins (see above); 2) to study the construction of the barrow, the working process and organization, and; 3) to get an impression of the surrounding landscape through different scientific analyses (Holst et al. 2004:12–13).

To answer these and related questions, members of the Skelhøj project produced a large number of plans of the barrow during excavation (Figure 2.8); a total of 200 plans were produced in all (Holst et al. 2004:14). Because of the profound

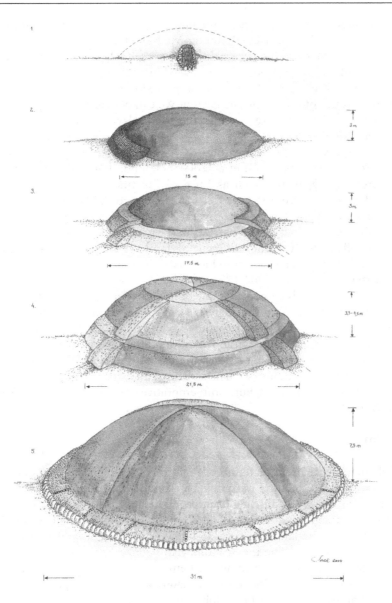

Figure 2.9 Reconstruction by Svend Aage Knudsen of the different building phases of Skelhøj (After Holst et al. 2004:fig. 7)

level of documentation the team were able to understand the complex architecture of the barrow and reconstruct the construction sequence of the monument. Firstly the ground had been cleansed by fire, a common trait known from many excavations of burial monuments from Early Bronze Age Scandinavia (e.g. Goldhahn 1999; Lundborg 1972; Marstrander 1963:318). Then an oak coffin was placed on the ground, which later was covered by a small cairn. After that the building of the barrow took place (Figure 2.9).

The entire barrow at Skelhøj seems to have been constructed during a single prolonged burial ceremony (see Goldhahn 1999 for another example of this). This interpretation is in line with the experiments on the 'iron core/capsule' from barrows analyzed by the Skelhøj project (Breuning-Madsen et al. 2001), as well as different architectural details from the excavated barrow itself. One such detail is that there were a series of different rows of stones placed in order that they radiated out from the inner part of the barrow. These 'rays' appeared in the same position in different stratigraphic layers of the turf in the barrow. We can conclude that the workers who added each layer of turf were aware of the overall layout and plan of the barrow (Holst et al. 2004:16, Fig. 4).

Another observation that underlines this interpretation is that the barrow was built in different sections (Holst et al. 2004:17), a building technique known from other barrows in Denmark, such as Lusehøj (Thrane 1984). The same sections could be documented from the interior of the cairn to the last layer of turf on the barrow's exterior. Different teams of workers appear to have been responsible for building different sections of the barrow; and each section of the barrow seems to have been built using turf from different parts of the surrounding landscape. The different working teams also seem to have used different ramps in the construction of the barrow (Holst et al. 2004:17).

The Skelhøj project is a good example of the broader perspective I wish to argue for – a shift in perspective in the analysis of mortuary monuments to include both *the dead and the living*. The strictly planned construction of the barrow, the use of large amounts of water in the burial ritual, the different working groups visible in the carefully documented turf sections, the use of turf from different parts of the landscape all speak of the monument as a socially constructed memory, not only commemorating the deceased, but commemorative of the participants in the funeral ceremony itself.

Sagaholm

It is likely that the different materials brought together in a monument like Skelhøj, with its intricate architectural morphology, carried social and ideological connotations, although these are difficult to interpret in the present. However, there are some ways of taking this further. As different kinds of monuments were placed in different places in the landscape, we do know that different landscapes were used for different purposes during the Scandinavian Bronze Age; barrows and cairns are usually situated on higher elevations, settlements and heaps of fire-cracked stone are usually placed on well-drained land below, while ritual deposits and rock art are situated at lower altitudes (after Johansen 1993):

High	Prehistoric remains	Elements
	heaven	
	burials	*mountain/ridge*
	settlements	*sand, moraine*
	rock art	*clay*
	ritual deposit	*water*
	underworld	
Low		

This very general pattern is well recognized within the Scandinavian Bronze Age (e.g. Bengtsson 2004; Eriksen 2003; Gerdin 1999; Jensen 1997; Johansen 1993;

Figure 2.10 The Sagaholm barrow during the excavation 1971 (Photo: Anders Wihlborg/ Jönköping County Museum [after Goldhahn 1999])

Kjellén and Hyenstrand 1977; Kristiansen and Larsson 2005; Larsson 1986; Ling 2005; Runcis 1999; Thedéen 2004; Wahlgren 2002; Wrigglesworth 2005). Typically different kinds of landscapes are interpreted as having different meanings or connotations. Rather than treating this pattern as the self-evident conclusion or end result of interpretation, we can instead adopt this pattern as a framework of analysis by considering the possibility that different elements of the landscape were juxtaposed or brought together in a monument. Monuments were then explicitly and meaningful composed.

This interpretative possibility is illustrated by the fascinating Sagaholm barrow from Småland, Sweden (Goldhahn 1999; 2000; 2005; Randsborg 1993; Wihlborg 1978). The Sagaholm barrow was excavated in the early 1970s and it was found to be about 24 metres across and about 4 metres high (Goldhahn 1999). The most fascinating thing about this barrow is the central kerb, which was decorated with rock art (Figure 2.10). Each slab in the kerb has been quarried and reshaped by pecking, with the purpose of fitting each slab in the final kerb. Originally there were about 100 slabs in the partly ruined barrow, and the slabs have been arranged so that the kerb tilted slightly outwards from the centre of the monument.

The slabs in this decorated kerb all consist of a reddish sandstone known as the geological Visingsö formation (Goldhahn 1999:134–9). This sandstone was not found naturally in the vicinity of the Sagaholm barrow, and during the Bronze Age the only place where this particular bedrock outcropped was on the island of Visningsö, around 30 kilometres from Sagaholm. Some of the slabs from Sagaholm still display a water-polished surface, which may indicate that they had originally been quarried at the water's edge (Goldhahn 1999:135, Fig. 6.14). At several places on the island of Visingsö, it is still possible to find 'natural slabs' at the water's edge,

Figure 2.11   The engraved slabs from the Sagaholm barrow had probably been quarried at the liminal zone between lake and land on Visningsö (Photo: Harry Bergenblad [after Goldhahn 1999])

similar in size and shape to the kerbstones from Sagaholm. It is probable that the slabs were quarried from a similar location.

These observations suggest that the position of the sandstone slabs in the Sagaholm barrow replicate their original position in the landscape. The landscape was re-created within the monument itself. The liminal position of the slabs in the landscape, situated between the world of the living and the watery underworld (Figure 2.11), was likewise recreated in the monument. In the monument the slabs were used to create a liminal space between the world of the living and the deceased (Figure 2.10, 2.13). The reddish sandstone created a boundary between the known and the unknown. The original location of the sandstone, then, was of decisive importance to how it came to be used within the monument.

The images from the Sagaholm kerb were pecked, ground, carved or outlined on the side facing the participants of the funeral ceremony. The images mostly depict horses. All the animals but one are facing to the right of the observer. The latter may be of significance as this is how the sun's daily journey is depicted on the famous ritual gear from Trundholm, Denmark and on several rock art images from different parts of Scandinavia. In earlier works, I have interpreted the horses and the kerb from Sagaholm as a materialized metaphor for the cosmological myth concerning the sun and its daily journey (Goldhahn 1999; 2000; 2005), an interpretation supported in a general context by other scholars (e.g. Kaul 2004a). This myth is also possible to detect in other aspects of Bronze Age material culture, most notably as iconography on Danish bronze razors (Figure 2.12):

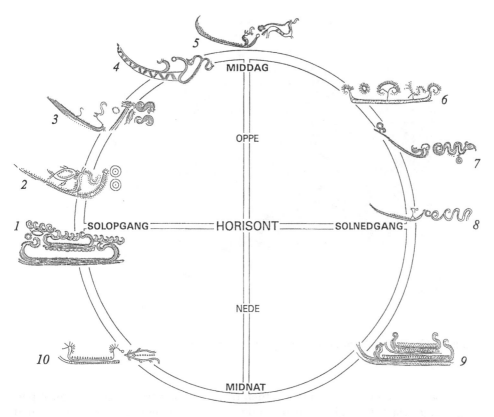

Figure 2.12 An illustration showing how the iconography on different bronze razors reflects the mythological story about the birth and re-birth of the sun during Late Bronze Age in Denmark (reworked after Kaul 2004b)

1: Sunrise. The fish pulls the rising sun up from the night-ship to the morning ship. 2: For a while, the fish was allowed to sail on with the ship. 3: The fish is to be devoured by a bird of prey. Stylized sun-horses(S-figures) are ready to fetch the sun. 4: Two sun-horses are about to pull the sun from the ship. 5: At noon the sun-horse has collected the sun from the ship. 6: In the afternoon the sun-horse lands with the sun on the sun-ship. 7: Some time after the sun-horse has landed, the sun is taken over by the snake from the afternoon-ship. 8: The snake is concealing the sun in its spiral curls. It will soon lead the sun down under the horizon. 9: Two night-ships sailing towards left. The sun is not visible, extinguished and dark on its voyage through the underworld. 10: A night ship followed by a fish swimming to the left. The fish is ready to fulfil its task at sunrise. The wheel has come full circle. (Kaul 2004b:131)

Given this perspective it seems as if the red colour of the slabs was of great importance. It is notable that the sun's life-course alters during the year, as does the appearance of the sun during its daily journey. At dusk the reddish sun shines from the underworld, and at dawn, the sun departs to this place from the world of the living (Figure 2.11). While this phenomenon occurs, the sun seems to changes its shape and colour. During the morning, the newly reborn sun seems to decrease in size, the colour of the sun changes from red to white, while over the day the heat from the sun increases. At dusk the opposite seems to occur. The deliberate choice

Figure 2.13   The Sagaholm barrow during the burial ceremony (Reconstruction by Hans Norberg [after Norberg 2004])

of red sandstone in Sagaholm could then be interpreted from a cosmological perspective, in which the red colour not only replicates the liminal state of the sun at dusk and dawn, but also the liminal state brought by death.

In the case of the Sagaholm barrow it is clear that the cosmology of the Bronze Age was dialectically related to the eschatology beliefs of society (Goldhahn 2000). A similar dialectic movement is suggested by the relationship between the monument in the landscape and the landscape materialized in the monument.

We have discussed the significance of death and cosmology in the Sagaholm barrow. We will turn now to the living (Figure 2.13). The stratigraphy of the Sagaholm barrow reflects a prolonged and complicated building process, with numerous intricate architectural features (Goldhahn 1999:99–139). The fact that the slabs were quarried at Visningsö, a total of about 5 metres[3] of rock, could be interpreted as a pronounced and conscious materialization of the living in the monument. Here it is important to underline the point that the agency and social strategies of the mourners and participants in the mortuary ritual were manifested in the construction of the monument (Figure 2.2, 2.7).

To analyze how different social groups and genders were manifested in a monument such as Sagaholm, we need to examine the images carved on the slabs in the central kerb. Even though the slabs originated from the same place in the landscape, the images added to the slabs are very different. This is especially obvious if we consider the ship images (see slab nos. 4, 6, 22, 25, 26, 32, 34; Goldhahn 1999), which each have their own style and are made with a variety of techniques; some are carved, others pecked or cut, while some are deeply pecked and ground. These observations suggest that the rock art from the Sagaholm barrow was made by different people who possessed differing knowledge and technical know-how (cf.

Bengtsson 2004:85–102; Coles 2005:9–14; Kristiansen 2002). Before discussing the implications of this it is important to compare Sagaholm with our next case study, Mjeltehaugen, Norway.

Mjeltehaugen

Together with Bredarör and Sagaholm, Mjeltehaugen on the island of Giske in western Norway constitutes one of the most prominent finds of rock art from a burial context in Scandinavia. The rock art was discovered in the 1840s, and after its discovery the excavators Wilhelm Christie and Anders Lorange excavated small areas of the monument and produced reports of their findings. Mjeltehaugen at this point in time was said to be around 30 metres across and about 2 metres high (Figure 2.14). The excavation reports are brief and provide different interpretations of the find contexts: according to Christie the decorated slabs covered '8 different cists', while Lorange stated that they originated from 'one cist constructed of 8 decorated slabs'. This discrepancy has been the source of differences of opinion (de Lange 1912; Mandt 1983; 1991; Mandt and Lødøen 2005; Marstrander 1963; Østmo 2005). Recently, Trond Linge has re-interpreted the slabs from Mjeltehaugen (2004). After a detailed analysis of the preserved slabs, and the available excavation reports, he suggests that the fragmented slabs once originated from two larger slabs that had covered four smaller cists (Linge 2005). Each cist had a ship image faced inwards towards the probable cremation burials (Figure 2.15).

The dating of the slabs has also been a subject of debate. Most researchers have argued for a date from the Neolithic or early Bronze Age period I (de Lange 1912; Mandt 1983; 1991; Marstrander 1963; Østmo 2005). However, based on

Figure 2.14 Mjeltehaugen from Giske in 1922 (Photo: Johannes Bøe/Bergen Museum)

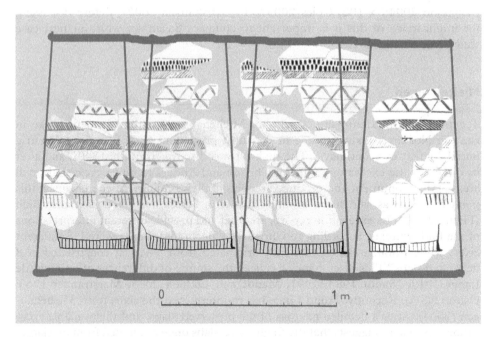

Figure 2.15 One of the decorated slabs from Mjeltehaugen which covered four smaller cists with cremated bones (After Linge 2005)

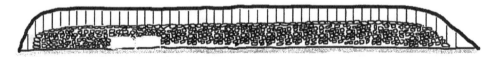

Figure 2.16 A tentative profile of the Mjeltehaugen (After Linge 2004)

similarities between the decorated slabs and the ornaments on different bronze objects, Linge suggest a dating to period II, 1500 to 1300 cal. BC. The argument over dating will almost certainly continue, but what matters is the monument itself. From the brief archaeological reports we know that the decorated cists in Mjelte-haugen were covered by an inner cairn, a cairn that was later covered by a turf barrow (Figure 2.16). Following the examples of Skelhøj and Sagaholm, the differ-ent building techniques and materials might be interpret as the result of a prolonged burial ceremony (Figure 2.16).

There are four different aspects of the Mjeltehaugen monument I want to emphasize here: 1) that barrows are unique to the area, and that the earthen barrow may express some sort of inter-regional identity; 2) the ship motifs on the slabs have a localized regional style and may be expressing some kind of regional warrior identity; 3) the cairn, the most common burial tradition in the area, may express a local group identity; and 4) these different identities are all manifested in the final monument.

Mjeltehaugen is the northernmost barrow dated to the Early Bronze Age in Europe. The barrow tradition was introduced to Scandinavia by the Single Grave Culture during the Middle Neolithic, but this tradition is unknown outside Jutland in Denmark (Ebbesen 2005; Hübner 2005). During the Early Bronze Age, approximately 1600 to 1100 cal. BC, barrows become more common outside Jutland, probably through influences from the continental Tumulus Culture. According to firm dendrochronology dating of the Danish oak coffins, the majority of Scandinavian barrows where built between 1425 to 1300 cal. BC (Jensen 1998; 2002). In Norway, barrows dating to the Bronze Age are most common on Jæren, Lista and Rogaland in the southwest (Møllerup 1992; Nordenborg Myhre 2004; Syvertsen 2003). The northernmost group of barrows is situated in Etne in the southern part of Hordaland (Fett 1963; Mandt 1972; Vevatne 1996). North of Etne, cairns are the dominant monumental burial tradition during the entire Bronze Age (Mandt 1991; Østerdal 1999; Rygh 1911; Ringstad 1987; Sognnes 2001; Wrigglesworth 2000). The only known monument that departs from this pattern is Mjeltehaugen.

Following the calculations of Baudou, it took around 710 working days to build Mjeltehaugen (cf. Ringstad 1987:138, 218), which reflects considerable time and effort. According to Linge's re-interpretation, it seems as though there are two different burial traditions that conjoin in the finished monuments; a) a local tradition of building cairns, followed by b) an inter-regional tradition of building barrows. The analogies with Skelhøj are obvious, but now we see how different kinds of social groups manifested themselves in the monument; local groups could be responsible for building the cairn, and inter-regional groups for building the barrow.

To widen our interpretation we must return to the rock art. Most of the images on the slabs from Mjeltehaugen are abstract and difficult to interpret (Figure 2.15). Both Marstrander (1963) and Malmer (1971) have suggested that they depict some sort of textiles, but while this interpretation is thought-provoking, well-preserved textiles from the Bronze Age do not confirm their interpretation; textiles are generally made by a different technique (Bender Jørgensen 1986; 1992; Hald 1980). The only motifs that are positively recognizable are those that depict ships. These all have very characteristic pronounced vertical prows. Some rock art researchers prefer to date this ship style to the Late Neolithic, sometimes between 2350 and 1700 cal. BC (Østmo 2005), but we lack any archaeological dating to support this. If this were correct, Mjeltehaugen would be an utterly unique phenomenon.

Here I wish to highlight the fact that similar abstract rock art motifs are well known from contemporary burial contexts dating to the early Bronze Age (1500 to 1100 cal. BC), both in Rogaland in the south (Nordenborg Myhre 2004; Syvertsen 2003), as well as Trøndelag in the north (Sognnes 2001). Following the ship chronology produced by Flemming Kaul, based on more than 800 ship images on different bronze items with secure dates, prows with animals heads such as those at Mjeltehaugen do not occur before 1500 cal. BC. The ships from Mjeltehaugen also have an extended keel in the stern, a typological trait only known from 1600 to 1300 cal. BC (Kaul 1998; 2003; 2005). A date for Mjeltehaugen of period II, between 1500 to 1300 cal. BC, therefore seems likely (see also Mandt and Lødøen 2005:127).

One reason for the difficulties in dating the ship images from Mjeltehaugen is their regional style (Figure 2.17), which is known from a region extending from Sunnfjord in the south to Trøndelag in the north (Linge 2004:102). Following Gro Mandt's (1991) research in the area, these particular ship images are known as type

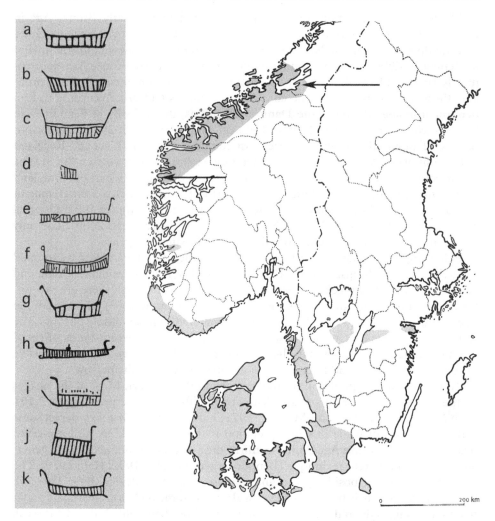

Figure 2.17 A figure showing the cognitive landscape of Mjeltehaugen. The possible quarries in Sunnfjord and Trøndelag have been marked by an arrow. The ship images are gathered from; (a) Auran; (b) Leirfall; (c) Røkke; (d) the burial slab from Skjervoll; (e) Mjeltehaugen; (f) Krabbestig; (g) Domba; (h) Unneset; (i) Leirvåg; (j) Leirvåg; (k) Vagndal in Hardanger. Light grey shows areas with known Bronze Age barrows in Scandinavia, dark grey areas where ship images similar to those depicted on the slabs from Mjeltehaugen are known. Cairns are to be found all around the coast of the Scandinavian peninsula (based on Askvik 1983; Linge 2004; Mandt 1983, 1991; Marstrander and Sognnes 1999; Nilsen 2005; Sognnes 2001)

A1. The distribution of these ships is interesting, as they are known from Leirvåg on the island of Atløy, and the rock art localities at Unneset, Domba and Krabbestig from the area south of Mjeltehaugen (e.g. Mandt 1991), and from the rock art sites at Leirfall, Auran, Røkke and Ydstines from Trøndelag in the north (e.g. Grønnesby 1998; Marstrander and Sognnes 1999; Sognnes 2001). This regional distribution suggests that the ship images express some form of regional identity, possibly the manifestation of some kind of warrior elite (Oestigaard and Goldhahn 2006).

The latter interpretation gains support from the fact that the burial slabs from Mjeltehaugen were made of an exotic bedrock unknown from the vicinity of the barrow (Linge 2004:101–2; Mandt 1983). The slabs are made out of a 'greenish-grey, fine-grained, schistose meta-greywacke with rusty, weathered layers rich in carbonate' (Askvik 1983:33), which only outcrops at Stavfjorden and Atløy in Sunnfjord in the south, and in the central parts of Trøndelag in the north (Figure 2.17). The two possible quarries for this bedrock, coincide, more or less, with the southern and northern limit of the regional ship motifs from Mjeltehaugen.

Both the engraved slabs from Sagaholm and Mjeltehaugen are therefore constructed from specifically chosen bedrock. The sandstones from Sagaholm were gathered some 30 kilometres away, and in the case of Mjeltehaugen, the distance was greater; the distance to Sunnfjord is about 100 kilometres, and it is about 250 kilometres to Trøndelag. Both of these journeys would have had to be made by boat, and Trond Linge has calculated that it took about three to five days each way (Linge 2004:103, cf. Vinner 2003). Considering that this area is one of the most dangerous waterways in northern Europe, with a lot of historically known ship wrecks (Linge 2004:103–5; Mandt 1983:30), the quarrying and gathering of slabs for the burial cist in Mjeltehaugen must have been a hazardous task which took several weeks to fulfil.

It is not possible from geological analysis alone to determine which area the slate slabs from Mjeltehaugen originated, and similar rock art ships are known from both areas. However, several circumstances suggest Trøndelag may be the likely area as similar cists with rock art are known from different cairns in this area, such as Steine, Rishaug and Skjervoll (Marstrander and Sognnes 1999; Sognnes 2001). The grave slabs from Skjervoll are made of an 'identical' bed rock (Askvik 1983:33) and the rock art from this slab is produced by a similar technique and style to that at Mjeltehaugen. We also know of several geometrical and abstract rock art images from this area that display considerable resemblance to the rock art from Mjeltehaugen, especially from the site at Leirfall in Stjørdal (Marstrander and Sognnes 1999; Nilsen 2005).

Even if circumstances speak for the Mjeltehaugen slabs being quarried in Trøndelag, it is possible that the presence of this bedrock in Sunnfjord was well known by those who built the monument, not least as the same bed rock is found in the same area as the rock art at Leirvåg where ships like those from Mjeltehaugen have been found (Mandt 1991; Wrigglesworth 2000). The observations above indicate that local, regional and inter-regional landscapes are manifested in Mjeltehaugen (Figure 2.17). The monument raised over the dead laid to rest in the eight cists in Mjeltehaugen was an explicitly materialized commemoration of the social identities of those who constructed the monument.

Conclusion: From Monuments in Landscape to Landscapes in Monument

The aim of this chapter was to demonstrate that altering our theoretical perspective from *the dead in the monument to the living who built the monument* and from *monuments in landscape to landscapes in monument* can broaden our understanding of death as a meaningful event in the past. The dead do not build monuments. The monumental burial practice of the Scandinavian Bronze Age is best understood as a monument to both the living and the dead. The position of the monuments in the landscape carries a history, and it is vital for our understanding of this ritual practice that the landscapes placed and materialized in monument are also considered of equal importance:

1) In the case of Bredarör we saw how the participants in the burial ritual manifested themselves on the decorated slabs. While the ontological status of the deceased changed on death, the social status of the living was also altered (cf. Figures 2.5 and 2.7).

2) In the case of the Skelhøj barrow, it was possible to show that different parts of one and the same monument were built of turf from different parts of the surrounding landscape, and that different parts of the barrow were built by different groups of labourers. While the barrow can be interpreted as a monument to the deceased, it can also be perceived as a commemoration to the labour forces that jointly built the monument. The monument of the dead was also a monument to the living.

3) In the case of Sagaholm, we saw that different individuals with different sex, gender, age, status and technical know-how may have manifested themselves on the decorated slabs in the kerb with rock art in general, and with different kind of ship styles in particular. The life-history of the stone slabs in the kerb also demonstrates the importance of considering the origin of the building materials in the surrounding landscape. I also argued that the colour of the slabs embodied cosmological knowledge as the red colour bore a resemblance to the sun's liminal state at dusk and dawn.

4) In the case of Mjeltehaugen, we saw how different local, regional and interregional burial traditions and ship styles were materialized in a single monument. It was argued that different social groups were responsible for building different parts of the monument. The quarried slabs, which most probably originated from Trøndelag in the north, emphasized the importance of the dialectical relationship between how monuments were materialized in the landscape and how different landscapes were materialized in the monument.

ACKNOWLEDGEMENTS

I would like to express my gratitude to the following people for helping me with thought-provoking discussions, pictures, criticisms and new perspectives concerning my thoughts on these issues; Terje Østigård, Terje Gansum, Flemming Kaul, Ulf Ragnesten, Trond Linge, Trond Lødøen, Gro Mandt, Kalle Sognnes, Hans Norberg, the members of the Skelhøj project, especially Mads Holst, Marianne Rasmussen, Svend Aage Knudsen, and Per Poulsen, and last but not least, Andy Jones.

REFERENCES

Aner, E., and K. Kersten 1973– Die funde der älteren Bronzezeit des nordischen kreises in Dänemark, Schleswig-Holstein und Niedersachsen. Bd I–XI. Neumünster: Karl Wacholtz Verlag.

Andersson, G. 2005 Gravspråk som religiös strategi. Valsta och Skälby i Attundaland under vikingatid och tidig medeltid. Stockholm: Riksantikvarieämbetet Arkeologiska Undersökningar, Skrifter No. 61.

Arnold, B., and N. L. Wicker, eds. 2001 Gender and the Archaeology of Death. Walnut Creek, CA: Alta Mira Press.

Artelius, T., and F. Svanberg, eds. 2005 Dealing with the Dead. Archaeological Perspectives on Prehistoric Scandinavian Burial Ritual. Stockholm: Riksantikvarieämbetet Arkeologiska Undersökningar, Skrifter No. 65.

Artelius, T. 2000 Bortglömda föreställningar. Begravningsritual och begravningsplats i halländsk yngre järnålder. Stockholm: Riksantikvarieämbetet Arkeologiska Undersökningar, Skrifter No. 36.

Askvik, H. 1983 Petrography of the Mjeltehaugen Slabs. Norwegian Archaeological Review 16(1):33.

Baudou, E. 1968 Forntida bebyggelse i Ångermanlands kustland. Arkiv för Norrländsk Hembygdsforskning XVII. Härnösand.

Bech, J. 2003 Fra fortidsminder til kulturmiljø – hvad Alstrup Krat og Hohøj gemte. Kulturministeriet, Kulturarvsstyrelsen og Miljøministeriet, Skov- og Naturstyrelsen i samarbejde med Kulturhistorisk Museum, Randers, Geologisk Institut, Aarhus Universitet, Nationalmuseet. Copenhagen.

Bender Jørgensen, L. 1986 Forhistoriske textiler i Skandinavien. Copenhagen: Nordiske Fortidsminder, Serie B: bd 9.

Bender Jørgensen, L. 1992 North European Textiles until AD 1000. Aarhus: Aarhus University Press.

Bengtsson, L. 2004 Bilder vid vatten. Kring hällristningar i Askum sn, Bohuslän. Gothenburg: Gotarc Serie C. Arkeologiska Skrifter No. 51.

Bergh, S. 1995 Landscape of the Monuments. A Study of the Passage Tombs in the Cúil Irra Region, Co. Sligo, Ireland. Stockholm: Riksantikvareiämbetet Arkeologiska Undersökningar, Skrifter No. 6.

Berntsson, A. 2005 Me and You and a Case of Beer. How the Bronze Age Barrows Were Built? Lund Archaeological Review 2004:21–4.

Binford, L. R. 1971 Mortuary Studies: Their Study and Potential. In Approaches to the Social Dimensions of Mortuary Studies. J. Brown, ed. Pp. 6–29. Washington, DC: Society for American Archaeology, Memoir No. 25.

Bloch, M., and J. Parry, eds. 1987 Death and Regeneration of Life. Cambridge: Cambridge University Press.

Boye, V. 1896 Fund af Egekister fra Bronzealderen i Danmark. Copenhagen: Andr. Fred. Høst and Søns Forlag.

Bradley, R. 1993 Altering the Earth. The Origins of Monuments in Britain and Continental Europe. Edinburgh: Society of Antiquities of Scotland, Monograph Series No. 8.

Bradley, R. 1998 The Significance of Monuments. On the Shaping of the Human Experience in Neolithic and Bronze Age Europe. London: Routledge.

Brueing-Madsen, H., M. K. Holst, and M. Rasmussen 2001 The Chemical Environment in a Burial Mound Shortly After Construction – An Archaeological-Pedological Experiment. Journal of Archaeological Science 28:691–7.

Burström, M. 1992 Rösesten – naturlig tillgång och kulturellt val. In Arkeologi i Värmland. Fornminnesinventeringen 1991 Säfle, Grums, Kils och Arvikas kommuner. L-E. Englund, ed. Pp. 40–3. Stockholm: Riksantikvarieämbetet.

Carlie, A. 1999 'Sacred White Stones'. On Traditions of Building White Stones into Graves. Lund Archaeological Review 5:41–58.

Carlsson, M. 2000 Stenåldersboplats och järnåldersgravfält vid Karleby. Södermanland, Östertälje socken, Gärtuna 3:1, Raä 10 och 17. Stockholm: Riksantikvarieämbetet Arkeologiska Undersökningar UV Mitt Stockholm, Rapport 1994:50.

Cederoth, S., C. Corlin, and J. Lindström, eds. 1988 On the Meaning of Death. Essays on Mortuary Rituals and Eschatological Beliefs. Uppsala: Uppsala Studies in Cultural Anthropology No. 8.

Chapman, R. W., I. Kinnes, and K. Randsborg, eds. 1981 The Archaeology of Death. Cambridge: Cambridge University Press.

Coles, J. 2005 Shadows from a Northern Past. Rock Carvings of Bohuslän and Østfold. Oxford: Oxbow.

Ebbesen, K. 2005 The Battle Axe Period. Copenhagen: Forfatterforlaget Attika.

Elfstrand, B. 1980 Järrnåldersgravar från Valle Härad. Västergötlands Fornminnesförenings Tidskrift 1979/1980:268–88.

Elfstrand, B. 1983 Ett märkligt gravfält i Varnhem. Fornlämning 40 Varnhems socken Västergötland. Stockholm: Riksantikvarieämbetet Rapport UV 1983:7.

Eriksen, E. 2003 Kosmografi i bronsealder – en analyse av det sørvestlige Sandefjord. Oslo: Opubl. hovedfagsoppgave famlagd vid arkeologiskt institutt vid Oslo universitet våren 2003.

Feldt, B. 2005 Synliga och osynliga gränser. Förändringar i gravritualen under yngre bronsålder-förromersk järnålder i Södermanland. Stockholm: Stockholm Studies in Archaeology No. 37.

Fernstål, L. 2005 Delar av en grav och glimtar av en tid. Om yngre romersk järnålder, Tuna i Badelunda i Västmanland och personen i grav X. Stockholm: Stockholm Studies in Archaeology No. 32.

Fett, P. 1963 Førhistoriske minne i Sunnhordaland. Etne prestegjeld. Bergen: Universitetet i Bergen, Historisk Museum.

Fleming, A. 1975 Tombs for the Living. Man 8:177–93.

Gansum, T. 2002 Fra jord til handling. In Plats och praxis. Studier av nordisk förkristen ritual. K. Jennbert, A. Andrén, and C. Raudvere, eds. Pp. 249–86. Lund: Nordic Academic Press/Vägar till Midgård No. 2.

Gansum, T. 2004 Hauger som konstruksjoner – arkeologiske forventninger gjennom 200 år. Gothenburg: Gotarc Serie B. Gothenburg Archaeological Thesis No. 33.

Gansum, T., G. B. Jerpåsen, and C. Keller 1996 Arkeologisk landskapsanalyse med visuelle metoder. Stavanger: AmS-Varia No. 28.

Gansum, T., and T. Oestigaard 2004 The Ritual Stratigraphy of Monuments That Matter. European Journal of Archaeology 7(1):61–79.

Gerdin, A-L. 1994 Svärd och säd från bronsåldern samt mycket annat – om nya spännande fynd i Tanum. Kungsbacka: Riksantikvarieämbetet Arkeologiska Undersökningar UV Väst, Småskrifter Nr 3.

Gerdin, A-L. 1999 Rösen. Uttryck för makt eller platser där himmel och jord möts i det kosmiska rummet. In Spiralens öga. M. Olausson, ed. Pp. 47–74. Stockholm: Riksantikvarieämbetet Avdelningen för Arkeologiska Undersökningar, Skrifter No. 25.

Glob, P. V. 1969 Danmarks helleristninger. Aarhus: Jysk Arkæologiskt Selskabs, Skrifter No. VII.

Goldhahn, J. 1999 Sagaholm – hällristningar och gravritual. Umeå: Studia Archaeologica Universitatis Umensis No. 11.

Goldhahn, J. 2000 Hällristningar, kosmologi och begravningsritual. Primitive Tider 2000:22–53.

Goldhahn, J. 2005 Från Sagaholm till Bredarör – hällbildsstudier 2000–2004. Gothenburg: Gotarc Serie C. Arkeologiska Skrifter No. 62.

Goldhahn, J. 2006 Hällbildsstudier i norra Europa – trender och tradition under det nya millenniet. Gothenburg: Gotarc Serie C. Arkeologiska Skrifter No. 64.

Grønnesby, G. 1998 Helleristningene på Skatval. Ritualer og sosial struktur. Trondheim: Gunneria No. 73.

Hald, M. 1980 Ancient Danish Textiles from Bogs and Burials. Copenhagen: Nationalmuseet.

Holst, M. K., H. Breuning-Madsen, and M. Rasmussen 2001 The South Scandinavian Barrows with Well-Preserved Oak-Log Coffins. Antiquity 75:126–36.

Holst, M. K., and M. Rasmussen 2002 Præsentation af Skelhøjprojektet. Lejre: Historisk-Arkæologisk Forsøgscenter. www.lejre-center.dk.

Holst, M. K., M. Rasmussen, and H. Breuning-Madsen 2004 Skelhøj. Et bygningsværk fra den ældre bronzealder. Nationalmuseets Arbejdsmark 2004:11–23.

Humphrey, S. C., and H. King, eds. 1981 Mortality and Immortality: The Anthropology and Archaeology of Death. London: Academic Press.

Hübner, E. 2005 Jungneolitische Gräber auf der Jütischen Halbinsel. Copenhagen: Nordiske Fortidsminder Serie B 24:1–3.

Hyenstrand, Å. 1980 Gravar – monument över levande. In Inventori in Honorem. En vänbok till Folke Hallberg. Å. Hyenstrand, ed. Pp. 240–4. Stockholm: Riksantikvarieämbetet.

Jensen, J. 1997 Fra Bronze- till Jernaldern – en kronologisk undersøgelse. Copenhagen: Nordiske Fortidsminder Serie B: bd 15.

Jensen, J. 1998 Manden i kisten. Hvad bronzealderens gravhøje gemte. Copenhagen: Gyldendal.

Jensen, J. 2002 Danmarks Oldtid. Bronzealder 2000–500 f Kr. Copenhagen: Gyldendal.

Johansen, B. 1993 Skärvstenshögar och sörmländsk bronsålder. Arkeologi i Sverige, Ny följd No. 2:99–118.

Johansen, K. L., S. T. Laursen, and M. K. Holst 2004 Spatial Patterns of Social Organization in the Early Bronze Age of South Scandinavia. Journal of Anthropological Archaeology 23:33–55.

Kaliff, A. 1997 Grav och kultplats. Eskatologiska föreställningar under yngre bronsålder och järnålder i Östergötland. Uppsala: AUN 24.

Kaliff, A., and T. Oestigaard 2004 Cultivating Corpses. A Comparative Approach to Disembodied Mortuary Remains. Current Swedish Archaeology 12:83–104.

Kaul, F. 1998 Ships on Bronzes. A Study in Bronze Age Religion and Iconography. Copenhagen: PNM Studies in Archaeology and History vol. 3.

Kaul, F. 2003 The Hjortspring Boat and Ship Iconography of the Bronze and Early Pre-Roman Iron Age. In Hjortspring – A Pre-Roman Iron Age Warship in Context. O. Crumlin-Pedersen and A. Trakadas, eds. Pp. 187–208. Roskilde: Ships and Boats of the North No. 5.

Kaul, F. 2004a Bronzealderens religion. Copenhagen: Nordiske Fortidsminder, Serie B: bd 22.

Kaul, F. 2004b Social and Religious Perceptions of the Ship in Bronze Age Northern Europe. The Dover Boat in Context: Society and Water Transport in Prehistoric Europe P. Clarke, ed. Pp. 122–37. Oxford: Oxbow.

Kaul, F. 2005 Skibet – myte og realitet. In Hellristninger. Billeder fra Bornholms bronzealder. F. Kaul, M. Stoltze, F. O. Nielsen, and G. Milstreu, ed. Pp. 75–94. Rønne: Bornholms Museum/Wormanium.

Kjeld Jensen, C., and K. Høilund Nielsen, eds. 1997 Burial and Society. The Chronological and Social Analysis of Archaeological Burial Data. Aarhus: Aarhus University Press.

Kjellén, E., and Å. Hyenstrand 1977 Upplands hällristningar. Uppsala: Upplands Fornminnesförenings Tidskrift No. 49.

Kristiansen, K. 1987 Centre and Periphery in Bronze Age Scandinavia. In Centre and Periphery in the Ancient World. M. Rowlands, M. T. Larsen, and K. Kristiansen, eds. Pp. 74–85. Cambridge: Cambridge University Press.

Kristiansen, K. 2002 Langfærder og helleristinger. In Situ 2000/2001:67–80.

Kristiansen, K. 2004 Kivikgraven, Wismarhornet, Simrisristningerne og den nordiske bronzealders begyndelse. In Prehistoric Pictures as Archaeological Source/Förhistoriska bilder som arkeologisk källa. G. Milstreu and H. Prøhl, ed. Pp. 69–83. Gothenburg: Gotarc Serie C. Arkeologiska Skrifter No. 50.

Kristiansen, K., and T. B. Larsson 2005 The Rise of Bronze Age Societies. Travels, Transmission and Transformations. Cambridge: Cambridge University Press.

Kyvik, G. 2005 Fenomenologiske persepktiver: gravritualer i bronsealder. Bergen: Universitetet i Bergen Arkeologiske Skrifter, Hovedfag/Master No. 1.

de Lange, E. 1912 Ornerte heller i norske bronsealdersgraver. Bergens Museums Aarbok 1912:3–36.

Larsson, L. 1993 Relationer till ett röse – några aspekter på Kiviksgraven. Bronsålderns gravhögar. L. Larsson, ed. Pp. 135–49. Lund: University of Lund Institute of Archaeology, Report Series No. 48.

Larsson, L. 2005 Från höglandskap till golflandskap. Arkeologi och naturvetenskap. Gyllenstiernska Krapperupstiftelsen Symposium nr 6 2003. C. Bunte, B. E. Berglund, and L. Larsson, eds. Pp. 145–62. Nyhamsläge.

Larsson, T. B. 1986 The Bronze Age Metalwork in Southern Sweden. Aspects of Social and Spatial Organization 1800–500 BC. Umeå: Archaeology and Environment 6.

Laursen, S. T., K. L. Johansen, M. K. Holst, and M. Rasmussen 2003 Høje, landskab og bosættelse. Rekognosceringer ved Tobøl-Plogstrup-højgruppen. Kuml 2003: 157–77.

Ling, J. 2005 The Fluidity of Rock Art. In Mellan sten och järn. Rapport från det 9:e nordiska bronsålderssymposiet, Göteborg 2003-10-09/12. J. Goldhahn, ed. Pp. 437–60. Gothenburg: Gotarc Serie C. Arkeologiska Skrifter No. 59.

Linge, T. E. 2004 Mjeltehaugen – fragment frå gravritual. Opublicerad hovedfagsoppgave framlagd vid Arkeologisk. Bergen: Institutt vid Bergens Universitet vår 2004.

Linge, T. E. 2005 Kammeranlegget i Mjeltehaugen – eit rekonstruksjonsforslag. In Mellan sten och järn. Rapport från det 9:e nordiska bronsålderssymposiet, Göteborg 2003-10-09/12. J. Goldhahn, ed. Pp. 537–70. Gothenburg: Gotarc Serie C. Arkeologiska Skrifter No. 59.

Lundborg, L. 1972 Undersökningar av bronsåldershögar och bronsåldersgavar i södra Halland Höks, Tönnersjö och Halmstads härader under åren 1854–1970. Halmstad: Hallands Museum.

Malmer, M. 1971 Bronsristningar. Kuml 1971:189–210.

Mandt, G. 1972 Bergbilder i Hordaland. Bergen: Årbok for Universitetet i Bergen. Humanistisk Serie 1970 No. 2.

Mandt, G. 1983 Tradition and Diffusion in West-Norwegian Rock Art. Mjeltehaugen Revisited. Norwegian Archaeological Review Vol 16 (1):14–32.

Mandt, G. 1991 Vestnorske ristninger i tid og rom. Kronologiske, korologiske og kontekstuelle studier. Bd 1–2. Bergen: Opubliserad doktorgradsavhandling framlagd vid arkeologiskt institutt vid Bergens universitet.

Mandt, G., and T. Lødøen 2005 Bergkunst. Helleristningar i Noreg. Oslo: Det Norske Samlaget.

Marstrander, S. 1963 Østfolds jordbruksristninger. Skjeberg. Oslo: Instituttet for Sammenlignende Kulturforskning Serie B: Skrifter LIII.

Marstrander, S., and K. Sognnes 1999 Trøndelags jordbruksristninger. Trondheim: Vitark No. 1. Acta Archaeologica Nidrosiensia.

Mauss, M. 1990 The Gift. London: Routledge.

Metcalf, P., and R. Huntington 1991 The Celebration of Death. The Anthropology of Mortuary Ritual. 2nd edn. Cambridge: Cambridge University Press.

Møllerup, O. 1992 Arkeologi, vern og museum. Stavanger: AmS-Varia 19.

Nilsen, T. B. 2005 Vedrørende en bergkunstlokalitet i Stjørdalen. En kaususstudie av Leirfallristningene, med fokus på kronologi og tolkning. Tronheim: Masteroppgave vid Institutt for Arkeologi og Religionsvitenskap, NTNU.

Nilsson Stutz, L. 2003 Embodied Rituals and Ritualized Bodies. Tracing Ritual Practices in Late Mesolithic Burials. Lund: Acta Archaeologica Lundensia No. 46.

Norberg, H. 2004 Presentation av historiskt material. Att skapa en interaktiv presentation om Sagaholmsgraven. Opubl. examensrapport vid Institutionen för Innovation, Design och Produktutveckling. Eskilstuna: Mälardalens Högskola.

Nordenborg Myhre, L. 1998 Fragmenter av en annen virkelighet. Stavanger: AmS-Småtrykk No. 46.

Nordenborg Myhre, L. 2004 Trialectic Archaeology. Monuments and Space in Southwest Norway 1700–500 BC. Stavanger: AmS-Skrifter 18.

Oestigaard, T. 1999 Cremation as Transformations: When the Dual Cultural Hypothesis Was Cremated and Carried Away in Urns. European Journal of Archaeology 2 (3):345–64.

Oestigaard, T., and J. Goldhahn 2006 From the Dead to the Living: Funeral Ceremonies as Transaction and Re-Negotiations. Norwegian Archaeological Review 39 (1).

Olivier, L. 1999 The Hochdorf 'Princely' Grave and the Question of the Nature of Archaeological Funerary Assemblages. In Time and Archaeology. T. Murray, ed. Pp. 109–38. London: Routledge.

Østerdal, A. 1999 Tid, rom og sted – bronsalderrøysene i Hordaland. Bergen: Opublisserad hovodfagsoppgave framlagd vid det arkeologiska institutt vid bergens Universitet.

Østmo, E. 2005 Over Skagerak i i steinalderen. Noen refleksjoner om oppfinnelsen av havgående fartøyer i Norden. Viking 2005:55–82.

Parker Pearson, M. 1999 The Archaeology of Death and Burial. College Station: Texas A&M University Press.

Ragnesten, U. 2005 En rösemiljö i Arendal på Hisingen i Göteborg – ett komplext rituellt område. In Mellan sten och järn. Rapport från det 9:e nordiska bronsålderssymposiet, Göteborg 2003-10-09/12. J. Goldhahn, ed. Pp. 353–83. Gothenburg: Gotarc Serie C. Arkeologiska Skrifter No. 59.

Randsborg, K. 1974 Social Stratification in Early Bronze Age Denmark. Prähistoriche Zeitschrift Bd 49:38–61.

Randsborg, K. 1993 Kivik. Archaeology and Iconography. Acta Archaeologica No. 64 (1).

Rausing, G. 1993 Mounds, Monuments and Social Mobility. In Bronsålderns gravhögar. L. Larsson, ed. Pp. 191–6. Lund: University of Lund Institute of Archaeology, Report Series No. 48.

Ringstad, B. 1987 Vestlandets største gravminner. Ett forsøk på lokalisering av forhistoriske maktsentra. Bergen: Opubl. Magistergradsavhandling framlagd vid Bergens Universitets Arkeologiske Institutt 1986.

Rowlands, M., and C. Tilley 2006 Monuments and Memorials. In Handbook of Material Culture. C. Tilley, W. Keane, S. Küchler, M. Rowlands, and P. Spyer, eds. Pp. 500–15. London: Sage.

Runcis, J. 1999 Den mytiska geografin. Reflektioner kring skärvstenshögar, mytologi och landskapsrum i Södermanland under bronsålder. Spiralens öga. M. Olausson, ed. Pp. 127–55. Stockholm: Riksantikvarieämbetet Avdelningen för Arkeologiska Undersökningar, Skrifter No. 25.

Runcis, J. 2002 Bärnstensbarnen. Bilder, berättelser, betraktelser. Stockholm: Riksantikvarieämbetet Arkeologiska Undersökningar, Skrifter No. 41.

Rundkvist, M. 2003 Barshalder 1/2. A Cemetery in Grötlingbo and Fide Parishes, Gotland, Sweden, c. AD 1–1100. Excavations and Finds 1826–1971. Stockholm: Stockholm Archaeological Reports No. 40.

Rygh, K. 1911 En gravplads fra broncealderen. Det Kgl. Norske Videnskabers Selskabs Skrifter No. 1:3–30.

Simonsen, M. F., and D. Vogt 2005 Fotsåleristninger i gravkontekst: Jong – et nytt funn fra Øst-Norge. In Mellan sten och järn. Rapport från det 9:e nordiska bronsålderssymposiet, Göteborg 2003-10-09/12. J. Goldhahn, ed. Pp. 473–87. Gothenburg: Gotarc Serie C. Arkeologiska Skrifter No. 59.

Sjögren, L. 2005 Minoiskt i norr? Om kulturella influenser från Kreta till Skandinavien. *In* Mellan sten och järn. Rapport från det 9:e nordiska bronsålderssymposiet, Göteborg 2003-10-09/12. J. Goldhahn, ed. Pp. 151–66. Gothenburg: Gotarc Serie C. Arkeologiska Skrifter No. 59.

Skoglund, P. 2005 Vardagens landskap. Lokala perspektiv på bronsålderns materiella kultur. Lund: Acta Archaeologica Lundensia Series in 8° No. 49.

Sköldebrand, M. 1997 Högby 87. En begravningsplats genom årtusenden. Linköping: Riksantikvarieämbetet Arkeoilogiska Undersökningar, UV Linköping Rapport 1997:6.

Skre, D. 1997 Raknehaugen. En empirisk loftsrydding. Viking 1997:7–42.

Sognnes, K. 2001 Prehistoric Imagery and Landscapes: Rock Art in Stjørdal, Trøndelag, Norway. Oxford: BAR International Series No. 998.

Stensköld, E. 2004 Att berätta en senneolitisk historia. Sten och metall i södra Sverige 2350–1700 f. Kr. Stockholm: Stockholm Studies in Archaeology No. 34.

Stjernquist, B. 1990 An Iron Age Settlement at Smedstorp, in South-East Scania. Meddelande från Lunds Universitets Historiska Museum 1989–1990:83–100.

Strömberg, B. 2005 Gravplats – gravfält. Platser att skapa minnen vid – plaster att minas vid. Gothenburg: Gotarc Series B. Gothenburg Archaeological Theses No. 35.

Svanberg, F. 2003 Decolonizing the Viking Age 1/2. Lund: Acta Archaeological Lundensia, Series in 8° No. 43.

Syvertsen, K. I. J. 2003 Ristninger i graver – graver med ristniger. Om ristningers mening i gravminner og gravritualer. En analyse av materiale fra Rogaland. Bergen: Opublicerad hovedfagsoppgave framlagd vid Arkeologisk Institutt vid Bergens Universitet våren 2003.

Tainter, J. 1978 Mortuary Practices and the Study of Prehistoric Social Systems. Archaeological Method and Theory 1:105–41.

Thedéen, S. 2004 Gränser i livet – gränser i landskapet. Generationsrelationer och rituella praktiker i södermanländska bronsålderslandskap. Stockholm: Stockholm Studies in Archaeology No. 33.

Theliander, C. 2005 Västergötlands kristnande. Religionsskifte och gravskickets förändring 700–1200. Gothenburg: Gotarc Serie B. Archaeological Theses No. 41.

Thrane, H. 1963 Hjulgraven fra Storehøj ved Tobøl i Ribe Amt. Kuml 1962:80–112.

Thrane, H. 1984 Lusehøj ved Voldtofte – en sydvestfynsk storhøj fra yngre broncealder. Odense: Fynske Studier XIII.

Thrane, H. 1990 The Mycenean Fascination: A Northerner's View. Orientalisch-Ägische Einflüsse in der Europäische Bronzezeit (Bader, T. red):165–80. Bonn: Römische-Germanisches Zentralmuseum, Monographien No. 15.

Tilley, C. 1994 A Phenomenology of the Landscape. Places, Paths and Monuments. Oxford: Berg.

Verlaeckt, K. 1993 The Kivik Petroglyphs. A Reassessment of Different Opinions. Germania 71:1–29.

Vevatne, K. 1996 Ristningar i Etne. Ein analyse av tid og rum. Bergen: Opubl. hovodfagsoppgave framlagd vid det arkeologiska institutt vid Bergens Universitet.

Victor, H. 2002 Med graven som granne. Om bronsålderns kulthus. Uppsala: AUN No. 30.

Vinner, M. 2003 Sea Trails. *In* Hjortspring – A Pre-Roman Iron Age Warship in Context. O. Crumlin-Pedersen and A. Trakadas, eds. Pp. 103–18. Roskilde: Ships and Boats of the North No. 5.

Wahlgren, K. H. 2002 Bilder av betydelse. Hällristningar och bronsålderslandskap i nordöstra Östergötland. Stockholm: Stockholm Studies in Archaeology No. 23.

Wason, P. K. 1994 The Archaeology of Rank. Cambridge: Cambridge University Press.

Westergaard, B. (with a contribution by Jan Bergström) 1987 Gravhög med skeppssättningar. Halland 1987:58–74.

Widholm, D. 1998 Rösen, ristningar, riter. Lund: Acta Archaeologica Lundesia, Series in Prima 4° No. 23.

Wihlborg, A. 1978 Sagaholm. A Bronze Age Barrow with Rock-Engravings. Meddelande från Lunds Universitets Historiska Museum 1977/1978:111–28.

Wrigglesworth, M. 2000 Ristninger og graver som sted. En visuell landskapsanalyse. Bergen: Opublisserad hovodfagsoppgave framlagd vid det arkeologiska institutt vid Bergens Universitet.

Wrigglesworth, M. 2005 Vognmotivet i vestnorsk broncealderkontekst. Mellan sten och järn. Rapport från det 9:e nordiska bronsålderssymposiet, Göteborg 2003-10-09/12 (Goldhahn, J. red):561–570. Gothenburg: Gotarc Serie C. Arkeologiska Skrifter No. 59.

2 (b)

Everything in its Right Place? On Selective Deposition, Landscape and the Construction of Identity in Later Prehistory

David Fontijn

This chapter will focus upon a particular problem of archaeological interpretation, namely that the interpretation of the activities of prehistoric communities depends upon which places in the landscape our analysis focuses upon; different places and activities carry with them particular understandings of society. The image of society evoked by a specific practice in one particular place can be very different from one based on activities carried out in another place; the analysis of specific places carry with them certain biases. Bronze Age sites in the southern Netherlands are a case in point.

The Middle Bronze Age (1800–1100 BC) is thought to herald the formation of an ordered and fixed 'agrarian' landscape. Both the settlement and burial evidence offer a view of society as being made up of isolated, peaceful and egalitarian local groups. It has been claimed that Bronze Age society and Bronze Age people's use of the landscape is by now fairly well understood. However, it is only recently that attention has been paid to comparing the evidence from different sorts of places in the landscape.

All over the region large numbers of bronze objects have been found in wet places, like swamps and rivers. Recent research has shown that these objects were deliberately deposited by Bronze Age communities, with the express intention to abandon them forever. The items sacrificed tend to be highly 'valuable' objects, many of which have been imported from distant regions. These include numerous axes, and ornaments in supra-regional styles, but also swords and spears, many of which show signs of having been used in battle. It is not only the deliberate abandonment or disposal of such special items that seems remarkable, but also the fact that it took place in a specific kind of environment: in wet places, beyond the confines of the humanly constructed landscape. It is striking that the analysis of objects deposited in rivers presents a very different picture of Bronze Age society to that normally obtained from the analysis of burials and settlements. Imported objects like swords denote violence, the celebration of martial ideals and the social significance of exchange relations with far-flung societies, quite unlike the picture of peaceful egalitarian communities obtained from settlements and burials. How are we to reconcile such different images of society reflected in practices carried out in wet places compared with those in burials and settlements? This chapter will deal with that problem.

A case study of the southern Netherlands during the Middle and Late Bronze Age (1800–800 BC) will serve to show how people differentiated between zones in the landscape. Charting the practice of selective deposition of metalwork, I will demonstrate how different types of places became imbued with different ideas and values through time.

Making Sense of the Prehistoric Landscape

The problem set out above seems first and foremost to be an empirical one. The evidence from settlements, burial monuments and bronze deposits tends to be spatially separated. Even though settlements have been uncovered in large-scale landscape excavations (Gerritsen 2003:26–9), the precise position of burial monuments in the settled landscape can rarely be documented. Problems in relating bronze finds to prehistoric land use are even worse. Only 4 per cent of bronze objects were found during 'professional' excavations (Fontijn 2002). The majority of bronzes were recovered by 'non-professionals' and for that reason more often than not lack substantial contextual evidence. The reliability of such finds has therefore been called into question in several European regions, to the extent that they were omitted from any discussion of the Bronze Age at all (Verlaeckt 1996: 6–7). Nevertheless, for the region under study here, an analysis of recorded finds shows that at least 69 per cent (661 objects) are reliable finds for which a depositional context can be reconstructed in varying degrees of detail (Fontijn 2002). In addition, this analysis also shows that the predominance of bronzes from wet places cannot be explained by selective preservation or occasional loss; they must have ended their lives in such places because prehistoric people deliberately left them there.

There are also problems of an epistemological nature. The seemingly 'rationally-ordered' agrarian settlements of Bronze Age northwest Europe are often considered to resonate with medieval or historical agrarian landscapes (Brück 1999:323). The emphasis on the 'familiar' aspects of Bronze Age agrarian landscape ignores the evidence of many 'unfamiliar' practices like the construction of barrows and metalwork deposition.

The biggest interpretative challenge seems to be the 'odd' metalwork finds from wet places. If their predominance in such places can only be explained by assuming that people deliberately deposited such scarce and valuable items for perpetuity, how are we to make sense of such 'wasteful' behaviour? As a matter of fact, such practices appear to have taken place in large parts of Europe for long periods of time (Bradley 1990; Kristiansen 1998; Needham 1989), particularly in non-metalliferous regions like the southern Netherlands, where all bronze had to be imported from a distance (Bradley 1990:132–5).

A widely-shared interpretation of such depositions is to see them as ritual acts of sacrifice, in which scarce (and therefore prestigious) goods were removed from society and offered to gods or supernatural entities. The function of such rituals is often seen as enhancing the political power of the owner who is thought to gain prestige in the eyes of his/her community by sacrificing valuables. Some archaeologists have argued that it may tacitly have served to create scarcity and therefore to uphold the prestigious value of bronze and hence the political role of those who based their power on the monopolization of access to bronze exchange networks (reviewed in Fontijn 2002:17–20).

Bronze Finds as Indicative of Ritual Places?

If bronze finds are recognized as the result of 'ritual' practices they may provide an important insight into the prehistoric perception of landscape. By mapping 'ritual' depositions we may define those areas prehistoric communities considered 'sacred' places. On the other hand, it might be argued that such an approach is inappropriate for non-modern societies and may even hamper our understanding of the evidence. If we use a term like 'ritual', we tacitly assume that a distinction between 'ritual' and 'profane' places and practices was relevant for the society in question (Bradley 2005). However, a ritual–profane distinction is historically situated in a rational way of thinking typical of the post-Enlightenement (Brück 1999). In this latter mode, 'practical' behaviour is a pre-supposed human trait, whereas 'ritual' behaviour is practice beyond functional requirement. Consequently 'ritual' becomes something that has to be proved by archaeologists, whereas practical action is assumed. Ritual action, in a way, equals irrationality. A survey of the way in which archaeologists have approached bronze deposits from the early 19th century until recent times exemplifies this (Fontijn 2002:13–22). The rational-economic perspective defines both the problem and its solutions. It asserts there is something 'strange' (i.e. economically irrational) about leaving 'valuable' metalwork in the ground. If this cannot be explained in a practical ('profane') way (as loss, discard or temporarily stored but never retrieved), only then does a 'ritual' interpretation become acceptable. Therefore, explanations of bronze deposition as practices that enhance prestige or create scarcity, transform the economically 'irrational' act into an economically rational activity.

We also need to consider whether the identification of places as 'ritual' adds something to our understanding of prehistoric landscape; whether the distinction between ritual and non-ritual is merely a 'taxonomic' and epistemologically anachronistic dichotomy (cf. Brück 1999). Firstly, patterns in the archaeological record itself provide clues that the prehistoric engagement with landscape was very differently constituted. With regard to bronze deposition, we have already seen an example of specific patterns in deposition. Particular types of objects appear to have ended up in particular locations, often in association with certain objects. This holds true for many more regions in Bronze Age Europe and cannot simply be explained by processes of post-depositional decay and recovery (Hundt 1955; Needham 1989). This alone suggests that deposition may have been based on a widely shared set of rules, and therefore must have been anything but an irrational practice.

Patterns of selective deposition also illustrate the problem of explaining such practices in terms of creation of prestige; if it was only metal content that mattered, how then are we to make sense of the fact that the bronzes deposited in – say – a burial, are different from those placed in a river? Patterns in the evidence suggest that the 'practical' and 'the ritual' may have even been linked. Large amounts of axes from 'ritual' wet places show traces of an intensive, practical use-life.

Approaching the Bronze Age Landscape: Selective Deposition

In what follows, it seems appropriate to ignore pre-conceived distinctions between ritual and the profane in order to focus on the selective patterns of deposition. Such patterns reflect widely-shared practices in which distinctions and similarities between places were expressed. We will take the deposition of swords as an example. In the southern Netherlands, swords and other weapons are conspicuously missing in a number of well-researched contexts, such as burials, in which they could easily have been preserved. They are however found, in large numbers, in the major rivers of the region. We will see later on that this trend is true for the entire region, and for a very long period of time. Situations in which particular objects were kept distinct from others in deposition indicate these objects are not just 'things', but valuables imbued with specific meanings (cf. Rowlands 1993:147). This is not only true of the objects themselves, but also of the places in which they are deposited. For example, the fact that swords were apparently preferably deposited in rivers encourages an interpretation of rivers as the 'proper' receptacle for swords.

It is important to realize that a significant proportion of the objects that were placed in rivers or marshes show traces of a long use-life and lengthy period of circulation (Figure 2.18). This suggests a situation in which objects did not carry special meanings from the beginning but only as the result of a particular life-path or cultural biography. Kopytoff (1986) points out how in every society there are often shared ideas on the particular life-paths certain objects should follow, just as such ideas exist for the careers of persons. Interestingly, many of the bronzes that were deposited must actually have been significant in the personal careers of individual persons. The construction of personal identities often involves the transformation of the self. Ethnographically, we know that material culture is often instrumental in the construction of such identities (Hoskins 1998). The fact that much of the deposited metalwork consists of body ornaments is suggestive of the mutual merging of the cultural biographies of objects and humans.

The same may hold true for the biographies of places. Only specific types of places were selected for depositional practices. These places not only share specific physical characteristics, but as we will see below, they may also have had specific histories which might have made them appropriate for a specific depositional act. I will now examine one particular pattern of selective deposition: the different ways in which paraphernalia related to personal identities were deposited, to analyze the implications for the construction of the identity of both places and communities.

The Role of Burial Practices and Burial Monuments in Landscape Organization

Burial monuments are an obvious starting point for studies of the prehistoric landscape, not least because many earthen round-barrows are visible in the present day. Although older Neolithic graves are occasionally known in the southern Netherlands, it is only from c.2600 BC onwards that the history of burial practices and their significance for the structuring of landscape can be analyzed in some detail. From that period, we are dealing with a mortuary tradition in which burials of individuals are visibly marked with earthen mounds or barrows (Drenth and Lohof 2005). Such barrows seem to have acted as focal points in the landscape for later

Figure 2.18 Bronze sword of type Rosnoën (c. 1300–1125 BC), found in a marsh near Kronenberg (length 53 cm). It was probably imported from western France. Impact marks on the blade and a completely reworked butt indicate that it was intensively used (Drawing by E. van Driel, University of Leiden)

burials, either inserted in the mound itself, as secondary graves (Figure 2.19), or in new mounds in their vicinity (Figure 2.20). Although interment under barrows must have been a rare event when it emerged during the Late Neolithic, increasing numbers of people were buried in such a way as the Bronze Age wore on, culminating in the Late Bronze Age and Early Iron Age urnfields, when true cemeteries emerged in which, in some cases, almost every member of a local group was buried under an individual mound (Fokkens 1997). Throughout the Bronze Age, burials were never wealthy or truly monumental like, for example, their Scandinavian contemporaries (see Goldhahn, this volume). Perhaps for that reason, Bronze Age burial rites in this region have always been seen as rather straightforward representations of society, in line with settlement evidence. However, following the approach discussed above, it will become apparent that the situation is more complex.

Let us begin by considering burial practice itself. Archaeological evidence, by its very nature, particularly sheds light on the final stages of the funerary sequence: the disposal of the bodily remains of the deceased deposited in the place where they were to remain. There are clear patterns to be observed in the way in which this was done, showing that there were culturally-specific ideas on the right way to treat and represent the bodily remains at this stage of the burial, ideas that were being reproduced, but also evaluated and negotiated in this very act (see Goldhahn, this volume). Among them may be ideas on the proper way of representing the deceased at this stage of the burial, as a particular kind of person, and on the values with which this identity was imbued. As discussed above, identity can be constructed using specific bodily adornment including appropriate paraphernalia and gifts supplied by the mourners. Circumstances of preservation are such that few perishable items (such as dress or clothing) will have survived in the archaeological record. Bronze items are the objects most frequently preserved. Arguably, these bronze objects

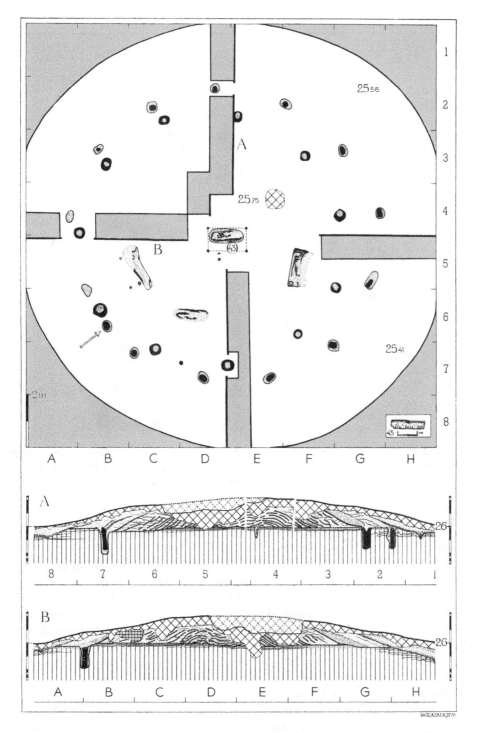

Figure 2.19 Middle Bronze Age barrow with primary and secondary interments. Toterfout-Halve Mijl, tumulus 5 (Source: Glasbergen 1954)

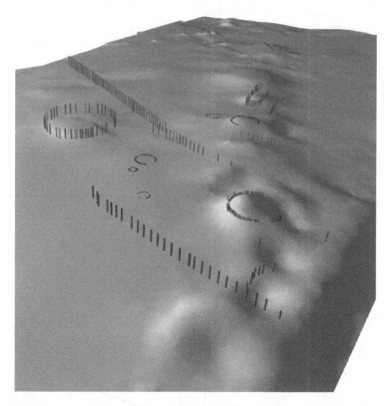

Figure 2.20 Reconstruction of the aligned Bronze Age barrows of Berghem-Zevenbergen. Shown are the barrows, some with post circles, and several prehistoric post alignments. The isolated barrow to the left dates to the Early Iron Age (Made by W. van der Laan, Archol BV, Leiden)

provide a clue for our understanding of the ideological meanings expressed in the burial.

The earliest burials are predominantly inhumation graves, but from the Middle Bronze Age onwards, the cremation rite gains importance until it becomes predominant in the Late Bronze Age urnfield period (Drenth and Lohof 2005). For cremation burials, it is important to realize that there are at least two moments at which a specific identity (which might leave observable traces) was expressed: when the body was displayed on the pyre, and when his or her remains were placed in the grave (Barrett 1994:119–20). It is important to realize that throughout the entire Middle and Late Bronze Age the provision of bronze items in burials is an exception. If bronzes are present they are usually body ornaments, dress fittings, toilet articles and sometimes small tools, generally simple – presumably locally made – items, executed in local styles (Fontijn 2002). A sample of urnfields, where several graves contained bronzes, and where the sex and age of the deceased could be determined, indicates that the social meaning of bronze items was idiosyncratic and local (ibid.: 197–208). For example, in one urnfield (Roermond-Mussenberg) bronzes are only known from the graves of females and children, and here there are indications that they served to distinguish between categories of women themselves; in another contemporary urnfield (Weert-Raak), bronzes are associated with males and females, but exclude children. The precise meaning of such items may escape us, but it is worth making the point that the identities constructed seem to be local (expressed in an occasionally idiosyncratic style) and to express local social concerns (i.e. that comparable items do not seem to relate to ideas on social identities that were widely shared among communities). We will see below that there is sufficient reason to suggest that this is a skewed representation of reality, expressing a concern with specific ideas and values, and ignoring others.

An important requirement for the biography of a specific place created by burial is whether the burial ritual resulted in a visible monument. Unless the mound was erased altogether (which rarely happened in the Bronze Age), the mound became a permanent feature of the landscape. As earthen round mounds were built over burials from the Late Neolithic until the Roman Period (and later) in this region, we might expect that a mound constructed in the Early Bronze Age would also be recognized as a mortuary monument for some period afterwards. Thus, construction of a mound was much more than the closing act of a funeral; it also formed a lasting artefact that would 'presence' the former occupants of the landscape.

Once created the majority of these mounds were re-used for burial. Were they also constructed for this purpose? Barrows constructed in the late Neolithic (2900–2000 BC) may be visibly similar to those from the much later Middle Bronze Age, but they had a very different role in the structuring of the landscape. Before the Middle Bronze Age, burials were only dug into existing barrows long after they had been erected. For those built during the Middle Bronze Age the number of secondary interments is not only considerably higher, but re-use took place with a much shorter time-interval, during the same or the following generation (Lohof 1994; Theunissen 1999). The Middle Bronze Age re-use of burial mounds reflects a situation in which it is likely that there was a genealogical link between consecutive burials (see Garwood 1991 for comparable discussion of genealogical links in the British Early and Middle Bronze Age).

The re-use of barrows from the Late Neolithic and Early Bronze Age can have only drawn on a form of cultural memory that was mythical at best (Bradley 2002; Lohof 1994:102). By contrast, it is difficult to find Middle Bronze Age barrows that were not re-used during the Middle Bronze Age, which may suggest that re-use was not coincidental, but part of a pre-ordained cultural notion on the appropriate biography of burial places (cf. Bradley 2002:86). Once constructed, a barrow would have been expected to serve as a place of burial for specific individuals from the same or following generation, until it was considered appropriate to cease using it and build or re-use another one.

The way in which this re-use took place was not as straightforward as it may seem. As collective graves, Middle Bronze Age barrows are often seen as the burial grounds of households, 'family barrows', constructed over the grave of the male head of family, with his relatives in secondary graves (Fokkens 1997:362). However, recent research shows that the number of people who were interred in such monuments would have only been 10 per cent or lower of the entire population (Lohof 1994; Theunissen 1999). The majority of people were buried elsewhere, in a manner that does not survive in the archaeological record. However, among the secondary graves in these barrows both sexes and all age categories are present. In addition, no true distinctions seem to have been made in terms of body treatment or grave gifts between the graves other than position in the grave, and primary graves do not seem to have been reserved for male adults (Fontijn and Cuijpers 2002;

Theunissen 1999). Summing up, a barrow cannot have been the true burial place of a family, but some sort of *pars pro toto*, evoking the *ideal* of a collective grave that was open to all ages and sex categories in the community.

In Late Bronze Age urnfields more people than before were buried under barrows in individual rather than collective grave monuments. Nevertheless, urnfields generally represent the graves of several households as an undifferentiated collective, although dispersed single-generation households were common in this period. This suggest that urnfields were a context for the expression of collectivity as a cultural value (Gerritsen 2003:243).

Placing recent graves next to older ones became increasingly important from the Middle Bronze Age on. New mounds were constructed on top of older ones, and new barrows placed in similar positions as existing ones, often resulting in regularly aligned groups of Middle Bronze Age barrows (Figure 2.20). The way in which this was done suggests that burial practices in barrows may well have accompanied a notion of tradition and repetition; the repetition of acts performed in the past. It is also in the Middle Bronze Age that older, Late Neolithic, barrows were re-used for burial on a considerable scale, suggesting that Middle Bronze Age communities explicitly attempted to establish links in the burial ritual with the monuments of a distant past. Although Late Neolithic burials were originally placed in isolated positions in the landscape (Drenth and Lohof 2005:433), several case studies show that they acquired a new role in the re-ordered landscape of the Middle Bronze Age, as they became foci for Middle Bronze Age barrow groups. These barrow groups often developed into extensive burial landscapes by the end of the Early Iron Age (Figure 2.21; Fontijn 1996).

Contrast: Depositing Valuables in Unaltered Places

If we base our understanding of society on the profuse evidence from burials, there would be little reason for viewing the Bronze Age inhabitants of the southern Netherlands other than as egalitarian and peaceful groups in which localism was pervasive. We can view the burial evidence in a different light if we combine it with an analysis of the large amount of metalwork found in watery places. The metalwork in watery contexts includes categories that are lacking in graves, like body ornaments in non-local styles and numerous weapons, occasionally including weapon sets. The weaponry and associated martial imagery particularly exemplify the point that a distinction was made between the deposits in graves and specific sorts of 'natural' places. From a European perspective, the picture of 'localism' and peacefulness denoted by the burial deposits is remarkable. Warrior graves containing a specific and supra-regionally shared set of paraphernalia and weapons, and the 'warrior ideal' that went with it, are generally considered as a defining characteristic of the European Bronze Age (Treherne 1995; see Hanks, this volume). Warrior graves are practically unknown in the Bronze Age of the southern Netherlands and northern Belgium. This is remarkable in view of the fact that it is precisely this same region for which there is plentiful evidence that swords, spears and even entire warrior outfits in supra-regional styles were current at that time, often in much higher quantities than in the adjacent regions (Fontijn 2002: table 11.2). The Overloon hoard is a good case in point: the hoard contains the equipment of at least two warriors including an ornament, placed in or directly near a stream (ibid.:103).

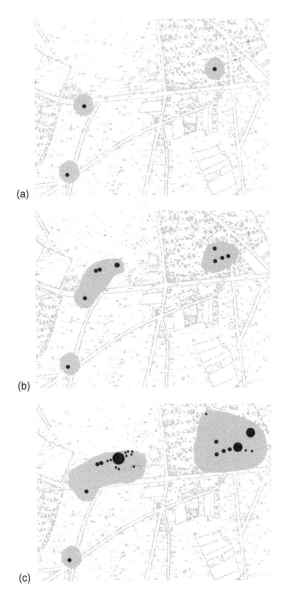

Figure 2.21 The development of the mortuary landscape in between Oss-Berghem-Schaaijk. (a) Late Neolithic (c.2500–2000 BC); (b) Middle Bronze Age (1800–1100 BC); (c) Late Bronze Age-Early Iron Age (1100–500 BC) (Source: Fokkens and Jansen 2004)

Comparable warrior equipment is known from burials in adjacent regions, but at Overloon we are dealing with a situation in which these paraphernalia were surrendered, and placed in a stream valley marsh. This may have happened at some stage in the life-cycle or at death (Figure 2.22). However, there is no evidence in the southern Netherlands, for Bronze Age burials in rivers or marshes accompanying such deposits (ibid:229–30).

Finds like the Overloon hoard imply several things. In marked contrast to the local identity expressed in burials, they show that there were people in the

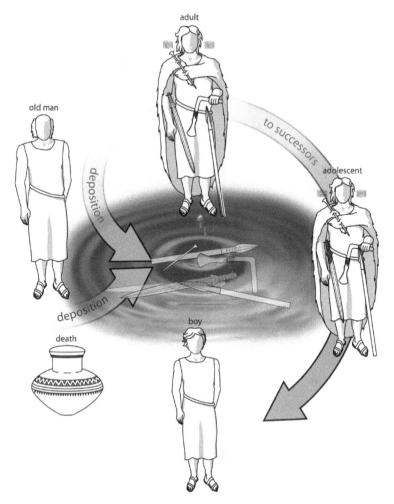

Figure 2.22 Hypothetical lifecycle of a warrior. Arrows indicate moments when martial paraphernalia might have been surrendered, either by giving them to a successor, or by depositing
them in a watery place. An alternative is to suppose that warriorhood was less related to stages
in the lifecycle, but more a temporary, context-dependent identity. In both models were weapons
periodically placed in rivers or marshes (Drawing by M. Oberendorff, University of Leiden)

southern Netherlands who knew about and adopted a particular kind of
imagery that was held in common by groups in several regions. In addition, the role
of body ornaments and dress fittings shows that such supra-regional personal
identities went hand in hand with a transformed bodily appearance. However,
the objects by which this transformation was achieved are almost exclusively
known from depositions in watery 'natural' places, rather than graves, or other locations in the cultivated agrarian landscape. The implication, then, must be that items
like weapons or special, supra-regionally styles of ornament were seen as imbued
with specific and circumscribed meanings that were not relevant (perhaps even
taboo) in the portrayal of the deceased in the grave. However, as will be demonstrated in more detail below, studies show that weaponry, and the paraphernalia of

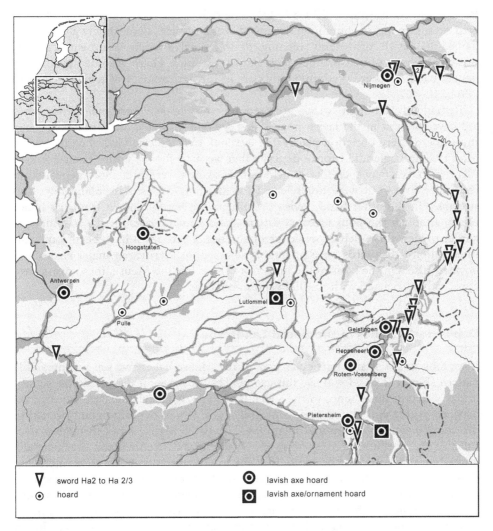

Figure 2.23   Distribution of sword deposits in relation to multiple-object hoards in the southern Netherlands (Source: Fontijn 2002:fig. 8.21)

warriorhood in particular, were adopted by these same communities, and were periodically removed from circulation to be deposited in specific sorts of places. If the set of weapons and ornaments were instrumental in the construction of a martial identity, then their deliberate removal by sacrifice may have implied its de-construction.

The way in which particular categories of bronzes were placed in the landscape shows that people did not only differentiate between burials and wet places; people also differentiated between different *types* of wet places, like between major rivers such as the Rhine or the Meuse on the one hand, and between swamps, peat bogs and small streams on the other. This implies that different types of watery places had different connotations. A first example comes from the study region as a whole. Figure 2.23 depicts the distribution of swords and that of rich hoards of the Late

Bronze Age Ha B3-phase (925–800 BC). The rich hoards generally consist of sock-eted axes, sometimes containing dozens of axes at a time, occasionally also accom-panied by lavish ornaments relating to the north-French 'Plainseau culture', presumably part of conspicuous high status costumes. There is some indirect evi-dence that these were predominantly part of the appearances of females (Fontijn 2002:239–46).

Remarkably although swords are predominantly known from major rivers they are never present in the lavish hoards that we find in inland sites, not even when these hoards were buried in places that overlook river valleys. These hoards are the most rich and splendid bronze deposits that we have for the entire Bronze Age in this region. We may therefore conclude that swords were preferably deposited in the major rivers but were not selected for the mass deposits in inland bogs and streams. On the other hand, lavish ornaments are hardly known from the major rivers, although the poor recovery circumstances in the rivers make it somewhat harder to view this solely as evidence of absence. There must have been some cul-tural notion that swords were preferably selected for sacrifice in major rivers, and nowhere else. On the basis of the finds from rivers like the Meuse, these rivers were apparently associated with martial values and ideas.

Depositional Zones in the Social Landscape

If we look in detail at a particular part of the Meuse Valley, we see a comparable pattern (Figure 2.24). I will use this example as the basis for discussing the signifi-cance of depositional zones in the social landscape, what relations are constructed between people and places, and, conversely, how acts of deposition contributed to the construction of communal identities. The River Meuse flows through a river valley with pronounced river terraces (Figure 2.24). Settlements are generally located on the loamy, fertile grounds of the middle terraces. Such areas, including those flanking the often steep-sided ridge of the higher terraces, are ringed by stream valleys and a variety of marshes. A map of the distribution of bronze finds in this landscape indicates that they were deposited in the River Meuse and/or its back-swamps and most wet, 'natural' places in the periphery of the settled area, with an occasional example of a bronze deposit in a dry location situated in a conspicuous high place. It is striking to see that swords in particular are missing from the inland bogs, but prevalent in the Meuse itself or its backswamp. For a group of people living near Echt during the Bronze Age, all wet zones were accessible, but clearly people used the river for different sorts of depositions than the inland marshes and stream valleys.

From the perspective of those who dwelt in the farming community, depositional zones must have been peripheral. If we take the house as 'the centre of the world' (see Boric, this volume and Gerritsen, this volume) and model the spatial distribu-tion of items in relation to it (Figure 2.25), then it is apparent that most bronzes were deposited at some distance from the agrarian land in the major rivers; in addi-tion objects with links to the supra-regional 'outer' world were deposited relatively far away. Objects that are more related to local identities tend to be deposited in places closer to the house. Interestingly, the deposits in burials or on or near farm-steads (Fontijn 2002:144–7) are also different from site to site, whereas those in the major rivers seem to have been much more formalized. For example, river

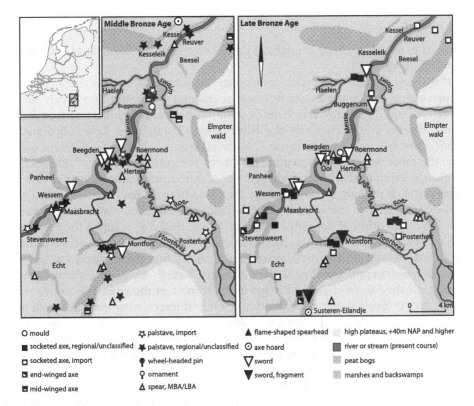

Middle Bronze Age ⊙

Kessel
Reuver
Kesseleik
Beesel
Haelen
Buggenum
Elmpter wald
Beegden
Roermond
Herten
Panheel
Wessem
Maasbracht
Stevensweert
Montfort
Posterholt
Echt

Late Bronze Age

Kessel
Reuver
Kesseleik
Beesel
Haelen
Buggenum
Elmpter wald
Beegden
Ool Roermond
Herten
Panheel
Wessem
Maasbracht
Stevensweert
Montfort
Posterholt
Echt
Susteren-Eilandje

0   4 km

○ mould
■ socketed axe, regional/unclassified
□ socketed axe, import
◣ end-winged axe
◪ mid-winged axe

✪ palstave, import
✯ palstave, regional/unclassified
● wheel-headed pin
○ ornament
△ spear, MBA/LBA

▲ flame-shaped spearhead
⊙ axe hoard
▽ sword
▼ sword, fragment

high plateaus, +40m NAP and higher
river or stream (present course)
peat bogs
marshes and backswamps

Figure 2.24 Deposition in the River Meuse and in the adjacent inland marshes in Midden-Limburg for the Middle and Late Bronze Age. Only contextualized finds are mapped (Source: Fontijn 2002: fig. 14.1)

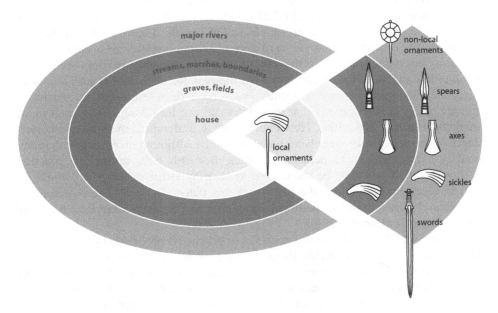

major rivers
streams, marshes, boundaries
graves, fields
house
local ornaments

non-local ornaments
spears
axes
sickles
swords

Figure 2.25 Deposition of different categories of objects in relation to the house (Drawing by M. Oberendorff, University of Leiden)

deposits in the Meuse bear similarities to those in the River Rhine in Mid-Germany (Torbrügge 1970–71).

If we now include other social groups in this perspective, it becomes clear that many streams and marshes are not only peripheral zones, but also divide up the habitable land. They may have been boundaries between territories or groups, but some streams, and particularly the River Meuse itself, must have functioned as connections between communities. The River Meuse is clearly of a different nature than the other waterways, as it must have been the common point of reference for all groups living in the Meuse Valley; it was also the practical connection with the outer world. It is likely that most of the imported bronzes that were deposited were initially imported to the southern Netherlands via this same river. If we consider that the distribution of deposited metalwork (Figure 2.24) mapped for the Meuse River catchment area probably represents only a fraction of what was actually being deposited on land during the Bronze Age, it shows that there is no focal or 'cult' place to which people travelled to deposit items. Rather, it seems as if many groups living near the Meuse deposited items in 'their' part of the river. It is entire zones rather than individual places that mattered. Deposition clearly took place from both sides of the rivers, and may also have been practised from boats on the river. Both sides of the large Echt-Montfort swamps seem to have been used, suggesting that different communities (living on the opposite side of the swamp?) visited the area; this must have happened repeatedly.

A comparison of the distribution of depositions in the Middle and Late Bronze Age shows a remarkable tradition in the practice. It is not just the same zones that were used for a very long time, they were also used in a similar way (e.g. the association between swords and the major river). This tradition in practice is surprising especially when we take into account the fact that depositions took place rarely. Calculations show that at its peak (at the end of the Late Bronze Age–beginning of the Iron Age) a figure of even one deposit per local group within 25 years would be an over-estimation (Fontijn 2002:214–15). The traditions of deposition echoes those long traditions observed in the placing of burials (Figure 2.21). In the case of burials we can argue that the tradition of practice relates to a concern with repeating ancestral acts. But in the case of burial monuments, barrows are permanent, visible places. This cannot have been the case for depositional sites in watery places. Although not many deposition sites have been excavated in northwest Europe, there are indications that these sites did not have long lasting man-made markers (Harding 2000:309). How then are we to understand the impressive time-depth in the use of such wet places for depositions? Although marshes are phenomenal as natural places, as depositional sites they only exist during the practice. Afterwards, they can only be recognized as such by virtue of religious knowledge and insider's knowledge on the history of this place. As such they represent an 'imaginary' rather than 'phenomenal' landscape in the terms described by social anthropologists (Hirsch 1995).

The social reality related to this tradition of practice is probably complex. Certain ideas on selective deposition, like the preference for depositing swords in rivers, were widely shared, even across several European regions (Torbrügge 1970–1). There are arguments that the sort of zones where this was practised had similar natural characteristics (e.g. at confluences of rivers, near elevations; Fontijn 2002:260–2). An inhabitant of another region may therefore well have recognized the confluence near Roermond as a proper place for a sword deposition. But this is different from knowing the precise historical meaning such a site had for the groups living there. Depositions cluster in *particular* stretches of rivers or swamps, not just in any wet zone. That the distribution of deposited objects resulting from such a long use of a swamp or river is rather diffuse may be explained by the absence of markers pointing out the exact position of earlier depositional locations, or alternatively, such precise knowledge was simply not seen as important. At any rate, such 'multiple deposition zones' suggest that for some cases deposition was determined by a wish to repeat acts done in the past. Insider knowledge on 'knowing the right place and the proper way of doing things' may even have functioned to create insiders and outsiders and thus to define membership of a 'sacrificial community'. The scenery and inaccessibility of depositional places like some inland bogs may well be in line with practices that involve secrecy, whereas deposits in major rivers may have involved much larger audiences. In this way, depositional sites not only provide people with an identity, people may also base their communal identities on such places.

Selective Deposition and its Consequences

Above, we have explored some of the characteristics of two widely shared and long-lived practices in which people interacted with and organized the landscape. We saw that practices of object deposition may have worked to differentiate between zones in the landscape. It may both reflect and construct specific views on the ideational ordering of the landscape. But can we make any further sense of the intentions associated with deposition?

In order to gain an increased understanding of deposition, we need to return to the meaning the deposited bronze items had for society. In every society, there is a tension between different but co-existing social realities (Fontijn 2002:273–4). The first is that of the local group, rooted in a sense of belonging to a specific locality. The second is the reality detached from locality, in which one's group is seen as part of a much wider, partly 'imagined' social whole. These views co-exist, but the second is potentially an ambiguous category, as it denotes the dependency of the local group on factors beyond their own control. What effectively links both realities is the imported item, in this case the bronze objects. This does not automatically imply that imported materials were necessarily treated differently, but in several European regions there are indeed indications that bronze, as a material, had added significance, especially in the non-metalliferous regions (Bradley 1990:132–5; Kristiansen 1998). We have seen that it is not only imported objects, but also specific idealized personal identities and their associated accoutrements that were widespread, like the warrior equipment that was deposited in the Overloon hoard. In the southern Netherlands, some people were in a way 'dressed internationally', claiming membership of far-flung 'imagined' communities. The Overloon example also enables us to reflect on the fact that imagery with such supra-regional affiliations is, in parts of Europe, often also related to warrior's appearances (see Hanks, this volume). We have seen that weaponry was rigidly kept apart in depositional practices. But weaponry may have been considered an ambiguous category in itself, as violence may be considered a transgressive, and therefore ambiguous, category implying a threat to social cohesion (Harrison 1995).

I will now continue by considering the way in which these objects were placed in the landscape. Many of the objects selected must already have had added significance as a result of their previous biographies. The act of deposition itself may have been a special event in which the biographies of people, the objects and the place coalesced. It will have been an event in which the objects and what they represented were emphasized and celebrated, and at the same time an act that would entail their disappearance from society altogether. At least in the case of a deposition in a grave, the location was marked with a monument, while in the case of deposition in watery places locations remain unmarked. Paradoxically, ethnographic analogies suggest that the intention behind such a removal of valuables from society need not have been to erase such objects and the cultural values they represent, but rather they may have served to create a 'memory in their absence' (Rowlands 1993:146), and thus to reproduce the special character of place, the object and the cultural values with which it was seen to be related. Our regional study illustrates that from the Middle Bronze Age onwards people kept on carrying out similar sorts of depositions – probably with considerable time-intervals in between – in the same unaltered watery places for a long time, without any written protocol on which to base their selection of places. This not only suggests that specific sorts of places came to be imbued with a certain identity, but also that these identities became increasingly 'fixed' as the Bronze Age wore on.

As meaningful objects themselves may have been considered as 'personified' (Bazelmans 1999:32–4), the distinction between placing objects in a swamp or on or next to the deceased need not be absolute. Yet, it is relevant to realize that in a burial a specific personal identity is created by the mourners by adorning the body with bronze ornaments. The biographies of object and the individual are 'fused' (in a literal sense during cremation). The ideological emphasis in such burial practices seems to be on local identities and on the representation of a community as a collective whole, and the places where such ideals were celebrated are often visibly marked.

When objects were deposited in a marsh or river we see the reverse: a personal identity was de-constructed, with the matching paraphernalia surrendered and removed from society forever. This may well have been a suitable practice for coping with objects that were seen as important and meaningful but also as ambiguous and circumscribed. They were placed in remote zones of the landscape that may have had a certain ambiguity: such watery zones were generally not altered by the human hand, and represent diffuse boundaries in a physical, social and perhaps also in a cosmological way (between the real and an 'under-world', cf. Bradley 2000:28–32)? Such a way of dealing with charged objects may well have been a long-term characteristic of deposition in this region. From the Early Neolithic onwards, there are examples of imported items (like flint or stone axes) that were kept separate from settlements and placed in watery sites (Fontijn 2002:247; Wentink 2006). It may be considered that the act of deliberately giving up or sacrificing a component of imported materials by incorporating them with the local landscape might have been a socially and religiously acceptable way of realigning the ambiguity of the item with the moral order at home (cf. Bloch and Parry 1989). This brings us to the intriguing question of how people conceptualized such depositional acts?

Defining deposition in terms of 'removal' implies a one-sided practice from the point of view of people. However, in non-modern communities, society as a whole is often seen as constituting both humans and ancestors, spirits and gods (Bazelmans 1999; Bird-David 1999; Ingold 2000). Land itself may also have been seen as imbued with personal characteristics, and evokes the prolongation of human nature (Pálsson 1996). Deposition may therefore imply a reciprocal logic of 'taking' and 'giving'. A conspicuous characteristic of depositions in wet places in this region is that objects show traces of use and are usually deposited in an undamaged state. Often the edges of swords, spears or axes have even been sharpened as if they still had to be used. This implies that deposition was not considered as 'destruction', but rather seen as the prolonging of the object's life-path or career. Axes that were intensively used to *alter* the land ('taking'), and clearly showing the traces thereof, were preferably placed in *unaltered* places. Could this mean that deposition was seen as some sort of 'giving back' and thus reflects the 'reciprocity' towards the land that Pálsson (1996) documented for some non-modern societies? It should be realized that the specific patterns of selective deposition can only be understood by considering a framework that encompasses a view of the object's original role and function; what it 'did' to the land. One widely accepted theory views depositions in wet places as sacrifices to 'gods', with specific types of places associated with specific spiritual entities (Bradley 2000). Historical sources on Germanic and Celtic practices suggest that watery places may have been conceptualized in such a way by Late Iron Age communities (Fontijn 2002:16–17, 267–8). However, in most European regions, depositional practices existed since the Early Neolithic, and it seems highly unlikely that it had the same meaning during thousands of years (Bradley 1990). As a matter of fact, Bronze Age depositions have characteristics that set them apart from those of the later Iron Age. We may, for example, think of the widely-shared selective nature of deposition, the fact that it was almost a Pan-European phenomenon, but also that Bronze Age deposition does not seem to have been focused on single 'cult places' like those we know from the Late Iron Age, but rather entire environmental zones like stretches of rivers. Although it seems likely that selective deposition was determined by a culturally-specific logic, it is more appropriate to see Iron Age sacrifices to personified gods as a historically-specific conceptualization of a, by then, age-old practice, rather than its very essence.

Deposition and the Construction of Identity

Throughout the southern Netherlands, depositional practices were carried out in which meaningful objects were placed in specific types of places and avoided in others. One anthropological theory of ritual practice states that ritual reveals ideological values at their deepest levels (Barraud and Platenkamp 1990:103). But a combination of the burial practice versus the deposition of items in rivers alone shows that the ideological values of localism and the representation of the group as a non socially stratified, peaceful whole played out in the burial ritual are not in line with the significance of martial identity, warfare and the supra-regional as symbolized by the objects placed in rivers. It seems as if particular values were emphasized in one context and denied in others. The use-traces on the numerous spearheads and simple bronze dress fittings deposited suggest that both were much-used items in the daily life of most local groups. The overwhelming majority are likely to have ended up in the melting pot in order to sustain a thriving local bronze industry. It is only on special occasions that such items were sacrificed in places in the landscape, but it is in these events that such categories seem to have been separated. Emphasizing warfare, martial values or membership of supra-regional networks in one context, and localism and collectivity in another, suggests that particular beliefs and understandings were relative to context, 'hence the need to maintain their spatial separation' (Thomas 1996:179).

Different depositional practices may also have involved different participants. We have already seen how participation itself may imply knowledge of 'the proper way of doing things' and even may have been instrumental in the construction of specific ('sacrificial') communities. Thus, deposition need not only be a practice that imbues places with a specific identity, but participation in the practice can also imbue people with a specific identity.

This chapter began by asking how activities in one place in the landscape could evoke a different image of society to those that took place in another. The answer to this question must be that society is not a self-contained entity with a few predominant values, but rather a heterogeneous whole enhancing several potentially conflicting ideas and values (Bazelmans 1999:42–3). People could adopt martial identities in one context (e.g. during the act of weapon deposition), yet define themselves as belonging to a more encompassing and undifferentiated social whole during burial practices (e.g. urnfields as collective cemeteries of several households). Selective deposition then, seems to have functioned to keep such objects, and particularly the ideologies they stood for, apart; both spatially (by depositing them in different parts of the landscape) and conceptually. As such, selective deposition may represent a system of resolving ideological and political tension stemming from different and sometimes even conflicting values present in every society (Fontijn 2002:279). If we are to get a better understanding of society, this calls for excavation and survey strategies that are sensitive to such heterogeneous orderings of landscape as constructed by prehistoric communities themselves instead of trying to grasp them in pre-conceived images of our own making such as 'ritual' versus 'profane' places.

REFERENCES

Barraud, C., and J. D. M. Platenkamp 1990 Rituals and the Comparison of Societies. Bijdragen tot Taal, Land en Volkenkunde KITLV 146:103–23.

Barrett, J. C. 1994 Fragments of Antiquity: An Archaeology of Social Life in Britain, 2900–1200 BC. Oxford: Blackwell.

Bazelmans, J. 1999 By Weapons Made Worthy. Lords, Retainers and Their Relationship in Beowulf. Amsterdam Archaeological Studies, 5. Amsterdam: Amsterdam University Press.

Bird-David, N. 1999 Animism Revisited: Personhood, Environment and Relational Epistemology. Current Anthropology 40:67–79.

Bloch, M., and J. Parry 1989 Introduction: Money and the Morality of Exchange. In Money and the Morality of Exchange. J. Parry and M. Bloch, eds. Pp. 1–31. Cambridge: Cambridge University Press.

Bradley, R. 1990 The Passage of Arms. An Archaeological Analysis of Prehistoric Hoards and Votive Deposits. Cambridge: Cambridge University Press.

Bradley, R. 2000 An Archaeology of Natural Places. London and New York: Routledge.

Bradley, R. 2002 The Past in Prehistoric Societies. London and New York: Routledge.

Bradley, R. 2005 Ritual and Domestic Life in Prehistoric Europe. London and New York: Routledge.

Brück, J. 1999 Ritual and Rationality: Some Problems of Interpretation in European Archaeology. European Journal of Archaeology 2:313–44.

Drenth, E., and E. Lohof 2005 Heuvels voor de doden. Begravingen en grafritueel in bekertijd, vroege en midden-bronstijd. In Nederland in de Prehistorie. L. P. Louwe Kooijmans, P. W. van den Broek, H. Fokkens, and A. van Gijn, eds. Pp. 433–54. Amsterdam: Bert Bakker.

Fokkens, H. 1997 The Genesis of Urnfields: Economic Crisis or Ideological Change? Antiquity 71:360–73.

Fokkens, H., and R. Jansen 2004 Het vorstengraf van Oss: een archeologische speurtocht naar een prehistorisch grafveld. Utrecht: Matrijs.

Fontijn, D. 1996 Socializing Landscape. Second Thoughts About the Cultural Biography of Urnfields. Archaeological Dialogues 3:77–87.

Fontijn, D. 2002 Sacrificial Landscapes. Cultural Biographies of Persons, Objects and 'Natural' Places in the Bronze Age of the Southern Netherlands, c.2300–600 BC. Analecta Praehistorica Leidensia 33/34:1–392.

Fontijn, D., and S. G. F. M. Cuijpers 2002 Revisiting Barrows: A Middle Bronze Age Burial Group at the Kops Plateau, Nijmegen. Berichten van de Rijksdienst voor het Oudheidkundig Bodemonderzoek 45:157–89.

Garwood, P. 1991 Ritual Tradition and the Reconstruction of Society. In Sacred and Profane. P. Garwood, D. Jennings, R. Skeates and J. Toms, eds. Pp. 10–32. Oxford: Oxford University Committee for Archaeology Monograph 32.

Gerritsen. F. 2003 Local Identities. Landscape and Community in the Late Prehistoric Meuse-Demer-Scheldt Region. Amsterdam Archaeological Studies 9. Amsterdam: Amsterdam University Press.

Glasbergen, W. 1954 Barrow Excavations in the Eight Beautitudes. The Bronze Age Cemetery between Toterfout and Halve Mijl, North Brabant I: The Excavations. Palaeohistoria 2:1–134, fig. 13.

Harding, A. F. 2000 European Societies in the Bronze Age. Cambridge World Archaeology. Cambridge: Cambridge University Press.

Harrison, S. 1995 Transformations of Identity in Sepik Warfare. In Shifting Contexts. Transformations in Anthropological Knowledge. Marilyn Strathern, ed. Pp. 81–97. London and New York: Routledge.

Hirsch, E. 1995 Introduction. Landscape: Between Place and Space. In The Anthropology of Landscape. Perspectives on Space and Place. Eric Hirsch and Michael O' Hanlon, eds. Pp. 1–30. Oxford Studies in Social and Cultural Anthropology. Oxford: Clarendon Press.

Hoskins, J. 1998 Biographical Objects. London and New York: Routledge.

Hundt, H.-J. 1955 Versuch zur Deutung der Depotfunde der Nordischen jüngeren Bronzezeit unter besonderer Berücksichtigung Mecklenburgs. Jahrbuch des Römisch-germanischen Zentralmuseums Mainz 2:95–140.

Ingold, T. 2000 The Perception of the Environment. London and New York: Routledge.

Kopytoff, I. 1986 The Cultural Biography of Things: Commoditisation as Process. In The Social Life of Things. Arjun Appadurai, ed. Pp. 64–91. Cambridge: Cambridge University Press.

Kristiansen, K. 1998 Europe Before History. Cambridge: Cambridge University Press.

Lohof, E. 1994 Tradition and Change. Burial Practices in the Late Neolithic and Bronze Age in the North-Eastern Netherlands. Archaeological Dialogues 1:98–118.

Pálsson, G. 1996 Human-Environmental Relations. Orientalism, Paternalism and Communalism. In Nature and Society: Anthropological Perspectives. P. Descola and G. Pálsson, eds. Pp. 63–81. London and New York: Routledge.

Needham, S. 1989 Selective Deposition in the British Early Bronze Age. World Archaeology 20:229–48.

Rowlands, M. 1993 The Role of Memory in the Transmission of Culture. World Archaeology 25:141–51.

Theunissen, L. 1999 Midden-Bronstijdsamenlevingen in het zuiden van de Lage Landen: een evaluatie van het begrip 'Hilversum-cultuur'. PhD dissertation, University of Leiden.

Thomas, J. 1996 Time, Culture and Identity. An Interpretive Archaeology. London and New York: Routledge.

Torbrügge, W. 1970/1971 Vor- und Frühgeschichtliche Flussfunde. Zur Ordnung und Bestimmung einer Denkmälergruppe. Berichte der Römisch Germanischen Kommission 51/52:1–146.

Treherne, P. 1995 The Warrior's Beauty: The Masculine Body and Self-Identity in Bronze-Age Europe. Journal of European Archaeology 3:105–44.

Verlaeckt, K. 1996 Between River and Barrow. A Reappraisal of Bronze Age Metalwork Found in the Province of East-Flanders (Belgium). BAR International Series 632. Oxford: Archaeopress.

Wentink, K. 2006 Ceci n'est pas une hache: Neolithic Depositions in the Northern Netherlands. Leiden: Microweb.

3

The Living House – Architecture, the Everyday and the Human Lifecycle

Introduction

Under the culture-historical paradigm settlement archaeology provided a means of mapping the geographical spread of culture groups. With the development of 'New Archaeology' and later contextual archaeology the analysis of settlements provided archaeologists with an important insight into the details of everyday lives. Rather than treating houses and settlements simply as the dwelling places of past peoples structured solely by economic principles, an alternative approach has emerged in which the house is seen as both a physical and symbolic structure. Houses reflect the symbolic principles of the people who inhabit them (Hodder 1990; Parker Pearson and Richards 1994); however houses are often also organizational units structured along lines of kinship and lineage (Joyce and Gillespie 2000). A perspective on houses that sees them as physical structures, symbolic structures, and organizational units provides archaeologists with a powerful analytical focus. It allows archaeologists to examine the physical construction of houses, the symbolic use of space, as well as to understand the lifecycle of houses (cycles of construction, use, rebuilding and destruction) according to principles of descent, residence and kinship. The house and the settlement emerge then as crucial focuses for prehistoric archaeology as their analysis provides an important window on the fundamental principles that structure the lifeways of prehistoric peoples. Furthermore the analysis of houses provides an important point of contrast with other social practices, such as the building of monuments and the deposition of artefacts (Bradley 2005).

The emergence of sedentary settlement is a characteristic of the Neolithic period. What is the role of the house in the important changes that herald the shift from hunting and gathering to sedentary agriculture? As we saw in the introduction, Ian Hodder (1990) argues for the primary importance of houses in the process of domestication marked by the Neolithic. In **Chapter 3 (a)** *Dusan Boric* investigates the role of houses in the shift from foraging and fishing to agriculture in the earliest Neolithic of the Balkans. He argues that houses emerge as important mnemonic focuses; as anchors for social memory around which social units organized themselves.

The 'wandering' settlements of the later prehistoric sequence in the Netherlands have often been assumed to be a prime example of settlement shift determined by economic principles: agricultural settlements moved on as land became exhausted. However, in **Chapter 3 (b)** *Fokke Gerritsen* takes an alternate view based on anthropological models of the house based on descent, kinship and memory. He instead argues for the significant role played by memory and kinship in cycles of rebuilding and settlement shift during the Iron Age of the Netherlands.

REFERENCES

Bradley, R. 2005 Ritual and Domestic Life in Prehistoric Europe. London: Routledge.

Hodder, I. 1990 The Domestication of Europe. Oxford: Blackwell.

Parker Pearson, M., and C. Richards 1994 Architecture and Social Order. London: Routledge.

Joyce, R. A., and S. D. Gillespie 2000 Beyond Kinship: Social and Material Reproduction in House Societies. Philadelphia: University of Pennsylvania Press.

3 (a)
First Households and 'House Societies' in European Prehistory

Dušan Borić

> Between 'narrated' time and 'constructed' space there are many analogies and overlappings. Neither reduces to the fragments of the universal time and space of geometers. But neither do they oppose a clear alternative to them. The act of configuration takes place at the point of rupture and suture of two levels of apprehension: constructed space is also geometrical, measurable, and calculable space. Its qualification as a lived place superimposes itself upon and is interwoven with its geometrical properties in the same way that narrated time weaves together cosmic and phenomenological time. Whether it be fixed space or space for dwelling, or place to be traversed, constructed space consists in a system of sites for major interactions of life. (Ricoeur 2004:150)

Can we imagine what our lives would be like without built spaces, i.e. houses we live in? Although during the Palaeolithic of Eurasia constructed open-air dwellings might have been as frequent as natural shelters with traces of human habitation, the house, as we know it, becomes a more visible feature of the European archaeological record only with the onset of the Neolithic period. This change from *dwelling* to *building* (cf. Ingold 2000), concomitant with changes in social relations, has frequently been seen as a difference between societies that construct elaborate built environments and those who do not. This chapter will examine both dwelling and building perspectives, and will consider the conditions that promote an emphasis on elaborately constructed spaces found in the archaeological record of the Mesolithic and Neolithic southeast Europe (Figures 3.1 and 3.6). In this region built environments appear for the first time in European prehistory. Specific historical trajectories for such a situation are examined by arguing for a continuing interaction between southwest Asian and southeast European communities within a wide 'culture area'. At the same time, certain local Mesolithic communities in Europe develop a rich and original architectural vocabulary by exhibiting the first signs of the formation of the 'house society' type of social institution (*sensu* Lévi-Strauss). Through architecture they made explicit symbolic links to both the environment they inhabited and their lived bodies. In the later phases of the Neolithic the household becomes the focal point of social interactions, with a likely continuing importance of the 'house society' social structure. The social significance of constructed spaces as they developed in southeast and central Europe during the Neolithic prefigure the major paradigm of social existence (the house and the household) that will persist as a dominant feature well into later European prehistory.

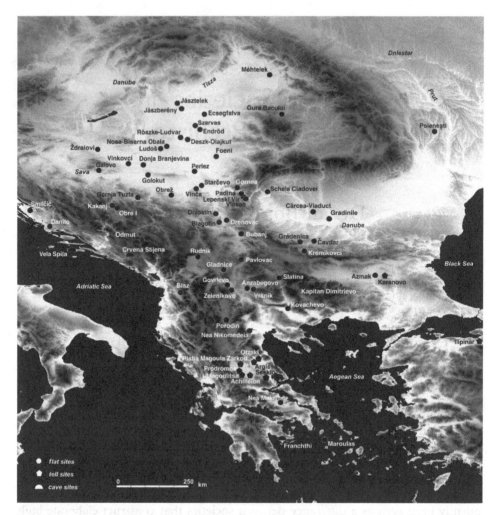

Figure 3.1 Map of southeast Europe showing the distribution of principal Mesolithic, Early and Middle Neolithic sites, 6300–5500 cal. BC

Household, 'House' and 'House Societies': Social and Symbolic Expressions

In the past decades, a sophisticated field of study has grown both in anthropology and archaeology that focuses on the social and symbolic aspects of the built environment and the household or simply the 'house'. One may be reluctant to use the term 'house' in an unproblematic way, since it assumes the baggage of culturally constructed sets of ideas about what houses mean in our present-day social contexts. However, for archaeologists it is important to develop an adequate theoretical framework for the study of domestic architecture and other built spaces and to facilitate ways of discussing what they can tell us about the existence of social institutions that constructed them.

One such framework is provided by a recent revival among socio-cultural anthropologists and archaeologists of Lévi-Strauss's concept of the 'house society' (*sociétés à maison*). Originally, Lévi-Strauss developed this concept as an alternative to traditional kinship categories when faced with the complexity of social ties and relationships in a wide array of societies across the globe (1983; 1987). Classic example of 'house societies' include the traditional societies of the northwest American coast (e.g. Marshall 2000) and medieval European and Japanese noble houses. In these contexts 'strict lineage rules for succession of inheritance did not apply . . . nor was house continuity dictated by the biology of reproduction' (Gillespie 2000:26). In such instances the house plays a role of a collective agency, as a social institution that may incorporate 'hereditary occupants, their close agnates and cognates, more distant relatives and affines, and even non-related clients' (Gillespie 2000:25). In Lévi-Strauss's own words, *la maison* is defined as a

> personne morale détentrice d'un domaine composé à la fois de biens matériels et immatériels, qui se perpétue par la transmission de son nom, de sa fortune et de ses titres en ligne réelle ou fictive, tenue pour légitime à la seule condition que cette continuité puisse s'exprimer dans le langage de la parenté ou de l'alliance, et, le plus souvent, des deux ensemble. (Lévi-Strauss 1979:47)

> moral person, keeper of a domain composed altogether of material and immaterial property, which perpetuates itself by the transmission of its name, of its fortune [destiny, chance] and of its titles in a real or fictive line, held as legitimate on the sole condition that this continuity can express itself in the language of kinship [descent] or of affinity [alliance], and, most often, of both together. (Lévi-Strauss 1987:152)

The importance of the house as a social institution in various ethnographic examples has prompted an interest among archaeologists. Archaeologists have attempted to recognize and document the examples of possible prehistoric house societies in those regions where elaborate physical buildings dominate the archaeological record (e.g. Chesson 2003; Joyce and Gillespie 2000; Kuijt 2000). Such a possibility becomes a powerful analytical and interpretive tool for archaeologists if a rigorous archaeological analysis is attempted. One justification for the use of the term 'house' is that it is an indigenous category much better suited to describe the reality of kinship ties and collective alliances than some imposed terminology, such as 'lineage' (Carsten 1997:23) or 'corporate group' (Lévi-Strauss 1987). It best describes the complex interplay of the significance of the house society social institution and its frequent reification in a physical building. Yet, not every site with building structures need indicate the existence of a 'house society' type of social institution.

Going beyond Lévi-Strauss's initial proposal, a number of researchers sought a more universal and less rigid framework for the study of houses and households in various social contexts, seeing the house as an active social agent whose existence does not necessarily need to lead to the formation of the type of house society social institution with hierarchical structure that Lévi-Strauss often described. Such a view of the house as a physical building that symbolically and metaphorically mediates between the human body and landscape by sometimes mirroring landmark features or by mapping the body onto architecture widens interpretive possibilities. Some of these recent approaches see houses as outer shells of a collective body that may objectify cosmological, genealogical and social relations in myriad ways. The house is seen as a microcosm that reflects and objectifies the structuring of cosmological orders (e.g. Bachelard 1964; Bourdieu 1990; Carsten and Hugh-Jones 1995;

Joyce and Gillespie 2000; Lévi-Strauss 1983; 1987; papers in Parker Pearson and Richards 1994; Rapoport 1994).

Two influential works in archaeology examined the historical trajectory of the appearance of the first huts and their importance for the domestication of social orders among human societies largely on the basis of archaeological data. In a social evolutionary context, Wilson (1988) argues that the material expression of the epiphenomenon of domestication can be traced to the construction of the first huts by Palaeolithic hunter-gatherers around 15,000 years ago. This process reaches another level with the onset of the Neolithic and the beginnings of farming life when built spaces created a world of boundaries and constraints, which fundamentally changed social order in human societies. According to Wilson, humanly built environments appeared as blueprints, on the one hand, for how the universe is organized, and, on the other hand, for channelling social norms in the structuring of daily life. This approach also emphasizes a difference between the conceptions of time in hunter-gatherer societies that lacked built environments, frequently characterizing them as 'timeless', as opposed to farming societies imbued with a 'sense of history'. However, the past that we will review below was far more complex.

By focusing on the process of the spread of agricultural communities and 'the Neolithic way of life' from western Asia to Europe, Hodder (1990) proposes a narrative that postulates a fundamental historical role for the concept of the house. The house is intimately tied to the process of domesticating plants and animals as well as people. The concept of the house as the central unit of production and social life becomes the vehicle of social change and the spread of domestication across Europe. Hodder suggested two structuring forces, which he termed *domus* and *agrios*. According to Hodder, *domus* was equated with home and domesticity and is primarily related to female gender while *agrios* is defined as a male principle that Hodder, among other things, relates to death and burial. While this approach has been criticized as overly structuralist and generalized, there remains a pervasive attraction in seeing the house as a focal point in structuring of social life with the start of the Neolithic (see Hodder 1998; Hodder and Cessford 2004; Borić n.d.; see below).

One of the early works in archaeological house-centred research provided a model of a cross-cultural generalization as a means of equating types of architectural organization with social structure. Models, such as those of Kent Flannery (1972; see also Flannery 1993), assumed the existence of two types of societies in Neolithic southwest Asia based on different architectural forms: curvilinear or rectangular. Social change was illustrated by architectural change as the curvilinear huts of the Natufian and PPNA (pre-Pottery Neolithic A) gave way to the rectangular buildings of PPNB (pre-Pottery Neolithic B) villages. The first type of society (compound-dwelling) is associated with communal storage, where all resources are distributed and shared amongst community members. This type of society corresponds with a large and extended family (often polygynous). The archaeological expectations for such social groups, according to Flannery, are either a large structure for the entire group or a series of smaller houses. This type of social group is recognized in the Natufian and PPNA settlements characterized by circular small huts. The second type of society (village) is one associated with the existence of private storage in each household. This is equated with a form of social organization where distinctive nuclear families can compete in the accumulation of 'wealth'. The archaeological expectation of the site plan for such village societies is 'one which has either widely spaced household units or closed-in feasting and storage areas, in order to avoid the jealousy and conflict which might arise from one household visibly having more than another' (Wiessner 1982:173 cited by Flannery 1993:111). Such a development is seen in the transition to the rectangular architecture of the PPNB. Some critiques of Flannery's model have read the argued change from circular to rectangular houses as a universal rule, arguing that it can hardly be a satisfactory explanation (Saidel 1993; Parker Pearson and Richards 1994:63). Flannery, on the other hand, responds to some of this criticism by insisting that 'the shape of architecture is trivial' in this case and that what matters is the minimal unit of production and storage that differentiates compound-dwelling from village type societies (1993:110, 113). We shall see below whether this model holds for the archaeological record of European prehistory.

However, an important critique of some of these approaches in the recent scholarship on houses has been raised. It is argued that some of the above-mentioned ethnographic examples, which archaeologists often readily rely on, produce a totalizing and frozen ethnographic snapshot that understands the structure of house space as a direct reflection of a particular social order. Such accounts do not take into consideration the subversive and fluid nature of material culture and instead favour a totalizing structure and assume that meanings are 'fixed' onto a particular building space in a synchronic way (Buchli 1999). However, this critique also reminds us that there are no simple translations between social order and architecture. Although the cumulative nature of the archaeological record may frequently seduce one to assume fixed meanings in built spaces in an overly structuralist manner, such interpretations may mask long processes of negotiation of unstable meanings. We must rather consider built spaces as social arenas, where the unfolding of daily life inscribes individual actors with individual microhistories. One should envision the negotiation of built space as a continuous process where 'boundaries are drawn only to be erased or redrawn in another place' (Carsten 1997:27).

One may suggest that as an analytical unit, the household occupies a particular position between two different scales – the individual human body that inhabits the space of a house on the one hand, and the projection of the house's corporate face as an embodiment of a collective agency in its interaction with other houses within a society, on the other hand (Gell 1998). The study of the building layout, position of features within a building, such as placement of burials within the domestic area, or objects of symbolic value, position of elaborate hearths or less permanent fire installations, etc., can all be used to discern the rich texture of the unfolding daily life as well as patterns of behaviour that in a more or less conscious way get transmitted through routinized practices over generations to form a specific cultural/dwelling identity. Yet, these practices are never fixed, and inherited elements of a tradition are always challenged and appropriated on the ground (cf. Habermas 1987).

In summary, one can single out three themes that could be considered in discerning social and symbolic dimensions of buildings in the archaeological record: 1) expression of a specific *cultural* identity (cf. Coudart 1994) in the building layout, frequently based on origin myths; 2) particular strategies of social stratification and differentiation through spatial patterning both between different households of a settlement and within a household; and 3) creation of an institution with collective agency that perpetuates the continuity of a descent group beyond the lives of individual house members (similar to Lévi-Strauss's 'house society' definition). These three elements will be examined more closely against the archaeological evidence of southeast and central European Neolithic.

Forager Houses: Capturing the Landscape

Mesolithic houses are usually elusive in the archaeological record of European Prehistory[1] However, the discovery of the sites in the Danube Gorges region of the north-central Balkans offers an unprecedented settlement record and we shall focus on this region in the discussion of 'Mesolithic' dwellings. The chronological sequence of the sites in this region covers the period from at least around ca. 9500 to 5500 cal. BC with the continuity in the occupation of the same locales and the maintenance of specific habitual practices (Borić and Miracle 2004; Radovanović 1996a). The best-known site from this region is Lepenski Vir, situated in the Upper Gorge of the Danube, while more elaborate architectural structures were also found at the neighbouring sites of Vlasac and Padina. It seems that the form of rectangular stone-lined hearths, which remained a constant feature of this regional sequence, appeared as early as ca. 9500 cal. BC. At present, it remains unclear whether these hearths were open-air features or they had some sort of light upper construction. During the Mesolithic period, burials were frequently found in association with these hearths (e.g. Srejović and Letica 1978).

Existing radiometric dates indicate that possibly around or somewhat prior to 7000 cal. BC the first structures with a trapezoidal layout appear at the site of Vlasac, as is the case with Dwelling 4 at this site (Borić n.d.; Srejović and Letica 1978). These features had their wider, entrance areas (2.5–4 m wide) facing the River Danube, while the narrow back sides (0.7–1.2 m) of the buildings were dug into the sloping terrace of the site and encircled by split stones (the sides of the trapezoidal base measured 3–3.5 m). Rectangular hearths were placed in the centre of each dwelling (Figure 3.2). In most cases, the building floor was covered with red crushed limestone mixed with sand. Also, red boulders were found as part of the back, narrow side of these hearths, marking the central, commanding position in the building.

Around 6200 cal. BC more elaborate structures with a trapezoidal layout were built at the upstream, neighbouring sites of Lepenski Vir and Padina (Jovanović 1969; 1987; Srejović 1972). Both sites were located on gentle sloping river terraces and had been sporadically occupied for already more than two millennia (from around 9500 cal. BC) before the start of more intensified building activities. These structures were similarly oriented to those found at Vlasac, with their wider ends facing the river and the narrow end dug into the loess sandy slope. The largest structure is 9 metres wide in its front part with the floor surface of approximately 36 metres^2 while most of the buildings are smaller, with 2.5–4 metre-wide entrance areas and floors of 5.5 to 28 metres^2. These buildings were in several cases placed above much older rectangular hearths and residues of earlier occupation in an intentional attempt to construct/re-invent social memory (Borić 2003). At Lepenski Vir, the levelled floor area was covered with a reddish limestone surface of substantial hardness. As a continuation of the same building practices seen at Vlasac, trapezoidal buildings at Lepenski Vir have rectangular stone-lined hearths in the centre of each building. Different from Vlasac, where one finds only several 'aniconic' (unornamented) boulders, at Lepenski Vir sandstone boulders began to

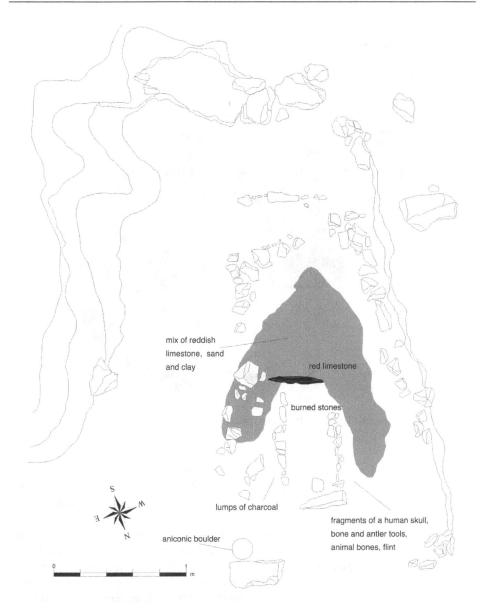

Figure 3.2   Dwelling 4 at Vlasac, Serbia, c.7000 cal. BC

be decorated with geometric motifs and were sometimes turned into the depiction of a fish–human hybrid being (Borić 2005b; Srejović and Babović 1983). These boulders and similarly decorated mortars became an important part of the interior of buildings, frequently placed at the back, narrow side of the hearth, i.e. in the central location of the building. In certain buildings, hearths were surrounded with A-shaped stone plaque supports that might have been part of a fire installation, but which also had a symbolic significance. The latter conclusion is based on one instance from House 40 at Lepenski Vir, where instead of stone plaques placed to form the shape of an A, one finds a human mandible turned upside down with a stone plaque placed between the two mandibular branches

Figure 3.3 Trapezoidal Treskavac Mountain situated in front of Lepenski Vir, Serbia

(Srejović 1972). Bearing in mind the practice of circulation of detached skulls and mandibles, the described instance may indicate that these A-supports might have symbolically stood for the absent members of a particular household: perhaps the deceased and ancestors.

   The commencement of more intensified building activity at Lepenski Vir coincides with the appearance of the first farming communities across the Balkans and is most frequently related to processes of interactions and conversions between local foragers in the Danube Gorges and the first farmers from the surrounding areas (e.g. Borić 2002; 2005a; Radovanović 1996a; 1996b; Tringham 2000a; Whittle 1996). This particular historical context is confined to the period between ca. 6200 to 5900 cal. BC (Borić and Dimitrijević n.d.). The importance granted to the Lepenski Vir locale in this process must have stemmed from its spatial position in front of the most prominent landmark in this micro-region – the trapezoidal mountain Treskavac, situated across the river (Figure 3.3). It seems that in an attempt to mobilize indigenous origin myths related to this landmark feature, the community in the Danube Gorges might have underlined the explicit links between this landmark as the *axis mundi* of its cosmology and the built spaces, which replicated the cosmological order (cf. Eliade 1957; Helms 1998; Rivière 1995). By mimicking its shape in the construction of buildings, the structures might have been seen to acquire the durability and permanence of the mountain itself (Borić 2003). Around this time, Lepenski Vir became the central place of this regional tradition on the basis of the concentration of objects and contexts that were charged with symbolic significance (e.g. Borić 2005b; Radovanović 1996a; Srejović 1972). An argument has been advanced that this elaboration of building space can be related to the emphasis on the local identity that might have been threatened by the newly arrived farming communities (Radovanović 1996b). Yet, it could also be that the process of architectural elaboration stemmed not only from the threat of losing one's identity but also from the desire to emulate the world of shared values and practices that the physical building embodied (see below).

The described architectural development in the Danube Gorges is the most illuminating example of the situatedness of *building* in *dwelling* that Ingold (2000) emphasizes by way of Heidegger (1971) in his discussion of the origins of architectural forms in human as well as animal worlds. In the Danube Gorges, the trapezoidal shape of the building does not seem to be first conceived in the mind as an immaterial template and consequently repeatedly built at Lepenski Vir and other sites as an external objectification of a master architect's mind. Instead, the shape and building arrangements were fundamentally grounded in the being-in-the-world of people inhabiting this region at these particular locales for several millennia. The examples of experimental building activity at Vlasac attest to this. As previously emphasized by Jovanović (1969), the trapezoidal building shape was also of practical value in constructing a dwelling structure in the specific topography that characterizes this riverine zone with steep cliffs and sloping terraces. It seems that it was at this particular historical juncture that the community in the region made a conscious effort to represent and underline their inherent ways of dwelling and building in a more elaborate and concrete way.

The three-dimensional reconstruction of the semi-subterranean buildings at Lepenski Vir (Figure 3.4) and other sites may underline the importance of the 'cave

Figure 3.4 Reconstruction of a typical building from Lepenski Vir, Serbia, c.6200–6000 cal. BC

trope' in conceptualizing ideas of the origin of the built shelter (cf. Srejović 1981:18). A connection between caves and dwellings in the first architectural villages of southwest Asia has been advanced in recent analyses that link the Upper Palaeolithic parietal art with a secluded atmosphere of buildings at the Early Neolithic site of Çatalhöyük in south-central Anatolia, characterized by abundantly painted and moulded images on their interior walls (Lewis-Williams 2004). Lewis-Williams's argument is that during the Upper Palaeolithic cave walls might have been conceptualized as the boundary between the everyday and the nether world from which spirit animals were released by the act of painting. In a similar way, building walls with painted and moulded images of animals and humans at Çatalhöyük might have acted as a membrane between different topological orders. The difference between 'natural' and 'constructed' ('cultural') spaces would thus appear blurred. Buildings at Lepenski Vir might have been perceived as 'natural' constructions like the trapezoidal mountain itself and, at the same time, 'constructed' ('cultural') for as much as the whole universe is constructed, including the Treskavac Mountain that they resembled.

While the appearance of architecture in the Danube Gorges has its roots in a particular way of dwelling that is strongly grounded in the local landscape, it seems that some elements of this architectural vocabulary and the timing of architectural developments relate to wider regional histories. One element of the architectural vocabulary from Lepenski Vir shared with chronologically earlier sites in the Levant and Anatolia is the construction of limestone floors of red colour, which characterize the PPNB period in the latter regions. In the Danube Gorges, the experimentation with this element is seen at Vlasac as early as 7000 cal. BC. Moreover, certain practices connected to buildings, such as placing burials (of infants in particular) within buildings and underneath floors, were shared with various contemporaneous communities in the Near East and the Balkans (Borić and Stefanović 2004). Even the principle of overlapping built structures observed at Lepenski Vir may allow us to consider it as an ersatz tell site, like the immense settlement mounds of southwest Asia with their continuous overlapping strata of occupation (cf. Borić n.d.; Sherratt 2005:143). This context may suggest that the Danube Gorges communities might have been part of communication networks of great antiquity that connected distant regions through the exchange of goods, values, practices and meanings. The 'house society' social organization might have operated in the Danube Gorges for several centuries if not a millennium prior to the arrival of pottery and domesticates owing to their contact with other communities of the eastern Mediterranean with a similar social organization (Borić n.d.; cf. Kuijt 2000). If the existence of such a widespread 'house society' social organization is accepted, the elaboration of the built space, which coincides with the appearance of the first migrants in the burial record of Lepenski Vir (Price and Borić forthcoming), is less a *resistance* to new Neolithic groups and individuals but rather a way of accommodating new alliances and forms of social relatedness. It is exactly the existence of the open and flexible 'house society' social organization stressed by Lévi-Strauss, which among other things involved the incorporation of 'foreign' blood, that might have allowed the indigenous community at Lepenski Vir to retain a number of elements of its cultural identity with deep roots in the past while partaking in the dramatically changed world of the Early Neolithic Balkans. Hence, the spread of the 'house society' social institution, characterized by flexible social arrangements beyond a kin group and by involving diverse and biologically unrelated communities, might have been an important element of the grand narrative of Mesolithic–Neolithic convergences across the Near East and Europe. Looking beyond the cliffs of the Danube Gorges, let's put this rather specific microregional example into a wider picture of the Early Neolithic Balkans.

Tell Building and the Physical House: Creation of Social Space in the Southern Balkans

The question of what the built environment of the Early Neolithic Balkans was like inevitably begs a question about the identity of these first Neolithic communities. At face value, the almost complete lack of open-air Mesolithic settlements in Thessaly in Greece and southern Bulgaria and large concentrations of Early Neolithic sites in these same regions from around 6300 cal. BC suggests that the first farming communities did not have Mesolithic predecessors and that they might have been migrant farmers from the Near East (e.g. van Andel and Runnels 1995). This theory is also backed by some striking similarities between the Neolithic communities of the Near East and the first farmers across the Balkans (Perlès 2001). Yet, we have already seen that in those places where the presence of local foragers is documented, such as the previously discussed sequence of the Danube Gorges, one may find some links to the 'Neolithic culture area' of the eastern Mediterranean throughout the Mesolithic period. These distant regions might have shared similar cultural practices. An alternative scenario to the colonization hypothesis envisioning the inscription of an Early Neolithic presence across an empty landscape in the southern Balkans would be to incorporate presently elusive Mesolithic presence (but see Kyparissi-Apostolika 2003) into the picture of the Neolithic spread in southeast Europe. Rather than seeing a uniform process of culture change, one should best argue for a mosaic of processes in which a significant impulse for transformations was, on the one hand, increasing mobility of human groups around 6300 cal. BC (Sherratt 2004), and, on the other hand, the participation of flexible and adaptable Late Mesolithic local foragers whose identities might not have fundamentally differed from those of early farmers (Borić 2002; 2005a; Whittle 1996; Whittle et al. 2002).

The first Neolithic buildings in Greece are associated with a process that also saw the formation of *tell* (artificial mounds) settlements with 2 to 4 metres of Early Neolithic stratigraphy; in the case of the site of Prodromos 3 there were 6 metres of stratigraphy with ten successive Early Neolithic levels (Perlès 2001:174). Such depths of occupation suggest that the communities who began occupying these locales around 6300 cal. BC by repeated building at the same location emphasized their attachment to a particular place in the given landscape. At the settlement level particular social groups within a community defined themselves in a similar way by delimiting their social spaces. Arguments have been made that tell settlements even at this nascent stage could have been perceived as important landmarks in the creation of a new social landscape (e.g. Chapman 2000). Across the Balkans one can discern an important differentiation in the type of settlements and constructions between the tell-dominated settlement pattern that characterizes the southern Balkans and largely 'flat' sites of the northern Balkan Early Neolithic (see below). The approximate division line runs from the west along the southern areas of Kosovo, northern areas of the FYR of Macedonia and south of the Stara Planina mountain range in Bulgaria.

Tell building represents the key similarity between the southern Balkans and the Near East along with the choice of techniques of building-construction and rectangular architecture (see Perlès 2001:Table 9.1). In Greece, one encounters a frequent use of wattle and daub technique associated with post-framed architecture with and without stone foundations (e.g. Elateia, Achilleion IIa-b, Prodromos, Argissa, Nea Nikomedeia), as well as occasional use of mud bricks placed directly on the ground without vertical timber frames (e.g. Magoulitsa, Otzaki, Sesklo), or placed on stone foundations (e.g. Argissa, Sesklo). These techniques were frequently changing from one to another phase of a settlement or even between buildings of a single phase. While these choices were made according to a particular tradition of building construction they must have depended on the local availability of particular materials used in constructions. Buildings varied in size: at Nea Nikomedeia in Macedonia they ranged from 6 by 8 metres to 11.8 by 13.6 metres in the case of the so-called 'shrine' building that also had internal posts (Pyke and Yiouni 1996), but at other sites buildings were rather small (see Perlès 2001:Table 9.1). These were usually one- and occasionally two-room buildings with gabled or flat roofs. The location of hearths and ovens within buildings varied considerably, while hearths and ovens were also found in the open-space around and between buildings (e.g. Achilleion, see Winn and Shimabuku 1989; see Kotsakis 1995).

Large tell sites were also found farther to the north and northeast in Bulgaria. The most prominent of these is Karanovo with up to 12 metres of Neolithic stratigraphy over 4 hectares and with three Early Neolithic building phases that show the continuity in the use of the same building location from one phase to another (Hiller and Nikolov 1997). As currently dated, the occupation of Karanovo does not start before 6000 cal. BC, which is also the start date for a comparable tell sequence at the site of Ilıpınar situated close to the Anatolian shores of the Sea of Marmara (Roodenberg et al. 1990). There were many other tells and 'flat' sites in Macedonia, such as Anzabegovo (Gimbutas 1976), Vršnik (Garašanin and Garašanin 1961), Porodin (Grbić et al. 1960), etc., and in Bulgaria, such as Kovachevo (Demoule and Lichardus-Itten 1994), Eleshnica, Chavdar, and other sites (see Thissen 2000). Buildings at most of these sites were rather small (7 by 7 m or smaller), post-framed, one-room, rectilinear surface structures. At Karanovo, there is a tendency for overcrowding of settlement space over time, which is followed by the erection of a post fence between certain areas of the village. It is not clear whether this particular situation can be related to Flannery's (1973, see above) village model of a household with closed-in storage and feasting area to avoid jealousy of other households. Still farther to the north, bordering with the Starčevo-Körös-Criş complex, is the site of Slatina, where a well-preserved surface structure (12.5 by 9.5 m) was found with evidence of a series of repairs (Nikolov 1992). The date is somewhat later for the occupation of this site in the century after 5800 BC. The uncovered building had a narrow room in the back, behind a large domed oven. Here a footed storage container was found, while in the main room a large amount of botanical remains and wooden 'beds' were encountered. There were internal post-framed partitions and screens. One is left to wonder whether these partitions were shielding this house's 'wealth' from the outside onlookers.

Although one finds certain similarities with the Near East, the architecture of the southern Balkans is far from a canonized building pattern as there are many examples of combined techniques of building-construction and original and innovative solutions. In addition, apart from the dominant form of surface rectilinear

Figure 3.5 House clay model from Porodin, Macedonia

architecture, in at least one instance at the site of Nea Makri in Attica, Greece one also finds a semi-subterranean rectangular dwelling feature with a hearth in the centre (Perlès 2001:184–5; Theocharis 1956). However, simple pit features found at various Early Neolithic sites across the southern Balkans where one finds no fire installations and which have once been interpreted as habitation structures are best understood as clay digging or refuse pits rather than dwellings (see below about 'pit-huts' of the northern Balkans).

That the conceptual and symbolic significance of the house represents a defining feature of the Early Neolithic in the Balkans is best proven through the proliferation of clay objects that represent miniature versions of buildings (cf. Bailey 1993). Some of these objects provide details of gabled roofs, construction weights that held the roof (Figure 3.5), wall decoration and bucrania, as well as divisions of the interior of building space, and, in this way, help immensely in our reconstructions of life-size buildings from the building rubble left to us. In particular, the oven and the chimney become emphasized on some of these objects. The significance of fire installations, ovens and hearths in the symbolic and religious universe of these Early/Middle Neolithic communities is seen through examples of rather monumental female clay figurines that might have been chimneys of real buildings (Jovanović 1991a). The emphasis on clay models of houses, which have no parallels in the Near East, may be important for understanding the nascent social importance of physical buildings and social and symbolic structures that enabled them. One may suggest that clay models at this early stage might have been an objectification of a particular social institution that was a novel feature of the social landscape across the Balkans. Here, the house is seen as a social institution approximating the Lévi-Strauss's *maison* and which might have been the common integrative medium for the establishment of the Neolithic 'way of life' across the region. This comes close to Hodder's concept of *domus* as the main structuring principle that pervades the daily conduct of individuals in the Neolithic (1990; 1998; see above). But instead of focusing on the idea of an autonomous household (cf. Whittle 1996:69–70), Lévi-Strauss's house model evokes the importance of interactions with other households in a community and with the outside world.

Although it remains impossible for us to penetrate into the fascinating complexity that must have characterized the kinship system of each Neolithic community, we may follow Lévi-Strauss in assuming that the house as a social institution signified beyond a kin-based group, in this way promoting an ethos of shared values and practices between diverse communities. Such an integrative house ideology that emphasized the continuity of belonging to the same past might have created a domino effect in the southern Balkans during the Early Neolithic. It connected communities over a large area and also exhibited signals of rivalry between households and settlements. But was such an assumed house ideology equally successful across the region? The following examples from the northern Balkans may muddy the picture.

Elusive Houses and Shifting Places: Starčevo-Körös-Criş Pottery Complex

Areas of the northern Balkans and the Great Hungarian Plains saw the development of a different settlement pattern from the southern Balkans. The culture–history tradition of local scholarship defines the Early and Middle Neolithic of the northern Balkans as Starčevo-Körös-Criş complex on the basis of a surprisingly uniform range of pottery forms, decoration and technology of pottery manufacturing. But there are also indications of more localized styles in the period from around 6200 to 5500 cal. BC (see Whittle et al. 2002; Whittle et al. 2005). The area that this complex covers extends in the south from the northern areas of FYR of Macedonia, Kosovo and central Serbia, western parts of Bosnia, northern Croatia, and into the Great Hungarian Plains and across the Carpathian Mountains in Romania.

With regard to the identification of architectural forms in this large region, the main debate has concentrated on the question of whether numerous pit features of largely single occupation sites can in certain instances be seen as semi-subterranean dwellings (Bailey 1999; Minichreiter 2001), or whether the surface buildings were the dominant habitation structure but most often invisible due to intensive erosion of single occupation sites, specially prone to the destruction by ploughing (Chapman 2000:86; Lichter 1993:24). Arguments have been put forth that argue for one or the other scenario but to date the resolution of this question awaits field projects that systematically target the problem. The absence of primary contexts (hearths, ovens, floors) within pits remains the main obstacle to accept pit-huts as the main type of habitation structure. On the other hand, across the study area there are some examples of surface rectilinear structures, such as surface concentrations of pottery and daub and fire installations discovered at the Starčevo site of Vinkovci in Croatia (Dizdar and Krznarić Škrivanko 2000), the Starčevo-Criş settlement of Poienești in Romania (Mantu 1991), surface buildings at the Körös sites of Nosa-Biserna Obala (Garašanin 1958) and Ludaš-Budžak (Sekereš 1967) in Serbia and Kotacpart-Vata tanya (Banner 1943:11), Tiszajenő (Tringham 1971: Figure 14/c) and Szolnok-Szanda (Kalicz and Raczky 1980–1:14–15) in Hungary, as well as other similar structures (e.g. Comşa 1978; Horváth 1989:85–6; Paul 1995). Moreover, a house clay model found at the site of Röszke-Ludvár is seen as an indication about the existence of buildings with vertically standing walls and gabled roofs in the northern Balkans too (Trogmayer 1966). The dimensions of preserved structures varied from 4–6 metres by 7–8 metres (Horváth 1989:86). These were flimsy and rather impermanent structures. At some sites, such as Nosa-Biserna Obala, a large number of clay storage silos were found associated with these structures.

The most visible architectural element found at every site of this period in the northern Balkans is daub. Daub is fired clay of building walls, floors and ovens. In the case of wall daub, it usually has visible parallel wattle impressions from the wooden construction of the building. This building-construction technique, known as wattle and daub, featured frequently across the northern Balkans at this time and was also encountered in the southern Balkans (see above). Fresh mud was applied to the wooden frame of poles and woven twigs, and left to dry. It seems that some building structures from this period were (intentionally?) burned down at the end of their use, which contributed to the preservation of daub in the archaeological record. One usually finds pieces of daub in various pit features and, if one accepts that these come from surface buildings, we should envision that pieces of building walls along with other cultural materials might have been pushed into existing clay-borrowing and/or refuse pits across the settlement. In this way, we observe a difference from the pattern encountered in the southern Balkans, where buildings are built over previous foundations, creating the physical verticality and maintaining the attachment to a particular location. Instead, communities of the central and northern Balkans chose to create a record of invisibility, concealing the residues of previous occupation. This creates the impression of an elusive built environment. There seems to have been a need to annul the trace of living at a particular location and to move to a new place, starting anew by building into virgin soil and starting from scratch. This pattern of behaviour is in accord with the short-lived nature of most of these sites, frequently occupied not longer than 100–200 years (e.g. Whittle 2005), which also could have contributed to a large number of sites across landscapes. Some of these sites might have been occupied, abandoned and reoccupied after a period of time (Whittle et al. 2002). Yet, there is a pronounced horizontal displacement of uncovered features that usually do not overlap, which all awakens the 'sense of ephemerality' (Thissen 2005). Since occasional burials are encountered at these sites, usually placed in pits and covered with other cultural materials (pottery, fragments of daub, animal bones etc., e.g. Leković 1985), one could suggest that the abandonment of individual building structures as well as settlements might have related to taboos about the pollution from death (Chapman 1994).

So, what does this very different Neolithic habitation pattern tell us about the social organization of these communities? Argument concerning the 'house society' social organization, previously argued for, is less applicable in this social setting. There seems to be a lot of mobility and little permanence (Whittle 1996; 2003; 2004), and perhaps the social structure of these groups is best understood as some kind of extended family or perhaps small kin-based groups with communal storage and equal distribution of resources. The hunter-gatherer ethic of sharing might have applied here despite the use of pottery and domestic stock, especially sheep and goat. These people might have been a mixture of Neolithic migrants and, mostly, local Mesolithic populations who swiftly took up the whole or parts of the 'Neolithic package'. Their identities must have in part relied on rooted forager social practices while their social organization might have been marked by a much greater fluidity and adaptability (cf. Cribb 1991). It contrasts with earlier described forager populations in the Danube Gorges characterized by a pronounced territoriality and interest in genealogical reckoning. It seems that over several hundred years Starčevo-Körös-Criş groups hesitated to fully accept the southern model of social existence in which the nesting image of a physical house was the main emblem. If the house institution is seen as having an outward projection of incorporating new groups and establishing new alliances, the hesitation to fully implement this model of social existence in Starčevo-Körös-Criş communities might have been the main reason for the halt of several hundred years in the spread of farming once it reached Trans-danubia around 6000 BC.

However, certain practices, such as intentional burning of buildings, structured deposition of red deer and aurochs' skulls (e.g. Makkay 1979), as well as occasional human burials and discarded figurines found in association with numerous pit features may also indicate similarities with those contemporaneous communities that were placing more emphasis on the verticality of physical houses and the creation of social genealogies. The patterns of deposition that were taking place across the Starčevo-Körös-Criş 'culture area' might have created slowly, over time, the sense of belonging to particular locales. At a particular historical juncture, people might have reformulated their origin myths. Around 5500 cal. BC, some of these mobile Neolithic shepherds start maintaining the continuity of dwelling at particular locales which contributed to the creation of the first real tell sites in the northern Balkans. Before we examine this process, we shall turn to a different cultural phenomenon with parallel social existence to the Late Neolithic of the Balkans. This newly emerging cultural area might have been closely related to a series of transformations among the late Starčevo communities on the fringes of the southeast European Neolithic world. Again, the physical building is set to take centre stage.

Communication, Conversion and Spread: The Mediating Longhouse

Parallel with transformations in the Starčevo-Körös area in the northern Balkans that led to highly visible changes in settlement layouts and pottery technology and establishment of the Vinča and Tisza cultures (see below), around 5500 cal. BC one finds the earliest longhouses in the region of Transdanubia (Bánffy 2004; 2005) of northwestern Hungary, northern Austria and southern Germany all the way to the middle Rhine (Gronenborn 1999). These *älteste* Linear Pottery culture (LBK from its German name *Linearbandkeramik*) settlements were not characterized by exceptionally large buildings that become the hallmark of this culture tradition especially toward its end around 4800 cal. BC (for review see Coudart 1998; Lüning 1988; Sommer 2001). The first longhouses did not exceed 20 metres in length, being usually around 15 metres long and 6–7 metres wide (in the later phase of the LBK the length of some buildings is even beyond 30 m). Yet, such large structures for the standards of the Balkan Neolithic represented a major change (cf. Lenneis 1997). These large post-framed buildings can be recognized by deep foundation ditches and rows of internal posts visible in the *loess* soil along with borrow pits for clay that flanked the sides of buildings. No intact floors have ever been preserved. There is also the adherence to the northern orientation in the earliest phase but which changes towards the northwest and west in the later phases outside of central Europe and closer to the Atlantic coast (Coudart 1998; cf. Bradley 2002:19–34). There are a number of quite diverse models proposed in order to explain this new and exceptional phenomenon but many questions remain open. Where did the tradition of longhouses originate from? Who were the people that built these large structures – expanding farmers or a mixture of local foragers and incoming farmers? What mechanism enabled the extent of the LBK distribution and its argued cultural cohesion from the middle Danube over central and western Europe, reaching the Paris basin in its later phase as well as regions across the Carpathian mountains in present-day Moldavia? What purpose did such large buildings serve? What type of social and kinship structure was housed in the LBK buildings?

Newly excavated and dated LBK settlements in western Hungary as well as those neighbouring the Tisza culture in the area west of the Danube (regional variant

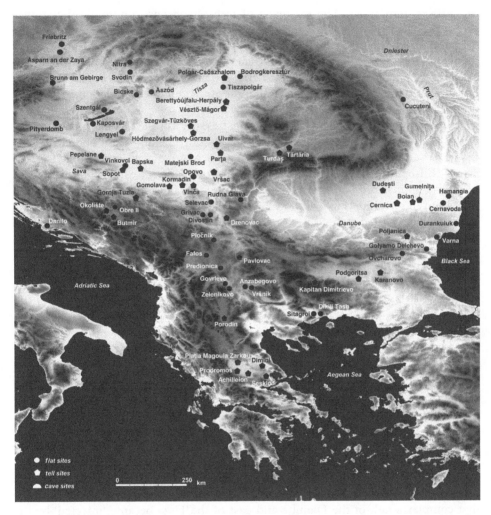

Figure 3.6 Map of southeast Europe showing the distribution of the principal Late Neolithic flat and tell sites and the early LBK settlements, c.5500–4500 cal. BC

known as Alföld Linear Pottery) may suggest that the area north of the Drava River and across the western part of the Great Hungarian Plain might have been the region where the LBK emerged (Figure 3.6). Earlier Starčevo settlements are known from this area up to the northern shores of Lake Balaton and the pottery from the recently excavated *älteste* LBK site of Szentgyörgyvölgy-Pityerdomb in Transdanubia shows dominant Starčevo traits mixed with LBK ornamental motifs (Bánffy 2004; 2005). If one accepts that Transdanubia and Alföld represent core areas from which the LBK evolved with its origin in the Starčevo-Körös populations of these regions, the inevitable question that follows is about the identity of the first longhouse builders. The colonization hypothesis in the case of the LBK holds that the increase of farming populations, which reached the Great Hungarian Plain around 6000 cal. BC, in the years after 5500 cal. BC, led to a pioneering 'conquest' of forager territories in the west (e.g. Bogucki 1995). Differently, a number of local Hungarian and Austrian scholars indicate that the forager populations that lived on the frontiers of the Neolithic world must have been involved in the emergence of the LBK communities. The existence of well-established communication routes across the Great Hungarian Plain in the distribution of Szentgál radiolarite in the west and obsidian in the east is frequently quoted in the absence of Mesolithic settlements. Also, Mesolithic trapezoidal transverse arrowheads and other technological traits characteristic of the earliest LBK 'are indicative not of casual borrowing, but of close contact with, if not assimilation of, Mesolithic populations' (Sommer 2001:254).

In recent years, Alasdair Whittle has most clearly voiced this alternative model of the LBK spread (1996:chapter 6; 2003:134–43). The argument about a demographic overflow that might have caused this new wave of farming spread across central Europe seems weak at present. Also, the rapidity of expansion might have been overemphasized in previous models as the early phase of the LBK might have lasted for almost 400 years (Sommer 2001:254), indicating a period that was long in the making. LBK longhouses, despite their large size and the huge effort put into their construction, might have been rather dispensable and ephemeral buildings as their life-span was rather short, perhaps only used over 25 years per house generation (Whittle 2003:140–1). Beyond the basic architectural uniformity and pottery forms and decoration, one also encounters important regional differences (Whittle 1996). If we allow that local foragers were involved in the process of the LBK spread, then one may see a long process of convergences in which new subsistence resources were adopted along with pottery, but the very structure of the longhouse becomes a new expression of 'an indigenous ethic of cooperation and integration' (Whittle 1996:150) that was the characteristic of local foragers. Rather than seeing the essential differences between what we see as ideal-type foragers and farmers (cf. Borić 2005a), we may envision that local forager groups understood the longhouse and new subsistence practices as perfectly suited to the continuation of their existence. Several centuries of co-existence with the world of Early Neolithic farmers at close proximity might have facilitated this quick take-up of new subsistence practices and reformulated ideologies.

It could be argued that due to presently unknown causes around 5500 cal. BC the Starčevo-Körös complex divided into two different cultural manifestations. The first complex south of the Danube and east of the Tisza became 'infected' by the attitudes that promoted an ideology that emphasized the attachment to a place under the influence of the southern Balkan ways of habitation (see below). The second tradition came into play with the LBK longhouses by which a different choice was made, the one oriented on the spread toward the northwestern areas of the continent and on pronounced mobility. In this way, the longhouse might have acted as an institution for attracting a larger social group 'with people of differing identities and pasts' (Whittle 2003:136). If we accept this mediating role of the longhouse one is left to wonder about the type of social and kinship organization that might have been housed in such a structure. Could it be that the longhouse to a large extent served for various types of communal gatherings that involved not only the kin-based group but a much larger community of affines, neighbours and guests?

Such is the case with the longhouses of northwest Amazonia (Hugh-Jones 1995). The longhouse or maloca of Tukanoan-speaking people that resembles the cosmological order of this community is a large structure that housed several different families. The physical structure is identified with its inhabitants and in particular its sponsor, i.e. leader, while those involved in the building of the house must recognize a particular social arrangement that was being maintained by such an act of building. Despite possible tensions and disputes, social norms promote 'the unity of the household as a group linked by co-residence, kinship, co-operation, and, especially, by the sharing of food' (Hugh-Jones 1995:231). Along with the importance of descent for this community, the ethos of consanguinity is expressed both in everyday life and in the context of ritual gatherings and dance feasts that are known as 'houses', serving to forge alliances between houses. What is created in this way is 'an open-ended regional system based on the exchange of women, goods and ritual services.' (Hugh-Jones 1995:249). And further, '[t]he origin myths of Tukanoans speak of their migration from the Milk River located downstream in the East. Their notion of house is always contextually defined; like the reflections in the mirrored hall, its nesting imagery can recede outwards to encompass ever wider groupings' (Hugh-Jones 1995:252).

Such a nesting imagery could be envisioned for the LBK longhouses that similarly might have been characterized by an open-ended system of settlements that searched for alliances among forager populations but also with other farming groups. The reality must have been characterized by complex identities. The longhouse possibly served to a large extent as a place for gatherings with ritual feasts and exchanges between diverse and biologically unrelated people who shared the ethos of consanguinity, which in particular must have related to food-sharing. There are some indications on the basis of strontium analyses that women might have come to some LBK settlements from upland forager sites (Price et al. 2001). It has also been argued that the orientation of the LBK houses as well as the routes of *Spondylus* acquisition along the Danube may indicate the existence of an origin myth that saw the community's descent from the east or southeast of Europe (Bradley 2002). The orthodox insistence upon adherence to such an origin myth and constant circulation and communication that held the newly established social groupings together over a large area might have been particularly important in regions with still strong indigenous presences. All this may indicate that the notion of the 'house' (*sensu* Lévi-Strauss) in the LBK context took on a new form, enabling complex arrangements between kin-based groups, affines and foreigners. The physical building represented 'an idiom of various kinds of social groupings' (Hugh-Jones 1995:248).

The abandonment of longhouses, being left to decay after a short span of their use, may resemble the practices characteristic of the Starčevo-Körös complex with regard to the abandonment of their sites of dwelling, perhaps upon the death of a leader of a social group embodied in a physical building. Occupation residues were concealed in various pits and ditches. The taboo on the pollution from death, which likely characterized the abandonment of Starčevo-Körös sites, similarly might have caused the abandonment of a particular longhouse in the early phase of the LBK. 'Abandoned by its people, the maloca dies along with its owner. Roof and walls rot away leaving the heavy hardwood columns, standing like bleached bones on a site full of memories, the histories of its residents' (Hugh-Jones 1995:247). After the dissolution of the LBK homogeneity in the 5th millennium cal. BC, longhouses must have remained an important feature of social memory. This is evident in the creation of elongated earthen long barrows in northwest Europe as ersatz longhouses (Hodder 1994; cf. Bradley 2002:30–6). Across the landscape one finds 'a series of monuments that seem like the ghosts of an older way of living' (Bradley 2002:33).

Maintaining the Continuity of Places: Late Neolithic Houses of the Balkans

As we have seen, around 5500 cal. BC typical LBK longhouses appeared for the first time, but the whole of southeast Europe and beyond was also affected by fundamental changes in the ways people inhabited the land and even in the shape and outlook of materialities that were being used. The causes for these shifts remain unknown. At the same time, first tell-settlements emerge across the northern Balkans, in particular on the banks of large rivers, such as the Danube, Sava and the Tisza and their tributaries, as well as in adjacent regions (Figure 3.6). It seems that certain sites that were occupied as single occupation sites in the previous period now become nodal points in an extended network of communication and exchanges. Such is the site of Vinča, the eponymous site of the culture group defined on the basis of a novel form of dark-polished pottery, also characterized by a unique style of figurines with mask-covered (triangular) faces as well as the first copper mining activities and early metallurgy presently known in Europe (e.g. Chapman 1981; Jovanović 1982; Schier 2005). The type-site of Vinča is situated on the banks of the Danube near Belgrade. The excavations at this site have been carried out in several phases for almost a century now, uncovering in the thickest parts of the sequence almost 9 metres of the vertical stratigraphy, with Vinča horizons dominating (Schier 1996; 2000; Stevanović and Jovanović 1996; Tasić 2005; Vasić 1932–6). The lowermost levels at Vinča belong to the Early Neolithic. The earliest occupation of this site is marked by pit features with the typical Starčevo pottery recognized at this level (Letica 1968). A group burial containing several individuals was found in a pit uncovered at this depth, although it is likely that this feature was dug in from the level overlaying the Starčevo horizon.

It is not clear what prompted people to change the previous pattern of inhabiting the region, which was characterized by shifting settlement locations. They attached importance to the Vinča locale rather than the neighbouring Early Neolithic type-site of Starčevo, across the Danube from Vinča. We should perhaps refrain from relying on the migration hypothesis of culture history to explain this culture change both in the type of settlement history that was being produced from around 5400 cal. BC as well as with regard to new pottery technology (but see Kozłowski 2004). Yet, by refusing the migrationist model the shift does not seem less enigmatic. One of the solutions could be that the choice in the location of tells-to-be depended on their place in the landscape, next to the main communication routes (cf. Sherratt 2004). The establishment of exchange networks seems to have been particularly related to major rivers as is indicated by the distribution of exotic goods, such as *Spondylus* (Müller 1997; Willms 1985), and the importance of this aspect may also be linked to the LBK world farther to the northwest. Intriguingly, with the start of this period previously discussed sites in the Danube Gorges, such as Lepenski Vir, are completely abandoned and no Late Neolithic settlements are known from this region for several hundred years.

In Thessaly, Greece and southern Bulgaria certain Early and Middle Neolithic tell sites were abandoned, and new Late Neolithic tell settlements built. There were also (dis)continuous occupations of the same sites throughout the period, such as the impressive sequences of Karanovo in Bulgaria and Sesklo in Thessaly. In the northern Balkans, similar to Vinča, the novel form of tell settlements became visible very quickly across the Carpathian Basin and along the lower Danube. Sites such as Gomolava (Brukner 1980; 1988), Gornja Tuzla, Okolište (Kujundžić-Vejzagić et al. 2004; http://www.dainst.org/index_930_de.html), Uivar (Schier and Draşovean 2004), Hódmezővásárhely-Gorza (Horváth 1987), Polgár-Csőszhalom (Raczky et al. 1994), Ovcharovo (Todorova et al. 1983), Golyamo Delchevo (Todorova et al. 1975), Dolnoslav (Radunceva 1991), Podgoritsa (Bailey et al. 1998), and others slowly emerge within their respective regional (culture) groups defined on the basis of regionally differentiated styles of pottery forms and decoration: Vinča, Szákálhat, Tisza, Hamangia, Gumelnita, Boian, etc. Large post-framed households were built with deep foundation trenches and with occasional indications of an upper storey under a thatched roof. The interior of buildings was also usually divided into several cells with one or more fire installations and domed ovens, granaries and areas of particular task-related activities. One also finds clay models of houses as was the characteristic of first tell settlements in the southern Balkans in the earlier period.

But there were also large flat sites in this social landscape, such as Selevac (Tringham and Krstić 1990), Divostin (McPheron and Srejović 1988), or Opovo (Tringham et al. 1992) in Serbia. These were sometimes shorter-lived occupations, yet the tell principle of buildings overlapping can be traced here too although with no creation of a tell's verticality. The similarity of practices at both tell and flat sites may warn us that calls for the monumentality of tells to be seen as the sign of the intention of their builders to mark the settlement location in the environment (e.g. Chapman 2000) could have been overemphasized in the recent scholarship and could be the outcome of our own obsession with visual perception. Habitual practices expressed in the sequence of house building, repairing, dismantling, burning (see below) and rebuilding by superimposing or overlapping the previous layout, through which eventful house and settlement histories were created, might have had more importance for the construction of social memory and ties to a place than the visibility of the tell from a distance. This is not to deny that over time certain sites might have acquired a more prominent standing in a wider community through the accumulation of memories and particular histories but this might not have been necessarily proportional to the height of a particular tell.

There are now good indications that the practice of intentional burning of abandoned buildings after a life cycle of their use was widespread in the Late Neolithic of the northern Balkans. To some extent, this practice might have begun already in the Early Neolithic (see above), but it became a very visible and elaborate (ritual?) act across southeast Europe only in the Late Neolithic (e.g. Chapman 1999; Stevanović 1997; Tringham 2000b; 2005). Even more surprising is that abandoned buildings were burned with their complete inventories of pottery and other artefacts left behind. This practice contributed to the preservation and great visibility of buildings and associated material culture. It seems that the act of building destruction was far from a profane activity. Through the act of intentional burning the whole sequence of life events associated with a particular building and materialities of daily life with specific memories attached to them was somehow 'sealed' beneath the rubble of burned mud walls. The mental template that activated this type of practice might have not differed greatly from the one previously described in relation to the Early Neolithic concealment of occupation residues within pit features. Although, when compared with the Early Neolithic, the change in the Late Neolithic is evident in insistence on the continuity of the building location by

Figure 3.7   Foundation trenches of the Vinča culture buildings at Gomolava, Serbia

superimposing, overlapping and cutting through previous buildings, the practices of intentional burning of houses and their inventories may bear profound similarities with the previous period in the need to start anew, to provide a fresh beginning (cf. Borić 2003 for the notion of repetition/recapitulation in relation to architectural features and 'material memory'). However, it should also be emphasized that the intentional burning of buildings is not evident at every Late Neolithic site in southeast Europe and certainly varied at particular times and due to special circumstances as evident in the vertical sequences of many tell sites. For instance, at the Vinča culture tell site of Gomolava, an older building horizon was recognized with large postholes and with deep foundation trenches visible in the loess soil (their size was 16 × 8 m), similar to those of central European LBK, and with no traces of intentional burning (Figure 3.7). This horizon was overlain with the horizon characterized by rectilinear burned buildings (Brukner 1980; 1988). It is also important to emphasize that the intentional house burning, which, if to be successful in turning wall mud into a hard daub rubble, must have lasted for several days, was more than the decision of an 'autonomous household' as the act of burning of a single building in a closely spaced village must have been of major concern for all neighbouring buildings (Whittle 1996:107).

Although it seems that most of the tell settlements were stable throughout the period from around 5400 to 4500 cal. BC, one also notices the construction and continuous repair of large fortification ditches. This practice may signal that there

Figure 3.8 House model and figurines from Platia Magoula Zarkou

might have existed inter-communal disputes that occasionally led to violent encounters. However, one could argue that this practice of constructing enclosures also related to the symbolic domain of defining the settlement limits of one community in relation to the outside, and the world of 'Otherness'. And this might have been another important aspect of being-in-the-Neolithic.

In Greece, one sees some type of differentiation and specialization within newly established settlements such as Dimini, with a hill-top position, that had several concentric walls encircling the settlement. There was an open central court encircled with buildings while concentrations of *Spondylus* shell items were found around the site (Andreou et al. 1996; Halstead 1993). At the neighbouring Sesklo, which has remained in use since the Early and Middle Neolithic, one finds a possible example of a large special-purpose, communal building measuring 20 by 9 metres, centrally placed in relation to other structures and with internal divisions, clay floors and a large rectangular hearth (Theocharis 1973). There were also less elaborately built new sites, such as Dikili Tash (Deshayes and Treuil 1992), and Sitagroi (Renfrew et al. 1986) in the Drama Plain of Thrace. One should envision a social landscape that tolerated different and sometimes conflicting ideas about permanence and continuity. One fascinating example from an old tell site in Thessaly, Platia Magoula Zarkou, is of particular relevance for the idea of the connection between a physical building and a social 'house' (Figure 3.8). Beneath the floor of a building related to the Tsangli phase at this site an unroofed house model was found with an oven, a partition screen wall and eight anthropomorphic figurines (Gallis 1985). These figurines could possibly be gendered as two male–female pairs and children (?) thus representing an ideal of generational continuity of a kin group – from a founding couple, i.e. grandparents (perhaps represented by the two largest figurines?), through the successful growth of another generation represented by the smaller male–female pair and their offspring. This deposit could be understood as a votive deposit that perhaps was prompted by the reproductive problems and misfortunes that the household might have endured.

In the central and northern Balkans, most of the buildings do not exhibit any major signs of differentiation among households. However, the case has been put forth for special purpose buildings, i.e. some type of 'shrines' at several sites. The argument primarily relies on the existence of rather large buildings with a number of internally divided cells. One of these 'special' buildings with raised 'altar'-like pedestals and life-size figurine heads and specially built granary areas was discovered at Parta in Romania (Rus and Lazarovici 1991), while another large, multi-celled building is known from the site of Gorsza in Hungary (Horváth 1987). In addition, a number of buildings have bucrania (plastered skulls of cattle) that were part of the architectural construction usually related to the entrance area, along with ornamented parts of the house façade and pedestalled (altar?) features (e.g. Kormadin, Figure 3.9; see Jovanović and Glišić 1960; Jovanović 1991b), as well as occasionally ornamented frontal surfaces of domed ovens found in some buildings (e.g. Vinča, see Vasić 1932–6). The bucranion as an architectural element was a prominent feature of Early Neolithic sites in Anatolia, most prominently known at Çatalhöyük over a millennium earlier than here-described sequences of the Late Neolithic Balkans. The re-appearance of this feature is another enigmatic element associated with the Vinča culture in particular. Yet, despite all of the mentioned 'special' features, it does not seem very easy to differentiate between buildings that might have had a communal or ritual role and other 'ordinary' buildings.

One may argue that the lack of more obvious communal and ritual buildings could indicate the absence of a central authority of the village and point to conditions of social contract where the regulation of acceptable behaviour and means of social interaction and reproduction were delegated to the house level (cf. Hodder and Cessford 2004), representing social groupings that might have identified with particular physical buildings. This brings us again back to the original definition of the 'house society' social organization à la Lévi-Strauss (see above), where the house as a collective entity takes over the role of controlling and disciplining its members and directing interactions with other individuals belonging to other 'houses' within a community or even in relation to people inhabiting other nearby or distant settlements.

Around mid-fifth millennium cal. BC this continuous development was temporarily disrupted in most of the areas covered by the Vinča and Tisza cultures of the central and northern Balkans. It seems that this change is related to new cultural formations defined as Early Copper Age Tiszapolgár and Bodrogkeresztúr culture groups originating from the upper reaches of the Tisza River. These mobile herders might have brought an end to some tell settlements, such as Vinča. The reason for this might have been to disrupt the monopoly that the Vinča culture might have had over copper mining and circulation of copper objects. These new cultural manifestations ceased to contribute to the visibility of a settlement record and

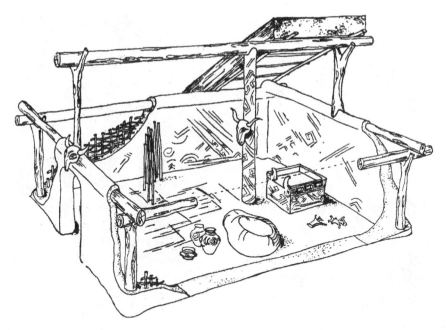

Figure 3.9 Reconstruction of a building from the Vinča culture site of Kormadin, Serbia, c.5000–4500 BC (After Jovanović 1991b)

instead became visible through large cemeteries consisting of single inhumation graves, sometimes placed on top of large, abandoned tells (e.g. Vinča, see Jevtić 1986). Despite these, from the perspective of house-centred research, 'intrusive' elements in the accumulation of the settlement record, the norm of living in large villages established in southeast Europe in particular during the Late Neolithic, will persist as a recurrent rule paradigm of social existence in later periods of European prehistory.

Conclusion

In this chapter, I argued that the social institution of the 'house society' remained a deeply rooted form of social organization throughout European prehistory despite the challenges of changing historical and political circumstances. One of the crucial roles of this type of social institution, most clearly associated with a physical building in the Neolithic, was to provide the continuity of a particular moral standing of a 'house' and to enable its social reproduction, which in reality required flexible social arrangements and incorporation of non-biologically related members, i.e. genetically and culturally unrelated 'Others'. This model of social organization, originating in the Near East, might have been already present in forager groups of the Danube Gorges in the course of the Mesolithic period. These groups were part of a wider 'culture area' with Neolithic communities of western Asia for several millennia. Towards the end of the 7th millennium cal. BC they readily elaborated aspects of their own built environment, rooted in local habits of *dwelling* in a particular landscape as a way of proving allegiance to the expanding Neolithic world.

Figure 3.10 Burned remains of a building with its inventory from the Vinča culture site of Pločnik, Serbia, c.5000 BC (Courtesy of D. Šljivar)

In other European regional contexts the connection of the physical building and the 'house' as a collective 'moral person' might have forged new identities and enabled the incorporation of local forager populations across the Balkans and central Europe into an extended network of newly promoted ideologies and Neolithic ways-of-being. A sense of thick material histories with named genealogies were being generated at particular nodal points that fixed communities' origin myths for considerable periods of time.

ACKNOWLEDGEMENTS

I would like to thank Penny Bickle, Daniela Hoffman, Boban Tripković, Marc Vander Linden and Alasdair Whittle for their useful comments on earlier drafts of this chapter. I am also grateful to Goce Naumov for providing the photograph of the house model from Porodin.

NOTE

1   In southeast Europe, dwelling structures were reported at several Mesolithic sites in the Jázság region on the northern fringe of the Great Hungarian Plain (Kertész 1996). There are a number of recorded huts from Early Mesolithic Maglemosian sites in northwestern Europe due to their good preservation in peat bogs. These huts usually have a hearth in the centre of a rectangular floor area made of bark (Bokelmann 1981; Grøn 1988; Larsson 1990; Nielsen 1997; Price 1987; Woodman 1981). Huts were also found at Late Mesolithic sites in the latter region. These huts were circular or were placed within natural depressions. During this period, in coastal areas, certain sites were also more permanent

aggregations with some elaborate constructions. However, one should remember that the examples of Mesolithic dwellings in northwestern Europe are not readily comparable to dwellings in the Danube Gorges on the sole condition of the two cultural phenomena being defined as 'Mesolithic'. One should historically contextualize the significance of building elaboration and associations in both regions since several thousand years divide these different sequences and the emphasis on building and aggregation might have been of different nature.

REFERENCES

Andreou, Stelios, Michael Fotiadis, and Kostas Kotsakis 1996 Review of Aegean Prehistory V: The Neolithic and Bronze Age of Northern Greece. American Journal of Archaeology 100:537–97.

Bachelard, Gaston 1964 The Poetics of Space. New York: Orion Press.

Bailey, Douglass W. 1990 The Living House: Signifying Continuity. In The Social Archaeology of Houses. Ross Samson, ed. Pp. 17–48. Edinburgh: Edinburgh University Press.

Bailey, Douglass W. 1993 Chronotypic Tension in Bulgarian Prehistory: 6500–3500 BC. World Archaeology 25:204–22.

Bailey, Douglass W. 1999 The Built Environment: Pit-Huts and Houses in the Neolithic. Documenta Praehistorica 26:153–62.

Bailey, Douglass W. 2000 Balkan Prehistory. Exclusion, Incorporation and Identity. London and New York: Routledge.

Bailey, Douglass W., Ruth E. Tringham, Jason Bass, Mirjan Stevanović, M. Hamilton, H. Neumann, I. Angelova, and A. Raduncheva 1998 Expanding the Dimensions of Early Agricultural Tells: The Podgoritsa Archaeological Project, Bulgaria. Journal of Field Archaeology 25(4):375–96.

Bánffy, Eszter 2004 The 6th-Millennium-BC Boundary in Western Transdanubia and its Role in the Central European Transition (Szentgyörgyvölgy-Pityerdomb settlement). Budapest: VAH 15.

Bánffy, Eszter 2005 The Early Neolithic Settlement at Szentgyörgyvölgy-Pityerdomb. Antaeus 28:175–216.

Banner, J. 1943 Az újabbkőkori lakóházkutatás mai állása Magyarországon (L'État actuel de la recherche des habitations néolithiques en Hongrie). Archaeologiai Értesitö 4:1–28.

Blier, S. P. 1987 The Anatomy of Architecture. Cambridge: Cambridge University Press.

Bogucki, Peter 1995 The Linear Pottery Culture of Central Europe. In The Emergence of Pottery: Technology and Innovation in Ancient Societies. W. K. Barnett and J. W. Hoopes, eds. Pp. 89–97. Washington and London: Smithsonian Institution Press.

Bokelmann, K. 1981 Duvensee, Wohnplatz 8. Offa 38:21–40.

Borić, Dušan 2002 The Lepenski Vir Conundrum: Reinterpretation of the Mesolithic and Neolithic Sequences in the Danube Gorges. Antiquity 76:1026–39.

Borić, Dušan 2003 'Deep Time' Metaphor: Mnemonic and Apotropaic Practices at Lepenski Vir. Journal of Social Archaeology 3(1):41–75.

Borić, Dušan 2005a Deconstructing Essentialisms: Unsettling Frontiers of the Mesolithic-Neolithic Balkans. In (Un)settling the Neolithic. Douglass Bailey, Alasdair Whittle, and Vicky Cummings, eds. Pp. 16–31. Oxford: Oxbow Books.

Borić, Dušan 2005b Body Metamorphosis and Animality: Volatile Bodies and Boulder Artworks from Lepenski Vir. Cambridge Archaeological Journal 15(1):35–69.

Borić, Dušan 2007 The House Between Grand Narratives and Microhistories. In The Durable House: House Society Models in Archaeology. Robin Beck, ed. Pp. 97–129. Carbondale: Center for Archaeological Investigation Press. Occasional Papers No. 35.

Borić, Dušan, and Sofija Stefanović 2004 Birth and Death: Infant Burials from Vlasac and Lepenski Vir. Antiquity 78(301):526–46.

Borić, Dušan, and Vesna Dimitrijević 2007 When Did the 'Neolithic Package' Reach Lepenski Vir? Radiometric and Faunal Evidence. Documenta Praehistorica 34:53–72.

Borić, Dušan, and Preston Miracle 2004 Mesolithic and Neolithic (Dis)continuities in the Danube Gorges: New AMS Dates from Padina and Hajdučka Vodenica (Serbia). Oxford Journal of Archaeology 23(4):341–71.

Bourdieu, Pierre 1990 The Kabyle House or the World Reversed. In The Logic of Practice. Pp. 271–319. Cambridge: Polity Press.

Bradley, Richard 2002 The Past in Prehistoric Societies. London and New York: Routledge.

Brukner, Bogdan 1980 Naselje vinčanske grupe na Gomolavi (neolitski i ranoeneolitski sloj). Izveštaj sa iskopavanja 1967–1976. g. Rad vojvodjanskih muzeja 26:5–55.

Brukner, Bogdan 1988 Die Siedlung der Vinča-Gruppe auf Gomolava (die Wohnschicht des spätneolithikums und frühäneolithikums – Gomolava Ia, Gomolava Ia-b und Gomolava Ib) und der Wohnhorizont des äneolithischen Humus (Gomolava II). In Gomolava – Chronologie und Stratigraphie der vorgeschichtlichen und antiken Kulturen der Donauniederung und Südosteuropas (Interlationales Symposium, Ruma 1986). Nikola Tasić and Jelka Petrović, eds. Pp. 19–38. Novi Sad: Vojvo anski muzej and Balkanološki institut SANU.

Buchli, Victor 1999 An Archaeology of Socialism. Oxford and New York: Berg.

Carsten, Janet 1997 The Heat of the Hearth. The Process of Kinship in a Malaya Fishing Community. Oxford: Clarendon Press.

Carsten, Janet, and Stephen Hugh-Jones, eds. 1995 About the House, Lévi-Strauss and Beyond. Cambridge: Cambridge University Press.

Chapman, John C. 1981 Vinča Culture of South-East Europe: Studies in Chronology, Economy and Society. BAR International Series 117:i–ii. Oxford: British Archaeological Reports.

Chapman, John C. 1993 Social Power in the Iron Gates Mesolithic. In Cultural Transformations and Interactions in Eastern Europe. John Chapman and Pavel Dolukhanov, eds. Pp. 71–121. Aldershot: Avebury.

Chapman, John C. 1994 The Living, the Dead and the Ancestors: Time, Life Cycles and the Mortuary Domain in Later European Prehistory. In Ritual and Remembrance: Responses to Death in Human Societies. J. Davies, ed. Pp. 40–85. Sheffield: Sheffield Academic Press.

Chapman, John C. 1999 Deliberate House-Burning in the Prehistory of Central and Eastern Europe. Glyfer och arkeologiska rum – en vänbok till Jarl Nordbladch. Anders Gustafsson and Hakan Karlsson, eds. Pp. 113–26. Gothenburg: Gothenburg University.

Chapman, John C. 2000 Fragmentation in Archaeology. People, Places and Broken Objects in the Prehistory of South-Eastern Europe. London and New York: Routledge.

Chesson, Meredith S. 2003 Households, Houses, Neighborhoods and Corporate Villages: Modeling the Early Bronze Age as a House Society. Journal of Mediterranean Archaeology 16(1):79–102.

Comşa, E. 1978 Contribution à l'étude de la culture Criş en Moldavie (le site de Glăvăneştii Vechi). Dacia 22:9–36.

Coudart, A. 1994 Maisons néolithiques, maisons de Nouvelle-Guinée. L'ethnologie comparée sur choix social et technique. In De la préhistoire aux missiles balistiques. L'intelligence sociale des techniques. B. Latour and P. Lemonnier, eds. Pp. 228–52. Paris: La Découverte.

Coudart, A. 1998 Architecture et société néolithique: l'unité et la variance de la maison danubienne. Paris: Éditions de la Maison des Sciences de L'Homme.

Cribb, Roger 1991 Nomads in Archaeology. Cambridge: Cambridge University Press.

Demoule, Jean-Paul, and Marion Lichardus-Itten 1994 Kovačevo. Rapport prélimininaire (Campagnes 1986–1993). Bulletin correspondance hellénique 118:561–618.

Deshayes, J., and R. Treuil 1992 Dikili Tasch: village préhistorique de Macedoine orientale. Paris and Athens: Ecole Francaise d'Athens.

Dizdar, Marko, and Maja Krznarić Škrivanko 2000 Prilog poznavanju arhitekture starčevačke kulture u Vinkovcima. Vijesnik Arheološkog muzeja u Zagrebu 32–33 (1999–2000): 7–22.

Eliade, Mirca 1957 The Sacred and the Profane. The Nature of Religion. New York: Harvest Books.

Flannery, Kent V. 1972 The Origins of the Village as Settlement Type in Mesoamerica and the Near East: A Comparative Study. In Man, Settlement and Urbanism. Peter J. Ucko, Ruth Tringham, and G. W. Dimbleby, eds. Pp. 23–53. London: Duckworth.

Flannery, Kent V. 1993 Will the Real Model Please Stand Up: Comments on Saidel's 'Round House or Square?' Journal of Mediterranean Archaeology 6(1):109–17.

Gallis, Kostas J. 1985 A Late Neolithic Foundation Offering from Thessaly. Antiquity 59:20–4.

Garašanin, Draga 1958 Die Siedlung der Starčevokultur in Nosa bei Subotica und das Problem der neolithischen Lehmscheunen. Bericht über den V Internationalen Kongress, Hamburg. Hamburg.

Garašanin, Milutin, and Draga Garašanin 1961 Neolitska naselba Vršnik, kaj selo Tarinci. Zbornik na Štipskot Naroden Muzej 2:123–45.

Garašanin, Milutin, and Ivana Radovanović 2001 A Pot in House 54 at Lepenski Vir I. Antiquity 75(287):118–25.

Gell, Alfred 1998 Art and Agency. An Anthropological Theory. Oxford: Clarendon Press.

Gillespie, Susan D. 2000 Lévi-Strauss. Maison and Société à maisons. In Beyond Kinship. Social and Material Reproduction in House Societies. Rosemary A. Joyce and Susan D. Gillespie, eds. Pp. 22–52. Philadelphia: University of Pennsylvania Press.

Gimbutas, Marija, ed. 1976 Neolithic Macedonia: As Reflected by Excavation at Anza, Southeast Yugoslavia. Los Angeles: The Institute of Archaeology, University of California at Los Angeles.

Grbić, Miodrag, S. Mačkić, B. Nađ, D. Simoska, and D. Stalio 1960 Porodin, Kasnoneolitsko Naselje na Tumbi kod Bitolja. Bitolj.

Grøn, O. 1988 Seasonal Variation in Maglemosian Group Size and Structure. Current Anthropology 28:303–17.

Gronenborn, Detlef 1999 A Variation of a Basic Theme: The Transition to Farming in Central Europe. Journal of World Prehistory 13(2):123–210.

Habermas, Jürgen 1987 The Philosophical Discourse of Modernity: Twelve Lectures. Cambridge: Polity Press.

Halstead, Paul 1993 Spondylus Shell Ornaments from Late Neolithic Dimini, Greece: Specialized Manufacture or Unequal Accumulation? Antiquity 67:603–9.

Heidegger, Martin 1971 Building Dwelling Thinking. In Poetry, Language, Thought. Pp. 145–61. New York: Harper and Row.

Helms, Mary W. 1998 Access to Origins: Affines, Ancestors, and Aristocrats. Austin: University of Texas Press.

Hiller, Stefan, and Vassil Nikolov, eds. 1997 Karanovo: Die Ausgrabungen im Südsektor 1984–1992. Horn: Ferdinand Berger & Söhne.

Hodder, Ian 1990 The Domestication of Europe. Structure and Contingency in Neolithic Societies. Oxford: Blackwell.

Hodder, Ian 1994 Architecture and Meaning: The Example of Neolithic Houses and Tombs. In Architecture and Order: Approaches to Social Space. Mike Parker Pearson and Colin Richards, eds. Pp. 73–86. London: Routledge.

Hodder, Ian 1998 The Domus: Some Problems Reconsidered. In Understanding the Neolithic of North-Western Europe. Mark Edmonds and Colin Richards, eds. Pp. 84–101. Glasgow: Cruithne Press.

Hodder, Ian, and Craig Cessford 2004 Daily Practice and Social Memory at Çatalhöyük. American Antiquity 69(1):17–40.

Horváth, Ferenc 1987 Hódmezővásárhely-Gorza: A Settlement of the Tisza Culture. *In* The Late Neolithic of the Tisza Region. Pál Raczky, ed. Pp. 31–46. Budapest-Szolnok: Kossuth Press.

Horváth, Ferenc 1989 A Survey on the Development of Neolithic Settlement Pattern and House Types in the Tisza Region. *In* Neolithic of Southeastern Europe and its Near Eastern Connections. Varia Archaeologica Hungarica II. Sándor Bökönyi, ed. Pp. 85–101. Budapest: Institute of Archaeology, Academy of Sciences.

Hugh-Jones, Stephen 1995 Inside-Out and Back-to-Front: The Androgynous House in Northwest Amazonia. *In* About the House, Lévi-Strauss and Beyond. Janet Carsten and Stephen Hugh-Jones, eds. Pp. 226–52. Cambridge: Cambridge University Press.

Ingold, Tim 2000 Building, Dwelling, Living: How Animals and People Make Themselves at Home in the World. *In* The Perception of the Environment. Essays on Livelihood, Dwelling and Skill. Tim Ingold, ed. Pp. 172–88. London and New York: Routledge.

Jevtić, Miloš 1986 Grobovi bakarnog doba iz Vinče. Starinar XXXVII:135–44.

Joyce, Rosmery A., and Susan D. Gillespie, eds. 2000 Beyond Kinship. Social and Material Reproduction in House Societies. Philadelphia: University of Pennsylvania Press.

Jovanović, Borislav 1969 Chronological Frames of the Iron Gate Group of the Early Neolithic Period. Archaeologica Iugoslavica 10:23–38.

Jovanović, Borislav 1982 Rudna Glava. Najstarije rudarstvo bakra na centralnom Balkanu. Bor-Beograd: Muzej rudarstva i metalurgije & Arheološki institut.

Jovanović, Borislav 1987 Die Architektur und Keramik der Siedlung Padina B am Eisernen Tor, Jugoslawien. Germania 65(1):1–16.

Jovanović, Borislav 1991a Arhitektonska plastika u Starcevackoj kulturi. Zbornik Narodnog muzeja XIV–1:53–64.

Jovanović, Borislav 1991b Die Kultplatze und Architektur in der Vinča-Kultur. Banatica 11:119–24.

Jovanović, Borislav, and Jovan Glišić 1960 Eneolitsko naselje na Kormadinu kod Jakova. Starinar XI:113–42.

Kalicz, Nándor, and Pál Raczky 1980–1 Siedlung der Körös-Kultur in Szolnok-Szanda. MittArchInst 10–11:13–24.

Kertész, Róbert 1996 The Mesolithic in the Great Hungarian Plain. *In* At the Fringes of Three Worlds: Hunter-Gatherers and Farmers in the Middle Tisza Valley. László Tálas, ed. Pp. 5–34. Szolnok: Damjanich Museum.

Kotsakis, Kostas 1995 The Use of Habitational Space in Neolithic Sesklo. *In* La Thessalie, Colloque international d'archéologie: 15 années de recherches (1975–1990), bilans et perspectives. J. C. Decourt, B. Helly, and Kostas Gallis, eds. Pp. 125–30. Athens: Tameion Archeologikon Poron.

Kozłowski, Janusz K. 2004 La néolithisation de la zone balkano-danubienne et l'occupation du territoire. *In* Transmission des savoirs et interactions culturelles. Paul-Louis van Berg, Philippe Jespers, and Florence Doyen, eds. Pp. 9–24. Brussells: Revue Civilisations.

Kuijt, Ian 2000 Near Eastern Neolithic Research. Directions and Trends. *In* Life in Neolithic Farming Communities. Social Organization, Identity, and Differentiation. Ian Kuijt, ed. Pp. 311–22. New York: Kluwer Academic/Plenum Publishers.

Kujundzič-Vejzagič, Zilka, Johannes Müller, K. Rassmann, and T. Schüler 2004 Okolište – Grabung und Geomagnetik eines zentralbosnischen Tells aus der ersten Hälfte des 5. vorchristlichen Jahrtausends. *In* Parerga Praehistorica: Jubiläumsschrift zur Prähistorischen Archäologie. 15 Jahre UPA. Universitätsforsch. Prähistorischen Archäologie 100. Bernard Hänsel, ed. Pp. 69–81. Bonn.

Kyparissi–Apostolika, Nina 2003 The Mesolithic in Theopetra Cave: Data on a Debated Period of Greek Prehistory. *In* The Greek Mesolithic: Problems and Perspective. Nena

Galanidou and Catherine Perlès, eds. Pp. 189–98. London: British School at Athens Studies 10.

Larsson, Lars 1990 The Mesolithic of Southern Scandinavia. Journal of World Prehistory 4:257–309.

Leković, Vladimir 1985 The Starčevo Mortuary Practices – New Perspectives. Godišnjak – Centar za Balkanološka Ispitivanja 27:157–72.

Lenneis, Eva 1997 Houseforms of the Central European Linear Pottery Culture and of the Balkan Early Neolithic – A Comparison. Poročilo o raziskovanju paleolitika, neolitika in eneolitika v Sloveniji 24:143–9.

Letica, Zagorka 1968 Starčevo and Körös at Vinča. Archaeologica Iugoslavica IX:11–18.

Lévi-Strauss, Claude 1979 La Voie des masques. Paris: Plon.

Lévi-Strauss, Claude 1983 The Way of the Masks. London: Jonathan Cape.

Lévi-Strauss, Claude 1987 Anthropology and Myth: Lectures 1951–1982. Oxford: Blackwell.

Lewis-Williams, David 2002 The Mind in the Cave: Consciousness and the Origins of Art. London: Thames and Hudson.

Lewis-Williams, David 2004 Constructing a Cosmos: Architecture, Power and Domestication at Çatalhöyük. Journal of Social Archaeology 4(1):28–59.

Lichter, Clemens 1993 Untersuchungen zu den Bauten des südosteuropäischen Neolithikums und Chalkolithikums. Buch am Erlbach: Verlag Marie L. Leidorf.

Lüning, Jens 1988 Frühe Bauern in Mitteleuropa im 6. und 5. Jahrtausend vor Chr. Jahrbuch des Römisch-Germanischen Zentralmuseums Mainz 35:27–93.

McPherron, Alen, and Dragoslav Srejović, eds. 1988. Divostin and the Neolithic of Central Serbia. Pittsburgh: University of Pittsburgh.

Makkay, János 1979 Foundation Sacrifices in Neolithic Houses of the Carpathian Basin. Valcamonica Symposium III (the Intellectual Expressions of Prehistoric Man: Art and Religion):157–67.

Mantu, Cornelia-Magda 1991 The Starčevo-Criş Settlement from Poieneşti (Vaslui County). Banatica 11:173–83.

Marshall, Yvonne 2000 Transformations of Nuu-chah-nulth Houses. In Beyond Kinship. Social and Material Reproduction in House Societies. Rosemary A. Joyce and Susan D. Gillespie, eds. Pp. 73–102. Philadelphia: University of Pennsylvania Press.

Minichreiter, Kornelija 2001 The Architecture of Early and Middle Neolithic Settlements of the Starčevo Culture in Northern Croatia. Documenta Preahistorica 28:199–214.

Müller, Johannes 1997 Neolithische und chalkolithische Spondylus-Artefakte. Ammerkunden zu Verbreitung, Tauschgebiet und sozialer Funktion. In Beitrage zur prähistorischen archäologie zwisches Nord- und Sudeuropa. Cornelia Becker, ed. Pp. 91–106. Espelkamp: Marie Leidorf.

Nielsen, E. 1997 Untersuchung einer Alt- und Mittelsteinzeitlichen Fundstelle in Wauwil-Obermoos. Heimatkunde des Wiggertals 54:47–65.

Nikolov, Vassil 1989 Das frühneolithische Haus von Sofia-Slatina: Eine Untersuchung zur vorgeschichlichen Bautechnik. Germania 67:1–49.

Parker Pearson, Mike, and Colin Richards 1994 Architecture and Order: Spatial Representation and Archaeology. In Architecture and Order: Approaches to Social Space. Mike Parker Pearson and Colin Richards, eds. Pp. 38–72. London: Routledge.

Paul, I. 1995 Vorgeschichtliche Untersuchungen in Siebenbürgen. Alba Iulia: Universitatea Alba Iulia.

Perlès, Catherine 2001 The Early Neolithic in Greece. The First Farming Communities in Europe. Cambridge: Cambridge University Press.

Price, T. Douglas 1987 The Mesolithic of Western Europe. Journal of World Prehistory 1:225–305.

Price, T. Douglas, and Dušan Borić forthcoming Foragers and Farmers in the Danube Gorges: Mobility, Interaction, and Exchange. Journal of Anthropological Archaeology.

Price, T. Douglas, R. Alex Bentley, J. Lüning, D. Gronenborn, and J. Wahl 2001 Prehistoric Human Migration in the Linearbandkeramik of Central Europe. Antiquity 75: 593–603.

Pyke, G., and Y. P. Yiouni 1996 The Excavation and the Ceramic Assemblage. *In* Nea Nikomedeia I: The Excavation of an Early Neolithic Village in Northern Greece. Robert J. Rodden and K. A. Wardle, eds. London: The British School at Athens.

Raczky, Pál, Walter Meier-Arendt, Katalin Kurucz, Zsigmond Hajdú, and Ágnes Szikora 1994 Polgár-Csőshalom: A Late Neolithic Settlement in the Upper Tisza Region and its Cultural Connections (Preliminary report). Jósa András Múzeum Évköyve 36:231–312.

Radovanović, Ivana 1996a The Iron Gates Mesolithic. Ann Arbor: International Monographs in Prehistory.

Radovanović, Ivana 1996b Kulturni identitet djerdapskog mezolita. Zbornik radova Narodnog muzeja XVI(1):39–47.

Raduncheva, A. 1991 Kurzer vorläufiger Bericht über die Ausgrabungen in Dolnoslav. *In* Kupferzeit als historische Epoche. Jan Lichardus, ed. Pp. 107–10. Bonn.

Rapoport, A. 1994 Spatial Organization and the Built Environment. *In* Companion Encyclopaedia of Anthropology: Humanity, Culture and Social Life. Tim Ingold, ed. Pp. 460–502. London: Routledge.

Renfrew, Colin, Marija Gimbutas, and Ernestine S. Elster, eds. 1986 Exacavations at Sitagroi: A Prehistoric Village in North-East Greece, I. Los Angeles: Institute of Archaeology, University of California, Los Angeles.

Ricoeur, Paul 2004 Memory, History, Forgetting. Chicago and London: The University of Chicago Press.

Rivière, Peter 1995 Houses, Places and People: Community and Continuity in Guiana. *In* About the House, Lévi-Strauss and Beyond. Janet Carsten and Stephen Hugh-Jones, eds. Pp. 189–205. Cambridge: Cambridge University Press.

Roodenberg, J., Laurens Thissen, and H. Buitenhuis 1990 Preliminary Report on the Archaeological Investigations at Ilıpınar in NW Anatolia. Anatolica 16:61–144.

Rus, Dana, and Gheorghe Lazarovici 1991 On the Developed Neolithic Architecture in Banat. Banatica 11:87–118.

Saidel, Benjamin Adam 1993 Round House or Square? Architectural Form and Socio-Economic Organization in the PPNB. Journal of Mediterranean Archaeology 6(1):65–108.

Schier, Wofram 1996 The Relative and Absolute Chronology of Vinča: New Evidence From the Type Site. *In* The Vinča Culture, its Role and Cultural Connections. Florin Drașovean, ed. Pp. 141–62. Timișoara: The Museum of Banat.

Schier, Wofram 2000 Measuring Change: The Neolithic Pottery Sequence of Vinča-Belo Brdo. Documenta Praehistorica 27:187–97.

Schier, Wofram 2005 Masken, Menschen, Rituale. Altag und Kult vor 7000 Jahren in der prähistorischen Siedlung von Uivar, Rumänien. Würzburg: Xpress.

Schier, Wolfram, and Florin Drașovean 2004 Vorbericht über rumänisch-deutschen Prospektionen und Ausgrabungen in der befestigten Tellsiedlung von Uivar, jud. Timiș, Rumänien (1998–2002). Praehistorische Zeitschrift 79:145–230.

Sekereš, Laszlo 1967 Ludoš-Budžak, ranoneolitsko naselje. Arheološki pregled 9:9–12.

Sherratt, Andrew 2004 Fractal Farmers: Patterns of Neolithic Origin and Dispersal. *In* Explaining Social Change: Studies in Honour of Colin Renfrew. John Cherry, Chris Scarre, and Stephen Shennan, eds. Pp. 53–63. Cambridge: The McDonald Institute for Archaeological Research.

Sherratt, Andrew 2005 Settling the Neolithic: A Digestiff. *In* (Un)settling the Neolithic. Douglass Bailey, Alasdair Whittle, and Vicky Cummings, eds. Pp. 140–6. Oxford: Oxbow Books.

Sommer, Ulrike 2001 Hear the Instruction of Thy Father, and Forsake not the Law of Thy Mother. Change and Persistence in the European Early Neolithic. Journal of Social Archaeology 1(2):244–70.

Srejović, Dragoslav 1972 Europe's First Monumental Sculpture: New Discoveries at Lepenski Vir. London: Thames and Hudson.

Srejović, Dragoslav 1981 Lepenski Vir: Menschenbilder einer frühen europäischen Kultur. Mainz am Rhein: Verlag Philipp von Zabern.

Srejović, Dragoslav, and Ljubinka Babović 1983 Umetnost Lepenskog Vira. Belgrade: Jugoslavija.

Srejović, Dragoslav, and Zagorka Letica 1978 Vlasac. Mezolitsko naselje u Djerdapu (I arheologija). Belgrade: Srpska akademija nauka i umetnosti.

Stevanović, Mirjana 1997 The Age of Clay: The Social Dynamics of House Destruction. Journal of Anthropological Archaeology 16:334–95.

Stevanović, Mirjana, and Borislav Jovanović 1996 Revisiting Vinča-Belo Brdo. Starinar 47:193–204.

Tasić, Nenad N. 2005 Vinča – The Third Glance (Excavations 1998–2002). In Prehistoric Archaeology and Anthropological Theory and Education, Reports of Prehistoric Research Projects 6–7. Lolita Nikolova, J. Fritz, and J. Higgins, eds. Pp. 1–8. Salt Lake City: Karlovo.

Theocharis, D. 1956 Nea Makri. Eine grosse neolithische Siedlung in der Nähe von Marathon. Mitteilungen der Deutschen Archäologischen Instituts 71:1–29.

Theocharis, D. 1973 Neolithic Greece. Athens: National Bank of Greece.

Thissen, Laurens 2000 A Chronological Framework for the Neolithisation of the Southern Balkans. In Karanovo III. Beiträge zum Neolithikum in Südosteuropa. S. Hiller and V. Nikolov, eds. Pp. 193–212. Vienna: Phoibos Verlag.

Thissen, Laurens 2005 The Role of Pottery in Agropastoralist Communities in Early Neolithic Southern Romania. In (Un)settling the Neolithic. Douglass Bailey, Alasdair Whittle, and Vicky Cummings, eds. Pp. 71–8. Oxford: Oxbow Books.

Todorova, Henrieta, S. Ivanov, V. Vasilev, M. Hopf, H. Quitta, and G. Kohl 1975 Selishtnata Mogila pri Golyamo Delchevo. Razkopi i Prouchvaniya 5. Sofia: Bulgarskata Akademija na Naukite.

Todorova, Henrieta, V. Vasilev, Z. Janusevic, M. Kovacheva, and P. Valev 1983 Ovcharovo. Razkopi i Prouchvaniya 9. Sofia: Bulgarskata Akademiya na Naukite.

Tringham, Ruth 1971 Hunters, Fishers and Farmers of Eastern Europe, 6000–3000 BC. London: Hutchison University Library.

Tringham, Ruth 2000a Southeastern Europe in the Transition to Agriculture in Europe: Bridge, Buffer or Mosaic. In Europe's First Farmers. T. Douglas Price, ed. Pp. 19–56. Cambridge: Cambridge University Press.

Tringham, Ruth 2000b The Continuous House: A View from a Deep Past. In Beyond Kinship. Social and Material Reproduction in House Societies. Rosemary A. Joyce and Susan D. Gillespie, eds. Pp. 115–34. Philadelphia: University of Pennsylvania Press.

Tringham, Ruth 2005 Weaving House Life and Death into Places: A Blueprint for a Hypermedia Narrative. In (Un)settling the Neolithic. Douglass Bailey, Alasdair Whittle, and Vicky Cummings, eds. Pp. 98–111. Oxford: Oxbow Books.

Tringham, Ruth E., Bogdan Brukner, Timothy Kaiser, Ksenija Borojević, Nerisa Russell, Peter Steli, Mirjana Stevanović, and Barbara Voytek 1992 Excavations at Opovo 1985–7: Socioeconomic Change in the Balkan Neolithic. Journal of Field Archaeology 19:351–86.

Tringham, Ruth E., and Dušan Krstić, eds. 1990 Selevac: A Neolithic Village in Yugoslavia. Los Angeles: UCLA.

Trogmayer, Ottó 1966 Ein neolitisches Hausmodellfragment von Röszke. AASzeg 10:11–26.

Vasić, Miloje M. 1932–6 Preistoriska Vinča I–IV. Beograd: Izdanje i štampa Državne štamparije Kraljevine Jugoslavije.

van Andel, Tjeerd, and Curtis Runnels 1995 The Earliest Farmers in Europe. Antiquity 69:481–500.

Whittle, Alasdair 1996 Europe in the Neolithic. The Creation of New Worlds. Cambridge: Cambridge University Press.

Whittle, Alasdair 1998 Fish, Faces and Fingers: Presences and Symbolic Identities in the Mesolithic-Neolithic Transition in the Carpathian Basin. Documenta praehistorica 25:133–50.

Whittle, Alasdair 2003 The Archaeology of People. Dimensions of Neolithic Life. London and New York: Routledge.

Whittle, Alasdair 2004 Connections in the Körös Culture World: Exchange as an Organising Principle. Antaeus 27:17–26.

Whittle, Alasdair 2005 Lived Experience in the Early Neolithic of the Great Hungarian Plain. In (Un)settling the Neolithic. Douglass Bailey, Alasdair Whittle, and Vicky Cummings, eds. Pp. 64–78. Oxford: Oxbow Books.

Whittle, Alasdair, László Bartosiewicz, Dušan Borić, Paul Pettitt, and Michael Richards 2002 In the Beginning: New Radiocarbon Dates for the Early Neolithic in Northern Serbia and South-East Hungary. Antaeus 25:63–117.

Whittle, Alasdair, László Bartosiewicz, Dušan Borić, Paul Pettitt, and Michael Richards 2005 New Radiocarbon Dates for the Early Neolithic in Northern Serbia and South-East Hungary. Antaeus 28:347–55.

Wiessner, P. 1982 Beyond Willow Smoke and Dogs' Tails: A Comment on Binford's Analysis of Hunter-Gatherer Settlement Systems. American Antiquity 47:171–8.

Willms, C. 1985 Neolitischer Spondylusschmuck: hundert Jahre Forschung. Germania 63:331–43.

Wilson, Peter 1988 The Domestication of the Human Species. New Haven: Yale University Press.

Winn, Sh., and D. Shimabuku 1989 Architecture and Sequence of Building Remains. In Achilleion, A Neolithic Settlement in Thessaly, Greece, 6400–5600 BC. Marija Gimbutas, Sh. Winn, and D. Shimabuku, eds. Pp. 32–68. Los Angeles: Institute of Archaeology, University of California, Los Angeles.

Woodman, Peter 1981 A Mesolithic Camp in Ireland. Scientific American 245:120–8.

3 (b)

Domestic Times: Houses and Temporalities in Late Prehistoric Europe

Fokke Gerritsen

Introduction

There are numerous reasons for archaeologists to choose houses as their object of study. As artefacts, their attraction lies in their large size and complexity; as locations in the landscape they are central places, from which the inhabitants build an understanding of the world they live in. Questions of household organization, settlement patterns and subsistence economy, age and gender relations, the organization of craft production, the practices of everyday life, or the relationship between architecture and cosmological order are just some of the many themes which could be, and have been, addressed by studying the archaeological record of prehistoric houses (e.g. Joyce and Gillespie 2000; Parker Pearson and Richards 1994).

This chapter looks at houses too, but approaches them from a slightly different perspective, the perspective of time and temporality. All archaeological inquiry is concerned with time, of course, in the sense of sequence, chronology, synchronic and diachronic similarity and difference. The study of those dimensions of time that were meaningful to people in the past is less well established in the discipline. Its significance for archaeology has been repeatedly stated (Gosden 1994; Ingold 1993; Lucas 2005), and the topic has been addressed in relation to monuments (Bradley and Williams 1998) and mortuary rituals (Williams 2003). The temporalities of social life as it takes place in and around houses have rarely been explored (for some exceptions, see Bradley 2002:58–81; Brück 1999; Gerritsen 1999). This chapter looks at 'domestic times' by asking two questions. What archaeological means do we have to study the temporalities of domestic life? And, how were houses involved in the construction of temporality in the past? The case studies presented to look at these questions come from Bronze Age and Iron Age northwest Europe.

Time, temporality, memory and domestic life are common terms, but they defy easy definition. Some also come with considerable 'baggage' in the form of meanings and connotations acquired through their varied usage in philosophy, history, the social and cognitive sciences, and in archaeology. The first short sections aim to clarify how these terms are used in this chapter.

Time, Temporality and Social Memory

The form of time that archaeologists are most accustomed to in their work is an abstract form of time which can be divided into successive, uniform units and measured as clock-time or calendrical periods. This is only one kind of temporality, however, one that occurs alongside and resonates with many other temporal frames of reference. Abstract time is often said to be opposed to substantial time. The latter is embedded in social life, human experience and perception. This distinction is useful, as long as one avoids the pitfall of pre-conceived categorizations that could easily follow from it: abstract and substantial time do not line up neatly with a distinction between the modern world and ancient society (Dietler and Herbich 1993; Lucas 2005:93–4), nor do they overlap with a distinction between universal time that proceeds independently of human observation and time as perceived and constructed in people's minds.

Temporalities, in the sense used in this chapter (akin to the meaning proposed by Tim Ingold 1993), typically come about in the interference of multiple dimensions of abstract and substantial, external and internalized time. Including clock-time, temporalities are humanly constructed, but through indissoluble interactions with the rhythms of astronomical phenomena (e.g. day and night, seasons, movement of sun and moon) and biological processes and cycles (e.g. the human lifespan, growth rates of plants and animals). Furthermore, on the human side of things, the construction of temporalities occurs in the interaction of cognitive processes and social practices.

Societies now and in the past make use of many temporalities simultaneously, but not always the same ones, and historical changes can be traced in their relative importance. The European High Middle Ages, for example, are sometimes described as a period when new forms of time consciousness and new systems of valuing time and work came about (e.g. Thrift 1996:169–212). This happened through the interplay of several factors. The ecclesiastical calendar had by this time merged with the seasonally organized agricultural calendar. The development of more accurate timekeeping devices and the increased use of church bells in the countryside brought about the expansion of monastic temporal regimes over the agrarian landscape and into daily work routines. An increased use of writing and record-keeping meant, furthermore, that new ways of using the past to organize production regimes entered society. Here, very clearly, one can see new temporalities emerging in the interaction between social, mental, technological and natural processes.

In everything we do, we draw on the past. We need the past to be able to function knowledgeably in the present and to sustain expectations about the future (Connerton 1989; Gosden 1994; Ingold 1996; Lowenthal 1985). The uses of the past take many forms. The bodily skills that we employ for habitual actions were learnt in the past, but can be applied without consciously invoking the moment when we first acquired them. Following daily routines or adhering to social conventions are forms of bringing the past to bear on the present which can, but do not always, establish a conscious relationship between the two. In some circumstances, however, adhering to (or breaking with) customs and traditions can be deliberate and politically charged. In other situations again, for example during a memorial service for a deceased relative, specific memories are represented, others probably left unmentioned.

The past, though, is not only what has happened, but also how people remember what has happened (Lowenthal in Ingold 1996:207). Drawing on the past to act in the present always involves the application of memory, and as a result the past is not an immutable phenomenon. It will be clear that the past in this definition is something else than recorded history; neither is it something that plays a role only in societies that chronicle events through writing. This form of the past that exists in the present has relevance in all societies. Which is not to say, however, that it is everywhere the same. The ways in which people connect past, present and future are culturally and historically situated (Gell 1992; Munn 1992).

The term memory is used here primarily in the sense of social memory (see Van Dyke and Alcock 2003). This differs from individual memory in that it is about the memories shared by a group of people and, even more importantly, about the social practices, the artefacts and places that are employed for their transmission (Connerton 1989; Halbwachs 1980; Rowlands 1993). When we claim that the past is made to serve a purpose in the present, it is often social memory that helps attain this goal. It provides a collective basis for the selection of what is forgotten and what is remembered. Following Connerton (1989), himself influenced by Maurice Halbwachs, many scholars agree that social memory relies on social practices, including the commemorative ceremonies and bodily practices of which some examples were given above. It is 'body-work' as much as 'mind-work', and the two cannot be neatly separated.

Social practices differ in the degree to which they involve mnemonic processes that are internal or external to the human body (Lucas 2005:77–8). Internal, or in Connerton's term 'incorporated', practices use skills and postures that are remembered through the habitual use of the body. Inscribed practices make use of external media instead, which can be written or iconographic materials, but can also be artefacts and places in a more general sense. This distinction is useful to think about the different ways in which memory and cultural knowledge are transmitted, but it is important to realize that incorporated and inscribed practices are not mutually exclusive. In a prehistoric situation, raising a barrow mound over a grave was an inscribing as well as an incorporating act: it 'inscribed' a durable place into the landscape, which allowed particular interpretations of the past to be made and certain memories to endure (even though the particular reading of the past need not have remained fixed for very long). But the project would fail without bodily skills and incorporated memories regarding the correct ways to raise a barrow.

Studying Domestic Temporalities

This chapter looks at houses as sites of social memory, but also explores links between houses and temporalities more broadly. The term 'house' is used here foremost to describe an archaeological entity. Unless explicitly stated, the term 'house' is not used here in its social sense, referring to the symbolic unity of a residence and its inhabitants (for archaeological examples of this perspective: Gerritsen in press; Joyce and Gillespie 2000).

What means do we have as archaeologists to find time in the static remains of houses? Of particular importance in this respect is the insight that social practices are temporally structured, including those practices that are involved in the building and inhabiting of houses. That is to say that practices follow certain rhythms and recur according to certain temporal schedules (Lucas 2005:67–71). Whenever social practices involve or produce artefacts and places (which is almost always the case), and whenever these are preserved in the archaeological record (much less frequently, of course), archaeologists have an opportunity to study these social practices and make inferences about the embedded temporalities.

These rhythms and periodicities are culturally defined and transmitted, and they can change through human agency. But they involve (and produce) materials and places that themselves also contain temporal dimensions, over which people do not always have control. The temporalities of domestic life in prehistoric agricultural societies, we can safely assume, were fundamentally affected by the cycles of the seasons, rates of depletion and regeneration of the cultivated soils, and the biological properties of plants and animals. This fact offers a fruitful way of studying domestic temporalities. But the real interest for archaeologists and anthropologists no doubt lies in the complex interactions between different kinds of temporal structures, and how these temporalities together form the historically specific temporal regimes of domestic life (Bourdieu 1990; Giles and Parker Pearson 1999).

In a recent article, Lin Foxhall (2000) has pointed out that whereas many archaeological contexts are created by the speedy flow of daily life in the past, archaeologists are accustomed to searching for long-term patterns. By focusing on durable and monumental places, they overlook the fact that for the people who used them their significance would have been primarily connected to short-term motivations and desires. Worshippers leaving votive offerings at a sanctuary, for example, were primarily interested in the short- and medium-term effects of their offering; archaeologists, on the other hand, emphasize the centuries' long existence of the architecture.

Foxhall's call for an archaeology of short-term time scales is quite reasonable, and would seem appropriate for domestic contexts where the daily concerns of individuals and households predominate. But the temporal approach to domestic life that I propose in this chapter is somewhat different. It rests on the notion that time cannot be neatly divided up into short-, medium- and long-term scales. In their domestic practices as much as in their mortuary or religious practices, people make use of and create many temporalities. Multiple time-scales resonate with each other in each of these (Ingold 1993). Surely, it was significant to the worshippers mentioned above that the way in which they expressed their short-term ambitions followed traditions that were passed on from previous generations.

One way of dealing with these multi-dimensional temporalities archaeologically is by using the concept of biography. This notion, derived from the anthropological literature on material culture, asserts that objects, like persons, lead a social life (Appadurai 1986; Kopytoff 1986). Objects absorb and produce meanings during their lifetime; they interact with and affect the people among whom they circulate, and thus generate their own life history. The recounting of this history in the form of a biography provides a means to gain insight into the social and cultural world of which the object was part (see Gosden and Marshall 1999 for discussion and archaeological examples). Moreover, as will be shown below, a biographical approach is well suited to bring out the temporally layered character of houses and domestic assemblages. This will be a guiding concept in the case studies that follow, first to look at a single example of an excavated Iron Age house, then to look at the temporalities of domestic architecture more generally.

A Short Biography of an Iron Age House

At a certain moment in the third century BC, a group of people constructed a farmhouse on a slightly elevated peat pillow behind the coastal sand ridges of the western Netherlands, in an area now called Bernisse on Voorne-Putten (Goossens 2002). They built the house according to the customs of the time (Figure 3.11A). It was a rectangular structure with three longitudinal rows of timber uprights in the interior, supporting the main load of the roof. Its size was close to average, with a length of 16.5 metres and a width of 6 metres. Normal for the period, too, was the particular division of the internal space: it had a dwelling section in the western part and a byre in the eastern part, separated by a passage with two entrances opposite each other in the long walls. The term 'longhouse' is commonly used to refer to this characteristic northwest European house type; more precise is the German term *Wohnstallhaus*.

There is rich evidence for the activities that took place during the period of occupation of the Bernisse house. At a certain moment, probably not long after the house was initially built, the inhabitants constructed a 9.5 metre-long extension against the short wall of the byre section, with a floor of layers of twigs, reeds and dung on top of larger branches (Figure 3.11B). Within the byre, layers of sand mixed with ash and reeds show that the floor had been repeatedly (periodically?) resurfaced. Thick dung layers in the byre and in the extension, containing cattle lice and mites, demonstrate that cattle were indeed kept indoors, at least during certain periods of the year. Broken pots were discarded in particular places. One concentration of potsherds was found along the outside of the northern wall of the byre, one inside in the extension, and a third to the southeast of the house. The house and associated artefacts together thus show practices of daily life that were spatially and temporally patterned, perhaps connected to daily and seasonal rhythms. The construction of an extension to the house was a one-time event, perhaps reflecting an increase in the number of cattle held by the inhabitants, which was unforeseen at the time of building.

It is difficult to say accurately how long the occupation lasted, but inevitably the time came when the house and its site were abandoned. Water levels rose and the house remains soon became covered by clayey sediments. Still within the pre-Roman Iron Age, the former house site was made suitable for crop cultivation by digging several drainage ditches (Figure 3.11C). Incidentally, these also cut through the (by then underground) levels of floors, dung and garbage, exposing cultural materials that perhaps briefly brought the house again to the awareness of the community.

Describing a house in terms of its biography brings out different aspects than more common approaches to houses. The study of house typology and typo-chronological development is an example. It is the study of long-term traditions and gradual evolution. This is an important aspect of house temporalities (and one that I will come back to below), but it is limited in that it looks for the true character of a building solely in its initial construction. A house biography, in contrast, works from the premise that the significance of the building lies in its full life-history, including its afterlife as a ruin or merely as a memory (Gerritsen 1999). And just like a person's life history is defined to a large extent by his or her interactions and relationships with the surrounding world, a biography of a house is also the story

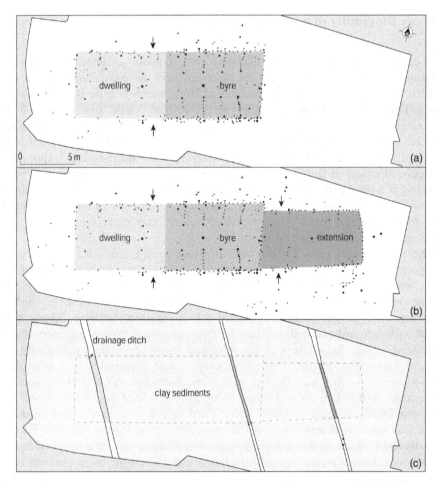

Figure 3.11 Middle Iron Age longhouse at Geervliet, Bernisse, Netherlands: (a) initial state; (b) with later extension; (c) Late Iron Age drainage ditches dug through the house site, exposing construction timbers and floor levels (Simplified after Goossens 2002:App. 1)

of the inhabitants, and of the landscape of which the house is part. These last aspects are largely missing from the brief biography of the Bernisse house above, but they will be explored through other examples below.

The house biography notion also differs from approaches to domestic spaces common in the literature on the archaeology of households and domestic activities (Allison 1999). These focus on the spatial patterning of domestic activities, and frame these within a restricted set of time-scales, for example of daily or seasonal practices. Domestic archaeological assemblages of late prehistoric farmsteads can inform us not only of these short time-scales, but also, and perhaps even more so, of the temporalities of the order of human life cycles and longer.

House Building and Social Memory

Building a house marks in many ways a new beginning. It is the start of a relationship between a building and its inhabitants, between a building and its surroundings and between the inhabitants and their surroundings. But just like any person's biography has a genealogical preamble, a new house marks a start merely in a relative sense. Requiring different forms of social memory (knowledge, skills, traditions and conventions), the building of any new house has its roots in the past. Some of these forms can be traced in the archaeological record.

Many of the bodily skills involved in the construction work were part of the habitual techniques that people would have applied on a regular basis. Preparing timbers and joining wood were not exclusive to house-building practices and undoubtedly belonged to the skills that were learned early in life from other members of the local community. But more specialized knowledge was required as well. In the case of the peat landscapes of the Bernisse region, this included specific techniques for creating structurally sound architecture that reached some 4 metres or more over the soft and unstable ground surface. Presumably, each building project served to pass on this kind of technical knowledge to a younger generation. Even though it required more conscious training than bodily skills, it may have been shared by a large segment of the population.

Going a step further, some archaeologists have proposed that building a longhouse in northwest and north Europe involved specialists whose architectural knowledge was shared and transmitted among a select group (Zimmermann 1988). Arguments for the presence of such specialists derive from observations of a high degree of consistency in the internal proportions of late prehistoric and early historic longhouses over large regions. Even though houses differed considerably in size and construction, many appear to have been laid out according to one of a restricted number of sets of rules regarding the proper proportions. These sets were remarkably widespread and conservative. Although this need not point unambiguously to specialist builders or restricted access to knowledge of architectural rules, it is quite interesting that careful effort was put into the maintenance of particular house-building conventions across time. Other elements were allowed to change more freely.

A similarly conservative element of longhouses, their defining characteristic in fact, was their function as a dwelling for both people and animals. These were domestic animals in the literal sense of the word. The longhouse (*Wohnstallhaus*) type has a history going back to at least the mid-second millennium (Arnoldussen and Fontijn in press), over a millennium before the Bernisse house was built. During those centuries and during many more since then, houses changed structurally and building techniques evolved (Figure 3.12). But the practice of stabling animals within the house remained a constant factor. How should we understand this phenomenon? In recent years the conviction has grown that explanations for this practice cannot be found in reasons of functionality alone (e.g. cattle keeping the house warm, easy manure collecting, or the warmth of the house increasing milk production; Zimmermann 1999). Social and ideological factors are now considered to have been more important, at least for later prehistoric longhouses (Fokkens 1999; Roymans 1999). The high symbolic and socio-political value of cattle for the Late Iron Age communities of northwest Europe was noted by classical authors, and the longhouse would seem to be an expression of this.

This ideological significance goes some way in explaining the conservative nature of longhouse building styles. In addition, however, the historical dimension may have been meaningful in a more direct sense. While it is highly unlikely that the Iron Age builders were aware of the absolute time-depth of the longhouse practice, it appears quite possible that it was meaningful to Iron Age house builders that they carried on a tradition which had begun long before them. The significance of a

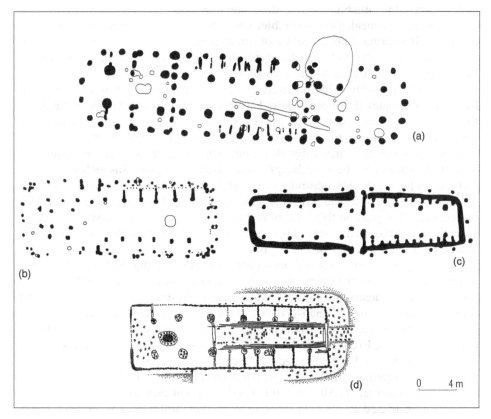

Figure 3.12 Examples of various types of longhouses with stall partitions in byre: (a) Legård, Denmark, Bronze Age (After Bech and Mikkelsen 1999:fig. 7); (b) Hijken, Netherlands, Iron Age (After Huijts 1992:fig. 68); (c) Grøntoft, Denmark, Iron Age (After Rindel 1999:fig. 8); (d) Feddersen Wierde, Germany, Roman Iron Age (After Haarnagel 1979:fig. 25)

tradition often lies in the link with a past that is deliberately maintained by replicating forms, styles, actions or words The factual temporal distance between that past and the present is less significant than the 'body of knowledge' that the past represents (Giles and Parker Pearson 1999). So not only was a longhouse an expression of the high symbolic value that the inhabitants attached to their animals, it also held cosmological significance. Typically, cosmologies make reference to a distant past, explaining why things are the way they are by invoking events, ancestors and non-human beings from a primordial era, for example through origin myths. In the case of prehistoric longhouses, the in-house byre commemorated this distant past in physical form, and at the same time the physical form (and the dwelling practices that accompanied it) served to carry on the associated values further into time.

Building Rhythms, Temporal Regimes and Household Identities

If connections between the Iron Age longhouse and its cosmologically grounded origins remain hazy, other domestic temporalities can be explored as well. A significant feature of the longhouse type of northwest Europe is that a house was built directly as a complete unit, with full-scale dwelling and byre sections. The great majority of late prehistoric houses also lack evidence for major modifications during their lifetime, the Bernisse house being unusual in this respect. The hipped roof construction of most house types was not particularly suited to enlargement, although archaeological cases show that it could be done. There were small secondary structures in the yard, mostly small four-post granaries, which could be increased in number and replaced as the need arose, but these were unsuitable for habitation or stabling. In effect, the initial building constituted the core of the house until its abandonment and demolition. It was maintained and repaired, but it did not develop over time.

The actual biography of each house is unique, of course. Excavated houses show considerable variation in the amount of repairs that were carried out, reflecting a range from briefly inhabited houses to ones whose life was made to last as long as possible. Nevertheless, some overall relation would have existed between the lifespan that was intended at the outset and the average duration of those 'lives'. Undoubtedly, people would have been aware that the decisions they made at the initial building stage affected the future of the building. The choice for the species or thickness of construction wood, for example, influenced the future history of maintenance and repairs to the building. It is difficult to imagine that people would consistently build houses that required constant repair to be able to last for a desired number of years; they would either build more frequently or would make more durable constructions. This 'built-at-once' character implies that people were aware of the maximum lifespan of a house at the time of its construction. In other words, a house was conceptualized at the time of building not solely as a physical, but also as a temporal entity.

How long did an average house biography take to unfold? Estimates for the number of years during which houses in late prehistoric northwest Europe were occupied are difficult to make. For the dry-land landscapes of this region, where sandy soils predominate, it is commonly assumed that houses had an average life of 20 to 40 years. This means that within small local communities, house building was an infrequent activity, and most people would have constructed a house for themselves no more than once or twice in their lifetime.

Building houses directly as complete units and making them last seem like sensible strategies to us. Other choices are possible, however. An alternative is a system whereby a farm begins as a single small structure, and where additional buildings of approximately the same size are constructed as the household grows, and as increasing resources permit. This system is well known ethnographically from Africa (Moore 1986). In yet another system, houses endure and individuals and families of a local community move into whichever available house best suits their current circumstances (Lane 1994). Different forms of dwelling practices lead to different architectural configurations, but also to different building rhythms and different kinds of house biographies. Each system goes together with a particular construction of time.

This can best be shown archaeologically by contrasting the longhouse traditions of northwest Europe with late prehistoric settlements in northern France and south and central Germany (Audouze and Büchsenschütz 1992:222–6; Joachim 1982). The latter often consist of numerous rather small and not very substantial structures (Figure 3.13). Significantly, it is difficult to distinguish between dwellings and

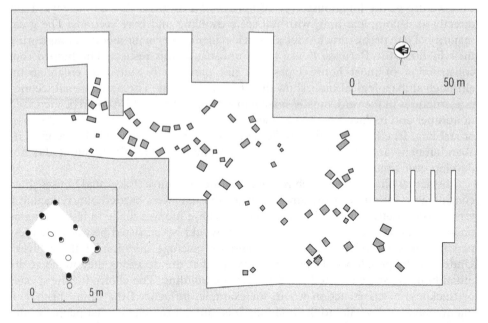

Figure 3.13 Late Iron Age occupation at Eschweiler, Germany. The inset shows one of the larger buildings, identified as a dwelling (Generalized plan after Joachim 1982:fig. 2)

buildings for other purposes, and individual structures may well have switched functions during their lifetime. This pattern reflects perhaps a system whereby farmsteads began as one small building, to which new 'modules' were added when extra space for dwelling, stabling or craft production was needed. This would have presented a flexible system, easily adaptable to expected or unforeseen circumstances and opportunities, and not requiring the kind of foresight that was involved in building a longhouse. In effect, the life-cycles of these farmsteads may not have had clear beginnings and endings.

The 'built-at-once' nature of longhouses was grounded in a very different temporal conceptualization of houses than a 'modular' building system. The building rhythm of longhouses consisted of comparatively long periods of occupation, punctuated by short phases of abandonment and new construction (although not necessarily simultaneously). With the 'modular' system, building would have been more of an ongoing process, frequently taking place within a local community.

There is a strong potential for a punctuated regime to become associated with socially significant transitions in the lives of people and local communities, certainly much larger than that of the ongoing building process of French or German Iron Age settlements. In an earlier publication, I have suggested for the southern Netherlands' Iron Age that the rhythm of building and abandoning ran parallel with the social cycles of formation, growth and dissolution of households (Gerritsen 1999). The formation of a household, for example through marriage, prompted the building of a new house, and conversely, the building process cemented the inhabitants into a social group with a shared sense of home. Given the estimated average lifespan of houses, the other end of the biography may have consisted not only of the abandonment of the house but also the dissolution of the household. This link between the biography of a house and that of its main inhabitants would have been a powerful element in the construction of both individual and family identities (building and people thus constituting a social house in the sense referred to above; Gerritsen in press). One can imagine that building a house for oneself marked the beginning of (a new stage in) adult life, while for others a house marked the place of birth and childhood. Few adults grew old in the house they were born in, and few houses survived their first generation of inhabitants.

Naturally, this model cannot be expected to be valid for the whole geographical extent and duration of the longhouse tradition. There was undoubtedly a great deal of regional and historical variation in the way in which house biographies and the lives and social identities of the inhabitants were linked. Using the biographical model as a starting point, a number of interesting questions can be raised to explore the background of this variation. For example, even though it is generally true that a late prehistoric longhouse did not go through major modifications once it was built, there are cases where this clearly happened. How should we interpret these variations? Were enlargements perhaps motivated by social competition within the community? What were the social implications of deviating from the 'normal' biography of a house? As a more concrete example, how should we understand the biographies of the houses of Noordbarge, a Late Iron Age and Early Roman period settlement in the northern Netherlands (Figure 3.14)? In contrast to the dominant building practices of the time, the life-histories of this set of houses appear to have been extended by a process of attaching additions to one of the short ends and

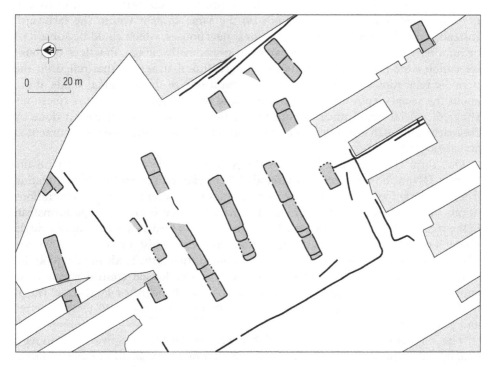

Figure 3.14   Enclosed settlement at Noordbarge, Netherlands (1st c. BC/1st c. AD) (Generalized after Harsema 2005:fig. 24.8)

gradually abandoning segments at the other end (Harsema 2005). How should we envisage in these cases the links between house biographies and the construction of social identities? These questions are raised to suggest something of the potential of a temporal perspective on houses, and cannot be explored further here. But the general point to make is that people organize the temporalities of their identities and life-cycles through their interactions with the material world and the temporalities contained in it.

Houses Moving Through the Landscape

The Bernisse house, to return to it once again, was erected at a previously uninhabited location. The inhabitants did not necessarily come from far away, but they were not locals either, quite strictly speaking. The reasons for the move away from the old location and to this new place may have been unforeseen, given that they lived in a wetland landscape where even minor changes in the natural drainage systems could cause flooding and have an obvious impact on local living conditions. But in itself, moving house locations was a common, even structural, phenomenon in the Bronze Age and Iron Age. This suggests that in Bernisse, too, the move to this location may well have taken place according to established routine. As archaeologists, we observe the spatial effects of this practice, but it is worth asking whether its temporal dimensions were not of equal importance. This means that we have to extend the temporal and spatial scales of analysis towards the landscapes of which the houses were part.

'Wandering' farmsteads are a well-known phenomenon in northwest European prehistory. Houses were rarely rebuilt on the same spot or within the farmyard. Instead, a new location was chosen for most new houses, which could be some tens or hundreds of metres or more away from previous dwellings. Practices of house relocation were probably integrated with agricultural strategies that relied on the periodic relocation of cultivated land. But returning to the argument made above about the social significance of house-building rhythms, we can also ask questions about the social significance of house relocation practices. This is easiest done by comparing, through examples, different forms of relocation that can be documented archaeologically.

One form is exemplified by the findings of large-scale excavations around the town of Oss in the southern Netherlands. These yielded several longhouses dating from the Early Iron Age, as well as more numerous locations where concentrations of pits or granaries suggest that there may have been an Early Iron Age farmstead in the vicinity (Figure 3.15; Schinkel 2005). Almost all farmsteads have only a single phase of occupation. In effect, the plan shows a collapsed history of about 300 years of periodic relocation, with never more than one or two farmsteads inhabited at the same time within the excavated sections. Our chronological control is not close enough to establish the actual 'route' of farmsteads through the landscape. But it is clear that house moving took place over distances of at least 100 to 150 metres and potentially much more.

The Late Bronze Age longhouses that were excavated at Spjald in Denmark equally represent several centuries of occupation of a very small number of farmsteads (Figure 3.16). One or two houses may have been rebuilt on the spot, but the general pattern is one of periodic relocation. Similar to the situation at Oss, the

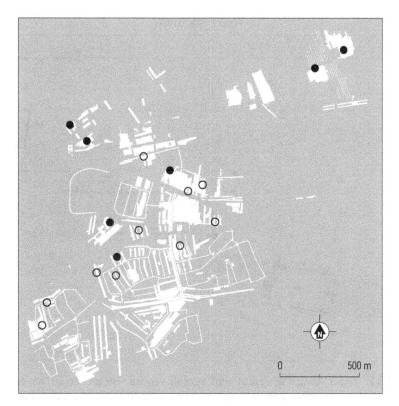

Figure 3.15 Early Iron Age farmyards at Oss, Netherlands. Black: longhouse present; open circle: concentration of Early Iron Age features, nearby presence of house suspected (Generalized plan after Schinkel 2005:fig. 23.3; Gerritsen 2003:fig. 3.17)

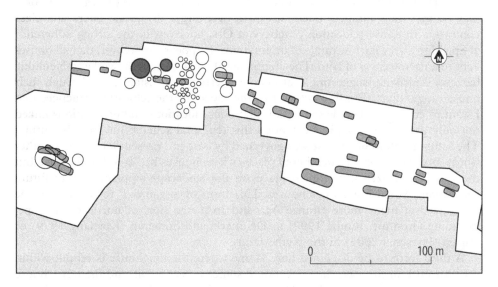

Figure 3.16 Late Bronze Age occupation at Spjald, Denmark. Grey: longhouses and secondary buildings; dark grey: Neolithic barrows; open circles: Iron Age cemetery (Generalized plan after Becker 1982:fig. 15)

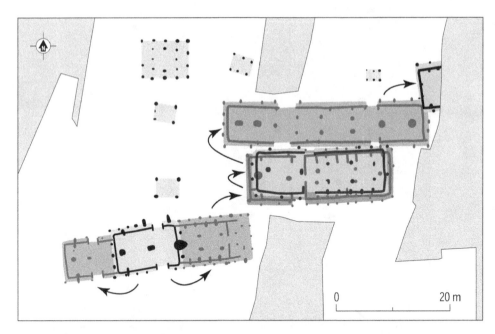

Figure 3.17 Native-Roman farmstead with multiple replacement phases at Oss, Netherlands. The arrows indicate the most likely sequence, based on artefacts and spatial distribution of houses. The oldest house is the small house in the southwest section (Compiled after Wesselingh 2000: figs. 96–9, 109–10, 188–92)

artefact finds do not make it possible to determine the exact sequence (Becker 1982:64). It may be that houses followed an east to west or west to east path, or it may be that they 'jumped' back and forth over larger distances. There is a clear contrast with house relocation practices at Oss, however, in the strong adherence at Spjald to a very narrow range of orientations. It appears, moreover, that all houses kept to a narrow strip of land. The alignment of houses towards two large Neolithic barrows is striking, suggesting that people referred to a distant past through their house orientations (Bradley 2002). But the aspect of the relocation practices that I want to emphasize here is the notion that house locations and orientations linked not only present to past, but extended this temporal scheme towards the future. The future location of a house was governed by past and present locations. In other words, people not only remembered places where houses had stood in the past, but they also recognized unoccupied places in the landscape as places where future generations would build their houses. This form of 'organized' relocation can be recognized at many more Bronze Age and Iron Age sites in northwest Europe, including Grøntoft (Rindel 1999) in Denmark, and Someren (Kortlang 1999) or Hijken (Harsema 2005) in the Netherlands.

A third form to be discussed here is one where the longhouse is rebuilt within the farmyard. In this case the relocation distance is very small, and the term 'house replacement' is more suitable. One farmstead for which a sequence of house replacements can be relatively securely reconstructed was found at Oss, dating from the Roman Period (Figure 3.17; Wesselingh 2000). The longhouse makes only minor shifts in location, maintains a single orientation throughout its multi-phase history, and at one stage is rebuilt on exactly the same spot as a predecessor. The adherence to one location appears to have been of great significance.

In a broad chronological overview, some general patterns in the relative impor-tance of the different forms of relocation and replacement can be pointed out. Throughout the Middle and Late Bronze Age, different forms of house relocation practices appear to have occurred side by side, and house replacement is not uncommon. A characteristic pattern among Bronze Age houses in the northern Netherlands is one where series of annexes extended the size of the house to monu-mental proportions, presumably lengthening its lifespan considerably too. During the earlier Iron Age, relocation of the form described for Oss was the most common pattern, followed over the course of the later (pre-Roman) Iron Age by a decrease in the emphasis on house relocation and a growing attachment of farmsteads and nucleated settlements to particular places (Gerritsen 2003:102–5). During the Roman period/Roman Iron Age, settlements with fixed locations dominate the northwest European rural landscape. In some regions of the longhouse tradition, multi-phase farmsteads and settlements appear already in the pre-Roman Iron Age, alongside 'wandering' farmsteads. Examples of later Iron Age sites with an emphasis on replacement rather than relocation are Nørre Fjand in Jutland, Denmark, and sites such as Boomburg and Ezinge in the salt marshes of north Germany and the Netherlands (plans and references to the primary literature in Müller-Wille 1977).

The examples of residential practices described here are grounded in factors such as local environmental conditions, agricultural practices and cultural tradi-tions. Even though these are thoroughly interconnected, I will focus here on the cultural aspects, and in particular on the ways in which different temporalities come about through these different practices of relocation and replacement. The practice of house replacement would have been well suited to express a sense of continuity, especially in the bond between a family and a home or home range (Gerritsen in press). If not the actual building itself, the home would have survived individuals and generations, incorporating the memories of past inhabitants in its biography. Suggesting an absence of change, rebuilding in the farmyard or on the exact site of the previous house could have been a form of commemoration, using the past to express claims for present and future. Interestingly, at about the same time at the end of the Late Iron Age that house replacement practices became more common in the southern Netherlands, house types with a much heavier construction than before appeared. Presumably, these were more durable and could be inhabited for longer periods than previous house types.

If house durability was connected to a strategy of maintaining lasting social enti-ties, it could be that house relocation practices served to attain the opposite. That is to say that moving away from a house location was done to establish discontinu-ity, emphasizing renewal and change over the ties between past and present genera-tions. I suggested above that the punctuated building rhythms of the longhouse tradition served to demarcate phases in human life-cycles. The transition to a new phase in life would have been marked all the more strongly if it also involved moving to a new place in the landscape. Rather than uphold memories in the landscape by adhering to particular inhabited places, a goal of house relocation may have been to avoid or even forget memories. An existing social configuration was substituted for a new one by a spatial reorganization of the landscape. Or, to put it slightly differently, new personal and collective identities were made possible by deliberately relinquishing previous ones.

There are indications that the break between old and new houses and old and new identities was sometimes given extra emphasis by leaving behind household goods at the old house site. In the southern Netherlands pits occur within or near some Iron Age houses that were filled with burnt artefacts, including complete ceramic vessels, grinding stones, spindle whorls, and loom weights (Gerritsen 1999; 2003:96–102). The placement of many of these pits, for example at locations where upright posts would have stood, indicates that they could only have been dug and filled at or after the abandonment of the house. It appears that, even though they were portable, these goods were apparently not considered moveable. The end of the biography of these objects did not extend beyond the closure of the relationship between house and inhabitants.

House relocation practices and house replacement practices thus appear to have been grounded in different sets of temporalities. The first was connected to temporalities based on renewal, relocation and the periodic relinquishing of identities, the second on continuity, durability and the maintenance of memories and identities. From a historical perspective, the gradual change from relocation towards replacement practices in the last centuries of the (pre-Roman) Iron Age signals profound changes in the temporal regimes of the domestic sphere.

Concluding Thoughts

Summarizing in a nutshell the points that these case studies have tried to make, one can say that prehistoric houses functioned as elements of social memory and temporalities in multiple and changing ways. They constituted material for the transmission of social memory through bodily and commemorative practices. The temporal rhythms of house building and demolition, house relocation and replacement provided the means to create or deny connections between past, present and future. In different places and at different times, prehistoric households and communities used houses in different ways to create time and history.

In this sense, domestic life in and around houses was based on specific temporalities, which probably differed to some extent from those that underpinned other spheres of life, such as mortuary or religious contexts. In fact, during the Late Bronze Age and Early Iron Age, 'wandering' farmsteads were accompanied in the dry-land landscapes of the Netherlands and northern Germany by collective cemeteries that symbolized all that contemporary houses did not: stable bonds between a local community, its collective ancestors and a territory, and collective identities that took precedence over individuals and short-lived generations. Within a single chronological phase, the cemetery and the domestic domain were constructed on very different but interconnected temporal principles.

Investigating the differences and resonances between the temporalities of different spheres of life can make a fruitful field of study. But one would need to be careful to avoid *a priori* assumptions about the different character of domestic and non-domestic life (Bradley 2005). The case studies have hopefully shown that it would be an oversimplification to draw a clear contrast between domestic life as being governed largely by habitual or non-discursive time or by the short-term concerns of daily life on the one hand, and other spheres of life as being the realm of monumental time, ancestors and durable cosmologies on the other.

Early on in this chapter, I remarked that temporalities come about in the mutual interactions between social, mental, physical and biological processes. The domestic temporalities that were described in the case studies are a case in point. A house itself is an artefact whose life-cycle is formed by people's culturally specific ideas on how a house biography should proceed, as much as by such natural phenomena as the decay rate of timbers and thatch and the cycles of birth and death of the inhabitants. As archaeologists we are good at turning the meagre remains that we excavate into three-dimensional houses in our minds. The further challenge is to think about these houses as temporal constructions.

REFERENCES

Allison, P., ed. 1999 The Archaeology of Household Activities. London: Routledge.

Appadurai, A. 1986 Introduction: Commodities and the Politics of Value. *In* The Social Life of Things. Commodities in Cultural Perspective. A. Appadurai, ed. Pp. 3–63. Cambridge: Cambridge University Press.

Arnoldussen, S., and D. Fontijn In press Toward Familiar Landscapes? On the Nature and Origin of Middle Bronze Age Landscapes in the Netherlands. Proceedings of the Prehistoric Society.

Audouze, F., and O. Büchsenschütz 1992 (1989) Towns, Villages and Countryside of Celtic Europe. From the Beginning of the Second Millennium to the End of the First Millennium BC. H. Cleere, trans. London: Batsford.

Bech, J.-H., and M. Mikkelsen 1999 Landscapes, Settlement and Subsistence in Bronze Age Thy, NW Denmark. *In* Settlement and Landscape. C. Fabech and J. Ringtved, eds. Pp. 69–78. Højbjerg: Jutland Archaeological Society.

Becker, C. J. 1982 Siedlungen der Bronzezeit und der vorrömischen Eisenzeit in Dänemark. Offa 39:53–71.

Bourdieu, P. 1990 (1980) The Logic of Practice. R. Nice, trans. Cambridge: Polity Press.

Bradley, R. 2002 The Past in Prehistoric Societies. London: Routledge.

Bradley, R. 2005 Ritual and Domestic Life in Prehistoric Europe. London: Routledge.

Bradley, R., and H. Williams, eds. 1998 The Past in the Past. The Reuse of Ancient Monuments. Theme Issue. World Archaeology 30/1.

Brück, J. 1999 Houses, Lifecycles and Deposition on Middle Bronze Age Settlements in Southern England. Proceedings of the Prehistoric Society 65:1–22.

Connerton, P. 1989 How Societies Remember. Cambridge: Cambridge University Press.

Dietler, M., and I. Herbich 1993 Living on Luo Time: Reckoning Sequence, Duration, History and Biography in a Rural African Society. World Archaeology 25:248–60.

Fokkens, H. 1999 Cattle and Martiality. Changing Relationships Between Man and Landscape in the Late Neolithic and the Bronze Age. *In* Settlement and Landscape. C. Fabech and J. Ringtved, eds. Pp. 35–44. Højbjerg: Jutland Archaeological Society.

Foxhall, L. 2000 The Running Sands of Time: Archaeology and the Short-Term. World Archaeology 31:484–98.

Gell, A. 1992 The Anthropology of Time. Cultural Constructions of Temporal Maps and Images. Oxford: Berg.

Gerritsen, F. 1999 To Build and to Abandon. The Cultural Biography of Late Prehistoric Houses and Farmsteads in the Southern Netherlands. Archaeological Dialogues 6:78–114.

Gerritsen, F. 2003 Local Identities. Landscape and Community in the Late Prehistoric Meuse-Demer-Scheldt Region. Amsterdam Archaeological Studies, 9. Amsterdam: Amsterdam University Press.

Gerritsen, F. In press Relocating the House. Social Transformations in Late Prehistoric Northern Europe. *In* The Durable House: House Society Models in Archaeology. Robin

Beck Jr., ed. Center for Archaeological Investigations, Occasional Paper No. 35. Carbondale: Southern Illinois University.

Giles, M., and M. Parker Pearson 1999 Learning to Live in the Iron Age. Dwelling and Praxis. *In* Northern Exposure. Interpretative Devolution and the Iron Ages in Britain. B. Bevan, ed. Pp. 217–31. Leicester Archaeology Monographs, 4. Leicester: Leicester University Press.

Goossens, T. A. 2002 Een Boerderij uit de Midden-IJzertijd bij Geervliet (gemeente Bernisse). BOOR Balans 5:31–61.

Gosden, C. 1994 Social Being and Time. Oxford: Blackwell.

Gosden, C., and Y. Marshall 1999 The Cultural Biography of Objects. World Archaeology 31:169–78.

Haarnagel, W. 1979 Die Grabung Feddersen Wierde. Methode, Hausbau, Siedlungs- und Wirtschaftsformen sowie Sozialstructur. Wiesbaden: Steiner Verlag.

Halbwachs, M. 1980 (1950) Collective Memory. Francis Ditter, Jr. and Vida Yazdi Ditter, trans. New York: Harper & Row.

Harsema, O. 2005 Boerderijen tussen de raatakkers. Nederzettingen op de noordelijke zandgronden. *In* Nederland in de Prehistorie. L. P. Louwe Kooijmans, P. W. van den Broeke, H. Fokkens, and A. van Gijn, eds. Pp. 543–56. Amsterdam: Bert Bakker.

Huijts, C. 1992 De voor-historische boerderijbouw in Drenthe. Reconstructiemodellen van 1300 vóór tot 1300 na Chr. Arnhem: SHBO.

Ingold, T. 1993 The Temporality of the Landscape. World Archaeology 25:152–74.

Ingold, T., ed. 1996 1992 Debate: The Past is a Foreign Country. *In* Key Debates in Anthropology. T. Ingold, ed. Pp. 199–248. London: Routledge.

Joachim, H.-E. 1982 Ländliche Siedlungen der vorrömischen Eisenzeit im rheinischen Raum. Offa 39:155–62.

Joyce, R., and S. Gillespie, eds. 2000 Beyond Kinship. Social and Material Reproduction in House Societies. Philadelphia: University of Pennsylvania Press.

Kopytoff, I. 1986 The Cultural Biography of Things: Commodization as a Process. *In* The Social Life of Things. A. Appadurai, ed. Pp. 64–91. Cambridge: Cambridge University Press.

Kortlang, F. 1999 The Iron Age Urnfield and Settlement from Someren-'Waterdael'. *In* Land and Ancestors. Cultural Dynamics in the Urnfield Period and the Middle Ages in the Southern Netherlands. F. Theuws and N. Roymans, eds. Pp. 133–98. Amsterdam Archaeological Studies, 4. Amsterdam: Amsterdam University Press.

Lane, P. 1994 The Temporal Structuring of Settlement Space among the Dogon of Mali: An Ethnoarchaeological Study. *In* Architecture and Order. Approaches to Social Space. M. Parker Pearson and C. Richards, eds. Pp. 196–216. London: Routledge.

Lowenthal, D. 1985 The Past is a Foreign Country. Cambridge: Cambridge University Press.

Lucas, G. 2005 The Archaeology of Time. London: Routledge.

Moore, H. 1986 Space, Text and Gender. An Anthropological Study of the Marakwet of Kenya. Cambridge: Cambridge University Press.

Müller-Wille, M. 1977 Bäuerliche Siedlungen der Bronze- und Eisenzeit in den Nordseegebieten. *In* Das Dorf der Eisenzeit und des frühen Mittelalters. Siedlungsform – wirtschaftliche Funktion – soziale Struktur. H. Jankuhn, R. Schützeichel, and F. Schwind, eds. Pp. 153–218. Göttingen: Akademie der Wissenschaften in Göttingen.

Munn, Nancy 1992 The Cultural Anthropology of Time: A Critical Essay. Annual Review of Anthropology 21:93–123.

Parker Pearson, M., and C. Richards 1994 Architecture and Order. London: Routledge.

Rindel, P. 1999 Development of the Village Community 500 BC–100 AD in West Jutland, Denmark. *In* Settlement and Landscape. C. Fabech and J. Ringtved, eds. Pp. 79–99. Højbjerg: Jutland Archaeological Society.

Rowlands, M. 1993 The Role of Memory in the Transmission of Culture. World Archaeology 25:141–51.

Roymans, N. 1999 Man, Cattle and the Supernatural in the Northwest European Plain. *In* Settlement and Landscape. C. Fabech and J. Ringtved, eds. Pp. 291–300. Højbjerg: Jutland Archaeological Society.

Schinkel, K. 2005 Buurtschappen in beweging. Nederzettingen in Zuid- en Midden-Nederland. *In* Nederland in de Prehistorie. L. P. Louwe Kooijmans, P. W. van den Broeke, H. Fokkens, and A. van Gijn, eds. Pp. 519–41. Amsterdam: Bert Bakker.

Thrift, N. 1996 Spatial Formations. London: Sage.

Van Dyke, R., and S. Alcock 2003 Archaeologies of Memory. Oxford: Blackwell.

Wesselingh, D. 2000 Native Neighbours. Local Settlement System and Social Structure in the Roman Period at Oss (The Netherlands). Analecta Praehistorica Leidensia, 32. Leiden: Faculty of Archaeology.

Williams, H., ed. 2003 Archaeologies of Remembrance. Death and Memory in Past Societies. New York: Kluwer/Plenum.

Zimmermann, W. H. 1988 Regelhafte Innengliederung prähistorischer Langhäuser in der Nordseeanraumerstaaten. Germania 66:464–88.

Zimmermann, W. H. 1999 Why Was Cattle-Stalling Introduced in Prehistory? The Significance of Byre and Stable and of Outwintering. *In* Settlement and Landscape. C. Fabech and J. Ringtved, eds. Pp. 301–18. Højbjerg: Jutland Archaeological Society.

4

Materiality, Technology and Transformation – The Emergence of Novel Technologies

Introduction

As we saw in the introduction technological change has been an important means of categorizing and defining prehistoric periods. While prehistoric archaeology has moved beyond the 'three age', or even the 'five age', system the technological division of prehistory still serves as a useful heuristic and we still speak in terms of the 'Neolithic', 'Bronze Age' and 'Iron Age'. Despite the critique of the 'three age' system there is no doubt that certain fundamental technological changes do occur during prehistory, although we no longer need to treat these as concomitant with major social and economic changes. Two major technological innovations are discussed in this chapter: the emergence of pottery during the Neolithic, and the emergence of metalworking, specifically copper and bronze working, during the Chalcolithic (Copper Age) and Bronze Age.

Rather than seeing these technological changes as the result of an inevitable evolutionary process or progression archaeologists are now considering the social implications of new technologies. Influenced by technological studies in anthropology and the strong French tradition of detailed technological analysis archaeologists are now beginning to consider precisely how new technologies are adopted and developed (Dobres 2000; Lemonnier 1993). How are techniques learnt and by whom? How is labour organized? How does the technology impact on certain sectors of society? In what senses does the adoption of a new technology create new forms of sociality? How does the new technology relate to previous technologies? These questions are not always easy to answer in a prehistoric context, nevertheless they are important ways forward. They enable archaeologists to escape the economic and technological determinism of previous approaches.

In **Chapter 4 (a)** *Dragos Georghiu* discusses the emergence of pottery technologies in Neolithic Europe. Taking a symbolic and social approach to the question he asks why a full pottery technology emerges in the Neolithic, while we have evidence for experimentation with fired clay as early as the Palaeolithic. His chapter provides a detailed analysis of the adoption and use of pottery in a series of regions in Neolithic Europe, and in each region he is careful to consider both the practical and symbolic implications of the new technology. In **Chapter 4 (b)** *Barbara Ottaway and Ben Roberts* provide an equally detailed study of the emergence and organization of metalworking technology during the earliest phases of the Central European Bronze Age, taking into account the practical, organizational and social implications of the technology.

BIBLIOGRAPHY

Dobres, M-A. 2000 Technology and Social Agency. Oxford: Blackwell.
Lemonnier, P. 1993 Technological Choices: Transformation in Material Culture Since the Neolithic. London: Routledge.

4 (a)
The Emergence of Pottery

Dragos Gheorghiu

Introduction: Grand Narrative vs. a Mosaic of Perceptions

A subject such as the emergence of pottery, and the discussion of ceramic technology, is undoubtedly perceived as a 'meta-narrative' (see Knapp 1996:131). We encounter difficulties in producing a grand narrative (cf. Tilley 1993:14) because of the complexity of the significant details, which are only revealed by detailed contextual analysis (see Tringham 2000).

All grand syntheses of European prehistory (Bailey 2000; Chapman 2001; Guilaine 2005; Kruk and Milisauskas 1999; Milisauskas 2002a; Perlès 2001; Whittle 1996) have approached the subject as *part* of general chapters on the Neolithic because ceramic technology was influenced by local custom (e.g. de Roever 2004; Gibson 2002; Muntoni 2003; Spataro 2002, etc.). Similarly, specialized events such as the 1993 SAA Meeting (see Barnett and Hoopes 1995), or synthesizing works (see Freestone and Gaimster 1997) dedicated to producing a global image (e.g. Cumberpatch and Blinkhorn 1997) of the emergence of pottery, approach the subject by segmenting it into regional traditions or Techno-Complexes.

Ceramics

The present text uses the generic term of 'ceramics' to designate all objects made of fired clay, from pottery and figurines to fired wattle and daub buildings. I employ this inclusive categorical term due to the technological isomorphism of different categories of objects.

From a cultural perspective, ceramics are the first plastic (malleable) material, a perfect medium of plastic representation and the basic material for skeuomorphs (in which one material is made to look like another, for example pots are sometimes made to look like baskets or metal containers). Ceramics are used in contemporary rituals and are used as utilitarian objects.

From a physical-chemical perspective ceramics are the final product of a pyro-technological sequence or 'rite of passage' which begins with the identification of the clay sources, the preparation of clay, the modelling of the shape of the object, the drying and the (pre- or post-firing) decoration, followed by firing and sometimes by post-firing processes (Livingstone Smith 2005:6ff.). In spite of the sophistication of contemporary analyses (Barclay 2001; Orton et al. 2001) or of experimental archaeology (Gibson 2002; Livingstone Smith et al. 2005; Volkova 2002, etc.) which allows the identification of the technological stages of the ceramic product in different traditions, one still cannot determine exactly the methods of firing (Gheorghiu 2002; Gosselain 2002; Livingstone Smith et al. 2005) in the prehistoric archaeological record.

Several theories have been offered to elucidate the emergence of pottery, from V. Gordon Childe (1951) who saw Neolithic pots as skeuomorphs of putative basketry containers. More recent theories have focused on the ability of clay to act as a detoxification agent in cooking certain plant foods (Arnold 1999:129, table 6.1, 135), the role of pots as prestige goods used in ritual displays (Hayden 1990; Hayden 1995), or pots as symbols of ethnicity and group identity (Armit and Finlayson 1995). In my opinion a study of the emergence of pottery must insist upon the symbolic aspects of the process, which can be witnessed as early as the first experiments with clay in the Palaeolithic.

Ceramics in Palaeolithic and Neolithic Europe

According to Pawlikovski et al. (2000) the earliest evidence of the emergence of ceramic technology in Europe as clay-lined structures (Karkanas et al. 2004:514; Koumouzelis et al. 2001; Pawlikovski et al. 2000) is to be found in the middle Aurignacian sequence dated 34–32 kyr BP at Klisoura cave 1, in the northwestern Peloponnese. Other examples for the use of ceramics in the Paleolithic come from Mas d'Azil and La Bouiche in the Pyrenees, but the largest ceramic inventory comes from the Moravian sites of Dolni Věstonice I and II and Pavlov I and II, with more than 10,000 ceramic fragments (Vandivier et al. 1989:1002).

The analysis of the *chaînes opératoires* of the ceramic figurines indicate that ceramics were used as a ritual and symbolic material, an assumption supported by the high-fracture rate of ceramic fragments resulting from the making of figurines from separate parts and the intentional thermal shock that caused the sudden destruction of the wet clay objects. This suggests a high interest in the ritual and symbolic process of constructing/deconstructing the objects than in creating a final product (Soffer et al. 1993:273). It is not an exaggeration to infer a potential magical nature to the process of construction/deconstruction of ceramic objects, a cultural trait that seems to re-emerge with the coming of pottery to Greece. All these abovementioned examples demonstrate the existence of a European Palaeolithic that produced ceramics without developing pottery (Vandivier et al. 1989:1002). The absence of pottery in Europe continues during the Mesolithic in contrast with other parts of the world.

It is not easy to superimpose prehistoric cultural processes on contemporary geography. Alongside Eastern and Western Europe I also include in my discussion an area which includes the Balkan Peninsula and western and central Anatolia. This can be seen as a single cultural area (Özdoğan 1993:177; although the definition of this as a cultural region is still controversial, e.g. Demoule 1993). Whatever the designation of the Balkans and Anatolia most archaeologists accept that there are relationships and connections between the two regions (Demoule 1993; Nandris 1970a; Perlès 2003:97; Wijnen 1993a). Furthermore the Balkans and Anatolia have important connections to mainland Europe during the Neolithic.

Recent theories (Özdoğan 2005:15; Perlès 2003:93) confirm the old supposition of migrant farmers from the Near East, colonists of multiple origins (Perlès 2003:101; 2005) as far as the aceramic stage (Özdogan 1997:21), and a period corresponding to the collapse of the Pre-Pottery Neolithic B (PPNB) in the Near East (Cauvin 1989:21; Cauvin 1997). It seems that the emergence of pottery in western Asia and later on in Europe was the result of a complex social process, still not fully understood, than of demographic pressure (see Cauvin 1989; Perlès 2001:53), therefore pottery technology appears to be the result of both cultural crisis and of cognitive changes invested in a new symbolic technology.

The Neolithic ceramic package common to western Asia and Europe, containing coarse pottery and monochrome pottery, 'cult tables' or clay boxes, steatopygious figurines (with exaggerated anatomical features), anthropomorphic or zoomorphic vessels, pintaderas (pottery stamps) and tokens (Özdoğan 2005:21), specific to western Asian cultures, was the result of a common ceramic technology and symbolism for the Balkan–Anatolian region.

For southeastern Europe a 'homogenous' model of demic (or population) migration cannot be accepted without also taking into account the contribution of Mesolithic foragers in the transition to the Neolithic (Tringham 2000:32), like the Crvena Stjena ceramics developed by foragers after contact and acculturation with traditions using pottery. The adoption of pottery technology by Mesolithic populations seems to have been more the result of a symbolic decision, rather than of a practical one.

Frameworks of Analysis

Not only do ceramics have a social symbolic value of display (see Bourdieu 1984:281) related to their role as objects of payment in bride-wealth, or their role as gifts and offerings during different ritual and social occasions, but the primary symbolism of pottery comes from its skeuomorphic and imitative character, by copying animals and plants, the human body and significant household or everyday objects. Symbolism also arises from the social practices in which pottery is involved, such as the process of food- and beverage-making.

In Neolithic Europe the emergence of pottery seems to have been a symbolic process associated with its use in social practices (Vitelli 1995:61) compared to western Asia where its adoption is associated with the skeuomorphic connections made between pots and other forms of material culture (Moore 1995:48).

The artistic elaboration of pottery can be treated as a signalling process for the expression of social identity (see Bowser 2000) or more precisely the signalling of social prestige (Bliege Bird and Smith 2005:233). Bliege Bird and Smith stress that decoration, style and quality of craftsmanship are messages related to a given community's politics of competition. Various archaeological (Dietler and Hayden 2001) and ethnographic (see Bowser 2000) examples relate the conspicuous use of pottery to its relationship with alcohol consumption and feasting. Indeed it is notable that the *chaîne opératoire* (technical sequence) of pottery-making often seems to have symbolic analogies with those of fermented beverages (see Jennings et al. 2005). It is worth noting that a number of authors have linked the emergence of pottery to the symbolic role of pottery in consumption practices, as consumption practices are often bound up with the signalling of prestige and communality (Chapman

1988:4; Hayden 2001:38). The present text will highlight the symbolic and social aspect of pottery use in all the Techno-Complexes discussed.

Since the 'Neolithic Revolution' seems to have been largely symbolic in nature (Cauvin 1997:271; Hodder 1990), this point of view shall be explored beside the analysis of rarity, prestige and status. Such a mode of analysis allows me to draw out the social choices and symbolism within the *chaîne opératoire* of ceramic technologies, as social practices are intimately bound up with the material symbolism of ceramic technologies.

As the objective of the present chapter is to discuss the relationship of pottery technology with the social and as many of the recent studies on ceramics (to cite only van der Leeuw 2002 and Spataro 2002) take either a *chaînes opératoires* (see Dobres 2000:173; Lemonnier 1996:546) or symbolic (see Cauvin 1997; Hodder 1982) perspective, throughout I have analyzed the relationship between the technological stages of production and different social aspects, such as ritual use and symbolism, which have not been previously discussed in association with ceramic technology.

Chaînes Opératoires

The *chaînes opératoires* of ceramic technology consists of the series of operations which transform raw material into final product; *chaînes opératoires* are composed of immutable stages, determined by physical laws. Besides the physical constraints we also have to take into account cultural choices where the producer can choose between alternative actions (see Lemonnier 1986:155; van der Leeuw 2002:240). For example, the process of firing involves the following physical immutable stages: the evacuation of molecular water; the calcinations of (intentionally or unintentionally added) organic materials; sintering (when temperatures rise at 800–1050°C); and vitrification at 1100–1300°C (see Kingery 1997:12). The *chaînes opératoires* can be perceived as sequential material operations (Dobres 2000:154) with fixed and flexible stages (Schlanger 1997:144). This is especially true of ceramic technology. The dual character of ceramic technology allows us to investigate both the technical process as well as ritual and symbolic action.

The originality of ceramic technology, compared to the previous materials and technologies used by prehistoric people was its additive character, a process consisting of a repetitive addition of materials which conferred a ritual character on the production sequence. Not only some of the stages, but the entire *chaînes opératoires* could become repetitive actions of symbolization (Gheorghiu 2005), since repetitive actions identified in the archaeological record are considered to have a ritual content (Gheorghiu 2001:19). Contrary to the common assumption that any ritualized action could be identified because of its lack of technical motivation (see Humphrey and Laidlaw 1994:158; Whitehouse 2002:46), any technical action could include a ritual dimension (see Lemonnier 2004:39). A *chaîne opératoire* could therefore be assimilated to a ritual action since it is similarly structured, and such an interpretation is essential to approaching prehistoric pottery.

The subjective stages within the technological process were culturally determined by the metaphorical paradigm of the social group and not by the artisan alone. Therefore the 'choice of the potter' (i.e. of an individual), identified in ethnoarchaeological case studies (see Gosselain 2002; Van der Leeuw 1997) seems to have been less operable in prehistoric societies where developing standardization issued from an increasing social control was influenced by the dominant metaphors of the time. Ceramic technology was in fact a 'choice of the community', at the same time functional and symbolic. Choice could have played a role in the affirmation of group identity.

The choice of temper is one among many symbolic choices during the process of manufacture of the clay object, being a subjective stage of operation. The act of choosing a technical variant is a symbolic action; the temper in the clay paste could be dung, sand, grog, crushed bones, calcite or flint, depending upon the symbol the community intends to transmit. Another good example of choice in pottery technology is the additive or extractive method of making the decoration.

People, Technology and Water

The southeastern European Neolithic is characterized by a short aceramic episode in Crete as well as Thessaly, at Argissa, Soufli, Gediki, and Sesklo around 6800 BC (see Guilaine 2005:47; for recent dates see Boyadziev 2002:237), followed by a slow process of ceramic technology diffusion from south to northwest as both C14 and recent mitochondrial and Y-chromosomal DNA studies (King and Underhill 2002:707) suggest. The spread of pottery technology, an important part of the Neolithic 'package' of the first colonists of Europe, was due to demic diffusion (van Andel and Runnels 1995) and trait-adoption diffusion (Gkiasta et al. 2003:59ff.), i.e. acculturation, and cultural contacts (Bar-Yosef 2003:76).

When discussing the pottery technology dispersal across Europe it is essential to observe the close relationship of the pottery Techno-Complexes with water (both coastal and inland waterways). It is possible to define:

- a continental Mediterranean Techno-Complex (Anatolia and mainland Greece) that spread along the rivers and hydrographic structures of the Balkans (Figure 4.1);
- a continental First Temperate Neolithic Techno-Complex (the Balkans and the Lower Danube), a first synthesis between agriculturalists and hunter-gatherers, which spread along the local hydrographic structures (Figure 4.2);
- a coastal Mediterranean Techno-Complex (Adriatic coast, Italy, Spain, Portugal) that spread by seafaring along the sea's shores (Figure 4.3);
- a continental Second Temperate Neolithic Techno-Complex (Central Europe), resulted from a second synthesis between agriculturalists and hunter-gatherers which spread mainly along the Danube hydrographic structure (Figure 4.4); and
- a continental ceramic Mesolithic Techno-Complex, that spread along the western European hydrographic structures (Figure 4.5).

There is no doubt that the advance of the Neolithic cultural 'package' and of pottery technology took place in Europe along two ways: the riverine valleys of the Danube and tributaries through Central Europe and along the Mediterranean coasts (Bar-Yosef 2003:76) beginning at 7000 BC. C14 dates infer a first colonization of the Mediterranean around 5900/5800 BC (Keroualin 2003:112) on the Italian coasts; a second stage of colonization, between 5800–5600 BC is mentioned on the

Iberian coasts, followed by Andalusia, south of Portugal and by the Atlantic coast around 5000 BC. The geographic pattern of distribution of domesticates and pottery along the Mediterranean coasts suggests a seafaring demic diffusion model (Zilhão 1993). It is also worth noting that the pottery technology of the coastal Mediterranean Techno-Complex was influenced by water symbolism, the profile of the marine *Cardium* shell being used as imprint pattern.

Around 5500 BC in western Europe the adoption of agriculture and pottery by Mesolithic populations, as the result of a strategy of social and ritual integration (Barnett 1995:81) of the new symbols of prestige, developed along the local riverine valleys. A similar spread of pottery technology along a hydrologic structure happened around 5300 BC along the River Rhone.

The Continental Mediterranean Technocomplex (Anatolia and Mainland Greece)

In western Asia and in Europe pottery emerges at the same moment, which can be dated around 8000 BP (Moore 1995:44), with a change in economy represented by the husbandry of sheep and goats (Moore 1995:40), and was preceded by small portable symbolic ceramic artefacts as seals and figurines (see Perlès 2003:101).

Plastering, an additive technique of making objects, seems to have been part of the technological Neolithic package of aceramic and ceramic cultures of this Techno-Complex, being used for objects (Perlès 2001:217) and for buildings (see Rodden 1965). In my opinion the method of plastering was preserved as a skeuomorph in the exaggerated way of slipping the coarse-ware walls with deep parallel grooves of barbotine, a technique which can be observed throughout the Neolithic (see also Mellaart 1965:60).

Early pottery had a small number of shapes and was divided into two categories: coarse and fine (Figure 4.1). If the coarse pottery's role was to be used for cooking, the fine pottery seems to have had a role in the consumption of specific food and drink. The differences between the two categories was not only aesthetic but also structural; the temper used was different as well as the method of finishing the surface of the vases.

The high degree of the burnishing of the surface of fine ware was specific for the pottery of this Techno-Complex. This was a method which could fill up the pores of vases' walls by sintering, to improve their capacity to contain liquids, and which transformed the value of the object by making it shine. Another way to improve the value of the vases was colour, which evolved from a monochrome stage to coloured slips and painting.

The monochrome horizon spread from Thessaly, at Achilleion, Argissa, Sesklo, Otzaki, Soufli, in Greece (Lazarovici 1996), in Bulgaria (Özdoğan 2005:21), within the hydrologic basin of the Lom River at Koprivec, Cerven, Olrovets 1, Poljanitsa, the hydrologic basin of the Iantra River, at Bjala (Todorova 1995:83–4) up to the Sturma River (Ursulescu 2000:82). This horizon was followed by another one characterized by white painted ceramics, which also followed the alluvial valley system of the Struma, Maritsa and Tunca rivers. Around 6000 BC in the Balkans along with the white pottery (at Anzabegovo-Vrsnic I, Galabnik I, Karanovo I, Starčevo) a dark painted pottery (using red, brown, black colours) is recorded

Figure 4.1 Greek Neolithic pottery (After Perlès 2001:215)

(Boyadziev 2002:237). A red slipped pottery horizon corresponding to Hacilar VI–V in Anatolia (Parzinger and Özdoğan 1995:14–15) generated the Sesklo, Karanovo and Starčevo traditions in Europe (Özdoğan 1989:205; Özdoğan 1997:27; Özdoğan 2005:23; Ursulescu 2000:84).

Greece

A characteristic of the Early and Middle Neolithic of Greece was the domination of fine pottery (Perlès 1992; Vitelli 1993a), and the fact that monochrome pottery predates coarse impressed ware by almost half a millennium (Hameau 1987; Pluciennik 1997:48).

The combination between monochrome and painting with a gradual development of the latter characterizes the Early Neolithic southern Greek pottery (Phelps 2004:29). Typical fine wares were the medium bowls and the bowls with ring feet (Phelps 2004:37). In the following period pottery was characterized by painted decoration and relief decoration as oval pellets or grooving and ribbing the wet surface of the vase and in a later phase by overlapping slip on painting (Phelps 2004:39). A high quality pottery with sintered slip, labelled *Urfirnis* (see Kunze 1931), characterizes the northeast Peloponnese Middle Neolithic. Wares with high feet with perforations to allow for the easier desiccation (drying) of the unfired objects (Vitelli 1993b) are now common.

The gritless paste for fine vases was made of levigated local clays (Winn and Shimabuku 1989:78) and the addition of grit characterized the medium and coarser containers (Phelps 2004:30; see also Vitelli 1993b:135–44). Community choice can be observed in the use of temper for the fine ware: crushed limestone or calcite followed by quartz in the Peloponnese, mica and mica schist at Sesklo, quartz at Achilleion, but also andesite, serpentine, feldspar, schist and possibly grog or plant fibres (Perlès 2001:211).

Different traditions of vase building are also an index of community choice; vases were made pressed in moulds and with the coil building method (Vitelli 1993b:97) at Franchti and Lerna, or by slab building in Macedonia, Thessaly, central Greece and Corinthia (Wijnen 1993b). A variability within the same technology can be observed: for example the coil building method in Macedonia, at Nea Nikomedeia and other later settlements was performed by positioning the coils on top of each other, a technique different from other parts of Greece where the coils partly covered each other (Perlès 2001:211). It is possible that the design of ring feet had also been motivated by the technology of formation, being the result of the positioning of a lump of clay on the middle protuberance of a *tournette* (slow motion wheel).

Characteristic for monochrome ceramics is a burnished surface. This is a time-consuming operation (Perlès 2001:213; Vitelli 1993b:97) to reduce porosity (Winn and Shimabuku 1989:79), which leaves the tool traces easily visible (Phelps 2004:31). In the Middle Neolithic one can notice a two-stage burnishing, before and after the slipping of the vase (Vitelli 1993b:8). Slip was applied to the vases' surface with the help of a brush or by dipping the vase into the solution (Winn and Shimabuku 1989:79). In the Middle Neolithic there is a propensity for slips rich in iron mineral oxides especially at Franchti (Vitelli 1993b:8). Nea Nikomedeia in Macedonia was a special case, where potters used a thick layer of slip (Perlès 2001:213).

Because of the variation in the colour of pottery, from the black monochrome to uneven red slips, this pottery was named Rainbow Ware, Buntpoliert, or Variegated (Phelps 2004:31), suggesting firing in an open structure where it is possible to create an oxidizing and a reduced atmosphere by quenching the fire. It is possible that dung was used as fuel (Vitelli 1993b:106), which produced temperatures under 800°C to protect the vases with calcite as temper. Björk (1995:67) reports, at Achilleion, temperatures of maximum 950°C which could be reached in closed ovens or kilns, which suggests advanced pottery firing. In the Middle Neolithic this technological ingenuity reaches a peak with the three-stage method of firing, which is an indication of a high degree of specialization (Vitelli 1995:56). Vitelli (1993b:200) states that at Franchti vases were fired individually being progressively stacked into the fire; a similar case is reported at Corinth (Perlès 2001:213).

The analysis of the symbolic meaning of the technological decisions would suggest that levigation (preparation of clay to produce an even mixture), the crushed temper, burnishing, the progressive positioning of vases in the fire and fire quenching could be analogous operations to those for producing bread or fermented beverages from cereals, a point of view which would connect the technology of fine pottery with its final ritual use in communal ceremonies. The image of cereals was modelled as relief decoration on the vases' surfaces as oval pellets. Such analogies could have had a magical character for the first makers and users of pottery.

Early Neolithic pottery technology suggests the ascendancy of standardization of the *chaînes opératoires* as for example the vases of uniform dimensions and shapes but with different tempers and different burnishing methods (Vitelli 1995:60), which can be viewed as a developing ritualized action. Additional evidence for the ritual role of pottery (Perlès and Vitelli 1999:103) could be the fact this pottery was *not* used for food preparation, and its dimensions were too small for food storage (Vitelli 1989:26–7). It is unlikely that this pottery possesses a 'functional' household role (Perlès and Vitelli 1999:98). One can infer that the role of pottery in the Early and Middle Neolithic was one of social presentation and rituality not related to food processing, consumption or storage, a supposition that relates to the community's choice to the magic power of the new technology (see Vitelli 1993a:253).

As early as the Middle Neolithic, southern Greece demonstrates a development of the standardization of the pottery technology first with the shapes and dimensions of wares followed by an increased homogeneity of pastes for fine wares and an increase in the scale of production (Vitelli 1993b:210).

In the Middle Neolithic pottery becomes the result of a craft specialization; it is possible that due to the analogies between cereal processing (see Crown and Wills 1995:248) and pottery and of the magical aspects of the combustion process, that potters could have had a special status within society, possibly related to shamanism (Vitelli 1995:60–2).

Painting which appeared on the most visible surfaces, the utilization of ring feet, as well as the extreme shiny surface polishing, could be connected with a greater propensity for display of these ceramic containers, probably with a social motivation of display on special occasions (Vitelli 1995:56), an assumption supported also by the limited number of pots (Perlès 2001:217) and the rising social role of the potters (Vitelli 1995:62). The ascendancy of vessels on ring feet could be perceived as a new mode of use and of visual perception of the vases, which is also underlined by the intensity of their burnishing. My interpretation of the vases with perforated support is they were for heating drinks (positioned on embers to heat the liquid contained) and could have been an index of a new community ritual.

Middle Neolithic homogenization of the fine wares in different settlements of the northeastern Peloponnese could have been the result of a practice of exogamy and the making of pottery by women (Cullen 1985:86; Pluciennik 1997:47). Alongside the production of pottery there was also a ritual micro-world of household objects, zoomorphic and anthropomorphic representations, and miniature clay vases being used in funerary ritual (Perlès 2001:268).

The Techno-Complex of fine polished ceramics which appeared relatively rapidly in Southern Greece, characterized by a complex technology with ritual significance continues northward to Thessaly and Macedonia and later continues towards the Balkans, diffusing the shapes of pottery and their associated ritual use.

By contrast, the Late Neolithic was characterized by a remarkable increase in the production of coarse ware which suggests the emergence of a different kind of production, different roles for pottery and a shift of ceramic technology from specialists to non-specialists (Vitelli 1993a:252).

The First Temperate Neolithic Technocomplex in Continental Europe

The difference between the Neolithic in Greece and the Balkans is due to the geographical-hydrologic context (Sherratt 1982) whose climatic determinism gave the name to the Techno-Complex as the First Temperate Neolithic (FTN) (Nandris 1970b). The FTN can be understood as a second wave of advance of a semi-sedentary society which created a new Techno-Complex by *adaptation* and *transformation* (see Renfrew 1987:154) of the parent economy. In addition, a new rituality emerges and alters the original pottery typology from the Near East. I shall address this below.

Starčevo

Starčevo, a homogeneous Techno-Complex spread over a large geographical region, is generally treated as a set of regionally distinct traditions like Anzabegovo-Vrsnik culture (Macedonia), the Karanovo culture (southern Bulgaria), the Kremikovci culture (western Bulgaria), the Criş culture (Romania), and the Körös culture (Hungary) (Manson 1995:65).

There are two well-defined categories of Starčevo pottery (Figure 4.2), the fine and the coarse; the first one is characterized by a large diversity of surface treat-

Figure 4.2 Starčevo pottery

ments (Spataro 2004:323) such as burnished monochrome ware, white-on-red or black-on-red painted, and the second one by vases covered by thick slips, with manifest traces of the fingers, nail impressions or impressed or appliqué cords (Manson 1995:67). Some of the fine wares, with or without pedestals and coloured with red slip, are shaped like poppy seeds, which could be interpreted as symbolically related to the content of vases. A large majority of the coarse ware had spherical or hemispherical shapes, and occasionally shouldered pots with cylindrical necks were produced. Alongside pottery, weights, spindle whorls, stamps, house models, 'altars' (or lamps), anthropomorphic and zoomorphic figurines are also components of the ceramic repertoire.

In the earliest stages of pottery production, painted pottery is present in a very small proportion and it is not present in all settlements (Manson 1995:73); later decorated pottery with white and dark colours and triangular, zigzags and curvilinear motifs as garlands and spirals becomes more frequent. The appearance of fine pottery demonstrates a gradual rise in the visibility and value of pottery in some community rituals. A specific shape for fine pottery is the cup with a highly perforated pedestal, which could be seen as an index of a continued community ritual from the south.

The coarse ware which dominates the Starcevo pottery (Manson 1995) was of a large dimension with thick walls as well as of medium size dimensions, the latter, the result of a similar technology of production, is characterized by thinner walls decorated with incisions, impressions and applied relief decorations. Some of the coarse ware of large dimensions had thicker bases to stabilize the pot; some medium size vessels had four small legs. Protuberances, sometimes horizontally or vertically perforated, or tunnel-like or band-like handles (Manson 1995:71) indicate the use of cord to suspend or transport these vases. It is possible that the large numbers of coarse ware vessels, with the probable function of storage or food preparation, could be an index of the adaptation of the potters of Starcevo communities to their new environment.

A continuation of the technological traditions from Greece could be detected in the making of fine grained paste (Manson 1995:71). One can observe in some areas a trend in time in the choice of non micritic, humic and micaceous local clays rich in fine alluvial quartz sand (Spataro 2003 [2004]:39), but there isn't any relationship detected between the paste and the vases' walls technology of finishing. Furthermore there is no relationship detected between the type of temper and the shape of the vases (see Spataro 2003 [2004]:40). The fine-grained paste was tempered with sand, mica and also with small pebbles (Manson 1995:71), but a new tendency is the use of chaff as temper for the coarse and semi-coarse pottery. I interpret the intensive use of the chaff (produced by using dried dung as temper, which explains the standardized dimension of the cut vegetal fibres) as a symbolic intention to express the community's economic adaptation to the new environment, which extended to cattle breeding and cereal cultivation. Dried dung used as temper increases the plasticity and workability of the paste, a uniform process of drying and firing, as well as a lightened weight and an increased thermal conductivity.

Starčevo technology seems to have been relatively homogenous over large geographic areas; for example the Transylvania and Banat regions were characterized by similar recipes for matrix and temper (Spataro 2004:332). Starčevo pottery is characterized by a tendency to thin the vases' walls, probably a technical process to improve resistance to thermal shock (Manson 1995:73) which could be seen as an increasing tendency for using pottery in the food making process. An index of a high skill technology and mass production in the manufacture of pottery can be seen in the round vases with thin walls and a small curved in surface on their bottom, probably being made on a slow potter wheel or *tournette* with a protuberance on its centre.

Slip covers the micro voids created after the combustion of the organic temper on the surface of the vase. Probably the vases were dipped into a larger vase filled with coloured slip; painting was executed with fine brushes.

All vases decorated with coloured slips were subject to an excessive burnishing process, their exterior perfectly polished expressing a very visible shine. High burnishing of this sort increases the visibility of the object and could relate to the enhanced social use of these vessels.

Fine monochrome ware is generally characterized by dark cores and very thin ceramic layers, as a result of rapid firings with low temperatures of maximum 600°C (Spataro 2003; Spataro 2004:39) only in a few instances did temperatures reach 850°C (Manson 1995:71). As for the fine ceramics with coloured slip, the rare fire-clouds on its surface (see Paul 1995:Table II, 3, 4 for the Pre-Criş tradition) could be interpreted as an oxidizing firing, possibly in ovens, simple kilns, or in large vessels fired in bonfires. These are likely to have been produced by an oxidizing fire in a close pyrostructure where vases were in close contact, rather than by direct contact with the fuel.

Current analyses do not allow the identification of a postfiring treatment of the Starčevo ware, but the large proportion of the coarse ware correlated with the development of plant cultivation, whose processing necessitates boiling to neutralize the toxins (see Arnold 1999:129), suggests a postfiring treatment for filling up the pores to increase the capacity of vases to hold liquids.

One can identify in the Starčevo communities a propensity for the choice of those variables that increase the thermal performance of vases (Manson 1995:73), from the thinning of the wares' walls to the gradual passage from organic temper to mineral temper. The use of dung as temper could have been a symbolic choice referring to the early Starčevo economy focused on cattle breeding, while the use of mineral temper could have referred to the taking into possession of new lands for cultivation. Such choice, together with the increase of the number of cooking ware, could be interpreted as an index of increased plant cultivation.

The fine ware decorated with coloured slips and paint could have had, as in Greece, a role in social display and use, but also probably for storing substances with a high social value. Their role seems to have increased in time as the complexity of their decoration and surface treatment increased, with extreme burnishing and complex painted patterns being the result of social preference. Some of the red slipped round vases from the Lower Danube region were shaped like poppy capsules, a symbolism that suggests a social and ritual utilization of red poppy, *Papaver somniferum*. In all subtraditions vases with high pedestals demonstrate the continuation of an earlier Anatolian–Aegean ritual tradition, while the reduction in the use of decorative patterns and categories of vases could be the result of a reduction in the visibility of those rituals or contexts that utilized pottery.

The Coastal Mediterranean Technocomplex

The Impressed Ware (IW) tradition which characterizes the first Neolithic communities of the Mediterranean spread over an extremely large coastal region and included different local traditions (Figure 4.3). Chronologically IW emerges in the last two centuries of the 8th millennium BP at the same time in Italy (the *impressa*) and on Croatia's littoral coasts (the *impresso*), but the diffusion on the Adriatic coast of Italy lasted a millennium (Spataro 2002:25). There is a demonstrated relationship between the ceramic traditions on both sides of the Adriatic from the Early Neolithic (Guilaine 2005:60). In time the *impresso* diffused to the inland and to the Pô plain since the *impressa* expanded to the Balkans (Keroulain 2003:130). In the Middle Neolithic we observe a diversity of local traditions, to cite only the Danilo *figulina* pottery from the Adriatic Balkans and the Ripoli pottery from central Italy. It seems that the impressed method was a technique using tools easily available for early colonists, which were replaced in time by a more complex technique involving painting.

There is still considerable debate about the kind of model that explains the spread of the Neolithic in the Adriatic region in the 7th millennium BP, the 'availability' model (as at Edera Cave) or the demic diffusion model (as in the Adriatic basin area), but the distribution of Impressed Ware pottery in the region infers a movement of population from southeast to northwest. It seems that the Mesolithic background for the ceramic traditions that appear in the Adriatic region was not significant (Spataro 2002:33).

The Impressed Ware Tradition

Impressed-ware ceramics have been discovered in open-air sites as well as in the many caves of the Dalmatian littoral. For example the Vela Jama cave produced an assemblage of three different phases, the oldest being characterized by coarse spherical and ovoid pots decorated both with finger and pinched impressions as well as with *Cardium* shell.

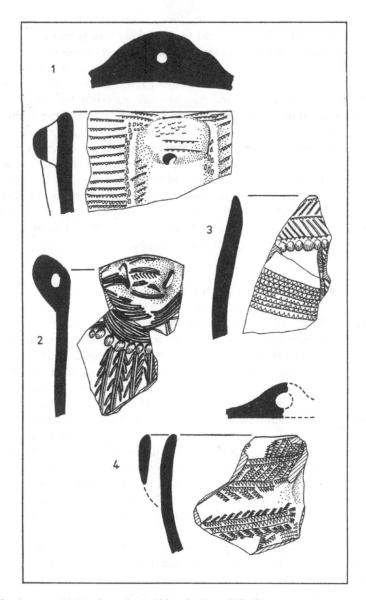

Figure 4.3   Impressed Ware from Spain (After Phillips 1975:69)

In some early settlements the ceramic paste had no inclusions, unlike the later Danilo and Hvar phases, when crushed calcite was used as temper (Spataro 2002:91). It is noteworthy to observe the existence of a technological tradition in the fabric of the ceramics of this site, which extends into the Middle Neolithic.

IW pottery was decorated with marine shells (*Cardium* and *Mytilus*), as well as with impressed finger and fingernail patterns, incisions being rare (Spataro 2002:73). Generally the IW pottery was fired in short firings, at low temperatures below 750°C. Generally the coarse pottery was fired in an oxidized atmosphere (Chapman et al. 1996:189), probably open fires.

Danilo/Hvar Traditions

The Adriatic Balkan Middle Neolithic was characterized by several pottery traditions, including the Danilo and Hvar Cultures of the Dalmatian Coast. Danilo fine pottery or *figulina* has similarities with central Italy (Spataro 2002:115), which suggests a relationship between the two sides of the Adriatic.

Chapman (1988) divides the Danilo ceramics into four major fabric groups: bichrome painted, dark burnished, with or without incised decoration, monochrome, red or buff, and coarse, with a variety of nuances. Characteristic of both traditions (Benac and Marjianovič 1993:138) are jars, deep cylindrical cups and hemispherical bowls decorated with geometric patterns. Hvar fine pottery was decorated with spiral patterns. *Figulina* pottery was characterized by a vitrified fine matrix, resulting from a long process of levigation (Spataro 2002:122).

The Danilo and Hvar pottery was primarily decorated with incised triangles and spiral patterns, sometimes filled with red colour, and later with meander patterns (Spataro 2002:75). In a later phase the decoration with circles and garlands become current as well as monochrome pottery. Pots were covered with a decorative white slip (Spataro 2002:114). At Danilo Bitinj, it seems that the painted pottery was made of imported clay and fired at low temperatures, but generally *figulina* fine pottery was fired over 850°C, which involves the use of kilns for this operation (Spataro 2002:91). Monochrome pottery was fired in quenched fires or ovens.

Cardium shell decoration could be considered symbolically related to water and navigation. This disappeared over time, being replaced with decoration of the cordons with fingernail impressions, a process which could be perceived as a gradual change in the symbolism of the colonists. One can perceive continuities in the technology of pottery-making between the Early and Middle Neolithic, the latter is characterized by new shapes and decorations, the result of the diversity of social activities (Chapman 1988:4). Among them, a new type of vessel, the high-pedestalled pot emerges in the Middle Neolithic, which may be an index of similarities with Greece, Starčevo or the Linearbandkeramik (LBK).

The division into different categories of pottery implies a diversification in the technologies of the community. For example in the Middle Neolithic one can identify two parallel technologies, one for coarse pottery, using local clay, with or without temper, and with low temperature firings, and a second for the *figulina* ware, more complex and time consuming, since the clays were the result of a long process of preparation, probably imported, and using higher temperatures for firing, probably with the use of kilns. One can assert that the separation of the domestic and ritual activities was performed through a diversification in pottery technology.

The Rapid Colonization of the Northern Mediterranean Coast

Between 5900/5800 BC, as a result of the rapid diffusion of seafaring colonists (Zilhão 1993) into the Mediterranean basin, there is a simultaneous emergence of different stylistic groups in the Impressed Ware Techno-Complex on the coasts of southern Italy, southern France and Spain; for example the Early Neolithic or *Impressa ligure* from Arene Candide, Italy, has analogies with Pont de Roque-Haute in Languedoc, France and with Caucade in Provence, France. Two different evolutions can be observed in the Mediterranean IW Techno-Complex: one rapid, which led to painted pottery, in the Adriatic and the eastern coast of Italy up to Sicily, and a second one which continues the impression method, from France to Portugal. In Italy IW spreads over a large region from the Tuscan islands to Sicily, where, after a 'pure impressed' ware phase (Pluciennik 1997:51), it develops into the Stentinello tradition (Keroualin 2003:114). In southern Italy, as with the Dalmatian coast (Chapman 1988:19), after a first phase of coarse pottery decorated with impressions for storage or cooking, new classes of fine pottery acknowledge the emergence of novel practices relating to drink and food consumption and feasting (Malone 1985; Pluciennik 1997:48).

In contrast with the variability from the Italian region, the Cardial ware of France was characterized by round-bottom vases with a limited variability, decorated with an alternation of impressed and unimpressed bands made with *Cardium* shell, diverse comb-like instruments, fingers or nails (Keroualin 2003:118).

Compared to its eastern neighbours, the Early Neolithic of France is a far more complex subject (Binder and Courtin 1986). For example at the Pendimoun site in Provence a pot decorated with shells and nails appears on an earlier level than Cardial ware (Binder et al. 1993). In northeast Spain the Montserrat or Cardial tradition (Colliga 1998:769) developed a limited typology of round and hemispherical shapes with a similar decoration and the same technology of production as in southern France.

There is an uneven spread of shell decoration on the Iberian peninsula: rarity in the south and profusion on the Atlantic coasts (Guilaine 2005:87). The occurrence of early pottery of good quality in Spain, which was replaced in time by a pottery of a lesser quality, as well as the reduction of the diversity of ceramic types (Guilaine 2005:82), could have been the result of an interaction with the autochthonous population. In time, shell decoration declined with the new phase of the Epicardial.

Southern Italian Impressed Ware

Southern Italian Impressed coarse ware materialized in the shape of baskets skeuomorphs (see Tiné 1983:Table 126), the result of local manufacture (Pluciennik 1997:47). The second phase, of the southeast Italian early Neolithic, is characterized by painted pottery, or *figulina*, but the dominant class remains impressed ceramics.

While the Early Neolithic ware employed local clays, Middle Neolithic painted *figulina* pottery also used non-local clays (Muntoni 1999a:88) obtained from a minimum 30-kilometre distance, indicating that pottery was not solely a domestic activity but had acquired a new social dimension (Muntoni 1999b:241). There is no choice visible in the utilization of temper for the Early Neolithic vases, their paste incorporating local inclusions (Williams 1980) with variable granularity, but for the Middle Neolithic pottery inclusions like calcite for coarse ware (Muntoni 1999a:242) were intentionally added (Muntoni 1999a:88). As mineral tempers offer the pot good mechanical resistance, heat conductivity and diffusion (Skibo et al. 1989), one can infer that coarse ware was employed for cooking. The construction of coarse ware employed the coil building method (Muntoni 1999a:244), and the vases were decorated using the *Cardium* shell as impressing instrument (Muntoni 2003:56).

Painting transformed the decorative patterns by reducing the decorated areas to the most visible surface of the vases and by replacing the points with lines, parallel or crossed, under the shape of chevrons and zigzags. The red, brown or white pigments necessitate a lighter-coloured background and therefore imposed a new technique of firing.

Not only was the painted *figulina* pottery characterized by well-burnished surfaces but the undecorated Early Neolithic ware also had burnished surfaces, as a method of sealing or waterproofing and to increase the strength of the walls of the pottery (Muntoni 1999a:244).

The variability in the light colours of the incised pottery is an index of combustion in the oxidizing atmosphere of open firings (Muntoni 2003:58), at low temperatures under 700–800°C (Cassano et al. 1995; Pluciennik 1997:47). *Figulina* fine ware was fired at higher temperatures, up to 1000°C, only in an oxidized atmosphere and in closed combustion structures like kilns (for the use of kilns in the Cardial see Roudil 2003:515ff.).

The first incised pottery from the south of Italy (like the Tavoliere region) is expressed in a primary phase with pots with the skeuomorphic shape of wickerwork storage containers, decorated over their entire surface with impressions (Tiné 1983: Plate 126), and in a second phase, with the emergence of fine painted pottery or *figulina*, the shapes tend to be more portable, therefore with a different ritual function.

The pottery of the southern Italian Neolithic seems to have occurred in cult or ritual contexts (Pluciennik 1997:48ff.), where fine and painted pottery prevailed, or in graves (Muntoni 1999a:241), where whole vessels or intentionally fragmented vessels were offered as funerary goods (Robb 1994).

With the advent of the *figulina* wares there is evidence of the emergence of circulation networks for raw and finished materials. Another consequence of the appearance of *figulina* pottery is the transformation from domestic production to technical specialization. At the level of the *chaînes opératoires* one can observe standardization over time, an elaboration, and an eventual rise in technical ability in ceramic production (Muntoni 2003:323).

Linear Pottery – Or the Second Temperate Neolithic

The end of the Starčevo-Criş-Körös First Temperate Neolithic Techno-Complex corresponds with the appearance of the Linear Pottery (LP) or Linearbandkeramik (LBK) or Rubané, the result of the acculturation or rapid transformation and fusion of the Mesolithic populations (Otte 1996:95; Whittle 1996:150ff.), which I have labelled as the Second Temperate Neolithic (Figure 4.4). In the Transdanubian region there is evidence of two centuries stasis between 5750 and 5500 BC in the dispersal of the ceramic cultures of the First Temperate Neolithic, probably due to interaction with local populations (Keroualin 2003:111).

Radiocarbon dates (Lenneis et al. 1996) support the theory of two initial ceramic groups in central Europe that generated the LP culture, a western one named LP Alföld and the Transdanubian LP (Keroualin 2003:123) that dispersed along the axis of large rivers (Lenneis 1989; Lüning et al. 1989; for river as trade routes; see also Milisauskas 2002b:165) across a large geographic area where ceramics were not previously present, with the exception of the western part where two anomalous local ceramic traditions, Limburg and La Hoguette, suggest a Mesolithic pottery tradition in direct association (Bogucki 1995:89) with farmer communities. There

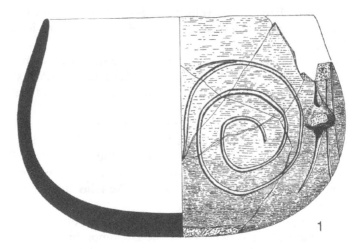

Figure 4.4 Linearbandkeramik pottery

was also interaction with the Cardial Techno-Complex in the west of Europe (Otte 1996:96; Scarre 1992) and with a second wave of diffusion of ceramic cultures from the Near East in the Danubian–Carpathian area (Ursulescu 1991) up to the upper Dniester region of the Western Ukraine (Dergachev et al. 1991:14).

An early phase of dispersal of the LP in central Europe comprised western Hungary, north and eastern Austria, Slovakia, the Czech Republic and southern and central Germany (Lüning et al. 1989:fig. 1), and was followed by a second phase of extension into southern Poland, the Rhineland, and into the Hainault region of Belgium (Constantin 1985:54) and the Paris Basin (Raemaekers 1999:131). Probably the uniformity of the Techno-Complex was due to its distinct origin although the process of conversion of the FTN into LP is not yet fully understood (Whittle 1996:150). There are several names for the second phase regional variant: Ačkovy in Bohemia, Zofipole in southern Poland and Flomborn in Germany (Bogucki 1995:91). The second phase had a specific decorative design the so-called 'music-notes' (Notenkopf) style. A late phase was characterized by a more baroque decoration and regional variability.

The LP Techno-Complex represented the end of the tradition of painted pottery; the incised lines, simple or filled with pigment, were now the main method of decoration. In an early phase flat-based bowls, with different tempers, incised with curves and linear patterns (Whittle 1996:157), seem to have been an influence from FTN communities. The shapes of some vessels, like the globular bowls, infer a multifunctional use, like storage, transport or food preparation (Bogucki 1995:93), and the simple or perforated buttons suggest a propensity for suspending the vases.

The relative uniformity of the shapes and decoration of pottery in the LP Techno-Complex and the analogies with the western Mesolithic traditions could have been the result of a continued tradition of translating into ceramics the shapes of the containers of preceding mobile populations. There is a regional variation in time of the decorative patterns incised in Moravia and southern Poland derived from the curvilinear music-note ware (Bogucki 1995:91). There is evidence of the use of white pigment in the western region of the Techno-Complex to infill incisions (Modderman 1988), and of the use of graphite in the southeast, at the interface with Starčevo.

Both fine and coarse ware were made of local argillaceous clays (Modderman 1988), from different sources of acquisition (Bosquet et al. 2005:104). The decorated pottery had thin walls and was not tempered; on the contrary, undecorated pottery was frequently tempered with sand, grit or grog (Raemaekers 1999:137). Different organic and mineral tempers were used as cultural markers (Bosquet et al. 2005:104).

Diverse methods were used to raise the walls of vases, from the hammering of a piece of clay (Constantin 1994:249) to the coil-building method (Van Berg 1996:38). The complex decorative patterns necessitated a correct partition of the vase's surface. It is possible that the round shape of the bowls was the result of a decision to increase the thermal shock resistance of the pottery (Tite and Kilikoglou 2002:1) and at the same time a design adaptation for mobile communities. There are examples of awkward modelling supposed to have been done by apprentices (Van Berg 1996:46) and of high quality, done by specialized potters. Open firing seems to have been the most common technique, with an average temperature of 700–800°C (Milisauskas 2001:193).

'Diversity in uniformity' (Modderman 1988) is the paradox that characterizes the LP Techno-Complex, for example the diversity of the *chaînes opératoires* in a single context (Bosquet et al. 2005:112) versus the apparent stability of the regional styles. The remarkable homogeneity of the ancient LP could have been the result of a prevailing traditionalism (Price and Keely 1996:97). Ceramic production seems to have been the preserve of specialized persons and pots appear to have been produced by a single potter for many villages, suggesting the existence of networks of exchange (Milisauskas 2002b:165) and of exogamy (Bogucki 1995:95).

It seems that the technology of the First Temperate Neolithic communities was continued in the pottery of the early stage of the new Techno-Complex, like the use of chaff (dung?) as temper (Maxim 1999:68), the decoration of coarse pottery with impressed bands, or pedestalled cups, and the offering of pottery as grave goods (Milisauskas 2002b:181), but in time the new *chaînes opératoires* formed a completely new identity for the Techno-Complex. The extensive use of sand as temper, besides increasing functional efficiency, could have been a symbolic choice of the LP communities to express their relationship with water in an analogous way to the IW communities.

The major difference with this Techno-Complex was the use of incisions (a very simple technique which I consider to have been the community choice of a population with a high mobility, similar to that of the Impressed Ware Techno-Complex) and the extensive use of round shapes for pottery. It seems that pottery did not obviously reflect status or gender differences (Milisauskas 2002b:182) like in other Techno-Complexes, and this may be one reason why the LP communities did not produce a really fine ceramics, like the *figulina*. In the western part of the Techno-Complex, there is evidence of poppy cultivation (Bakels 1991), a product which could have been exported together with pottery into the hunter-gatherer world.

The Continental Ceramic Mesolithic

In 6th-millennium western Europe we can observe the indigenous production and use of pottery in hunter-gatherer societies (Lichardus-Itten 1986; Van Berg and Cauwe 2000:33; Van Berg and Cahen 1986). I have already mentioned La Hoguette (Jeunesse 1987) and Limburg pottery from France and the Netherlands; we also need to consider Swifterbant pottery (Raemaekers 1999), another indigenous

Figure 4.5   Ertebolle pottery from Tybrind Vig, Denmark (After Mithen 2001:101)

ceramic style from the Netherlands (Figure 4.5). A variant of the Swifterbant tradition is the Doel, in Belgium, which appears in a late Mesolithic context (Crombé et al. 2002:700).

The La Hoguette pottery tradition was discovered in eastern France (Jeunesse 1986), Dutch and Belgian Limbourg and western Germany (Lüning et al. 1989:fig. 1–2), and predated the LP Techno-Complex (Raemaekers 1999:136). La Hoguette seems to be an unambiguous example of pottery adoption by Meso-lithic communities, the Neolithic influ-ences probably coming from the Cardial tradition (approx. 5500 BC), and Limburg the result of Epicardial influences around 5500 BC (see Keroualin 2003:141). By contrast, Limburg pottery emerges in LP milieus and extends across a large geo-graphic region, from the Paris basin, the Netherlands (Modderman et al. 1970), up to western Germany (Raemaekers 1999:136). The Swifterbant tradition extended in the area of the wetlands between the Scheldt and Elbe rivers, covering parts of the Netherlands and western Germany (Raemaekers 1999:11). It was suggested that La Hoguette pottery could be the source of the Swifterbant pottery style (Hogestijn and Peeters 1996:112), since they both have conically shaped-pots and bowls, but the differences in the *chaînes opératoires* of tempering and the difference in decorative patterns suggest this hypothesis is unlikely (Raemaekers 1999:136). At the same time the differences between the technologies of Limburg and LP pot-teries necessitate against any connection between them (Van Berg 1990:175).

The purely Mesolithic character of these ceramic cultures has been challenged (see Whittle 1996:152), being perceived as the result of the recent Cardial/ancient Epicardial influences, for La Hoguette, and a final Mesolithic with Epicardial influ-ences for Limburg pottery (Keroualin 2003:141). These ceramic cultures exist in a dynamic relationship with Neolithic societies. They compel us to consider a fresh perspective on the relations of contact and the cultural transfers between non-Neo-lithic and western European Neolithic societies (cf. Thomas 1996). Contacts between hunter-gatherers and farmers were of a varied nature (see Spielman and Eder 1994:304–5), and probably included the exchange of domestic carbohydrates (Peter-son 1978:335) or opiate products (Price and Keely 1996; Raemaekers 1999:138). The products of LP farmers were therefore exchanged together with pottery.

La Hoguette pottery is represented by conical vases and bowls with perforated lugs and undulated cordons on the body, with incisions on them or on the body of the vases (Jeunesse 1986:43; Van Berg 1990:163). I believe the cordons represent skeuomorphs of the ropes for suspending the vases. A pure ritual function for the vases with conical bottom has been suggested (Nicod et al. 1996:87).

Limbourg pottery was characterized by vases with round bases, with round or elliptic knobs, sometimes perforated (see Jeunesse et al. 1991:48–9), and the Swift-erbant pottery had pointed, round, sagging or flat bases, with S-shaped profiles, rim decoration being characteristic for this tradition (Raemaekers 1999:108).

The choice of hunter-gatherer communities could be identified in the selection of temper; therefore crushed bone is the symbolic option which defines the *chaîne opératoire* of both La Hoguette and Limburg pottery. Apart from crushed bones, La Hoguette pottery was tempered with sand, grit, grog (Raemaekers 1999:137), shell (Jeunesse et al. 1998:44), or hematite (Van Berg 1990:430). Limburg pottery was tempered with crushed bone too in variable proportion (Van Berg 1990:429), but also with sand, grit, or grog.

As for the Swifterbant pottery, the tempering agents were the same as in the Neolithic agrarian Techno-Complexes: organic material, grit (mostly quartz) or sand (De Roever 1979). The pottery from Doel was tempered mainly with grog and organic material (Crombé et al. 2002:701).

The technique of modelling was probably a symbolic marker-like decoration. La Hoguette vases were built with coil-building N-joints; its banded decoration was made with comb. In eastern France, the incisions were replaced by impressed cordons with small impressions with the shape of cereal grains, a characteristic which can be attributed to a southern influence (Keroualin 2003:136). The pattern of the cordons could have been a skeuomorph representing a net of ropes that suspended the vase. Limburg pottery used coil-building with N-joints, sometimes badly fixed (Jeunesse et al. 1998:46); its decoration was with U or V-shaped incisions (Manen 2002). The Swifterbant method of vase-making was also the coil building, with frequent H-joints, but also with N and Z and the decoration was executed with the aid of spatulas and by nail impressions (Raemaekers 1999:30, Table 3.3). By contrast the Doel pottery decoration is limited, and mainly consists of oblique impressions of fingernails or spatulas on top of the rim (Crombé et al. 2002:701).

La Hoguette pottery was generally fired in an oxidized atmosphere on the exterior and reduced atmosphere on the interior (Jeunesse et al. 1998:44), which suggests a positioning upside down of the vases in the bonfire. Limburg pottery was fired insufficiently in an oxidized atmosphere, at low temperatures, which left a black core in the walls of the vases (Jeunesse et al. 1998:46).

Late Mesolithic Europe was characterized by a selective adoption of the Neolithic package (see Bogucki 1987:2; Zvelebil and Dolukhanov 1991:264), i.e. pottery was adopted *before* other components. For example the Swifterbant and the Danish and southern Swedish Ertebølle traditions of northwest Europe represent the emergence of pottery earlier than domesticates (Raemaekers 1999:186, fig. 5.1). Examples of pottery from hunter-gatherer contexts come from Lepenski Vir I (Borić and Stefanović 2004:536) or Montenegro (Tringham 2000:27) in the Balkans, from Tuscany (Barker 1996), and from the coasts of southern France and the Netherlands (Vermeersch 1996). The character of the hunter-gatherer pottery was of medium quality, with a minimum of constraints on the *chaîne opératoire*, which suggests the absence of a specialization in this new craft, the absence of 'prestige' ceramics, and multifunctional and probably multi-ritual functions for the reduced number of types of vases. The shapes and dimensions of vases as well as the presence of skeuomorphic cord decoration is an index of high transportability.

Conclusion: From Skeuomorphs to 'Pottery as Pottery'

Pottery was ascribed to the social realm from its very beginning because of its magical, symbolic and ritual character. Symbols were hidden inside the *chaînes opératoires*, but were visible in the decoration, in the shape of the pottery and prob-ably in the way it was handled. Social choices could be detected in the symbolic, subjective stages within the *chaînes opératoires* of the technology of making and their change could represent major social transformations.

In the Early Neolithic pottery was the most efficient and rapid solution for a first phase of colonization of foreign lands. Since pottery was made from local soils, its production could represent a symbolic taking into possession of new places, literally incorporating new places within its fabric.

If Early Neolithic pottery was a skeuomorph, from the Middle Neolithic pottery became a class of its own: *pottery as pottery*. With the emergence of Middle Neolithic pottery technology pottery was transformed into a commodity, which emitted obvious messages concerning the social visibility of the individual and the commu-nity's politics of celebration or competition.

The analogies between the *chaînes opératories* of pottery-making and those of processing grains, for example, suggest a symbolic and ritual relationship between the two procedures, pottery from now on being directly associated with the process of fermentation. The production and consumption of fermented bever-ages (sometimes in conjunction with narcotic substances; Sherratt 1991:234) could have been among the causes of the high social visibility of pottery. One can note the early manifestation of fine highly decorated pottery as cups and bowls which precede the coarse pottery for cooking, which could be related to a new social practice of drinking. I consider that drinking cultures in Europe emerged as soon as the introduction of pottery, at the same time in agricultural cultures and, as trait adoption, in the hunter-gatherers' cultures, where pottery precedes other elements of the Neolithic package. As soon as the utilization of pottery extends outside the domestic zone, such as in the case of funerary and other community rituals, one can witness the beginning of a process of modelling the social that will continue for millennia.

ACKNOWLEDGEMENTS

The author would like to thank to the following who helped him with documenta-tion: Bogdan Capruciu, Dr Aracelli Martin Colliga, Dr Armand Desbat, Dr Andy Jones, Dr Italo Muntoni, Dr Judith Regenye, Dr John Robb, Dr Paulien de Roever, Professor Ralph Rowlett, Dr Marie-Chantal Frère Sautot, Dr Michaela Spataro, Professor Olga Soffer, Dr Peter Staedler, Dr Nenad Tasic and Professor Karen Vitelli. Last, but not least, my gratitude goes to Dr Andy Jones, Deirdre Ilkson and Louise Spencely for their kind support during the elaboration of this text.

REFERENCES

Armit, I., and B. Finlayson 1995 Social Strategies and Economic Change: Pottery in Context. *In* The Emergence of Pottery. Technology and Innovation in Ancient Societies. W. K. Barnett and J. W. Hoopes, eds. Pp. 267–76. Washington, DC: Smithsonian Institution Press.

Arnold, D. E. 1999 Ceramic Theory and Cultural Process. Cambridge: Cambridge University Press.

Bailey, D. W. 2000 Balkan Prehistory. Exclusion, Incorporation and Identity. London: Routledge.

Bakels, C. C. 1991 The Crops of the Rössen Culture. *In* Palaeoethnobotany and Archaeology. International Work-Group for Palaeoetnobotany 8th Symposium, Nitra-Nové Vozkany 1989. E. Hajnalova, ed. Pp. 23–7. Acta Interdisciplinaria Archaeologica 7.

Barclay, K. 2001 Scientific Analysis of Archaeological Ceramics. Oxford: Oxbow Books.

Barnett, W. 1995 Putting the Pot Before the Horse. Earliest Ceramics and the Neolithic Transition in the Western Mediterranean. *In* The Emergence of Pottery. Technology and Innovation in Ancient Societies. W. K. Barnett and J. W. Hoopes, eds. Pp. 79–88. Washington, DC: Smithsonian Institution Press.

Barnett, W. K., and J. W. Hoopes, eds. 1995 The Emergence of Pottery. Technology and Innovation in Ancient Societies. Washington, DC: Smithsonian Institution Press.

Bar-Yosef, O. 2003 Away from Home: Prehistoric Colonizations, Exchanges and Diffusions in the Mediterranean Basin. *In* Exchanges et diffusion dans la préhistoire Méditerranéenne. B. Vandermeersch, ed. Pp. 71–81. Paris: CTHS.

Benac, A., and B. Marijanovic 1993 Les Balkans du Nord-Ouest. *In* Atlas du Néolithique Européen, Vol. 1. L'Europe Orientale. J. K. Kozlovwski, ed. Pp. 127–50. ERAUL 45.

Binder, D., J.-E. Brochier, H. Duday, D. Helmer, P. Marinval, S. Thiébault, and J. Wattez 1993 L'Abri Pendimoun à Castellar (Alpes-Maritimes): Nouvelles données sur le complexe culturel de la Céramique Imprimée Méditérranéenne dans son contexte stratigraphique. Gallia Préhistorique 35:177–251.

Binder, D., and J. Courtin 1986 Les styles céramiques du Néolithique ancien provençal. Nouvelles migraines taxinomiques? *In* Le Néolithique de la France. J.-P. Demoule and J. Guilaine, eds. Pp. 83–93. Paris: Picard.

Björk, C. I. 1995 Early Pottery in Greece: A Technological and Functional Analysis of the Evidence from Neolithic Achilleion, Thessaly. Jonsered: Paul Aströms Förlag (SIMA 115).

Bliege Bird, R., and E. A. Smith 2005 Signaling Theory, Strategic Interaction and Symbolic Capital. Current Anthropology 46(2):221–48.

Bogucki, P. 1987 The Establishment of Agrarian Communities on the North European Plain. Current Anthropology 28:1–24.

Bogucki, P. 1995 The Linear Pottery Culture of Central Europe. *In* The Emergence of Pottery. Technology and Innovation in Ancient Societies. W. K. Barnett and J. W. Hoopes, eds. Pp. 89–97. Washington, DC: Smithsonian Institution Press.

Borić, D., and S. Stefanović 2004 Birth and Death: Infant Burials from Vlasac and Lepenski Vir. Antiquity 301(78):526–46.

Bosquet, D., H. Fock, and A. Livingstone-Smith 2005 La Chaîne opératoire de la céramique Rubanée: Première tentative de reconstruction. *In* Pottery Manufacturing Processes: Reconstitution and Interpretation. A. Livingstone Smith, D. Bosquet, and R. Martineau, eds. Pp. 103–14. Oxford: Archaeopress, British Archaeological Reports, International Series 1349.

Bourdieu, P. 1984 Distinction: A Social Critique of the Judgment of Taste. Cambridge, MA: Harvard University Press.

Bowser, B. 2000 From Pottery to Politics: An Ethnoarchaeological Study of Political Factionalism, Ethnicity, and Domestic Pottery Style in the Ecuadorian Amazon. Journal of Archaeological Method and Theory 7:219–48.

Boyadziev, Y. 2002 The Role of Absolute Chronology in Clarifying the Neolithization of the Eastern Half of the Balkan Peninsula. Abstracts Book, VIII EAA Annual Meeting. 24–9 September 2002, Thessaloniki, Greece, p. 237.

Cassano, S. M., C. Gratziu, C. Meucci, S. Marini, and I. Muntoni 1995 Analisi technologiche di impasti ceramici dal villagio di Masseria Candelara. Scienze dell' Antichita 8:40–9.

Cauvin, J. 1989 La néolithisation au Lévant et sa première diffusion. *In* Néolithisations: Proche et Moyen Orient, Méditerranée Orientale, Nord de l'Afrique, Europe Méridionale,

Chine, Amérique du Sud. O. Aurenche and J. Cauvin, eds. Pp. 3–32. Oxford: British Archaeological Reports, International Series 516.

Cauvin, J. 1997 Naissance des divinités – naissance de l'agriculture. Paris: Flammarion.

Chapman, J. 1988 Ceramic Production and Social Differentiation: The Dalmatian Neolithic and the Western Mediterranean. Journal of Mediterranean Archaeology 1(2):3–25.

Chapman, J. 2001 Fragmentation in Archaeology. People, Places and Broken Objects in the Prehistory of South Eastern Europe. London and New York: Routledge.

Chapman, J., R. Shiel, and J. Batovic 1996 The Changing Face of Dalmatia. Archaeological and Ecological Studies in a Mediterranean Landscape. London: The Society of Antiquaries, Research Report 54: Cassel.

Childe, V. G. 1951 Man Makes Himself. London: New American Library of World Literature.

Colliga, A. M. 1998 Le Nord-est de la peninsule Ibérique (et les Baléares). In Atlas du Néolithique Européen, Vol. 2, L'Europe occidentale. J. Guilaine, ed. Pp. 763–824. ERAUL 46.

Constantin, C. 1985 Fin du Rubané, céramique du Limbourg et post- Rubané. Le Néolithique le plus ancien du Bassin Parisien et en Hainaut. Oxford: British Archaeological Reports, International Series 273.

Constantin, C. 1994 Structure des productions céramiques et chaînes opératoires. In Actes des XIVèmes rencontres internationales d'archéologie et d'historie d'Antibes, 21–23 Octobre 1993. D. Binder and J. Courtin, eds. Pp. 243–53.

Contenson, H. de, and L. C. Courtois 1979 A propos des vases en chaux: Recherches sur leur fabrication et leur origine. Paléorient 5:177–82.

Crombé, Ph., Y. Perdaen, J. Sergant, J.-P. Van Roeyen, and M. Van Strydonck 2002 The Mesolithic-Neolithic Transition in the Sandy Lowlands of Belgium: New Evidence. Antiquity 76:699–706.

Crown, P. L., and W. H. Wills 1995 Economic Intensification and the Origins of Ceramic Containers in the American Southwest. In The Emergence of Pottery: Technology and Innovation in Ancient Societies. W. K. Barnett and J. W. Hoopes, eds. Pp. 241–54. Washington, DC: Smithsonian Institution Press.

Cullen, T. 1985 Social Implications of Ceramic Style in the Neolithic Peloponnese. In Ancient Technology to Modern Science. W. Kingery, ed. Pp. 77–100. Columbus: American Ceramic Society.

Cumberpatch, C. G., and P. W. Blinkhorn, eds. 1997 Not So Much a Pot, More a Way of Life. Oxford: Oxbow Monograph 83.

De Roever, J. P. 1979 The Pottery from Swifterbant-Duch Ertebølle? (Swifterbant Contribution 11). Helinium 19:13–36.

De Roever, J. P. 2004 Swifterbant-Aardewerk. Een analyse van de neolitische nederzettingen bij Swifterbant, 5e millennium voor Christus. Gröningen: Gröningen University.

Demoule, J.-P. 1993 Anatolie et Balkans: la logique évolutive du Néolithique egéen. Anatolica XIX:1–17.

Dergachev, V., A. Sherratt, and O. Larina 1991 Recent Results of Neolithic Research in Moldavia (USSR). Oxford Journal of Archeology 10:1–16.

Dietler, M., and B. Hayden 2001 Digesting the Feast – Good to Eat, Good to Drink, Good to Think: An Introduction. In Feasts: Archaeological and Ethnographic Perspectives on Food, Politics, and Power. M. Dietler and B. Hayden, eds. Pp. 1–20. Washington, DC: Smithsonian Institution Press.

Dobres, M.-A. 2000 Technology and Social Agency. Outlining a Practice Framework for Archaeology. Oxford: Blackwell.

Freestone, I., and D. Gaimster, eds. 1997 Pottery in the Making. World Ceramic Traditions. London: British Museum Press.

Gheorghiu, D. 2001 Tropes in Material Culture. In Material, Virtual and Temporal Compositions; On the Relationship between Objects. D. Gheorghiu, ed. Pp. 17–26. Oxford: Archaeopress, British Archaeological Reports, International Series 953.

Gheorghiu, D. 2002 Fire and Air Draught: Experimenting Chalcolithic Pyroinstruments. *In* Fire in Archaeology. D. Gheorghiu, ed. Pp. 83–94. Oxford: Archaeopress, British Archaeological Reports, International Series 1089.

Gheorghiu, D. 2005 Symbolic Technologies. http://www.semioticon.com/virtuals/archaeology/arch.htm.

Gibson, A. 2002 Prehistoric Pottery in Britain and Ireland. Stroud: Tempus.

Gkiasta, M., T. Russel, S. Shennan and J. Steele 2003 Neolithic Transition in Europe: The Radiocarbon Record Revisited. Antiquity 77(295):45–62.

Gosselain, O. P. 2002 Poteries du Cameroun méridional. Styles techniques et rapports à l'identité. Paris: CNRS Editions.

Gourdin, W. H., and W. D. Kingery 1975 The Beginnings of Pyrotechnology: Neolithic and Egyptian Lime Plaster. Journal of Field Archaeology 2:133–50.

Guilaine, J. 2005 La mer partagée. La Méditerranée avant l'écriture 7000–2000 avant Jésus-Christ. Paris: Hachette.

Hameau, P. 1987 Le Niveau à céramique imprimée dans le Néolithique grec. *In* Premières communautés paysannes en Méditerranée Occidentale. J. J. Guilaine, J. Courtin, J.-L. Roudil, and J.-L. Vernet, eds. Pp. 329–34. Paris: CNRS.

Hayden, B. 1990 Nimrods, Pickers, Pluckers, and Planters: The Origins of Food Production. Journal of Anthropological Achaeology:31–69.

Hayden, B. 1995 The Emergence of Prestige: Technologies and Pottery. *In* The Emergence of Pottery. Technology and Innovation in Ancient Societies. W. K. Barnett and J. W. Hoopes, eds. Pp. 257–66. Washington, DC: Smithsonian Institution Press.

Hayden, B. 2001 Fabulous Feasts: A Prolegomenon to the Importance of Feasting. *In* Feasts: Archaeological and Ethnographic Perspectives on Food, Politics, and Power. M. Dietler and B. Hayden, eds. Pp. 23–64. Washington, DC: Smithsonian Institution Press.

Hodder, I. 1982 Symbols in Action. Cambridge: Cambridge University Press.

Hodder, I. 1990 The Domestication of Europe. Cambridge: Cambridge University Press.

Hogestijn, W. J., and H. Peeters 1996 De opgraving van de mesolithische/vroeg-neolithische bewoningsresten van de vindplaats 'Hoge Vaart' bij Almere (Prov. Fl.), Een blik op een duistere periode van de Nederlandse prehistorie. Archeologie 7:80–113.

Humphrey, C., and J. Laidlaw 1994 Naven ou le donner à voir. Essai d'interprétation de l'action rituelle. Paris: Edition du CNRS/Edition de la Maison des sciences de l'homme.

Jennings, J., K. L. Antrobus, S. J. Atencio, E. Glavich, R. Johnson, G. Loffer, and C. Luu 2005 'Drinking Beer in a Blissful Mood'. Alcohol Production, Operational Chains, and Feasting in the Ancient World. Current Anthropology 46(2):275–303.

Jeunesse, C. 1986 Rapports avec le Néolithique ancien d'Alsace de la céramique 'danubienne' de La Hoguette (à Fontenay-le-Marmion, Calvados), Actes du Xe Colloque interrégional sur le Néolithique, Caen, 30 septembre–2 octobre 1983. Revue Archéologique de L'Ouest. Supplément 1:41–50.

Jeunesse, C. 1987 La Céramique de la Hoguette. Un nouvel élément non-rubané' du Neolithiqie ancien de l'Europe du Nord-Ouest. Cahiers Alsaciens 30:5ff.

Jeunesse, C., P.-Y. Nicod, P.-L. Van Berg, and J.-L. Voruz 1998 Nouveaux témoins d'âge néolithique ancien entre Rhône et Rhin, Le Néolithique du centre-ouest de la France, Actes du XVIIIe Colloque interrégional sur le Néolithique, Poitiers 1994, pp. 43–78.

Karkanas, P., M. Koumouzelis, J. K. Kozlowski, V. Sitlivy, K. Sobczyk, F. Berna, and S. Weiner 2004 The Earliest Evidence for Clay Hearths: Aurignacian Features in Klisoura Cave 1, Southern Greece. Antiquity 301(78):513–25.

Keroualin, M. de 2003 Genèse et diffusion de l'agriculture en Europe. Agriculteurs-Chasseurs-Pasteurs. Paris: Éditions Errance.

King R., and P. A. Underhill 2002 Congruent Distribution of Neolithic Painted Pottery and Ceramic Figurines with Y-Chromosome Lineages. Antiquity 76:707–14.

Kingery, D. 1997 Operational Principles of Ceramic Kilns. *In* The Prehistory and History of Ceramic Kilns, vol. VII. P. Rice, ed. Pp. 11–19. Westerville: The American Ceramic Society.

Knapp, A. B. 1996 Archaeology Without Gravity: Postmodernism and the Past. Journal of Archaeological Method and Theory 3:127–58.

Koumouzelis, M., B. Ginter, K. Kozlovski, M. Pawlikowski, O. Bar-Yosef, R. M. Albert, M. Litynska-Zajac, E. Stworzewicz, P. Wojtal, G. Lipecki, T. Tomek, Z. M. Bochenski, and A. Pazdur 2001 The Early Upper Paleolithic in Greece: The Excavations in Klisoura Cave. Journal of Archaeological Science 28:515–39.

Kruk, J., and S. Milisauskas 1999 The Rise and Fall of Neolithic Societies. Krakow: Polskiej Akademii Nauk.

Kunze, E. 1931 Orchomenos II. Die Neolitische Keramic, Muenchen.

Lazarovici, G. 1996 The Process of Neolithization and the Development of the First Neolithic Civilization in the Balkans. *In* XIII UISPP, Section 9, Colloqium XVII, Forli. Pp. 21–38.

Lemonnier, P. 1986 The Study of Material Culture Today: Toward an Anthropology of Technical Systems. Journal of Anthropological Archaeology 5:147–86.

Lemonnier, P. 1996 Technology. *In* Encyclopedia of Social and Cultural Anthropology. A. Barnard and J. Spencer, eds. Pp. 544–7. London: Routledge.

Lemonnier, P. 2004 Mythiques chaînes opératoires. Téchniques et culture 43–4:25–43.

Lenneis, E. 1989 Zum Forshungstand der Ältesen Bandkeramik in Österreich. Archäologisches Korresspondenzblatt 19:23–36.

Lenneis, E., P. Stadler, and H. Windl 1996 Neue 14C-daten zum Frühneolithikum in Österreich. Préhistoire Européenne 8:97–116.

Lichardus-Itten, M. 1986 Premières influences méditerranéennes dans le Néolithique du Basin Parisien. *In* Le Néolithique de la France: Hommage a G. Bailloud. Pp. 147–60. Paris: Piccard.

Livingstone Smith, A. 2005 Introduction. *In* Pottery Manufacturing Process: Reconstitution and Interpretation. A. Livingstone Smith, D. Bosquet, and R. Martineau, eds. Pp. 5–11. Oxford: Archaeopress, British Archaeological Reports, International Series 1349.

Livingstone Smith, A., D. Bosquet, and R. Martineau, eds. 2005 Pottery Manufacturing Process: Reconstitution and Interpretation. Oxford: Archaeopress, British Archaeological Reports, International Series 1349.

Lüning, J. 1991 Die Anfänge der Landwirtschaft vor 7000 Jahren: Ausgrabungen in Friedberg-Bruchenbrücken. *In* Archäologie der Wetterau: Aspekte der Forschung. V. Rupp, ed. Pp. 95–106. Friedberg: Verlag der Bindernagelschen Buchhandlung.

Lüning, J., U. Kloos, and S. Albert (with contributions by J. Eckert and Chr. Stein) 1989 Westliche Nachbarn der bandkeramischen Kultur: Die Keramikgruppen La Hoguette und Limburg. Germania 67:335–420.

Malone, C. 1985 Pots, Prestige and Ritual in Neolithic Southern Italy. *In* Papers in Italian Archaeology IV: Prehistory. C. Malone and S. Stoddart, eds. Pp. 118–51. Oxford: British Archaeological Reports, International Series 244.

Manen, C. 2002 Structures et identité des styles céramiques du Néolithique ancien entre Rhine et Ebre. Gallia Préhistoire 44:121–65.

Manson, J. I. 1995 Starčevo Pottery and Neolithic Development in the Central Balkans. *In* The Emergence of Pottery. Technology and Innovation in Ancient Societies. W. Barnett and J. W. Hoopes, eds. Pp. 65–77. Washington, DC: Smithsonian Institution Press.

Maxim, Z. 1999 Neo-Eneoliticul din Transilvania. Cluj-Napoca: Muzeul National de Istorie a Transilvaniei.

Mellaart, J. 1965 Earliest Civilizations of the Near East. London: Thames and Hudson.

Milisauskas, S. 2001 Linear Pottery. Linearbandkeramik (LBK) Culture. *In* Encyclopedia of Prehistory. Vol. 4: Europe. P. Peregrine and M. Ember, eds. Pp. 191–7. New York: Kluwer Academic and Plenum Publishers.

Milisauskas, S., ed. 2002a European Prehistory. A Survey. New York: Kluwer Academic Press and Plenum Press.

Milisauskas, S. 2002b Early Neolithic. The First Farmers in Europe. *In* European Prehistory. A Survey. S. Milisauskas, ed. Pp. 143–92. New York: Kluwer Academic and Plenum Publishers.

Mithen, S. 2001 The Mesolithic Age. *In* The Oxford Illustrated History of Prehistoric Europe. B. Cunliffe, ed. Pp. 79–135. Oxford: Oxford University Press.

Modderman, P. J. R. 1970 Linierbandkeramik aus Elsloo und Stein, Nederlandse Oudheden. Analecta Praehistorica Leidensia 3.

Modderman, P. J. R. 1988 The Linear Pottery Culture: Diversity in Uniformity. Berichten van de Rijksdienst voor het Oudheidkunding Bodemonderzock 38. Pp. 63–139.

Moore, A. M. T. 1995 The Inception of Potting in Western Asia and its Impact on Economy and Society. *In* The Emergence of Pottery. Technology and Innovation in Ancient Societies. W. K. Barnett and J. W. Hoopes, eds. Pp. 39–53. Washington, DC: Smithsonian Institution Press.

Muntoni, I. 1999a Le ceramiche Neolitiche del Tavoliere in uno studio archeometrico. *In* Fonti di informazione e contesto archeologico. Manufatti ceramici e neolitizzazione meridionale. E. Ingravallo, ed. Lecce: Mario Congedo.

Muntoni, I. 1999b From Ceramic Production to Vessel Use: A Multi-Level Approach to the Neolithic Communities of the Tavoliere (Southern Italy). *In* Ethno-Analogy and the Reconstruction of Prehistoric Artifact Use and Production. L. R. Owen and M. Porr, eds. Pp. 237–54. Tübingen: Mo Vince.

Muntoni, I. 2003 Modellare l'argilla. Vasai del Neolitico antico e medio nelle Murge pugliesi. Florence: Instituto Italiano di Preistoria e Protoistoria.

Nandris, J. 1970a The Development and Relationships of the Earlier Greek Neolithic. Man 5(2):192–213.

Nandris, J. 1970b Groundwater as a Factor in the First Temperate Neolithic Settlement of the Koros Region. Zbornik Narodnok Muzeja (Beograd) 6:59–73.

Nicod, P.-Y., J.-L. Voruz, C. Jeunesse, and P. -L. Van Berg 1996 Entre Rhône et Rhin au Néolithique ancien. *In* La Bourgogne entre les basins Rhénan, Rhodanien et Parisien: Carrefour ou frontière?. Actes du XVIIIe Colloque interrégional sur le Néolithique, Dijon, 25–27 octobre 1991, Supplément à la Revue Archéologique de l'Est:85–94.

Orton, C., P. Tyers, and A. Vince 2001 Pottery in Archaeology. Cambridge: Cambridge University Press.

Otte, M. 1996 Contacts Rubané-Cardial. *In* La Bourgogne entre les bassins rhénan, rhodanien et parisien: carrefour ou frontiere? Actes du Colloque de Dijon, 14ème Supplément à la Revue Archéologique de l'Est:95–9.

Özdoğan, M. 1989 Neolithic Cultures of Northwestern Turkey. A General Appraisal of the Evidence and Some Considerations. *In* Neolithic of Southeastern Europe and its Near Eastern Connections. S. Bokony, ed. Pp. 201–15. Budapest: Instituti Archaeologici Academiae Scienticum Hungaricae.

Özdoğan, M. 1993 Vinca and Anatolia: A New Look at the Very Old Problem (or Redefining Vinca Culture from the Perspective of Near Eastern Tradition). Anatolica XIX:173–93.

Özdoğan, M. 1997 The Beginning of Neolithic Economies in Southeastern Europe: An Anatolian Perspective. Journal of European Archaeology 5:1–33.

Özdoğan, M. 2005 The Expansion of the Neolithic Way of Life: What We Know and What We Do Not Know. *In* How Did Farming Reach Europe? Anatolian–European Relations from the Second Half of the 7th Through the First Half of the 6th Millennium cal. BC. C. Lichter, ed. Pp. 13–27. Oxford: Oxbow Books.

Parzinger, H., and M. Özdoğan 1995 Vortrag zur Jahressitzung 1995 der Roemish-Germanischen Komission. Die Ausgrabungen in Kirklareli (Turkisch-Thrakien) und ihre Bedeutung fuer die Kulturbeziehungen zwischen Anatolien und dem Balkan vom

Neolitikum bis zur Frueh bronzenzeit, Bericht der Roemish-Germanischen Komission des Deutschen Archaeologischen Instituts 76:5–29. Frankfurt am Main.

Paul, I. 1995 Vorgeschichtliche Untersuchungen in Siebenbuergen. Alba Iulia: Bibliotheca Universitatis Apulensis.

Pawlikowski, M., M. Koumouzelis, B. Ginter, and K. Kozlowski 2000 Emerging Ceramic Technology in Structured Aurignacian Hearths at Klisoura Cave I in Greece. Archaeology, Ethnology & Anthropology of Eurasia 4:19–29.

Perlès, C. 1992 Systems of Exchange and Organization of Production in Neolithic Greece. Journal of Mediterranean Archaeology 5(2):115–64.

Perlès, C. 2001 The Early Neolithic in Greece. The First Farming Communities in Europe. Cambridge: Cambridge University Press.

Perlès, C. 2003 Le rôle du Proche-Orient dans la néolithisation de la Grèce. In Echanges et diffusion dans la préhistoire Méditerranéenne. B. Vandermeersch, ed. Pp. 91–104. Paris: CTHS.

Perlès, C. 2005 From the Near East to Greece: Let's Reverse the Focus – Cultural Elements That Did Not Transfer. In BYZAS 2. How Did Farming Reach Europe? Anatolian-European Relations from the Second Half of the 7th Through the First Half of the 6th Millennium Cal. BC. C. Lichter, ed. Pp. 275–90. Istanbul: Veröffentlichungen des Deutschen Archäologischen Instituts Istanbul.

Perlès, C., and K. Vitelli 1999 Craft Specialization in the Neolithic of Greece. In Neolithic Society in Greece. P. Halstead, ed. Pp. 96–107. Sheffield: Sheffield Academic Press.

Peterson, J. T. 1978 Hunter-Gatherers/Farmer Exchange. American Anthropology 80: 335–51.

Phelps, B. 2004 The Neolithic Pottery Sequences in Southern Greece. Oxford: Archaeopress, British Archaeological Reports, International Series 1259.

Phillips, P. 1975 Early Farmers of West Mediterranean Europe. London: Hutchinson.

Pluciennik, M. Z. 1997 Historical, Geographical and Anthropological Imaginations: Early Ceramics in Southern Italy. In Not So Much a Pot, More a Way of Life. C. G. Cumperpatch and P. W. Blinkhorn, eds. Pp. 37–56. Oxford: Oxbow Monograph 83.

Price, T. D., and L. H. Keely 1996 The Spread of Farming into Europe North of the Alps. In Last Hunters – First Farmers. New Perspectives on Prehistoric Transition to Agriculture. T. D. Price and A. B. Gebauer, eds. Pp. 95–126. Santa Fe: School of American Research Press.

Raemaekers, D. C. M. 1999 The Articulation of a 'New Neolithic'. The Meaning of the Swifterbant Culture for the Process of Neolithization in the Western Part of the North European Plain (4900–3400 BC). Monograph, Faculty of Archaeology, University of Leiden.

Renfrew, C. 1987 Archaeology and Language. The Puzzle of Indo-European Origins. London: Penguin.

Robb, J. 1994 Burial and Social Reproduction in the Peninsular Italian Neolithic. Journal of Mediterranean Archaeology 7:27–71.

Rodden, R. J. 1965 Nea Nikomedeia, an Early Neolithic Village in Greece. Scientific American 212:83–91.

Roudil, J.-L. 2003 Les foyers du Néolithique ancien (Cardial) de la Baume d'Oulen (Labastide-de-Virac/Le Garn, Gard, Ardèche, France). In Le Feu domestique et ses structures au Néolithique et aux Ages des métaux. M.-C. Frère-Sautot, ed. Pp. 515–23. Montagnac: Monique Mergoil.

Scarre, C. 1992 The Early Neolithic of Western France and Megalithic Origins in Atlantic Europe. Oxford Journal of Archaeology 11(2):121–54.

Schlanger, N. 1997 Mindful Technology: Unleashing the Chaîne Opératoire for an Archaeology of Mind. In The Ancient Mind. Elements of Cognitive Archaeology. C. Renfrew and E. B. W. Zubrow, eds. Pp. 143–51. Cambridge: Cambridge University Press.

Sherratt, A. 1982 Mobile Resources: Settlements and Exchange in Early Agricultural Europe. *In* Ranking, Resource and Exchange. C. Renfrew and S. Shennan, eds. Pp. 13–26. Cambridge: Cambridge University Press.

Sherratt, A. 1991 Palaeobotany: From Crops to Cuisine. *In* Paleoecologia e arqueologia II. Trabalhos dedicados a A. R. Pinto de Silva. F. Queiroga and A. P. Dinis, eds. Pp. 221–39. Vila Nova de Famalicao.

Skibo, J. M., M. B. Schiffer, and K. C. Reid 1989 Organic-Tempered Pottery: An Experimental Study. American Antiquity 54:122–46.

Soffer, O., P. Vandivier, and J. Svoboda 1993 The Pyrotechnology of Performance Art: Moravian Venuses and Wolverines. *In* Before Lascaux. The Complete Record of the Early Upper Paleolithic. H. Knecht, A. Pike-Tay, and R. White, eds. Pp. 259–77. Boca Raton: CRP Press.

Spataro, M. 2002 The First Farming Communities of the Adriatic: Pottery Production and Circulation in the Early and Middle Neolithic. Trieste: Edizioni Svevo.

Spataro, M. 2003(2004) Early Neolithic Pottery Production in the Balkans: Minero-Petrographic Analyses of the Ceramics from the Starčevo-Criş Site of Foeni-Salas (Banat-Romania). Atti Soc. Protohist. Friuli-V.G., Trieste, XIV:25–43.

Spataro, M. 2004 Differences and Similarities in the Pottery Production of the Early Neolithic Starčevo-Criş and Impressed Ware Cultures. Rivista di Scienze Preistoriche LIV:323–35.

Spielman, K. A., and J. F. Eder 1994 Hunters and Farmers: Then and Now. Annual Review of Anthropology 23:303–23.

Thomas, J. 1996 The Cultural Context of the First Use of Domesticates in Continental Central and Northwestern Europe. *In* The Origins and Spread of Agriculture and Pastoralism in Eurasia. D. R. Harris, ed. Pp. 310–22. London: UCL Press.

Tilley, C., ed. 1993 Interpretative Archaeology. Oxford: Berg.

Tiné, S. 1983 Passo di Corvo e la civilita Neolitica del Tavoliere, Genova.

Tite, M., and V. Kilikoglou 2002 Do We Understand Pots and Is There an Ideal Cooking Pot? *In* Modern Trends in Scientific Studies on Ancient Ceramics. V. Kilikoglu, A. Hein, and Y. Maniatis, eds. Pp. 1–8. Oxford: Archaeopress, British Archaeological Reports, International Series 1011.

Todorova, H. 1995 The Neolithic, Eneolithic and Transitional Period in Bulgarian Prehistory. *In* Prehistoric Bulgaria (Monographs in World Archaeology 22). D. Bailey and I. Panayotov, eds. Pp. 79–98. Madison: Prehistory Press.

Tringham, R. 2000 Southeastern Europe in the Transition to Agriculture in Europe: Bridge, Buffer, or Mosaic. *In* Europe's First Farmers. D. T. Price, ed. Pp. 19–56. Cambridge: Cambridge University Press.

Ursulescu, N. 1991 La civilization de la céramique rubanée dans les régions orientales de la Roumanie. *In* Le Paléolithique et le Néolithique de la Roumanie en contexte européen. Pp. 188–224. Iassi: Universitatea Al. I. Cuza.

Ursulescu, N. 2000 Neolitizarea teritoriului Romaniei in context sud-est European si Anatolian. *In* Contributii privind neoliticul si eneoliticul din regiunile est-carpatice ale Romaniei. Pp. 75–220. Iassi: Universitatea Al. I. Cuza.

Van Andel, T. J., and C. N. Runnels 1995 The Earliest Farmers in Europe. Antiquity 69:481–500.

Van Berg, P.-L. 1990 Céramique du Limbourg et Néolithization en Europe du Nord-Ouest. *In* Rubané et Cardial. D. Cahen and M. Otte, eds. Pp. 161–208. Etudes et recherches archéologiques de l'Université de Liège 39.

Van Berg, P.-L. 1996 Gauches, joueurs et apprentis: production des marges dans la céramique rubanée occidentale. *In* La Bourgogne entre bassins rhénan, rhodanien et parisien: carrefour ou frontière? Actes du XVIIIème Colloque Interrégional sur le Néolithique, Dijon, 25–27 octobre 1991, Supplément à la Revue Archéologique de l'Est:29–53.

Van Berg, P.-L., and D. Cahen 1986 Relations sud-nord au Néolithique ancien en Europe occidentale (II), Actes du XIIème Colloque interrégional sur le Néolithique, Metz, pp. 3–32.

Van Berg, P.-L., and N. Cauwe 2000 Les plus anciennes céramiques d'Asie et leurs relations avec la péninsule européenne. In Les Vivants, les morts et les autres. P.-L. Van Berg, P. Jespers, and F. Doyen, eds. Civilisations XLVII(1–2):25–40.

Van der Leeuw, S. E. 1997 Cognitive Aspects of 'Technique'. In The Ancient Mind. Elements of Cognitive Archaeology. C. Renfrew and E. B. W. Zubrow, eds. Pp. 135–42. Cambridge: Cambridge University Press.

Van der Leeuw, S. E. 2002 Giving the Potter a Choice. In Technical Choices. Transformations in Material Cultures Since the Neolithic. P. Lemonnier, ed. Pp. 238–88. London: Routledge.

Vandivier, P., O. Soffer, B. Klima, and K. Svoboda 1989 The Origin of Ceramic Technology at Dolni Věstonice, Czechoslovakia. Science 246:1002–8.

Vermeersch, P. M. 1996 Mesolithic in the Benelux, South of the Rhine. In The Mesolithic. K. Kozlowski and C. Tozzi, eds. Pp. 33–9. Forli: IUPPS, ABACO.

Vitelli, K. 1989 Were Pots First Made for Foods? Doubts from Franchti. World Archaeology 21(1):17–29.

Vitelli, K. 1993a Power to the Potters: Comments on Perlès' 'Systems of Exchange and Organization of Production in Neolithic Greece'. Journal of Mediterranean Archaeology 6(2):247–57.

Vitelli, K. 1993b Franchti Neolithic Pottery, vol. 1. In Excavations at Franchti Cave, Greece. T. W. Jacobsen, ed. Bloomington: Indiana University Press.

Vitelli, K. 1995 Pots, Potters, and the Shaping of Greek Neolithic Society. In The Emergence of Pottery. Technology and Innovation in Ancient Societies. W. K. Barnett and J. W. Hoopes, eds. Pp. 55–63. Washington, DC: Smithsonian Institution Press.

Volkova, H. V. 2002 Role of Experiment in Reconstruction of the Fatyanovo Pottery Technology. In Modern Trends in Scientific Studies on Ancient Ceramics. V. Kilikoglu, A. Hein, Y. Maniatis, eds. Pp. 95–102. Oxford: Archaeopress, British Archaeological Reports, International Series 1011.

Whitehouse, H. 2002 Conjectures, Refutations, and Verification: Towards a Testable Theory of 'Modes of Religiosity'. Journal of Ritual Studies 16:44–59.

Whittle, A. 1996 Europe in the Neolithic. The Creation of New Worlds. Cambridge: Cambridge University Press.

Wijnen, M. H. 1993a Neolithic Pottery from Sesklo. Technological Aspects. In La Thessalie. Quinze années de recherche archéologiques, 1975–1990, Bilans et perspectives. J. C. Decours, B. Helly, and K. Gallis, eds. Pp. 149–54. Athens, Kapon: Ministry of Culture.

Wijnen, M. H. 1993b Early Ceramics: Local Manufacture Versus Widespread Distribution. In Anatolia and the Balkans. J. Roodenber, ed. Pp. 319–31. Anatolica 19.

Williams, J. 1980 Appendice VII: A Petrological Examination of the Prehistoric Pottery from the Excavations in the Castello and the Diana Plain of Lipari. In Meligunis Lipara. Vol. V. L. Bernabo Brea and M. Cavalier, eds. Pp. 845–68. Palermo.

Winn, S., and D. Shimabuku 1989 Pottery. In Achileion, a Neolithic Settlement in Thessaly, Greece, 6400–5600 BC. M. Gimbutas, S. Winn, and D. Shimabuku, eds. Los Angeles: Monumenta Archaeologica 14, Institute of Archaeology, UCLA.

Zilhão, J. 1993 The Spread of Agro-Pastoral Economies Across Mediterranean Europe: A View from the Far West. Journal of Mediterranean Archaeology 6:5–63.

Zvelebil, M., and P. Dolukhanov 1991 The Transition to Farming in Eastern Europe. Journal of World Prehistory 5:233–78.

4 (b)
The Emergence of Metalworking

Barbara S. Ottaway and Ben Roberts

Technological changes and material innovations provide the chronological framework through which social change and transformation in prehistory are understood. In essence it is these shifts, rather than continuity, that largely construct our framework for understanding the past. (Sofaer-Derevenski and Stig-Sørensen in press)

Introduction

The emergence of metalworking is one of the most intensively investigated and debated areas in prehistory. The ubiquity of prehistoric copper, gold and bronze objects has meant that, together with ceramics, metal has provided a chronological backbone to later European prehistory as well as an important avenue of archaeological investigation into the behaviour of prehistoric communities. To understand how this occurred, it is necessary to explore the continuing influence of the three broad approaches that have influenced the development of research into prehistoric metal.

The desire to place an object in a chronological framework, provenance it to a region or an ore source or establish how it is made is manifested in the earliest research into prehistoric metals that dates from the late 18th–early 19th century. At this time, the first experiments were performed on metal artefacts to determine their authenticity and antiquity (Craddock 1995; Goodway 1991), and the cataloguing and classification of bronze objects were used to shape the understanding of prehistory (Trigger 1989). During the late 19th century and early 20th century, metallurgical analyses were being reported in archaeological circles whilst vast typological schemes and corpora of metal objects were being published and debated (e.g. Montelius 1903). The establishment of 'archaeometallurgy' as a unique discipline during the mid- to late 20th century sees the continuation of this strong empirical tradition. The integration of fieldwork, laboratory analysis and experimental replication that underpins much modern investigation into prehistoric metals may be still developing (Killick 2001), but for many projects the fundamental aims remain the same.

Theories concerning the influence of metal on prehistoric societies were advanced throughout the 19th century as the distinct 'ages' of copper, bronze and iron became accepted as facts. Pervasive throughout the works of many influential scholars is the equation of metallurgical abilities with social complexity. These ideas were developed most profoundly by the great prehistorian V. Gordon Childe (1944; 1958) who placed the 'spread' of metalworking innovations and the existence of mobile metal specialists at the heart of his immensely influential schemes of social evolution and class construction. Consequently, in discussing fundamental issues such as social complexity, trade and exchange, and craft specialization, metallurgical evidence is still frequently cited by prehistorians.

In studying metals' production, use and deposition it became clear that the prehistoric communities had been presented with a number of choices. Archaeologists and archaeometallurgists have been trying to look at metal artifacts and analytical results from the perspective of prehistoric communities to understand and explain the choices that were taken. This paradigmatic shift came about through anthropological and ethnographic research of modern metallurgical traditions, which revealed the intricate social and symbolic dimensions of metallurgical processes and the uses of metal objects (e.g. Bisson et al. 2000; Herbert 1984; 1993) that are frequently lacking in archaeological interpretations (Budd and Taylor 1995). The intellectual foundations for exploring these dimensions of prehistoric metallurgy were laid by archaeometallurgists interested in cultural expression through technology (e.g. Lechtman 1977; Smith 1977) and by anthropologists looking into the meanings communicated through technology and material culture (e.g. Appadurai 1986; Lemmonier 1986; Pfaffenberger 1988).

The impact and influence of the empirical approach on the emergence of metalworking in Europe has been profound. It has provided the technological basis for understanding prehistoric metallurgy that has allowed many of the theories generated by prehistorians such as V. Gordon Childe and his intellectual descendents to be evaluated. However, despite the rapid growth in interpreting prehistoric technologies and material cultures from socially-embedded perspectives (e.g. Dobres and Hoffman 1999; Ehrhardt 2005; Gosden and Marshall 1999; Kingery and Lubar1993; Lechtman 1996a; 1996b; Lemmonier 1993; Schiffer 2001; Sillar and Tite 2000), its application to European prehistoric metallurgy has been limited to relatively few scholars (e.g. Doonan 1999; Ottaway 2001; Sofear-Derevenski and Stig-Sørensen 2002; in press; Vandkilde 1996).

This chapter draws upon each of these approaches to analyze the archaeometallurgical, archaeological and geological evidence for each aspect of the metallurgical cycle (Figure 4.6), which includes the initial prospection for the ore, ore processing, smelting and/or alloying, casting and/or shaping of the metal object, acquisition, use and/or recycling and the final deposition of the object. Investigating each individual stage can go beyond simply identifying *what* occurred in order to look at *why* certain choices were made and others were not (Needham 2004; Ottaway 2001). The scope of this study encompasses the earliest appearances of copper, copper-base alloys, gold and silver in Europe. It seeks to address the following questions: When did people first use metal? What metalworking technology did they possess? Where did the objects and knowledge come from? What roles did metal objects and production practices play in the lives of prehistoric communities? How should the transmission, adoption and development of metal objects and metallurgical practices be understood? Whilst it is obviously not possible within the constraints of this chapter to give a comprehensive catalogue of evidence, case studies ranging throughout Europe will be employed.

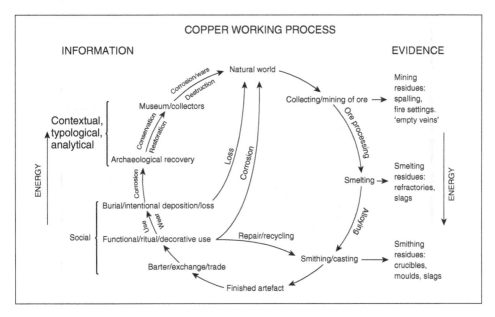

Figure 4.6 Metallurgical cycle (After Ottaway 2001:fig. 1)

Ores, Origins and Chronologies

The study of the emergence of metalworking in Europe tends to be overshadowed by debates concerning evidence for the earliest metallurgical phenomena in a particular region. The application of modern excavation techniques, the recognition and analysis of metallurgical debris and the increasing number of calibrated radiocarbon dates has ensured that these debates remain ongoing. The picture presented here could change rapidly with new finds and new dates, as has been demonstrated by the recent discovery of an early copper production site at Brixlegg, Austria (Höppner et al. 2005). The use of dates in (calibrated) millennia BC and the deliberate avoidance of prehistoric nomenclature in this chapter are due to a wish to avoid the confusion that such labels tend to inject. For instance, the Eneolithic of the Balkans and Italy, the Copper Age of Hungary, the Chalcolithic of Iberia and France but also the late Neolithic of Central Europe, Britain and Ireland all denote periods where the use of metal had become established.

The earliest evidence for copper in Europe, as shown on the map and accompanying table (Figure 4.7 and Table 4.1) indicates that the appearance of objects, mines and the remains of smelting and working is by no means a uniform 'spread' and neither is the presence of objects dependant upon the proximity of ore sources. The primacy of Anatolia is undisputed, with beads shaped from native (i.e. naturally-occurring) copper dating as early as the 8th millennium BC at Cayonu Tepesi (Maddin et al. 1999; Ozdogan and Ozgodan 1999). In eastern and central Europe, the sporadic appearance of early copper artefacts, in the form of fishhooks and beads, occurs from the late 6th millennium BC (Tringham and Krstic 1990). These metal artefacts in both regions are earlier than the first evidence of copper mining, smelting and casting, thus preceding what is here denoted by the term 'metallurgy'.

Figure 4.7 Earliest evidence for copper mentioned in the text

Table 4.1 Sites with the earliest evidence for copper in Europe mentioned in the text and on Figure 4.7

Site	Evidence	Radiocarbon dating	Reference
Rudna Glava	Extraction	c.4980–4670 cal. BC	Jovanovic and Ottaway (1976)
Brixlegg	Smelting	c.3960–3650 cal. BC	Höppner et al. (2005)
Monte Loreto	Extraction	c.3500 cal. BC	Pearce and Maggi (2005)
La Capitelle du Broum	Smelting	c.3100–2700 cal. BC	Ambert et al. (2002)
Kargaly	Extraction Processing Smelting	Late 4th–early 3rd mill. BC	Chernykh (2003)
Ross Island	Extraction Processing Roasting/Smelting?	c.2400–1800 cal. BC	O'Brien (2004)
Great Orme	Extraction Processing	c1800–1000 cal. BC	Wager (2001)

There is currently no clear indication whether Renfrew's assertion (1969; 1973) of the independent origins of metallurgy in southeast Europe still stands. It is suspicious that copper smelting appears synchronically in southeast Europe, Iran and the southern Levant in the mid–late 5th millennium BC a few hundred years after the established beginning of copper smelting in Anatolia (Thornton 2001). Hopefully, future studies of the earliest metalworking in these areas, including ongoing archaeometallurgical surveys in eastern Anatolia and the Caucasus, will provide clarification. The claim of an independent invention of metallurgy in southern Iberia (Renfrew 1967; 1973) might be reinforced by the early–mid-5th millennium BC date for the copper slag fragment at Cerro Virtud in southeast Spain (Ruiz-Taboada and Montero-Ruiz 1999). However, this slag fragment pre-dates the earliest copper artefacts and other evidence of metallurgy in the region by almost a millennium (Montero-Ruiz 1994; 2005), thus remaining an isolated and problematic piece of evidence.

Arsenical copper, probably the earliest intentional copper-base alloy in Eurasia, appears throughout Europe from at least the 4th millennium BC. It should be noted that whereas some of these are intentionally produced alloys, others may be the result of accidental smelting of copper ores with arsenic impurities. Similarly, the earliest evidence for tin bronze (i.e. copper and tin alloys) is a single piece of slag from Hungary, reportedly dating to the late 5th millennium BC (Glumac and Todd 1991). However, as this find predates the earliest occurrences of copper-tin alloys in this region by over a millennium, it may well be an isolated case of accidental mixed smelting of copper ores with other tin-bearing ores. Further west, individual objects made of copper with low additions of tin appear in Montenegro, central Germany, northern Italy and northern Spain during the earlier 3rd millennium BC (Fernandez Miranda et al. 1995; Krause 2003:210; Müller 2001:278; Primas 2002). Thus, whilst the ability to create tin bronze can be demonstrated at an early date, the adoption and production of bronzes with consistently high percentages of tin only occurred significantly later in these areas (Pare 2000), in contrast to the very rapid transition from the use of pure or arsenical copper to tin bronze in Britain and Ireland during the late 3rd millennium BC (Needham 1996; O'Brien 2004). These widely differing rates of adoption do not appear to be related to the distance away from the relatively scarce tin ores throughout Europe (Figure 4.8b) (Pernicka 1998). Rather it appears to relate to regional preference (Guimlia-Mair and Lo Schiavo 2003; Primas 2002). The appearance of tin bronze in western Europe and areas up to the western edge of the Carpathians is well covered by regional studies, but its occurrence in the Carpathian Basin has to be re-evaluated in the light of new chronological data. Following this, the pathway(s) of the transmission of tin alloying into central Europe *is* confirmed as both influences from the west Mediterranean and the Carpathians can be demonstrated (Krause 2003:241).

The earliest exploitation and working of 'native' gold occurs in southeast Europe and subsequently throughout eastern Europe during the mid 5th–4th millennium BC, as demonstrated most spectacularly at Varna in eastern Bulgaria (Makkay 1991; Renfrew 1986). As the earliest gold objects found further east only date to the 4th and early 3rd millennium BC (Gopher et al. 1990), it would appear that gold working arose independently in the region (Renfrew 1986). Gold objects are found on the southern and western coastal areas of the Iberian peninsula and southern France with some frequency by the early 3rd millennium BC (Elèure 1982; Pingel 1989). It is only during the mid–late 3rd millennium BC that gold is present in central

(a)

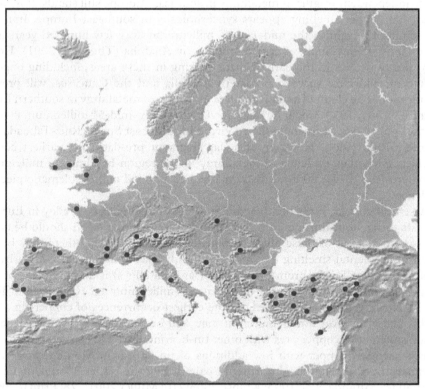

Figure 4.8a Copper sources

Europe (Hartmann 1970; 1982), northern France (Elèure 1982), Ireland and Britain (Eogan 1994; Taylor 1980), despite the presence of accessible sources throughout these regions that could have been exploited earlier. Gold is rarely alloyed with copper despite the fact that the two are easily melted together to produce a metal known as *tumbaga* as in Central and South America. This possibly occurred in Ireland during the late 3rd/early 2nd millennium BC (Taylor 1980) though the evidence is not entirely clear. The apparent restrictions on the mixing of gold and copper may reflect the differing values or different conceptions of the materials in prehistoric communities.

The earliest appearance of silver objects in Europe occurs in a spectacular deposit from Alepotrypa cave in southern Greece dated to the mid 5th–early 4th millennium BC (Muhly 2002). Meanwhile, in the central Mediterranean, silver and copper objects and evidence for production are concentrated in Sardinia during the late 4th–early 3rd millennium BC (Lo Schiavo 1988; Lo Schiavo et al. 2005; Skeates 1994). Although silver objects do occur in northern Italy, Romania and northern Bulgaria throughout this period, it is only in the late 3rd millennium BC that silver becomes widespread (Primas 1995). Silver, which occurs rarely in native form, can also be extracted from argentiferous lead ores such as galena and cerrusite (Figure 4.8c) even as a by-product of lead smelting.

There is a sporadic presence of lead objects throughout Europe such as in southeast Europe from the early 4th millennium BC (McGeehan-Liritzis 1983), southeast

(b)

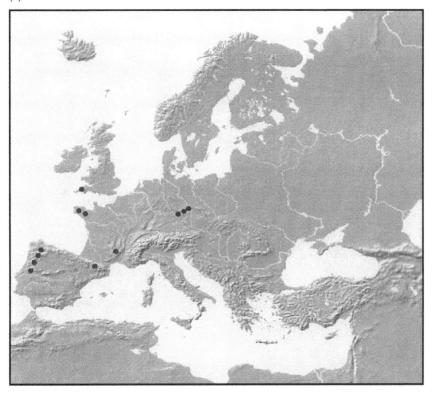

Figure 4.8b Tin sources

France from the late 4th millennium BC where it is contemporary with the earliest copper (Guilaine 1991), and northern England from the early 3rd millennium BC (Hunter and Davis 1994). As lead does not occur naturally, these occurrences represent the smelting of lead ores. In addition, lead was frequently alloyed with copper throughout the Bronze Age in order to increase the fluidity of the bronze for casting purposes. Its lower smelting temperature relative to copper ores means that it might have been the earliest smelted metal though the evidence is sparse and it has received little scholarly attention.

Prospection

The prospection and exploitation of copper ores for their use as pigments or ornaments, such as in Anatolia from the 9th to the 8th millennium BC (Schoop 1995), and in southeast Europe from the early–mid-6th millennium BC at sites such as Zmajevac (Glumac 1991) and Lepenski Vir (Jovanovic 1982), pre-dates the evidence of metal objects or metallurgical practices in these regions. This implies a shift in the purpose of ore prospection and meaning of the ores themselves, whose symbolic potential is only beginning to be recognized (Boivin and Owoc 2004). With the adoption of metalworking the distinctive colours of the various types of ore (Table 4.2) and their respective sources (Figure 4.8a–d) may well have been

(c)

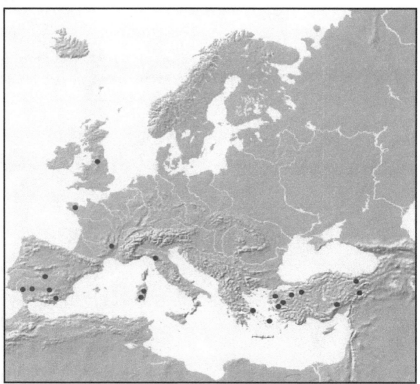

Figure 4.8c   Silver/lead sources

important in their selection or rejection (e.g. Jovanovic & Ottaway 1976). Smelting the oxidic ores of copper, such as the green and blue malachite and azurite, requires different treatment to that of copper sulphides, such as black–golden brown chalcopyrite, and this would have been recognized. The widespread distribution and colouring of copper ores throughout Europe (Figure 4.8a) would have facilitated the transmission of prospecting knowledge.

Unlike copper ores, which are often found in proximity to native copper deposits, tin ores such as cassiterite and stannite (Figure 4.8b) give little indication, other than by their heaviness, of their metallurgical potential. Most tin ores are found in streambeds as placer deposits, which result from the weathering of the parent rock. The visual anonymity of the mineral together with the relative rarity of tin sources in Europe means that the successful prospection for tin ore would have required prior knowledge that may well have been gained from afar.

Silver, which can occur in native form, was probably mostly extracted from the argentiferous lead ores such as galena and cerussite (Figure 4.8c) as at the mines of Laurion in Greece (Gale and Stos-Gale 1981), or as jarosite as in the south of Spain at Rio Tinto and Tharsis (Craddock 1995:213). However, there is as yet no evidence for early prehistoric prospection for native silver or for any of these ores in Europe, even though the minerals are distinctive in their appearance. Gold metal, like tin ores, is often found as 'nuggets' in alluvial placer deposits or as veins in less accessible quartz rock. However, gold's brilliant, corrosion-

(d)

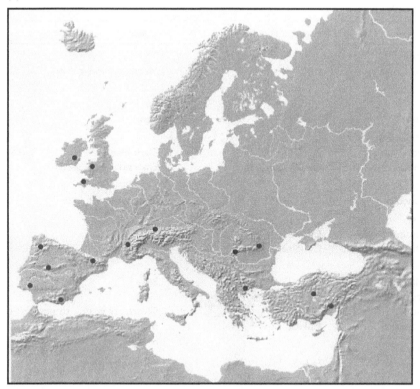

Figure 4.8d Gold sources

resistant lustre, in combination with its easy identification in stream beds (especially in areas where large nuggets occurred, such as Transylvania in Romania (Tylecote 1987:47), made its early prospection much less challenging than that of tin ores (Figure 4.8d).

Extraction

The accessibility of a particular ore determined the character of its extraction. It is very probable that in the case of copper ores extraction initially took the form of collecting surface outcrops, as is thought to have occurred throughout Iberia (Rovira and Ambert 2002). However, due to the nature of the activity, the evidence for this is hard to date reliably and is frequently obliterated by later mining processes. The evidence for early gold extraction in Europe is virtually non-existent (Weisgerber & Pernicka 1995), and that of early tin is very sparse (Meredith 1998; Penhallurick 1986). It is probable that the earliest gold and tin derived from placer deposits and surface collection, both of which will have left very ephemeral evidence.

It is only when ore sources were repeatedly exploited both by above ground mining (creating pits and 'Pingen') and by deep mining (creating shafts and galleries) that the evidence becomes less tentative. Pits or 'Pingen' and their resultant spoil would have been visible in the landscape, as at the early 3rd millennium BC

Table 4.2 Formula and colour of some of the most important ores of copper, arsenic, tin, gold, silver and lead

Ore Type	Chemical Formula	Colour
Copper		
Native Copper	Cu	Metallic yellow-golden
Copper Oxides		
Tenorite	CuO	Black
Cuprite	Cu_2O	Red
Copper Carbonates		
Azurite	$2CuCO_3Cu(OH)_4$	Dark blue
Malachite	$CuCO_3Cu(OH)_4$	Emerald – dark green
Copper Silicate		
Chrysocolla	$CuSiO_3H_2O$	Light turquoise blue
Fahlores		
Tennantite	$Cu_{12}As_4S_{13}$	Black/grey
Tetrahedrite	$Cu_{12}Sb_4S_{13}$	Black/grey
Copper Sulphides		
Covellite	CuS	Blue
Chalcocite	Cu_2S	Grey
Bornite	Cu_5FeS_4	Silver/grey tarnish to peacock colours
Chalcopyrite	$CuFeS_2$	Brassy yellow
Arsenic		
Arsenopyrite	$FeAsS$	Silver/grey/white
Tin		
Cassiterite	SnO_2	Brown/black/grey
Stannite	Cu_2FeSnS_4	Black/grey
Gold		
Native Gold	Au	Metallic golden-yellow
Lead		
Galena	PbS	Silver/black/lead grey
Cerussite	$PbCO_3$	White/yellow brown/grey
Silver		
Native silver	Ag	Metallic silver
Argentite	Ag_2S	Lead grey/black
Jarosite	$XFe_3[(OH)_6(SO_4)_2]$ X can be Ag, K, Na, or Pb	Yellow/dark brown

site of Pioch Farrus, France (Ambert 1996). Prehistoric mine shafts can be very extensive, as at the 5th millennium BC copper mine of Rudna Glava in Serbia, where they were up to 25 metres deep (Jovanovic 1982).

The tools employed in the extraction of the ore, such as stone hammers, antler picks and cattle bone scapulae, are frequently encountered at many mining sites (Pascale 2003; Weisgerber and Pernicka 1995). These often provide the initial indicators of a prehistoric mining site in the vicinity due to the non-local nature of the materials frequently used to make the tools. The rare discovery of tools made of more perishable materials, such as the wooden shovels, wedges and a pick handle from Libiola, Italy (Maggi and Del Lucchese 1988), the deer antler picks from El Aramo and El Milagro, Spain (De Blas 1998), or the wooden launder used to run water out of the mining shafts as found in Wales (Timberlake 2003), demonstrate that the range of tools employed was far broader than is usually represented by the archaeological record.

Experimental replications in extracting ore using hafted stone hammers and antler picks have revealed that having the hammer impact on the ore and the antler pick prise it from the rock face proved highly effective (e.g. Craddock 1990; Timberlake 2003). The durability of the tools, the ability to repair broken ones, the size of the support team to carry out the repairs and the accessibility and availability of the raw material to do so, would have influenced the pace of the extraction. In certain instances, this method was combined with the use of fire-setting to loosen the rock, as is demonstrated by the extraction surfaces at Ross Island, Ireland, in the late 3rd millennium BC (O'Brien 2004). Experimental replications revealed that this technique required a thorough understanding of the local rock as well as careful control over the fire and fuel supply (O'Brien 1994).

In relation to the exploitation of surface outcrops, the following of ore-bearing veins through underground extraction required not only a dramatic increase of labour, but also the organization and expertise needed to facilitate the movement of miners and their equipment, to provide adequate ventilation, illumination and drainage, and to bring the ore to the surface, all whilst ensuring that the underground structures did not collapse. It seems probable that the experience gained through the underground extraction of flint, stone and minerals, all of which began prior to the extraction of metalliferous ores, might have provided knowledge that would aid in such risky subterranean activities. These sites include the 6th-millennium-BC flint mine at Wittlingen, near Stuttgart, in Germany (Keefer 1993), the 5th-millennium-BC variscite mine at Can Tintorer, Spain (Blasco et al. 1998), and the 5th-millennium-BC haematite mine in the Black Forest of Germany (Goldenberg et al. 2003).

Surface, open cast or underground extraction of copper ore rarely occurred in the vicinity of settlements due to the frequent location of metalliferrous ore sources in relatively inhospitable or inaccessible terrain. This means that, in many instances, expeditions had to be organized to extract the ore. The debris and natural resources surrounding a mine provide indications as to the nature of the expeditions. Thus, an early copper-mining expedition may well have required mobilizing labour, assembling equipment and tools, making baskets or skin bags for carrying the ore, organizing a supply of food and fresh water, and potentially negotiating access to the mine. However, in areas where ubiquitous and easily-obtainable copper sources were present, as in southern Iberia (Hunt-Ortiz 2003; Montero-Ruiz 1994), there may well have been considerably less effort involved in such activities.

The religious beliefs and social dynamics that underlay seasonal and permanent mining communities have been rarely addressed in archaeometallurgy despite the recognized potential of such studies in archaeology (e.g. Kassianidou and Knapp 2005; Knapp et al. 1998; Topping and Lynott 2005) and in earlier anthropological research (e.g. Godoy 1985; Nash 1982). The excavation of complete vessels and unused hammerstones hidden under stone-built cases in the 5th-millennium-BC mine at Rudna Glava, Serbia (Jovanovic 1982), and the presence of numerous potential but unused stone tools which had been specially selected and brought up from the beach to the Great Orme copper mine in Wales during the 2nd millennium BC (Gale 1995), provide tantalizing glimpses of the ritual practices apparently integral to the mining process. It is tempting, given their ubiquity in recorded pre-industrial mining practices (e.g. Nash 1982), to explain these features as aspects of votive offerings given in return for the ore extracted and to ensure future supply.

The evidence for the creation, organization and identity of mining 'communities of labour' (Wager 2002:47) can be sparse and ambiguous. Interpretations tend to rely on the logistic requirements involved together with related assumptions regarding the division of labour. This gap in understanding is often expressed in the depictions of miners who, following anthropological observations, are usually men, while the ore processors are women and children despite several recorded exceptions in the ethnographic record (e.g. Herbert 1984:44). Given the narrowness of galleries and shafts in mines such as at Rudna Glava or the Great Orme, Wales (Dutton and Fasham 1994), where only very small adults or children could have passed through, and the absence of any reason why women might not have been involved in the extraction process, this perception has to be revised. The earlier workings of previous expeditions would have been visible to any arrivals and may well have influenced where that expedition worked. The expansion of mining activity during the 3rd and 2nd millennia BC increased the demands and organizational complexity of such undertakings, thereby fundamentally changing the social dynamics.

This can be seen in the existence of mining communities during the Bronze Age that subsisted solely through the trade of copper ores as at the Klinglberg, Austria (Shennan 1998; 1999), and Kargaly in the southern Urals of Russia (Chernykh 1992:2003). In the latter case, malachite and azurite were first exploited during the late 4th to early 3rd millennium BC, although the peak appears to have been in the 2nd millennium BC, at which time at least 20 settlements were located within the area of ore deposits. One of these settlements, the recently excavated site of Gornyj, was occupied year-round in spite of extremely low winter temperatures, hot summer winds and a dearth of fuel. It contained living quarters, areas of ore processing and areas where some smelting and casting of heavy copper tools were carried out. Much of the unsmelted ore seems to have been exchanged for animals as testified by the vast quantity of predominantly cattle bones that far exceeded the nutritional needs of the settlement's occupants. Extensive underground passages within the settlement, unconnected to mining activities but nevertheless requiring additional communal effort, all imply a close-knit community existing in harsh working and living conditions but with thriving social and religious practices (Chernykh 2003).

Processing

The early processing or 'beneficiation' of extracted copper ore to separate the copper-rich minerals from the host rock, or gangue, would have been small-scale (like the early extraction process) and would have been done by hand-sorting. The presence of stone tools, usually made from non-local rock with surfaces often having concave impressions from crushing the ore, and piles of small pieces of crushed gangue nearby, can provide evidence for this process. The striking colours of the copper ores and the familiarity of crushing and grinding actions that would have derived from the treatment of arable crops meant that little experience and no new knowledge would have been required of the participants. The influence of ore processing on the final composition and thus on the properties of the metal may also have been recognized (Merkel 1985). The ore extracted during early mining expeditions was often transported away from the mine to nearby settlements and worked there as at Belovode, a recently excavated Vinca settlement near the copper mine of Rudna Glava (Sljivar and Jacanovic 1996). However, beneficiation in some of the later periods did also take place near the mine; for instance, the presence of a similar number of stone tools used for mining and for ore processing in the direct vicinity of the Bronze Age mine at Brandergang in Austria indicates that the two processes were carried out spatially close to one another (Gale and Ottaway 1990).

Given the temporary nature of the early ore expeditions and the labour-intensive character of the ore processing, it is possible that individuals not involved in the extraction of the ore were dedicated to the beneficiation. Although hand-sorting of crushed ore may well have been sufficient initially, the increase in the volume of ore extracted and the advent of the grinding of ore, which resulted in material too fine to be hand-sorted, required the use of a more mechanical method such as the gravity separation technique (Craddock 1995). In this process, the ore is washed so that the lighter gangue becomes suspended in a flow of water and is carried away, while the denser mineral sinks and can be periodically retrieved. At Ffynnon Rhufeinig, Wales, 800 metres from the Bronze Age mine of Great Orme, a survey and excavation found just such an ore-processing site (Wager 1997) which has now been dated to the first half of the 2nd millennium BC, the same period in which the mine was in operation.

The movement of the extracted and processed ore to the place where it was to be smelted, especially in the volumes being produced in later periods, would have required considerable labour and organization, whether it occurred over land or sea. The situation of smelting sites close to ore sources, as in the Bronze Age sites in the Trentino in Italy (Hohlmann 1997:106), or at La Capitelle du Broum in southeast France in the early 3rd millennium BC (Ambert et al. 2002; 2005) is therefore not surprising. However, it is probable that, as in the cases of Gornyj, Russia (Chernykh 2003), and Klinglberg, Austria (Shennan 1998; 1999), processed but not smelted ore was also exchanged with other communities.

Smelting

Smelting converts crushed, and preferably well-beneficiated, metalliferous ores to metal. It requires a containing structure (e.g. a hollow in the ground with or without clay lining, a crucible or a furnace), a good supply of fuel (e.g. charcoal), and some way to conduct and control air directly to the fuel (e.g. naturally by strong steady wind or artificially with the help of blowpipes, tuyères or bellows) in order to reach the necessary temperature (commonly >1000°C) and right conditions (e.g. reducing atmosphere). Some ores require the addition of a flux, such as iron oxides or sand, which helps the metal to separate from the gangue by facilitating the formation of slag.

Copper sulphide ores cannot be reduced to metal through the single-phase process under reducing conditions the way copper oxide and carbonate ores can.

There are several ways in which copper sulphides could have been treated. For example, the smelting process could have been preceded by several cycles of roasting (Craddock 1989; 1995:136) to drive off the sulphur and convert the ores into copper oxides which can then be smelted to produce the metallic copper under reducing conditions. Alternatively, it has been shown experimentally that copper oxide and sulphide ores could have been mixed together in the smelt to create self-reducing conditions, a process known as 'co-smelting' (Rostoker et al. 1989). More recently it has been suggested that copper sulphide ores might also have been smelted in a simple one-phase process without prior roasting (Lorscheider et al. 2003).

The assumption that the production of copper followed a linear evolutionary development based on the mastery by prehistoric smiths of increasingly more challenging technological processes prevailed until recently in archaeological and archaeometallurgical discussions (Tylecote 1987). In this model, the use of native copper preceded the smelting of copper oxide and copper carbonate ores, which was followed by the smelting of copper sulphide ores and the introduction of alloying. This evolutionary model now needs to be revised for the following reasons: it has been realized that native copper, once melted, cannot be distinguished from smelted copper (Wayman and Duke 1999). This makes it probable that native copper continued to be used long after the invention and/or adoption of smelting technology. Furthermore, the recent discoveries that sulphide copper ores were smelted in the late 5th to early 4th millennium BC in east Bulgaria (Ryndina et al. 1999), in the second half of the 5th millennium BC in Austria (Höppner et al. 2005), the early 3rd millennium BC in southeast France (Ambert et al. 2002), and in the mid-3rd millennium BC in southwest Ireland (O'Brien 2004) potentially indicate that at least some prehistoric smiths were able to smelt all types of copper ores at the very beginnings of metallurgy in each region (Bourgarit 2007).

The archaeological and archaeometallurgical evidence for early smelting can be ephemeral. The careful processing and smelting of highly-concentrated copper carbonate ore could have meant that there was little gangue attached to the mineral particles and thus only minimal amounts of slag would have formed (Craddock 1989; 1995; 1999). This could explain the dramatic under-representation of copper slag in certain regions and periods such as Britain in the Bronze Age (Barber 2003). Experimental replications have demonstrated that smelting could have occurred in a pit within a flat ceramic vessel and a directed air supply (e.g. Timberlake 2003). This would render the process archaeologically almost undetectable. In such cases it is only through the recognition of small pieces of slag retrieved during careful excavation or by sieving as, for instance, at the 5th–4th-millennium-BC settlement of Selevac (Tringham & Krstic 1990), that early smelting evidence can be recovered. More substantial evidence for the smelting of copper ore ranges from ceramic vessels, as have been found in Austria (Lippert 1992), Iberia and southeast France (Gomez-Ramos 1996; Müller et al. 2004; Rovira & Ambert 2002), to stone settings as in the Trentino in Italy (Hohlmann 1997:105), perforated furnaces as found at Chrysocamino on Crete (Betancourt 2005), and whole batteries of stone furnaces as seen in Austria and Italy during the 2nd millennium BC (Cierny et al. 2004; Doonan et al. 1996).

The importance of the composition, condition and supply of fuel has been highlighted in recent years due to modern smelting experiments. Craddock (2001) argues that the discovery and use of charcoal in early copper smelting was certainly crucial for obtaining high temperatures in certain areas and providing a source of carbon monoxide for reducing the ore.

Remains of smelting processes from early periods show that the liquid copper was often trapped in the solidifying slag, which then had to be crushed in order to obtain the copper prills. A better understanding of beneficiation and fluxing, and the achievement of greater pyrotechnological control of the smelting process, led to the separation of slag and copper so that slag no longer had to be broken up. Consequently, mounds of large 'cakes' of slag are often found near the smelting sites of the Late Bronze Age, as for instance at Ramsau in Austria (Doonan et al. 1996). Copper collected in the form of prills had to be re-melted to form larger metal pieces which could then be worked or cast into a shape. Copper smelted from complex ores might have been refined to remove oxide inclusions, which make the metal very brittle, and other impurities, such as arsenic, antimony and bismuth. This process could be carried out in an open crucible either by blowing air over the surface (Hauptmann 2007), or by stirring the molten metal with a greenwood stick. The refining process leaves behind inhomogeneous, gassy crucible slag (Craddock 1995:203). In later periods refining might have been carried out in small furnaces.

The development and social acceptance of the smelting process may have been aided in part by earlier pyrotechnological experiences, such as fire-hardening wood, heating lithics to ease fracturing, or firing ceramics (Craddock 2001; Gheorghiu this volume). As smelting experiments have shown, even 'simple' smelting technology needed to be carried out within a fairly narrow margin of error or else the entire process would fail. Being proficient in smelting would require verbal instruction and visual demonstration under experienced individuals or groups for a successful transfer of knowledge. Recognizing the correct raw materials and memorizing the sequence and timing of actions and addition of substances may well have been facilitated by the use of songs, rituals and taboos (Budd and Taylor 1995; Rowlands and Warnier 1993). The inevitable or deliberate restriction of such crucial knowledge could have ensured that it remained in the hands of a few select groups of metal producers, who only passed on their craft to people of their choosing. The relationships of copper smelters to their prehistoric communities are ill-defined and understudied beyond the identification and discussion of graves thought to be those of metalworkers (e.g. Bátora 2002; Bertemes and Heyd 2002) and specialist metal production sites such as Almizaraque (Müller et al. 2004). The influence of the African ethnographic record, which approaches smelting from a symbolic and religious perspective and which has noted that smelters can be either powerful men or community outcasts (e.g. Bisson et al. 2000; Rowlands 1971) has been pervasive in recent years.

Evidence for the smelting of tin ores is elusive (Meredith 1998). Due to the high purity of the main mineral, cassiterite (Table 4.2) slag is not usually formed, which makes tin production difficult to locate in the archaeological record. Thus, the tin slag found in a burial dating to c.1500 BC at Caerloggas, southwest England (Salter 1997), and the small tin beads from an Early Bronze Age burial of a young woman at Buxheim in Bavaria, south Germany (Ottaway 2001:fig. 7) are rare finds indeed. It is postulated that the technique for early smelting of tin ores involved heating in a crucible covered with charcoal to a temperature of about 1000°C (Craddock 1995:132; Tylecote 1987:140). Whilst the relative rarity of tin ores (Figure 4.8b) may well have restricted access, the knowledge and ability to undertake the process would have been comparable to copper smelting.

Although silver does occur in its native form, most of the prehistoric silver in Europe was probably smelted from argentiferous lead ores, such as galena (Figure 4.8c). The process is essentially a two-stage one in which smelting at high temperature under reducing conditions was followed by cupellation, a lead-soaking process (Tylecote 1987:89) which involved heating the smelted metal to about 1000°C in a strong current of air (Craddock 1995:221). This oxidized the lead to form a litharge, or lead oxide, leaving the refined silver floating on top. The mid 5th–early 4th-millennium-BC date for the silver objects at Alepotrypa Cave, southern Greece (Muhly 2002:78) and the late 4th–early 3rd-millennium-BC date for silver objects in Sardinia (Lo Schiavo 1988; Skeates 1994) are contemporary with the earliest copper smelting in each region.

Alloying

One of metal's most valuable and intriguing characteristics is that it can be mixed or 'alloyed' with another metal to alter the composition and the properties of the final material. The major early alloys are of copper and arsenic to form arsenical copper, known also as arsenic bronze, and copper and tin to form (tin) bronze. Leaded bronzes appear in the Bronze Age. Other minerals, such as antimony, silver, nickel and bismuth, can also be found in early copper objects, but these usually originate from smelting fahlores (which naturally contain these minerals). Such products are not alloys *per se* in that 'alloys' are defined as the deliberate admixtures of two or more metals. Arsenical copper constitutes the earliest known copper alloy throughout Europe. The extent to which it was accidentally or intentionally produced has been the subject of ongoing debate (e.g. Budd and Ottaway 1995; Hauptmann and Weisgerber 1985; Lechtman 1996a; Müller et al. 2007). The presence of arsenic can, in comparison to pure copper, slightly lower the melting point, improve the quality of the cast, increase the hardness of the metal through cold-working (i.e. hammering while at room temperature) (Figure 4.9, where cold-working is expressed as reduction in thickness), improve the ability to be hot-worked repeatedly (i.e. hammered while heated), and alter the colour to a more silvery appearance compared to the red colour of pure copper (Northover 1989). The issue lies in whether arsenical copper was obtained by the intentional mixed smelting of copper minerals with ores rich in arsenic, by the deliberate selection of certain copper ores with high arsenic impurities, by the intentional mixing of certain metal types, or whether there was insufficient recognition of the process resulting in more random and haphazard metal compositions. In all but the last scenario, the communication between smith and smelter would have to be a close one, assuming that the smithing and smelting were carried out by different people.

Similar to the production of arsenic bronzes, tin bronzes could have been made by: mixing tin and copper oxide ores in a crucible or furnace, co-smelting copper sulphide ores with tin oxide ores (Rostoker and Dvorak 1991), adding tin oxides to liquid copper (Hauptmann and Weisgerber 1985), or by smelting tin oxides to obtain metallic tin, and then adding this product to metallic, *molten* copper under reducing conditions (Tylecote 1987:143). Although traditionally assumed to be a genuine (i.e. 'intentional') alloy, recent research has demonstrated that the careful smelting of a rare copper-containing tin sulphide ore (i.e. stannite, see Table 4.2), or of even rarer deposits containing both copper and tin oxides as found in Iberia and central Asia (e.g. Borroffka et al. 2002; Parzinger 2002; Parzinger and Boroffka 2003; Rovira and Montero-Ruíz 2002), could produce a tin bronze.

Nevertheless, the production of tin bronze in Europe would most probably have been achieved through the deliberate alloying of copper with tin ores or metal, requiring considerable knowledge of, as well as access to, either through negotiation or through distant exchange networks, relatively scarce tin sources (Figure 4.8b). Although tin bronze possesses many properties similar to arsenical copper, important differences do exist. Substantial hardening can be achieved in unworked cast tin bronzes up to 13 per cent tin, whereas arsenic bronzes achieve only a modest hardening through alloying alone (Lechtman 1996a). Furthermore, the brittle nature of tin bronze can be overcome up to a certain point by cycles of hammering, or cold working, followed by the application of heat, or annealing. In contrast, arsenical copper is highly ductile and can be cold worked and annealed repeatedly without becoming brittle (Figure 4.9), making it ideal for sheet copper.

The discussion about the degree of control being exerted over the composition of prehistoric metal objects and the extent to which this can be identified from the compositional evidence stretches far beyond debates concerning alloying. The vast programmes of compositional analysis from Stuttgart (Junghans et al. 1960; 1968; 1974), and Moscow (Chernykh 1992), and the project of re-evaluation and extension of the analytical programme in the 1990s (Krause and Pernicka 1996) was dedicated to the quest of provenancing objects to specific copper and (to a lesser extent) gold sources (e.g. Hartmann 1970; 1982; Watling et al. 1999). Although there are many critics of this approach (e.g. Tylecote 1970; Wilson and Pollard 2001), the interpretation of these analyses does allow the tentative identification of regional compositional groupings (Liversage 1994; Needham 2002) and broader metallurgical provinces (Chernykh 1992). Combined with new radiocarbon dates, such analyses have helped to build a detailed picture of the technological side of early metallurgy in Europe by providing the foundation for further investigation and interpretation of this huge and accessible data set.

Provenance studies have been underpinned by combining compositional analysis and lead isotope analysis, which has proven to be a useful tool in characterizing copper sources and including (or more often excluding) them as possible sources for particular metal artefacts. So far this combination has been used in southeast Europe for early copper objects (Gale et al. 1991; Pernicka 1987; 1997; Pernicka et al. 1993) and in the Aegean and northwest Anatolia for tin bronze artefacts of the Early Bronze Age (Pernicka 1990; Pernicka et al. 2003; Stos-Gale 1992). All these analytical results can be used to support studies of prehistoric communication, exchange and social interaction at local, regional and broader spatial and temporal scales.

Working, Casting and Finishing

The earliest copper artefacts, such as the copper needle from Trestiana, Romania (Glumac 1991), and the awl from Neszmley, Hungary (Bognar-Kutzian 1976), both dated to the late 6th millennium BC, were hammered to shape. Hammering without heating (i.e. cold-working) serves to shape metal and/or to increase the hardness of the metal, for instance on a cutting edge. The application of heat (i.e. annealing) and more hammering allow the metal to be further worked and hardened without

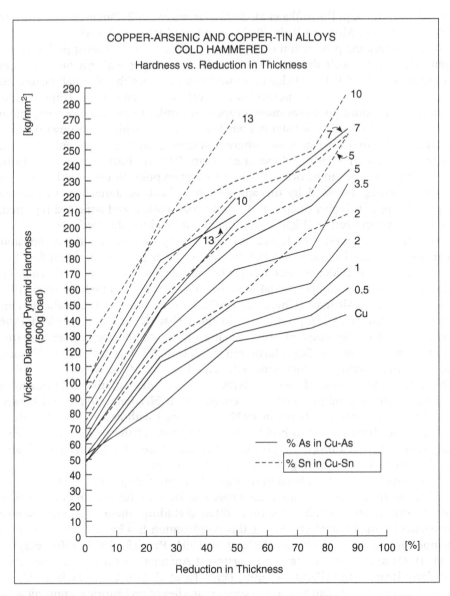

Figure 4.9 Comparison of the work-hardening behaviour of cold-hammered copper-arsenic and copper-tin alloys (After Lechtman 1996)

cracking. Studying the microstructure of a metal artefact by metallographic analysis (Scott 1991; Wang and Ottaway 2004) can determine whether or not an object has been cast (Figure 4.10a), hammered or annealed (Figure 4.10b). This analytical technique has great potential to unlock information about how different communities chose to produce their metal objects (Kienlin 2006; Northover 1996). Similarly, xero-radiography of complex metal artefacts has the potential to reveal the stages in the construction process and if multiple pieces of metal were used as has recently been shown on the Nebra sky disc (Lehmann et al. 2005).

(a)

Figure 4.10a As-cast 10 per cent tin bronze showing pronounced dendrites (Wang and Ottaway 2004). Image width 1.3 mm

(b)

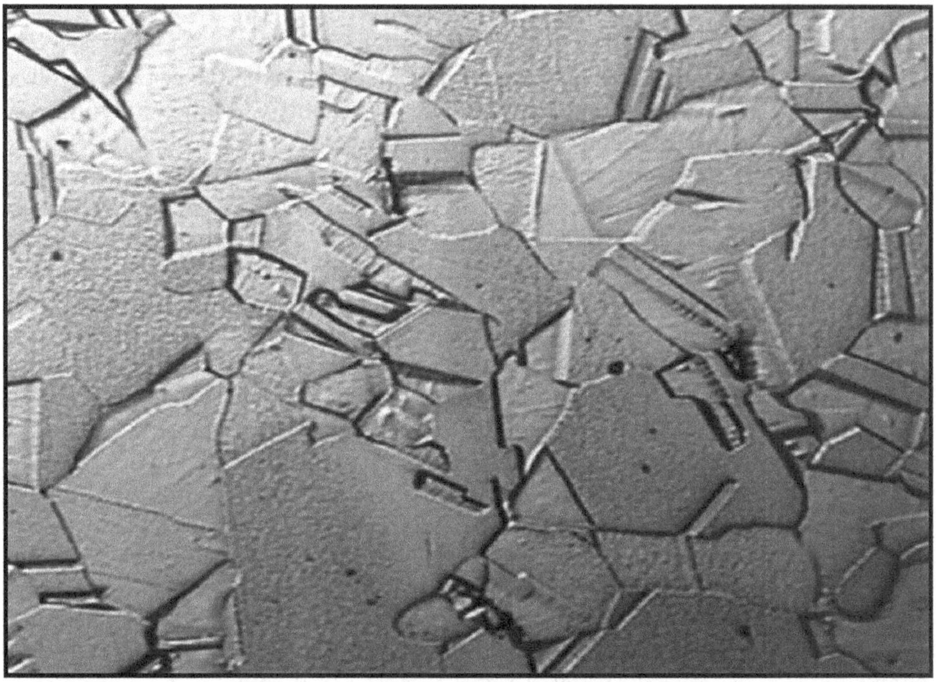

Figure 4.10b Cold-worked and annealed 6 per cent tin bronze (Wang and Ottaway 2004). Image width 0.13 mm

Pouring molten metal into pre-shaped forms, or moulds, enabled complex shapes to be obtained. Moulds, both open and two-part closed ones, were made of a variety of materials including stone, sand, clay or metal (Wang and Ottaway 2004). Moulds are under-represented in the archaeological record when compared to the number of extant metal objects. This would suggest that many moulds were made from perishable materials such as clay, which can disintegrate depending on the temperature at which it was fired prior to casting (Ottaway 2003), or sand which falls apart entirely after the casting is completed (Ottaway and Seibel 1998). Such moulds were either hand-formed or carved to shape, or formed using the lost wax (*cire perdue*) method. This latter method entails creating the object form in wax and encasing it in clay. The application of heat melts the wax and bakes the clay leaving a negative mould into which molten metal can be poured.

After casting an object and exposing it to further shaping or hardening processes, the finishing of a metal object's surface through the use of sand, grit, water, fleeces and textiles over periods of diligent and careful grinding and polishing seems to have been important (Nakou 1995). This can be seen on the copper axe accompanying 'Ötzi', the mid–late-4th-millennium-BC 'Iceman' discovered in the Alps (Spindler 2001), which had even been polished on the section covered by the haft and which thus would not have been visible to the casual observer. The further decoration of metal through the engraving of lines, the scribing of dots or impressing the surface to create shapes in relief (*repoussée*), such as seen on the copper disc found in Neolithic contexts in Lake Constance, Germany, or on many gold objects, with a variety of punches, scribes and chisels (e.g. Armbruster 2000) is evidenced throughout Europe.

Use

The use of metal objects and the activities in which they would have been involved is conventionally assumed from the form, which is thought to follow the function. The tripartite division of metal objects into weapons, tools and ornaments is based upon the more modern visual correlate, its depositional context and/or the position of the object on the body in a burial. Labels for artefacts such as 'shields', which are argued to have no defensive abilities (Coles 1962), and 'basket earrings', which may or may not have been worn on the ears (Russel 1990; Sherratt 1986), were assigned by antiquarians and accepted into modern literature. These typologies immediately run into trouble when confronted by ubiquitous metal artefacts such as daggers, which can serve as weapons, tools or ornaments of status in differing contexts.

Such issues can be addressed through the recording of use-wear on metal objects by low-magnification microscopy and the careful comparison of these traces to those left on modern replications after various activities were performed with them (e.g. Bridgford 1997; Kienlin and Ottaway 1998; Kristiansen 1978:2002; Roberts and Ottaway 2004). The fact that many metal objects had to be re-sharpened means that use-wear analysis mainly looks at the final activities carried out with that object just before deposition. For example, copper and bronze flanged axes, which were deposited in graves in the north-alpine region during the late 3rd to early 2nd millennium BC, were assumed to be status symbols whilst their counterparts encountered in the landscape and erroneously labelled 'stray finds' were thought to be simply tools (Abels 1972). This hypothesis has been contradicted by use-wear analysis which demonstrated that axes in graves had been subjected to heavy use before deposition (Kienlin and Ottaway 1998). The study of the use of metal objects is therefore not only crucial to understanding their roles in prehistoric communities, but also to understanding the underlying reasons for their acquisition and deposition.

Circulation, Recycling and Deposition

Although evidence for the recycling of metals is hard to identify archaeologically and archaeometallurgically, there is nothing to indicate that communities would not have been aware of this practice and did not employ it. Objects were deposited in conditions varying from pristine to heavily-used, thereby contradicting any notions that they were simply discarded when thoroughly worn (Roberts and Ottaway 2004; see Fontijn, this volume). Therefore, the majority of metal objects discovered in settlements, pits, caves, wells, rivers, lakes and fields throughout Europe *has* to be understood as the result of deliberate depositions (see Fontijn, this volume). Explanations for this 'hoarding' phenomenon have been proposed by many scholars that have ranged from votive offerings, competitions for prestige to the storage or dumping of bronze supplies (see Bradley 1998; Fontijn 2002). In contrast, those metal objects found accompanying bodies or cremations are usually interpreted in terms of the identity of those with whom they have been placed. Whatever the underlying reasons, these copper, silver, gold and especially bronze objects were neither recovered nor recycled. Consequently, there is an unavoidable bias in the perception of metal use in the past towards periods and regions where higher metal deposition, rather than recycling, occurred which can seriously distort interpretations (Needham 2001; Taylor 1999). Whilst certain objects would appear to have been made for deposition, the removal of tools, weapons and ornaments from use and circulation meant that more had to be acquired.

The presence of metal objects, even in regions which have neither ore sources nor evidence for metal production, required extensive communication and transport networks either based on or actively involved in the metals trade (Shennan 1986; 1993; Sherratt 1976; 1993). The increase in the scale and complexity of bronze metal production and consumption throughout Europe during the second millennium BC implies that the circulation of bronze reached immense proportions. The exceptional recovery of shipwrecks carrying metal objects, as at Langdon Bay, southeast England (Muckleroy 1981), provides rare insights into the movement of metal. The unique convertibility of metal through the recycling process meant that any object could be an 'ingot' and could either be melted down and re-cast in a new form according to local and regional cultural considerations or incorporated by communities in their original shape. The identification of certain metal objects thought to be produced for transport, melting and re-shaping – such as oxhide metal ingots in the Mediterranean (Kassianidou and Knapp 2005), rings, 'ribs', ingot torcs and even flat axes in central Europe (Butler 2002; Krause and Pernicka 1998), or socketed axes in northwest Europe (Briard 1993) – serve to stimulate further debates concerning the relationship between metal production and trade. The importance of this fluidity in influencing prehistoric exchange dynamics has been emphasized by Sherratt (1993) and Shennan (1993; 1999) who stress that the existence of a convertible, widely-accepted and standardized material enabled social and economic diversification and intensification.

Discussion

It has become clear during the discussion of the data presented here that the emergence of metallurgy in Europe is not a continuous, evolutionary or logical progress, but one that owed much to good channels of communication, effective transfer of skills, local adaptation and regional choices and preferences. Whereas some regions see the initial appearance and use of metal objects without any evidence for local metallurgical know-how, other areas have single- or dual-function sites, presenting evidence for specific stages only in the metallurgical production cycle. Such areas include mining and beneficiation but not smelting sites at the Great Orme in Wales, smelting of copper ores without mining or further working of the metal at Chrysokamino in Crete (Betancourt 2005), and local smithing but not mining or smelting in the North European Plain and Switzerland (Ottaway 1973; Ottaway and Strahm 1975). In other regions, such as the Trentino in Italy, there is evidence for all stages involved in the production cycle from mining, beneficiation and smelting to smithing (Cierny 2003).

To explain the emergence of metalworking in Europe first requires a reassessment of interpretations that have come to be accepted regardless of the actual archaeological, archaeometallurgical or anthropological evidence. The importance and potential of metal for transforming agriculture, warfare, economics and social relations are self-evident to the modern Western mindset. It is evident therefore that underlying many interpretations is the belief that the possession of metal objects and the knowledge and ability to create them would have been inherently desirable to prehistoric communities. The passive acceptance and adoption of each subsequent 'innovation' in the metallurgical production process, increasing the efficiency of production or enhancing the properties of the object, would be inevitable as the benefits would be 'obvious', thereby encouraging it to diffuse across Europe. Such models lead to the assumption that the accumulation of metal objects or the control and exploitation of metal production would be of fundamental importance to prehistoric individuals and groups able to use this 'wealth' to demonstrate their 'elite' status. Whilst there may well be evidence in certain regions or periods to support this, and given that few scholars propose alternative theories concerning the relationship of metal to the broader dynamics of prehistoric societies (e.g. Strahm 1994), these assumptions tend to go unchallenged. At a broader scale, the proposed connection of particular metal objects or production practices to an archaeological 'culture', as exemplified by references to Beaker Culture and Funnel Beaker Culture metal artefacts, serves only to locate the evidence in space and time rather than explain its presence.

The presence of the earliest metal objects throughout Europe was a consequence of local, regional and interregional networks of communication and exchange that prehistoric communities depended upon to find partners or acquire livestock, locally unobtainable goods and information. It is important to re-emphasize that early copper or gold objects were not necessarily superior to wood, bone, flint and ceramics for performing everyday tasks. Rather, their colour, lustre and malleability provided the foundations for the initial attraction that led to their deliberate and continual acquisition. The fact that the earliest known metal objects throughout many regions of Europe are beads, rings and earrings, designed to be worn in life as well as in death, would seem to support the importance of visual expression. The potential difficulties in acquiring further objects should not be seen as a natural impediment to their continued acquisition as this may well have formed an integral aspect of the attraction. Defining the motivations of prehistoric individuals and communities for the acquisition of metal objects and metallurgical knowledge that would occur after their incorporation throughout Europe would be to ignore the incorporation and use of metal in very different economic, social and religious dynamics that underlay these prehistoric societies.

Although it is easy to imagine how knowledge of the manipulation of a metal object through the application of hammering and heating could come about through local experimentation with the new material, it is more difficult to imagine numerous indigenous inventions of the smelting process across Europe. Indeed, the ability to extract copper from the ore would have required a combination of learning, presumably from metallurgically knowledgeable individuals or groups, and practical experience. Partial understandings of the metallurgical practices could not be responsible for success. Once the basic knowledge of the metallurgical processes had been gained, archaeological evidence points to many regional variations indicating adaptation of the learned process to fit local resources and cultural styles and beliefs.

The perceptions and roles of metalworkers in prehistoric communities are hard to define. It is perhaps erroneous to discuss individuals in certain aspects of the production given the collective nature of so many of the metallurgical processes, including the ore prospection, extraction, processing and transport. The existence of even a part-time metalworker required the commitment of the broader community to aid in the production and acquisition of the objects. The shaping of early metal objects to replicate existing forms made in other materials, and the considerable variation in the early metal object forms and alloys being produced in regions throughout Europe, undoubtedly reflect differences in local community standards and desires rather than the individual leanings of metalworkers (e.g. Ottaway 1973: fig 12). It is the cultural understandings constructed by prehistoric communities regarding metal objects and production practices that are being expressed. It is only through this process of social negotiation that prehistoric communities approached the appearance of the new material or innovation (Ottaway 2001; Sofaer-Derevenski and Stig-Sørensen 2002; in press) despite the potential for new forms to be achieved.

ACKNOWLEDGEMENTS

A version of this paper was presented at the conference *Metallurgy: A Touchstone for Cross-Cultural Interaction* held at the British Museum 28–30th April 2005 and we are very grateful to the suggestions and comments we received there. We especially would like to thank Roland Müller, Maribel Martínez Navarrete and Chris Thornton for their detailed reviews of earlier drafts. The opinions and any mistakes remain our own.

REFERENCES

Abels, B.-U. 1972 Die Randleistenbeile in Baden-Württemberg, dem Elsass, der Franche-Comte und der Schweiz. Prähistorische Bronzefunde IX, 4.

Ambert, P. 1996 Cabrières-Hérault et le contexte régional du dévelopment de la première métallurgie du cuivre en France (III° millénaire avant J.C.). Archéologie en Languedoc 20:1–70.

Ambert, P., L. Bouquet, J.-L. Guendon, and D. Mischka 2005 La Capitelle du Broum (district minier de Cabrières-Péret, Hérault): établissement industriel de l'aurore de la métallurgie française (3100–2400 BC). *In* La première métallurgie en France et dans les pays limitrophes. Paul Ambert and Jean Vaquer, eds. Pp. 83–96. Paris: Mémoire de la Société Préhistorique Française 37.

Ambert, P., J. Coularou, C. Cert, J.-L. Guendon, D. Bourgarit, B. Mille, N. Houlès, and B. Baumes 2002 Le plus vieil établissement de metallurgistes de France (III millénaire av J.-C.): Péret (Hérault). Comptes Rendu Palevol 1:67–74.

Appadurai, A., ed. 1986 The Social Life of Things. Cambridge: Cambridge University Press.

Armbruster, B. 2000 Goldschmiedekunst und Bronzetechnik: Studien zum Metallhandwerk der Atlantischen Bronzezeit auf der Iberischen Halbinsel. Montagnac: M. Mergoil.

Barber, M. 2003 Bronze in the Bronze Age: Metalwork and Society in Britain c. 2500–800 BC. Stroud: Tempus.

Bátora, J. 2002 Contribution to the Problem of 'Craftsmen' Graves at the End of Aeneolithic and in the Early Bronze Age in Central, Western and Eastern Europe. Slovenská Archeológia, 50/2:179–228.

Bertemes, F., and V. Heyd 2002 Der Übergang Kupferzeit/Frühbronzezeit am Nordwestrand des Karpatenbeckens – kulturgeschichtliche und paläometallurgische Betrachtungen. *In* Die Anfänge der Metallurgie in der Alten Welt. M. Bartelheim, R. Krause, and E. Pernicka, eds. Pp. 185–229. Rahden: Leidorf.

Betancourt, P. 2005 Chrysokamino 1: The Minoan Estate. Hesperia Supplements 36. Princeton: ASCSA Publications.

Bisson, M., T. Childs, P. De Barros, A. Holl, and J. Vogel 2000 Ancient African Metallurgy: The Socio-Cultural Context. Lanham: Altamira Press.

Blasco, A., M. J. Villalba, and M. Edo 1998 Explotación. manufactura, distribución y uso como bien de prestigio de la 'calaíta' en el Neolítico: el ejemplo del complejo de Can Tintorer. *In* Minerales y metales en la prehistoria reciente: algunos testimonios de su explotación y laboreo en la Península Ibérica. Germán Delibes de Castro, ed. Pp. 41–70. Studia Arqueológica 88. Valladolid: Universidad de Valladolid.

Bognar-Kutzian, I. 1976 On the Origins of Early Copper-Processing in Europe. *In* To Illustrate the Monuments, V. Megaw, ed. Pp. 69–76. London: Thames and Hudson.

Boivin, N., and M.-A. Owoc 2004 Soil, Stones, and Symbols: Cultural Perceptions of the Mineral World. London: University College London.

Boroffka, N., J. Cierny, J. Lutz, H. Parzinger, E. Pernicka, and G. Weisgerber 2002 Bronze Age Tin from Central Asia: Preliminary Notes. *In* Ancient Interactions: East and West in Eurasia. K. Boyle, C. Renfrew, and M. Levine, eds. Pp. 135–60. Cambridge: McDonald Institute of Archaeological Research.

Bourgarit, D. 2007 Chalcolithic Copper Smelting. *In* Metals and Mines: Studies in Archaeometallurgy. S. La Niece, D. Hook, and P. Craddock, eds. Pp. 3–14. London: Archetype and British Museum.

Bradley, R. 1998 A Passage of Arms: An Archaeological Analysis of Prehistoric Hoards and Votive Deposits. Oxford: Oxbow.

Briard, J. 1993 Relations Between Brittany and Great Britain During the Bronze Age. *In* Trade and Exchange in Prehistoric Europe. C. Scarre and F. Healy, eds. Pp. 183–9. Oxford: Oxbow.

Bridgford, S. 1997 Mightier Than the Pen? An Edgewise Look at Irish Bronze Age Swords. *In* Material Harm: Archaeological Studies of War and Violence. J. Carman, ed. Pp. 95–115. Glasgow: Cruithne Press.

Budd, P., and B. Ottaway 1995 Arsenical Copper: Chance or Choice? *In* Ancient Mining and Metallurgy in Southeast Europe. Bora Jovanovic, ed. Pp. 95–102. Belgrade: Bor.

Budd, P., and T. Taylor 1995 The Faerie Smith Meets the Bronze Industry: Magic Versus Science in the Interpretation of Prehistoric Metal-Making. World Archaeology 27:133–43.

Butler, J. 2002 Ingots and Insights: Reflections of Rings and Ribs. *In* The Beginnings of Metallurgy in the Old World. M. Bartelheim, E. Pernicka, and R. Krause, eds. Pp. 229–43. Rahden/Westf: Marie Leidorf.

Chernykh, E. 1992 Ancient Metallurgy in the USSR. Cambridge: Cambridge University Press.

Chernykh, E. 2003 Die vorgeschischtlichen Montanreviere an der Grenze von Europa und Asien: Das Produktionszentrum Kargaly. *In* Man and Mining – Mensch und Bergbau: Studies in Honour of Gerd Weisgerber. T. Stöllner, G. Körlin, G. Steffens, and J. Cierny, eds. Pp. 79–92. Der Anschnitt Beiheft 16. Bochum: Deutsches Bergbau Museum.

Childe, V. G. 1944 Archaeological Ages as Technological Stages. Journal of the Royal Anthropological Institute of Great Britain and Ireland 74:7–24.

Childe, V. G. 1958 The Prehistory of European Society. London: Pelican.

Childs, T., and D. Killick 1993 Indigenous African Metallurgy: Nature and Culture. Annual Review of Anthropology 22:317–37.

Cierny, J. 2003 Vier Dinge verderben ein Bergwerk – welche Ereignisse haben die Bergwerkproduktion in der Frühzeit beeinflusst? *In* Man and Mining – Mensch und Bergbau: Studies in Honour of Gerd Weisgerber. T. Stöllner, G. Körlin, G. Steffens, and J. Cierny, eds. Pp. 93–102. Der Anschnitt Beiheft 16. Bochum: Deutsches Bergbau Museum.

Cierny, J., F. Marzatico, R. Perini, and G. Weisgerber 2004 Der spätbronzezeitliche Verhüttungsplatz Acqua Fredda am Passo Redebus (Trentino). *In* Alpenkupfer: Rame delle Alpi. G. Weisgerber, and G. Goldenberg, eds. Pp. 155–64. Der Anschnitt Beiheft 17. Bochum: Deutsches Bergbau Museum.

Coles, J. 1962 European Bronze Age Shields. Proceedings of the Prehistoric Society 38:156–90.

Craddock, B. 1990 The Experimental Hafting of Stone Mining Hammers. *In* Early Mining in the British Isles. Peter Crew and Simon Crew, eds. Pp. 58–9. Snowdonia: Plas Tan y Bwlch.

Craddock, P. 1989 The Scientific Investigation of Early Mining and Metallurgy. *In* Scientific Analysis in Archaeology and its Interpretation. J. Henderson, ed. Pp. 178–213. Oxford: Oxford University Press.

Craddock, P. 1995 Early Metal Mining and Production. Edinburgh: Edinburgh University Press.

Craddock, P. 1999 Paradigms of Metallurgical Innovation in Prehistoric Europe. *In* The Beginnings of Metallurgy. A. Hauptmann, E. Pernicka, T. Rehren, and Ü. Yalçin, eds. Pp. 175–92. Bochum: Deutsches Bergbau Museum.

Craddock, P. 2001 From Hearth to Furnace: Evidences for the Earliest Metal Smelting Technologies in the Eastern Mediterranean. Palaeorient 26:151–65.

De Blas Cortina, M. A. 1998 Producción e intercambio de metal: la singularidad de las minas de cobre prehistóricas del Aramo y El Milagro (Asturias). *In* Minerales y metales en la prehistoria reciente: algunos testimonios de su explotación y laboreo en la Península Ibérica. Germán Delibes de Castro, ed. Pp. 71–104. Studia Arqueológica 88. Valladolid: Universidad de Valladolid.

Dobres, M.-A., and C. Hoffman 1999 The Social Dynamics of Technology. Practice, Politics, and World Views. Washington, DC: Smithsonian Institution Press.

Doonan, R. 1999 Copper Production in the Eastern Alps during the Bronze Age: Technological Change and the Unintended Consequences of Social Reorganization. *In* Metals in Antiquity. S. Young, M. Pollard, P. Budd, and R. Ixer, eds. Pp. 72–7. British Archaeological Reports (International Series) 792. Oxford: Archaeopress.

Doonan, R., S. Klemm, B. Ottaway, G. Sperl, and H. Weinek 1996 The East Alpine Bronze Age Copper Smelting Process: Evidence from the Ramsau Valley, Eisenerz, Austria. *In* Archaeometry 94: Proceedings of the 29th International Symposium of Archaeometry. S. Demerci, A. Ozer, and G. Summers, eds. Pp. 17–22. Ankara: Tübïtak.

Dutton, A., and P. Fasham 1994 Prehistoric Copper Mining on the Great Orme, Llandudno, Gwynedd. Proceedings of the Prehistoric Society 60:245–86.

Ehrhardt, K. 2005 European Metals in Native Hands: Rethinking Technological Change 1640–1683. Tuscaloosa: University of Alabama Press.

Elèure, C. 1982 Les Ors Préhistoriques. Paris

Eogan, G. 1994 The Accomplished Art: Gold and Gold-Working in Britain and Ireland during the Bronze Age (c. 2300–650 BC). Oxford: Oxbow Monograph 42.

Fernández Miranda, M., Ignacio Montero-Ruíz, and Salvador Rovira 1999 Los Primeros Objectos de Bronce en el occidente del Europa. Trabajos de Prehistoria 52(1):57–69.

Fontijn, D. 2002 Sacrificial Landscapes: Cultural Biographies of Persons, Objects and Natural Places in the Bronze Age of Southern Netherlands, c. 2300–600 cal. BC. Annalecta Praehistoria Leidensia 33–34.

Gale, D., and B. Ottaway 1990 An Early Mining Site in the Mitterberg Ore Region of Austria. *In* Early Mining in the British Isles. Peter Crew and Simon Crew, eds. Pp. 36–8. Snowdonia: Plas Tan y Bwlch.

Gale, N. H., and Z. A. Stos-Gale 1981 Cycladic Lead and Silver Metallurgy. Annual of the British School at Athens 76:169–224.

Gale, N. H., Z. A. Stos-Gale, P. Lilov, M. Dimitrov, and T. Todorov 1991 Recent Studies of Eneolithic Copper Ores and Artefacts in Bulgaria. *In* Découverte du Metal. J.-P. Mohen, ed. Pp. 49–76. Paris: Picard.

Glumac, P. 1991 The Advent of Metallurgy in Prehistoric Southeast Europe. PhD dissertation, University of California at Berkeley.

Glumac, P., and J. Todd 1991 Early Metallurgy in Southeast Europe: The Evidence for Production. *In* Recent Trends in Archaeometallurgical Research 8.1. P. Glumac, ed. Pp. 8–19. Philadelphia: MASCA Research Papers in Science and Archaeology.

Godoy, R. 1985 Mining: Anthropological Perspectives. Annual Review of Anthropology 14:199–217.

Goldenberg, G., A. Maass, G. Steffens, and H. Steuer 2003 Haematite Mining during the Linear Ceramics Culture in the Area of the Black Forest, South West Germany. *In* Man and Mining-Mensch und Bergbau: Studies in Honour of Gerd Weisgerber. T. Stöllner, G. Körlin, G. Steffens, and J. Cierny, eds. Pp. 179–86. Der Anschnitt Beiheft 16. Bochum: Deutsches Bergbau Museum.

Gómez-Ramos, P. 1996 Hornos de reducción de cobre y bronce en la pre y protohistoria de la península Ibérica. Trabajos de Prehistoria 53(1):127–43.

Goodway, M. 1991 Archaeometallurgy: Evidence of a Paradigm Shift? *In* Material Issues in Art and Archaeology II. P. Vandiver, J. Druzik, and G. X. Wheeler, eds. Pp. 705–12. Pittsburgh: Materials Research Society.

Gopher, A., T. Tsuk, S. Shalev, and R. Gophna 1990 Earliest Gold Artifacts in the Levant. Current Anthropology 31(4):436–43.

Gosden, C., and Y. Marshall, eds. 1999 The Cultural Biographies of Objects. World Archaeology 31.

Guilaine, J. 1991 Roquemengarde et les débuts de la métallurgie en France méditerranéenne. *In* Découverte du métal. C. Eluère and J. P. Mohen, eds. Pp. 279–94. Paris: Picard.

Guimlia-Mair, A. 2005 Copper and Copper Alloys in the South-Eastern Alps: An Overview. Archaeometry 47(2):275–92.

Guimlia-Mair, A., and F. Lo Schiavo, eds. 2003 Le problème de l'étain à l'origine de la métallurgie/The Problem of Early Tin: Acts of the XIVth UISPP Congress, University of Liège, Belgium, 2–8 September 2001. British Archaeological Reports (International Series) 1199. Oxford: Archaeopress.

Hartmann, A. 1970 Prähistorische Goldfunde aus Europa: Spektralanalytische Untersuchungen und deren Auswertung. Studien zu den Anfängen der Metallurgie 3. Berlin: Mann.

Hartmann, A. 1982 Prähistorische Goldfunde aus Europa: Spektralanalytische Untersuchungen und deren Auswertung. Studien zu den Anfängen der Metallurgie 5. Berlin: Mann.

Hauptmann, A. 2007 The Archaeometallurgy of Copper: Evidence from Faynan, Jordan. Berlin: Springer Verlag.

Hauptmann, A., and G. Weisgerber 1985 Vom Kupfer zur Bronze: Beiträge zum frühesten Berg- und Hüttenwesen. *In* Archäologische Bronzen, antike Kunst, moderne Technik. H. Born, ed. Pp. 16–36. Berlin: Reimer.

Herbert, E. 1984 Red Gold of Africa. Copper in Precolonial History and Culture. Madison: University of Wisconsin Press.

Herbert, E. 1993 Iron, Gender, and Power: Rituals of Transformation in African Societies. Bloomington: Indiana University Press.

Hohlmann, B. 1997 Beitrag zur spätbronzezeitlichen Kupfermetallurgie im Trentino (Südalpen) im Vergleich mit anderen prähistorischen Kupferschlacken aus dem Alpenraum. Dissertation, Ruhr University, Bochum.

Höppner, B., M. Bartelheim, M. Husijmans, R. Krauss, K. Martinek, E. Pernicka, and R. Schwab 2005 Prehistoric Copper Production in the Inn Valley, Austria, and the Earliest Copper Production in Central Europe. Archaeometry 47(2):293–315.

Hunter, F., and M. Davis 1994 Early Bronze Age Lead – A Unique Necklace from Southeast Scotland. Antiquity 68:824–30.

Hunt-Ortiz, M. 2003 Prehistoric Mining and Metallurgy in South-West Iberian Peninsula. British Archaeological Reports (International Series 1188). Oxford: Archaeopress.

Jovanovic, B. 1982 Rudna Glava: Najstarije Rudarstvo Bakra na Centralnom Balkanu. Bor-Beograd: Muzej Rudarstva Metalurgije, Arheoloski Institut, Posebnaizdanja, Knjiga 17.

Jovanovic, B., and B. Ottaway 1976 Copper Mining and Metallurgy in the Vinca Group. Antiquity 50:104–13.

Junghans, S., E. Sangmeister, and M. Schröder 1960 Metallanalysen kupferzeitlicher und frühbronzezeitlicher Bondenfunde aus Europa. Studien zu den Anfängen der Metallurgie 1. Berlin: Mann.

Junghans, S., E. Sangmeister, and M. Schröder 1968 Kupfer und Bronze in der frühen Metallzeit Europas. Die Materialgruppen beim Stand von 12000 Analysen. Studien zu den Anfängen der Metallurgie 2/1–3. Berlin: Mann.

Junghans, S., E. Sangmeister, and M. Schröder 1974 Kupfer und Bronze in der frühen Metallzeit Europas. Katalog der Analysen Nr. 10041–22000 (mit Nachuntersuchungen der Analysen Nr. 1010040). Studien zu den Anfängen der Metallurgie 2/4. Berlin: Mann.

Kassianidou, V., and A. B. Knapp 2005 Archaeometallurgy in the Mediterranean: The Social Context of Mining, Technology and Trade. *In* The Archaeology of Mediterranean Prehistory. A. B. Knapp and E. Blake, eds. Pp. 215–51. Oxford: Blackwell.

Keefer, E. 1993 Steinzeit. Württembergisches Landesmuseum Stuttgart. Stuttgart: Theiss.

Kienlin, T., and B. Ottaway 1998 Flanged Axes of the North-Alpine Region: An Assessment of the Possibilities of Use-Wear Analysis on Metal Artefacts. *In* L'Ateletian bronzier en Europe du xx au viii siècle avant notre ère, C. Mordant, M. Perno, and V. Rychner, eds. Pp. 271–86. Paris: Comité des taraux historiques et scientifique.

Kienlin, T. L., E. Bischoff, and H. Bischoff 2006 Copper and Bronze during the Eneolithic and Early Bronze Age: A Metallographic Examination of Axes from the North Alpine Region. Archaeometry 48(3):453–68.

Killick, D. 2001 Science and Speculation in the Origins of Extractive Metallurgy. *In* Handbook of Archaeological Sciences. Don Brothwell and Mark Pollard, eds. Pp. 483–92. London: Wiley.

Kingery, W. D., and S. Lubar, eds. 1993 History from Things: Essays on Material Culture. Washington, DC: Smithsonian Institution Press.

Knapp, A. B., V. Pigott, and E. Herbert, eds. 1998 Social Approaches to an Industrial Past: The Archaeology and Anthropology of Mining. London: Routledge.

Krause, R. 2003 Studien zur kupfer- und frühbronzezeitlichen Metallurgie zwischen Karpatenbecken und Ostsee. Vorgeschichtliche Forschungen 24. Rahden/Westf: Marie Leidorf.

Krause, R., and E. Pernicka 1996 Das neue Stuttgarter Metallanalysenprojekt 'SMAP'. Archäologisches Nachrichtenblatt 1:274–91.

Krause, R., and E. Pernicka 1998 The Function of Ingot Torques and their Relation with Early Bronze Age Copper Trade. In L'Ateletian bronzier en Europe du xx au viii siècle avant notre ère. C. Mordant, M. Perno, and V. Rychner, eds. Pp. 219–25. Paris: Comité des taraux historiques et scientifique.

Kristiansen, K. 1978 The Consumption of Wealth in Bronze Age Denmark: A Study in the Dynamics of Economic Processes in Tribal Societies. In New Directions in Scandinavian Archaeology. K. Kristiansen and C. Paludan-Müller, eds. Pp. 158–91. Copenhagen: National Museum of Denmark.

Kristiansen, K. 2002 The Tale of the Sword – Swords and Swordfighters in Bronze Age Europe. Oxford Journal of Archaeology 21(4):319–32.

Lechtman, H. 1977 Style in Technology: Some Early Thoughts. In Material Culture: Styles, Organization, and Dynamics of Technology. Heather Lecthman and Robert Merrill, eds. Pp. 3–20. St Paul: West Publishing Co.

Lechtman, H. 1996a Arsenic Bronze: Dirty Copper or Chosen Alloy? A View from the Americas. Journal of Field Archaeology 23:477–514.

Lechtman, H. 1996b Cloth and Metal: The Culture of Technology. In Andean Art at Dumbarton Oaks. E. Boone, ed. Pp. 33–43. Washington, DC: Dumbarton Oaks Research Library and Collection.

Lehmann, E., P. Vontobel, E. Deschler-Erb, and M. Soares 2005 Non-Invasive Studies of Objects from Cultural Heritage. Nuclear Instruments and Methods in Physics Research A 542:68–75.

Lehrberger, G. 1995 The Gold Deposits of Europe: An Overview of the Possible Metal Sources for Prehistoric Gold Objects. In Prehistoric Gold in Europe: Mines, Metallurgy and Manufacture. G. Morteani, and P. Northover, eds. Pp. 115–44. New York: Kluwer.

Lemmonier, P. 1986 The Study of Material Culture Today: Toward an Anthropology of Technical Systems. Journal of Anthropological Archaeology 5:147–86.

Lemmonier, P., ed. 1993 Technological Choices: Transformation in Material Culture since the Neolithic. London: Routledge.

Lippert, A. 1992 Der Götschenberg bei Bischofshofen: Eine Ur- und Frühgeschichtliche Höhensiedlung im Salzachpongau. Vienna: Verlag der Österreichischen Akademie der Wissenschaften.

Liversage, D. 1994 Interpreting the Compositional Patterns in Ancient Bronze: The Carpathian Basin. Acta Archaeologica 65:57–134.

Lo Schiavo, F. 1988 Early Metallurgy in Sardinia. In The Beginnings of the Use of Metals and Alloys. R. Maddin, ed. 92–103. Cambridge, MA: MIT Press.

Lo Schiavo, F., A. Giumlia-Mair, and R. Valera 2005 Archaeometallurgy in Sardinia: From the Origin to the Beginning of Early Iron Age. Monographies Instrumentum 30. Montagnac: Monique Mergoil.

Lorscheider, F., A. Mass, and D. Steiniger 2003 Frühe Kupferproduktion – archäologischer Befund und Experiment: Versuche zur Fahlerzverhüttung in einem einzigen Ofen. In Man and Mining – Mensch und Bergbau: Studies in Honour of Gerd Weisgerber. T. Stöllner, G. Körlin, G. Steffens, and J. Cierny, eds. Pp. 301–8. Der Anschnitt Beiheft 16. Bochum: Deutsches Bergbau Museum.

Maddin, R., J. Muhly, and T. Stech 1999 Early Metalworking at Cayonu. *In* The Beginnings of Metallurgy. A. Hauptmann, E. Pernicka, T. Rehren, and Ü. Yalcin, eds. Pp. 37–44. Der Anschnitt Beiheft 9. Bochum: Deutsches Bergbau Museum.

Maggi, R., and A. Del Lucchese 1988 Aspects of the Early Copper Age in Liguria. Rassegna di Archaeologia 7:331–8.

Maggi, R., and M. Pearce 2005 Mid-Fourth Millennium Copper Mining in Liguria, North-West Italy: The Earliest Known Copper Mines in Western Europe. Antiquity 79:66–77.

Makkay, J. 1991 The Most Ancient Gold and Silver in Central and South-east Europe. *In* Decouverte du Metal. J. P. Mohen, ed. Pp. 119–30. Paris: Picard.

McGeehan-Liritzis, V. 1983 The Relationship Between Metalwork, Copper Sources, and the Evidence for Settlement in the Greek Late Neolithic and Early Bronze Age. Oxford Journal of Archaeology 2.2:147–80.

Meredith, C. 1998 An Archaeometallurgical Survey of Ancient Tin Mines and Smelting Sites in Spain and Portugal. British Archaeological Reports, International Series 714. Oxford: Archaeopress.

Merkel, J. 1985 Ore Beneficiation during the Late Bronze Age/Early Iron Age at Timna, Israel. MASCA Journal 3(5):164–9.

Montelius, O. 1903 Die älteren Kulturperioden im Orient und Europa. Stockholm.

Montero-Ruiz, I. 1994 El origen de la Metalurgia en el Sureste Peninsula. Almeria: Instituto de Estudios Almerienses.

Montero-Ruiz, I. 2005 Métallurgie ancienne dans la Péninsule Ibérique. *In* La première métallurgie en France et dans les pays limitrophes. P. Ambert and J. Vaquer, eds. Pp. 187–94. Paris: Mémoire de la Société Préhistorique Française 37.

Muckleroy, K. 1981 Middle Bronze Age Trade Between Britain and Europe: A Martime Perspective. Proceedings of the Prehistoric Society 47:275–97.

Muhly, J. 2002 Early Metallurgy in Greece and Cyprus. *In* Anatolian Metal II. Ü. Yalçin, ed. Pp. 77–82. Der Anschnitt, Beiheft 15. Bochum: Deutches Bergbau Museum.

Müller, J. 2001 Soziochronologische Studien zum Jung- und Spätneolithikum im Mittelelbe-Saale Gebiet (4100–2700 v.Chr). Vorgeschichtliche Forschungene 21. Rahden/Westf: Marie Leidorf.

Müller, J. 2002 Modelle zur Einführung der Zinnbronzetechnologie und zur sozialen Differenzierung der mitteleuropäischen Frühbronzezeit. *In* Vom Endneolithikum zur Frühbronzezeit: Muster sozialen Wandels? J. Müller, ed. Pp. 267–89. Universitätsforschung zur prähistorischen Archäologie 90. Bonn: Habelt.

Müller, R., G. Goldenberg, M. Bartelheim, M. Kunst, and E. Pernicka 2007 Zambujal and the Beginnings of Metallurgy in Southern Portugal. In Metals and Mines: Studies in Archaeometallurgy. S. La Niece, D. Hook, and P. Craddock, eds. Pp. 15–26. London: Archetype and British Museum.

Müller, R., T. Rehren, and S. Rovira 2004 Almizaraque and the Early Copper Metallurgy of Southeast Spain: New Data. Madrider Mitteilungen 45:33–56.

Nakou, G. 1995 The Cutting Edge: A New Look at Early Aegean Metallurgy. Journal of Mediterranean Archaeology 8(2):1–32.

Nash, J. 1982 We Eat the Mines and the Mines Eat Us: Dependency and Exploitation in Bolivian Tin Mines. New York: Columbia University Press.

Needham, S. 1996 Chronology and Periodisation in the British Bronze Age. Acta Archaeologica 67:121–40.

Needham, S. 2001 When Expediency Broaches Ritual Intention: The Flow of Metal Between Systemic and Buried Domains. Journal Royal Anthropological Institute 7:275–98.

Needham, S. 2002 Analytical Implications for Beaker Metallurgy in North-West Europe. *In* The Beginnings of Metallurgy in the Old World. M. Bartelheim, E. Pernicka, and R. Krause, eds. Pp. 99–133. Rahden/Westf: Marie Leidorf.

Needham, S. 2004 Migdale-Marnoch: Sunburst of Scottish Metallurgy. In The Neolithic and Early Bronze Age of Scotland in their European Context. I. Shepherd and G. Barclay, eds. Pp. 217–45. Edinburgh: Royal Society of Antiquaries of Scotland.

Northover, P. 1989 Properties and Use of Arsenic-Copper Alloys. In Old World Archaeometallurgy. A. Hauptmann, E. Pernicka, and G. Wagner, eds. Pp. 111–18. Der Anschnitt Beiheft 7. Bochum: Deutsches Bergbau Museum.

Northover, P. 1996 From Stone to Bronze. H. Vandkilde, ed. Pp. 321–67. Moesgard: Jutland Archaeological Society.

O'Brien, W. 1994 Mount Gabriel: Bronze Age Mining in Ireland. Galway: National University of Ireland.

O'Brien, W. 2004 Ross Island: Mining, Metal and Society in Early Ireland. Galway: National University of Ireland.

Ottaway, B. 1973 The Earliest Copper Ornaments in Northern Europe. Proceedings of the Prehistoric Society 39:294–331.

Ottaway, B. 1994 Prähistorische Archäometallurgie. Espelkamp: Marie Leidorf.

Ottaway, B. 2001 Innovation, Production and Specialisation in Early Prehistoric Copper Metallurgy. European Journal of Archaeology 4(1):87–112.

Ottaway, B. 2003 Experimentelle Archaeometallurgy. In Man and Mining – Mensch und Bergbau: Studies in Honour of Gerd Weisgerber. T. Stöllner, G. Körlin, G. Steffens, and J. Cierny, eds. Pp. 341–7. Der Anschnitt Beiheft 16. Bochum: Deutsches Bergbau Museum.

Ottaway, B., and S. Seibel 1998 Dust in the Wind: Experimental Casting of Bronze in Sand Moulds. In Paléométallurgie des cuivres: Actes du colloque de Bourg-en-Bresse et Beaune, 17–18 Oct. 1997. M.-C. Frère-Sautot, ed. Pp. 59–63. Monographies Intrumentum 5. Montagnac: Monique Mergoil.

Ottaway, B., and C. Strahm 1975 Swiss Neolithic Copper Beads: Currency, Ornaments or Prestige Items? World Archaeology 6(3):307–21.

Ozdogan, M., and M. Ozgodan 1999 Archaeological Evidence on the Early Metallurgy at Cayonu Tepesi. In The Beginnings of Metallurgy. A. Hauptmann, E. Pernicka, T. Rehren, and Ü. Yalcin, eds. Pp. 13–22. Bochum: Der Anschnitt Beiheft 9.

Pare, C. 2000 Bronze and the Bronze Age. In Metals Make the World go Round. C. Pare, ed. Pp. 1–38. Oxford: Oxbow Books.

Parzinger, H. 2002 Das Zinn in der Bronzezeit Eurasiens. In Anatolian Metal II. U. Yalcin, ed. Pp. 159–77. Der Anschnitt 15. Bochum: Deutsches Bergbau Museum.

Parzinger, H., and N. Boroffka 2003 Das Zinn der Bronzezeit in MittelasienI. Archologie in Iran und Turan. Mainz am Rhein: Verlag Philp von Zaubern.

Pascale De, A. 2003 'Hammerstones from early copper mines': sintesi dei ritrovamenti nell' Europa e mel Mediterraneo orientale e prime considerazioni sui mazzuoli di Monte Loreto (IV millennio BC – Liguria). Rivista di Studi Liguri 69:5–42.

Penhallurick, R. 1986 Tin in Antiquity. London: Institute of Metals.

Pernicka, E. 1987 Erzlagerstätten in der Ägäis und ihre Ausbeutung im Altertum: Geochemische Untersuchungen zur Herkunftsbestimmung archäologischer Metallobjekte. Jahrbuch des Römisch-Germanischen Zentralmuseums 34:607–714.

Pernicka, E. 1990 Gewinnung und Verbreitung der Metalle in prähistorischer Zeit. Jahrbuch des Römisch-Germanischen Zentralmuseums 37(1):21–129.

Pernicka, E. 1997 Prehistoric Copper in Bulgaria: Its Composition and Provenance. Eurasia Antiqua 3:41–180.

Pernicka, E. 1998 Die Ausbreitung der Zinnbronze im 3. Jahrtausend. In Mensch und Umwelt in der Bronzezeit Europas. B. Hänsel, ed. Pp. 135–47. Kiel: Oetker-Voges Verlag.

Pernicka, E., F. Begemann, S. Schmitt-Strecker, and G. Wagner 1993 Eneolithic and Early Bronze Age Copper Artefacts from the Balkans and their Relation to Serbian Copper Ores. Praehistorische Zeitschrift 68:1–54.

Pernicka, E., C. Eibner, Ö. Öztunali, and G. Wagner 2003 Early Bronze Age Metallurgy in the Northeast Aegean. *In* Ancient Troia and the Troad: Scientific Approaches. G. Wagner, E. Pernicka, and H. P. Uerpmann, eds. Pp. 143–72. Berlin: Springer-Verlag.

Pfaffenberger, B. 1988 Fetishized Objects and Humanised Nature: Toward an Anthropology of Technology. Man 23:236–52.

Pingel, V. 1989 Zum Beginn der Goldmetallurgie auf der Iberischen Halbinsel. *In* Old World Archaeometallurgy. A. Hauptmann, E. Pernicka, and G. Wagner, eds. Pp. 227–34. Der Anschnitt Beiheft 7. Bochum: Deutsches Bergbau Museum.

Primas, M. 1995 Gold and Silver during the 3rd Mill. Cal. BC. *In* Prehistoric Gold in Europe: Mines, Metallurgy and Manufacture. G. Morteani and P. Northover, eds. Pp. 77–93. New York: Kluwer.

Primas, M. 2002 Early Tin Bronze in Central and Southern Europe. *In* The Beginnings of Metallurgy in the Old World. M. Bartelheim, E. Pernicka, and R. Krause, eds. Pp. 303–14. Rahden/Westf: Marie Leidorf.

Renfrew, C. 1967 Colonialism and Megalithismus. Antiquity 41:276–88.

Renfrew, C. 1969 The Autonomy of the South-East European Copper Age. Proceedings of the Prehistoric Society 35:12–47.

Renfrew, C. 1973 Before Civilization: The Radiocarbon Revolution and Prehistoric Europe. London: Jonathan Cape.

Renfrew, C. 1986 Varna and the Emergence of Wealth in Prehistoric Europe. *In* Social Life of Things: Commodities in a Cultural Perspective. A. Appadurai, ed. Pp. 141–68. Cambridge: Cambridge University Press.

Roberts, B., and B. Ottaway 2004 The Use and Significance of Socketed Axes during the Late Bronze Age. European Journal of Archaeology 6(2):119–40.

Rostocker, W., and J. Dvorak 1991 Some Experiments with Co-smelting to Copper Alloys. Archaeomaterials 5:5–20.

Rostoker, W., V. Pigott, and J. Dvorak 1989 Direct Reduction of Copper Metal by Oxide-Sulphide Mineral Interaction. Archaeomaterials 3:69–87.

Rovira, S., and P. Ambert 2002 Vasijas cerámicas para reducir minerales de cobre en la península Ibérica y en la francia meridonal. Trabajos de Prehistoria 59(1):89–105.

Rovira, S., and I. Montero-Ruíz 2002 Natural Tin-Bronze Alloy in Iberian Peninsula Metallurgy: Potentiality and Reality. *In* Le problème de l'étain à l'origine de la métallurgie/The Problem of Early Tin Colloque/Symposium. A. Giumlia-Mair and F. Lo Schiavo, eds. Pp. 15–22. British Archaeological Reports S1199. Oxford: Archaeopress.

Rowlands, M. 1971 The Archaeological Interpretation of Prehistoric Metalworking. World Archaeology 3(2):210–34.

Rowlands, M., and J.-P. Warnier 1993 The Magical Production of Iron in the Cameroon Grassfields. *In* The Archaeology of Africa: Food, Metals and Towns. B. Andah, A. Okpoko, T. Shaw, and P. Sinclair, eds. Pp. 512–50. London: Routledge.

Ruíz-Taboada, A., and I. Montero-Ruíz 1999 The Oldest Metallurgy in Western Europe. Antiquity 73:897–903.

Russel, A. 1990 Two Beaker Burials from Chilbolton, Hampshire. Proceedings of the Prehistoric Society 56:153–72.

Ryndina, N., G. Indenbaum, and V. Kolosova 1999 Copper Production from Polymetallic Sulphide Ores in the Northeastern Balkan Eneolithic Culture. Journal of Archaeological Science 26:1059–68.

Salter, C. 1997 A Note on the Tin Slags from Caerloggas Down, Cornwall and the Upper Merrivale Blowing House. *In* Prehistoric Extractive Metallurgy in Cornwall. P. Budd and D. Gale, eds. Pp. 45–50. Truro: Cornwall Archaeological Unit.

Schiffer, M., ed. 2001 Anthropological Perspectives on Technology. Albuquerque: University of New Mexico Press.

Schoop, U.-D. 1995 Die Geburt des Hephaistos: Technologie und Kulturgeschichte neolithischer Metallverwendung im Vorderen Orient. Espelkamp: Marie Leidorf.

Scott, D. 1991 Metallography and Microstructure of Ancient and Historic Metals. Los Angeles: Getty Conservation Institute.

Shennan, S. 1986 Central Europe in the Third Millennium BC: An Evolutionary Trajectory for the Beginning of the European Bronze Age. Journal of Anthropological Archaeology 5:115–46.

Shennan, S. 1993 Commodities, Transactions and Growth in the Central European Early Bronze Age. Journal of European Archaeology 1(2):59–72.

Shennan, S. 1998 Producing Copper in the Eastern Alps during the Second Millennium BC. In Social Approaches to an Industrial Past. A. B. Knapp, V. Piggott, and E. Herbert, eds. Pp. 191–204. London: Routledge.

Shennan, S. 1999 Cost Benefit and Value in the Organization of Early European Copper Production. Antiquity 73:352–63.

Sherratt, A. 1976 Resources, Technology and Trade: An Essay on Early European Metallurgy. In Problems in Social and Economic Archaeology. I. Longworth, G. Sieveking, and K. Wilson, eds. Pp. 557–81. London: Duckworth.

Sherratt, A. 1986 The Radley 'Earrings' Revised. Oxford Journal of Archaeology 5:61–6.

Sherratt, A. 1993 What Would a Bronze Age World System Look Like? Relations Between Temperate Europe and the Mediterranean in Later Prehistory. Journal of European Archaeology 1:1–57.

Sillar, B., and M. Tite 2000 The Challenge of 'Technological Choices' for Material Science Approaches in Archaeology. Archaeometry 42(1):2–20.

Skeates, R. 1994 Early Metal Use in the Central Mediterranean Region. Accordia Research Papers 4:5–47.

Sljivar, D., and D. Jacanovic 1996 Veliko Laole, Belovode: Vinca Culture Settlement in Northeastern Serbia. Préhistoire Européenne 8:175–88.

Smith, C. S. 1977 Metallurgy as a Human Experience: An Essay on Man's Relationship to his Materials in Science and Practice Throughout History. Metals Park: American Society for Metals.

Sofaer-Derevenski, J., and M.-L. Stig-Sørensen 2002 Becoming Cultural: Society and the Incorporation of Bronze. In Metals and Society: Papers from a Session Held at the European Association of Archaeologists Sixth Annual Meeting in Lisbon 2000. B. Ottaway and E. Wager, eds. Pp. 117–22. British Archaeological Reports International Series) 1061. Oxford: Archaeopress.

Sofaer-Derevenski, J., and M.-L. Stig-Sørensen In press Technological Change as Social Change: The Introduction of Metal in Europe. In Continuity – Discontinuity: Transition Periods in European Prehistory. M. Bartelheim, and V. Heyd, eds. Rahden/Westf: Marie Leidorf.

Spindler, K. 2001 The Man in the Ice. London: Weidenfield and Nicholson.

Stos-Gale, Z. A. 1992 The Origin of Metal Objects from the Early Bronze Age Site of Thermi on the Island of Lesbos. Oxford Journal of Archaeology 11(2):155–77.

Strahm, C. 1994 Die Anfänge der Metallurgie in Mitteleuropa. Helvetia Archaeologica 25:2–39.

Taylor, J. 1980 Bronze Age Goldwork of the British Isles. Cambridge: Cambridge University Press.

Taylor, T. 1999 Envaluing Metal: Theorizing the Eneolithic 'Hiatus'. In Metals in Antiquity. S. Young, M. Pollard, P. Budd, and R. Ixer, eds. Pp. 22–32. British Archaeological Reports (International series) 792. Oxford: Archaeopress.

Thornton, C. 2001 The Domestication of Metal: A Reassessment of the Early Use of Copper Minerals and Metal in Anatolia and Southeastern Europe. University of Cambridge M. Phil. Thesis.

Timberlake, S. 2003 Excavations on Copa Hill, Cwmystwyth (1986–1999); An Early Bronze Age Copper Mine within the Uplands of Central Wales. British Archaeological Reports (British Series) 348. Oxford: Archaeopress.

Topping, P., and M. Lynott 2005 The Cultural Landscape and Prehistoric Mines. Oxford: Oxbow Books.

Trigger, B. 1989 A History of Archaeological Thought. Cambridge: Cambridge University Press.

Tringham, R., and D. Krstic, eds. 1990 Selevac: A Neolithic Village in Yugoslavia. Los Angeles: UCLA.

Tylecote, R. 1970 The Composition of Metal Artifacts: A Guide to Provenance? Antiquity 44:19–25.

Tylecote, R. 1987 An Early History of Metallurgy in Europe. London: Longman.

Vandkilde, H. 1996 From Stone to Bronze. The Metalwork of the Late Neolithic and Earliest Bronze Age in Denmark. Jutland: Jutland Archaeological Society Publications and Aarhus University Press.

Wager, E. 1997 Ffynnon Rufeinig. Great Orme Exploration Society 1:6–9.

Wager, E. 2002 Mining as Social Process: A Case Study from the Great Orme, North Wales. *In* Metals and Society: Papers from a Session Held at the European Association of Archaeologists Sixth Annual Meeting in Lisbon 2000. B. Ottaway and E. Wager, eds. Pp. 45–9. British Archaeological Reports (International Series) 1061. Oxford: Archaeopress.

Wang, Q., and B. Ottaway 2004 Casting Experiments and Microstructure of Archaeologically Relevant Bronzes. British Archaeological Reports (International Series) 1331. Oxford: Archaeopress.

Watling, R. J., J. Taylor, R. J. Chapman, R. B. Warner, M. Cahill, and R. C. Leake 1999 The Application of Laser Ablation Inductively Coupled Plasma Mass Spectrometry (LA-ICP-MS) for Establishing the Provenance of Gold Ores and Artefacts. *In* Metals in Antiquity. P. Budd, and S. Young, eds. Pp. 53–63. Oxford: Archaeopress.

Wayman, M., and J. Duke 1999 The Effects of Melting on Native Copper. *In* The Beginnings of Metallurgy. A. Hauptmann, E. Pernicka, T. Rehren, and Ü. Yalçin, eds. Pp. 55–63. Bochum: Deutsches Bergbau Museum.

Weisgerber, G., and E. Pernicka 1995 Ore Mining in Prehistoric Europe: A Short Overview. *In* Prehistoric Gold in Europe: Mines, Metallurgy and Manufacture. G. Morteani and P. Northover, eds. Pp. 115–44. New York: Kluwer.

Wilson, L., and A. M. Pollard 2001 The Provenance Hypothesis. *In* Handbook of Archaeological Sciences. Don Brothwell and Mark Pollard, eds. Pp. 507–18. London: Wiley.

5

Death, Remembrance and the Past

Introduction

The archaeology of death is a perennially important topic (Parker Pearson 1999). For 'New' archaeologists the structure and content of graves was analyzed in the hope of understanding social organization. This perspective placed the figure of the corpse at centre stage, and interpreted the contents and structure of the grave as if the corpse sought to express social identity and structure. This view is based upon a fallacy. It is not the corpse that orchestrates the burial, it is the mourners who organize and structure burial ritual. If we are to understand how burial rituals are used to express social identity, and how they relate to social organization we need to take on the perspective of the mourners, rather than the corpse. This change in perspective led a later generation of archaeologists to analyze burial ritual in terms of the dynamics of social power (Barrett 1996; Parker Pearson 1999). Coupled with a detailed analysis of mortuary ritual based on a close reading of the anthropology of death, this perspective has largely transformed the way in which mortuary data is now analyzed. Nevertheless, this power-based perspective has tended to treat funerary rituals simply as an arena for the exercise and display of social power, and has overlooked the emotive significance of death (Tarlow 1999). Closer attention to the emotive qualities of mortuary rituals has led archaeologists to consider the role of remembrance in relation to death rituals.

The topic of memory has grown in significance in archaeology over the last decade (Bradley 2002; Van Dyke and Alcock 2003), while some attention has been paid to the role of memory in everyday contexts much of this literature has focused upon remembrance in mortuary contexts (Williams 2003). By considering the role of memory archaeologists are now paying more attention to the emotive role of mortuary rituals and are considering the social and emotive impact on prehistoric societies in more detail. In doing so they are gaining a closer knowledge, and writing richer accounts, of specific prehistoric societies.

In **Chapter 5 (a)** *Katina Lillios* provides an excellent overview of the recent literature on memory both in archaeology and cognate disciplines. She goes on to discuss the role of a class of artefacts – decorated slate plaques – from Neolithic and Chalcolithic (Copper Age) mortuary contexts in Portugal and Spain. She argues for a re-analysis of these objects in terms of their role as genealogical records. Her analysis shows that decoration on these objects is systematic, and is likely to constitute a record of the relationships between people buried in the communal *tholos* tombs of early prehistoric Iberia.

In an equally detailed account in **Chapter 5 (b)** *Bryan Hanks* discusses the role of remembrance in the representation of warrior identities in the later prehistoric sequence of Europe, and especially the *kurgan* burials of the later prehistoric Russian steppes. He analyzes the patterns and sequence of burial to argue for the central place that mortuary ritual plays, both in the expression of remembrance and the exercise of power.

Both Lillios and Hanks emphasize the importance of detailed contextual studies of both the structure and sequence of mortuary contexts, and the close analysis of the artefacts buried with the dead. These studies indicate that a discussion of memory is central to the proper analysis of mortuary archaeology and how critical the role of remembrance is to the negotiation of power in mortuary arenas.

REFERENCES

Barrett, J. C. 1996 The Living, the Dead and the Ancestors: Neolithic and Early Bronze Age Mortuary Practices. *In* Contemporary Archaeology in Theory: A Reader. R. W. Preucel and I. Hodder, eds. Pp. 394–412. Oxford: Blackwell.

Bradley, R. 2002 The Past in Prehistoric Societies. London: Routledge.

Parker Pearson, M. 1999 The Archaeology of Death and Burial. Stroud: Sutton.

Tarlow, S. 1999 Bereavement and Commemoration. Oxford: Blackwell.

Van Dyke, R., and S. Alcock 2003 Archaeologies of Memory. Oxford: Blackwell.

Williams, H. 2003 Archaeologies of Remembrance: Death and Memory in Past Societies. New York: Kluwer Academic/Plenum Press.

5 (a)
Engaging Memories of European Prehistory

Katina T. Lillios

Introduction

During the Neolithic of western Europe human groups engaged in a distinctive set of mnemonic practices that centred on funerary rituals performed at collective burial monuments. At these 'stages for the performance of ritual' (Barrett 1994) Neolithic peoples orchestrated their memories by manipulating objects, architecture, bodies, animals, and fire. The death of a person set in motion a series of decisions, negotiations, and rituals – the preparation of the body, the determination of the appropriate monument for burial, the selection of objects to be buried with the dead, and feasting. Some bodies went through further processing, such as defleshing, secondary burial, sorting of the skeletal elements, and burning. Throughout these rites, specialists or kin engaged with the dead in lengthy and intimate ways, provoking new memories, new acts of forgetting, and ultimately, new identities. The burial monuments themselves also had complex biographies. Burial structures were sometimes annexed, and elements of earlier monuments, such as menhirs, were sometimes incorporated. These mnemonic practices, in addition to having therapeutic properties, could also be used politically to create new pasts in accordance with changing visions of the present and future. The long histories of bodies, objects, and monuments of the Neolithic shaped the actions, beliefs, and identities of individuals and groups for hundreds of years, as they continue to do to this day.

The Seduction of Memory

The last few centuries of human existence have seen social cataclysms and upheavals on a monumental scale. The European colonial projects, slavery, world and civil wars, genocide, mass migration, and the creation of new nation-states have produced dislocations and disjunctures rarely experienced before in the history of humanity. In this historical context, memory has been deployed as an instrument of redemption, a therapeutic bridge and a weapon of repression (Climo and Cattell 2002; Fortier 2000; Hall 2001; Rappaport 1998; Saunders 2004; Shackel 2000; Watson 1994; Werbner 1998; Zerubavel 1995). The development of communication technologies has rendered these cataclysms not only the domains of those groups immediately involved but part of the collective history of our global community. The need for healing from these collective wounds as well as the opportunities afforded to individuals and groups within emerging power structures have fueled the academic interest in social memory (Zerubavel 2003:38). The apocalyptic anxieties of a new calendrical cycle – the turn of the millennial clock (Gould 1997) – have also, no doubt, contributed to the popular and scholarly concern with mnemonic bridging.

As memory transcends and fuses segmented social realities, so has memory studies brought diverse scholars, in an otherwise highly fractious and specialized professional landscape, together in 'a nonparadigmatic, transdisciplinary, centerless enterprise' (Olick and Robbins 1998:105). The relationship between the academic study of memory and collective memory is, thus, an intimate one. And because of this, a self-consciousness and reflexivity in the scholarly study of memory is imperative. For example, the particular flavour of memory conceived by scholars is a heavy memory, a memory redolent with grief, suffering and loss. Sometimes this memory takes a lighter form as nostalgia, longing or sentimentality (Lowenthal 1985; Stewart 1993). Whatever the flavour, memory is almost always construed as backward thinking, unrepeatable and linear. However, notions of time are dynamic and culturally relative (Dietler and Herbich 1993), and these are inextricably linked to how memory is structured and temporalized. For the Maori, for example, the past was viewed as before one, and they were said to face their ancestors (Thomas 1995:59). Furthermore, members of industrial societies often constitute memory as individually experienced and owned. Indeed, Sennett suggested that modern capitalism encourages people to view memory as private property, and when such memories are disturbing, they are often individually suffered and not shared collectively (Sennett 1998). Also, the memories observed and objectified are those constructed by a literate social group – academics – who place a high premium on literacy, often viewed as the material and superior counterpart of memory (Fuller 2001; Goody 1977; Ong 1982; Parry 1985). As Goody pointed out 'As members of a written culture we tend to read back our own memory procedures onto oral cultures. We look at oral cultures through literate eyes, whereas we need to look at orality from within' (Goody 1998:85). We might debate the inherent essentialism in Goody's admonition or our ability to look at 'orality from within', though his words caution us against intellectual complacency in our study of memory practices. Finally, and likely related to our privileging of literacy, our discussions of memory and material mnemonics often privilege the sense of vision in the creation of memories. Scholars refer to how ancient people's awareness of landscapes, colour, light, space or monuments provoked and constructed memories. If we are archaeologists, our livelihood depends on our ability to be productive while gazing at computer screens, reading books, examining artefacts, staring down microscopes and interpreting graphs. However, this development of our visual processing is perhaps done at the expense of recognizing the role of other bodily experiences and senses – touch, smell, sound, taste, movement and emotions – in eliciting and shaping memories, both in the past and in the present (Hamilakis et al. 2001; Meskell 1996; Seremetakis 1996).

Many archaeologists have, since the 1990s, devoted themselves to the study of memory and material mnemonics, particularly for the prehistoric record in Europe. Useful summaries are found in Holtorf (2000–4), Bradley (2002), Whittle (2003: Ch. 5), Van Dyke and Alcock (2003), Williams (2003), and Herzfeld (2003). As with historians, anthropologists, and art historians (Battaglia 1983; 1992; Bloch 1998; Climo and Cattell 2002; Connerton 1989; Fentress and Wickham 1992; Halbwachs 1980 [1951]; Hoskins 1998; Küchler 1988; Kwint et al. 1995; Nora 1989; 1996–8; Schama 1995; Yates 1966; Zerubavel 2003), archaeologists have worked to define, identify and classify mnemonic practices, to explore how memories are materialized, and to determine the agency of objects in constituting memory. The most recent work has centred on applying the notions of agency and practice of Bourdieu (1977), Giddens (1979; 1984), and Gell (1998) and the phenomenology of Heidegger (1971) towards apprehending the 'continuous and interactive process of engagement between person and world' (Jones 2004a:203). Some archaeologists are also considering the full range of bodily senses that can activate memory, such as colour and light (Bradley 1988; Jones 1999; 2004a and b; Jones and McGregor 2002), sound (Watson and Keating 1999), and texture (Cummings 2002).

A concern for memory and mnemonic practices in archaeology is related to and, in some cases, predicated on intellectual currents in the archaeological study of agency (Dobres and Robb 2002), time and biography (Bradley 1991; Gilchrist 2000; Gosden 1994; Gosden and Marshall 1999; Holtorf 1996; Lucas 2005; Robb 2002; Thomas 1996), personhood (Fowler 2004; Whittle 2003), and identity politics (Díaz-Andreu and Champion 1996; Jones 1997; Kohl and Fawcett 1995). The thousands of enduring and visible monuments of the Neolithic that are scattered throughout the countryside, some even preserved in the towns and cities of Europe, have also certainly shaped the importance of memory studies in European prehistory (Holtorf 2000–4).

The archaeological concern to identify 'the past in the past' – the search for instances of remembering and forgetting in ancient peoples – is, perhaps, the ultimate form of humanizing the past Other. To 21st-century Euro-Americans, memory is entangled in the construction of personhood. Those illnesses that compromise and ultimately dissolve memory, such as Alzheimer's, threaten a person's identity more so than most other physical ailments. Discerning the memory practices of our ancestors is perhaps the closest we will ever get to that ancient Other on the other side of the temporal glass. Whatever the motivation, the archaeological study of memory is a particularly poignant act. We seek to understand in the ancient Other precisely those actions to which we devote our lives: the imposition of order on the material traces of past lives. Memory is seductive, indeed.

Life and Death in Early Prehistoric Europe

There is a vast literature devoted to the Neolithic of Europe, and western Europe in particular (Barrett 1994; Bogucki 1988; Bradley 1998; Edmonds 1999; Hodder 1990; Price 2000; Richards 2003; Thomas 1991; Whittle 1989; 1996; 2003). I use the term Neolithic inclusively to cover the broad period during which human populations became fully sedentary and agricultural. Thus, it includes the period known as the Copper Age or Eneolithic in some regions. In this section, I provide a summary of the basic lifeways of these ancient peoples and outline in greater detail the evidence for the Iberian Peninsula. I highlight those aspects of cultural behaviour that are most relevant to contextualizing mnemonic practices, including population mobility, sociopolitical structures and economic life.

Between 6000–2000 BC, human populations in western Europe were engaged in a complex reorganization of their physical and social landscapes. Indigenous hunters and foragers during the Neolithic found themselves increasingly in contact with agricultural peoples, their crops (wheat, barley), animals (cattle, sheep, goat, pigs) and material culture (polished stone axes, ceramics). Immigrant groups of farmers found themselves dealing with new landscapes, peoples and resources (Gregg 1988). Throughout this period in Europe, human groups continued to hunt wild animals, such as rabbit, boar, ibex and red deer, to forage wild plants and to fish. While some encounters between foragers and farmers were likely productive and peaceful, involving the exchange of food, goods or marriage partners, others resulted in violent conflict (Keeley 1997).

Early Neolithic settlement occupations in western Europe vary markedly by region, reflecting different environmental constraints, building materials and social groupings (Darvill and Thomas 1996). Some of these sites are simple round or oval depressions in the soil or caves and rockshelters. Others appear to have been more permanently settled farmsteads and villages. In the late Neolithic, settlement aggregation sites emerged. Walls, palisades, towers and ditches enclosing settlements may have functioned as defence or as refuges for human groups, but they may also have served as corrals for animal domesticates or as symbolic markers of space and territory.

Scholars have been critical of the notion of a Neolithic package – the suite of domesticates, ceramics and sedentism that Childe (1952) and others used to characterize the revolutionary changes brought about by farming. In much of Europe, as Thomas (1991) argued, human groups continued to practise a foraging economy throughout much of the Neolithic and remained highly mobile. These people remained 'tethered but still often fluid and unstable' (Whittle 2003:40). Regular and extensive trade in polished stones, shells and ceramics also point to a high degree of mobility (Barnett 1990). Recent isotopic studies and AMS dates, however, challenge this gradualist model for much of northern Europe, and suggest that the adoption of agriculture may have been a much quicker process than previously imagined (Bonsall et al. 2002; Rowley-Conwy 2004; Schulting and Richards 2002).

Some of the tethers that bound Neolithic peoples to the landscape were, no doubt, the monuments they built to their collective dead. Sometimes they housed their dead in megalithic structures, such as long-barrows, dolmens and passage graves; sometimes they placed their dead in caves (natural and artificial) and rockshelters. Although collective burials are generally viewed as a distinctly Neolithic phenomenon, some Mesolithic peoples also buried their dead collectively (Cauwe 2001). In general, adult women and men, as well as children, were often buried together. At Fussell's Lodge long-barrow, in southern England, the bones of adult women and men, children and cattle were buried, with the remains of some individuals reordered or combined (Whittle 2003:34–5). Towards the end of the Neolithic and at the beginning of the Bronze Age, individual inhumations become increasingly common, though there is some reuse of Neolithic tombs, which I discuss further below.

The collective inhumations of the Neolithic are often thought to indicate a strong sense of corporate identity, at least at death. The segregation of bones by age and sex in many tombs, such as Fussell's Lodge and other sites (Shanks and Tilley 1982), suggest, however, that individual social distinctions during life may have been carried over and reproduced at death. Indeed, some archaeologists have argued that the corporate nature of megalithic tombs masked internal social conflict and competition (Chapman 1981). Certainly skeletal remains of the Neolithic bear witness to violent deaths, either as a result of ritual sacrifice or conflict, such as the mass grave at Roaix, France (Christensen 2004; Keeley 1996:38) and Talheim, Germany (Wahl and König 1987).

These behavioural changes that occurred between the earlier and later Neolithic can be broadly understood as a shift from an immediate to a delayed economy. Woodburn (1982) and Meillassoux (1972) developed these ideas through their ethnographic fieldwork in Africa. They posited that as human groups become increasingly reliant on plant and animal domesticates and less mobile, they become increasingly oriented to the future in order to manage these delayed-return economies. To ensure the successful continuation of this new mode of production and the systems of hierarchy that emerge, they become increasingly concerned with materializing and legitimating their ancestors, descent groups and genealogies in enduring forms. This model has guided many studies of the European Neolithic and even later periods such as the Iron Age (such as Arnold and Murray 2002; Bradley 2002; Chapman 1981; Edmonds 1999; Parker Pearson and Ramilisonina 1998; Tilley 1996). Recently, however, Whitley critiqued this 'obsession with ancestors' (Whitley 2002; see also responses in Pitts 2003 and Whitley 2003). Indeed the problem is part of a broader debate in anthropology on the universality (or not) of ancestor worship (Steadman et al. 1996). I take the view that all cultural groups have an interest in their origins, though not all individuals in these groups might share that interest. How ancestry and origins are defined, constructed and materialized, though, vary greatly and change over time. Indeed, the archaeological and ethnographic evidence suggest that material mnemonics become important symbolic capital used to manage production and reproduction during periods of crisis or profound social change (Lillios 1999).

The Neolithics of the Iberian Peninsula

Beginning in the 6th millennium BC, human groups living on the Iberian Peninsula underwent a series of social and economic transformations stimulated by the introduction of plant and animal domesticates (Arias 1999; Bernabeu Aubán and Orozco-Köhler 1999; Chapman 1990; Gilman and Thornes 1985; Jorge 1999; Kunst 2001) and marked archaeologically in some regions by the appearance of cardial shell-decorated ceramics. Whether these transformations occurred as a result of colonization by Mediterranean maritime peoples, the trade of foodstuffs without population movement or some combination of these processes is debated (Jackes et al. 1997; Peña-Chocarro et al. 2005; Richards 2003; Zilhão 1993; 2001). The speed of the uptake of domesticates is also disputed. Some scholars envision a long and gradual integration of domesticates by hunting and foraging peoples, lasting around 1,000 years. Zilhão has argued, however, that if only radiocarbon dates on short-life samples for Early Neolithic sites are taken into account, this uptake actually took no more than six generations, and thus was a fairly rapid process (Zilhão 2001).

As with much of Western Europe, settlement evidence for the earliest farming populations is rather sparse on the Iberian Peninsula. Recent excavations of open air and cave sites are, however, increasing this number. These include Vale Pincel I (Silva and Soares 1981), Caldeirão (Zilhão 1992), Laranjal de Cabeço das Pias (Carvalho and Zilhão 1994), São Pedro de Canaferrim (Simões 1999), and Valada do Mato, in Portugal (Diniz 2001) and La Lámpara and La Revilla del Campo in Spain (Michael Kunst, personal communication).

Although the precise dates are still unclear, it appears that some hundreds of years following the earliest appearance of domesticates, human groups began to construct megalithic tombs to bury their dead (Leisner 1965; 1998; Leisner and Leisner 1943; 1951; 1956; 1959). As in earlier periods, they also used caves and rockshelters. Some of the earliest of these megalithic burials, such as Poço da Gateira in Portugal, were individual inhumations. These tombs, as well as some of the settlements of the period, such as Valada do Mato (Diniz 2001) and Xarez 12 (Gonçalves 1999a:39–40), were found with material culture typically associated with hunting and foraging peoples, such as microliths. This has led some archaeologists to argue that indigenous foraging communities built the first megaliths (Leisner and Leisner 1951). One might also propose, however, that 'immigrant' farming groups acquired or reproduced some of these local goods as a way to demonstrate affiliation with the 'natives' and to legitimate their claim to land and space. As always, it is dangerous to equate material culture with peoples.

While during the Neolithic animal herding and agriculture were practised in many enclaves of the Peninsula, particularly those not occupied by hunters and foragers, it was not until the later Neolithic that a fully agricultural and sedentary lifestyle was established. Groups farmed wheat and barley, and supplemented their agricultural base by herding sheep, goat, cattle and pigs, hunting wild game (such as boar and deer), gathering wild plants and plant products (such as acorns), fishing and collecting shellfish, particularly along the Atlantic and Mediterranean coasts. Harrison (1985) argued that during the later Neolithic, Iberia underwent a Secondary Products Revolution, as did other regions of prehistoric Europe. Animal domesticates began to be used for their secondary products (dairy products, traction, transportation), and viticulture and woodland management were carried out.

During the later Neolithic, human groups occupied caves, rockshelters and open-air sites, particularly on hilltops at the confluence of rivers. Some of these hilltop sites were walled and had circular/semi-circular towers or bastions built into their walls. These sites include Zambujal (Sangmeister and Schubart 1981) and Leceia in Portugal (Cardoso 1997), and Almizaraque (Delibes et al. 1986) and Terrera Ventura (Gusi 1986) in Spain. Most settlements are about 1 hectare, with population estimates ranging from a dozen to over 1,000 individuals. There are, however, larger sites, such as Los Millares in Spain (5 ha), and some exceptionally large sites, many along the Guadiana River. These include Perdigões in Portugal (16 ha) (Lago et al. 1998), San Blas in Spain (30 ha) (Hurtado 2004), Ferreira do Alentejo in Portugal (50 ha) (Arnaud 1993), La Pijotilla in Spain (80 ha) (Hurtado 1986), and Marroquíes Bajos in Spain (113 ha) (Zafra et al. 1999). Díaz-del-Río (2004) hypothesized that these sites' variability might be explained by their different histories of fusion/fission cycles that characterize segmentary societies. Other scholars have begun to question the monolithic designation of these sites as settlements and suggest that their symbolic and phenomenological qualities be addressed, such as how they structured vision and visibility, constrained human actions and delimited space (Jorge 2003).

Although the exact evolutionary sequence is still disputed, it appears that over the course of the 4th and 3rd millennium BC Neolithic peoples in the Iberian Peninsula buried their dead collectively in rock-cut tombs, corbel-vaulted tombs (or tholoi), and passage graves. Hundreds of these tombs dot the Portuguese and Spanish countryside, though their largest concentrations are in the northwestern and southern regions of the peninsula. Some regions are so densely filled with these tombs – such as the Alentejo province of southern Portugal – that archaeologists have traditionally viewed them as landscapes to the dead or ancestral geographies. Nonetheless, recent research has indicated that residential occupations are sometimes associated with these burials or are within a few kilometres distance (Boaventura 2001; Gonçalves 2000). Thus, the activities of the living were often spatially integrated with the remains of the dead. These later tombs, unlike earlier tombs, generally had passages that allowed for repeated access to the dead. Bradley (1998) has termed these 'open graves', and suggested the construction of these monuments signals a change towards ancestor worship and was linked to the beginnings of agropastoralism. Such a model is consistent with the ideas of Meillassoux and Woodburn and may be broadly correct, but as Jorge (1999:64) noted, the empirical evidence is lacking in Portugal.

Funerary rites during the later Neolithic of Iberia included both primary burials and the secondary treatment of the corpse (Gonçalves 1999a and b). In the case of secondary burials, clusters of bone groups, such as crania or long bones, were buried together. At the passage grave of Perdigões, in Portugal, cranial bones were generally found along the walls of the chamber (Lago et al. 1998:79). The bones and artefacts found with these dead are sometimes coloured with ochre. Fires were sometimes also set within the tomb chamber, probably to purify the interior of the tomb (Rojo-Guerra and Kunst 2002). Offerings were placed with the deceased, some of which were especially made to accompany the dead. These included polished stone axes and adzes (which are regularly found unused), flint blades, arrowheads, stone beads, undecorated globular ceramics, and plaques made of slate, schist and sandstone. These plaques, sometimes found on the body of the dead and engraved with geometric designs and anthropo-/zoomorphic imagery, have long intrigued archaeologists, who have generally interpreted them as Mother Goddess figures (Gonçalves 1999a). Based on analyses of over 1,100 plaques in the Engraved Stone Plaque Registry and Inquiry Tool (ESPRIT) (Lillios 2004a), there is compelling evidence to suggest that the plaques may, in fact, have functioned as mnemonics of lineage histories (Lillios 2002; 2003; 2004b). In this light, the tombs in which they are housed may also be viewed as memory archives or sites of memory storage (Hendon 2000).

The variability in tomb types, the size, location and visibility of these tombs, the number of individuals buried within them and the quantity and quality of goods found with these individuals all suggest that later Neolithic societies differentiated their members. For example, those individuals buried within some of the larger megaliths, such as the Anta Grande do Zambujeiro, in Portugal (Kalb 1981; Silva and Parreira 1990), with its 6-metre-high orthostats, were likely of a higher status than those housed in smaller megaliths. At the megalithic cemetery/settlement site of Los Millares, Spain, the tombs with the highest proportion of prestige goods were located closest to the settlement (Chapman 1990).

There is both direct and indirect evidence for violent conflict during the Iberian Copper Age (Kunst 2000). The construction of elaborate systems of fortification with bastions, sometimes involving multiple lines of dry-stone walls (such as at Los Millares and Zambujal), suggests there was a need for defence and heightened political tensions. Weaponry, such as copper daggers, as well as painted images of armed people in caves, are also suggestive of militarism. More direct evidence of violent conflict has been found in the burials at the Hipogeo de Longar and at San Juan ante Portam Latinam in Spain. At the Hipogeo de Longar, a tomb in which at least 112 individuals of different ages and sexes were buried with few grave goods, four individuals were found with arrowheads embedded in their skeletons. At San Juan ante Portam Latinam, 289 individuals were discovered, and nine had arrowheads in them.

At the end of the later Neolithic in Iberia, many settlements were abandoned. The causes of these discontinuities are unclear, but they may be related to climatic and environmental change, social conflict, and/or a realignment of the political order (Lillios 1993). Individual burials became the new norm, perhaps reflecting a new social order in which the memory of individuals took precedence over the memory of groups.

Traces of Memory in the European Past

Memory is a material reality as well as a social practice. That is, the evocation of past behaviours and the construction of individual and collective memories involve social and psychological needs. But these evocations require and generate the stimulation of the bodily senses and, often, the use of material culture. Thus, archaeologists do have access to traces of some mnemonic practices. For archaeologists to invoke memory, two conditions are generally satisfied. First, there is an indication of sequential behaviour; that is, first A, then B. Furthermore, there is usually the demonstration that A was still visible when B occurred (Blake 2003:94; Hingley 1996:232–3). In addition to these two conditions, archaeologists often attempt to demonstrate that there was no 'rational, economic, practical' reason for these behaviours (Hingley 1996:232). By eliminating such materialist conditions, idealist explanations, such as memory, are then to be inferred. What makes any case compelling is a patterning and regularity in the kinds of objects that are heirloomed, the kinds of landscapes that appear to be mimicked, and the kinds of monuments that are reused.

In this section, I examine the archaeological evidence for mnemonic practices in the Neolithic of western Europe. I discuss some of the better-known examples from northern and central Europe, and then present in more detail case studies from the Iberian Peninsula. Because of the nature of memory studies, which transcend traditional chronological boundaries, I also consider later practices that involve Neolithic sites or objects. For the Neolithic of western Europe, broadly defined, these practices are of four types.

1. Reuse and/or transformation of burial monuments
2. Curation of artefacts and human remains
3. Inscriptive recording
4. Mimesis

In this discussion, I also explore some of the possible performative, phenomenological qualities of these practices. Which bodily senses were stimulated in the creation, engagement or experience of these mnemonics? Who engaged in the creation of these objects or in the orchestration of these mnemonic practices? Who was the intended audience? What was the level of agency and intentionality suggested by these practices? What kinds of intended and unintended consequences or structuring qualities did these practices elicit?

Reuse and/or Transformation of Burial Monuments

The continued reuse or transformation of funerary structures for sometimes hundreds of years practically defines the European Neolithic. Studies of the collective nature of death at this time, and the multiplicity of bodies in a shared and confined space, have long played a central role in European prehistory. Perhaps in contrast to the funerary rituals of the highly individualistic societies that archaeologists come from, attentive to maintaining the discreteness of bodies at death, Neolithic practices with their jumbling, sorting and removal of human bones come as a bit of a shock.

The long histories of use and rebuilding of Neolithic tombs and monuments are widely attested. Stonehenge is the most famous example, with a long biography extending from the Neolithic through the Early Bronze Age (3100–1600 BC) (Cleal et al. 1995). Indeed, some archaeologists would argue that the life of Stonehenge continues to this day, as archaeologists, neo-pagans, English Heritage officials and local landowners contest their claims to the proper use of the Stonehenge landscape (Bender 1998; Holtorf 2005). The complex histories of the sites of Petit Chasseur in the southern Alps (Bradley 2002; Gallay 1995), Balnuaran of Clava in Scotland (Bradley 2000a; 2002), Aosta in Italy (Bradley 2002; Mezzena 1998), and megalithic sites in Mecklenburg-Vorpommern, Germany (Holtorf 2000–4), serve as powerful testimonies of the longevity and dynamism of Neolithic monuments. In Brittany, prehistorians have long noted that portions of menhirs were often reused, covered or concealed in the building of megalithic monuments (Bradley 2002; Cassen 2000; Giot 1987). One of the most compelling cases is the discovery of two conjoining fragments of a carved stone found 3 kilometres apart, one at the passage grave La Table des Marchand and the other at the chambered tomb at Gavrinis.

During the Iron Age of Scotland, Neolithic tombs were visited and explored, as Iron Age pottery in these tombs attests (Hingley 1996). These later activities do not appear to be the result of long-term occupation, given the lack of hearths associated with these remains. It is unclear, however, whether Iron Age peoples engaged in feasting, disposal of household goods or short-term occupation at these Neolithic sites. In some cases, whatever Neolithic remains were in tomb were removed (Hingley 1996:232). Sometimes the tomb was also altered and rebuilt; sometimes it was used as a house. This close association between Iron Age peoples and Neolithic material culture has been suggested as the basis for the use of Neolithic decorative motifs (lattice, herringbone, etc.) on Iron Age ceramics (Hingley 1996:240).

In the Iberian Peninsula, as in other regions of Europe, megaliths also have long biographies, some still continuing their 'useful' lives in recent times as Christian chapels (São Dinis and São Brissos, in Portugal for example), pig sties, chicken coops (Leisner and Leisner 1959:167, 319–20), and as sites inspiring discussions of monument life-histories (Holtorf 2002). In central and northwestern Iberia, megaliths are regularly found with Early Bronze Age deposits. At the Anta 2 do Couto da Espanhola in Portugal, later Neolithic and Bronze Age artefacts attest to such an enduring use (Cardoso et al. 2000). Similarly, menhir fragments were sometimes incorporated in passage graves, as at Vale de Rodrigo 2 (Larsson 2001). The building of annexes is another feature of Iberian megalithic sites. The sites of Comenda 2 and Farisoa 1, Portugal, each began as a passage grave and later had a tholos annexed (Gonçalves 1999a:18–19; Leisner and Leisner 1951:Est. X and XIV) (Figures 5.1a and 5.1b). At the burial complex of Olival da Pega 2 (OP2), Gonçalves documented such a series of rebuildings (Gonçalves 1999a:90–111). The first monument constructed was a large passage grave (OP2a), with 16 metres of its corridor preserved. After OP2a was built, the tholos OP2b was annexed. In the construction of OP2b, changes and the removal of stones from the original passage grave were made, presumably to facilitate access. Following this, another tholos, OP2d, was added to the other side of the passage of OP2, and a microtholos, OP2e, was annexed to OP2d. The final funerary deposit of the complex (OP2c) was placed to the exterior of the complex.

It is also important to note that OP2 is located just 300 metres from Olival da Pega 1, one of the largest megalithic tombs in Iberia (Leisner and Leisner 1951:252). Its main chamber is 4 × 5.6 metres in diameter, the tallest stela in its chamber is

(a)

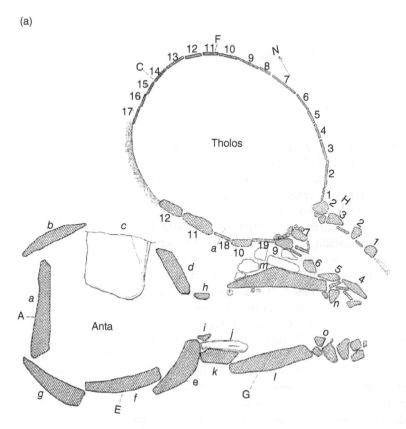

Figure 5.1 Dynamic Monuments: (a) Farisoa (Anta I and Tholos) (Leisner and Leisner 1951:Est. XIV); (b) Comenda (Anta 2 and Tholos) (Leisner and Leisner 1951:Est. X)

(b)

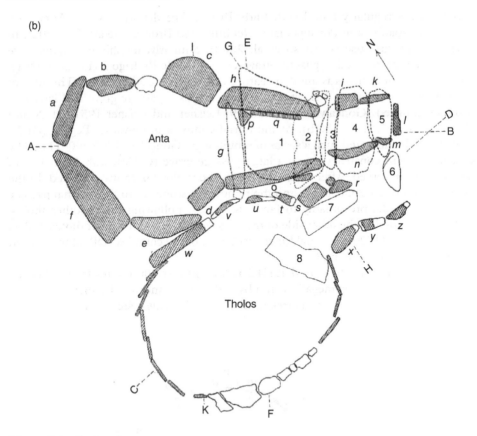

Figure 5.1 *Continued*

4.4 metres high, and its corridor was at least 8.6 metres long. Many individuals were found with 134 slate plaques and other artefacts (Gonçalves 1999a; Leisner and Leisner 1951:236–52). What is the relationship between these two tombs? What would precipitate the creation of one tomb so close to another? One possible interpretation is that new tombs were constructed 'in response to competition, opportunity, or the increasing tenuousness of ancestral ties' (Bloch 1971).

Another compelling case for the enduring memory of space is found at Escoural in Portugal (Araújo and Lejeune 1995; Silva and Araújo 1995). Its long history is likely due, at least in part, to it being an unusual feature in the landscape (Bradley 2000b). Although situated in a granitic landscape, Escoural is a limestone cave formed owing to unusual metamorphic and crystallization processes. Within the 30 chambers of the cave are remains of human use spanning nearly 50,000 years. The earliest use dates to the Middle Palaeolithic. During the Upper Palaeolithic, human groups painted and engraved the interior of the cave with bovids and horses. In the Early Neolithic, people buried some of their dead in the cave. Then, by the later Neolithic, the cave was sealed, a large tholos was constructed some 600 metres outside the cave, and a fortified settlement established immediately on the hillock over the cave. No later Neolithic materials have been found inside the cave.

How might we interpret this sequence of behaviours at Escoural? Some scholars have argued that 'foreign' colonizers established the later Neolithic settlement on the cave site in an act of symbolic desecration and violent forgetting (Gomes et al. 1983–4). Such an interpretation may, however, be more reflective of contemporary sensibilities about the treatment of the past and the dead. We avoid building over cemeteries and stepping on graves. We also know all too well about the establishment of Christian altars, shrines and churches over indigenous monuments and shrines, most in flagrant and violent acts of cultural erasure associated with colonialism. But, in the case of the later Neolithic of the Iberian Peninsula there is no evidence for large-scale colonization. We might, therefore, also consider an alternate interpretation. If great power was derived from this space, we could also imagine there was a conscious desire to appropriate the power of such an anomalous, ancient and possibly dangerous spot for the living. This seems consistent with another important fact. The tholos of Escoural has the largest number of slate plaques found anywhere in the Iberian Peninsula, with 167 (Santos and Ferreira 1969). Perhaps Late Neolithic people believed this massive cave, this odd feature in the landscape, to be an *axis mundi* (Eliade 1954), a place of orientation and communication between the land of the dead and the living, as caves so often are (Brady and Prufer 2005). Perhaps its force was so great that they sealed the cave to harness its power and protect themselves from it, securing the power they may have derived from it.

The Curation of Artefacts and Human Remains

This class of mnemonics includes portable objects that were curated or recycled over multiple generations. As with the reuse of architectural features, archaeologists often demonstrate that the functional qualities of the object were outlived, and thus the only possible reason for the object's circulation was its symbolic qualities. Patterned biographies also serve as clues to whether a class of object was perceived as a special class of heirloom. For example, Kristiansen compared two classes of Early Bronze Age swords of Denmark and determined that their biographies were significantly different. Flange-hilted swords had clear traces of wear and re-sharpening, whereas the full-hilted swords did not and were interpreted as regalia (Kristiansen 1984 in Bradley 2002:54–5). Determining whether an object is continuously used or circulated or whether it was discovered and then curated is certainly a challenge (Bradley 2002:53), but minimally requires the use of a biographical approach (Kopytoff 1986) and good temporal control. Curated objects during the Neolithic of Europe include stone tools, ceramics and human remains.

Skeates suggested that stone axe amulets from later Neolithic sites in mainland Italy, Malta, Sicily and Sardinia were heirlooms (Skeates 1995). Some appear to have begun their lives as larger functional objects, such as adzes, and that, over time, those made of distinctive stones or associated with ancestors of note were transformed by further polishing and perforation and made into pendants. Cleal argued that Grooved Wear ceramics of the later Neolithic of Britain also had long biographies. Compared to other ceramics of the period, Grooved Wear pots had four times the incidence of repair and many that were repaired were formally deposited at henges, suggestive of their distinctive biographies (Cleal 1988).

The engraved slate plaques were also recycled. Over 30 recycled plaques have been found in tombs, and they occur as plaque fragments that were re-polished on their broken edge, re-perforated, or re-engraved on their obverse side (Gonçalves et al. 2003; Lillios 2002:138–9; 2004a) (Figure. 5.2). Plaque recycling may

Figure 5.2   Recycled plaques: (a) Olival da Pega (Leisner and Leisner 1951:Est. XXVIII, 31); (b) Comenda da Igreja, obverse and reverse (Leisner and Leisner 1959:tab. 27, 1, 78); (c) Ribeira de Oliveiras (Leisner and Leisner 1959:tab. 34, 9, 2); (d) Carvão (Leisner and Leisner 1959:tab. 34, 6, 4); (e) Antões 3 (Leisner and Leisner 1959:tab. 19, 3, 9); (f) Alcogulo 3 (Leisner and Leisner 1959:tab. 3, 3, 2); (g) Folha das Barradas (Leisner 1965:tab. 34, 3); (h) Monte Abraão (Leisner 1965: tab. 56, 100); (i) Palmela (Leisner 1965:tab. 111, 43); (j) Alcanena (Correia 1921:fig. 28); (k) Lapa do Bugio (Cardoso 1992:Est. 15, 16)

represent curio collecting, a fairly innocent reuse of an object that caught a visitor's eye. However, given the monumentality of megalithic spaces and the density of objects and human remains, this innocence seems unlikely for most recycled plaques. Rather, these cases suggest the appropriation and/or the resistance of the power of an individual formerly associated with a plaque. Thus, they may speak to acts that transformed an inalienable possession to an alienable possession, or 'defeats of hierarchy' (Mills 2004; Weiner 1992). That these recycled plaques are relatively rare,

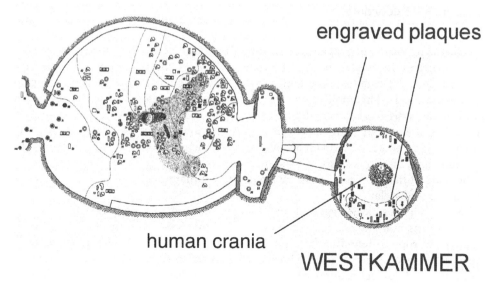

engraved plaques

human crania

WESTKAMMER

Figure 5.3 Praia das Maçãs, Portugal. Slate plaques and group of crania in Westkammer (From Leisner et al. 1969:pl. B.)

despite the fact that tombs were regularly revisited, may also speak to the perceived potency of the objects.

Another set of objects that were likely to have been curated or circulated are cranial discs (rounded pieces of human cranial bones). These have been found at a number of megalithic sites in Europe, such as the Coizard hypogea in the Marne (Mohen 1990:229). Found with these amulets were trepanned human skulls, the possible 'sources' of these amulets. Trepanation was also practised among Neolithic peoples of the Iberian Peninsula. Cranial disks were found at Olival da Pega 1 and 2 (Gonçalves 1999a), and trepanned skulls were found at the sites of Casa da Moura, Furninha (Cardoso 2002:218; Delgado 1880), and Pedrinha (Gama and Cunha 2003), and in Spain at Ciempozuelos (Liesau von Lettow-Vorbeck and Pastor Abascal 2003). The deposition of cranial discs in burials suggests that trepanning was not always a clinical practice, but may have been associated with the production of ancestral relics (Arnott et al. 2003; Piggott 1940). Direct dating of the discs as well as their associated skulls, both trepanned and not, would determine whether these were curated objects or heirlooms. The mobility of human skeletal remains in the Iberian Neolithic attests to the potency of the human body and particularly the skull. This practice is consistent with the separation of skulls in mortuary contexts, as noted earlier. A particularly illustrative example of a skull group was found in the western chamber (Westkammer) at the artificial cave of Praia das Maçãs, near Lisbon, Portugal (Leisner et al. 1965) (Figure 5.3). Interestingly, the engraved slate plaques from this site were all found in this chamber, which was also the oldest section of the tomb. The chronological and spatial organization of the site strongly suggest that the Westkammer was a focal space, and that the engraved plaques were important materializations of ancestral skulls, or at least were closely associated to those individuals.

Inscriptive Recording

While the recording of genealogies, histories, myths and other narratives in materialized forms undoubtedly involve the highest level of intentionality, they are also
nevertheless difficult to prove and even more challenging to ascribe meaning to
(Houston 2004). The application of semiotics, the investigation of *chaîne opératoires*
and the analysis of sketches, drafts, corrections and errors in a large data set can
provide some guidance. In ancient times, the manufacture of such records probably
involved a small set of individuals, and their audience was likely also restricted to
an elite class of religious specialists, members of a sodality or another elite group.
The scale of these objects might be small and intimate or they might be public, as
in the case of stelai.

Some scholars have suggested that the common motifs found on stelai and portable objects point to the existence of a megalithic 'code' during the Neolithic of
western Europe (Bueno Ramírez and Balbín Behrmann 1998). While some relatively
fixed set of meanings may indeed have been involved in such objects, we are on more
solid methodological ground when we focus on a discreet set of objects within a
particular region. Again, I wish to return to the engraved plaques of the Iberian
Peninsula and, in particular, the Classic plaques (also known in the literature as the
geometric plaques). This plaque type is the most abundant and extensively distributed plaque type. Nearly 70 per cent plaques of the catalogued plaques in ESPRIT
are Classic, and they have been found in tombs from the west coast of Portugal to
southwestern Spain (Lillios 2004a and b). What is most striking about these plaques
is their conservative compositional grammar. They are divided into two design fields:
a narrower one-third (top) and a wider bottom two-thirds (base). Separating the top
and base is either a single horizontal line or single or multiple horizontal bands. The
base is where the decorative elements are concentrated, and one or more of six
repeating geometric motifs or vertical or horizontal registers are found here: checkerboard, vertical bands, triangles, chevrons, herringbones and zigzags. The most
common motifs are triangles (68%). In contrast to their compositional conservatism,
the Classic plaques vary greatly in engraving styles, suggesting that many individuals
using a shared design template were involved in their production.

When the plaques are examined for evidence of design regularities (e.g., regular
spacing of registers and design motifs), some plaques show attempts to 'squeeze in'
registers. These 'squeezed in' registers are smaller in their spacing or in the straight-
ness of their lines, or were drawn after the other registers, as suggested by a different
technique or engraving style (Lillios 2004a:cat. nos. 36, 205, 33, 603, for example).
On other plaques, the opposite situation is suggested; there was ample room to create
an additional register, but this was not done (Lillios 2004a:cat. nos. 43, 103, 264,
487, for example). There are also plaques with preliminary sketches on one side and
a completed design on the other, such as the stunning example from Dolmen das
Conchadas, in Portugal. This plaque has an unfinished sketch with four horizontal
lines on one side, while the other side has a finished drawing of a Classic plaque with
three registers (Figure 5.4). Qualitative evidence such as this strongly suggests that
the number of registers was a key feature of the plaques' design.

When the plaques are analyzed by their provenance and compared regionally,
other intriguing patterns emerge. First, most plaques are found in sequences. That
is, plaques generally occur in series by motifs and numbers of registers – such as

(a)   (b)

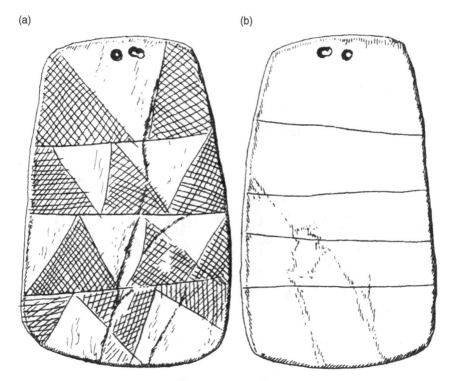

Figure 5.4 Dolmen das Conchadas, Portugal: (a) obverse; and (b) reverse (Leisner and Leisner 1965:tab. 27, 64)

the sequence of two-, three-, four-, and five-registered triangle plaques. Although there are sequences among the chevron, zigzag and checkerboard plaques, these continuities are most common among the triangle plaques (Figure 5.5A–M).

This combination of evidence – in the plaques' *chaîne opératoires*, formal structure, distribution and close association with individuals suggest they recorded something about the social identity of the deceased. I have hypothesized that the number of design registers recorded the number of generations that separated the deceased from a founding ancestor (Lillios 2002; 2003; 2004b). Thus, a person buried with a four-registered triangle plaque was four generations removed from an important founding ancestor of the 'triangle' clan. Clearly, this model is a first approximation of what was likely a more complex recording system, which will hopefully be refined and tested with DNA studies. Given that the plaques tend to be found in passage graves or other open graves, and thus were revisited, it seems quite plausible that, whatever their precise meaning, they were meant to be consulted by later peoples for important decisions, such as who had the right to be buried in the tomb.

Mimesis

Finally, I would like to briefly discuss a class of behaviours known as mimesis, or imitation. These are materialized behaviours that cite or reference imagery from the

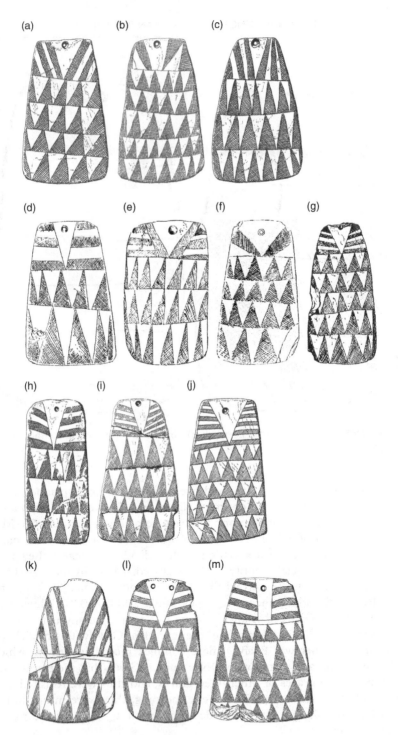

Figure 5.5 Plaque sequences: (a) Leisner 1965:tab. 39, 109; (b) Leisner 1965:tab. 39, 112; (c) Leisner 1965:tab. 39, 115; (d) Santos and Ferreira 1969:fig. 6; (e) Santos and Ferreira 1969:fig. 7, 73; (f) Santos and Ferreira 1969:fig. 7, 71; (g) Santos and Ferreira 1969:fig. 6, 65; (h) Leisner 1965:tab. 27, 69; (i) Leisner 1965: tab. 27, 66; (j) Leisner 1965: tab. 27, 67; (k) Almagro Basch 1961–2:fig. 17; (l) Almagro Basch 1961–2:fig. 8; (m) Almagro Basch 1961–2:fig. 5

natural or cultural landscape in new media. Indeed, some of these behaviours challenge the notion of universal boundaries separating the natural and the cultural. They also point to the agency and apotropaic qualities of material world and art (Boric 2003; Gell 1998). These cases are perhaps the most difficult to demonstrate, as the level of intentionality and degree to which the behaviour was conscious can always be disputed. I consider three categories of such behaviour: architecture referencing landscapes, architecture copying earlier architecture and material culture evoking other material culture in new media (media transferral or skeuomorphs).

In the first case, of architecture emulating landscapes, there are examples from different regions and phases of the Neolithic. Boric suggested that the trapezoidal houses at Lepenski Vir, in southeast Europe, mnemonically evoked the Treskavac Mountain on the other side of the Danube, facing the site (Boric 2003). In this mimesis, the houses acquired the power of the mountain. Similarly Tilley (1996) argued that the portal dolmens of Bodmin Moor in Britain mimicked the granitic tors of the surrounding landscape.

The regular orientation of structures has also been suggested as a kind of mnemonic referencing. Bradley noted that early Neolithic houses of central Europe were regularly oriented to the east. Not finding a good functional reason for such an orientation, he suggested that these early farming peoples built their houses oriented to their place of origins (Bradley 2001). Similarly, throughout the Neolithic of the west Mediterranean, megaliths have been shown to be regularly oriented to the east, at approximately the axis of the midwinter sunrise (Hoskin 2001). However, megalithic tombs on the Balearic Islands tend to face the west. Bradley's model of ancestral origins seems to find some support in the anomalous data for the Balearics, as people would have likely populated the islands from the Iberian mainland to the west.

A second class of mnemonic behaviours is suggested by architectural mimesis. Bradley and others suggest that the later Neolithic long mounds and enclosures of central and western Europe imitate the form of, and sometimes were even built over, early Neolithic longhouses (Bradley 1998; 2002). In Portugal, later Neolithic populations constructed megalithic burials – dolmens – using the locally available stone, limestone (Leisner 1965) – with the same architectonic plan as the Alentejo megaliths (Rui Boaventura, personal communication). What is intriguing about this practice of dolmen construction in the Lisbon Peninsula is that there were ample 'natural' spaces in which it would have been easier to bury the dead, such as caves and rockshelters, and indeed these were sometimes used. Might immigrants from the Alentejo have built these dolmens to reproduce their ancestral architecture? One might also imagine nouveau-elites of the Lisbon area built these tombs in a strategy to appropriate the status of an 'exotic' and 'archaic' architectural style.

Media transference or skeuomorphs are another form of mnemonic behaviour. The classic examples are the Danish daggers mimicking in flint the more prestigious and less accessible bronze daggers, down to the stitching of the leather handle-coverings (Stafford 1998). Harrison also suggested that Beaker ceramics exemplified the transferral of textile weaves onto the ceramic medium (Harrison 1974:105).

In the Iberian Peninsula, the formal similarities between the engraved plaques and Neolithic polished stone axes have occasionally been noted (Leisner and Leisner 1951). They are roughly the same colour – both dark grey/black – the same size –

that of a human hand – and the same form – trapezoidal or rectangular. Polished stone tools predate the use of slate plaques but continued to be used at the same time as the plaques. Their raw materials, amphibolite and slate, are sourced to the same region, the Alentejo of Portugal. And, experimental studies have shown that the technology and physical actions required to make a slate plaque are nearly identical to manufacturing a polished stone tool, although making an engraved plaque takes far less time (Woods and Lillios in press). I suggest that the plaques referenced axes, which were potent visual metaphors for these Neolithic peoples, as they were throughout western Europe (Edmonds 1995; Skeates 2002; Tilley 1999). A plaque evoked 'axe-ness', with its power to transform a forest into a field, to transform nature into culture and to transform a live and threatening enemy into a dead and safe enemy. An axe evoked strength and durability. An axe was a tool essential in the construction of social and cultural personhood. Axes made one human. An object made of slate in the form of an axe offered a rich potential for inscribing and materializing a suite of qualities and information relating to the durability or identity of an individual or group. A slate plaque may have been the ideal symbolic palette for creating enduring memories in ancient Iberia.

Conclusions and the Futures of Memory

Human groups during the Neolithic of Europe were involved in complex transformations of their social, physical and cognitive world. They explored new landscapes, interacted with new people, engaged with new plants and animals, lived in new kinds of houses and communities and related to their dead in new ways. If current dates for the shift to an agricultural lifestyle are correct for Europe, these transformations might have taken place over only six generations. And, given that it is likely that three generations were alive at a given time, these changes would have been quite perceptible. The shock of the new could well have instigated profound changes to mnemonic practices. The archaeology of Neolithic Europe suggests such transformations, in the reuse of sacred objects, the circulation of the remains of the dead, the mimesis of ancestral landscapes and rituals that brought the living and dead together in liminal spaces that both ordered and transcended time, by mobilizing 'deep time' (Boric 2003). There is indeed something almost obsessive about the repetitive and iterative qualities of the memory practices of Neolithic peoples. Perhaps they, like us, felt a collective anxiety about what the future might hold.

REFERENCES

Almagro Basch, M. 1961–2 Un ajuar dolménico excepcional procedente de la Granja de Céspedes de Badajoz. *In* Homenaje a C. Mergelina. Pp. 35–82. Murcia: Universidad de Murcia.

Araújo, A. C., and M. Lejeune 1995 Gruta do Escoural: Necrópole Neolítica e Arte Rupestre Paleolítica. Lisbon: Instituto Português do Património Arquitectónico e Arqueológico.

Arias, P. 1999 The Origins of the Neolithic along the Atlantic Coast of Continental Europe: A Survey. Journal of World Prehistory 13(4):403–64.

Arnaud, J. 1993 O povoado calcolítico de Porto Torrão (Ferreira do Alentejo): síntese das investigações realizadas. Vipasca. Arqueologia e Historia 2:41–60.

Arnold, B., and M. L. Murray 2002 A Landscape of Ancestors in Southwest Germany. Antiquity 76(292):321–2.

Arnott, R., S. Finger, and C. U. M. Smith, eds. 2003 Trepanation. History, Discovery, Theory. Lisse, The Netherlands: Swets and Zeitlinger.

Barnett, W. K. 1990 Small-Scale Transport of Early Neolithic Pottery in the West Mediterranean. Antiquity 64(245):859–65.

Barrett, J. C. 1994 Fragments from Antiquity: An Archaeology of Social Life in Britain, 2900–1200 BC. Oxford: Blackwell.

Battaglia, D. 1983 Projecting Personhood in Melanesia: The Dialectics of Artefact Symbolism on Sabarl Island Society. Man 18:289–304.

Battaglia, D. 1992 The Body in the Gift: Memory and Forgetting in Sabarl Mortuary Exchange. American Ethnologist 19(1):3–18.

Bender, B. 1998 Stonehenge: Making Space. Oxford: Berg.

Bernabeu-Aubán, J., and T. Orozco-Köhler, eds. 1999 Actes del II Congrés del Neolític a la Península Ibèrica. València: Universitat de València.

Blake, E. 2003 The Familiar Honeycomb: Byzantine Era Reuse of Sicily's Prehistoric Rock-Cut Tombs. In Archaeologies of Memory. R. Van Dyke and S. Alcock, eds. Pp. 203–20. Oxford: Blackwell.

Bloch, M. 1971 Placing the Dead: Tombs, Ancestral Villages, and Kinship Organization in Madagascar. London: Seminar Press.

Bloch, M. 1998 How We Think They Think: Anthropological Approaches to Cognition, Memory, and Literacy. Boulder, CO: Westview Press.

Boaventura, R. 2001 O Sítio Calcolítico do Pombal (Monforte). Lisbon: Instituto Português de Arqueologia.

Bogucki, P. 1988 Forest Farmers and Stockherders. Cambridge: Cambridge University Press.

Bonsall, C., M. G. Macklin, D. E. Anderson, and R. W. Payton 2002 Climate Change and the Adoption of Agriculture in North-West Europe. European Journal of Archaeology 5(1):9–23.

Boric, D. 2003 'Deep Time' Metaphor: Mnemonic and Apotropaic Practices at Lepenski Vir. Journal of Social Archaeology 3(1):46–74.

Bourdieu, P. 1977 Outline of a Theory of Practice. Cambridge: Cambridge University Press.

Bradley, R. 1988 Darkness and Light in the Design of Megalithic Tombs. Oxford Journal of Archaeology 8:251–9.

Bradley, R. 1991 Ritual, Time and History. World Archaeology 23(2):209–19.

Bradley, R. 1998 The Significance of Monuments: On the Shaping of Human Experience in Neolithic and Bronze Age Europe. New York: Routledge.

Bradley, R. 2000a The Good Stones: A New Investigation of the Clava Cairns. Edinburgh: Society of Antiquaries of Scotland.

Bradley, R. 2000b The Archaeology of Natural Places. London: Routledge.

Bradley, R. 2001 Orientations and Origins: A Symbolic Dimension to the Long House in Neolithic Europe. Antiquity 75(287):50–8.

Bradley, R. 2002 The Past in Prehistoric Societies. London: Routledge.

Brady, J. E., and K. M. Prufer, eds. 2005 In the Maw of the Earth Monster: Studies of Mesoamerican Ritual Cave Use. Austin: University of Texas Press.

Bueno Ramírez, P., and R. de Balbin Behrmann 1992 L'art mégalithique dans la Péninsula Ibérique – une vue d'ensemble. L'Anthropologie 96(2–3):499–572.

Bueno Ramírez, P., and R. de Balbin Behrmann 1998 The Origin of the Megalithic Decorative System: Graphics Versus Architecture. Journal of Iberian Archaeology 0:53–67.

Cardoso, J. L. 1992 A Lapa do Bugio. Setubal Arqueologica IX–X:89–225.

Cardoso, J. L. 1997 O Povoado de Leceia (Oeiras), Sentinela do Tejo no Terceiro Milénio a. C. Lisbon: Museu Nacional de Arqueologia.

Cardoso, J. L. 2002 Pré-História de Portugal. Lisbon: Verbo.

Cardoso, J. L., F. Ribeiro Henriques, and J. C. Caninas 2000 Arquitectura, espólio, e rituais de dois monumentos megalíticos da Beira Interior: Estudo comparado. *In* Muitas Antas, Pouca Gente? V. S. Gonçalves, ed. Pp. 195–214. Lisbon: Instituto Português de Arqueologia.

Carvalho, A. M. Faustino de, and J. Zilhão 1994 O povoado Neolítico do Laranjal de Cabeço das Pias (Vale da Serra, Torres Novas). *In* Actas das V Jornada Arqueológicas (Lisboa, 1993). Pp. 53–67. Lisbon: Associação dos Arqueólogos Portugueses.

Cassen, S. 2000 Stelae Reused in the Passage Graves of Western France: History of Research and Sexualisation of the Carvings. *In* Neolithic Orkney in its European Context. A. Ritchie, ed. Pp. 233–46. Cambridge: McDonald Institute for Archaeological Research.

Cauwe, N. 2001 Skeletons in Motion, Ancestors in Action: Early Mesolithic Collective Tombs in Southern Belgium. Cambridge Archaeological Journal 11(2):146–63.

Chapman, R. 1981 The Emergence of Formal Disposal Areas and the Problem of Megalithic Tombs in Prehistoric Europe. *In* The Archaeology of Death. R. Chapman, I. Kinnes, and K. Randsborg, eds. Pp. 71–81. Cambridge: Cambridge University Press.

Chapman, R. 1990 Emerging Complexity: The Later Prehistory of South-East Spain, Iberia and the West Mediterranean. Cambridge: Cambridge University Press.

Childe, V. G. 1952 New Light on the Most Ancient East (4th edn., rewritten). London: Routledge and Kegan Paul.

Christensen, J. 2004 Warfare in the European Neolithic. Acta Archaeologica 75:129–56.

Cleal, R. M. J. 1988 The Occurrence of Drilled Holes in Later Neolithic Pottery. Oxford Journal of Archaeology 7:139–45.

Cleal, R. M. J., K. Walker, and R. Montague 1995 Stonehenge in its Landscape: Twentieth-Century Excavations. London: English Heritage.

Climo, J. J., and M. G. Cattell, eds. 2002 Social Memory and History: Anthropological Perspectives. Walnut Creek: Altamira Press.

Connerton, P. 1989 How Societies Remember. Cambridge: Cambridge University Press.

Correia, V. 1921 El Neolítico de Pavía. Madrid: Museo Nacional de Ciencias Naturales.

Cummings, V. 2002 Experiencing Texture and Transformation in the British Neolithic. Oxford Journal of Archaeology 21(3):249–61.

Darvill, T., and J. Thomas, eds. 1996 Neolithic Houses in Northwest Europe and Beyond. Oxford: Oxbow.

Delgado, J. F. N. 1880 La grotte de Furninha à Peniche. Congrès Internationale d'Anthropologie et d'Archeologie. Pp. 107–78. Lisbon.

Delibes, G., M. Fernández-Miranda, M. D. Fernández-Posse, and C. Martín Morales 1986 El poblado de Almizaraque. *In* Homenaje a Luis Siret (Cuevas de Almanzora, 1984). Pp. 167–77. Seville.

Díaz-Andreu, M., and T. Champion, eds. 1996 Nationalism and Archaeology in Europe. London: UCL Press.

Díaz-del-Río, P. 2004 Copper Age Ditched Enclosures in Central Iberia. Oxford Journal of Archaeology 23(2):107–21.

Dietler, M., and I. Herbich 1993 Living on Luo Time: Reckoning Sequence, Duration, History and Biography in a Rural African Society. World Archaeology 25(2):248–60.

Diniz, M. 2001 O sítio neolítico da Valada do Mato, Évora: problemas e perspectivas. Revista Portuguesa de Arqueologia 3(1):45–59.

Dobres, M.-A., and J. Robb, ed. 2002 Agency in Archaeology. London: Routledge.

Edmonds, M. 1995 Stone Tools and Society. London: Batsford.

Edmonds, M. 1999 Ancestral Geographies of the Neolithic. London: Routledge.

Eliade, M. 1954 Cosmos and History: The Myth of the Eternal Return. Princeton: Princeton University Press.

Fentress, J., and C. Wickham, eds. 1992 Social Memory: New Perspectives on the Past. Oxford: Blackwell.

Fortier, A.-M. 2000 Migrant Belongings: Memory, Space, Identity. New York: Berg.

Fowler, C. 2004 The Archaeology of Personhood: An Anthropological Approach. London: Routledge.

Fuller, C. J. 2001 Orality, Literacy, and Memorization: Priestly Education in Contemporary South India. Modern Asian Studies 35(1):1–31.

Gallay, A. 1995 Les stèles anthropomorphes du site mégalithique du Petit-Chasseur à Sion (Valais, Suisse). Notizie Archeologische Bergomensi 3:167–94.

Gama, R. P., and E. Cunha 2003 A Neolithic Case of Cranial Trepanation (Eira Pedrinha, Portugal). *In* Trepanation. History, Discovery, Theory. R. Arnott, S. Finger, and C. U. M. Smith, eds. Lisse, The Netherlands: Swets & Zeitlinger.

Gell, A. 1998 Art and Agency: An Anthropological Theory. Oxford: Clarendon Press.

Giddens, A. 1979 Central Problems in Social Theory. Berkeley: University of California Press.

Giddens, A. 1984 The Constitution of Society. Berkeley: University of California Press.

Gilchrist, R. 2000 Archaeological Biographies: Realizing Human Lifecycles, -Courses and -Histories. World Archaeology 31(3):325–8.

Gilman, A., and J. B. Thornes 1985 Land-Use and Prehistory in South-East Spain. London: George Allen and Unwin.

Giot, P.-R. 1987 Barnenez, Carn, Guenoc. Rennes: Université de Rennes.

Gomes, R. V., M. Varela Gomes, and M. Farinha dos Santos 1983–4 Resumos de intervenções em Escoural (Montemor-o-Novo). Clio/Arqueologia 1:77–8.

Gonçalves, V. S. 1999a Reguengos de Monsaraz: Territórios Megalíticos. Lisbon: Câmara Municipal de Reguengos de Monsaraz.

Gonçalves, V. S. 1999b Time, Landscape and Burials 1. Megalithic Rites of Ancient Peasant Societies in Central and Southern Portugal: An Initial Review. Journal of Iberian Archaeology 1:83–109.

Gonçalves, V. S., ed. 2000 Muitas Antas, Pouca Gente? Actas do I Colóquio Internacional Sobre Megalitismo. Lisbon: Instituto Português de Arqueologia.

Gonçalves, V. S., A. Pereira, and M. Andrade 2003 A propósito do reaproveitamento de algumas placas de xisto gravadas da região de Évora. O Arqueólogo Português 21:209–44.

Goody, J. 1977 The Domestication of the Savage Mind. Cambridge: Cambridge University Press.

Goody, J. 1998 Memory in Oral Tradition. *In* Memory. P. Fara and K. Patterson, eds. Pp. 73–94. Cambridge: Cambridge University Press.

Gosden, C. 1994 Social Being and Time. Oxford: Blackwell.

Gosden, C., and Y. Marshall 1999 The Cultural Biography of Objects. World Archaeology 31(2):169–78.

Gregg, S. A. 1988 Foragers and Farmers: Population Interaction and Agricultural Expansion in Prehistoric Europe. Chicago: University of Chicago Press.

Gould, S. J. 1997 Questioning the Millennium. New York: Harmony Books.

Gusi Jener, F. 1986 El yacimiento de Terrera Ventura (Tabernas) y su relacion con la Cultura de Almería. *In* Homenaje a Luis Siret. Pp. 192–5. Seville.

Halbwachs, M. 1980 (1951) The Collective Memory. New York: Harper and Row.

Hall, M. 2001 Social Archaeology and the Theatres of Memory. Journal of Social Archaeology 1(1):50–61.

Hamilakis, Y., M. Pluciennik, and S. Tarlow, eds. 2001 Thinking Through the Body: Archaeologies of Corporeality. New York: Kluwer/Plenum.

Harrison, R. J. 1974. Origins of the Bell Beaker Cultures. Antiquity 48:99–109.

Harrison, R. J. 1985 The 'Policultivo Ganadero', or the Secondary Products Revolution in Spanish Agriculture, 5000–1000 BC. Proceedings of the Prehistoric Society 51: 75–102.

Heidegger, M., ed. 1971 Poetry, Landscape, Thought. New York: Harper and Row.

Hendon, J. A. 2000 Having and Holding: Storage, Memory, Knowledge, and Social Relations. American Anthropologist 102(1):42–53.

Herzfeld, M. 2003 Whatever Happened to 'Influence'? The Anxieties of Memory. Archaeological Dialogues 10:191–203.

Hingley, R. 1996 Ancestors and Identity in the Later Prehistory of Atlantic Scotland: The Reuse and Reinvention of Neolithic Monuments and Material Culture. World Archaeology 28(2):231–43.

Hodder, I. 1990 The Domestication of Europe: Structure and Contingency in Neolithic Societies. Oxford: Blackwell.

Holtorf, C. 1996 Towards a Chronology of Megaliths: Understanding Monumental Time and Cultural Memory. Journal of European Archaeology 4:119–52.

Holtorf, C. 2000–4 Monumental Past: The Life-Histories of Megalithic Monuments in Mecklenburg-Vorpommern (Germany). Electronic document. https://tspace.library.utoronto.ca/handle/1807/245.

Holtorf, C. 2002 Excavations at Monte da Igreja near Évora (Portugal). From the Life-History of a Monument to Re-Uses of Ancient Objects. Journal of Iberian Archaeology 4:177–201.

Holtorf, C. 2005 From Stonehenge to Las Vegas: Archaeology as Popular Culture. Walnut Creek: Altamira Press.

Hoskin, M. 2001 Tombs, Temples and Their Orientations: A New Perspective on Mediterranean Prehistory. Bognor Regis: Ocarina Books.

Hoskins, J. 1998 Biographical Objects. New York: Routledge.

Houston, S. 2004 The Archaeology of Communication Technologies. Annual Review of Anthropology 33:223–50.

Hurtado Pérez, V. 1986 El Calcolítico en la Cuenca Media del Guadiana y la necrópolis de La Pijotilla. Arqueología 14:51–75.

Hurtado Pérez, V. 2004 San Blas. The Discovery of a Large Chalcolithic Settlement by the Guadiana River. Journal of Iberian Archaeology 6:93–116.

Jackes, M., D. Lubell, and C. Meiklejohn 1997 On Physical Anthropological Aspects of the Mesolithic–Neolithic Transition in the Iberian Peninsula. Current Anthropology 38:839–46.

Jones, A. 1999 Local Colour: Megalithic Architecture and Colour Symbolism in Neolithic Arran. Oxford Journal of Archaeology 18(4):339–50.

Jones, A. 2004a By Way of Illustration: Art, Memory and Materiality in the Irish Sea and Beyond. In The Neolithic of the Irish Sea: Materiality and Traditions of Practice. V. Cumming and C. Fowler, eds. Pp. 202–13. Oxford: Oxbow.

Jones, A. 2004b Matter and Memory: Colour, Remembrance and the Neolithic/Bronze Age Transition. In Rethinking Materiality: The Engagement of Mind with the Material World. C. Gosden, E. DeMarrais, and C. Renfrew, eds. Pp. 167–78. Cambridge: McDonald Institute for Archaeological Research.

Jones, A., and G. MacGregor, eds. 2002 Colouring the Past: The Significance of Colour in Archaeological Research. Oxford: Berg.

Jones, S. 1997 The Archaeology of Ethnicity. London: Routledge.

Jorge, S. O. 1999 Domesticating the Land: The First Agricultural Communities in Portugal. Journal of Iberian Archaeology 2:43–98.

Jorge, S. O. 2003 Revisiting Some Earlier Papers on the Late Prehistoric Walled Settlements of the Iberian Peninsula. Journal of Iberian Archaeology 5:89–135.

Kalb, P. 1981 Zur relativen chronologie portugiesischer megalithgräber. Madrider Mitteilungen 22:55–77.

Keeley, L. H. 1996 War Before Civilization. Oxford: Oxford University Press.

Keeley, L. H. 1997 Frontier Warfare in the Early Neolithic. In Troubled Times: Violence and Warfare in the Past. D. L. Martin and D. W. Frayer, eds. Pp. 303–19. Amsterdam: Gordon and Breach Publishers.

Kohl, P., and C. Fawcett, eds. 1995 Nationalism, Politics, and the Practice of Archaeology. Cambridge: Cambridge University Press.

Kopytoff, I. 1986 The Cultural Biography of Things: Commoditization as Process. *In* The Social Life of Things. A. Appadurai, ed. Pp. 64–91. Cambridge: Cambridge University Press.

Kristiansen, K. 1984 Krieger und Haüptlinge in der Bronzezeit Dänemarks. Ein Beitrag zur Geschichte des bronzezeitlichen Schwertes. Jahrbuch des Römisch-Germanischen Zentralmuseum Mainz 31:187–208.

Küchler, S. 1988 Malangan: Objects, Sacrifice and the Production of Memory. American Ethnologist 15(4):625–37.

Kunst, M. 2000 A guerra no calcolítico na Península Ibérica. ERA Arqueologia 2:128–42.

Kunst, M. 2001 Das Neolitikum der Iberischen Halbinsel. *In* Hispania Antiqua. Tilo Ulbert, ed. Pp. 37–66. Mainz: Verlag Philipp von Zabern.

Kwint, M., C. Breward, and J. Aynley, eds. 1995 Material Memories: Design and Evocation. Oxford: Berg.

Lago, M., C. Duarte, A. Valera, J. Albergaria, F. Almeida, and A. Faustino Carvalho 1998 Povoado dos Perdigões (Reguengos de Monsaraz): dados preliminaries dos trabalhos arqueológicos realizados em 1997. Revista Portuguesa de Arqueologia 1(1):45–152.

Larsson, L. 2001 Decorated Facade? A Stone with Carvings from the Megalithic Tomb Vale de Rodrigo, Monument 2, Alentejo, Southern Portugal. Journal of Iberian Archaeology 3:35–46.

Leisner, G., and V. Leisner 1943 Die Megalithgräber der Iberischen Halbinsel. Der Süden. Volume 1, 1. Berlin: Walter de Gruyter.

Leisner, G., and V. Leisner 1951 Antas do Concelho de Reguengos de Monsaraz. Lisbon: Uniarch.

Leisner, G., and V. Leisner 1956 Die Megalithgräber der Iberischen Halbinsel. Der Westen. Berlin: Walter de Gruyter.

Leisner, G., and V. Leisner 1959 Die Megalithgräber der Iberischen Halbinsel. Der Westen. Berlin: Walter de Gruyter.

Leisner, V. 1965 Die Megalithgräber der Iberischen Halbinsel. Der Westen. Berlin: Walter de Gruyter.

Leisner, V. 1998 Die Megalithgraber der Iberischen Halbinsel: Der Westen. Madrider Forschungen Vol. I, 4. Berlin: Walter de Gruyter.

Leisner, V., G. Zbyszewski, and O. da Veiga Ferreira 1965 Les monuments préhistoriques de Praia das Maçãs et de Casainhos. Lisbon: Serviços Geológicos de Portugal.

Liesau von Lettow-Vorbeck, C., and I. Pastor Abascal 2003 The Ciempozuelos Necropolis Skull: A Case of Double Trepanation? International Journal of Osteoarchaeology 13:213–21.

Lillios, K. T. 1993 Regional Settlement Abandonment at the End of the Copper Age in the Lowlands of West-Central Portugal. *In* Abandonment of Settlements and Regions: Ethno-Archaeological and Archaeological Approaches. C. Cameron and S. Tomka, eds. Pp. 110–20. Cambridge: Cambridge University Press.

Lillios, K. T. 1999 Objects of Memory: The Ethnography and Archaeology of Heirlooms. Journal of Archaeological Method and Theory 6(3):235–62.

Lillios, K. T. 2002 Some New Views of the Engraved Slate Plaques of Southwest Iberia. Revista Portuguesa de Arqueologia 5(2):135–51.

Lillios, K. T. 2003 Creating Memory in Prehistory: The Engraved Slate Plaques of Southwest Iberia. *In* Archaeologies of Memory. R. Van Dyke and S. Alcock, eds. Pp. 129–50. Oxford: Blackwell.

Lillios, K. T. 2004a The Engraved Stone Plaque Registry and Inquiry Tool, ESPRIT. Electronic document. http://research2.its.uiowa.edu/iberian/.

Lillios, K. T. 2004b Lives of Stone, Lives of People: Re-Viewing the Engraved Plaques of Copper Age Iberia. European Journal of Archaeology 7(2):125–58.

Lowenthal, D. 1985 The Past is a Foreign Country. Cambridge: Cambridge University Press.

Lucas, G. 2005 The Archaeology of Time. London: Routledge.

Meillassoux, C. 1972 From Reproduction to Production. Economy and Society 1:93–105.

Meskell, L. 1996 The Somatisation of Archaeology: Discourses, Institutions, Corporeality. Norwegian Archaeological Review 29(1):1–16.

Mezzena, F. 1998 Le stele antropomorfe dell'area megalitica di Aosta. In Dei di Pietra: La Grande Statuaria del III Milenio aC. F. Mezzena, ed. Pp. 91–121. Skira: Regione Autonoma Valle d'Aosta.

Mills, B. 2004 The Establishment and Defeat of Hierarchy: Inalienable Possessions and the History of Collective Prestige Structures in the Pueblo Southwest. American Anthropologist 106(2):238–51.

Mohen, J.-P. 1990 The World of Megaliths. New York: Facts on File.

Nora, P. 1989 Between Memory and History. Representations 26(3):9–25.

Nora, P. 1996–8 Realms of Memory: The Construction of the French Past. New York: Columbia University Press.

Olick, J., and J. Robbins 1998 Social Memory Studies: From 'Collective Memory' to the Historical Sociology of Mnemonic Practices. Annual Review of Sociology 24:105–240.

Ong, W. 1982 Orality and Literacy: The Technologizing of the Word. London: Methuen.

Parker Pearson, M., and Ramilisonina 1998 Stonehenge for the Ancestors: The Stones Pass on the Message. Antiquity 72(276):308–26.

Parry, J. 1985 The Brahmanical Tradition and the Technology of the Intellect. In Reason and Morality. J. Overing, ed. Pp. 200–25. London: Tavistock.

Peña-Chocarro, L., L. Zapata, M. J. Iriarte, M. González Morales, and L. Guy Straus 2005 The Oldest Agriculture in Northern Atlantic Spain: New Evidence from El Mirón Cave (Ramales de la Victoria, Cantabria). Journal of Archaeological Science 12:579–87.

Piggott, S. 1940 A Trepanned Skull of the Beaker Period from Dorset and the Practice of Trepanning in Prehistoric Europe. Proceedings of the Prehistoric Society 3:112–32.

Pitts, M. 2003 Don't Knock the Ancestors. Antiquity 77(295):172–8.

Price, T. D., ed. 2000 Europe's First Farmers. Cambridge: Cambridge University Press.

Rappaport, J. 1998 The Politics of Memory: Native Historical Interpretations in the Colombian Andes. Durham: Duke University Press.

Richards, M. 2003 The Neolithic Invasion of Europe. Annual Review of Anthropology 32:135–62.

Robb, J. 2002 Time and Biography: Osteobiography of the Italian Neolithic Lifespan. In Thinking Through the Body: Archaeologies of Corporeality. Y. Hamilakis, M. Pluciennik, and S. Tarlow, eds. Pp. 153–71. New York: Kluwer/Plenum.

Rojo-Guerra, M. A., and M. Kunst, eds. 2002 Sobre el Significado del Fuego en los Rituales Funerarios del Neolítico. Valladolid: Universidad de Valladolid.

Rowley-Conwy, P. 2004 How the West Was Lost: A Reconsideration of Agricultural Origins in Britain, Ireland, and Southern Scandinavia. Current Anthropology 45(S83).

Sangmeister, E., and H. Schubart 1981 Zambujal, die Grabungen 1964 bis 1973. Mainz am Rhein: P. von Zabern.

Santos, M. F. dos, and O. da Veiga Ferreira 1969 O monumento eneolítico de Santiago do Escoural. O Arqueólogo Português 3:37–62.

Saunders, N. J., ed. 2004 Matters of Conflict: Material Culture, Memory and the First World War. London: Routledge.

Schama, S. 1995 Landscape and Memory. New York: Knopf.

Schulting, R. J., and M. P. Richards 2002 The Wet, the Wild and the Domesticated: The Mesolithic–Neolithic Transition on the West Coast of Scotland. European Journal of Archaeology 5(2):147–89.

Sennett, R. 1998 Disturbing Memories. In Memory. P. Fara and K. Patterson, eds. Pp. 10–26. Cambridge: Cambridge University Press.

Seremetakis, C. N. 1996 The Senses Still. Chicago: The University of Chicago Press.

Shackel, P. A. 2000 Archaeology and Created Memory: Public History in a National Park. New York: Kluwer.

Shanks, M., and C. Tilley 1982 Ideology, Power, and Ritual Communication: A Reinterpretation of Neolithic Mortuary Practice. In Symbolic and Structural Archaeology. I. Hodder, ed. Pp. 129–54. Cambridge: Cambridge University.

Silva, A. C., and A. C. Araújo 1995 Gruta do Escoural. Lisbon: Instituto Português do Património Arquitectónico e Arqueológico.

Silva, A. C., and R. Parreira 1990 A Colecção Arqueológica do Hospital Distrital de Évora. Évora: Instituto Português do Património Cultural.

Silva, C. T. da, and J. Soares 1981 Pré-História da Area de Sines. Lisbon: Gabinete da Area de Sines.

Simões, T. 1999 O Sitio Neolítico de São Pedro de Canaferrim, Sintra. Lisbon: Institute Português de Arqueologia.

Skeates, R. 1995 Animate Objects: A Biography of Prehistoric 'Axe-Amulets' in the Central Mediterranean Region. Proceedings of the Prehistoric Society 61:279–301.

Skeates, R. 2002 Axe Aesthetics: Stone Axes and Visual Culture in Prehistoric Malta. Oxford Journal of Archaeology 21(1):13–22.

Stafford, M. 1998 In Search of Hindsgavl: Experiments in the Production of Neolithic Danish Flint Daggers. Antiquity 72:338–49.

Steadman, L. B., C. T. Palmer, and C. F. Tilley 1996 The Universality of Ancestor Worship. Ethnology 35:63–76.

Stewart, S. 1993 On Longing: Narratives of the Miniature, the Gigantic, the Souvenir, the Collection. Durham, NC: Duke University Press.

Thomas, J. 1991 Rethinking the Neolithic. Cambridge: Cambridge University Press.

Thomas, J. 1996 Time, Culture and Identity: An Interpretive Archaeology. London: Routledge.

Thomas, N. 1995 Oceanic Art. London: Thames and Hudson.

Tilley, C. 1996 The Powers of Rocks: Topography and Monument Construction on Bodmin Moor. World Archaeology 28(2):161–76.

Tilley, C. 1999 Metaphor and Material Culture. Oxford: Blackwell.

Van Dyke, R., and S. E. Alcock 2003 Archaeologies of Memory: An Introduction. In Archaeologies of Memory. R. Van Dyke and S. E. Alcock, eds. Pp. 1–13. Oxford: Routledge.

Wahl, J., and H. König 1987 Anthropologisch-Traumologische untersuchung der Menschlichen Skelettreste aus dem Bandkeramischen Massengrab bei Talheim, Kreis Heilbronn. Fundberichte aus Baden-Wurtemberg 12:65–193.

Watson, A., and D. Keating 1999 Architecture and Sound: An Acoustic Analysis of Megalithic Monuments in Prehistoric Britain. Antiquity 73(280):325–36.

Watson, R. S., ed. 1994 Memory, History, and Opposition under State Socialism. Santa Fe: School of American Research.

Weiner, A. 1992 Inalienable Possessions: The Paradox of Keeping-While-Giving. Berkeley: University of California Press.

Werbner, R., ed. 1998 Memory and the Postcolony: African Anthropology and the Critique of Power. London: Zed Books.

Whitley, J. 2002 Too Many Ancestors. Antiquity 76(291):119–26.

Whitley, J. 2003 Response to Mike Pitt's 'Don't Knock the Ancestors'. Antiquity 77(286):401.

Whittle, A. 1989 Problems in Neolithic Archaeology. Cambridge: Cambridge University Press.

Whittle, A. 1996 Europe in the Neolithic: The Creation of New Worlds. Cambridge: Cambridge University Press.

Whittle, A. 2003 The Archaeology of People: Dimensions of Neolithic Life. London: Routledge.

Williams, H., ed. 2003 Archaeologies of Remembrance: Death and Memory in Past Societies. New York: Kluwer Academic/Plenum.

Woodburn, J. 1982 Social Dimensions of Death in Four African Hunting and Gathering Societies. *In* Death and the Regeneration of Life. M. Bloch and J. Parry, eds. Pp. 187–210. Cambridge: Cambridge University Press.

Woods, A. D., and K. T. Lillios In press Wearing Stone: Experimental Use-Wear Analysis of the Iberian Engraved Slate Plaques. *In* Proceedings of the IV Iberian Archaeological Congress (Faro 2004).

Yates, F. 1966 The Art of Memory. London: Routledge and Kegan Paul.

Zafra, N., F. Hornos, and M. Castro 1999 Una macro-aldea en el origen del modo de vida campesino: Marroquíes Bajos (Jaén) c. 2500–2000 cal ANE. Trabajos de Prehistoria 56(1):77–102.

Zerubavel, E. 2003 Time Maps: Collective Memory and the Social Shape of the Past. Chicago: University of Chicago Press.

Zerubavel, Y. 1995 Recovered Roots: Collective Memory and the Making of Israeli National Tradition. Chicago: University of Chicago Press.

Zilhão, J. 1992 Gruta do Caldeirão. O Neolítico Antigo. Lisbon: Instituto Português de Arqueologia.

Zilhão, J. 1993 The Spread of Agro-Pastoral Economies Across Mediterranean Europe: A View from the Far West. Journal of Mediterranean Archaeology 6:5–63.

Zilhão, J. 2001 Radiocarbon Evidence for Maritime Pioneer Colonization at the Origins of Farming in West Mediterranean Europe. Proceedings of the National Academy of Sciences 98(24):14180–5.

5 (b)
The Past in Later Prehistory

Bryan Hanks

Introduction

The late prehistoric period of temperate Europe, spanning approximately the late third through first millennia bc, represents a period of dynamic social change. As the previous chapter examined for the earlier phases of European prehistory, the connection between death, landscape and ancestor-veneration provided a vibrant forum for the living wherein the celebration of the deceased served importantly in the articulation and perpetuation of cultural tradition and social practice. It is clear from the widespread and variable nature of prehistoric monuments in Europe that funerary events represented highly charged moments of human intentionality, commemoration and bereavement (Barrett 1994; Bradley 1998; 2000; Chapman 2000). For archaeologists, the physical traces of these events provide a unique corpus of material for investigating the complex relationship between social memory, ritual practice and the construction of funerary tombs and monument complexes (Holtorf 1998; Mizoguchi 1993; Williams 2003).

This chapter will investigate these themes in order to examine the broader patterns connected with death and remembrance among late prehistoric societies and to explore how the role of memory coalesced with new forms of identity and social commemoration. While the living play a critical role in the choices made during funerary events, the burial of social members also reflects elements of the life history and significance of the deceased within early societies as well (Parker Pearson 1993; 1999:5–11). The preparation of the corpse, its placement and orientation and the inclusion of personal objects and other material items during the process of interment can reveal complex actions of meaning whereby the social memory of the deceased is rearticulated through mnemonic display and ritual action (Jones 2003; Williams 2006:20). Such evidence reveals important elements of both individual and corporate identity construction and renegotiation.

In consideration of the late prehistoric period in Europe, one of the most important material patterns is evidence for the increasing scale of institutionalized warfare between communities. Settlement fortifications, weaponry, armor and new forms of mortuary practice all combine to reflect distinct changes in the technology, material culture and social prestige surrounding what has been interpreted as the materialization of a distinctive warrior lifestyle and ideology (Harding 2000:271; Kristiansen & Larsson 2005:246; Treherne 1995). Physical representations of these important social transitions appear in the form of rock art, anthropomorphic standing stones and new categories of bodily aesthetics reflected through objects of adornment, dress and the expressive efficacy of weaponry and armour. Such materiality and its relationship to new forms of social practices connected with violence and warfare, at both the individual and societal scales of human action, form an important arena for archaeological interpretation. This chapter, therefore, will not focus on the specific culture-historical patterns found in temperate Europe at this time, but will instead examine the complex relationship between the themes of warrior identity, social commemoration and new forms of funerary practice. This approach will offer a comparative perspective for interpreting the widespread trend in greater elaboration of funerary monument construction and warrior lifestyle characteristics that become evident across much of Eurasia during the late prehistoric period.

Monuments, Memory and Society

Halbwachs (1992) has argued that *social memory* is a collective phenomenon largely constructed through the active negotiation of what is chosen to be remembered and what is to be forgotten by a society. From this perspective, the past is understood as a fluid construct that is continually rewritten as the commemoration of specific past events highlights their role in the articulation of present day identities and historical conditions. Within our own contemporary world one of the most powerful categories of commemoration is the war monument, which stands as a potent reminder of the impact that 20th-century warfare and the tragedy of human sacrifice has had on modern culture and society.

For example, from a distinctly Eurasian perspective, one of the most imposing monuments of WWII is the colossal memorial complex of Mamayev Kurgan, which is located in the present day city of Volgograd (Stalingrad), Russian Federation. Standing proudly atop the memorial complex is the great allegorical statue *Rodina Mat' Zovyot* ('The Motherland Calls'), which memorializes the substantial sacrifice of soldiers and citizens during the Battle for Stalingrad. This battle, which took place against the German Sixth Army from August 1942 to February 1943, is an event that has been cited as the *single largest battle* in human history, with casualty estimates ranging from 1.7 to 2 million. The *Rodina Mat' Zovyot*, a freestanding concrete statue 85 metres in height, including the raised 33-metre metal sword, dominates the surrounding landscape and has provided a focal point of active social commemoration for nearly 40 years.

The Mamayev Hill memorial complex, arguably one of the most impressive in all of Eurasia, recites the tragic events that took place at this very location and attempts to memorialize the almost unfathomable scale of human loss endured by the Soviet people. Historically situated, the monument reflects the intense power of ideology, nationalism and *place* in the minds of the living. In aggregate, the various elements of the monument effectively embody the sacrifice of both the individual and the collective and, like most nationalistic war memorials, moves beyond its own place in time to link the past with the contemporary through commemorative practices undertaken at the site. This transcendence of time – connecting place with past and present – is most effectively captured in a statement taken from the official website for the monument:

> Here on the Mamayev Hill lies the invisible connection between the generations. Veterans recall the hard days of trials – the days of the war, share with younger generations their experiences of being the true citizens and defenders of their country, teach the young how to stay faithful to the traditions of the old. Such events never pass without leaving a certain impact on the people. After each meeting young people become morally stronger, they become infected by that gigantic emotional force that the veterans have. This emotional force is love to the motherland and its people. The flow of time can't kill our glorious past. The voice of history, just like the will of the passed away and the living veterans, brings simple and clear truth to the young generations – a human being is born to live. (State Heritage Website, Mamayev Kurgan)

Memorials of modern-day warfare provide a unique and significant commentary on our past by encapsulating the ultimate sacrifices made through war and the dynamism of nation-state building (Rowlands 1993; Saunders 2003). The commemoration of these events, their locations and their place in time through holiday observances and ceremonial events are an essential element in the fabric of our own contemporary social memory and reflect the dramatic social conditions we have passed through to reach our own moment in time. Such monuments also serve to reinforce social and cultural concepts of honour, glory and sacrifice through their construction, physical settings and use. While written history may provide rich details of wartime events, it is an entirely different matter to actually visit the site of a large commemorative complex. Halbwachs would consider this memory production a social phenomenon and as such well anchored within larger society. However, each of us who has felt the powerful emotion of visiting memorials clearly have individual emotive responses that both stimulate and structure our understanding of the past as well as the memory of events that have shaped our history. While social memory may be strongly rooted in the collective, it is experienced first and foremost through individual perception and experience.

This important scalar relationship between memory at the social level and the experiential individual level has particular significance for the archaeologist, as the majority of the human past is set among societies of oral rather than written traditions. As Goody (2000) has suggested, the dynamic process of memory production among non-literate societies plays an especially important role in the preservation of tradition and cultural practice. When considering this, an important distinction can be made between *inscribed* memory practices, which are physically manifested through such objects as monuments, iconography or texts, and what we may think of as *embodied* memory, which is created through enactment, ritual and bodily performance, and as such are highly mutable and transient (Connerton 1989; Rowlands 1993). However, both areas of memory production can be explored archaeologically and as Van Dyke and Alcock have suggested, the overlapping categories of 'ritual behaviors, narratives, objects and representations, and places' are perhaps the most accessible for archaeological study (2003:6). Certainly, material objects and their contextual settings have long been the focus of archaeological thought, although the performative nature of ritual activity has been more resistant to archaeological interpretation. Nevertheless, in recent years archaeologists have increasingly turned to the study of performance and its connection to the power of spectacle and theatricality within social life in order to investigate the power of embodied ritual practices in early societies (e.g. Bergman and Kondoleon 1999; Inomata and Coben 2006; Pearson & Shanks 2001).

Funerary events by their very nature form an important category of such practices, as they are often structured through significant public or communal participation, such as monument construction, processional activities, sacrifice and feasting. While such activities have often been highlighted in terms of political intention and authority (DeMarrais, Castillo, & Earle 1996; Parker Pearson 1982; 1984), these events also can be viewed as dynamic performances that generate spectacle and emotional response among participants (Metcalf & Huntington 1991:43; Tarlow 1999:20). From this point of view, funerary practices can be seen both as loci for the memorialization of the deceased and as significant settings for the creation of memory through the performative aspects of viewing and participation.

Although memory has become an important topic within recent theoretical archaeology, scholars have infrequently considered aspects of memory creation through *psychological* responses to death and participation in funerary events (for notable exceptions see Kus 1992 and Tarlow 1999). Rather, archaeologists have focused more on theories of phenomenology, embodiment and sociological approaches to death and burial. For example, in a recent edited volume entitled *Archaeologies of Remembrance: Death and Memory in Past Societies,* Williams states that the main inspiration for the book, 'comes from the work of Halbwachs (1992), arguing that memory is a social, not a psychological phenomenon, and can reside in society rather than simply in the heads of individuals' (2003:6). Such a perspective has placed an important emphasis on the materiality of the corpse and the mnemonic properties of objects and physical settings as media for the creation of collective social memory through funerary activities (ibid.). Such approaches have been extremely productive in acknowledging the efficacy of memory (re)production within prehistoric societies; however, it is important not to exclude the role of memory production at the individual level. Judging from recent trends in theoretical archaeology, which have routinely emphasized human agents in the past, it seems rather contradictory that many current approaches to memory would chose to focus more intently on how memory functions within larger social structures instead of at the individual level. Perhaps this is a result of the enduring stigma that archaeological interpretation cannot find its way into the 'minds of people in the past', but rather must be content with examining broader patterns of social practice.

In contrast to recent archaeological approaches to social memory, a considerable amount of scholarly attention in the social sciences has been directed towards the psychological characteristics of memory within individuals and their connection with broader aspects of memory production at the societal level (e.g. Beike, Lampinen, & Behrend 2004; Nilsson & Ohta 2006). Two important themes that have received considerable attention, which may have particular relevance for the archaeologists seeking to understand the intersection between death, burial and social memory production, are what have been termed *autobiographical memories* and *flashbulb memories.*

Autobiographical memory has been seen as a crucial component in the reflexive narrative construction of 'self' and therefore figures prominently in the negotiation of one's own social awareness and identity formation throughout an individual's lifetime (Conway 1990; Singer, Jefferson & Blagov 2006; Wang & Conway 2006:10). From this point of view, various institutionalized stages and events, such as *rites de passage* within an individual's life history, provide a crucial structure for long-term memory and the perception of personal pasts and their connection with the contemporary. Based on cognitive studies, long-term autobiographical memories most often have an experiential connection whereby individuals remember more effectively events or processes in which they were either personally involved or which had a dramatic impact on their community or larger society. Of these, flashbulb memories are perhaps the most powerful (Conway 1995; Pezdek 2006). For example, within American society the attack on Pearl Harbour, the assassination of President John F. Kennedy and more recently the terrorist attacks of September 11th all serve as pivotal points in American history. Furthermore, because of their lasting impact on larger society, they also represent episodic memory events for people who were alive when they happened and as such factor significantly into the construction of individual narrative memory. For example, if asked, most people would be able to vividly describe the context of where they were and what they were doing at the exact moment they first learned of or witnessed in real time the tragic events of September 11th.

As archaeologists, we may take such psychological processes and events for granted within our own society of today. However, when considering changing patterns of material evidence in the past that connect with death and social commemoration it is important to consider more thoroughly how processes of memory work at different scales and as a result impact both individual and collective memory production. For the remainder of this chapter, these issues will be examined through a more focused approach to the relationship between memory and the material patterns and events connected with warfare, death and the social commemoration of warriors in later European prehistory.

Archaeological Perspectives of Death and Burial

As the discussion in the previous chapter examined in detail, archaeologists increasingly have turned to the subject of memory as an important theme of research and interpretation in recent years. Studies of death and burial have been one of the primary areas of emphasis as prehistoric mortuary practices provide an important perspective on how people of the past engaged in the commemoration of recently deceased community members as well as known and mythologized ancestors (Williams 2003:3). In context, however, this recent emphasis on memory within archaeological study reflects just one of many important shifts in intellectual thought over the past four decades relating to the scalar relationship between individual perception and action and how it both contributes to and is influenced by larger societal structures.

The study of death and burial underwent a radical theoretical shift in the 1970s, as many archaeologists began to focus more intently on the reconstruction of past social structures and in particular on themes relating to rank, status and role. Drawing comparatively on ethnographic analogies, cross-cultural generalizations became a crucial component in the development of the New Archaeology (Processual Archaeology), and what became labelled as middle-range theory, for connecting the 'static' archaeological record of the past with the active nature of human behaviour in the present (Binford 1971; Brown 1981; Saxe 1970; Tainter 1978).

Such approaches were criticized in the 1980s and early 1990s as being too positivist in nature and for underemphasizing the dynamic nature of human intentionality, or agency, within processes of death and burial (Hodder 1982; Parker Pearson 1982; 1999; Shanks & Tilley 1982). The emergence of this post-processualist critique followed similar intellectual trends in cultural anthropology and other social sciences that placed emphasis on *agency* theory (Giddens 1984) and *practice* theory (Bourdieu 1977; 1984) as important categories of human action. As a result of this trend, many archaeologists focused more intently on the role of the living in controlling and manipulating the mortuary event (Härke 1997; Parker Pearson 1993). Such approaches were effective in highlighting certain aspects of social power and ideology within early ritual traditions. The view that the 'dead do not bury themselves' became representative of a new direction in archaeological thought for investigating the complex relationships that exist between the living and the dead through the process of burial and ancestor commemoration. Contemporaneous developments in feminist theory and gender studies also added significantly to the burgeoning new focus within archaeological studies that sought to more effectively illuminate individual human agency in the past.

Over the past decade or so, many archaeologists have attempted to move beyond the rather arbitrary category of *agents* and their *agency* in an attempt to focus more explicitly on concepts of personhood, life history and individual identity in the past (Edmonds 1999; Fowler 2002; 2004; Hodder 1999:132–7; Whittle 2003). Such approaches border on being almost empathetic in nature, as they have attempted to push beyond broader perceptions of faceless agents to provide a more humanistic perception of the past and the nature of past people's lives.

In considering the impact of these trends in the study of death and burial, it is clear that recent developments in the osteological study of human remains potentially offer an important new range of data for the reconstruction of individual life-histories (Robb 2002; Sofaer 2006:63). For example, remarkable improvements in the study of bone chemistry, such as ancient DNA, trace elements and stable isotopes, have provided richly detailed information on migration, dietary patterns and biological relationships within sample populations. Coupled with more conventional studies, such as skeletal growth and development, biomechanical activity markers and physical trauma, osteoarchaeology provides a unique window into accumulative events within the life history of individuals. In fact, Saul and Saul (1989) have suggested the term *osteobiography* as a more appropriate term for the study of the human skeleton as being a reflection of lifetime histories and biological events.

Nevertheless, even with rapid new developments in the study of human remains there remains a strong disjunction between theory and method. As Sofaer has stated, few osteoarchaeologists have attempted to engage with more recent trends in theoretical archaeology which treat the body as something beyond mere artefact or object (2006:24). By contrast, theoretical archaeologies have focused increasingly on concepts of embodiment, corporeality and materiality and their relationship to ontological constructions of the body (e.g. Hamilakis, Pluciennik, & Tarlow 2002; Meskell 2000). One of the most interesting connections between such conceptual approaches and recent methodological developments in osteoarchaeology is the possibility of examining the life-cycles of individuals more closely (Gilchrist 2004; Robb 2002). By focusing on the duration of events of single life-histories, a stronger commitment is made to the interpretation of shorter scales of human history and ultimately the meaning and significance of individual lives in the past (Gilchrist 2000:235).

With this potential convergence of new methodological approaches and theoretical trends, it would seem that we are standing at the threshold of a novel multidisciplinary approach to reconstructing people's lives in the past. Such a project provides a much stronger footing for examining the contribution of individuals within early societies and therefore seems poised to push beyond the boundaries of conventional social models for interpreting the past. Nevertheless, while such integrative approaches are tantalizing in their potentiality, they are unfortunately the exception rather than the standard for many studies in European prehistory. In fact, it seems that in many ways we are really only just beginning to comprehend the potential of the past as we continually push theoretically and methodologically towards a more humanistic understanding of past lives and how they contributed to historically contingent social structures. In the next section, I briefly review the broader trends of societal attitudes and practices surrounding death in the Bronze to Early Iron Age and then focus more specifically on the link between new forms of warrior identity and the patterns of social commemoration for these individuals.

Death and Burial in Later European Prehistory

The Neolithic to Bronze Age transition, which occurred in various phases across the European continent from approximately the 4th to 3rd millennia bc, has been understood as a dramatic shift in social, material and economic conditions. As the previous chapter examined, the Neolithic is characterized by the emergence and diffusion of domestication and agriculture in conjunction with increasingly complex relationships between communities, land and their ancestors. Such developments are broadly reflected in the construction of funerary monuments and ritual settings, such as large megalithic tombs and enclosures, across much of western Europe and the British Isles. Such sites and associated ritual practices have been interpreted as reflecting the strong emphasis placed on corporate identities and collective ritual activities by societies of this period (Barrett 1990; 1994; Bradley 1998).

By the late 3rd and early 2nd millennia bc, major transformations began to occur between regions of temperate Europe as individuals and communities were drawn into greater interactive networks of communication, trade and cultural exchange. One of the most significant characteristics of this dynamic new setting was the emergence of mortuary patterns that placed much greater emphasis on individuals within societies and the material nature of their identities (Kristiansen 1984a; Kristiansen & Larsson 2005; Shennan 1982; 1986; Sherratt 1994; Treherne 1995). Disposal patterns for the dead developed as specific traditions within various regions, with flat inhumation, mounded inhumation and cremation being three of the most common categories (Harding 2000:76). With the rise of mounded inhumation (barrows) in some areas in the Early Bronze Age a clear connection with earlier Neolithic ritual landscapes is apparent. In Britain, for example, scholars have suggested that even with the incorporation of new patterns of mortuary practice, the placement of the inhumed dead in grave pits covered by earthen barrows formed an important 'field of discourse' between communities of the present and the dead of the ancestral past (Barrett 1994; Garwood 1991; Mizoguchi 1993). From this perspective, even with changing forms of interment connected with new social processes, there was a strong connection being maintained with previous lineages through ritual activities set within known and understood ancestral landscapes (Barrett 1994:125; Garwood 1991:17).

Other interpretations, however, have stressed that the appearance of new burial rites and new categories of material culture, particularly the deposition of personal prestige items, was indicative of emerging social inequalities within societies and that the placement of barrows within earlier Neolithic ritual landscapes was a distinct form of status legitimization (e.g. Bintliff 1984; Bradley 1984). Control over the production and circulation of early metals, prestige objects and subsistence resources are typically cited as evidence for increasing socio-economic status differentiation and the materialization of social elites within Early Bronze Age societies (Gilman 1981; Kristiansen 1984a; Milisauskas 1978; Rowlands 1980).

Significant culture-historical horizons connected with such trends include the Baden, Yamnaya, Globular Amphora and Corded Ware for Central and Eastern Europe and the Bell Beaker and Wessex cultures for western Europe and the British Isles (for detailed discussions see Coles & Harding 1979; Harding 2000; Sherratt 1994). In many cases the burial patterns connected with many of these archaeological cultures reveal the inhumation of single individuals with personal items and prestige goods including daggers and axes. For example, the widespread nature of the Bell Beaker phenomenon from Spain to the British Isles has long been the focus of scholarly debate. Considered by earlier generations of archaeologists to be evidence for the migration of specific cultural groups or specialists, in recent years the distribution of beakers has been viewed as more closely connected with the spread of new forms of social practice, including the consumption of alcohol through the use of small bell-shaped handle-less pots (Sherratt 1987; Sherratt 1994:253). In addition to the deposit of such new pottery types with the dead, many burials also contained weaponry items such as flint or metal (initially copper and then bronze) daggers, triangular barbed-and-tanged flint arrowheads, and stone wrist guards connected with archery (Figure 5.6). As Sherratt has suggested, this particular *package* of objects represents both the movement of new social practices and attitudes between élite members of communities as well as the possible mobility of certain individual specialists between regions (1994:250–6).

By the Late Bronze Age, ostentatious burials reflecting a well-expressed martial character became much more widespread within the Aegean, continental Europe and Eurasian steppe and suggest that the intensity of warfare and its technology and symbolism, with congruent societal practices and perceptions, steadily evolved in new directions (Figure 5.7). These developments have been traditionally characterized, particularly in the Aegean region, as the beginning of the age of Homeric heroes and legends. Often viewed as a widespread warrior-grave pattern that developed by the Late Bronze Age, which it is argued existed almost unchanged to early historic times, such burials have been seen as indicative of the emergence of 'chiefly' societies supported by a retinue of full-time or part-time warrior specialists (Harding 2000:274; Kristiansen 1982; Randsborg 1973; Shennan 1993). These interpretations have emphasized the rise in status and social power of elite warriors as a crucial factor in the widespread emergence of early ranked societies within the European and Eurasian regions.

While it is certain that these early warriors gained and controlled considerable social status and power through the obtainment and use of weaponry and other prestige items, other scholars have suggested that warrior identity and the masculine ethos that surrounded this lifestyle was more reflective of broader transformations

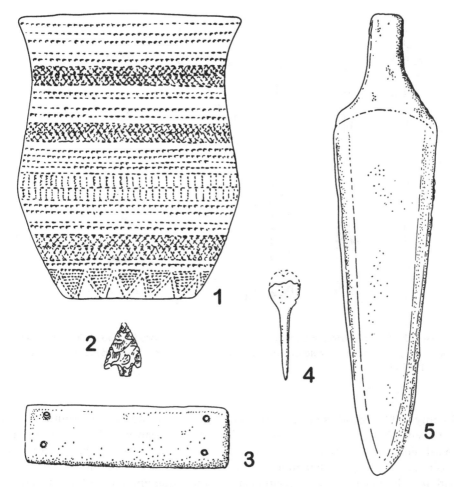

Figure 5.6 Objects from a Bell-Beaker grave, dating to the beginning of the second millennium bc at Roundway, Wiltshire, England: 1. Beaker; 2. flint arrowheads; 3. archer's wrist guard; 4. copper pin; 5. copper tanged knife-dagger (After Piggot 1965:99)

in gender categorization and body identity (Sørensen 1991; 1992; Treherne 1995). For example, it has been suggested that new social categories materialized through the active articulation of objects as the range of variation between gendered categories of masculinity and femininity became increasingly redefined within societies. Importantly, these gendered categories have been seen as not necessarily dependent on biological sex but instead as social categories that were mapped through material culture and its varying symbolism in the creation of new social identities (Gilchrist 1999; 2004; Yates 1993).

These views have had a profound impact on our understanding of the complexity surrounding achieved versus ascribed statuses in the formation and maintenance of warrior elites and their lineages in late prehistoric Europe. For example, regarding the Early Iron Age transition, Bettina Arnold's important study of the changing status roles of women in Early Hallstatt society has provided an important perspective on the dynamic relationship between frameworks of social power, gender and

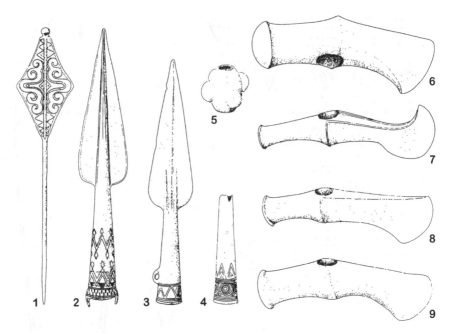

Figure 5.7 Part of hoard, mid-second millennium BC from Borodino, South Russia: 1. silver pin; 2–4. silver spear-heads with gold ornament; 5. alabaster mace-head; 6–9. jadeite battled axes (After Piggot 1965:131)

identity (1995). Studies such as Arnold's indicate that we must be cautious in our treatment of the masculine 'warrior' elite social category and its relationship to social hierarchy and power within periods of vibrant historical change. Such perspectives also suggest that more nuanced understandings of the role of warfare within early societies and its relationship to the social and cultural construction of 'warriors' must be set within specific socio-historical contexts.

In recent years, a number of studies have succeeded in offering a much broader theoretical treatment of such issues through more focused assessments of violence, warfare and martial symbolism and their changing social and material contexts (Carmen & Harding 1999; Harding 2007; Gilchrist 2003; Kristiansen & Larsson 2005; Osgood, Monks, & Toms 2000). Therefore, in order to evaluate the important relationship between the death of warriors and patterns of social commemoration in late prehistoric Europe, it will be helpful to first try and disentangle some of the conceptual problems surrounding the 'warrior' category.

Disentangling the Warrior

One of the most frequently cited works on late prehistoric warriors is, 'The Warrior's Beauty: The Masculine Body and Self-Identity in Bronze-Age Europe', by Paul Treherne (1995). Connecting with many of the theoretical issues noted above, Treherne's article focuses on the patterns of material culture linked to the emergence of high-status warriors and new forms of social practices that constituted the warrior *lifestyle*. Treherne suggests that there were four main material categories that can be recognized from mortuary contexts: 1) *warfare* as reflected by the deposit of weaponry; 2) *alcohol* consumption (drinking vessels); 3) *riding/driving* technology (e.g. chariots and wagons and later horse riding); and 4) *bodily ornamentation* (e.g. tweezers, razors, mirrors, objects of adornment, etc.) (1995:108). These specific sets of material objects, and the social practices they signified, represented an aggregation of both foreign and local elements through a process of *bricolage* (after Levi-Strauss 1966), whereby individuals actively constructed new forms of individual and shared identity reified through prestigious material items and activities. As Treherne suggests, such practices led to the development of a 'differentiated warrior ideology' that widely permeated societies and ultimately led to an increasingly prominent status group within many European communities (1995:109).

Based on Treherne's argument, one of the key elements of societal transformation is the emergence of cultural attitudes surrounding the warrior's body and its signification through *masculinity* and *beauty*, which he suggests are ordered around the ethos of violence and warfare (1995:124–7). With clear evidence for the increasing scale of individual combat in the late prehistoric period, the use of new weapons led to new types of interpersonal combat that had profound implications on cultural perceptions of the body as a locus of both power and weakness (Frank 1991; Shanks 1993; Theweleit 1989). The concurrent development of social values connected with glory and honour in battle frequently have been focused on as important by scholars, especially in the context of the commemoration in death of the lifestyle and ethos of the warrior. For example, in a similar discussion on the commemoration of Greek warriors, Vernant suggests that it is only through a *beautiful* death that the warrior can attain a form of enduring immortality within social memory (1991:57).

However, it may be argued that this tendency to view prehistoric warfare in such quixotic terms has greatly oversimplified the nature of the warrior category and has placed undue significance on the 'warrior's beauty' and on perceptions of an 'honourable' death within later prehistoric societies. Perhaps the roots of this perspective lay within studies of the Iron Age period, in particular the archaic and classical periods of Greece and historical evidence on Bronze Age warfare taken from written sources such as the Homeric epics. The backward projection of classical-period cultural attitudes and social commemoration rites (e.g. hero cults, war memorials, victory monuments, etc.) has in many ways influenced our perception of Bronze Age warfare. Therefore, the question of whether such perspectives are appropriate for interpreting Bronze Age societies is important as it influences our understanding of the relationship between certain forms of institutionalized conflict and the actual nature of the warrior category and its social meaning during this period. In more general terms, there has been a strong tendency in the scholarly literature to glorify warriors and to emphasize their hierarchical status within Bronze Age societies. For example, as Anthony Harding has so poignantly noted:

> The Bronze Age has long suffered from being viewed through eyes that romanticize its character, perhaps because of the Homeric associations that are commonly adduced. In such a society, war is considered glorious, and prowess in battle of enormous importance. We can survey such a scene from the comfort of our studies without having to stop to consider its sordidness and brutality. (2000:272)

In trying to disentangle this concept of the warrior in later European prehistory, one must consider carefully idealized perceptions of the warrior as opposed to the actual characteristics of a lifestyle of violence, as noted by Harding above. From a completely different perspective, it is possible to consider late prehistoric warriors as also existing at the edge of their own ordered societies. Drawing on Dumezil (1973) and Littleton's (1987) discussions of Indo-European myths and world view, Deborah Shepherd has suggested that because of the warrior's role as protector of the ordered community against the 'Other', this situated the warrior conceptually closer to the Other than his/her actual community (1999:219). Such a liminal position at the 'edge' of societies was perhaps reinforced by the ethos of violence that surrounded and permeated the lifestyle of the warrior.

More nuanced anthropological perspectives also may be helpful in rethinking the nature of the warrior category. For example, bioarchaeological research may provide a much stronger multidisciplinary approach to the social interpretation of warfare and its connection with societies. An excellent example of this is Robb's (1997) diachronic study of changing patterns of trauma in prehistoric Italy. This study investigated osteological evidence and changing trauma patterns between males and females to suggest that over time gendered roles became more fixed and women were less likely to be involved in activities of conflict and violence. Interdisciplinary approaches such as this offer several lines of empirical evidence in which to evaluate changing 'social' versus 'biological' realities of gender, status and physical violence among communities (Robb 1997; 2002).

Cross-cultural anthropological studies may also be informative for developing more nuanced theories of warrior identity. For example, the cultivation of warriors through various age-grade transitions into adulthood is well known ethnographically; however, this view of the life-cycle of the warrior and the psychoanalytical aspects of a life of violence and how it contributes to the construction of both identity and the formation of an 'ethos' has infrequently been discussed for prehistoric periods. An exception to this would be a critique of the Treherne article noted above, wherein Gilchrist suggests that Treherne (1995) 'presents a static picture of the masculine body, with the idealized image of the warrior at the height of his prowess. At what ages did the male gain and relinquish his warrior identity, and how was material culture used to mark such transitions? How did the warrior interrelate with other males of different ages, social roles, and ethnicities?' (2004:143). These are important questions, as they consider the category of 'warrior' in terms of the important dimensions of age and gender as well as culturally constructed practices. Such a view also acknowledges the active role of 'social time' – in this case the subjectively experienced life-cycle and its relationship to individual memory and identity construction (Gilchrist 2004:150).

Such issues bring us back once again to the significance of memory and its connection to social commemoration among Bronze Age societies. While we must be cautious in making bold generalizations about these societies through our interpretations of the mortuary record, this category of material evidence nevertheless represents an extremely important reflection of how the living chose to memorialize the warrior life-style of that time.

'Technologies' of Memory

Focusing on Late Neolithic to Early Bronze Age funerary practices, Andy Jones has suggested an important connection between the creation of social memory through ritualized mortuary activity and the use of material objects in specific sequences or patterns (2003:69). Analogous to the *chaîne opératoire* of technological production, Jones suggests that it is through the mnemonic characteristics of objects that a 'technology of remembrance' is created. This view places emphasis not only on the nature of objects to store and recite information but also on the process of memory production created through the social practices of remembering and forgetting. Such a process sets the embodied ritual action of the living and the materiality of the mortuary setting within a broader field of transformative action for both the disposal and commemoration of the deceased.

Williams has reconsidered this transformative process through Metcalf and Huntingdon's (1991) use of Hertz's 'theory of death' (1960), where it is suggested that an important tripartite relationship exists between the living (mourners), the corpse and the soul of the deceased (2006:20–1). Through the process of ritual action, and the use of material culture, the mourners transform the corpse and in so doing reconstitute social memories of the deceased (ibid.). The key physical elements within this process include the body of the deceased, specific combinations of material objects, and the design and use of the mortuary setting itself.

Recent scholarly tends within the social sciences have framed the body as the primary locus for cultural, sensory and physical engagement with the world (e.g. Featherstone et al. 1991; Polhemus 1988; Turner 1984). Such theoretical underpinnings are of special significance for mortuary archaeology as they provide a useful framework for interpreting the variety of responses to ontological security and cultural beliefs in the afterlife (Parker Pearson 1999:45). What is of particular importance here, within the context of the intersection between corpse, mourners and material culture through a 'technology of remembrance' process, is the treatment of the corpse through the various stages of the funerary event. For example, disposal patterns for the deceased in Late Bronze Age Europe took a variety of forms, ranging from the placement of certain individuals into bog contexts in northern Europe (to be forgotten forever?), to the construction of elaborate vaulted funerary tombs presumably for ruling lineages in the Aegean, to the cremation of the corpse and the placement of the remains in mortuary urns, cists or grave pit contexts.

Of particular interest in regards to disposal practices in temperate Europe is the cremation of the body, as such treatment reflects a distinct difference in cultural attitudes about preservation and the afterlife. A variety of cremation rites were practised in various locations in Europe during the Neolithic and Early Bronze Age and became the most common pattern of disposal in Britain during the Middle Bronze Age (Harding 2000:111). However, the progressive trend towards cremation in central Europe by the Late Bronze Age, including warrior individuals, is most clearly reflected in the Urnfield rites (Figure 5.8). This development represents an important transition in cultural attitudes towards the body of the deceased and remains largely unexplained in terms of its historical meaning. In fact, 'bi-ritual' simultaneous activities in the form of inhumation and cremation rites exist within several Urnfield cemeteries and seem to indicate an interplay of complex attitudes concerning bodily preservation, disposal and the afterlife (Harding 2000:111–13).

In most cases, the rite of cremation has also been interpreted as a constitutive element within the bodily aesthetics that surrounded the Bronze Age warrior lifestyle. As noted above in the discussion of Treherne's article on the 'warrior's beauty', the display, adornment and treatment of the body factored prominently within the warrior's lifestyle whereby the bodily aesthetics and practices honoured in life were also to be reflected in death. Such practices may also have had an important

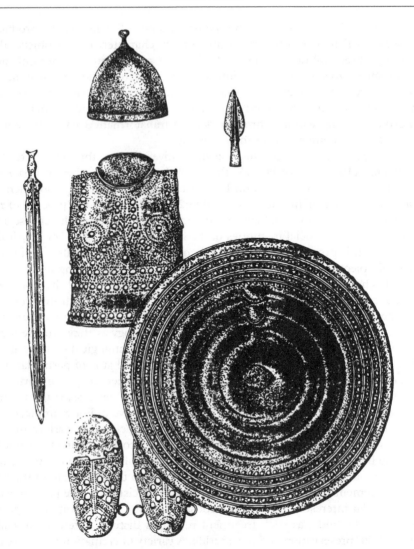

Figure 5.8 'Chiefly' Urnfield warriors from the Danube region, based on military gear recovered from burials and hoards (After Kristiansen 1998:116)

sociological role to play in the confrontation and acceptance of death by the living. As Treherne states, 'the culmination of a beautiful death in funerary rites fixes a place for the deceased both in the landscape and the minds of others and as such is one way to obviate the horror and anonymity of death's threshold' (1995:123). Treherne's perspective clearly draws inspiration from the *Iliad* and more generally from classical Greek responses to death and burial.

According to Vernant, the death of the warrior in the Greek world elicited a two-stage process of bodily preparation and treatment. As described in both the *Iliad* and *Odyssey* the body is first 'beautified; it is washed with warm water to cleanse it of soil and stain; its wounds are effaced with an unguent; the skin, rubbed with oil, takes on a special sheen; perfumed and adorned with precious materials, the corpse is then laid out on a litter to be viewed and mourned by the dead man's near and dear ones' (1991:69). In the second stage, and in the true Homeric tradition, 'the corpse is then burned on a pyre whose flames consume all that is made of flesh and blood, that is, everything both edible and subject to decay and thus attached to that ephemeral kind of existence where life and death are inextricably mingled' (ibid.).

This view of the practices surrounding the death and burial of Greek warriors is informative; however, we should be cautious of accepting it as too broad a generalization of warriors and societal responses to their death. The tendency to place too much attention on the aesthetics of beauty and glory surrounding the Greek warrior ideal may not be appropriate for other responses to death and burial of warriors in other social settings, particularly if one considers the reality of interpersonal combat. While specific damage to the body, such as the face and head, can vary widely according to cultural practice or warfare technologies (Walker 2001), the taking of trophy heads, scalping and extreme trauma to various parts of the body are certainly characteristics of early warfare. In consideration of these physical realities, how might societies have dealt with concepts of bodily aesthetics and the identity of the dead when warriors suffered such physical carnage or simply were not recoverable from the battlefield? Would societal responses through mortuary treatment have varied in conjunction with the type of death and/or mutilation of the corpse? Was the essence of the warrior so contained in the physicality of appearance and identity, that the loss or damage of these characteristics significantly impacted the way in which the dead were treated in the funerary rite? Could the trend towards widespread cremation practices in the Late Bronze Age signal a response to the changing scale and nature of combat? Unfortunately, such questions are extremely difficult to address with available evidence, but are nonetheless important when considering the changing practices and technologies of warfare and subsequent societal responses to the treatment and disposal of the dead.

Materiality of the warrior

In addition to the mortuary treatment of the warrior's body in the Bronze Age, it is important to consider other practices that may have related to practices of remembrance and the cultural symbolism surrounding objects of warfare and the warrior's life-style. Archaeological evidence from the Middle to Late Bronze Age provides strong evidence for the pervasive symbolism of warrior identity (Figure 5.9) within Europe and the similarity of its expression through specific categories of material objects (Kristiansen and Larsson 2005) Although the origins of warfare have deep roots extending back well before the Bronze Age (Keeley 1996; Walker 2001), the placement of weaponry such as daggers, axes and archery items into the graves of individuals in the Early Bronze Age signalled an important transition in the construction of individual identity. By the Late Bronze Age, the inclusion of expertly crafted swords, helmets, shields and other forms of armour, in addition to costly riding and traction technological elements, formed an important corpus of material items that contributed to the unique lifestyle and identity of elite warrior individuals and their lineages. In investigating these patterns, it is important to consider the varying fields of symbolism that existed for the use and disposal of certain categories of martial objects. Such areas of practice would include: rock art, anthropomorphic stelae and deposition of weaponry in other contexts.

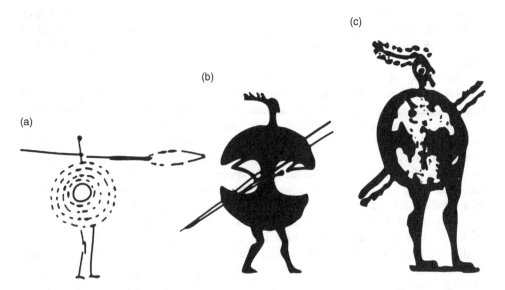

Figure 5.9a–c Bronze Age warriors with lances and shields (Kristiansen 1998)

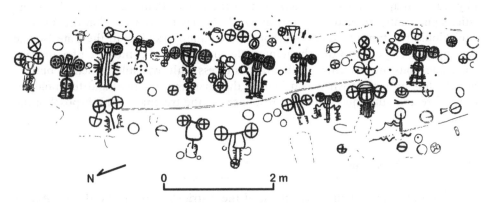

Figure 5.10 Rock art illustrating chariot groups from Fränarp, Sweden (After Coles 2002)

Rock art

One of the most enigmatic categories of material culture relating to late prehistoric warfare and warrior activities is rock art. Numerous rock art panels have been analyzed from northern Italy, southern France, Scandinavia, northwest Spain and the British Isles (for review see Harding 2000:335–48). While it is difficult to ascertain the exact intention of many of the rock art panels, they nevertheless provide important details and scenes of Bronze Age life with frequent depictions of human combat, weaponry, wheeled vehicles and boats (Figure 5.10).

Much has been made of the connection between weaponry symbolism and male 'masculinity' that is believed to have prominently emerged in the Bronze Age (Yates 1993). However, a number of different theoretical approaches have been used in the study of rock art and it is likely that many of the panels represent a palimpsest of activity and like any form of 'art' may have had multiple meanings over the course of their use and interpretation (e.g. Anati 1960; 1961; Bradley 1997; Coles 1993; Tilley 1991). Nevertheless, the depictions of warriors and warfare technologies may have played an important role in mnemonic recollection and for structuring the recounting of real events and individuals and/or mythologized ancestral pasts. While solid panel and portable rock art remain ambiguous in our understanding of the memorialization of real past events and individuals, the placement of stone sculptures or anthropomorphic stone stelae either near graves or in areas of apparent ritual activities does indicate an important relationship between societies and their memorialization of specific individuals (see Harrison 2004 for a comprehensive overview of this).

Anthropomorphic stelae

The placement of carved stones to mark the graves of what are presumed to be warriors was a common practice within Europe from the Copper Age onwards. In focusing on such markers attributed to the Bronze Age, the patterned repetition of weaponry, armor and chariots dominate many of the compositions (Figure 5.11). While the repetitious nature of such objects reinforces the widespread nature and symbolism of warfare and its technology for this time period, we must consider more carefully how the creation and placement of statue-menhirs and grave stelae connected with practices of memorialization. The use of such objects, particularly the permanence of stone markers, appears to signal a strong emphasis on the temporal duration of memory connected with specific individual commemoration. While we may interpret the application of certain categories of weaponry as diffused generic symbolism, they may have had much stronger connections with individual lives and histories and therefore may have formed an important element in the 'technology of remembrance' created around the deceased. What is particularly striking, from a comparative view, is the widespread nature of this practice. Stretching from Italy all the way across Eurasia to Mongolia, the use of anthropomorphic standing stones with applied weaponry symbolism became a very common element in the burial of individuals from the Copper Age onwards in Europe and from approximately the middle of the second millennium bc in eastern Eurasia.

We can interpret that the construction of large tumuli for the dead within the landscape signalled the importance of the deceased; however, once this process was completed the actual physicality of the individual was no longer visible once the body was cremated and/or interred within the tumulus. As such, a number of questions can be asked of the significance and meaning of grave stelae. For example, were stelae used as an important anthropomorphic portal for communication, interaction and subsequent commemoration of the deceased? Did the application of combinations of motifs on the stelae act as important mnemonic devices for recalling the individual character, exploits and life-events of the deceased? Can we consider the use of such stones in conjunction with the construction of graves and tumuli as a part of more complex 'technology of memory' practices? There are, of course, no straightforward answers to these questions, however the seemingly temporal permanence and anthropomorphic nature of stelae suggest an important connection with the commemoration of individual ancestors and clearly deserve more elaborate theoretical treatment in future studies of late prehistoric memory practices.

Weaponry and its symbolism

One of the defining characteristics of Bronze Age warrior identity, whether real or articulated during the mortuary event, was the placement of weaponry items with

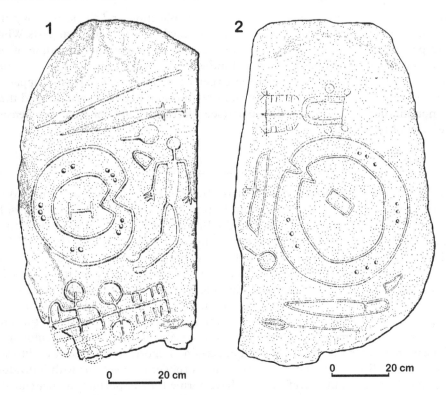

Figure 5.11 Shields and helmet on Iberian grave stelae: 1. Solana de Cabañas, Logrosan, Caceres; 2. Torrejon del Rubio (After Harding 2000:286 [Almagro 1966])

the deceased. In particular, much attention has been placed on sword production and use by Bronze Age societies and whether such implements acted as purely symbolic prestige items in some cases or were actively employed in battle in others. Use-wear analysis has been employed in several instances and has indicated a wide range of wear patterning from pristine blades that apparently were never used in combat to well worn blades indicative of heavy use and reconditioning (Harding 2000:281; 2007:109; Kristiansen 1984b). Thus, the picture that emerges is one where the use of weaponry items occurred in a variety of social contexts ranging from actual combat to the efficacy of such implements as a likely form of prestige and wealth.

In addition to the recovery of weaponry from Bronze Age graves, the placement of shields, lances, swords and other war-related objects in what have been perceived as 'hoards' and 'votive' deposits is one of the defining characteristics of the European Bronze Age. As noted above, the symbolism of such objects figures prominently on rock-art panels and grave stelae in many areas of Europe and Eurasia, but the interpretation of groups of objects found in pits and watery contexts has stimulated a tremendous amount of scholarly discussion over the social and economic meaning of these practices (see Harding 2000:Ch. 10).

The deposition of bronze objects included items other than weaponry, of course, such as sickles, axes, bracelets and fragmentary stock pieces. The aggregation of such objects may have related to the economic hoarding and protection of metal wealth for later trade or smelting and recasting. However, the increase in the deposition of weaponry objects in the Late Bronze Age, particularly in bogs and rivers, has been regularly discussed in terms of votive activities and their social meanings and contexts (Bradley 1984; 1990; Levy 1982; 1991).

Scant evidence exists in the Bronze Age of temperate Europe for what we might consider to be cult centers or specific constructions for ritual practices and this has placed much more emphasis on the significance of rock art and 'votive' deposits and their connection to religion and ritual (Harding 2000:309). Such practices also appear to have had strong connections with the materialism and symbolism surrounding warriors and their lineages. For example, the production, use and disposal of weaponry objects such as swords may have been strongly infused with cultural meaning wherein the objects themselves had 'biographies' of ownership across generations. While the disposal of such objects in watery contexts may have connected with some form of sacrifice or commemoration, the very context of their disposal also suggests attitudes of 'forgetting', wherein objects were taken out of social circulation to be lost forever to the human realm. Such activities may have related to tributes to the ancestors or as a characteristic of war and the sacrifice of objects taken from the defeated.

Therefore, while it is clear that Bronze Age societies re-articulated prominent characteristics of warrior identity (i.e. weaponry, riding/driving technology, feasting/drinking and personal objects) through a 'technology of remembrance' process, the characteristics of this life-style and its commemoration diffused beyond the mortuary setting. For example, Kristiansen and Larsson have argued for a much broader context for the use of rock art sites and 'votive' activities as being part of a cosmological order that structured ritual practices within specific landscape settings (2005:356). Such a view places emphasis on the active nature of warrior prestige identity, its relationship to broader societal belief systems and their reconstitution through ritual action within the landscape.

In this last section, I would like to examine the important shift in the nature of funerary activities and social commemoration which occurred in the Early Iron Age. A greater emphasis will be placed on the eastern European and Eurasian steppe area, as these regions have been infrequently turned to within traditional treatments of European later prehistory.

Large Scale Funerary Practices of the Early Iron Age

By the middle of the first millennium bc, societies began depositing objects in ritual settings on a much greater scale than in earlier periods (Wells 2001:70). Such practices occurred in the context of funerals but also within specially constructed ritual structures and settings, such as the rectangular enclosure at the cemetery of Vix in France (ibid.). This enclosure, some 200 metres southwest of the famous 'princess of Vix' burial, was defined by a rectangular ditch of approximately 23 metres on each side. The enclosure contained a single entrance point with two carved stone figures of a male and female placed nearby. Inside the enclosure, large quantities of animal bone remains and pottery appear to indicate feasting or other large scale communal activities (Chaume et al. 1995; Chaume 1997; Wells 2001:48). Other enclosures like that of Gournay-sur Aronde in northern France, which dates to approximately the 4th century bc, also indicate broader-scale feasting and ceremonial activities (Brunaux 1996).

Charlotte Fabech (1991) has suggested that this increase in the scale of ritual activity and participation of societal members signals an important transformation in the way that communities viewed themselves in terms of group identity and social structure. Such a view has important implications for the interpretation of the large elite tombs from this period as well, as scholars must consider such constructions not simply in terms of social power and hierarchical structure but also as important moments in changing historical conditions (Babić 2002). For example, as Peter Wells has stated:

> In the dynamic and fluid social context of Early Iron Age Europe, we need to understand rich burials not as reflections of a static hierarchical society, but as representations of moments within a process of social expression and display among the living. These graves are complex structures, and they express identity on different levels. (Wells 2001:46)

These social processes associated with the Early Iron Age, as noted by Wells, have stimulated great discussion on issues of ethnicity and identity, in part due to the interaction between the classical literate societies of Greece and Rome and their descriptions and perceptions of 'barbarian' tribes in temperate Europe. In recent years, archaeologists have steadily moved away from a focus on culture-historical frameworks of interpretation in order to consider more carefully the dynamic processes of group interaction and identity formation which occurred at the late prehistoric to early historic period in Europe (Jones 1997).

Certainly one of the most important catalysts for societal transformation in Early Iron Age Europe was the expanding influence of trade interaction that stemmed from the Mediterranean region. The movement of new commodities and material items were readily adopted and re-articulated in new expressive ways by Iron Age communities within Europe. Social status and prestige undoubtedly played an important part in the obtainment, use and display of new categories of material culture, such as Greek pottery, bronze drinking vessels, statuary, and exotic jewelry and other ornamentation. Large 'princely' tombs of the Early Iron Age reflect the aggregation of a variety of imported prestige items as elites rearticulated their identities in the face of changing social, cultural and material conditions (Arnold 2001; Babić 2002; Dietler 1994).

An important theoretical construct for understanding this dynamic setting in the face of greater societal interaction is that of the 'tribal zone', offered by Ferguson and Whitehead (1992). Through several comparative anthropological studies, they suggest that in cases where more politically centralized states come into contact with non-state 'tribal' level societies a dynamic zone of interaction is created (ibid.; see also Wells 2001:31–3). This asymmetrical relationship thus sets in motion a vibrant series of conflicts and institutionalized warfare driven by elements of materialism and individual agency. Such characteristics of human action, coupled with new forms of military technology and its symbolism, like mounted warfare, may have set the stage for important social and cultural transitions within Early Iron Age societies across the Eurasian region (Renfrew 1998).

It is an intriguing fact that in the first half of the first millennium bc, with a clear rise in the use of horses for individual mobility in warfare, the construction of immense tombs with large deposits of sacrificed animals (including humans on occasion), large scale feasting and the concentration of substantial labour to construct such complexes is in evidence from parts of central and eastern Europe all the way across the Eurasian steppe to Mongolia (Hanks 2001; 2003). Such a wide-spread pattern indicates that profound changes occurred in the relationship between societies and the character and scale of their commemoration of specific individuals upon their death. While it is rather straightforward to consider that such practices were simply an expression of higher levels of social status achieved through more expansive territorial power or control, we should also consider more carefully what role such commemoration practices actually played among the living. For example, was this simply a form of aggrandizement on the part of specific lineages relating to the maintenance of ascribed status? Or, is it possible to suggest that complex aspects of spectacle and ritual performance connected with the construction and use of such funerary complexes were being accentuated and developed in new ways for more powerful and lasting social memory production? If so, what did this mean in terms of new forms of societal organization and development? In considering these questions, it is useful to turn to some of the more elaborate complexes of the Iron Age, which occur in the east European steppe zone and in the region just north of the Caucasus Mountains.

Two of the largest Iron Age mortuary complexes that have been excavated, which have been associated with the emergence of the Scythian groups in the north Pontic steppe region, are the Kostromskaya Kurgan and Kurgan 1 connected to the Ulski Aul cemetery. Both of these sites are situated in the northern Caucasus region and were excavated in the late 19th to early 20th centuries. The Kostromskaya Kurgan complex was comprised of a large earthen mound which covered a four post wooden superstructure (Figure 5.12). Within the interior upper and lower chambers of the complex, excavators recovered the remains of 22 sacrificed horses, 13 human skeletons and a single human burial in the lower chamber (Minns 1971 [1913]:227).

Kurgan 1 from the Ulski Aul cemetery is even more startling in terms of the number of sacrificed horses and interment of human skeletons (Figure 5.13). This immense barrow construction was approximately 15 metres in height and contained over 400 horse skeletons and numerous human individuals. The exact number and precise context of the remains is difficult to ascertain because of the degree of disturbance at the site through early looting activities, however, the scale of construction and conspicuous consumption relating to sacrifice is remarkable (Minns 1971 [1913]:22).

Similar mortuary constructions, in varying degrees of complexity and scale of investment, exist just at the edge of the geographical boundaries of eastern Europe (i.e. Ural Mountains of Russia) in the forest steppe of the western Siberian plateau, the steppe zone of the southern Urals (e.g. Filipovka), and in the Sayan-Altai Mountains (e.g. Arzhan I and II) (see Bokovenko 1996; Davis-Kimball et al. 1995; Koryakova 1996; Rolle 1989 for discussions). Unfortunately, it is beyond the scope of this chapter to discuss these sites in detail; however, what is important in the context of this chapter's theme is the widespread nature and intense scale of ritual activity at these sites.

On one hand, it is rather easy to consider the significance of these sites in terms of specific historical political actions. For example, the largest of the Eurasian steppe tombs may be interpreted as reflecting the death of important chieftains who headed some form of larger supra-tribal organization and territorial control (Bokovenko 1996). Such processes can be imagined with the initial emergence of new forms of mobility and military technology where an escalation of territorial

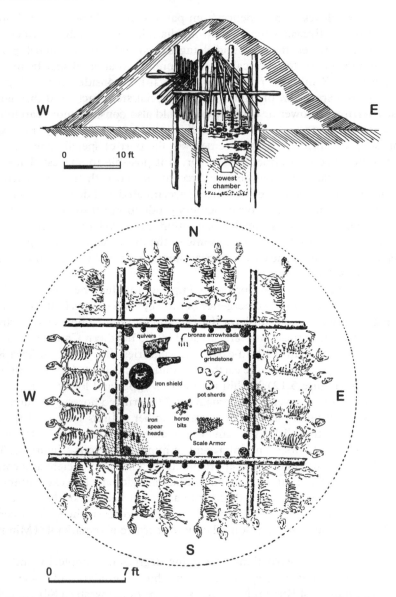

Figure 5.12 Kostromskaya Kurgan, northern Caucasus. Twenty-two sacrificed horses, lower chamber, four post superstructure, 13 human skeletons and single burial in the lower pit (After Minns [1971:227] first published 1913)

expansion was the likely result by certain groups. Such socio-political processes for the Early Iron Age in the Eurasian steppe zone have been discussed effectively in other publications and do not need to be readdressed here (e.g. Koryakova 1996; Kradin 2002). However, it is important to look beyond these sites as static indicators of wealth and power in order to consider them as dynamic loci for ritual action, performance and social memory production. The size and complexity of some of the sites indicate that significant numbers of people were brought together to carry out their construction, perhaps taking several days or weeks to accomplish. Such

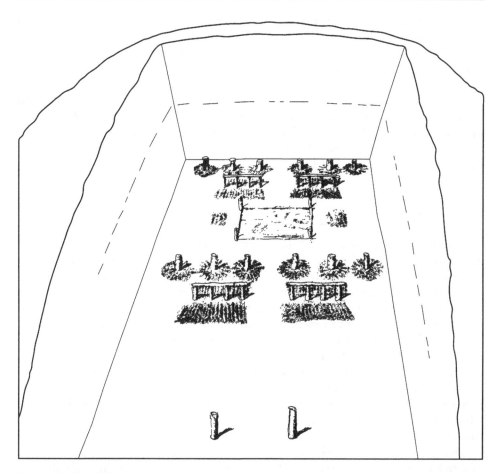

Figure 5.13   Ulski Aul, Kurgan 1, northern Caucasus, 15-meter-high barrow, a little over 400 horses sacrificed, numerous humans, number uncertain due to heavy disturbance from looting (After Minns [1971:227] first published 1913)

'public events' may have consolidated people from surrounding territories into short temporal 'communities' where participation in the construction of the sites and in large-scale conspicuous consumption and sacrifice produced strong individual as well as broader social memory production. Such activities have been widely discussed for the Neolithic of western Europe and the construction of megalithic monuments where a particular emphasis has been made on how the nature of monument construction both structures and mediates the social relations of the participants (Barrett 1994; Bradley 1998). Similar views have been employed for large-scale tomb construction in the European Iron Age, but unfortunately have not been discussed so productively in Eurasian steppe studies.

In considering the key differences between Bronze and Iron Age commemorative practices as discussed in this chapter, it is clear that broader transformative patterns occurred in both the scale and nature of warfare, death and social commemoration. Bronze Age attitudes surrounding warrior status and the lifestyle of these individuals appear to have focused strongly on the individual identity and the prestige surrounding military symbolism. The transition in the Early Iron Age towards large-scale funerary monuments and the creation of specific places of cult activities, ritual practice and social feasting suggests a more active role for societal participants and may relate to stronger connections with group and territorial identities, and larger-scale aspects of participation in the performance and theatricality of death and commemoration rites. How such social practices connect with changes in the nature of warfare and its material and symbolic dimensions at both the individual and societal levels have yet to be examined more theoretically. However, the significance of social memory and its connection with changing practices of tomb construction and memorial practices offer an important approach to these complex processes in the late prehistoric period of Europe.

Conclusion

This chapter has presented a broad view of the complex relationship between changing forms of prehistoric social commemoration and perceptions of warrior identity in late prehistoric Europe. As suggested, it is important to move in a direction that leads towards more nuanced interpretations of how and why societies chose to commemorate warriors and their lifestyles in the ways that they did and how these commemorative practices connect with broader social transformations. Such approaches should focus on being more historically contingent in the interpretation of the linkages between changes in the technology of warfare and in social responses to varying scales of violence and conflict. While one must be cautious in making sweeping interpretations of such societies from an evaluation of mortuary patterns, there appears to be ample evidence for significant changes in the way in which societies signalled the importance of warrior identity through the construction of tombs and complexes that honoured these individuals.

The study of warfare during the Bronze and Iron Ages has had a long tradition of scholarship in Europe, however it is only in recent years that more attention is being placed on the relationship of warfare to cultural responses to this category of practice. Numerous works have challenged scholars to reconsider existing evidence for long traditions of violence and warfare stretching well into the human past and to re-evaluate their historical meanings (e.g. Carmen and Harding 1999; Keeley 1996; Martin and Frayer 1997; Vencl 1999). In building on these excellent studies, scholars should work towards more nuanced theoretical interpretations of how the nature of warrior identity, and changing historical perceptions of this category, contributed to processes of social change and development. The contribution of recent trends in the theory of memory production and connected themes of materiality will most certainly offer an important perspective within such future studies.

REFERENCES

Anati, Emmanuel 1960 La Grande Roche de Naquane. Archives de l'Institut de paléontology humaine, Mémoire 31. Paris: Masson and Cie.
Anati, Emmanuel 1961 Camonica Valley. A Depiction of Village Live in the Alps from Neolithic Times to the Birth of Christ as Revealed by Thousands of Newly Found Rock Carvings. New York: Knopf.

Arnold, Bettina 1995 Honorary Males or Women of Substance? Gender, Status, and Power in Iron-Age Europe. Journal of European Archaeology 3(2):153–68.

Arnold, Bettina 2001 The Limits of Agency in the Analysis of Elite Iron Age Celtic Burials. Journal of Social Archaeology 1(2):210–24.

Babić, Staša 2002 'Princely Graves' of the Central Balkans – A Critical History of Research. European Journal of Archaeology 5(1):70–88.

Barrett, John 1990 The Monumentality of Death: The Character of Early Bronze Age Mortuary Mounds in Southern Britain. World Archaeology 22(2):179–89.

Barrett, John 1994 Fragments from Antiquity. Oxford: Blackwell.

Beike, Denise, James Lampinen, and Douglas Behrend, eds. 2004 The Self and Memory. New York: Psychology Press.

Bergman, Bettina, and Christine Kondoleon, eds. 1999 The Art of Ancient Spectacle. New Haven: Yale University Press.

Binford, Lewis 1971 Mortuary Practices: Their Study and Their Potential. American Antiquity 3(2):6–29.

Bintlinff, John, ed. 1984 European Social Evolution: Archaeological Perspectives. Bradford: University of Bradford.

Bokovenko, Nikolai 1996 Asian Influence on European Scythia. Ancient Civilizations from Scythia to Siberia: An International Journal of Comparative Studies in History and Archaeology 3(1):97–122.

Bourdieu, Pierre 1977 Outline of a Theory of Practice. Cambridge: Cambridge University Press.

Bourdieu, Pierre 1984 Distinction: A Social Critique of the Judgment of Taste. London: Routledge and Kegan Paul.

Bradley, Richard 1984 The Social Foundations of Prehistoric Britain. London: Longman.

Bradley, Richard 1990 The Passage of Arms: An Archaeological Analysis of Prehistoric Hoards and Votive Deposits. Cambridge: Cambridge University Press.

Bradley, Richard 1997 Rock Art and the Prehistory of Atlantic Europe: Signing the Land. London: Routledge.

Bradley, Richard 1998 The Significance of Monuments: On the Shaping of Human Experience in Neolithic and Bronze Age Europe. London: Routledge.

Bradley, Richard 2000 An Archaeology of Natural Places. London: Routledge.

Brown, James 1981 The Search for Rank in Prehistoric Burials. In The Archaeology of Death. Robert Chapman, Ian Kinnes, and Klavs Randsborg, eds. Pp. 25–37. Cambridge: Cambridge University Press.

Brunaux, Jean-Louis 1996 Les religiouns gauloises: Rituels celtiques de la Gaule indépendante. Paris: Éditions Errance.

Carmen, John, and Anthony Harding, eds. 1999 Ancient Warfare: Archaeological Perspectives. Stroud: Sutton.

Chapman, John 2000 Tensions at Funerals: Social Practices and the Subversion of Community Structure in Later Hungarian Prehistory. In Agency in Archaeology. Marcia-Anne Dobres and John Robb, eds. Pp. 21–33. London: Routledge.

Chaume, Bruno 1997 Vix, Le Mont Lassois: État de nos connaissances sur le site princier et son environnement. In Vix et les éphèmères principautés celtiques. Patrice Brun and Bruno Chaume, eds. Pp. 185–200. Paris: Éditions Errance.

Chaume, Bruno, Laurent Olivier, and Walter Reinhard 1995 Das keltische Heiligtum von Vix. In Heiligtümer und Opferkulte der Kelten. A. Haffner, ed. Pp. 43–50. Stuttgart: Konrad Theiss.

Coles, John 1993 Boats on the Rocks. In A Spirit of Enquiry. Essays for Ted Wright. John Coles, Valerie Fenwick, and Gillian Hutchinson, eds. Pp. 23–31. London: National Maritime Museum.

Coles, John 2002 Chariots of the Gods? Landscape and Imagery at Frännarp, Sweden. Proceedings of the Prehistoric Society 68:215–46.

Coles, John, and Anthony Harding 1979 The Bronze Age in Europe. New York: St. Martin's Press.

Connerton, Paul 1989 How Societies Remember. Cambridge: Cambridge University Press.

Conway, Martin 1990 Autobiographical Memory: An Introduction. Philadelphia: Open University Press.

Conway, Martin 1995 Flashbulb Memories. Hove: Lawrence Erlbaum Associates.

Davis-Kimball, Jeannine, Vladimir Bashilov, and Leonid Yablonsky, eds. 1995 Nomads in the Eurasian Steppes in the Early Iron Age. Berkeley: Zinat Press.

DeMarrais, Elizabeth, Luis Castillo, and Tim Earle 1996 Ideology, Materialization, and Power Strategies. Current Anthropology 37:15–31.

Dietler, Michael 1994 The Iron Age in Mediterranean France: Colonial Encounters, Entanglements, and Transformations. Journal of World Prehistory 11:269–358.

Dumezil, G. 1973 Gods of the Ancient Northmen. Einar Haugen, ed. and trans. Los Angeles: University of California Press. Publications of the UCLA Center for the Study of Comparative Folklore and Mythology 3.

Edmonds, Mark 1999 Ancestral Geographies of the Neolithic: Landscape, Monuments and Memory. London: Routledge.

Fabech, Charlotte 1991 Samfundorganisation religiøse ceremonier og regional variation. In Samfundorganisation og Regional Variation. Charlote Fabech and Jytte Ringtved, eds. Pp. 283–352. Aarhus: Jysk Arkaeologick Selskab.

Featherstone, M. M. Hepworth, and B. Turner, eds. 1991 The Body: Social Process and Culture Theory. London: Sage.

Ferguson, Brian, and Neil Whitehead, eds. 1992 War in the Tribal Zone: Expanding States and Indigenous Warfare. Santa Fe: School of American Research Press.

Fowler, Chris 2002 Body Parts: Personhood and Materiality in the Manx Neolithic. In Thinking through the Body: Archaeologies of Corporeality. Yannis Hamilakis, Mark Pluciennik and Sarah Tarlow, eds. Pp. 47–69. London: Kluwer Academic.

Fowler, Chris 2004 The Archaeology of Personhood: An Anthropological Approach. London: Routledge.

Frank, Arthur 1991 For a Sociology of the Body: An Analytical Review. In The Body: Social Process and Culture Theory. Mike Featherstone, Mike Hepworth, and Brian Turner, eds. Pp. 36–102. London: Sage.

Garwood, Paul 1991 Ritual Tradition and the Reconstitution of Society. In Sacred and Profane: Proceedings of a Conference on Archaeology, Ritual and Religion. Paul Garwood, David Jennings, Robin Skeates, and Judith Toms, eds. Pp. 10–32. Oxford: Oxbow.

Giddens, Anthony 1984 The Constitution of Society: Outline of the Theory of Structuration. Cambridge: Polity.

Gilchrist, Roberta 1999 Gender and Archaeology: Contesting the Past. London: Routledge.

Gilchrist, Roberta, ed. 2000 Human Lifecyles. Special Issue of World Archaeology 31(3).

Gilchrist, Roberta, ed. 2003 The Social Commemoration of Warfare. World Archaeology 35(1).

Gilchrist, Roberta 2004 Archaeology and the Life Course: A Time and Age for Gender. In A Companion to Social Archaeology. Lynn Meskell and Robert Preucel, eds. Pp. 142–60. Oxford: Blackwell.

Gilman, Antonio 1981 The Development of Social Stratification in Bronze Age Europe. Current Anthropology 22:1–23.

Goody, J. 2000 The Power of the Written Tradition. Washington: Smithsonian Institution Press.

Halbwachs, Maurice 1992(1950) On Collective Memory. L. A. Coser, ed. and trans. Chicago: University of Chicago Press.

Hamilakis, Yannis, Mark Pluciennik, and Sarah Tarlow, eds. 2002 Thinking Through the Body: Archaeologies of Corporeality. London: Kluwer Academic.

Hanks, Bryan 2001 Kurgan Burials of the Eurasian Iron Age – Ideological Constructs and the Process of Rituality. *In* Holy Ground: Theoretical Issues Relating to the Landscape and Material Culture of Ritual Space Objects. Adam Smith and Alison Brookes, eds. Pp. 39–48. Oxford: Archaeopress. BAR Series S956.

Hanks, Bryan 2003 The Eurasian Steppe 'Nomadic World' of the First Millennium bc: Inherent Problems within the Study of Iron Age Nomadic Groups. *In* Ancient Interactions: East and West in Eurasia. Katie Boyle, Colin Renfrew, and Marsha Levine, eds. Pp. 183–97. Cambridge: McDonald Institute Monographs.

Harding, Anthony 2000 European Societies in the Bronze Age. Cambridge: Cambridge University Press.

Harding, Anthony 2007 Warriors and Weapons in Bronze Age Europe. Budapest: Archaeolingua Series Minor.

Härke, Heinrich 1997 The Nature of Burial Data. *In* Burial and Society. Claus Nielsen and Karen Nielsen, eds. Pp. 19–27. Aarhus: Aarhus University Press.

Harrison, Richard 2004 Symbols and Warriors: Images of the European Bronze Age. Bristol: Western Academic & Specialist Press Limited.

Hertz, Robert 1960 Death and the Right Hand. London: Cohen and West.

Hodder, Ian 1982 The Present Past. London: Batsford.

Hodder, Ian 1999 The Archaeological Process: An Introduction. Oxford: Blackwell.

Holtorf, Cornelius 1998 The Life-Histories of Megaliths in Mecklenburg-Vorpommern (Germany). World Archaeology 30(1):45–66.

Inomata, Takeshi, and Lawrence Coben 2006 Archaeology of Performance: Theaters of Power, Community, and Politics. Oxford: AltaMira Press.

Jones, Andrew 2003 Technologies of Remembrance. *In* Archaeologies of Remembrance: Death and Memory in Past Societies. Howard Williams, ed. Pp. 65–88. New York: Kluwer/Plenum.

Jones, Siân 1997 The Archaeology of Ethnicity: Constructing Identities in the Past and the Present. London: Routledge.

Keeley, Lawrence 1996 War before Civilization: The Myth of the Peaceful Savage. Oxford: Oxford University Press.

Koryakova, Ludmila 1996 Social Trends in Temperate Eurasia during the Second and First Millennia bc. Journal of European Archaeology 4:243–80.

Kradin, Nikolay 2002 Nomadism, Evolution and World-Systems: Pastoral Societies in Theories of Historical Development. Journal of World-Systems Research, VIII, III: 368–99.

Kristiansen, Kristian 1982 The Formation of Tribal Systems in Later European Prehistory: Northern Europe, 4000–500 bc. *In* Theory and Explanation in Archaeology. Colin Renfrew, Michael Rowlands, and Barbara Seagraves, eds. Pp. 241–80. London: Academic Press.

Kristiansen, Kristian 1984a Ideology and Material Culture: An Archaeological Perspective. *In* Marxist Perspectives in Archaeology. Matthew Spriggs, ed. Pp. 72–100. Cambridge: Cambridge University Press.

Kristiansen, Kristian 1984b Krieger und Häuptlinge in der Bronzezeit Dänemarks. Ein Beitrag zur Geschichte des bronzezeitlichen Schwertes. Jahrbuch des Römisch-Germanischen Zentralmuseums 31:187–208.

Kristiansen, Kristian 1998 Europe before History. Cambridge: Cambridge University Press.

Kristiansen, Kristian, and Thomas Larsson 2005 The Rise of Bronze Age Society: Travels, Transmission and Transformations. Cambridge: Cambridge University Press.

Kus, Susan 1992 Towards an Archaeology of Body and Soul. *In* Representations in Archaeology. Jean-Claude Gardin and Christopher Peebles, eds. Pp. 168–77. Bloomington: Indiana University Press.

Levi-Strauss, Claude 1966 The Savage Mind. Chicago: University of Chicago Press.

Levy, Janet 1982 Social and Religious Organization in Bronze Age Denmark. The Analysis of Ritual Hoard Finds. Oxford: British Archaeological Reports (International Series 124).

Levy, Janet 1991 Metalworking Technology and Craft Specialization in Bronze Age Denmark. Archaeomaterials 5:55–74.

Littleton, C. Scott 1987 War and Warriors. In Encyclopedia of Religion, Vol. 15. M. Eliade, ed. Pp. 339–49. New York: Macmillan.

Martin, Deborah, and David Frayer, eds. 1997 Troubled Times: Osteological and Archaeological Evidence of Violence. New York: Gordon and Breach.

Melcalf, P., and R. Huntington 1991 Celebrations of Death: The Anthropology of Mortuary Ritual (2nd edn.). Cambridge: Cambridge University Press.

Meskell, Lynn 2000 Writing the Body in Archaeology. In Reading the Body: Representations and Remains in the Archaeological Record. Alison Rautman, ed. Pp. 13–21. Philadelphia: University of Pennsylvania Press.

Milisauskas, Sarunas 1978 European Prehistory. London: Academic Press.

Minns, Ellis 1971(1913) Scythians and Greeks: A Survey of Ancient History and Archaeology on the North Coast of the Euxine from the Danube to the Caucasus. New York: Biblio and Tannen.

Mizoguchi, Kochi 1993 Time in the Reproduction of Mortuary Practices. World Archaeology 25(2):223–35.

Nilsson, Lars-Göran, and Nobuo Ohta 2006 Memory and Society: Psychological Perspectives. New York: Psychology Press.

Osgood, Richard, Sarah Monks, and Judith Toms, eds. 2000 Bronze Age Warfare. Stroud: Sutton.

Parker Pearson, Mike 1982 Mortuary Practices, Society and Ideology: An Ethnoarchaeological Study. In Symbolic and Structural Archaeology. Ian Hodder, ed. Pp. 99–114. Cambridge: Cambridge University Press.

Parker Pearson, Mike 1984 Social Change, Ideology and the Archaeological Record. In Marxist Perspectives in Archaeology. Matthew Spriggs, ed. Pp. 59–71. Cambridge: Cambridge University Press.

Parker Pearson, Mike 1993 The Powerful Dead: Relationships Between the Living and the Dead. Cambridge Archaeological Journal 3:203–29.

Parker Pearson, Mike 1999 The Archaeology of Death and Burial. Stroud: Sutton.

Pearson, Mike, and Michael Shanks 2001 Theater/Archaeology. London: Routledge.

Pezdek, Kathy 2006 Memory for the Events of September 11, 2001. In Memory and Society: Psychological Perspectives. Lars-Göran Nillson and Nobuo Ohta, eds. Pp. 65–85. New York: Psychology Press.

Piggot, Stuart 1965 Ancient Europe: From the Beginnings of Agriculture to Classical Antiquity. Chicago: Aldine Publishing Company.

Polhemus, Ted 1988 Body Styles. London: Lennard Books.

Randsborg, Klavs 1973 Wealth and Social Structure as Reflected in Bronze Age Burials: A Quantitative Approach. In The Explanation of Culture Change. Colin Renfrew, ed. Pp. 565–70. London: Duckworth.

Renfrew, Colin 1998 All the King's Horses. In Creativity in Human Evolution and Prehistory. Steven Mithen, ed. Pp. 260–84. London: Routledge.

Robb, John 1997 Violence and Gender in Early Italy. In Troubled Times: Osteological and Archaeological Evidence of Violence. Deborah Martin and David Frayer, eds. Pp. 108–41. New York: Gordon and Breach.

Robb, John 2002 Time and Biography: Osteobiography of the Italian Neolithic Lifespan. In Thinking Through the Body: Archaeologies of Corporeality. Yannis Hamilakis, Mark Pluciennik, and Sarah Tarlow, eds. Pp. 153–71. London: Kluwer Academic.

Rolle, Renate 1989 The World of the Scythians. Los Angeles: University of California Press.

Rowlands, Michael 1980 Kinship, Alliance and Exchange in the European Bronze Age. *In* Settlement and Society in the British Late Bronze Age. John Barrett and Richard Bradley, eds. Pp. 15–55. Oxford: British Archaeological Reports (British Series 83).

Rowlands, Michael 1993 The Role of Memory in the Transmission of Culture. World Archaeology 25(2):141–51.

Saxe, Arthur 1970 Social Dimensions of Mortuary Practices. Unpublished PhD thesis, University of Michigan.

Saul, Frank, and Julie Saul 1989 Osteobiography: A Maya Example. *In* Reconstruction of Life from the Skeleton. Mehemet dşcan and Kenneth Kennedy, eds. Pp. 287–301. New York: Alan R. Liss.

Saunders, N. 1993 Crucifix, Calvary, and Cross: Materiality and Spirituality in Great War Landscapes. World Archaeology 35(1):7–21.

Shanks, Michael 1993 Style and the Design of a Perfume Jar from an Archaic Greek City State. Journal of European Archaeology 1:77–106.

Shanks, Michael, and Chris Tilley 1982 Ideology, Symbolic Power and Ritual Communication. *In* Symbolic and Structural Archaeology. Ian Hodder, ed. Pp. 129–54. Cambridge: Cambridge University Press.

Shennan, Stephen 1982 Exchange and Ranking: The Role of Amber in the Earlier Bronze Age of Europe. *In* Ranking, Resource and Exchange. Colin Renfrew and Stephen Shennan, eds. Pp. 33–45. Cambridge: Cambridge University Press.

Shennan, Stephen 1986 Central Europe in the Third Millennium bc: An Evolutionary Trajectory for the Beginning of the European Bronze Age. Journal of Anthropological Archaeology 5:115–46.

Shennan, Stephen 1993 Settlement and Social Change in Central Europe, 3500–1500 BC. Journal of World Prehistory 7(2):121–61.

Shepherd, Deborah 1999 The Elusive Warrior Maiden Tradition – Bearing Weapons in Anglo-Saxon Society. *In* Ancient Warfare. John Carman and Anthony Harding, eds. Pp. 219–43. Stroud: Sutton.

Sherratt, Andrew 1987 Cups That Cheered. *In* Bell Beakers of the Western Mediterranean. William Waldren and Rex Kennard, eds. Pp. 81–113. Oxford: British Archaeological Reports (International Series 331).

Sherratt, Andrew 1994 The Emergence of Elites: Earlier Bronze Age Europe, 2500–1300 BC. *In* The Oxford Illustrated Prehistory of Europe. Barry Cunliffe, ed. Pp. 244–76. Oxford: Oxford University Press.

Singer, Jefferson, and Pavel Blagov 2006 The Integrative Function of Narrative Processing: Autobiographical Memory, Self-Defining Memories, and the Life Story of Identity. *In* The Self and Memory. Denise Beike, James Lampinen, and Douglas Behrend, eds. Pp. 117–38. New York: Psychology Press.

Sofaer, Joanna 2006 The Body as Material Culture: A Theoretical Osteoarchaeology. Cambridge: Cambridge University Press.

Sørensen, Marie-Louise Stig 1992 Gender Archaeology and Scandinavian Bronze Age Studies. Norwegian Archaeological Review 25:31–49.

Tainter, Joseph 1978 Mortuary Practices and the Study of Prehistoric Social Systems. *In* Advances in Archaeological Theory. Michael Schiffer, ed. Pp. 105–41. London: Academic Press.

Tarlow, Sarah 1999 Bereavement and Commemoration: An Archaeology of Mortality. Oxford: Blackwell.

Theweleit, Klaus 1989 Male Fantasies, Vol. 2, Male Bodies: Psychoanalyzing the White Terror. Minneapolis: University of Minnesota Press.

Tilley, Chris 1991 Material Culture and Text. The Art of Ambiguity. London: Routledge.

Treherne, Paul 1995 The Warrior's Beauty: The Masculine Body and Self-Identity in Bronze Age Europe. Journal of European Archaeology 3(1):105–44.

Turner, Bryan 1984 The Body and Society: Exploration in Social Theory. Oxford: Blackwell.

Van Dyke, Ruth, and Susan Alcock 2003 Archaeologies of Memory: An Introduction. *In* Archaeologies of Memory. Ruth Van Dyke and Susan Alcock, eds. Pp. 8–13. Oxford: Blackwell.

Van Dyke, Ruth, and Susan Alcock, eds. 2003 Archaeologies of Memory. Oxford: Blackwell.

Vencl, Slavomil 1999 Stone Age Warfare. *In* Ancient Warfare: Archaeological Perspectives. John Carman and Anthony Harding, eds. Pp. 57–72. Stroud: Sutton.

Vernant, Jean-Pierre 1991 Mortals and Immortals: Collected Essays. Froma Zeitlin, ed. Princeton: Princeton University Press.

Walker, Phillip 2001 A Bioarchaeological Perspective on the History of Violence. Annual Review of Anthropology 30:573–96.

Wang, Q., and M. Conway 2006 Autobiographical Memory, Self, and Culture. *In* Memory and Society: Psychological Perspectives. Lars-Göran Nilsson and Nobuo Ohta, eds. Pp. 9–27. New York: Psychology Press.

Wells, Peter 2001 Beyond Celts, Germans and Scythians. London: Duckworth.

Whittle, Alasdair 2003 The Archaeology of People: Dimensions of Neolithic Life. London: Routledge.

Williams, Howard, ed. 2003 Archaeologies of Remembrance: Death and Memory in Past Societies. New York: Kluwer Academic.

Williams, Howard 2006 Death and Memory in Early Medieval Britain. Cambridge: Cambridge University Press.

Yates, Tim 1993 Frameworks for an Archaeology of the Body. *In* Interpretive Archaeology. C. Tilley, ed. Pp. 31–72. Oxford: Berg.

OTHER REFERENCE

Mamayev Kurgan, official website: http://mamayevhill.volgadmin.ru/11_n.htm.

6

Identity, Community, the Body and the Person

Introduction

That prehistoric people are not simply subject to the forces of evolution, and that culture does not simply play an adaptive role have been subjects of fierce debate. One aspect of this debate has been to argue for the signal importance of agency: of prehistoric peoples' abilities to act knowledgeably and with free will (albeit constrained by the dispositions of specific cultural contexts). Agency-centred approaches recognize that humans make choices, possess intentions and take actions (Barrett 1994; Dobres and Robb 2000). One of the key components of agency theory is the realization that actions are taken within a given cultural or historical framework. Culture shapes individual actions, while individual actions also serve to reproduce culture. By considering agency archaeologists give greater consideration to the relationship between individuals and society. Overall we see closer attention paid to the nature of the individual in recent archaeological accounts.

Alongside a consideration of how culture shapes individuals, and how individuals shape culture archaeologists, along with anthropologists, sociologists and other social theorists have begun to pay more attention to the body (Meskell 1996; Meskell and Joyce 2003). Human bodies are not seen as biologically given, but as being culturally shaped. The task of archaeologists is to map how bodies are culturally shaped and produced in different prehistoric societies.

In addition to a discussion of prehistoric bodies, the constitution of prehistoric people has also been the subject of critical scrutiny. While agency theory has placed emphasis upon the individual, the very concept of the individual has been questioned in prehistoric contexts. Through a close reading of the anthropology of Southern India, Melanesia and Mesoamerica it has been noted that the individual is a historically specific concept, which emerges in the modern West. The idea of autonomous people free to act and do as they choose is a product of modernity (Thomas 2004). In many of the non-western contexts mentioned above the idea of an individual separate or distinct from other people and their environment is simply alien: in these contexts people do not begin and end at the boundary of their bodies, rather people are made up of their social and environmental relationships. Components of a person's body may be considered to be embodied by artefacts or by the bodies of other people. The analysis and critique of the use of the individual in archaeological research has led to the call for an archaeology of personhood which reconsiders the many dimensions of being a person in prehistory (Fowler 2004; Jones 2005; Whittle 2003). Just as with bodies, people are also culturally constituted. There are many ways in which these issues can be considered. The most common is the analysis of bodies and considerations of personhood in mortuary contexts (Chapman 2000a; Fowler 2003; Thomas 2001), while the analysis of the structure and use of space (Houston and Stuart 1998) and the role of ideas of personhood in systems of exchange are also important (Chapman 2000b) The analysis of prehistoric persons and the cultural constitution of bodies is a research strand which, arguably, has emerged and developed with the increased discussion of prehistoric agency.

In **Chapter 6 (a)** *Dani Hoffman* and *Alasdair Whittle* discuss the varying dimensions of personhood in the Neolithic of central and western Europe. They investigate a variety of data including houses, settlements, burial and artefact exchange, and examine the way in which archaeologists might approach Neolithic bodies at a variety of scales.

In **Chapter 6 (b)** *Ing-Marie Back-Danielssen* analyzes the characteristics of the person in Late Iron Age Scandinavia, using both textual and archaeological sources to argue that persons are distributed entities constituted in a series of transactions or exchanges between humans and the spiritual or divine world.

These chapters importantly show that a 'one-size-fits-all' approach to prehistoric individuals, bodies or persons is unwarranted. Rather a detailed reading of the archaeological data, coupled with the analytical frameworks of anthropology, indicate the variety of ways in which people and bodies were made during prehistory.

REFERENCES

Barrett, J. C. 1994 Fragments from Antiquity: An Archaeology of Social Life in Britain 2900–1200 BC. Blackwell: Oxford.

Chapman, J. 2000a Tension at Funerals: Social Practices and the Subversion of Community Structure in Later Hungarian Prehistory. *In* Agency in Archaeology. M.-A. Dobres and J. E. Robb, eds. Pp. 169–95. Routledge: London.

Chapman, J. 2000b Fragmentation in Archaeology. Routledge: London.

Dobres, M-A., and J. E Robb 2000 Agency in Archaeology. Routledge: London.

Fowler, C. 2003 Rates of (Ex)change: Decay and Growth, Memory and the Transformation of the Dead in Early Neolithic Britain. *In* Archaeologies of Remembrance: Death and Memory in Past Societies. H. Williams, ed. Pp. 45–63. Kluwer Academic/Plenum Press: New York.

Fowler, C. 2004 The Archaeology of Personhood. Routledge: London.

Houston, S. D., and D. Stuart 1998 The Ancient Maya Self: Personhood and Portraiture in the Classic Period. RES 33:73–101.

Jones, A. 2005 Lives in Fragments?: Personhood and the European Neolithic. Journal of Social Archaeology 5 (2):193–217.

Meskell, L. 1996 The Somatization of Archaeology: Institutions, Discourses, Corporeality. Norwegian Archaeological Review 29 (1):1–16.

Meskell, L. M., and R. A. Joyce 2003 Embodied Lives: Figuring Ancient Maya and Egyptian Experience. Routledge: London.

Thomas, J. 2001 Death, Identity and the Body in Neolithic Britain. Journal of the Royal Anthropological Institute 6:653–68.

Thomas, J. 2004 Archaeology and Modernity. Routledge: London.

Whittle, A. 2003 The Archaeology of People: Dimensions of Neolithic Life. Routledge: London.

6 (a)
Neolithic Bodies

Daniela Hofmann and Alasdair Whittle

Bodies That Matter in the Neolithic

There are many questions we want to ask of Neolithic bodies. From our world, from our bodies, we want to catch something of theirs: to report on the visceral corporeality of Neolithic existence. How did the Neolithic *feel?* We have not yet developed a satisfactory language of Neolithic experience, and so it is hard to talk about what it would have been like to feel clay between the fingers, making pots, or with the cow's udder during milking, or the flesh, blood and bone of animals during butchery, or with bread and porridge between the teeth. We do not know how to really imagine being at the end of a hafted axe, clearing trees, travelling long distances to the axe source to acquire raw material, or passing long hours grinding out the desired, sensuous, smooth finish. Yet the embodied sensations of axe on wood, for example, may have become part of the history of the blade, its feel and emotional connotations, contributing to the stories told as axe blades were gifted from person to person, or eventually deposited in funeral rites. What did the Neolithic *look like?* We would like to be able to evoke something of posture and gesture, the ways men walked and women walked, and the 'numb imperatives' of routine action, as Pierre Bourdieu put it (1990:69). We could reflect on how people used their bodies as symbols, conscious or unthought, blatant or subtle. The signs of allegiance, descent and history or even the aesthetic of Neolithic beauty remain under-researched topics, but ones for which an engagement with the human body is central. How then was the Neolithic *embodied?* Here, issues of the sense of self and personal identity in the Neolithic are central, especially since we cannot assume that personhood was co-terminous with individual bodies, as is often claimed for the modern west. We must investigate whether the singular person at times divided or fragmented, shared, merged or united with others, present or past. There is also the question of differences between men and women, and indeed any other categories of person that there have been. And finally, one cannot assume that these ideas remained constant through the millennia of the Neolithic in Europe.

How might all or any of this be possible within Neolithic archaeology? In many ways, our subject has taken the body and the person for granted. That is now changing, but change is coming in a rush; typically, archaeology is catching up with debates carried on in other subjects. One anthropological work has referred to the

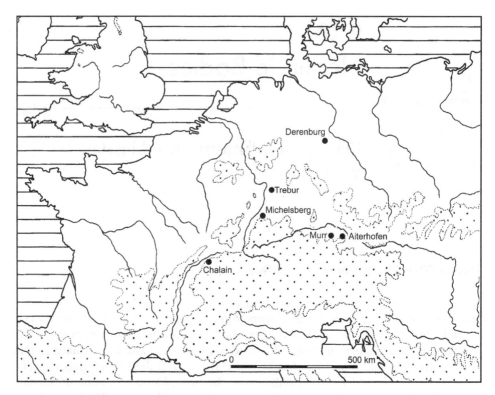

Figure 6.1   Map of central Europe showing main sites mentioned in the text (Drawing by Howard Mason and Ian Dennis)

way in which notions of the body have replaced notions of the person in that discipline (Strathern and Lambek 1998:5), whereas archaeology is now dealing with both simultaneously, and there is a danger of being over-influenced by fashion and trend. Other subjects have summarized the fruitful potential of regarding the body as the locus of social practice, as symbol and metaphor, as artefact, as fount of experience (Csordas 1990; 1993; 1999; Featherstone et al. 1991; Turner 1996). Archaeology has begun to absorb these approaches (e.g. Fowler 2004; Hamilakis et al. 2002; Lucas 1996; Meskell 1996; Meskell and Joyce 2003; Sofaer 2006; Treherne 1995). Following these sources, therefore, we want neither to separate the body from the mind, nor to promote some kind of universal, essential or natural Neolithic body, and we want to avoid seeing the body – or better, bodies plural – as a passive medium on to which predetermined or preformed social norms were inscribed. This also means that we are unsure where the limits of body study lie, but to turn the question at the start of this paragraph around, is any archaeology of the Neolithic now possible which ignores the body?

For the sake of coherence within a short chapter, we are going to confine our case studies largely to central and western Europe, from the 6th to the 4th millennia cal. BC, and we have selected examples that we believe serve to show how much more there is to be done in the matter of Neolithic bodies (Figure 6.1). We will begin with routines, then look at the presentation of the singular body in death rituals, which raises questions of personhood, move to fragmented and multiple bodies encountered in other contexts of deposition, and end by considering some aspects of representation. Of course, these are not neatly separable and bounded areas of experience: bodies feel, act and look at the same time, a challenge to how we write archaeology, which we can only take up partially here. Everywhere we can find difference, and the limitless possibilities of Neolithic bodies set a long agenda.

Routines: The Alpine Foreland Lake Villages

If gestures, postures and habitual ways of moving are integral for the embodiment of identity, then consideration must be given to the bulk of everyday routines. Habitual ways of moving and acting sediment into the body, leading to the reproduction of collectively held ideas of appropriateness through the mannerisms and comportment of individuals. In archaeological writing, these ideas are most often developed with reference to Bourdieu and the concept of the *habitus* (Bourdieu 1990), although they are also present in the dwelling perspective (Ingold 2000) and other approaches (e.g. Gamble 1999; Goffman 1967; Sofaer 2006). For the purpose of illustration, we have here chosen a setting renowned for the extraordinary preservation of many different kinds of material and with the potential for very precise dating: the Neolithic lake villages of the Alpine region. From their discovery in 1854 (Schlichtherle 1997; Speck 1990), Alpine marsh and lake villages have attracted the attention of scholars because of the wealth of artefacts and architectural evidence preserved in waterlogged conditions. In many cases, dendrochronology also permits a very tight dating of building phases and abandonment horizons (e.g. Ruoff 2004; Schlichtherle 2004). The wealth of syntheses and site reports (e.g. Jacomet et al. 2005; Pétrequin 1997a; 1997b; Schibler et al. 1997b; special section in *Berichte der Römisch-Germanischen Kommission* 1990) also provides the potential – so far largely unrealized – for writing an archaeology of daily life and routine embodiment. Chronologically, the earliest Alpine lake villages appear around 4300 BC in both northern Italy and southwest Germany/eastern Switzerland (Menotti 2004; Strahm 1997). They are established in locations often avoided by potential earlier Neolithic settlers, such as the Bandkeramik (see also Whittle 2003:144). Subsequently, lake villages are also established in western Switzerland, southeastern France, and parts of Bavaria, Austria and Slovenia, where the phenomenon can persist well into the Bronze Age (up until c.800 BC) (Strahm 1997). Many good examples exist but the settlement we have chosen here is Chalain 3, situated on a small, frequently flooded island near the shore of Lake Chalain in the French Jura. It is one of a series of sites here and on the neighbouring Lake Clairvaux, and the region has been extensively investigated (Pétrequin 1986; 1997a; 1997b; Pétrequin and Bailly 2004). Occupation of the Chalain 3 site begins around 3185 BC, a good half millennium after the first local lake villages. Like many other sites, Chalain undergoes several cycles of occupation, destruction or abandonment and cultural re-orientations, with activity finally ceasing around 2700 BC (Affolter et al. 1997; Pétrequin 1997c). Our focus here is on the oldest phase, VIII. At this point, the village consists of a group of 10–15 houses arranged in rows and protected by a palisade on the landward side. Occupation lasts about 20 years, before a hiatus and eventual re-occupation (Affolter et al. 1997; Pétrequin 1997c). Pierre Pétrequin has called this kind of setting a 'forest Neolithic', characterized by its short tenures of place and diverse subsistence

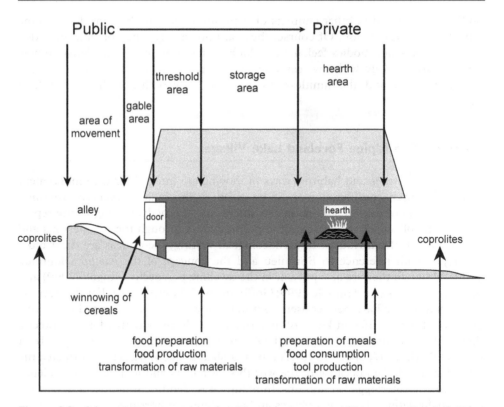

Figure 6.2 Schematic representation of activity areas in a phase VIII house at Chalain 3 (After Arbogast et al. 1997:599, fig. 12)

activities. We want to discuss this one specific example, but use it to hint at routines that may have occurred widely elsewhere. Houses at Chalain are very uniform, both in terms of dimensions (3.5–4 m wide, 10–12 m long) and in terms of layout. In phase VIII, there is a hearth towards the back of the house and a storage/sleeping area towards the front. No marked partition between the two areas is visible (Arbo-gast et al. 1997:595). Given the relative lack of spatial complexity, temporal orga-nization may have become important for different activities carried out in the house, the same space being used by different people throughout the day (Rapoport 1990:13–15). Also, in intimate settings where people interact daily, appropriate spaces for segregated activities need not be explicitly marked (Kent 1990:149; Rapoport 1990:17). They are a matter of habit, of the position of one's body in the right place, moving in the appropriate ways. Artefact distribution patterns (Figure 6.2) suggest that at Chalain food preparation and consumption took place around the hearth, alongside activities requiring light, such as woodworking. Messy tasks or those requiring space, such as winnowing or butchery, were carried out near the door or just outside, while some multi-purpose tools such as scrapers show no marked concentrations (Arbogast et al. 1997:588–94). Most meals were probably communal, as pots with traces of food residues are generally large, open bowls. Smaller forms are much rarer (Baudais and Delattre 1997:529–32; Giligny 1997), and household members probably shared food from the same vessel.

On this basis, we can envisage a household group engaged in a variety of activi-ties. During the day, most of the stronger members could be undertaking agricultural tasks or looking after livestock, perhaps leaving mainly children and the elderly to fish, manufacture or play. Later in the day, when more household members return, the interior of the house would be cleared of production debris, a meal prepared and shared. This is a time for more intense sociality when the house is busy with many people. Manufacturing activities may still continue alongside chatting, eating or sleeping. Thus, at different times there is the potential for different experiences and the embodiment of skills. Transhumance may have occurred at some seasons of the year (Pétrequin 1997c:50), the body strengthening on long marches after the herds, perhaps becoming tanned or coming to bear other visible marks of this engagement, alongside the invisible 'muscular consciousness' (Bachelard 1964) of the terrain and its paths. By shaping and forming the body, such activities can become crucial for a sense of, for instance, gendered identity (see also Parker Pearson 2000).[1] At other times, the emphasis may be on the consuming body, in close physical proximity to others around a hearth, or the communal experiences of sleeping very close to others in a cramped space (Whittle 2003:145). In this setting, there may be intimacy alongside separation signalized through gestures, such as who has the right to eat first, or in the relative position around the fire. This is only one of many possible images. The precise details of engagement will vary, for instance with different labour requirements throughout the day or year, at some times perhaps involving large numbers of people working together (see Jacomet et al. 1990). Some authors have seen this as a life of grindingly hard and unremitting labour, principally on agricultural tasks (Schibler et al. 1997a), and it may have been so at times. Nevertheless, there is probably scope for considerable seasonal and yearly variation, and people in these settings did other things besides cultivate cereals. The frequent cycles of abandonment and relocation of villages and the implication of frequent collaborative building projects are also of interest here. Seasonal patterns in lake water-levels, too, must be mentioned, allowing or closing off certain kinds of movement. This can tie in with patterns of social aggregation, feasting and consumption which could contrast with relative isolation or scarcity at other times of the year (Sené 1997), as elaborated in an ethnographic setting by Mark Harris (1998; 2000). Thus, the active, well-fed, adorned body of a large summer gathering may become a paler, thinner and confined body over the winter months. This could tie in with the ever-increasing literature on emotional states, also experienced through the body and liable to change in such drastically different social settings (Harris 2000; Tarlow 2000; Whittle 2003). It is interesting here also to speculate on the emotional corollaries of living so closely with others; a possible ideal of harmonious existence may be threatened by resentment or other negative emotions, hard to avoid in situations of close physical proximity in which others are not only seen and heard, but also touched and felt. Perhaps thinking of work routines and communal meals also leads to a vision of a too sanitized past, one without dirt, squalor, pain and illness, but also without passions and deeply felt desires. Addressing these ideas requires different ways of writing about archaeology, a challenge we still need to adequately problematize as a discipline. In addition, there are subtle differences in activity patterns between households at Chalain 3. In phase VIII, one house is consistently set apart from the others by the consumption of different kinds of foodstuffs and the use of different tools, such as boar's tusks and beaver incisors (Arbogast et al. 1997). Did these embodied, routine activities in this particular household, the different patterns of coming and going, and the consumption of different foods and use of different artefacts set its members apart from the community at large, while outwardly the house itself looked no different?

Routines: The Iceman

The famous Iceman met his death some two centuries earlier than Chalain 3, and on the south side of the Alps, quite far away from the French Jura. But in many ways, he belongs to the same kind of world, and illustrates dimensions so far only touched upon. We will not rehearse the details of his discovery, analysis or equipment, since they are well known and accessible (e.g. W. Müller et al. 2003; Spindler 1994; Spindler et al. 1995). We have raised doubts already about whether Neolithic life was unrelentingly hard, but the Iceman certainly shows previous injuries to his ribs, and his fingernails indicate stress in the months leading up to his death (Capasso 1995). At least as interesting was the combination of independence and inter-dependence that he shows. We have so far stressed the communality of Neolithic existence, and the bodily routines of close, shared living. Here was someone dressed and equipped for the cold and for high places, whether or not he was alone (which most narratives assume). At the same time, pollen and food remains indicate that this was a figure in direct contact with lowland, agricultural communities. The Iceman may have been a specialist of some kind, possibly connected with copper working as well as with other tasks, but it does not look as though he was a hermit. While he was found high in the Alps, and may thus have travelled far over the passes towards the north, the most recent scientific analysis suggests that he died within perhaps some 50 kilometres of where he may have been born (W. Müller et al. 2003); on the move, he was nonetheless rooted. The body of the Iceman bears only a few applied markings on it, on back and legs: to our eyes rather modest. This Neolithic body at any rate was not itself extravagantly decorated. Was his identity more obviously presented not just through his tasks and reputation but also through his clothing and appearance, through his preference for leather and garments in layers? There are rather few human remains and burial sites in the Neolithic archaeology of the Alpine foreland (in itself an under-considered topic: did the intense communality among the living foster forgetting of the dead?),[2] and it is thus hard to put this dimension of the Iceman further into context. If the Iceman overlaps in date with the decorated stelae of the southern Alpine valleys, that may be one way to contextualize him and emphasize his distinctiveness (John Robb, pers. comm.). Comparison with the presentation of identity in the contemporary Remedello culture cemeteries of the Po Valley is another (Spindler 1994: Whittle 1996), but that is taking us beyond our geographical area. To look further now at the presentation of the body in death, we will turn first to the LBK of the 6th millennium cal. BC.

The Body in Cemeteries

The LBK or Linearbandkeramik (c.5500–4900 cal. BC) was the first Neolithic culture of central and western Europe, appearing in the river valleys and on good soils in the middle of the 6th millennium cal. BC, starting a tradition of longhouse life that lasted well into the 5th millennium. Its longhouse settlements (another extremely fruitful field for thinking about the routines of daily life) have often been excavated, and close to some have been found smaller and larger groupings of individual graves. Study of the LBK has tended to be dominated by regional analysis on the one hand, and by the results of certain pre-eminent projects and sites on the other, such as Elsloo in Dutch Limburg, Langweiler on the Aldenhovener Platte in northwest Germany or Bylany in Bohemia. Some of the well known settlement sites or areas have substantial cemeteries adjacent, such as Niedermerz close to the Langweiler sites of the Aldenhovener Platte or Elsloo. Their bone preservation, however, is poor. Other larger and smaller cemeteries, with better bone preservation, are often less closely associated with detailed settlement studies (e.g. Lüning and Stehli 1994; Modderman 1970; Pavlu 2000; Whittle 1996). LBK cemeteries varied in size, from 10–20 graves right up to the hundreds found at Schwetzingen (Behrends 1990; 1997; Jeunesse 1997). Generally the graves in them contained individuals, of all ages and both sexes,[3] placed carefully in varying positions, and often provided with pots and other artefacts. It is likely, given the numbers involved, that the dead represented in LBK cemeteries were only a selection of local populations. Groupings among the graves might represent households (Grygiel 1994:74; Nieszery 1995; Pavúk 1972; van de Velde 1979; Veit 1996), or the individual grave might in some way have stood for the notion of house or household (notions of death perhaps linking the two). Cemeteries are also not the only places in which LBK people disposed of their dead, who are found interred in isolated or grouped graves on settlements themselves, and as fragmented bodies in settlement pits, enclosure ditches and also caves; the dead could also of course have been treated in archaeologically invisible ways (Jeunesse 1997: Orschiedt 1999; Veit 1993; 1996). A further example is the mass grave at Talheim, Baden-Württemberg, in southwest Germany, where the whole bodies of adult men and women, and children, had been pitched into a pit, having been beaten to death by axe and adze blows to the head (Wahl and König 1987). All these contexts may have been highly charged with emotional and social significance, and we cannot assume that the cemeteries were representative or neutral mirrors of their diverse contexts. By choosing the cemetery context here, we want to explore two complementary dimensions: the body as a vehicle for display and the body as situated in a network of artefacts. Our first example is the LBK cemetery of Aiterhofen, in the comparatively less well-known area of Lower Bavaria. Aiterhofen is a large burial ground, comprising 160 well-preserved inhumations and 65 cremations. Here, as with other LBK sites, the first interpretation offered was one of static male and female grave good assemblages (Jeunesse 1997; Nieszery 1995). However, on closer inspection, the picture is much more nuanced. Grave goods with a gendered connotation, such as objects made from *Spondylus* shell, are mostly with adult men between 20 and 40 years of age. Later in life, these ornaments, imported from far to the east, are increasingly combined with more idiosyncratic and locally available material, such as fox mandibles and river shells. For the older age group, the materials used for men and women increasingly overlap, breaking down the clearer distinctions between the sexes in the adult age range (Hofmann 2006).

Grave good associations are hence not static; rather, different associations are seen as appropriate for people of different ages, introducing a dynamic element in which grave goods and ageing bodies bring each other's identities into being. Perhaps the best example are the *Spondylus* armrings (Figure 6.3a). These are generally worn on the upper arm of adult men, but also buried with some children.

(a)   (b)

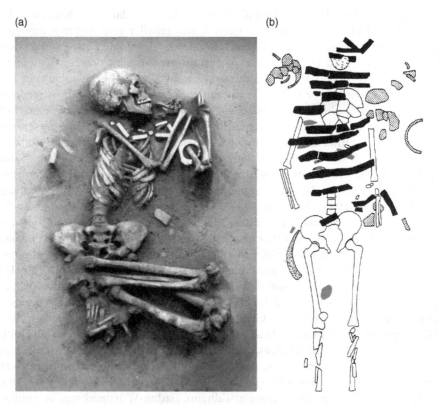

Figure 6.3 Bodies in cemeteries: (a) Burial 41 at Aiterhofen of a 10–12 year old child with *Spondylus* arm ring, beads and various stone tools (with kind permission of the Bayerisches Landesamt für Denkmalpflege); (b) Burial 70 at Trebur of an adult man with cow ribs (black) covering the upper body (After Spatz and von den Driesch 2001:fig. 1)

The diameter of the children's rings is very small. Those for adults are larger, but still so narrow that they could not have been taken off without breaking them (Nieszery 1995:85). Nieszery (1995:185f) suggests that the rings were conferred upon an individual at an early age and continuously worn. At some point, probably during an initiation ceremony in late childhood, smaller rings were broken and substituted for larger ones, again continuously worn thereafter.[4] The growth and maturation of the body, biologically a continuous process, is hence marked out and acknowledged culturally through non-local *Spondylus* armrings. In turn, the conferred adult identity is literally embodied in feeling and observing the rings becoming ever tighter around the arm, and then perhaps loosening as muscle substance decreased in older age. Identity thus seems to reside in the interplay of artefacts and bodies.

In some cases, the distinctions between artefacts and bodies are even more artificial or broken down completely. Perhaps the most obvious example is cremation, also carried out at Aiterhofen (Nieszery 1995). During cremation, a charged performance providing a rich sensual experience for the mourners (Williams 2004), the mortal body is fragmented and physically mixed with air and flames, but also with wood from the pyre, the remains of grave goods and even of animal bodies, as in the contemporary Stephansposching cemetery, also in Lower Bavaria (Schmotz

1992). Our second example is the 5th-millennium-cal.-BC cemetery of Trebur, in Hessen in central Germany. This serves to illustrate change through time, and thus the culturally dependent character of the presentation and treatment of the human body in mortuary rituals, and also shows increasingly strong connections between human and animal bodies. Trebur has some 128 graves. They have been assigned to two of the local post- LBK cultural groups: Hinkelstein and Großgartach. Traditionally, the Großgartach grouping has been seen to succeed Hinkelstein (Eisenhauer 1999; Spatz 1996). However, radiocarbon dates on Trebur skeletons now strongly suggest they overlap (J. Müller 2002; 2003).[5] This is especially interesting as the two culture groups are very distinct spatially within the cemetery. Essentially, a central and tightly packed core of Hinkelstein inhumations is surrounded by more loosely spaced Großgartach burials (J. Müller 2003; Spatz 1999). The available radiocarbon evidence suggests that the cemetery developed from three distinct foci. Overall, it thus seems as though two distinct 'identity groupings' (J. Müller 2003) used the cemetery simultaneously, but were distinguished from each other spatially and through the burial rite. The Hinkelstein dead are closely packed, but have many, diverse grave goods. Großgartach inhumations have comparatively fewer goods, and distances between graves are larger (J. Müller 2003; Spatz 1999). Hinkelstein individuals identified as those richest in grave-good quantity and quality are located at the centre of the cemetery, at the borderline between the Hinkelstein and Großgartach areas (Spatz 1999:pl. 186). This has been interpreted as deliberate signalling from one identity group to another, a display of wealth and power (J. Müller 2003). In such a model, the individual body becomes a vehicle for messages vital to the body politic, in this case about ethnic identity. Body position has also been brought into this perspective. In the LBK, inhumations were often crouched and had varying orientations (although the majority had their heads towards the southeast). In the Hinkelstein phase, there is a shift to extended bodies in a supine position, without exception oriented with heads to the southeast.[6] The grave good spectrum also changes (see below), as does pottery decoration. This has been seen as the sign of a rapid and wholesale religious re-orientation. Due to a perceived crisis at the end of the LBK, people are seen as adopting new norms and ideologies by establishing a new, very strict religion with rigidly enforced rules; this guaranteed community cohesion in a volatile world in the throes of change (Spatz 1999; 2003). This opens interesting perspectives on the body as part of a larger collectivity. A multitude of bodies is here used to make a point about group cohesion and to tie in with new cosmological principles. The body and its stereotypical treatment in death is a solidified expression of the concerns of living bodies and their political and religious convictions. Again, however, such ideas can be criticized for their lack of a sense of process, and a lack of greater fluidity between identities or even between categories such as the body and the associated objects. At Trebur, this point can best be made with the animal remains often found in graves. Animals and ornaments manufactured from animal teeth or bones are extremely rare in the LBK (Jeunesse 1997), but very prominent in the Middle Neolithic (Jeunesse and Arbogast 1997; Jockenhövel and Knoche 2003; J. Müller 2003; Sidéra 2000; von den Driesch 1999). Previously this has been linked to changing conceptions between fixed categories of domestic and wild throughout the Neolithic (Hodder 1990) or to a perceived revival of a Mesolithic substrate at this time and hence an increased symbolic importance especially of wild animals (Jeunesse and Arbogast 1997; Sidéra 2000; 2003). In contrast, the relationship between animal and human bodies in the graves can be emphasized. Clothing and ornaments could be described as 'second skins' for the deceased, and the focus on animals here is interesting. But the instances in which animal bodies almost completely cover over the human bodies in the graves are particularly striking. In 21 graves at Trebur, all in the Hinkelstein group, large portions of cattle thorax were placed over the deceased, mostly covering the head and upper body. This was generally the last item to be placed with the dead person and covered not only the most individual and recognizable body part – the face – but also the majority of the grave goods, which had equally mostly been placed around the upper body (Spatz 1999). Here, for the onlookers at the graveside, the animal and human bodies were becoming hard to tell apart, one potentially substituting for or subsuming the other[7] (Figure 6.3b). Instances like these help to break down the perceived, but perhaps unhelpful, distinctions between animal, human and object[8] and shake up our static models. As in the LBK case, other funerary practices also existed alongside cemeteries. These involved the fragmentation of human bodies and their mixing with animal bones and objects, for instance in the south German caves of Hanseles Hohl and Hohlenstein (Orschiedt 1999; 2002). Here, the bounded body as a vehicle for identity display is completely dissolved, a point developed in more detail in the next section.

Fragmented and Multiple Bodies

From the examples considered so far, it is easy to assume that the intact, singular body was the norm, against which fragmented or dissolved remains can be evaluated, but it is important to stress the multiplicity of forms of disposal from the LBK onwards. There came a time, however, after the LBK and its tradition had ended in the middle of the 5th millennium cal. BC, when – in typically diverse ways – fragmented and multiple bodies are much more frequently encountered in central and western Europe. We could have illustrated this by any number of examples from the phenomenon of barrows, cairns, passage graves and other constructions connected with the treatment of the dead which are found on the broad sweep of the 'Atlantic façade', from Iberia to southern Scandinavia. These are very well known, however, and we want to keep some geographical coherence in our examples, so we will look at enclosures and chambered graves in the area of the Rhineland and the Middle Saale-Elbe area of eastern Germany. Interrupted ditch systems are also found very widely in western Europe at this time, from central–west France to southern Scandinavia (and including southern Britain). Those of the Michelsberg culture, centred on the Rhineland, should date to the later 5th and earlier 4th millennia cal. BC. These were not the first enclosures, since there are varieties already in the LBK, to be succeeded by the more formal enclosures ('rondels' or *Kreisgrabenanlagen*) of the earlier 5th millennium cal. BC in central Europe (Andersen 1997; Petrasch 1990; Trnka 1991). Few of all these enclosures need be seen, in our view, as defensive, and can better be thought of as loci for special gatherings and ritual. As places of assembly, they could bring people in numbers together, for both building and use. The many significances of these locations must have included a sense of the collective labour involved in their construction. Gatherings may have brought in people from far beyond purely local communities, so these sites were also the scene for the presentation of unfamiliar faces and bodies, and the exchange of materials of distant origin. If assembly was a form of negotiation of identity, it is important to stress that – in strong contrast to both the earlier longhouse world of the LBK and the contemporary settlements of the Alpine foreland – this was a time when settlement was probably largely dispersed and impermanent; settlements are recognized by pits and other features rather than by concentrations of houses. In this perhaps more fluid social world, connections and relationships must have been of key importance. At enclosures, human remains are a recurrent find. Some take the form of intact skeletons, and it is clear that some more or less formal burials or funerals took place at these enclosures. In many other cases, however, more isolated human remains are found in both ditches and pits. It is possible that in some cases these are simply the disturbed remains of burials, but the recurrence of human bones on their own strongly suggests that these were part of a separate or further process. Enclosures were places where bodies or skeletons could be transformed, manipulated or circulated. These places of labour, assembly and exchange were also the loci for the distribution of human remains. The connections may have been complex, but it is hard not to think of the treatment of human remains as one important medium for the creation of relationships among dispersed communities. Michelsberg-Untergrombach itself, near Karlsruhe on the east side of the middle Rhine, is a fine example of these possibilities (Andersen 1997; Lüning 1968; Maier 1962). A partially interrupted ditch, running for at least 400 metres, encircles part of a low hilltop; other Michelsberg enclosures in the general area are more complex still (Andersen 1997:fig. 223). There are over 160 pits within the long arc defined by the ditch. What appear to be deliberately placed deposits were put in both the ditch and the pits. Recurrent materials deposited include animal bone, sherds of pottery and daub. Some 20 of the pits, mostly just inside the ditch, also contained human remains. There were also some human remains placed in the ditch itself. Some 170 bones represent perhaps 35–45 people; there are 15 skulls (Andersen 1997:199–200; Lüning 1968). Pit 50 had the skeleton of an old woman, but most others show very partial remains. In Pit 14 parts of a human skeleton, including a skull, were mixed with the bones of both domesticated and wild cattle, sherds from 15 pots, and daub (Andersen 1997:199–200) (Figure 6.4). The potential symbolism is rich, the partial human remains being intermingled both with different categories of animals and the residues of living (whether from daily life or special events).

Our second brief example takes us north to the Middle Saale-Elbe area. Through the 4th millennium cal. BC there are many, varied mortuary practices; burial mounds with cists are found as well as ordinary graves, and human remains again turn up in settlement contexts (J. Müller 2001:fig. 261). By the later 4th millennium cal. BC a tradition of small rectangular wooden or stone chambers had emerged. These contain some cremated remains but principally grouped inhumations. As usual, there is much variety but often 20 or more people are represented. The multiple bodies, whether deposited in one go or accumulated over time, form a single collectivity, individuals merging in death to express the solidarity of the social group, be it based on residence, alliance or kinship. Far from all these remains are intact, and there is debate about the processes involved. Some bodies may have dissolved elsewhere before being brought to the mortuary constructions, while in others, such as Derenburg-Löwenberg, Kreis Wernigerode, it is possible that there were complex transformations, including the variable use of fire, *within* these structures (J. Müller 2001:332–6). If human remains at enclosures in some way stand

Figure 6.4   Pit 14 at Michelsberg-Untergrombach, containing parts of a human skeleton, animal skulls and bone, sherds and daub (Maier 1962:fig. 18)

for distributed identities here was a more concentrated mode of merging of identity, within what may have been more tightly defined groups.

Body Representations

Finally, consideration of the body would not be complete without a brief look at its representation in other media. Again, the list of potential case studies is long, including depictions in Iberian rock art (Bradley 2002; Diaz-Andreu 2002; Fairén 2004), the statue menhirs of France and northern Italy (D'Anna et al. 1997; Dondio 1995:208–11), and the vast corpus of clay figurines from Neolithic cultures in southeastern Europe (Bailey 2005; Bánffy 1991; Gimbutas 1974; 1991; Talalay 1993; Tringham 1971), to name but a few. Here, we have chosen to return to the clay depictions of the LBK. This provides the opportunity to link representations of humans and their treatment to other kinds of evidence, such as the burial record. In contrast to the situation in southeast Europe, LBK clay figurines are relatively rare: an interesting and ill-understood difference. As a consequence, for a long time it has been accepted practice to explicitly refer to southeast European parallels and suggest an interpretation as mother goddesses (Höckmann 1965; 1972; 1985; 1987; Kaufmann 1989; Wunn 2001; 2002). The mother goddess argument has been criticized at length elsewhere (Bailey 2005; Conkey and Tringham 1995; Lesure 2002; Meskell 1995; Tringham and Conkey 1998), and this need not be repeated here.

More recently, it has been proposed that figurines are more likely to represent a community's ancestors, and LBK hairstyles and clothing have been recreated on the basis of their representation on figurines (Lüning 2005; 2006). As Douglass Bailey has pointed out in his recent study of Balkan examples, such discursive explanations are not going to get us very far. Ultimately, we will never know what exactly a figurine depicted, let alone what the different lines or decorations on it are meant to represent. It is likely that meanings were complex and ambiguous in the past, and they cannot easily be recovered now. A more fruitful line of enquiry is to investigate the material and representational characteristics of LBK figurines with a view to what this tells us about conceptions of bodies (Bailey 2005). LBK figurines are, for the most part at least, asexual (for some exceptions, see Höckmann 1985; Landesamt für Archäologie Sachsen 2003; Maurer 1982). Also, they are not detailed or anatomically correct representations of humans; while each has a unique and individual facial expression, for instance, features are generally abstracted or crudely modelled. In some cases, we cannot even be sure of the straightforward humanity of the depiction. Figures like the sheep/human head from Niederesch-bach, Hesse (Figure 6.5a), the paw from Sallach, Bavaria, or the bird-like Eilsleben figurine (Hampel 1989; Kaufmann 1989; Reinecke 1977) are hard to pin down in this respect. Indeed, those figurines which we interpret as explicitly human are part of a continuum of depictions linking humans, human/animal hybrids and fully zoomorphic representations, such as figures of cattle and pigs. There are also links with containers; from figurines incorporating pots, such as holding bowls, we can make connections with pottery with applied human or animal faces, as at Ober-piebing, Bavaria, with face-pots as at Stuttgart-Bad Cannstadt in southwest Germany and ultimately with widely used decorative motifs which may represent abstract human depictions (Reinecke 1977; Stöckl 2002).[9] In this context, we can also dwell on the use of clay as a material to model the body. Ethnographically, clay and pottery can often come to stand for humans or as containing ancestors, souls and so on (Barley 1995; Breton 2006). In the LBK case, the material qualities of clay could be important for its use in depictions. Clay is malleable, it allows the incor-poration of various substances as temper, such as ground grain in the figurine from Rockenberg, Hessen (Höckmann 1987), it can be decorated and it is finally hard-ened and transformed by fire. When hard, it can also be broken easily, and indeed figurines are never found whole. This has led some to suggest that fragmentation was deliberate, as often it does not happen at the weakest points of the figure or the breaks have subsequently been treated (Kaufmann 1976; Maurer 1982; Schade-Lindig 2002a). Most figurines are then discarded with household waste.[10] Interest-ingly, links can be drawn to LBK funerary practice, where some of these elements resurface. The practice of settlement burial, for instance, is widespread in the LBK, as already noted (Veit 1993; 1996). Subsequent to their interment, complete bodies decompose and may also be broken down through accidental disturbance in the course of settlement activities, mixing with household waste.

Occasionally, such fragmented remains are then reburied, such as the child skull from Quedlinburg, eastern Germany, covered by an inverted pot (Siemoneit 1997). Thus, the human body would be experienced as fragmentable and partible, and in some cases these concepts are explicitly drawn on in ritual. This is the case with cremations, mentioned above, a multi-sensory spectacle in which the human body is broken down on the pyre in front of onlookers and mixed with charred wood, artefacts and occasionally animal remains (Schmotz 1992; Williams 2004). In some

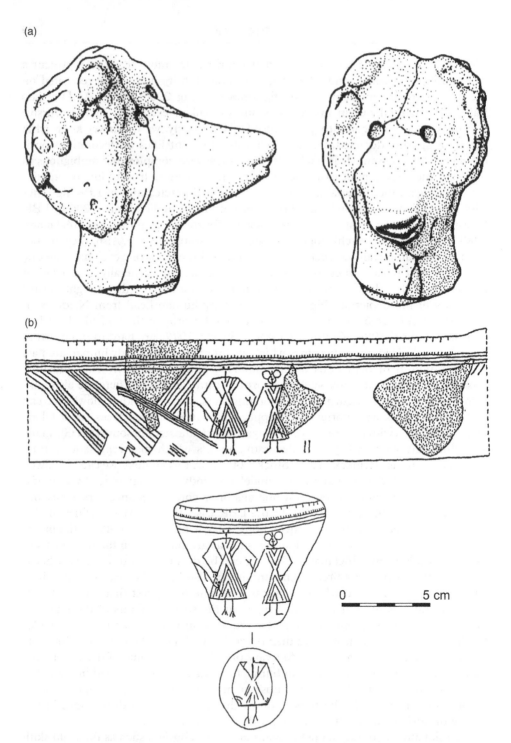

Figure 6.5 Represented bodies: (a) The Niedereschbach figurine, height c.4 cm (with kind permission of the Denkmalamt Frankfurt am Main); (b) The Murr wedding beaker (Neumair 1996:pl. XVI)

cases, such as the Jungfernhöhle in northern Bavaria, bodies were left to decompose
and the fragmented remains thrown into a cave alongside broken pottery and animal
bone (Kunkel 1955; Orschiedt 1999). Figurines thus draw out more explicitly what
can also be observed in parts of the total spectrum of funerary practice: bodies can
be ambiguous and fluid, combining human and animal characteristics. Boundaries
between objects and bodies can also be blurred, and these ideas are driven home
through fragmentations and admixture of various elements or by creating hybrid
depictions. The sliding scale linking people and pots is particularly evocative here:
are humans being metaphorically likened to containers, receptacles for substances?
Is this the same idea behind the incorporation of grain as temper at Rockenberg?
And is the fragmentation of buried bodies and of figurines linked with the release
of such substances or powers? These strands offer promising possibilities for further
investigation (see also Hofmann 2005), but what need to be drawn out here are the
implications for concepts of the human body. LBK figurines are not static depictions of naturalistic bodies. Rather, their making and use provided ways of drawing
links between various kinds of bodies: those of humans, animals, vessels and perhaps
other entities we can no longer recognize. They suggest the LBK body, beyond its
presentation in individual, bounded graves, as enmeshed in a wider universe without
any clear dividing lines between categories regarded as separate in today's western
world. As such, they question whether an archaeology of the (human) body can
ever stop at the boundary of an individual's skin. These ideas about bodies seem
very different from those prevalent in Bavaria in the late 5th into the early 4th millennium cal. BC. At this time, the LBK way of life in longhouses had long vanished,
eventually to be replaced by the archaeologically still under-researched Münchshöfen culture (MH, c.4500–3900 cal. BC). There are no known houses from this
culture, suggesting that constructions were probably slight, as noted already for the
Michelsberg horizon. Burial in cemeteries was also no longer practised. The few
inhumations come from the settlement context and are often interred in circumstances suggesting extraordinary events, such as multiple bodies arranged crosswise
on top of each other or the burial of disarticulated remains (Böhm 1998; Böhm
and Pielmeyer 1993; Kreiner 1995; 2001). The most abundant artefact category is
pottery, generally decorated with elaborate abstract designs such as lozenges (Süß
1976). Interestingly, this trend towards abstract motifs is also visible in Breton and
Irish passage graves. In spite of our limited knowledge, MH representations provide
a strong contrast to the earlier LBK material. The so-called 'wedding beaker' from
Murr, near Freising in Upper Bavaria, is particularly striking (Neumair 1996)
(Figure 6.5b). This small, 6.5-centimetre-high item bears the only incised depiction
of humans known from the MH, although humans can also be depicted as figurines
and anthropomorphic vessels (Kreiner and Pleyer 1999; Petrasch and Schmotz
1989). It shows two schematic figures walking arm in arm, both dressed and surrounded by groups of shorter and longer lines. The right figure is slightly smaller
and is holding the arm of its taller counterpart, which resulted in their interpretation as a female and a male figure respectively. The female figure shows an elaborate
hairstyle, while the face of the male is very abstracted. A third, headless figure
adorns the bottom of the vessel (Neumair 1996:51–5, 86). The excavators interpret
this vessel as a special ritual beaker used during wedding ceremonies, with the
smaller picture on the base showing the wish for children (Neumair 1996:53).
However, we cannot be sure that the relationship represented is that of a conjugal
couple. It is just as possible, although admittedly less romantic, to postulate

different age sets in their respective costume, such as a mother/father and daughter/son, or indeed no family relationship at all, or one not in line with modern binary definitions of gender. Rather than settling on too specific an explanation, therefore, we could simply remark that this MH vessel shows a specific relationship between two clearly defined persons, most likely exhibiting secondary gender or age characteristics in the form of costume and hairstyle. If these are a 'male' and 'female' figure, the size difference is also important, as sexual dimorphism is not pronounced in Münchshöfen skeletal material. Indeed, both sexes are so gracile that they are hard to tell apart anthropologically (Schröter 1996:109f). The size difference depicted on the beaker would thus show a strongly idealized version of what the relationship between men and women should be, rather than being strictly naturalistic. Thus, although the figures themselves are unique, they do not try to show specific individuals with their defining traits; rather, they show stereotypical personae in a stereotypical relationship to each other and to their environment. The medium of the depiction, pottery, is also significant here. At a time when elaborate architecture and status display in graves are largely absent, much effort is invested in the production of highly accomplished pottery, and it can be argued that this is now central for the establishment and maintenance of social relationships through serving food and drink (Hofmann 2006). The Murr beaker could be a statement about just such a relationship.

Human depictions are only one way by which MH people defined their place in the world, and ideally other kinds of evidence, such as burial, should be investigated in more detail. However, they suggest that relationships may have been more explicitly embodied in gesture, dress or posture.

Nevertheless, it seems premature to try to understand the significance of MH bodies without also considering their place in a wider universe of substances and metaphors, of new routines, new ways of consumption and new ways of burial.

Conclusion

We have tried to give an idea of the rich evidence available for thinking about Neolithic bodies, and have deliberately chosen examples that may be less familiar to non-continental readers. We have sought to show the potential for thinking about embodied routines, the ways in which bodies were inextricably caught up in the performance of identity, and various kinds of representation of the human form. We have highlighted the singular and the collective, the intact and dissolved, and have tried to draw attention to the recurrent intermingling of human and animal. Everywhere we see diversity, and we want to stress 'bodies' in the plural at any one time and in any one context. We want to highlight the need to combine different strands of evidence. We have tried to hint at change through time, by drawing on examples from the 6th to the 4th millennia cal. BC, and one aspect of diversity is clearly the lack of fixed or static conceptions of the body and identity.

Further studies could try to break down the divisions between our subheadings. For example, one could tackle how the embodied experience of building an enclosure could relate to the later treatment of human bodies within its circuit, layering embodied meanings and histories onto the same site. Similarly, a discussion of figurines could focus not just on representational aspects, but also on how the clay felt, during and after manufacture, and on the sensations of handling and breaking it.

The Murr beaker, too, has performative dimensions in its making and the incision of the figures, in its use for the preparation and consumption of beverages, and finally in its deposition.

Whether there is also a wider, coherent 'grand narrative' here – a history of Neolithic bodies through to the 3rd millennium cal. BC, and beyond, region by region or across central and western Europe as a whole – we prefer to leave open, and it is certainly beyond the short discussion possible here. The Iceman, for example, has been used as a convenient illustration of underlying structural development and conceptions of the individual in the later 4th millennium cal. BC (e.g. Hodder 2000), but we think this is far too neat. Figures like the Iceman may have existed much earlier in the circum-Alpine zone.

We find it hard to fence off a 'body subject', and do not want to overemphasize mind-less bodies. But routines, embodiment, identity and representation seem important approaches that we cannot now ignore. Perhaps it is now time to find the words or media to tackle the embodied feel of the axe on timber: the way in which the sharp blow, properly executed, might have perfectly expressed active, perhaps beautiful, prowess and skill; the manner in which each successive cut might have embedded into the tree, on its way to the longhouse or settlement, a whole set of distributed relationships; or the style in which the rise and fall of the axe might have evoked both past and future, such that the axe user experienced history literally in and through the hands.

ACKNOWLEDGEMENTS

We would like to thank Miranda Aldhouse-Green, Alex Bayliss, Dušan Boric, Penny Bickle, Amy Bogaard, Oliver Harris, Frances Healy, Lesley McFadyen, Bronwen Price and John Robb for their insightful criticism of earlier drafts. Thanks also to Howard Mason for Figure 6.1 and to Ian Dennis for his help with Figures 6.1, 6.2 and 6.3b. Furthermore, we would like to thank Dr. Andrea Hampel (Denkmalamt Frankfurt), Dr. Silvia Codreanu-Windauer (Bayerisches Landesamt für Denkmalpflege) and Dr. Susanne Reiter (Landesamt für Denkmalpflege Baden-Württemberg) for their assistance in gaining permission to reproduce copyrighted material. Erwin Neumair (Archäologischer Verein im Landkreis Freising e.V.) kindly allowed us to use his illustration of the Murr wedding beaker.

NOTES

1 Different activities can come to inscribe the body directly, in the form of muscle attachments and stress patterns on the skeleton (Sofaer 2006).

2 For exceptions see Lenzburg, and the intriguing megalithic graves in the Upper Rhône at Sion (Gallay 1990; Wyss 1967).

3 However, children, especially neonates, are generally under-represented, although more so in some sites than others. Occasionally, there is also a tendency to bury more men than women in cemeteries. Women and children, on the other hand, dominate in the settlement context (Jeunesse 1997; Orschiedt 1998; Siemoneit 1997; Veit 1993; 1996).

4 Interestingly, in the Marne area and Alsace, *Spondylus* armrings in graves are often broken and scattered all over the body (Jeunesse 2003:29), thus potentially mirroring practices at rites of passage during life.

5 New radiocarbon evidence suggests that Hinkelstein ceramics were manufactured between about 5000–4600 cal. BC and the Großgartach style was in use from 4900 to cal. 4500 BC (J. Müller 2003). There were, however, problems with the radiocarbon samples sent to one of the laboratories, where not all traces of modern carbon may have been removed. Thus, the absolute dates may have to be corrected. However, as the error consistently occurred in all samples, the relative sequence of graves is reliable (J. Müller 2003).

6 Some of the Großgartach graves are oriented in the exact opposite direction, i.e. with the head to the northwest. Interestingly, these graves cluster in the area of the cemetery closest to the Hinkelstein burials (Spatz 1999).

7 There is, however, a striking distinction between wild animal bone and teeth used for ornaments and domestic animal bone used as a food offering and to cover the body (Spatz and von den Driesch 2001).

8 Artefacts themselves can be likened to human bodies. This is the case in our present classification of pottery into 'neck', 'body' etc (Miranda Aldhouse-Green, pers. comm.), and has, for instance, been suggested by Tilley (1999) for Neolithic axes.

9 Stöckl's (2002) arguments must, however, be treated with caution. While he shows some clearly human depictions, it is far less certain that abstract motifs, such as V- and M-shapes or spirals, should also represent humans, especially as some of his comparative material comes from other time periods or geographically remote areas. To argue for a single meaning for all symbolism also disregards the potential for multiple, ambiguous or changeable meanings.

10 Recently, an LBK settlement with an extraordinary number of figurines has been excavated at Nieder-Mörlen in Hessen, and some figurines there seem to have been part of more structured deposits. However, the majority was still discarded with household waste (Schade-Lindig 2002a; 2002b).

REFERENCES

Affolter, J., R.-M. Arbogast, N. Delattre, F. Giligny, A. Maire, A.-M. Pétrequin, P. Pétrequin, and J.-L. Voruz 1997 Synthèse 3: Dynamique d'expansion culturelle et croissance démographique. *In* Les sites littoraux néolithiques de Clairvaux-les-lacs et de Chalain (Jura) III. Chalain station 3. 3200–2900 av. J.-C. Vol. 2. P. Pétrequin, ed. Pp. 563–75. Paris: Editions de la Maison des Sciences de l'Homme.

Andersen, N. H. 1997 The Sarup Enclosures, Volume 1: The Funnel Beaker Culture of the Sarup Site Including Two Causewayed Camps Compared to the Contemporary Settlements in the Area and Other European Enclosures. Mosegaard: Jysk Arkæologisk Selskab.

Arbogast, R.-M., V. Beugnier, N. Delattre, F. Gilligny, A. Maitre, A.-M. Pétrequin, and P. Pétrequin 1997 La répartition des témoins et le fonctionnement de la cellule domestique. *In* Les sites littoraux néolithiques de Clairvaux-les-lacs et de Chalain (Jura) III. Chalain station 3. 3200–2900 av. J.-C., Vol. 2. P. Pétrequin, ed. Pp. 583–639. Paris: Editions de la Maison des Sciences de l'Homme.

Bachelard, G. 1964 The Poetics of Space. Boston: Beacon Press.

Bailey, D. W. 2005 Prehistoric Figurines. Representation and Corporeality in the Neolithic. London: Routledge.

Bánffy, E. 1991 Cult and Archaeological Context in Middle and South-East Europe in the Neolithic and the Chalcolithic. Antaeus 19–20:183–249.

Barley, N. 1995 Dancing on the Grave: Encounters with Death. London: John Murray.

Baudais, D., and N. Delattre 1997 Les objets en bois. *In* Les sites littoraux néolithiques de Clairvaux-les-lacs et de Chalain (Jura) III. Chalain station 3. 3200–2900 av. J.-C. Vol. 2. P. Pétrequin, ed. Pp. 529–44. Paris: Editions de la Maison des Sciences de l'Homme.

Behrends, R.-H. 1990 Ein Gräberfeld der Bandkeramik von Schwetzingen, Rhein-Neckar-Kreis. Archäologische Ausgrabungen in Baden-Württemberg 1989:45–8.

Behrends, R.-H. 1997 La nécropole rubanée de Schwetzingen. *In* Le Néolithique Danubien et ses marges entre Rhin et Seine. Actes du 22ème colloque interrégional sur le Néolithique. C. Jeunesse, ed. Pp. 17–29. Strasbourg: Cahiers de l'Association pour la Promotion de la Recherche archéologique en Alsace.

Böhm, K. 1998 Münchshöfener Bestattungen in Ostbayern. *In* Archäologische Arbeitsgemeinschaft Ostbayern/West- und Südböhmen. 7. Treffen 11.-14. Juni 1997 in Landau an der Isar. J. Michálek, K. Schmotz, and M. Zápotocká, eds. Pp. 47–59. Rahden: Marie Leidorf.

Böhm, K., and R. Pielmeier 1993 Der älteste Metallfund Altbayerns in einem Doppelgrab der Münchshöfener Gruppe aus Straubing, Niederbayern. Das Archäologische Jahr in Bayern 1993:40–2.

Bourdieu, P. 1990 The Logic of Practice. Stanford: Stanford University Press.

Bradley, R. 2002 Access, Style and Imagery: The Audience for Prehistoric Rock Art in Atlantic Spain and Portugal, 4000–2000 BC. Oxford Journal of Archaeology 21:231–47.

Breton, S., ed. 2006 Qu'est ce qu'un corps? Paris: Flammarion.

Capasso, L. 1995 Ungueal Morphology and Pathology of the "Ice Man". *In* Der Mann im Eis: neue Funde und Ergebnisse. K. Spindler, E. Rastbichler-Zissernig, H. Wilfing, D. zur Nedden, and H. Nothdurfter, eds. Pp. 231–9. Vienna: Springer.

Conkey, M., and R. Tringham 1995 Archaeology and the Goddess: Exploring the Contours of Feminist Archaeology. *In* Feminisms in the Academy. D. Stanton and A. Stewart, eds. Pp. 199–247. Ann Arbor: University of Michigan Press.

Csordas, T. J. 1990 Embodiment as a Paradigm for Anthropology. Ethos 18:5–47.

Csordas, T. J. 1993 Somatic Modes of Attention. Cultural Anthropology 8:135–56.

Csordas, T. J. 1999 The Body's Career in Anthropology. *In* Anthropological Theory Today. H. L. Moore, ed. Pp. 172–205. Cambridge: Polity.

D'Anna, A., X. Gutherz, and L. Jallot 1997 L'art mégalithique dans le Midi de la France: Les stèles anthropomorphes et les statues-menhirs néolithiques. Revue Archéologique de l'Ouest 8:179–93.

Diaz-Andreu, M. 2002 Marking the Landscape: Iberian Post-Palaeolithic Art, Identities and the Sacred. *In* European Landscapes of Rock-Art. G. Nash and C. Chippindale, eds. Pp. 158–75. London: Routledge.

Dondio, W. 1995 La regione Atesina nella preistoria. Volume Primo: Il Trentino-Alto Adige e le zone limitrofe dalle origini all'età del rame. Bolzano: Edition Rætia.

Eisenhauer, U. 1999 Kulturwandel als Innovationsprozeß: Die fünf großen 'W' und die Verbreitung des Mittelneolithikums in Südwestdeutschland. Archäologische Informationen 22:215–39.

Fairén, S. 2004 Rock Art and the Transition to Farming. The Neolithic Landscape of the Central Mediterranean Coast of Spain. Oxford Journal of Archaeology 23:1–19.

Featherstone, M., M. Hepworth, and B. Turner, eds. 1991 The Body. Social Process and Cultural Theory. London: Sage Publications.

Fowler, C. 2004 The Archaeology of Personhood: An Anthropological Approach. London: Routledge.

Gallay, A. 1990 Historique des recherches enterprises sur le nécropole mégalithique du Petit-Chasseur à Sion (Valais, Suisse). *In* Autour de Jean Arnal. J. Guilaine and X. Gutherz, eds. Pp. 335–57. Montpellier: Premières Communautés Paysannes.

Gamble, C. 1999 The Palaeolithic Societies of Europe. Cambridge: Cambridge University Press.

Giligny, F. 1997 La ceramique de Chalain 3. *In* Les sites littoraux néolithiques de Clairvaux-les-lacs et de Chalain (Jura) III. Chalain station 3. 3200–2900 av. J.-C. Vol. 2. P. Pétrequin, ed. Pp. 327–62. Paris: Editions de la Maison des Sciences de l'Homme.

Gimbutas, M. 1974 The Gods and Goddesses of Old Europe. London: Thames and Hudson.

Gimbutas, M. 1991 The Civilization of the Goddess. San Francisco: HarperSanFrancisco.

Goffman, E. 1967 Interaction and Ritual. Essays on Face-to-Face Behaviour. Harmondsworth: Penguin.

Grygiel, R. 1994 Untersuchungen zur Gesellschaftsorganisation des Früh–und Mittelneolithikums Mitteleuropas. *In* Internationales Symposium über die Lengyel-Kultur 1888–1988. Znojmo-Kravska-Tešetice 3.–7.10.1988. P. Košturík, ed. Pp. 43–77. Brno-Kódž: Masarykova Univerzita.

Hamilakis, Y., M. Pluciennik, and S. Tarlow 2002 Introduction: Thinking Through the Body. *In* Thinking Through the Body: Archaeologies of Corporeality. Y. Hamilakis, M. Pluciennik, and S. Tarlow, eds. Pp. 1–21. Kluwer Academic/Plenum: New York/Dordrecht.

Hampel, A. 1989 Bemerkenswerte Fundstücke aus der linienbandkeramischen Siedlung in Frankfurt a. M. – Niedereschbach. Germania 67:149–57.

Harris, M. 1998 The Rhythm of Life on the Amazon Floodplain: Seasonality and Sociality in a Riverine Village. Journal of the Royal Anthropological Institute 4:65–82.

Harris, M. 2000 Life on the Amazon. The Anthropology of a Brazilian Peasant Village. Oxford: Oxford University Press.

Höckmann, O. 1965 Menschliche Darstellungen in der bandkeramischen Kultur. Jahrbuch des Römisch-Germanischen Zentralmuseums Mainz 12:1–34.

Höckmann, O. 1972 Andeutungen zu Religion und Kultus in der bandkeramischen Kultur. Alba Regia 12:187–209.

Höckmann, O. 1985 Ein ungewöhnlicher neolithischer Statuettenkopf aus Rockenberg, Wetteraukreis. Jahrbuch des Römisch-Germanischen Zentralmuseums Mainz 32:92–107.

Höckmann, O. 1987 Gemeinsamkeiten in der Plastik der Linearkeramik und der Cucuteni-Kultur. *In* La civilisation de Cucuteni en contexte Européen. Session Scientifique Iasi-Piatra Neamt 1984. M. Petrescu-Dîmbouita, ed. Pp. 89–97. Iasi: Université Al. I. Cuza.

Hodder, I. 1990 The Domestication of Europe. Structure and Contingency in Neolithic Societies. Oxford: Blackwell.

Hodder, I. 2000 Agency and Individuals in Long-Term Process. *In* Agency in Archaeology. M.-A. Dobres and J. Robb, eds. Pp. 21–33. London: Routledge.

Hofmann, D. 2005 Fragments of Power: LBK Figurines and the Mortuary Record. *In* Elements of Being: Mentalities, Identities and Movements. D. Hofmann, J. Mills, and A. Cochrane, eds. Pp. 58–70. Oxford: British Archaeological Reports.

Hofmann, D. 2006 Being Neolithic: Life, Death and Transformation in Neolithic Lower Bavaria. Unpublished PhD thesis, Cardiff University.

Ingold, T. 2000 The Perception of the Environment. Essays in Livelihood, Dwelling and Skill. London: Routledge.

Jacomet, S., C. Brombacher, and M. Dick 1990 Ackerbau, Sammelwirtschaft und Umwelt. *In* Die ersten Bauern. Pfahlbaubefunde Europas. Band 1. M. Höneisen, ed. Pp. 81–90. Zürich: Schweizerisches Landesmuseum.

Jacomet, S., U. Leuzinger, and J. Schibler, eds. 2005 Die jungsteinzeitliche Seeufersiedlung Arbon Bleiche 3: Umwelt und Wirtschaft. Archäologie im Thurgau 12. Frauenfeld: Dept. für Erziehung und Kultur des Kantons Thurgau.

Jeunesse, C. 1997 Pratiques funéraires au Néolithique ancien. Sépultures et nécropoles danubiennes 5500–4900 av. J.-C. Paris: Editions Errance.

Jeunesse, C. 2003 Les pratiques funéraires du Néolithique ancien danubien et l'identité rubanée: découvertes recentes, nouvelles tendances de la recherche. *In* Les pratiques funéraires néolithiques avant 3500 av. J.-C. en France et dans les régions limitrophes. Saint-Germain-en-Laye 15–17 juin 2001. P. Chambon and J. Leclerc, eds. Pp. 19–32. Paris: Société Préhistorique Française.

Jeunesse, C., and R.-M. Arbogast 1997 A propos du statut de la chasse au Néolithique moyen. La faune sauvage dans les déchets domestiques et dans les mobiliers funéraires. *In* Le Néolithique Danubien et ses marges entre Rhin et Seine. Actes du 22ème colloque interrégional sur le Néolithique. C. Jeunesse, ed. Pp. 81–102. Strasbourg: Cahiers de l'Association pour la Promotion de la Recherche archéologique en Alsace.

Jockenhövel, A., and B. Knoche 2003 Zur Rolle des Hirsches im neolithischen Europa. *In* Archäologische Perspektiven. Analysen und Interpretationen im Wandel. Festschrift für Jens Lüning zum 65. Geburtstag. J. Eckert, U. Eisenhauer, and A. Zimmermann, eds. Pp. 195–223. Rahden: Marie Leidorf.

Kaufmann, D. 1976 Linienbandkeramische Kultgegenstände aus dem Elbe-Saale Gebiet. Jahresschrift für mitteldeutsche Vorgeschichte 60:61–96.

Kaufmann, D. 1989 Kultische Äußerungen im Frühneolithikum des Elbe-Saale Gebietes. *In* Religion und Kult in ur- und frühgeschichtlicher Zeit. F. Schlette and D. Kaufmann, eds. Pp. 111–39. Berlin: Akademie-Verlag.

Kent, S. 1990 A Cross-Cultural Study of Segmentation, Architecture and the Use of Space. *In* Domestic Architecture and the Use of Space. An Interdisciplinary Cross-Cultural Study. S. Kent, ed. Pp. 127–52. Cambridge: Cambridge University Press.

Kreiner, L. 1995 Grabfunde der Münchshöfener Kultur im Landkreis Dingolfing-Landau. *In* Vorträge des 13. Niederbayerischen Archäologentages. K. Schmotz, ed. Pp. 71–84. Espelkamp: Marie Leidorf.

Kreiner, L. 2001 Die Ausgrabungen in der Trasse der Erdgasleitung zwischen Mödling und Landau. *In* Archäologie im Landkreis Dingolfing-Landau Band 1. L. Kreiner, ed. Pp. 52–74. Eichendorf: Eichendorf Verlag.

Kreiner, L., and R. Pleyer 1999 Die "Venus von Aufhausen" – Ein besonderes Gefäß der Münchshöfener Kultur. *In* Vorträge des 17. Niederbayerischen Archäologentages. K. Schmotz, ed. Pp. 55–69. Rahden: Marie Leidorf.

Kunkel, O. 1955 Die Jungfernhöhle bei Tiefenellern. Eine neolithische Kultstätte auf dem fränkischen Jura bei Bamberg. Münchner Beiträge zur Ur- und Frühgeschichte 5:1–138.

Landesamt für Archäologie Sachsen 2003 Der "Adonis von Zschernitz". Die älteste männliche Tonfigur Europas. www.archsax.sachsen.de/aktuelles/21082003.html.

Lesure, R. 2002 The Goddess Diffracted. Thinking About the Figurines of Early Villages. Current Anthropology 43:587–610.

Lucas, G. M. 1996 Of Death and Debt. A History of the Body in Neolithic and Early Bronze Age Yorkshire. Journal of European Archaeology 4:99–118.

Lüning, J. 1968 Die Michelsberger Kultur. Ihre Funde in zeitlicher und räumlicher Gliederung. Bericht der Römisch-Germanischen Kommission 48:1–350.

Lüning, J. 2005 Wine Weltpremiere: Kleider machen Leute – Kopfputz, Hüte und Schmuck ebenfalls. *In* Die Bandkeramiker. Erste Steinzeitbauern in Deutschland. Bilder einer Ausstellung beim Hessentag in Heppenheim/Bergstraße im Juni 2004. J. Lüning, ed. Pp. 213–71. Rahden: Marie Leidorf.

Lüning, J. 2006 Haare, Hüte, Hosenanzüge: Trachten der Bandkeramik und ihre Rolle im Ahnenkult. *In* Lebendige Vergangenheit: vom archäologischen Experiment zur Zeitreise. E. Keefer, ed. Pp. 52–64. Stuttgart: Theiss.

Lüning, J., and P. Stehli, eds. 1994 Die Bandkeramik im Merzbachtal auf der Aldenhofener Platte. Cologne: Rheinland-Verlag GmbH.

Maier, R. A. 1962 Fragen zu neolithischen Erdwerken Südbayerns. Jahresbericht der Bayerischen Bodendenkmalpflege:5–12.

Maurer, H. 1982 Neolithische Kultobjekte aus dem niederösterreichischen Manhartsbergbereich. Ein Beitrag zur jungsteinzeitlichen Geistesgeschichte. Mannus-Bibliothek Band 19. Hückeswagen: Gesellschaft für Vor- und Frühgeschichte.

Menotti, F., ed. 2004 Living on the Lake in Prehistoric Europe: 150 Years of Lake-Dwelling Research. London: Routledge.

Meskell, L. 1995 Goddess, Gimbutas and 'New Age' Archaeology. Antiquity 69:74–86.

Meskell, L. 1996 The Somatization of Archaeology: Institutions, Discourses, Corporeality. Norwegian Archaeological Review 29(1):1–16.

Meskell, L. M., and R. A. Joyce 2003 Embodied Lives: Figuring Ancient Maya and Egyptian Experience. London: Routledge.

Modderman, P. 1970 Linearbandkeramik aus Elsoo und Stein. Leiden: Leiden University Press.

Müller, J. 2001 Soziochronologische Studien zum Jung- und Spätneolithikum im Mittelelbe-Saale-Gebiet (4100–2700 v.Chr.). Rahden: Marie Leidorf.

Müller, J. 2002 Zur Belegungsabfolge des Gräberfeldes von Trebur: Argumente der typologieunabhängigen Datierungen. www.jungsteinsite.de; accessed November 2006.

Müller, J. 2003 Zur Belegungsabfolge des Gräberfeldes von Trebur: Argumente der typologieunabhängigen Datierungen. Prähistorische Zeitschrift 77:148–58.

Müller, W., H. Fricke, A. N. Halliday, M. T. McCulloch, and J.-A. Wartho 2003 Origin and Migration of the Alpine Iceman. Science 302:862–6.

Neumair, E. 1996 Murr – eine bedeutende Zentralsiedlung der jungsteinzeitlichen Münch-shöfener Kultur. Bericht über die Grabungskampagne 1995/96. Archäologie im Landkreis Freising 5:9–89.

Nieszery, N. 1995 Linearbandkeramische Gräberfelder in Bayern. Internationale Archäologie 16. Espelkamp: Marie Leidorf.

Orschiedt, J. 1998 Bandkeramische Siedlungsbestattungen in Südwestdeutschland. Archäol-ogische und anthropologische Befunde. Internationale Archäologie 43. Rahden: Marie Leidorf.

Orschiedt, J. 1999 Manipulationen an menschlichen Skelettresten. Taphonomische Prozesse, Sekundärbestattungen oder Kannibalismus? Tübingen: Mo Vince Verlag.

Orschiedt, J. 2002 Die 'Knochentrümmerstätte' im Hohlenstein-Stadel. Ein Beitrag zur Bestattungspraxis im frühen Jungneolithikum. In Varia Neolithica II. Beiträge zur Ur- und Frühgeschichte Mitteleuropas 32. H.-J. Beier, ed. Pp. 131–9. Weissbach: Beier and Beran.

Parker Pearson, M. 2000 Eating Money. Archaeological Dialogues 7:217–32.

Pavlu, I. 2000 Life on a Neolithic Site. Bylany – Situational Analysis of Artefacts. Prague: Institute of Archaeology, Czech Academy of Sciences.

Pavúk, J. 1972 Zum Problem der Gräberfelder mit der Linienbandkeramik. Alba Regia 12:123–30.

Petrasch, J. 1990 Mittelneolithische Kreisgrabenanlagen in Mitteleuropa. Bericht der Römisch-Germanischen Kommission 71:407–564.

Petrasch, J., and K. Schmotz 1989 Ein neues Idolfragment der Münchshöfener Kultur aus Niederbayern. Germania 67:158–61.

Pétrequin, P., ed. 1986 Les sites littoraux néolithiques de Clairvaux-les-lacs (Jura). Problé-matique générale. L'exemple de la station III. Paris: Editions de la Maison des Sciences de l'Homme.

Pétrequin, P., ed. 1997a Les sites littoraux néolithiques de Clairvaux-les-lacs et de Chalain (Jura) III. Chalain station 3. 3200–2900 av. J.-C. Vol. 1. Paris: Editions de la Maison des Sciences de l'Homme.

Pétrequin, P., ed. 1997b Les sites littoraux néolithiques de Clairvaux-les-lacs et de Chalain (Jura) III. Chalain station 3. 3200–2900 av. J.-C. Vol. 2. Paris: Editions de la Maison des Sciences de l'Homme.

Pétrequin, P. 1997c Stratigraphie et strategie de fouille. In Les sites littoraux néolithiques de Clairvaux-les-lacs et de Chalain (Jura) III. Chalain station 3. 3200–2900 av. J.-C. Vol. 1. P. Pétrequin, ed. Pp. 37–54. Paris: Editions de la Maison des Sciences de l'Homme.

Pétrequin, P., and M. Bailly 2004 Lake-Dwelling Research in France: From Climate to Demography. In Living on the Lake in Prehistoric Europe: 150 Years of Lake-Dwelling Research. F. Menotti, ed. Pp. 36–49. London: Routledge.

Rapoport, A. 1990 Systems of Activities and Systems of Settings. In Domestic Architecture and the Use of Space. An Interdisciplinary Cross-Cultural Study. S. Kent, ed. Pp. 9–20. Cambridge: Cambridge University Press.

Reinecke, K. 1977 Neue Funde der Linearbandkeramik aus Niederbayern. Archäologisches Korrespondenzblatt 7:201–10.

Ruoff, U. 2004 Lake-Dwelling Studies in Switzerland since 'Meilen 1854'. *In* Living on the Lake in Prehistoric Europe: 150 years of Lake-Dwelling Research. F. Menotti, ed. Pp. 9–21. London: Routledge.

Schade-Lindig, S. 2002a Idol- und Sonderfunde der bandkeramischen Siedlung von Bad Nauheim–Nieder-Mörlen "Auf dem Hempler" (Wetteraukreis). Germania 80: 47–114.

Schade-Lindig, S. 2002b Idole und sonderbar verfüllte Gruben aus der bandkeramischen Siedlung "Hempler" in Bad Nauheim–Nieder-Mörlen. *In* Varia Neolithica II. Beiträge zur Ur- und Frühgeschichte Mitteleuropas 32. H.-J. Beier, ed. Pp. 99–115. Weissbach: Beier and Beran.

Schibler, J., S. Jacomet, H. Hüster-Plogmann, and C. Brombacher 1997a Economic Crash in the 37th and 36th Centuries Cal. BC in Neolithic Lake Shore Sites in Switzerland. Anthropozoologica 25/26:553–70.

Schibler, J., H. Hüster-Plogmann, S. Jacomet, C. Brombacher, E. Gross-Klee, and A. Rast-Eicher 1997b Ökonomie und Ökologie neolithischer und bronzezeitlicher Ufersiedlungen am Zürichsee. Zürich: Monographien der Kantonsarchäologie Zürich.

Schlichtherle, H. 1997 Pfahlbauten rund um die Alpen. *In* Pfahlbauten rund um die Alpen. H. Schlichtherle, ed. Pp. 7–14. Stuttgart: Theiss.

Schlichtherle, H. 2004 Lake-Dwellings in South-Western Germany: History of Research and Contemporary Perspectives. *In* Living on the Lake in Prehistoric Europe: 150 Years of Lake-Dwelling Research. F. Menotti, ed. Pp. 21–35. London: Routledge.

Schmotz, K. 1992 Das bandkeramische Gräberfeld von Stephansposching. Archäologische Denkmäler im Landkreis Deggendorf, Heft 7. Deggendorf: Ebner.

Schröter, P. 1996 Zu den menschlichen Skelettfunden aus der Neolithischen Siedlung von Murr, Landkreis Freising. Archäologie im Landkreis Freising, Heft 5:107–11.

Sené, G. 1997 Les coprolithes du néolithique final de Clairvaux-les-lacs et de Chalain. *In* Les sites littoraux néolithiques de Clairvauxles-lacs et de Chalain (Jura) III. Chalain station 3. 3200–2900 av. J.-C. Vol. 2. P. Pétrequin, ed. Pp. 747–56. Paris: Editions de la Maison des Sciences de l'Homme.

Sidéra, I. 2000 Animaux domestiques, bêtes sauvages et objets en matières animales du Rubané au Michelsberg. De l'économie aux symboles, des techniques à la culture. Gallia Préhistoire 42:107–94.

Sidéra, I. 2003 De l'usage des produits de la chasse pour différencier des hommes. Fonctions votive et sociale de la chasse au Néolithique ancien et moyen du Bassin Parisien. *In* Les pratiques funéraires néolithiques avant 3500 av. J.-C. en France et dans les régions limitrophes. Saint-Germain-en-Laye 15–17 juin 2001. P. Chambon and J. Leclerc, eds. Pp. 91–8. Paris: Société Préhistorique Française.

Siemoneit, B. 1997 Das Kind in der Linienbandkeramik. Befunde aus Gräberfeldern und Siedlungen in Mitteleuropa. Internationale Archäologie 42. Rahden: Marie Leidorf.

Sofaer, J. 2006 The Body as Material Culture. A Theoretical Osteoarchaeology. Cambridge: Cambridge University Press.

Spatz, H. 1996 Beiträge zum Kulturenkomplex Hink elstein, Großgartach, Rössen: der keramische Fundstoff des Mittelneolithikums aus dem mittleren Neckarland und seine zeitliche Gliederung. Stuttgart: Theiss.

Spatz, H. 1999 Das mittelneolithische Gräberfeld von Trebur, Kreis Groß-Gerau. Wiesbaden: Selbstverlag des Landesamtes für Denkmalpflege Hessen.

Spatz, H. 2003 Hinkelstein: eine Sekte als Initiator des Mittelneolithikums? *In* Archäologische Perspektiven. Analysen und Interpretationen im Wandel. Festschrift für Jens Lüning zum 65. Geburtstag. J. Eckert, U. Eisenhauer, and A. Zimmermann, eds. Pp. 575–87. Rahden: Marie Leidorf.

Spatz, H., and A. von den Driesch 2001 Zu den tierischen Beigaben aus dem Hinkelsteiner und Grossgartacher Gräberfeld von Trebur, Kr. Gross-Gerau. *In* Rôle et statut de la chasse dans le Néolithique ancien danubien (5500–4900 av. J.-C.). Premières rencontres danubiennes Strasbourg 20 et 21 novembre 1996. R.-M. Arbogast, C. Jeunesse, and J. Schibler, eds. Pp. 113–28. Rahden: Marie Leidorf.

Speck, J. 1990 Zur Geschichte der Pfahlbauforschung. *In* Die ersten Bauern. Pfahlbaubefunde Europas. Band 1. M. Höneisen, ed. Pp. 9–19. Zürich: Schweizerisches Landesmuseum.

Spindler, K. 1994 The Man in the Ice. The Amazing Inside Story of the 5000-Year-Old Body Found Trapped in a Glacier in the Alps. London: Weidenfeld and Nicolson.

Spindler, K., E. Rastbichler-Zissernig, H. Wilfing, D. zur Nedden, and H. Nothdurfter, eds. 1995 Der Mann im Eis: neue Funde und Ergebnisse. Springer: Vienna.

Stöckl, H. 2002 Hatten bandkeramische Gefäßverzierungen eine symbolische Bedeutung im Bereich des Kultes? *In* Varia Neolithica II. Beiträge zur Ur- und Frühgeschichte Mitteleuropas 32. H.-J. Beier, ed. Pp. 63–97. Weissbach: Beier and Beran.

Strahm, C. 1997 Chronologie der Pfahlbauten. *In* Pfahlbauten rund um die Alpen. H. Schlichtherle, ed. Pp. 124–6. Stuttgart: Theiss.

Strathern, A., and M. Lambek 1998 Introduction. Embodying Sociality: Africanist-Melanesianist Comparisons. *In* Bodies and Persons: Comparative Perspectives from Africa and Melanesia. M. Lambek and A. Strathern, eds. Pp. 1–25. Cambridge: Cambridge University Press.

Süß, L. 1976 Zur Münchshöfener Gruppe in Bayern. *In* Die Anfänge des Neolithikums vom Orient bis Nordeuropa. Teil Vb Westliches Mitteleuropa. H. Schwabedissen, ed. Pp. 1–121. Cologne: Böhlau Verlag.

Talalay, L. 1993 Deities, Dolls and Devices: Neolithic Figurines from Franchthi Cave, Greece. Bloomington: Indiana University Press.

Tarlow, S. 2000 Emotion in Archaeology. Current Anthropology 41:713–46.

Tilley, C. 1999 Metaphor and Material Culture. Oxford: Blackwell.

Treherne, P. 1995 The Warrior's Beauty: The Masculine Body and Self-Identity in Bronze Age Europe. Journal of European Archaeology 3:105–44.

Tringham, R. 1971 Hunters, Fishers and Farmers of Eastern Europe, 6000–3000 BC. London: Hutchinson.

Tringham, R., and M. Conkey 1998 Rethinking Figurines: A Critical View from Archaeology of Gimbutas, the 'Goddess' and Popular Culture. *In* Ancient Goddesses: The Myths and the Evidence. L. Goodison and C. Morris, eds. Pp. 22–45. London: British Museum Press.

Trnka, G. 1991 Studien zu mittelneolithischen Kreisgrabenanlagen. Vienna: Verlag der Österreichischen Akademie der Wissenschaften.

Turner, B. S. 1996 The Body and Society: Explorations in Social Theory (2nd edn.). London: Sage Publications.

van de Velde, P. 1979 On Bandkeramik Social Structure. Analecta Praehistorica Leidensia 12:1–242.

Veit, U. 1993 Burials within Settlements of the Linienbandkeramik and Stichbandkeramik Cultures of Central Europe. On the Social Construction of Death in Early-Neolithic Society. Journal of European Archaeology 1:107–40.

Veit, U. 1996 Studien zum Problem der Siedlungsbestattung im europäischen Neolithikum. Tübinger Schriften zur ur- und frühgeschichtlichen Archäologie. Münster: Waxmann.

von den Driesch, A. 1999 Die tierischen Beigaben aus dem Gräberfeld des älteren Mittelneolithikums von Trebur, Kreis Groß-Gerau. *In* Das mittelneolithische Gräberfeld von Trebur, Kreis Groß-Gerau. Band I: Textteil. H. Spatz, ed. Pp. 355–72. Wiesbaden: Selbstverlag des Landesamtes für Denkmalpflege Hessen.

Wahl, J., and H. König 1987 Traumatologische Untersuchung der menschlichen Skelettreste aus dem bandkeramischen Massengrab bei Talheim, Kreis Heilbronn. Fundberichte aus Baden-Württemberg 12:67–193.

Whittle, A. 1996 Europe in the Neolithic: The Creation of New Worlds. Cambridge: Cambridge University Press.

Whittle, A. 2003 The Archaeology of People. Dimensions of Neolithic life. London: Routledge.

Williams, H. 2004 Death Warmed Up. The Agency of Bodies and Bones in Early Anglo-Saxon Cremation Rites. Journal of Material Culture 9:263–91.

Wunn, I. 2001 Götter, Mütter, Ahnenkult. Religionsentwicklung in der Jungsteinzeit. Beiheft der Archäologischen Mitteilungen aus Nordwestdeutschland Nr. 36. Rahden: Marie Leidorf.

Wunn, I. 2002 Religiöse Symbole im Neolithikum – ihre Entschlüsselung und Bedeutung. In Varia Neolithica II. Beiträge zur Ur- und Frühgeschichte Mitteleuropas 32. H.-J. Beier, ed. Pp. 35–54. Weissbach: Beier and Beran.

Wyss, R. 1967 Ein jungsteinzeitliches Hockergräberfeld mit Kollektivbestattungen bei Lenzburg, Kt. Aargau. Germania 45:20–34.

6 (b)

Bodies and Identities in the Scandinavian Late Iron Age

Ing-Marie Back Danielsson

Introduction

Debates surrounding personal and communal identities are matters of urgency amongst contemporary communities. These discussions are equally important in archaeology, as it is concerned with the analysis of the lifeways of people living in the past. Such analyses necessarily involve scrutiny of the concepts of identity, the body and the person. This chapter begins by reflecting on the contemporary significance of issues of identity and the body, before examining the construction of identities and bodies and the processes by which identities become related to, and are expressed through, bodies. It is argued that identity and body are far from being fixed and stable entities; rather, they should be seen as ongoing processes, things constructed, constructing and always contextual. What is more, bodies are constantly intertwined and interacting with things and beings, creating a multitude of bodies, identities and personhoods. In this manner the production, perception and conception of bodies and identities may vary according to time, place and community. In what follows, examples of what constituted a person during the late Iron Age in Scandinavia are presented, as well as suggestions about how the world/ cosmos was created, built around and reliant upon relationships among human beings, animals and things. I argue that by acknowledging and embracing the manifold expressions of body, identity and person, a creative potential is realized, inviting different interpretations of the past and, therefore, the present.

The Contemporary Significance of Identity

From its inception archaeology has been involved with the creation and categorization of identities and peoples. For instance, archaeology has (consciously as well as subconsciously) aided nations in recognizing their pasts by identifying and categorizing material remains as belonging to specific national groups (cf. Geary 2002; Kohl and Fawcett 1995; Thomas 2004; Wells 2001). This identification has then been used in more obvious political arenas. For instance, archaeological evidence was employed in order to define the border between Germany and Poland after the

First World War, since it was believed to show how ancient tribes were located geographically (Wiwjorra 1995:175 in Thomas 2004:110). A more recent example is the ongoing Swedish judicial process between the Saami and forest farmers. Here, archaeological evidence is used by both the Saami and the forest farmers to claim their respective ancient rights to the forest regions, today owned by the forest farmers (e.g. Anth 2002; a parallel may be seen with the controversies during the last centuries in North America between colonizing European Americans and Native Americans, especially since the passing of NAGPRA, the Native American Graves Protection and Repatriation Act, in 1990).

Archaeology also contributes to identities in a more direct bodily manner, since bodies are excavated frequently. Osteological (or physical anthropological) body morphology in various states of decay – and more recently DNA analyses – are applied in order to ascertain scientific information about the deceased being, such as sex and perhaps race. Fragments of clothes and objects accompanying the deceased are commonly also used to identify the being's sex, gender, social status, and so on. I maintain that these procedures in the end are less about gaining information and data, but are rather more about creating identities, not only of past people, but also of present people. These identities, or our modes of categorization, may have had nothing at all to do with prehistoric realities (see for example Back Danielsson 2002; 2007 and below, Boyd 1997, Fowler 2002; 2004; Hodder 1997; Thomas 2002; 2004:63). I would like to suggest instead that categorization is important for us today, and may be described as part of our modernist impulse to create order among things and beings (Thomas 2004). This ordering is far from neutral, objective and value-free, but is an expression of how our lives and existences are (and will be) structured. Within archaeology such categorization and ordering has resulted in universal and essentialist categories such as hunter-gatherers, farmers and warriors (see Pluciennik this volume; Hanks, this volume) – which often include a preponderance of ascriptions of men as active in stereotypical ways (e.g. Ceasar 1999, cf. Alberti 2006). Elisabeth Arwill-Nordbladh (1998) in her research on the interpretation of Viking-Age women in archaeology concluded that there is a strong relationship between contemporary gender ideology and presentations of prehistoric women. In both these ways, by helping and supporting nations or different ethnic groups to find 'their' past, and by supplying more individual-centred sex- and gender-related information, archaeology's identification processes can be argued to be irreducibly political (S. Jones 1997:11 in Thomas 2004:110–11).

I argue that by stressing and acknowledging different forms of realities, bodies and identities it is possible for archaeology to connect to present-day issues of discrimination, harassment, sexism, hostility towards immigrants, and so on. By pointing to the shortcomings of interpretations which rely on asymmetric dualisms and universalisms/essentialisms, it is possible to engage with a different and unfamiliar past, and perhaps a different future. One might also state that everybody living today is alien to the constructions of bodies, identities and relationships that were prevalent in different parts of prehistory. Consequently, as a blond Scandinavian who can trace her genealogy as far back as to 17th century through written sources, I am certainly not linked in any special way with people who lived, for instance, during the Viking Age (c.800–1050 AD). This internationally renowned era is otherwise held dear and continues to be essential for the creation of national identities in Sweden, Norway, Denmark and Iceland. However the way the bodies and the lives of the Vikings were perceived and constructed are as strange to me as they would be to an immigrant to Sweden. Questions that then arise are what kinds of relationships, things and substances may have constituted identities, bodies, persons and communities in Scandinavia during the Viking Age and the late Iron Age (AD 400–1050)? What bodies, things and/or substances made up a person? In what follows, I consider how these complex relationships have been interpreted and explored in a series of case studies from the Scandinavian Late Iron Age. I concentrate on the remains of human bodies, and from there work my way through the possible constructions of person and identity, and also examine how these constructions are interrelated with the community and/or cosmos.

Bodies and Identities

During the last 30 years the body has been analyzed and theorized within a host of academic disciplines. Archaeology, it is claimed, came late to the topic of the body, where the number of works published on bodies shows an increase only in the last 15 years (Joyce 2005:141). Debates on bodies and societies have gained inspiration from, for instance, the phenomenology of Merleau-Ponty, feminist philosophy from Simone de Beauvoir to Judith Butler, and Michel Foucault's history of systems of knowledge (e.g. Hamilakis et al. 2002; Meskell and Joyce 2003; Montserrat 1998; Rautman 2000).

The body is pivotal when it comes to identity, since identity is performed through the body and bodily actions. Such actions may be constituted by reflected and unreflected bodily movements, everyday behaviours and habits, sexual orientation, speech, choices of clothing, bodily modifications (tattooing, scarification, piercing, make-up, hair dying, etc.), choice of relationships, modes of subsistence, and so on. The explanations for expressions of identities vary with different understandings of the body. In Chris Shilling's terms (2003), these understandings may roughly be characterized as either a view of the body as naturalistic or as socially constructed. A naturalistic body is understood as a 'pre-social, biological basis on which the superstructures of the self and society are founded' (Shilling 2003:37). An individual in this perspective would view their natural body as that which defines their capacities and limitations. As such, a naturalistic perspective would contend that, for instance, gender inequalities are due to men's inherently superior bodies. In contrast, the opposing view holds that the body is socially constructed, shaped and engendered within different discourses. In this context discourse is defined as the systems that determine the production of knowledge and meaning. Discourses comprise 'language, images, unspoken beliefs and prejudices, laws and scientific concepts, and all other means by which human values are communicated, "naturalized", and reproduced' (Hall 2003:65). The view of the body as biologically determined has been challenged by the work of Thomas Laqueur (1990), who demonstrates the historical contingency of the notion of sexual dimorphism. Another pioneer of the historical study of the body is Michel Foucault.

Foucault (e.g. 1970; 1980) is exceptional in the way he has examined the body and how power relations shape the performing body, its gestures and daily actions. This suggests that the reasons for gender inequalities are not to be sought in an alleged natural body, but instead within power relations, where dominant power structures represented by science, systems of laws, schools, healthcare, and so on, produce what might be perceived as the normal state of affairs. Judith Butler (1993) draws from the work of Foucault when she argues that the materiality of the body is the effect of power relations.

What these different strands have in common is their response to the Western tradition of the Cartesian dualism of an (active) mind and a (passive) body, which affects the way the materiality of the body is understood. A division into mind/body leaves the materiality of the body as unquestionable and the nature of the body as 'fixed in biology' (Thomas 2002:33). Alternatively, if there is no natural body, then it follows that in the past there must have been alternative materializations, 'resulting in bodies that were lived and experienced in ways which would be quite unfamiliar to us' (Thomas 2002:38). Consequently, the way the body is apprehended – whether as natural or as socially constructed – has great implications for how societies and (differences between) people may be interpreted and is therefore an important issue to archaeology. Therefore even aspects of the body as biologically 'obvious' as sexual characteristics have to be reconsidered when analyzing past bodies (cf. Nordbladh and Yates 1990).

We will shift now from the discussion of bodies, to the issue of embodiment. Merleau-Ponty (1962), in his phenomenology of perception, emphasized the embodied existence of the cognisant person: a person always perceives the world from the viewpoint of their body. Equally, recent archaeological works on bodies have placed an emphasis on the body as a site of lived experience, where static conceptions of the body as 'a public, legible surface' are abandoned (Joyce 2005:139). In particular Meskell (1996; 1998; 2000; 2001) and Joyce (1993; 1998; 2004), separately and jointly (Meskell and Joyce 2003), have explored the analysis of lived embodiment, and have drawn inspiration from phenomenology and feminism. Meskell has focused on the embodied lives and personhoods of ancient Egypt (1999; 2002) and Joyce on those of pre-Columbian Mesoamerica (2001a). The body and embodied experiences as themes of interest have also been investigated in archaeology in a plethora of topics including sex and gender (e.g. Alberti 2001; Joyce 2001a and b; Milledge Nelson 2006; Stig-Sørensen 1991; 2000), sexuality (e.g. Schmidt and Voss 2000), masculinity (e.g. Alberti 2006; Caesar 1999; Treherne 1995; Yates 1993), consumption (e.g. Boyd 2002; Hamilakis 1999; 2002; A. Jones 1999), the senses (e.g. Houston and Taube 2000; Kus 1992; Watson and Keating 1999), emotions (e.g. Meskell 1999; Tarlow 1999; 2000; 2002), and figural representations (e.g. Back Danielsson 2002; 2007; German 2000; Joyce 2000; 2001b; 2003; Palka 2002).

This chapter focuses on embodied personhoods; as such concepts related to Western understandings of the body, such as individual and person, are re-examined. Recent explorations of embodied personhood have been undertaken by, for example, Fowler (2002; 2004), Joyce (2004), Looper (2003), Meskell (2001), Meskell and Joyce (2003), and Thomas (2002). Like the biological notion of sexual dimorphism, discussed above, the concept of the individual has also been argued to be historically contingent. The notion of the individual is allied with the rise of capitalist notions of property, and with a jural definition of the person held to be responsible by law. These definitions emerged with the Enlightenment, and the rise of a capitalist 'enterprise culture' (Douglas 1992). A number of authors have noted that the concept of the Western individual whose boundaries are defined by the limits of their bodies needs to be reconsidered in other cultural contexts (Douglas 1992; Strathern 1988; Wagner 2001). For example, the anthropological literature on Melanesia offers a fresh perspective on the Western individual as the primary definition of the person (Strathern 1988; Wagner 2001). Melanesian conceptions of the person stand in contrast to those of the West. The Melanesian person is made up of the totality of their social relations. Since this is the case the boundaries of the human body do not define the boundaries of the person. The intentionality and agency of such persons is extended, often through the medium of material culture (Battaglia 1991; Gell 1998) to the extent that objects may be considered to be external components of the person (e.g. Gell 1998; Munn 1986). This relational model of personhood has been characterized as *dividual*, to distinguish it from the Western *individual*. Dividuality refers to the partible and divisible aspects of a person's agency, whereby one's identity may be strategically attached, detached or permeated with someone or something else (cf. Fowler 2004:8–9; Strassburg 2000:26–7; Strathern 1988). Accordingly, the boundaries of a body do not necessarily equate to the individual or person (A. Jones 2002:161). I will consider these notions further when I interpret the various contexts from which burnt human and animal bones have been recovered in Late Iron Age Scandinavia. Consequently, socio-cultural elaborations and interpretations of identities, bodies, persons and communities are favoured in this chapter, since they are considered to enable more diverse and interesting interpretations of prehistoric communities and people. Although these are also expressions of our Western, modern world, they are a more fruitful way of engaging with the heterogeneous ways of being human expressed through archaeological materials, where difference is not a threat but a possibility.

Death, Transformative Powers and Regeneration in Late Iron Age Scandinavia

The treatment of dead bodies consistently leaves clues about how a community in a specific context regarded, (de)constructed and (re)processed body, identities and persons (e.g. Fowler 2004:160–1; Svanberg 2003a and b).

In the following section I focus on parts of the Iron Age in Scandinavia, mainly c.400–1050 AD, but also connect to early Anglo-Saxon (c.450–600 AD) cremation rites, as these have a great deal in common with burial procedures practised in parts of Scandinavia. The area in focus is the large Mälardalen region in Sweden, although other areas in Scandinavia will be mentioned. This presentation serves to demonstrate how a body or a person was constructed or perceived in certain contexts and how delicately the concepts of body, identity and community are interwoven. It is further suggestive of the potential of an archaeology of bodies and embodiments.

The cremated bones of animals and human beings were deliberately deposited in specific places for the period and place under consideration. Burial grounds are of course one obvious example where bones were deposited in meaningful and culturally specific ways. The burials of the Early Iron Age (c.400 BC–400 AD) in the large Mälardalen region in Sweden may be characterized as being rather homogenous in the sense that these rarely are equipped with artefacts and/or animal bones (Bennett 1987:21). The small quantity of burnt human bones that has been unearthed within mounds or small cairns had been cleansed and crushed to an amorphous mass prior to deposition. It has been suggested that these ways of dealing with death and transformation were means of letting the deceased become part of a collective group of undefined ancestors (Ericsson and Runcis 1995). In

Figure 6.6 Typical Late Iron Age mounds of the region Mälardalen in Sweden (Photo: N. Lagergren, ATA [the Antiquarian Topographical Archives])

the succeeding periods communities in Scandinavia underwent major changes, transformations that are expressed in the archaeological record in a variety of ways. For example, settlements were abandoned and moved, new names were given to farms and cultivated areas, languages changed and the treatment and deposition of dead bodies became more heterogeneous. The alterations were not sudden, but took place over the course of a couple of hundred years. Mounds, enclosing cremation layers and ceramic urns within which artefacts and burnt bones of humans and animals may be recovered, are generally found in the Late Iron Age (Bennett 1987:21), (Figure 6.6). By contrast, the cremation rites contemporary with the early Anglo-Saxon period involved picking out specific burnt bones from the pyre and depositing them, occasionally with artefacts, in an urn which was then placed in a communal burial site (Williams 2004). The places where the cremations took place and the places where the urns were buried were thus not the same, whereas as this was mostly the case in large parts of Late Iron Age Scandinavia.

It is also significant that within Late Iron Age burials archaeologists have concluded that bones are 'missing', since the quantity of burnt bones from a human, for instance, is always lower than it would have been, if a complete human body had been left in the cremation layers. An adult human body – when cremated – generates c.2 to 2.5 kilograms of burnt bones (Holck 1987). By contrast, the burials from representative (Late) Iron Age grave-fields in Mälardalen thought to represent only one human being contained an average of 267.9 grams (Sigvallius 1994:28). It is also the case that complete cremated animals were not always deposited within burials (e.g. Iregren 1972; Sigvallius 1994). This suggests that large quantities of burnt bones – both from animals and humans – were removed from the pyres and taken elsewhere. I argue that the absence of bones in burial contexts instead may be explained by their presence in other contexts (cf. Gansum 2004a and b). Importantly, it is only when the concepts of the body, the person and the individual are scrutinized and reconsidered that the Scandinavian Late Iron Age mode of dealing with, and distributing, bones becomes more understandable.

The most probable explanation is that burnt bones were removed after the cremation for purposes other than burial. And indeed, as we shall see, burnt bones have surfaced in other contexts, such as in connection to iron workings and the production of ceramics. Burnt bones may equally have been used in the production of glass beads, giving the beads a whitish colour (Sode 1996). I suggest that along with the changes in the communities between the Early and Late Iron Age new ways of being emerged, as demonstrated by the change in burial procedures, which involved not only humans but also animals and things. In particular, it seems to have been important in certain pivotal circumstances to have constantly intermingled things and beings, and that it was during such transitional stages that this intermingling was made possible. These new relationships among animals, humans and things are not only expressed in the contexts of burials, but are in evidence in other contexts as well, presented below. Further, they show how the relationships in the specific contexts are not only constitutive of persons, but also demonstrate how the same relationships may tell a great deal about a community and its cosmos.

Terje Oestigaard (2000) has recently interpreted bodies in burial contexts from Late Iron Age Norway as gifts prepared and served in different ways such as raw, cooked and burnt. The gifts were then subsequently put in appropriate wrappings, for instance in cauldrons or in urns. He considers these 'composites' to have been edible meals and gifts to gods, who, by accepting the holy meals, legitimized the social order, thus giving the preparation and giving of divine food great cosmological significance. From the point of view of the deceased, a safe journey to the land of the dead is promised by this holy consumption, and the spirit thus becomes benevolent. Much of Terje Oestigaard's reasoning builds on the fact that the excavated dead bodies, or rather body fragments, show great variation as regards the degree of burning (sometimes they are not burnt at all, indicating they were served raw). This is not only true for cremation funerals in Iron Age Scandinavia, but also for early Anglo-Saxon cremations. Although the cremation techniques of the time seem to have been remarkably efficient (e.g. Williams 2004:281) some parts of the deposited bones were exposed to lower temperatures, resulting in bones with varying colours, giving some a bluish tone, for example. The great variation in the degree of burning has been described by anatomist Per Holck (1987:131) as imperfect cremations due to a lack of oxygen. These bones, commonly described by archaeologists as being poorly burnt – hinting at unsuccessful funeral pyres – may however have been considered vital, and therefore purposeful, in other transformative processes. These processes have a great deal in common with burial and pyre procedures in that they are highly transformative, where beings of various sorts are returned to life by transformative agencies or forces such as fire and air or breath. We will now consider other contexts in which burnt bones have been retrieved.

Recycling Bones: Bone Temper in Ceramics

There are other contexts from which burnt bones have been retrieved. Through excavations of prehistoric remains we know that cremated body parts were re-used and re-integrated in other material contexts, into new practices and performances. For example, fragmentized burnt bones were used as temper in ceramic vessels (Stilborg 2001). As with regenerating or processing once-living (human) beings into possible ancestors, the transformation of formable, wet or moist clay tempered with fragmented animal and/or human burnt bones to give the composite a solidity or backbone, required a kiln or bonfire and a sufficient air supply. In the ancient Nordic cultures in particular, the addition of air or breath in progenerative actions was considered necessary to the creation of life (Steinsland 1990). Breath, thought, blood and godly appearances were all powers of the soul essential for the creation of human beings, and according to the medieval text *Voluspà*, these powers were conferred on humans by the gods.

To temper ceramic vessels with bones is a phenomenon that is known from north European pottery as early as the Neolithic and onwards (Stilborg 2001:400). The meanings ascribed to the use of bone temper will have varied during the course of time. From a modern functionalistic viewpoint bone temper appears a viable choice to attain an adjustable and plastic (malleable) clay body and helps to facilitate a more even drying process, for instance. However, the employment of bone temper had almost disappeared prior to the Early Iron Age. This suggests that the Iron Age people made an active choice when they brought bone temper into play again. Analyses of temper in pottery have primarily been conducted on materials from southern Scandinavia. In the Gudme-Lundeborg area on the Danish island of Funen bone temper was found only in fine-ware vessels that had been locally produced (Stilborg 2001:401). The majority of the pottery was recovered in cremation burials, where they acted as funerary urns. Fragments of such pottery were also recovered in what the archaeological excavators labelled as rubbish pits at the settlement of Gudme. One sherd was also found in another context at the trading site of Lundeborg, where it had been re-shaped as a pendant. In order to produce ceramic vessels, soft and moist clay was mixed with finely crushed bones, and then modelled to the desired shape. When dried, the transformative power of fire, together with the correct quantity of air, would turn the composite into a ceramic pot – or (alternatively) would give birth to a new member of the household. It is difficult to say whether the fine-ware vessels were produced primarily to become funerary urns. I would like to propose however that the choice of vessels with bones as temper in burial contexts was deliberate and purposeful. This conclusion is underlined by the argument presented by anthropologist Robert Hertz (1960:60), who notes that there is a close connection between the soul and the urn with the bones as the spiritual signifier of the charnel house (Hertz 1960 in Oestigaard 2000:50). The urn therefore embodies the deceased physically and spiritually.

Other places where burnt fragmented bones have been unearthed are in cooking pits, hearths, forges and on property borders (Gansum 2004a:43–4; Gansum 2004b:139). Bones of humans and animals have been encountered in the furrow between two buildings in the Viking-Age town of Birka, Sweden. One deposit contains parts of a cow skull with both horns intact, bones from the wings of an eider and a large human shoulder blade, allegedly from the body of a very sturdy man (Ambrosiani and Erikson 1993:15–17). Together with the bones were a few amulet rings of iron. The furrow acted as a boundary between the two buildings, and in one of them smithing activities had probably taken place. Terje Gansum has elegantly examined the roles of the bones in connection with the transformation of iron to steel in iron forges (2004a). I will focus on this practice below.

Recycling Bones: Burnt Bones in Iron Workings

The way in which iron was produced in Scandinavia during the Iron Age involved the extraction of bloomery iron from bog ore. This iron was comparatively soft in its raw state (like wet clay and human flesh). In order to make the iron hard – that is, to turn it into steel – it needed to be carbonized (Gansum 2004a:42). A clay oven was constructed where the necessary ingredients were brought together. Of importance was a sufficient air supply during the transformation process from ore to iron, accomplished through the use of bellows. The extensive analysis of the literature on iron smithing, the evaluation of archaeological materials and experimentation with an experienced smith has led Terje Gansum (2004a and b) to suggest the probable use of bone coal to carbonize bloomery iron. The use of bone coal in carbonizing processes is known from at least the Early Iron Age (c.400 BC–400 AD). Bone coal consists of the previously mentioned poorly burnt bones, which are bluish in tone, residue of the cremation process. Such bones are easily recognizable in funeral pyres, hearths and so on. Our modern way of describing the phenomenon of turning iron into steel, informed by science, would be something like: when the temperature inside a presumed clay cage/oven reaches 720°C the carbon within the bone coal starts to move from the bones to the iron. The carbon may penetrate the surface of the iron to a depth of as much as 3 millimetres, hardening it and enabling a sharp edge to be achieved, such as that on a sword. An Iron Age way of describing the same procedure may have concentrated on what we would describe as the deep symbolic meanings. By mingling soft iron with ancestral and/or animal bones (where the animal bones might have indicated ancestry as well), the heated intercourse produced in the forge ultimately resulted in a birth of, for instance, a sword, which carried the strength and characteristics of the chosen parents; a new 'person' was literally forged. Several anthropological and ethnographic studies have emphasized that notions of sexual intercourse and birth are commonly interlinked with the production of iron (e.g. Haaland 2004). Terje Gansum (2004a:49) considers it most likely that iron production at this time and place was associated with sexuality. For instance, the forge could be envisioned as a womb giving birth, and indeed what was delivered might have been perceived as a kin person with social qualities (Figure 6.7). We know from the *Poetic Edda* and the medieval sagas that swords actually had names. Some could even speak, sing and guide the hand and shanks of their awestruck wielders. Siv Kristoffersen (1995, cf. Hedeager 1997) has suggested that items composed of intermingled human and animal parts are ontologically indivisible from the person who wore them.

Randi Barndon (2004) provides a good ethnographic example of how ovens or furnaces may be connected to human bodies and bodily practices ethnographically. She has concluded that ideas about bodies and furnaces for iron workings among the Tanzanian Pangwa and Fipa are based on similar notions of thermodynamics, well-being and morality. For instance, both bodies and furnaces 'were treated with the same set of homeopathic medicines and magic' (Barndon 2004:35). Furnaces were considered no different from human beings, and they were cared for like humans and were likewise bound by the same rules of conducts regarding – for example – taboos against sexual intercourse. Both furnace and human bodies were perceived as containers for vital forces, consisting of body fluids and of course cold and hot substances that would have to be balanced correctly to achieve a healthy

Figure 6.7 A smelting furnace from the Late Iron Age/Middle Ages, Norway (Photo: Jan Henning Larsen)

desirable outcome (Figure 6.8). As a result, one might say that there would be no ontological difference between a human (body) and a non-human (furnace).

Bones and Ancestral Powers

Returning to Late Iron Age Scandinavian cremations, occasionally bones and the artefacts from burial mounds were sought after. Through archaeological excavations it is evident that burial mounds were opened shortly after their construction (e.g. Brendalsmo and Røthe 1992), anything from a few years to decades after initial burial. Terje Gansum (2004a and b) has suggested that these re-excavations of mounds were for the purposeful retrieval of bones. In this way, ancestral power was literally appropriated for occasions such as carbonizing iron, where bone coal was a necessary ingredient. Brendalsmo and Røthe (1992) have interpreted these retrievals or re-excavations as the possible recovery of items with magical power and those associated with necromancy. I would like to add that reasons for the 'delay' in recovering what must have been interpreted as objects with immense power could be that the burial of the deceased somehow was not successful, and countermeasures to stop the possible spectre had to be taken (Falk 1913). Or perhaps the deceased needed to be 'processed' for a period with animals and artefacts in the burial mound, which acted as a maturation chamber. In any case, we may assume that what was represented or created through the burial procedures was treated and regarded as a living entity. Howard Williams has recently stressed

Figure 6.8 A Pangwa iron smelting furnace decorated with female breasts (Photo: Randi Barndon)

that the agency of the dead needs to be considered in greater depth by archaeologists, and that '. . . the dead body can be conceptualized as a node in a nexus of social relationships, objects and exchanges through which personhood and remembrance are distributed and constituted' (Williams 2004:267). Through studying early Anglo-Saxon cremation rites he also suggests that by collecting certain human and/or animal bones and/or artefacts from a pyre and depositing them in a burial urn a new body – and a new personality depending on what was deposited in the urn – was created. The container might even be perceived as a metaphorical skin for the ancestral body. Within Late Iron Age Scandinavian contexts, there are several indicators that the deceased being or ancestor that dwelled in the burial mound had agency and was considered communicable. This is not only evident from the practice of opening burial mounds, but also from medieval sagas, Edda poems and laws, since they frequently refer to communication between living and dead beings (Brendalsmo and Røthe 1992:102). In particular, I think it is worth noting that the new Christian Gulating Law from the mid-13th century AD strictly forbade (heathen) activities such as grave digging. It also forbade sitting on mounds and asking the burial dwellers questions about the future or reasons for mishaps. This suggests that during the Late Iron Age relatives or kin of the deceased visited the mound on certain occasions to communicate with their ancestors. Communication with ancestors is also suggested by the way some burial mounds have been structured. They appear to have entrances connected to them, commonly called 'gates' that often are oriented to the southwest, inviting reciprocal communication between the living and the dead (e.g. Back Danielsson 2003). In his extensive work on Late Iron Age societies in Scandinavia the Russian historian Aron Gurevich (e.g. 1985) has emphasized that the living and the dead of the time did not live in two separate worlds, but in fact co-existed in one world, where the past, the present and the future were all interwoven into one fabric.

Animal and Body Parts in Other Contexts

I will now briefly examine other contexts where humans and animals intermingled during the Late Iron Age. In the Nordic animal style I (dating to c.475 AD) there is an abundance of mixing animals and human body parts. It has been suggested that the animal ornamentation illustrated mythical layers that were connected to animals within the Nordic world of ideas (e.g. Hedeager 1997; Kristoffersen 1995). Since the mixing of animals and humans were primarily represented on items of gold (Gansum 2004a:51), it might be suggested that only the people who could express such metamorphoses through having relationships with skilled and revered smiths had control over the mythical traditions and stories that were expressed, recounted or associated with the intermingling of humans and animals on the arte-facts. It is also worth noting that the (re-)appearance during the Iron Age of bone-tempered ceramic vessels recounted earlier was manifested in fine-ware pottery, perhaps also implying that not everybody had equal access to cosmic exchanges and relationships.

The emergence of the animal style I is concurrent with the changes in burial customs between the Early and the Late Iron Ages, detectable in the Mälardalen region and in large parts of the rest of Scandinavia. In later periods the animal ornamentation develops further and is evident on a number of excavated objects. It is only at the onset of the Middle Ages that the animal ornamentation's bent, stretched and sometimes squeezed horses, boars, lizards, birds etc. are replaced by winged dragons and outstanding vegetable ornamentation (Thunmark-Nylén 1995:49). But these belong to what has been coined 'Romanesque art' and the influence of Christianity, a period of time that lies outside the scope of the current chapter. Briefly this change within the Scandinavian communities also affected the ways in which bodies were treated after death. Inhumations became common, and complete human bodies without the participation of animals were usually buried in churchyards. Body parts were not scattered, circulated or perceived as necessary ingredients for the functioning of the cosmos, communities or kinship systems to the same extent as earlier. Rather, these concepts were given altogether new meanings.

If we turn to the history of religion, we also gain support for the fact that human beings and animals were interlinked during the Late Iron Age. For instance, all human beings had a *hugr*, a dimension of their soul, which under certain conditions could act on its own (Steinsland 1990:62). Commonly, it would materialize itself in the form of an animal. Gifted humans could practice this form of shape shifting, and Neil Price (2002) has recently explored the ways in which shape shifting, *sejd* or shamanism was expressed during the Viking Age in Scandinavia. Another dimen-sion of the soul was represented by the *fylgja*, which could be observed either in a female or in an animal shape. The *fylgja* as an animal gestalt has been interpreted as reflecting a genuinely Nordic perception of the soul, and it was born with the human and functioned like his/her alter ego (Steinsland 1990:62–3). The *fylgja* could never be killed or hurt, and only revealed itself in dreams or to clairvoyant people. It died when the human passed on. The relationship and interdependence between humans and animals is likewise expressed in Late Iron Age names of humans. A person could be named Björn, which means bear, as well as Ulf or Ylva, meaning wolf (Hedeager 2004:232–3).

I have maintained that the mixing of animal and human bones with (in) other substances could be realized foremost at transformational stages and places, such as at burials and the manufacturing of ceramics and steel. Other evidence also sup-ports this idea. Sven Isaksson (2000; see also Isaksson, Hjulström and Wojnar Johansson 2004) has analyzed food residues from pottery, recovered from Late Iron

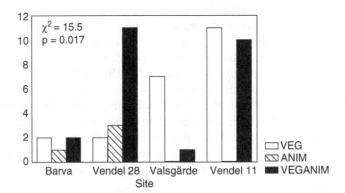

Figure 6.9 Frequencies of shards with lipids characterized as vegetable (VEG), animal (ANIM) and mixtures (VEGANIM). Shards analyzed from cemeteries (Barva and Vendel 28) demonstrated a higher relative degree of lipids of animal origin than shards of settlements (Valsgärde and Vendel 11) (Source: Isaksson 2000:19, paper VII)

Age cemeteries and settlements in the Mälardalen region. In both contexts, the pottery had been used for cooking only vegetables, or only animals or a combination of the two (Figure 6.9). However, whereas the ceramic urns placed in burials largely showed lipid traces (fats) of animals (more than 50 per cent), the ceramic vessels at settlements had very few (less than ten per cent of) pots with lipid traces of only animals. These vessels had instead been used for cooking vegetables or a mixture of vegetables and animal products. This suggests that the appropriate context for intermingling and establishing different sorts of relationships varied depending on social situation and place. Traces of iron production, furnaces, cooking pits and apparent ceramic ovens are all features that have been encountered on or in close proximity to burial grounds (Gansum 2004a:45). The regeneration or processing of the dead in order to give birth to ancestors obviously required the participation of animals to a large extent. The birth of steel and ceramic vessels likewise could require body parts. At settlements, the circulation of other substances, or vegetable foodstuffs, through bodies (human and non-human) was of importance.

Conclusion

During the Late Iron Age in Scandinavia, the existence of an animal element within a person was probably not perceived as odd. Moreover, a person need not have been manifested in human form, but could also have been non-human object, such as a sword, or perhaps a fine-ware ceramic vessel. The different elements that constituted a person could be processed during certain transformational stages, which were carried out in specific places. In all three transformational processes where bones were recycled – from clay to ceramics, from corpse to ancestor, from soft iron to steel – it is likely that the procedures necessarily involved substantial knowledge and that the (re)productions of the various bodies were ritualized and regulated spheres. Contrary to the idea of Howard Williams (2004:273) that early Anglo-Saxon cremation rites differed substantially from those of pottery making and iron workings, I think instead it is fruitful to consider their similarities as regards substances, transformational elements and places for enactments in the Late Iron Age Scandinavian cases. Further, the idea of (ancestral) human and animal bones circulating within varying communal contexts emphasizes not only the role of the bones as mediums of (re)birth, but also how the world/cosmos was created, built around and relied upon the exchange and relationships between human beings, animals and artefacts.

ACKNOWLEDGEMENTS

I would like to thank Andy Jones for inviting me to write in this volume and for making valuable comments on an earlier draft of this chapter. Equally I am grateful to the series editors for commenting on the paper. Ben Alberti, Jimmy Strassburg, Alex Gill, Marta Lindeberg and Elisabet Sandqvist are also thanked for commenting on an earlier version of the work. Ben Alberti has kindly revised my English. I also gratefully acknowledge support from the Birgit and Gad Rausing Foundation.

REFERENCES

Alberti, B. 2001 Faience Goddesses and Ivory Bull-Leapers: The Aesthetics of Sexual Difference at Late Bronze Age Knossos. World Archaeology Vol. 33:189–205.

Alberti, B. 2006 Archaeology, Men, and Masculinities. *In* Handbook of Gender in Archaeology. S. Milledge Nelson, ed. Pp. 401–34. Lanham: AltaMira Press.

Ambrosiani, B., and B. G. Erikson 1993 Birka vikingastaden. Höganäs: Wiken.

Anth, P. 2002 Samer hoppas HD ska lösa tvist om renbete. Dagens Nyheter February 16: A10.

Arwill-Nordbladh, E. 1998 Genuskonstruktioner i vikingatid. Förr och nu. Constructions of Gender in the Nordic Viking Age: Past and Today. Göteborg: Göteborg University.

Back Danielsson, I.-M. 2002 (Un)Masking Gender – Gold Foil (Dis)Embodiments in Late Iron Age Scandinavia. In Thinking Through the Body. Archaeologies of Corporeality. Y. Hamilakis, M. Pluciennik, and S. Tarlow, eds. Pp. 179–99. New York: Kluwer Academic/ Plenum Publishers.

Back Danielsson, I.-M. 2003 Ingenious Ignition. 'Flame, I'm Gonna Live Forever' and Other Movie Rhythms Shaking Late Iron Age Bodies on the Road. *In* Scandinavian Archaeological Practice – In Theory. Proceedings from the 6th Nordic TAG, Oslo 2001. J. Bergstøl, ed. Pp. 40–57. Oslo: Oslo University.

Back Danielsson, I.-M. 2007 Masking Moments. The Transitions of Bodies and Beings in Late Iron Age Scandinavia. Stockholm: Stockholm University.

Barndon, R. 2004 A Discussion of Magic and Medicines in East African Iron Working: Actors and Artefacts in Technology. Norwegian Archaeological Review 37(1):21–40.

Battaglia, D. 1991 The Body in the Gift: Memory and Forgetting in Sabarl Mortuary Exchanges, American Ethnologist 19:3–18.

Bennett, A. 1987 Graven. Religiös och social symbol. Strukturer i folkvandringstidens gravskick i Mälarområdet. Stockholm: Stockholm University.

Boyd, B. 2002 Ways of Eating/Ways of Being in the Later Epipalaeolithic (Natufian) Levant. In Thinking Through the Body. Archaeologies of Corporeality. Y. Hamilakis, M. Pluciennik, and S. Tarlow, eds. Pp. 137–52. New York: Kluwer Academic/Plenum Publishers.

Brendalsmo, J., and G. Røthe 1992 Haugbrot eller de levendes forhold til de døde – en komparativ analyse. META 1–2:84–119.

Butler, J. 1993 Bodies That Matter. On the Discursive Limits of 'Sex'. New York: Routledge.

Caesar, C. 1999 The Construction of Masculinity – The Driving Force of History: A New Way of Understanding Change in the Past. Lund Archaeological Review 5:117–36.

Chapman, J. 2000 Fragmentation in Archaeology. People, Places and Broken Objects in the Prehistory of South-Eastern Europe. London and New York: Routledge.

Douglas, M. 1992 The Person in an Enterprise Culture. In Understanding the Enterprise Culture: Themes in the Work of Mary Douglas. S. H. Heap and A. Ross, eds. Pp. 41–62. Edinburgh University Press: Edinburgh.

Ericsson, A., and J. Runcis 1995 Teoretiska perspektiv på gravundersökningar i Söderman-land. Stockholm: Riksantikvarieämbetet.

Falk, H. 1913 Begravelseterminologien i den oldnorsk-islandske litteratur. In Festskrift til Alf Torp. Pp. 1–18. Oslo: Aschehoug.

Foucault, M. 1970 The Order of Things. An Archaeology of the Human Sciences. New York: Vintage Books.

Foucault, M. 1980 Power/Knowledge, Selected Interviews and Other Writings 1972–1977. Brighton: Harvester.

Fowler, C. 2002 Body Parts: Personhood and Materiality in the Manx Neolithic. In Thinking Through the Body. Archaeologies of Corporeality. Y. Hamilakis, M. Pluciennik, and S. Tarlow, eds. Pp. 47–69. New York: Kluwer Academic/Plenum Publishers.

Fowler, C. 2004 The Archaeology of Personhood. An Anthropological Approach. London and New York: Routledge.

Gansum, T. 2004a Role of the Bones – from Iron to Steel. Norwegian Archaeological Review 37(1):41–57.

Gansum, T. 2004b Jernets fødsel og dødens stål. Rituell bruk av bein. In Minne och myt. Konsten att skapa det förflutna. Vägar till Midgård 5. Åsa Berggren, Stefan Arvidsson and Ann-Mari Hållans, eds. Pp. 121–55. Lund: Nordic Academic Press.

Geary, P. J. 2002 The Myth of Nations. The Medieval Origins of Europe. Princeton and Oxford: Princeton University Press.

Gell, A. 1998 Art and Agency: An Anthropological Theory. Oxford: Clarendon.

German, S. C. 2000 The Human Form in the Late Bronze Age Aegean. In Reading the Body: Representations and Remains in the Archaeological Record. A. E. Rautman, ed. Pp. 95–110. Philadelphia: University of Pennsylvania Press

Gurevich, A. 1985 Categories of Medieval Culture. London: Routledge and Kegan Paul.

Haaland, R. 2004 Technology, Transformation and Symbolism: Ethnographic Perspectives on European Iron Working. Norwegian Archaeological Review 37(1):1–19.

Hall, D. E. 2003 Queer Theories. Basingstoke and New York: Palgrave Macmillan.

Hamilakis, Y. 1999 Food Technologies/Technologies of the Body: The Social Context of Wine and Oil Production and Consumption in Bronze Age Crete. World Archaeology 13:38–54.

Hamilakis, Y. 2002 The Past Oral History: Towards an Archaeology of the Senses. In Thinking Through the Body. Archaeologies of Corporeality. Y. Hamilakis, M. Pluciennik, and S. Tarlow, eds. Pp. 121–36. New York: Kluwer Academic/Plenum Publishers.

Hamilakis, Y., M. Pluciennik, and S. Tarlow, eds. 2002 Thinking Through the Body. Archae-ologies of Corporeality. New York: Kluwer Academic/Plenum Publishers.

Haraway, D. 1990 [1985] A Manifesto for Cyborgs: Science, Technology and Socialist Feminism in the 1980s. In Feminism/Postmodernism. Linda J. Nicholson, ed. Pp. 190–233. New York and London: Routledge.

Haraway, D. 2003 The Companion Species Manifesto: Dogs, People and Significant Other-ness. Chicago: Prickly Paradigm.

Hedeager, L. 1997 Skygger af en anden virkelighed: oldnordiske myter. Köpenhamn: Samleren.

Hertz, R. 1960 Death and the Right Hand. Glencoe: Free Press.

Hodder, I. 1997 Commentary: The Gender Screen. *In* Invisible People and Processes. Writing Gender and Childhood into European Archaeology. J. Moore and S. Eleanor, eds. Pp. 75–8. London: Leicester University Press.

Holck, P. 1987 Cremated Bones: A Medical Anthropological Study of an Archaeological Material on Cremation Burials. Oslo: University of Oslo.

Houston, S., and K. A. Taube 2000 An Archaeology of the Senses: Perceptual Psychology in Classic Maya Art, Writing, and Architecture. Cambridge Archaeological Journal 10:261–94.

Iregren, E. 1972 Vårby och Vårberg II. Studie av kremerat människo- och djurbensmaterial från järnåldern. Stockholm: Stockholm University.

Isaksson, S. 2000 Food and Rank in Early Medieval Time. Stockholm: Stockholm University.

Isaksson, S., B. Hjulström, and M. Wojnar Johansson 2004 The Analyses of Soil Organic Material and Metal Elements in Cultural Layers and Ceramics. *In* Halvdanshaugen: arkeologi, historie og naturvitenskap. H. Larsen and P. Rolfsen, eds. Pp. 311–28. Oslo: Universitetets kulturhistoriske museer.

Jones, A. 1999 The World on a Plate: Ceramics, Food Technology and Cosmology in Neolithic Orkney. World Archaeology 31(1):55–77.

Jones, A. 2002 A Biography of Colour: Colour, Material Histories and Personhood in the Early Bronze Age of Britain and Ireland. *In* Colouring the Past. The Significance of Colour in Archaeological Research. A. Jones and G. MacGregor, eds. Pp. 159–74. Oxford and New York: Berg.

Jones, S. 1997 The Archaeology of Ethnicity: Constructing Identities in the Past and the Present. London: Routledge.

Joyce, R. A. 1993 Embodying Personhood in Prehispanic Costa Rica. Wellesley: Davis Museum and Cultural Center.

Joyce, R. A. 1998 Performing the Body in Prehispanic Central America. Res 33:147–65.

Joyce, R. A. 2000 Girling the Girl and Boying the Boy: The Production of Adulthood in Ancient Mesoamerica. World Archaeology 31:473–83.

Joyce, R. A. 2001a Gender and Power in Prehispanic Mesoamerica. Austin: University of Texas Press.

Joyce, R. A. 2001b Negotiating Sex and Gender in Classic Maya society. *In* Gender in Pre-Hispanic America. C. F. Klein, ed. Pp. 109–41. Washington, DC: Dumbarton Oaks.

Joyce, R. A. 2003 Concrete Memories: Fragments of the Past in the Classic Maya Present (500–1000AD). *In* Archaeologies of Memory. S. E. Alcock and R. van Dyke, eds. Pp. 104–125. Oxford: Blackwell.

Joyce, R. A. 2004 Embodied Subjectivity: Gender, Femininity, Masculinity, Sexuality. *In* A Companion to Social Archaeology. L. M. Meskell and R. W. Preucel, eds. Pp. 89–95. Oxford: Blackwell.

Joyce, R. A. 2005 Archaeology of the Body. The Annual Review of Anthropology 2005, vol. 34:139–58.

Kohl, P. L., and C. Fawcett, eds. 1995 Nationalism, Politics, and the Practice of Archaeology. Cambridge: Cambridge University Press.

Kristoffersen, S. 1995 Transformation in Migration Period Animal Art. *Norwegian Archaeological Review* 28(1):1–17.

Kus, S. 1992 Toward an Archaeology of Body and Soul. *In* Representations in Archaeology. J.-C. Gardin and C. S. Peebles, eds. Pp. 168–177. Bloomington: Indiana University Press.

Laqueur, T. 1990 Making Sex: Body and Gender from the Greeks to Freud. London and Cambridge, MA: Harvard University Press.

Latour, B. 1988 The Prince for Machines as well as for Machinations. *In* Technology and Social Process. B. Elliott, ed. Pp. 20–43. Edinburgh: Edinburgh University Press.

Looper, M. G. 2003 From Inscribed Bodies to Distributed Persons: Contextualizing Tairona Figural Images in Performance. Cambridge Archaeological Journal 13:25–40.

Merleau-Ponty, M. 1962 Phenomenology of Perception. London: Routledge.

Meskell, L. M. 1996 The Somatization of Archaeology: Institutions, Discourses, Corporeality. Norwegian Archaeological Review 29:1–16.

Meskell, L. M. 1998 The Irresistible Body and the Seduction of Archaeology. *In* Changing Bodies, Changing Meanings: Studies on the Human Body in Antiquity. D. Montserrat, ed. Pp. 139–61. London: Routledge.

Meskell, L. M. 1999 Archaeologies of Social Life: Age, Sex and Class in Ancient Egypt. Oxford: Blackwell.

Meskell, L. M. 2000 Writing the Body in Archaeology. *In* Reading the Body: Representations and Remains in the Archaeological Record. A. Rautman, ed. Pp. 13–21. Philadelphia: University of Pennsylvania Press.

Meskell, L. M. 2001 Archaeologies of Identity. *In* Archaeological Theory Today. I. Hodder, ed. Pp. 187–213 Cambridge, UK: Polity.

Meskell, L. M. 2002 Private Life in New Kingdom Egypt. Princeton: Princeton University Press.

Meskell, L. M., and R. A. Joyce 2003 Embodied Lives: Figuring Ancient Maya and Egyptian Experience. London: Routledge.

Milledge Nelson, S., ed. 2006 Handbook of Gender in Archaeology. Lanham: AltaMira Press.

Montserrat, D., ed. 1998 Changing Bodies, Changing Meanings: Studies on the Human Body in Antiquity. London: Routledge.

Munn, N. 1986 The Fame of Gawa: A Symbolic Study of Value Transformation in a Massim Society. Cambridge: Cambridge University Press.

Nordbladh, J., and T. Yates 1990 This Perfect Body, This Virgin Text: Between Sex and Gender in Archaeology. *In* Archaeology After Structuralism. I. Bapty and T. Yates, eds. Pp. 222–37. London: Routledge.

Oestigaard, T. 2000 Sacrifices of Raw, Cooked and Burnt Humans. Norwegian Archaeological Review 33(1):41–58.

Palka, J. W. 2002 Left/Right Symbolism and the Body in Ancient Maya Iconography and Culture. Latin American Antiquity 13:419–43.

Price, N. 2002 The Viking Way. Religion and War in Late Iron Age Scandinavia. Uppsala: Uppsala University.

Rautman, A. E., ed. 2000 Reading the Body: Representations and Remains in the Archaeological Record. Philadelphia: University of Pennsylvania Press.

Schmidt, R., and B. Voss, eds. 2000 Archaeologies of Sexuality. London: Routledge.

Shilling, C. 2003 [1993] The Body and Social Theory. London: Sage Publications.

Sigvallius, B. 1994 Funeral Pyres. Iron Age Cremations in North Spånga. Stockholm: Stockholm University.

Sode, Torben 1996 Anatolske glasperler. København: Thot.

Steinsland, G. 1990 Antropologiske og eskatologiske ideer i førkristen nordisk religion. Collegium Medivale 1:59–72. Oslo.

Stig-Sørensen, M.-L. 1991 Construction of gender through appearance. *In* The Archaeology of Gender: Proceedings of the Twenty-Second Annual Conference of the Archaeological Association of the Unviersity of Calgary. D. Walde and N. D. Willows, eds. Pp. 121–9. Calgary: University, Archaeological Association of the University of Calgary.

Stig-Sørensen, M.-L. 2000 Gender Archaeology. Cambridge, UK: Polity.

Stilborg, O. 2001 Temper for the Sake of Coherence: Analyses of Bone- and Chaff-Tempered Ceramics from Iron Age Scandinavia. European Journal of Archaeology 4(3):398–404.

Strassburg, J. 2000 Shamanic Shadows. One Hundred Generations of Undead Subversion in Southern Scandinavia, 7,000–4,000 BC. Stockholm: Stockholm University.

Strathern, M. 1988 The Gender of the Gift. Berkeley: University of California Press.

Svanberg, F. 2003a Decolonizing the Viking Age 1. Stockholm: Almqvist and Wiksell International.

Svanberg, F. 2003b Decolonizing the Viking Age 2. Death Rituals in South-East Scandinavia AD 800–1000. Stockholm: Almqvist and Wiksell.

Tarlow, S. 1999 Bereavement and Commemoration: An Archaeology of Mortality. Oxford: Blackwell.

Tarlow, S. 2000 Emotion in Archaeology. Current Anthropology 41:713–46.

Tarlow, S. 2002 The Aesthetic Corpse in Nineteenth-Century Britain. Thinking Through the Body. Archaeologies of Corporeality. Y. Hamilakis, M. Pluciennik, and S. Tarlow, eds. Pp. 85–98. New York: Kluwer Academic/Plenum Publishers.

Thomas, J. 2002 Archaeology's Humanism and the Materiality of the Body. *In* Thinking Through the Body. Archaeologies of Corporeality. Y. Hamilakis, M. Pluciennik, and S. Tarlow, eds. Pp. 29–45. New York: Kluwer Academic/Plenum Publishers.

Thomas, J. 2004 Archaeology and Modernity. London and New York: Routledge.

Thunmark-Nylén, L. 1995 Djurornamentik. *In* Vikingatidens ABC. C. Orrling, ed. Pp. 49. Stockholm: Statens historiska museer.

Treherne, P. 1995 The Warrior's Beauty: The Masculine Body and Self-Identity in Bronze-Age Europe. Journal of European Archaeology 3:105–44.

Wagner, R. 2001 An Anthropology of the Subject: Holographic Worldview in New Guinea and its Meaning for the World of Anthropology. Berkeley: University of California Press.

Watson, A., and D. Keating 1999 Architecture and Sound: An Acoustic Analysis of Megalithic Monuments in Prehistoric Britain. Antiquity 73:325–36.

Wells, P. 2001 Beyond Celts, Germans and Scythians: Archaeology and Identity in Iron Age Europe. London: Duckworth.

Williams, H. 2004 Death Warmed Up. Journal of Material Culture 9(3):263–91.

Wiwjorra, I. 1995 German Archaeology and its Relation to Nationalism and Racism. *In* Nationalism and Archaeology in Europe. M. Díaz-Andreu and T. Champion, eds. Pp. 164–88. London: UCL Press.

Yates, T. 1993 Frameworks for an Archaeology of the Body. *In* Interpretative Archaeology. C. Tilley, ed. Pp. 31–72. Oxford: Berg.

7

Interaction, Trade and Exchange

Introduction

One of the central tenets of culture-historical archaeology was to examine the impact of external cultures upon a given culture group. The influence of external cultures was seen as a prime motivator of social change. As such the movement of culture groups and the exchange of goods and ideas between them were seen to be crucial areas of enquiry. This said it was not until the development of science-based archaeology, coupled with the rigorous intellectual frameworks of New Archaeology, that the analysis of exchange began to be studied systematically. It was now not only possible to source artefacts and begin to analyze exchange networks, but it was also possible to describe and model them theoretically.

The ability of New Archaeology to predict types of exchange from the patterns of exchanged objects was called into question by Contextual archaeologists. Nevertheless, the study of exchange has flourished over the past two decades, with some archaeologists developing New Archaeology's interest in exchange through the study of peer polity interaction (Renfrew and Cherry 1986), or the study of world systems theory and the analysis of core–periphery relationships (Champion 1989). Indeed these models have been developed to provide holistic pictures of the interactions between different regions of prehistoric Europe, especially Bronze Age and Iron Age Europe (Kristiansen 1998).

One of the major achievements of these approaches has been to develop an understanding of exchange as a form of network in which goods and people move in multiple directions. This network approach has largely been retained by Contextual Archaeology although a significant development has been a deeper consideration of the nature of relationships created by exchange, and a more nuanced definition of modes of exchange. Many of these definitions have arisen from a close reading of the anthropological literature on exchange. Here the most basic distinction is between commodity exchange and gift exchange (Gregory 1982). Commodity exchange is the exchange of goods and materials in which no social tie or obligation is created between exchange partners. By contrast, gift exchange is a form of diplomacy in which the exchange of goods or materials is specifically designed to create social ties and obligations. Gift-exchange relationships may extend over a person's lifetime. These two forms of exchange have often been used by anthropologists to characterize different types of society. Despite this more recent studies point out that many societies practice both forms of exchange, in different social contexts (Thomas 1995). One development of this perspective on exchange is the realization that artefacts and people are closely intertwined in many gift-based relationships, to the extent that artefacts are often considered to possess life; the lives of artefacts change over their life-cycle. They are born, live and are destroyed in the same way as people. The treatment of artefacts at different stages of their lives is indicative of the kinds of exchange relationships in which they are involved.

This perspective has led archaeologists to examine the cultural biography of things in a variety of settings, most notably the European Neolithic (Bradley and Edmonds 1993; Jones 2000; Thomas 1996; Tilley 1996). Gift-exchange relationships not only conceive a close connection between people and things, they also promote a quite different model of the person (Strathern 1988). The exchange of artefacts is one way in which relationships are produced between people, to the extent that artefacts may come to stand for part of a person; models of exchange and models of people are interlocked then. Here the subject of exchange is closely related to the subject of personhood and the body discussed in Chapter 6. The close relationship between models of exchange and conceptions of the person has been discussed in detail by John Chapman (2000) for the Balkan Neolithic and Copper Age. He argues that the peculiar practice of fragmenting objects served to create relations between people during this period, and analyzes the use of different kinds of objects in differing types of relationships. In **Chapter 7 (a)** *John Chapman* discusses the differences in modes of exchange across Europe from the Late Mesolithic to the Early Bronze Age. He argues for a nexus of relationships between people, places and exotic things which form the framework for understanding exchange across early prehistoric Europe. Notably he emphasizes the significance, and growing interest in, 'the exotic' from the Late Mesolithic to the Early Bronze Age.

In **Chapter 7 (b)** *Peter Wells* analyzes the network of exchange relationships in central Europe from the Late Bronze Age to Late Iron Age, charting the shifting relationships between communities over this period of time. Taking an extensive view of exchange he shows how local relationships of exchange alter over time as societies are affected by large scale social changes, such as the emergence of the Roman world.

REFERENCES

Bradley, R., and M. Edmonds 1993 Interpreting the Axe Trade. Cambridge: Cambridge University Press.

Champion, T. C. 1989 Centre and Periphery. London: Unwin Hyman.

Chapman, J. 2000 Fragmentation in Archaeology. London: Routledge.

Gregory, C. A. 1982 Gifts and Commodities. London: Academic Press.

Jones, A. 2000 Life after Death: Monuments, Material Culture and Social Change in Neolithic Orkney. *In* Neolithic Orkney in its European Context. A. Ritchie, ed. Pp. 127–38. Cambridge: McDonald Institute Monographs.

Kristiansen, K. 1998 Europe before History. Cambridge: Cambridge University Press.

Renfrew, C., and J. Cherry 1986 Peer Polity Interaction and Socio-Political Change. Cambridge: Cambridge University Press.

Strathern, M. 1988 The Gender of the Gift. Berkeley: University of California Press.

Thomas, J. 1996 Time, Culture and Identity: An Interpretative Archaeology. London: Routledge.
Thomas, N. 1995 Entangled Objects. Harvard: Harvard University Press.
Tilley, C. 1996 An Ethnography of the Neolithic. Cambridge: Cambridge University Press.

7 (a)

Approaches to Trade and Exchange in Earlier Prehistory (Late Mesolithic–Early Bronze Age)

John Chapman

Introduction

The history of trade and exchange studies in prehistoric research is dominated by cyclical peaks and troughs. After a strong start in early processualist times, a deep decline in interest set in, particularly among post-processualists, although those telling grand narratives upheld the significance of trade and exchange against sharp theoretical and methodological criticism. However, more recently, a revival in material culture studies has stimulated a new wave of research in which concerns over the creation of personhood and identity (see Chapter 6) have re-focused on the significance of traded and exotic objects and their relationships to local persons. What has not yet been developed is a trajectory for earlier European prehistory, in which local insights into value, authority, prestige and fame are juxtaposed or contrasted with broader issues of inter-regional, millennial cultural change. In this chapter, an attempt will be made to relate persons, places and exotic things to each other and to their mutually constructed values across a range of time-places. The questions I seek to answer include:

- Firstly, can we draw meaningful distinctions between the terms 'exchange', 'trade' and 'barter'?
- Secondly, are there differences between 'gifts' and 'commodities', especially in relation to the personal contents of things?
- Thirdly, how was value created across a range of different communities, each using different forms of material culture?
- Fourthly, to what extent was the consumption of exotic things a necessary and sufficient condition for the emergence of inequalities?
- Finally, to what extent was trade and exchange marginal or central to cultural change in prehistoric Europe?

Terms

There has been much debate over the difference between the terms 'trade' and 'exchange' and their main associations: two-way trade in alienable commodities – things unconnected to persons – and two-way exchange of inalienable gifts – things with an intrinsic link to their producer. However, in view of archaeological difficulties in the identification of mechanisms of interaction, I propose to make no distinction between the terms 'trade' and 'exchange'. Concerning two other important terms, barter is taken to form a sub-set of trade and exchange, whereby goods cross cultural boundaries in a two-way transaction, while 'acquisition' is considered a one-way process whereby long-distance specialists gain exotic objects, often facilitated by giving gifts. A sharp distinction between gifts and commodities seems inappropriate (Gregory 1982), since 'commodities' can carry personal values and 'gifts' can be made for gain; moreover, objects can change from being a gift to a commodity during their lifetime. Appadurai (1986) notes that a commodity was not a particular kind of thing – rather that commodities were things in a particular situation, namely the stage in an object's life where its future consisted of exchangeability for some other thing. Moreover, in societies with more commoditization, there was a greater chance for a thing to enter into a commodity situation (see also Kopytoff 1986).

Previous Research

An expansion in research into trade and exchange began in the mid-1950s, based on the growing realization that even the least complex societies could not exist in isolation. Building on his early studies of obsidian and *Spondylus* trade routes, Renfrew (pro)claimed that 'trade can be studied', meaning that the objects of trade could be identified, their sources determined by modern analytical techniques and that quantitative methods permitted generalizations about distribution patterns (Renfrew 1975:3), leading to inferences about social organization. These four questions set the processualist agenda for trade and exchange.

The first two questions have not been superseded even today: it is still important to characterize the sources used to create a lithic assemblage through scientific analysis based on field studies of as many sources as possible. Nonetheless, a large number of provenancing questions remain unsettled. But while some analytical techniques have proven their worth (e.g., neutron activation analysis), others are more hotly debated than any non-scientific archaeological issue (e.g., lead isotope analysis of Mediterranean Bronze Age metalwork). However, the underlying issue of the desirability of knowing the sources of a site assemblage has not been questioned.

This is not the case with modes of acquisition and social inferences, where each question has led to contentious debates from the 1980s onwards. Renfrew himself beat a retreat from his ambitious scheme of identifying spatial signatures for each of the ten modes of obtaining resources at a distance (Renfrew 1975), while still maintaining the importance of the three modes most relevant to earlier prehistoric societies – down-the-line exchange, redistribution and prestige goods trade. Two contrasting responses to the question 'how?' could be characterized as engagement and total denial. It became clear that the graphs defining modes of acquisition could be varied by introducing variations in any important social and settlement variable, rendering them less than accurate predictors of exchange practices. This problem led to calls for better data collection, which was helpful but did not resolve the issue.

The gauntlet of total rejection of previous trade and exchange studies was thrown down by Ian Hodder (1984:26), who argued: 'It is simply impossible to test whether prehistoric artefacts moved from source to destination by exchange from person to person or whether, on the other hand, individuals went directly to the source.' The implication of this claim was clearly that social inferences drawn upon such shaky foundations as the modes of acquisition of distant objects were quite inadmissible. Hodder's status among post-processualists and the parallel rejection of scientific and mathematical archaeology by Shanks and Tilley were two important reasons for the neglect of trade and exchange in post-processual writing, except for Hodder and Tilley's more empirical studies, where exchange played a key role. Insofar as trade and exchange studies relied on mathematical reason, it was relegated to the positivist dustbin and the majority of interpretative monographs made minimal or no explicit mention of trade and exchange.

To a large extent, trade and exchange studies became marginalized and impotent in the post-processualist period – turning into the baby that was thrown out with the bathwater because of allegedly insuperable methodological problems. For if trade – once the cutting edge of social interpretation – cannot be related to social structure, what can trade tell us?

The reconciliation of trade and exchange studies with interpretative archaeology began with the recognition that the meanings of exchange and interchange themselves were more important than inferences of sociological information. In any case, societies can use a number of different forms and scales of exchange in their search for exotic items. To lose the graphical means of distinguishing modes of acquisition was liberating and led to a more realistic stance, whereby the more regularly an exotic item occurred on a remote site and the greater the distance between source and consumer, the less likely was direct procurement, or indeed warfare and raiding, and the more likely some form of exchange network.

A second salient starting-point for renewed dialogue was the recognition that communities often emphasized exotic things to the neglect of comparable and adequate local sources. By travelling far, a hitherto mundane object was automatically transformed into something special, whatever the means of movement. Moreover, in their journeys, exotic things and their meanings could be transformed in different contexts, becoming alienable commodities or inalienable gifts, depending upon the relationship between giver and receiver. An important process sustaining relationships between people and things was enchainment – the objectification of social relations between people using inalienable objects that continue to be personally linked to individuals. Notions of the changing biography of things have moved the debate further from earlier, sterile typological debates as to whether objects were commodities or gifts, prestige goods or utilitarian objects and whether they moved in open exchange or in relatively closed spheres of exchange (Edmonds 1999). The renewed debate over structure and agency in archaeology has also meant that we can begin to transcend debates over the causative priority of growing social inequality over increasing elite prestige goods trade or vice versa, in favour of the emergent, reflexive properties of both (Dobres & Robb 1999). This more flexible attitude to objects and their relations to people and places suggests that trade and exchange can find their place in an interpretative archaeology – an outcome well summarized by Broodbank (2000): 'Trade may represent only one of several conjunctures between power, distance and knowledge but it provides an invaluable insight into a wider discourse.' It is to this wider discourse that we now turn, through the prism of recent advances in social anthropology and material culture studies.

The Global and the Local: Flavours of Exoticity

The worldview of prehistoric communities may usefully be divided into three zones: the familiar world of our own settlement and community area; the strange world of foreign or alien places, beings and things; and, in between the others, the world of otherness, inhabited by people not belonging to our community but who shared our artefacts and symbols (Neustupny 1998). The boundaries between these zones were permeable, crossed by people and things but not by everyone in the community. In societies without specialized trading institutions most exchange was on an individual level, in social networks wider than the kinship or residential network. Trading partnerships confirming ties of alliance or kinship would have grown up over time through the exchange of inalienable objects, whereby the personal links between the producer and the thing was not lost and the quality of the relationship was emphasized. In prehistoric Europe, some inalienable objects were exchanged as deliberately broken fragments (Chapman 2000). The objects thus took with them a memory of both maker and place of origin – but they could be used and disposed of by the new owner much as she pleased. Exchanged objects could also have acted as measures of value (the worth of the person giving), media of value (the means by which the value is realized) and sometimes embodiments of value, if not the origins of those values. These values and meanings would have been worked out through performance in specific places, with changing values always possible. A person's fame would have been inter-dependent upon the fame of the objects which s/he exchanged within the familiar and the 'other' zones. Sometimes, however, communities acquired such objects from still further afield.

The remote and dangerous world of foreign places was the source of extraordinary materials and things which could confer significant renown on the local community by the prestige of the thing itself, the skills and characteristics of the acquirer and the powerful nature of the distant place. Helms (1993) has explored the prowess of the long-distance specialist in surviving the rigours of the alien zone and returning home with things that embodied the existential power and energy of the distant, the strange, even the cosmological. Helms makes a powerful case for one-way acquisition in transactions that emphasize the quality of the things rather than that of the relationship. She also maintains that skilled crafting and artistic production are akin to long-distance acquisition, emphasizing that creativity is an ordering of nature for cultural purposes. This suggests at least three routes to the production of elite value in both hierarchical *and* non-hierarchical societies. But locally found or made objects, which sustained enchained relations between exchange partners, were also vital for social reproduction, as well as for identity-formation at an individual, household or corporate group level.

How different were the three zones for communities living in different parts of Europe? Clarke's observation that European economic development was complex and uneven because of the great diversity of habitats, the mosaic of micro- and macro-environments and the nested tessellation of soils, flora and fauna (Clarke 1979:268) suggest the likelihood of extreme differences both within and between local and foreign zones. Some communities lived in extensive plains, never seeing mountains in their lives. Others created their worlds on islands, in river gorges and near spectacular mountain peaks, with all of the symbolic potential of such sea- and landscapes. But 'resources' were never culturally neutral, pertaining only to economy or geology. For a Neolithic plains-dweller, a marine shell ornament presenced a mysterious and alien force – the sea – while the local gold-bearing alluvial sands remained a 'value-less' object, until new social demands and technologies made this an embodied 'resource' for her Bronze Age descendants. Once achieved, knowledge of the foreign zone often led to a desire for its incorporation into local lifeways. This 'local domestication' of the exotic was a major benefit of prehistoric trade – the values of the exotic underpin this narrative.

Exchange Networks Within and Between Foragers and Early Farmers (7000–4000 BC)

Although forager archaeology is dominated by concerns over lithic technology, environmental change and settlement mobility, startling evidence for forager exchange exists for both the Early and the Late Mesolithic, suggesting that knowledge of the exotic was both widespread and vital for social reproduction. A study of western European mortuary ornaments reveals that each forager region is characterized by a different suite of personal ornaments, most of which were exotic to the region in question (Constandse-Westermann and Newell 1988). These objects were exchanged hand-to-hand, over distances of up to 600 kilometres, accumulating long and complex personal biographies as they moved, with their final act a statement of identity relating the newly-dead to their corporate group. Increasing intensity and complexity of the exchange network is documented for the Late Mesolithic period (Figure 7.1). We are lacking comparable studies in eastern Europe but long-distance movement of shells are documented into areas of dense forager settlement, such as the Danube gorges. These exchanges are paralleled in ethnography, where shells maintain their identities and meanings across cultural boundaries.

Nested within such long-distance exchanges were two scales of lithic distribution. Social territories across a wide zone of western and southern Europe have been defined on the basis of lithics acquired direct from a common source over a radius of 20–50 kilometres. This pattern suggests regular movement between the local and the 'other' zone by foragers, with exchange within these zones. A well-attested example of acquisition is the direct procurement of obsidian from the unoccupied island of Melos, in the Cyclades. The occurrence of small quantities of lithics over distances between 150 and 650 kilometres from their source indicates exchange or acquisition networks stretching far into the foreign zone. Even in the Late Mesolithic, however, areas such as southeastern Italy were exporting obsidian without receiving exotic lithics in return; we cannot assume that exoticity was universally valued or readily attained. But the long-distance movement of greenstone and diabase tools from Mesolithic (and later Neolithic) quarries in western Norway up to 650 kilometres to the south indicates a significant accumulation

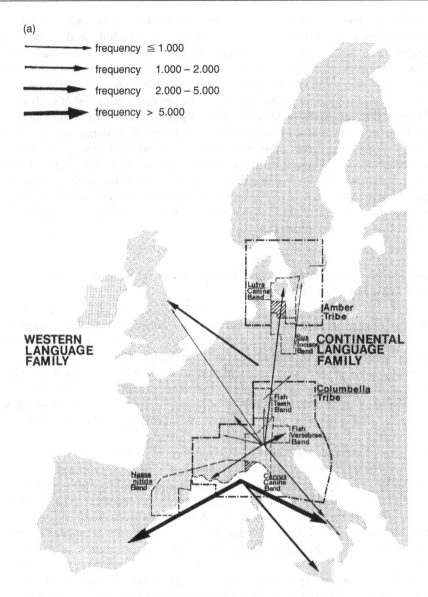

Figure 7.1 Extra-territorial ornament exchange in the Early Mesolithic (a) and Late Mesolithic (b) of western Europe (Source: Constandse-Westermann & Newell 1988:figs. 13–14)

of knowledge of the foreign zone and a high valuation of its objects by local foragers.

What becomes clear from the movement of shells and lithics in the Late Mesolithic is a widespread practice of domesticating the exotic, transforming not only many objects into things of high social value but also the reputation of persons acquiring, trading and consuming them. The contrasts between the exchange of lithics and shell ornaments raises the possibility of nested exchange spheres at this time. It is salutary to recognize that this suite of social practices pre-dated the emergence of Neolithic lifeways in every part of Europe.

(b)

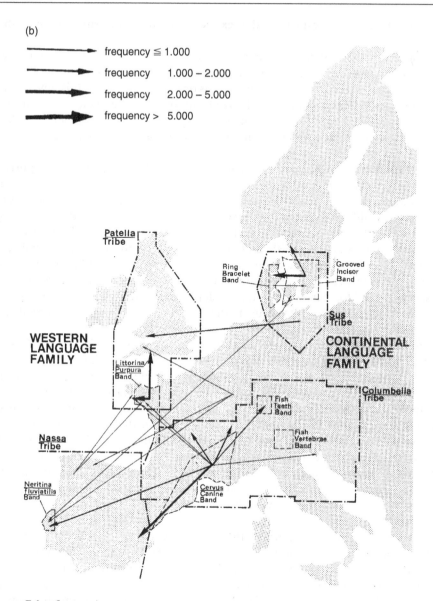

frequency ≤ 1.000
frequency   1.000 – 2.000
frequency   2.000 – 5.000
frequency > 5.000

Figure 7.1 *Continued*

The emergence of farming is one of the most significant changes in European prehistory. To the extent that the adoption of Neolithic lifeways in Europe is characterized by close bio-social relations with a narrow range of mostly Near Eastern domesticated plants and animals, the two fundamental features of the spread of the Neolithic comprised encounters between either incoming newcomers and foreign places (the diffusionist model) and/or between local foragers and exotic species, not to mention objects (the indigenist model): in short, exoticity lies at the heart of both encounters. However, this description of the Neolithic is clearly inappropriate for much of the 'Forest Neolithic' of eastern and northeastern Europe, with its distinctive combination of locally produced pottery and ground stone tools with minimal Oriental domesticates: the exotic was not a priority amongst these foragers.

Tringham (2000:45) usefully views the spread of the Neolithic as a two-way process of change, in which both agriculturalists and foragers were transformed. But to what extent were such transformations driven by exchange? It is now possible to identify several cases of lithic exchange from foragers to early farmers, although foragers rarely exchanged shell ornaments with their farming partners. We could add venison, wild boar meat and salmon steaks to this list, as well as useful social, navigational and ecological information. In the other direction, beefsteaks, mutton chops, alcoholic beverages, dairy products, unleavened bread and perhaps porridge were on the farming menu for foragers to savour. But the key change of emphasis with domesticates was from dead animals to live animals – the opportunity to accumulate wealth on the hoof, by conserving, raiding and trading. A good example of two-way exchanges between foragers and farmers occurred in the Bug-Dniestr zone, where Cris pottery, polished stone axes, cereals and domestic animals were imported in exchange for the foragers' pointed-based pottery and perhaps persons wearing distinctive red deer teeth and boar's tusk jewellery. In such exchange contexts, farmers and foragers would have developed enchained social relations, opening the way to increased sociability, information exchange and perhaps eventually new ways of creating personhood.

The fact that the vast majority of stone, bone or antler tools was used by the hands that made them does not diminish the significance of the small number of exotic finds that gained demonstrable fame and brought renown to those enjoying their attractions. Very occasionally, items journeyed from such a vast distance, even in comparison with other exotic things, that they merit special mention. The necklace of polished stone beads found at Lepenski Vir in the Iron Gates Gorge was made of paligorskite – a rare rock type known only from the Urals and Anatolia. Equally, the nephrite sceptre and axes in the western Bulgarian Early Neolithic site of Gălăbnik that probably derived from a central Asian source implied ancestral value and cosmological significance accumulated through mega-voyages lasting decades, if not longer, and passing through dozens of owners before reaching its final 'home'.

If we can recognize continuity in the social practices of long-distance exchange of exotics between foragers and farmers, to what extent are there communalities in their exchange networks? Three of the clearest cases concern maritime exchange. The Cycladic island of Melos remained without permanent settlement in the Early Neolithic, indicating the likelihood of continued direct procurement of obsidian. Here, Perlès (2001) has documented an expansion in seafaring activities in the Early Neolithic to cover exchange throughout Greece by specialist traders and obsidian-knappers. In the central Mediterranean, the Late Mesolithic network of shared personal ornaments bore a close resemblance to distributions of obsidian and decorated Cardial pottery, suggesting an intensification of exchange along trusted, ancestral routes. Thirdly, the western Norwegian coastal exchange networks for diabase and greenstone were expanded in the Neolithic. An excellent example of overland continuity concerns the exchange of Szentgál radiolarite from western Hungary into Moravia and Slovakia in both Late Mesolithic and the Earliest Neolithic (Linearbandkeramik), together with a huge Neolithic expansion, with pieces reaching distances of over 1,000 kilometres (Mateiciucová 2004) (Figure 7.2).

(a)

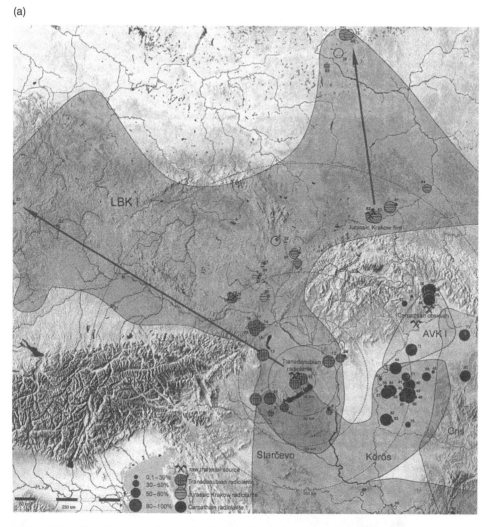

Figure 7.2 Distribution of Szentgál radiolarite from the Bakony Mountains, Western Hungary in the Mesolithic (a) and Early Neolithic (b) (Source: Matieciuková 2004:figs. 7–8)

Such cases indicate that profound changes were often linked to continuities in exchange networks from foragers to farmers, involving especially large-scale distribution of particular high-quality raw materials. Often dominant in the total lithic assemblage, these distant materials were preferred to local flints of adequate quality, reinforcing the importance of exotic things for a wide variety of everyday tasks carried out by most of the community. Such practices narrowed the difference between 'utilitarian' tools and 'exotic' prestige goods through the widespread sharing of cultural knowledge about foreign zones, that in turn transformed community identity.

A second difference in early farming exchange was the increased number of available sources – not only lithic but also shells and potting clay – collectively allowing a greater choice of materials which led to more varied patterns of acquisition and greater variations through time than hitherto. A concomitant development

(b)

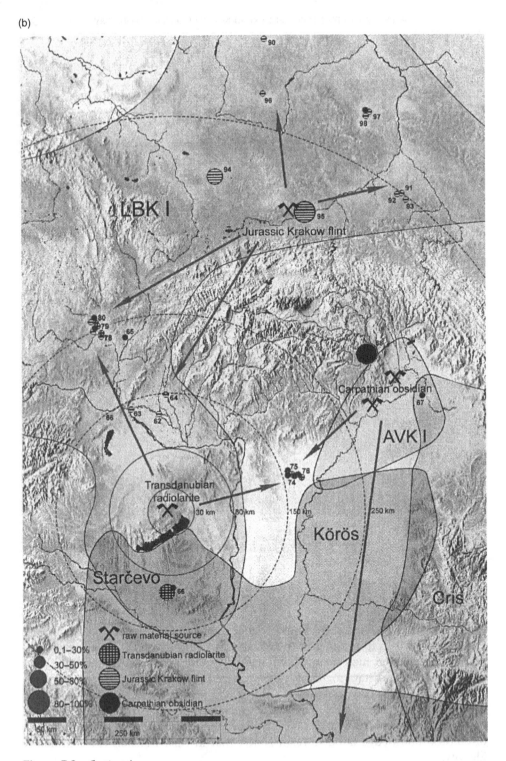

Figure 7.2 *Continued*

was the selection of a wider range of criteria for object value among early farming groups, based sometimes on the size of beads or the length of axes, sometimes on a widespread colour preference – pale or dark polished stone bracelets in Iberia, green bracelets in southern France and northern Italy (Harrison & Köhler 2001).

The dynamic and rapid evolution of these exchange networks gave differential opportunities to certain sites over their neighbours. For example, high-quality exotic lithics reached only some of the earliest Bandkeramik settlements but eastern Carpathian sites relied on local sources, unable to break into enchained long-distance networks. In some extreme cases, cultural choices led to the creation of an exclusion zone, for example in the case of obsidian, which was never exchanged into Iberia. By contrast, one can discern a pattern of selective exchange into socially differentiated settlement clusters, such as the Iron Gates Gorge fishing sites on the Danube, Apennine cave sites such as Grotta Scaloria, or the enclave of Bandkeramik sites in Kujavia.

There can be no doubting the diversity of distributions of different objects within specific regions in the early farming period. Perlès (2001) identifies different patterns for pottery, lithics and prestige ornaments in Greece. Tilley (1996) proposes four distributions for southern Scandinavia – copper and amber, flint axes, decorated pottery and ground stone polygonal battle-axes; while the converse distribution of exotic lithics (decreasing with time) and Mediterranean shell ornaments (increasing with time) in early farming sites in central Europe suggests another example. Whether or not these patterns imply the existence of separate exchange spheres for each class of object is still hotly debated. What we can surely infer is the complexification of material identities in many early farming communities, in which certain individuals were more closely identified with exotic valuables than others. There is some evidence to suggest such differences operated at the inter-site as well as the inter-personal level, with enchained exchanges potentially leading to indebtedness and inequality.

This study has revealed a perhaps unsuspected, but widespread, attachment to exotic objects throughout the Mesolithic and Early Neolithic periods. An important part in the differential emergence of both forager and farmer lifeways was the variable capacity of persons and corporate groups to develop enchained exchange relations using exotic goods.

The Intensification of Engagement with the Exotic (5000–2500 BC)

A key aspect of mixed farming, in comparison to foraging, was the greatly expanded range of sites that groups could occupy permanently. Aided greatly by the hitherto untapped reservoir of Holocene soil fertility, this potential was actualized in the periods following early farming, with two results – a steady increase in population, with a concomitant increasing demand for exotics, and a denser web of settlements, in interfluvial as well as upland locations, closer to each other and thereby with enhanced communications and exchange opportunities. The location of some places at key points in the exchange network could have formed the basis for inter-household or inter-community inequalities but not differences at the regional level.

Such a scenario, however, is attested in only half of Europe – mostly the southeast and the Mediterranean, with Greek and Balkan tell villages and Mediterranean open villages. In eastern Europe, the peak of this trend is reached in the Tripolye mega-sites, with populations in thousands living in sites covering up to 450 hectares. Such stable settlement networks stimulated the growth in the value of local places, the deepening of ancestral roots and the need for exotic objects for personhood. But in much of the remainder of Europe in the 4th and 3rd millennia, we witness what Thomas (1996) has termed the 'mesolithization' of central (and western) Europe, with far less sedentary occupation than hitherto, as well as smaller sites, more reliance on wild resources, more exchange and more homogenous artefact distributions. The main differentiation was created at enclosed central places, marked by seasonal ceremonies involving exotic objects. To what extent did the exchange networks of these two contrasting types of settlement structures differ in scale, meaning and significance?

One characteristic of the sedentary Mediterranean zone was the increasing range of exotic materials in circulation. Peltenburg (1991) lists seven exotic materials traded in Copper Age Cyprus, with a further six in local exchange. This diversity would have stimulated the formation of even more complex personal and group identities than in the Neolithic. At the same time, there was a long-term trend for communities to acquire the finest materials possible, as with the highest-quality (Lipari) obsidian by Late Neolithic groups in north Italy and the long-distance exchange of green-blue variscite ornaments in the Iberian Late Neolithic.

In the tell-dominated landscape of much of Greece and the Balkans, changing preferences for exotic materials can be seen at regional and inter-regional levels. The Vinca group of the central Balkans exemplifies changes through the life-cycle of village communities over the 5th millennium BC, with an early focus of exotic items on the centrally located Vinca tell leading to an expansion in the diversity of materials, the number of objects traded and the distance over which they were exchanged, in turn followed by a contraction to a suite of poorly integrated interactions (Chapman 1981). Likewise, in the Great Hungarian Plain, lacking in rocks and minerals except alluvial gold, a complex pattern of lithic exchange brought chronologically different suites of exotics to the central plain from surrounding uplands (Biró 1998). Insofar as the acquisition of objects was central to the classification of people, the plains settlers defined themselves through their consumption of exotic lithics, at first exclusively in settlements, later increasingly in rich grave assemblages.

Thirty generations passed before the demand for copper reached its Balkan apogee. Recent programmes of lead isotope analysis have provided major new insights into the distribution of Balkan Chalcolithic copper objects (Gale et al. 2000; Pernicka et al. 1993; 1997). The excavation of two 5th-millennium-BC copper mines – Rudna Glava in Serbia and Ai Bunar in Bulgaria – indicates the large scale of production for exchange – a scale not to be repeated until the *Fahlerz* boom of the late 3rd millennium BC. Despite the widespread local availability of copper sources, there was a strong preference for objects made of exotic copper, even near the mines. Peaks of exotic diversity occurred at the Dolnoslav tell and the Varna cemetery (Figure 7.3). By the end of the 5th millennium BC, the large Majdanpek source in northeast Serbia expanded its distribution to cover much of north Bulgaria, while Ai Bunar copper was preferred in northeast Bulgaria and eastwards across the north Pontic forest steppe, as far as the Volga. This mode of production declined in the 4th millennium BC to be replaced by the smaller-scale creation of arsenical copper objects.

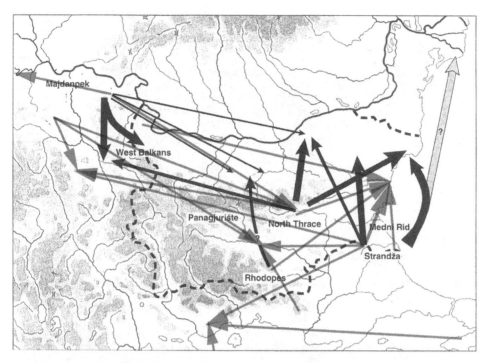

Figure 7.3 The distribution of copper from Balkan sources in the Chalcolithic period (Based on information in Pernicka et al. 1997 [black arrows]; Dimitrov 2002; Gale et al. 2002; Pernicka et al. 1993; Stos 2003 [all remaining = grey arrows])

The climax of exotic acquisition must surely be the Varna cemetery, with a huge diversity of materials buried with the world's earliest assemblage of gold-work. Nephrite hair-ornaments (Figure 7.4) from as far away as central Asia (?Afghanistan), marble beakers and *Spondylus* from the Aegean, copper from four Balkan sources, mined flint from north Bulgaria, gold and facetted carnelian beads from unknown sources – these represent the principal exotic materials deposited in the outstandingly rich graves. The accumulation of copper things from three different sources and other exotics in a single grave contributed to their complex mortuary narratives, recounted by the living in competitive display, ceremonial gift-giving and alliance-building. Many Varna grave goods exhibit the combination of fine crafting, artistic production and exotic origins that characterize elite values.

In the less sedentary zone of northern and western Europe, the very finest, most colourful materials travelled over distances rarely encountered further south – Grand Pressigny flint 900 kilometres from central France, jadeite axes a similar distance from the southeast Alps (Figure 7.5), and Senonian flint axes linking Danish farmers with foragers 1,000 kilometres to the north. The narrower range of materials in exchange networks in this zone is perhaps related to a series of long-term commitments to specific material of high value from particular renowned places. This is especially true of the flint mines that had far longer biographies than almost any contemporary settlement, developing as key symbolic foci in a landscape of dispersed homesteads.

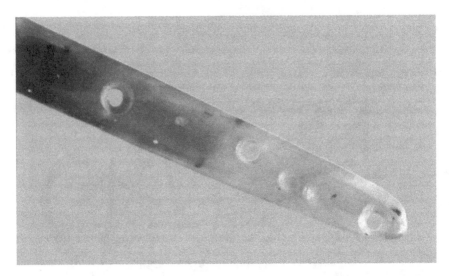

Figure 7.4 Nephrite hair-ornament, Varna II cemetery, Middle Chalcolithic, Bulgaria (Source: Kostov et al. 2003:fig. 2)

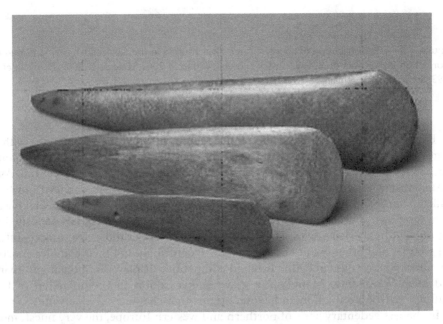

Figure 7.5 Jadeite axes, Middle Neolithic passage graves, Brittany (Source: Musée de Préhistoire de Carnac)

The paradox of the flint mines of the North European Plain lies in the huge quantities of axes produced in comparison with the general lack of their accumulation. De Groothe's (1997) reconstruction of the logistics of the Rijckholt mine in Belgium suggests a small workforce of four teams of four miners each for a month per annum could have extracted and produced rough-outs for the estimated millions of axes over 1,300 years – i.e., a long-term practice but small-scale at any

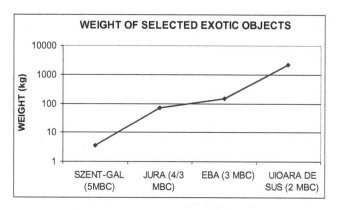

Figure 7.6 Selected weights of prehistoric exchange objects (Source: author)

given time, more concerned with local identity than with regional industry. These estimates suggest that Bradley and Edmonds (1993) are right to question the assumption of an exaggerated coherence in the axe trade. Even if long-distance specialists were critical in the acquisition of exotic axes, most people had a very partial knowledge of the wider exchange network, the meaning of the same axe differed in different regions and therefore axes may have circulated in different ways for different reasons.

There are clearly some major differences in exchange networks between more and less sedentary parts of Europe, with greater diversity of exotic materials in the Mediterranean and the southeast and more intensive exploitation and wider distribution of certain objects of high value in the centre, north and west. However, there are some important social practices shared all over Europe.

One aspect of the notion of the quantity of exchanged exotics concerns the size and weight of individual finds. While a 3.5-kilogram core of Szentgál radiolarite was clearly impressive for the early farming period, massive blocks of stone were being regularly moved to erect megaliths, as well as to move two or three decorated fragments of the same original stone to other megaliths up to 6 kilometres away, as in Brittany. But it must have been an astonishing achievement to back-pack a 70-kilogram block of granite across the Jura mountain range, prior to 3000 BC! The weights of (highly selected) finds grew logarithmically through European prehistory (Figure 7.6) – a sign of the increasing scale of the ordering of nature for cultural purposes.

Another communality is the increasing diversity in the contexts and strategies of exotic deposition. A contextual study of Balkan Copper Age deposition of exotica indicates exclusion from ritual contexts and incorporation into houses, intra-mural burials and hoards. This would suggest an inner core of non-mortuary ritual practices maintained as separate from the foreign zone, while exoticity contributed to identity formation in many other practices. A counterfactual case to the importance of exotics in mortuary contexts is found in the Portuguese Copper Age, where utilized axes made of exotic amphibolite were discarded in settlements while unused axes made of local stone were placed in graves. Here, the integration of exotic rock with everyday practices complemented the message of local ancestral links to the local land emphasized in the mortuary domain.

A final theme concerns the 4th-millennium-BC expansion in exchange networks linking the Balkans to Scandinavia. Krause (2003) has defined a sequence of exchange networks bringing metal to Scandinavia which is totally lacking in both copper and tin. The early dominance of Balkan–Carpathian metals was gradually replaced by a reliance on east Alpine arsenical copper, until a decline in north Alpine copper production brought a break in copper supplies from the south lasting 600 years. This example demonstrates the dramatic effects of the exhaustion of ores on local and long-distance identities and alliances. A re-orientation of Baltic amber exports to the south and east in this period apparently represented an unsuccessful attempt to re-engage metal supplies. It also documents an increasing awareness of the possibilities of the manipulation of exotics and suppliers living in the foreign zone.

Taking this topic one stage further, a shifting boundary can be defined between copper-using groups to the southeast and lithics-based societies to the northwest. Since there were no local copper sources for many of the lithics-based communities, it was difficult not only to transfer the raw materials and technology but also to generate demand for this unknown metal. Earlier exchange networks moving exotic goods between trusted trade partners in the Beaker network probably formed the main mechanism for the northwestward spread of copper-using over the rest of Europe. It was only later, in the late 3rd millennium BC, that trade in the reverse direction came into play, with the distribution of arsenical copper from Irish mines across much of western Europe. These arsenical copper networks were to lay the basis of long-term trusted hereditary networks for 2nd-millennium-BC trading.

Commodification and the Domestication of the 'Distant Exotic' (3000–1500 BC)

The European Early Bronze Age is the earliest period when commodity situations became common. While metal objects were strong candidates for commodities, other materials continued in traditional enchained relations. Amber, with its special colours and magical powers to generate electricity, was exchanged by west Baltic groups to northeast Baltic hunter-gatherer communities with minimal differentiation, as well as through many hands to arrive as heirlooms for Early Mycenean chiefs to deposit in the Shaft Graves (Beck & Shennan 1991) (Figure 7.7). However, that same amber was one of the few prestige materials *not* buried in south Scandinavian elite graves, because there were too many sources for effective centralized control of amber production. This example indicates two important properties of a 'commodity' – that it occurs in quantity but can be controlled and exploited by elites for inter-regional trade.

Other exotic materials exchanged on a small scale in this period included faience, shale and jet, ivory, chocolate flint and marble. These highly crafted, aesthetically beautiful materials formed the focus of continuing ceremonial gift-exchange, their concentration on a few sites helping to determine what Broodbank (2000) calls 'regimes of value' through their contribution to highly individual personal elite identities. There is a strong case for attached specialists working on several of these materials (amber, shale and gold) in the EBA of Brittany and Wessex; comparable craft specialization in silver, lead and marble is known from the Cycladic EBA. However, there is no evidence for elite control of material

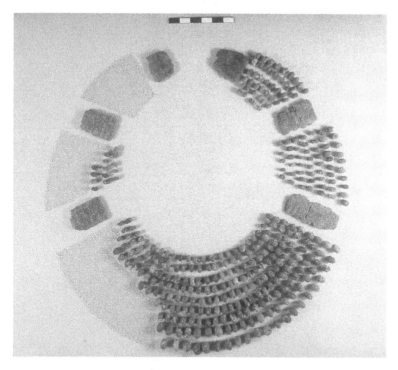

Figure 7.7 Amber necklace, Upton Lovell, Early Bronze Age grave, Wiltshire, England (Source: Devizes Museum)

sources in the Aegean. While these objects were the embodiment of cosmic order, exchanged in perhaps separate spheres from copper and bronze, what they *were not* was 'commodities'.

Sherratt (1993:14–17) has argued that, to be a commodity, the material must be desirable, able to change its form for local expression and be neither too common nor too rare. He rules out copper in favour of bronze, which was a locally produced, attractive and valued material with multiple uses – not a primitive valuable for use only in ceremonial prestations. However, recent advances in metallurgy have indicated the scarcity of standard tin bronze till after the peak of the central European Early Bronze Age, thus re-inserting copper objects into the equation.

The quantities in which copper and bronze objects have been found in central Europe show a regional 5-fold to 150-fold increase from the Corded Ware–Beaker horizon to the Early Bronze Age (Primas 1997). The development of deep mining to extract the sulphide ores of the eastern Alps introduced more metal than ever before into exchange networks, with unconstrained transactions in the core Alpine zone. The annual output from the largest Early Bronze Age mine – the Mitterberg, near Salzburg – has been estimated at 10 tons per annum, using a labour force of 100–400 workers. Much of this metal was converted into copper ingots (Ösenringe) of standardized weight for onward trade. Precisely because of their *general* exchange value, the significance of copper and bronze was felt in all aspects of local lifeways.

The huge quantities of metal in circulation led to the emergence of central Europe as a core with peripheries to the north and west. The Mitterberg copper

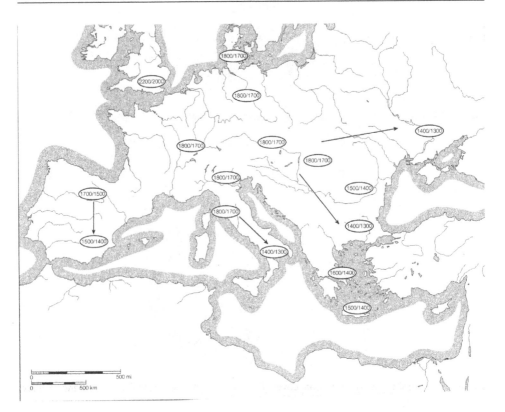

Figure 7.8 Chronological spread of the use of 'standard tin-bronze' across Europe (Source: Pare 2000:fig. 1.14)

has been identified as a major source for multi-directional, long-distance trade, supplying the majority of Scandinavian Bronze 1 and 2 objects, many objects in Hungary and Switzerland and many important hoards in France and Britain. Kristiansen (1987) has developed a convincing account of a intra-European core-periphery network, in which a metal-rich central European core exchanged copper for Baltic amber with a south Scandinavian periphery, which in turn became a focus for north Scandinavian outer margins. There are, however, few sources of usable tin in the eastern Alps and we have to look to the British Isles and Brittany for the main sources used in the Early Bronze Age. After 2000 BC, there was a radical re-organization of metalworking in Britain, with new copper mines and intensive exploitation of Cornish and Breton tin. From a European perspective, the earliest concentration of standard tin bronze is found in western Britain, dated to the late 3rd millennium BC. Cornish tin formed the basis for the widespread continental production of standard tin bronze in the 2nd millennium BC (Figure 7.8).

The Cornish–Breton tin trade to the south and east and the Alpine–Scandinavian copper axis were but two of the major metal trading networks in the Early Bronze Age. Another network linked the Aegean to the urban centres of the Near East but had hardly any impact on the rest of Europe. Even in the Early Bronze Age, north-eastern Aegean centres, such as the second 'city' of Troy, were importing tin bronze and copper objects whose sources have still not been matched in the Aegean, the Balkans or Anatolia – i.e. highly exotic objects. However, the rest of Europe was far in advance of the Aegean in terms of standard tin bronze, which was rare in the Aegean until after 1600 BC. The fact that Minoan palaces flourished with very little bronze clearly reveals that the adoption of standard tin bronze was a cultural choice in Europe, not a product of technological determinism.

Pare (2000) has refined the Childean explanation for the distinctiveness of the European Bronze Age, in which bronze was fundamental for economic production and social reproduction and the massive increase in trade, mostly for tin, lent itself to wider elite control than previously. While useful on a pan-European level, however, this idea needs contextualization within local processes of 'domestication'. We have seen that the 'local domestication' of the exotic – the acquisition of exotic objects and their incorporation into local structures of value – constituted a fundamental cultural practice from the Mesolithic onwards. The onset of bulk trade through trusted hereditary networks meant a hitherto unknown regularity in the appearance of exotic supplies that, even if it did not dispel the mystery of an Alpine dagger in Zealand, made it more familiar. In this way, commoditization of copper and bronze set in motion the 'domestication of the distant exotic', bringing the foreign zone closer to the local by a demystification of its products. Continuing over centuries, this process threatened the exotic basis of elite power, provoking the response of increased object differentiation by attached craftspeople, producing, for example, fine lost-wax-cast bronze swords.

One unintended consequence of the reliance on new metals was inequalities based not so much on individual settlements as on entire regions, depending on whether this development was compatible with local ideologies and, if so, whether regional groups developed access to wide-ranging elite-controlled exchange networks. This latter issue was often related to the extent of local sources of valuable material and the distance of an area from core zones or major exchange routes; it also concerned local potential for increasing production for exchange. A good example of contrasting trajectories is Brittany, where coastal settlers with access to widespread exchange networks accumulated British bronzes, Iberian copper and gold, Baltic amber and Central German metalwork (Sherratt 1994), while inland groups rejected exotica as incompatible with their ancestral megalithic traditions. Meanwhile, on the larger Cycladic islands, there was sufficient arable land for some groups – the 'landlubbers' – to rely on agricultural production, while maritime communities developed higher status as pirates or sea-traders, using longboats in the EBA and even larger sailing ships in the MBA to carry heavier cargoes (or larger pirate crews!) faster and further.

These examples portray a vibrant and changing suite of exchange networks, invariably based upon pre-existing exchange routes. Veneration of ancestors in the Bronze Age may have switched from the ancestral tells and megaliths of the Neolithic and Chalcolithic to those ancestral figures representing continuity in trusted hereditary exchange networks, with hereditary rights over resource-full places which proved of vital significance in exotic production. With the domestication of the foreign zone, however, there was a transformation in the ancestral significance of exotic objects, whose links to cosmic origins would have become weaker unless strengthened by fine crafting and aesthetic embellishment.

Just as the massive supplies of sulphide copper ores proved a massive stimulant to the extensive EBA exchange networks, so the decline in metal production at the end of the EBA had a drastic effect on settlement growth and unconstrained transactions (Shennan 1993). There were two widespread responses to this downturn.

Attempts to control the production of copper and bronze led to the establishment of Alpine hill forts and the creation of centralized production sites near ore sources. This development led to the intensification of direct links between the north Alpine zone and Scandinavia, with the breakdown of Danish–Carpathian networks. The second response was the exploitation of an inherent but neglected property of copper and bronze, viz., the production of new things by melting-down and recycling of old metalwork. The coeval expansion of two closely related pyrotechnological practices – the cremation of human bodies and the melting down of metal objects – strongly influenced new concepts of personhood (see Chapter 6). The increasing deposition of scrap metal hoards for re-cycling undermined many of the long-distance elite-dominated trade networks, which were replaced by shorter-distance down-the-line practices. However, such developments did not remove all elite control over metalwork but, rather, left elites to control supplies of weighed fragmentary bronze embodying ancestral tools, ornaments and weapons – a new form of hereditary possession that increased the significance of attached crafts – persons and special exotic gifts alike. A good example of this process is seen in the formation of a liminal area between the north Alpine and Atlantic metalworking areas in central France, dominated by hill forts with deposition of prestige goods made of metals from both areas. Elite consumption of other exotic non-commodities, such as amber, reached a peak in this period, especially in MBA France and the Mycenean Shaft-Graves, while the steep decline in the use of jet, shale and obsidian reduced the possibilities for individualized display. It was in the succeeding Late Bronze Age that a new, expansive cycle of long-distance trade began, with markedly different characteristics from those outlined for the Middle Bronze Age retraction (see Chapter 8a).

Conclusions and Future Directions

The results of this survey suggest three main conclusions. Firstly, the practice of local domestication of exotic materials and objects within settings designed to enhance the reputation of specific persons, households or corporate groups can be demonstrated for the entire five millennia. There can be little doubt that exotic objects made a significant difference to all kinds of society over this period, even those with few overt inequalities, because of the inherent value and aesthetic attractions of the things themselves. But the EBA commoditization of copper and bronze led to the demystification of the 'distant exotic', changing the balance between the local zone, the 'Other' zone and the foreign zone.

Secondly, there are important diachronic differences in the scale at which differences appear in the consumption of exoticity. In forager and early farming societies, different persons or households accumulated trading stocks of exotic objects but there were far fewer cases of such differences between settlements. Inter-settlement variations in access to exchange networks were distinctive features of the mature farming period but, in this phase, we also see major differences between the sites of a single region. It is with the emergence of EBA commoditization that we can first discern the creation of regional economies.

There are two main consequences arising from this growing scale of EBA exchange differentiation. The first concerns the relations between persons and the regional economic process – something beyond the control of, or awareness of, most individuals. The counterpoint of elite dependence upon exotic exchange was local attention to identities constructed in different ways – through an increasing focus on individualizing costumes and on personal histories expressed through exotic objects. Thirdly, economic differentiation led to the creation of new kinds of persons – miners, specialist gold-workers, pirates, musicians, sea-captains, expert weavers, cheese-makers and copper-smelters – that rarely existed before. The differentiation of personhood converged with the search for personal identities within a much larger exchange network to produce novel combinations of persons and objects.

REFERENCES

Appadurai, A. 1986 Introduction: Commodities and the Politics of Value. *In* The Social Life of Things. Commodities in Cultural Perspective. A. Appadurai, ed. Pp. 3–63. Cambridge: Cambridge University Press.

Beck, C., and S. Shennan 1991 Amber in Prehistoric Britain. Oxford: Oxbow Books.

Bíró, K. 1998 Lithic Implements and the Circulation of Raw Materials in the Great Hungarian Plain During the Late Neolithic Period. Budapest: Hungarian National Museum.

Bradley, R., and M. Edmonds 1993 Interpreting the Axe Trade: Production and Exchange in Neolithic Britain. Cambridge: Cambridge University Press.

Brodie, N. 1997 New Perspectives on the Bell Beaker Culture. Oxford Journal of Archaeology 16/3:297–314.

Broodbank, C. 1993 Ulysses Without Sails: Trade, Distance, Power and Knowledge in the Early Cyclades. World Archaeology 24/3:315–31.

Broodbank, C. 2000 An Island Archaeology of the Early Cyclades. Cambridge: Cambridge University Press.

Chapman, J. 1981 The Vinca Culture of South East Europe: Chronology, Economy, Society. I–117. Oxford: BAR.

Chapman, J. 2000 Fragmentation in Archaeology. London: Routledge.

Clarke, D. L. 1979 Trade and Industry in Barbarian Europe. *In* Analytical Archaeologist. Collected Papers of David L. Clarke, edited by his friends. Pp. 263–331. London: Methuen.

Constandse-Westermann, T., and R. Newell 1988 Patterns of Extraterritorial Ornaments Dispersion: An Approach to the Measurement of Mesolithic Exogamy. Supplemento della Rivista di Antropologia LXVI:75–126.

De Groothe, M. 1997 The Social Context of Neolithic Flint Mining in Europe. *In* Man and Flint. R. Schild and Z. Sulgostowska, eds. Pp. 70–5. Warsaw: Institute of Archaeology and Ethnology PAN.

Díaz-Andreu, M., and I. Montero 2000 Metallurgy and Social Dynamics in the Later Prehistory of Mediterranean Spain. *In* Metal Makes the World Go Round. The Supply and Circulation of Metals in Bronze Age Europe. C. F. E. Pare, ed. Pp. 116–32. Oxford: Oxbow Books.

Dimitrov, K. 2002 Die Metallfunde aus den Gräberfeldern von Durankulak. *In* Durankulak Band II. Die prähistorische Gräberfelder von Durankulak. H. Todorova, ed. Pp. 127–58. DAI. Sofia: Anubis.

Dobres, M.-A., and J. Robb, eds. 1999 Agency in Archaeology. London: Routledge.

Edmonds, M. 1995 Stone Tools and Society. London: Batsford.

Edmonds, M. 1999 Ancestral Geographies of the Neolithic. Landscapes, Monuments and Memory. London: Routledge.

Elster, E. S., and C. Renfrew, eds. 2003 Prehistoric Sitagroi: Excavations in Northeast Greece, 1968–1970. Volume 2: The Final Report. Monumenta Archaeologica 20. Los Angeles: UCLA Cotsen Institute of Archaeology.

Gale, N. H., S. Stos-Gale, A. Radouncheva, I. Ivanaov, P. Lilov, T. Todorov, and I. Panayotov 2000 Early Metallurgy in Bulgaria. Godishnik na Departament Arheologija NBU IV–V:102–68.

Godelier, M. 1999 The Enigma of the Gift. Cambridge: Polity Press.

Gregory, R. A. 1982 Gifts and Commodities. London: Academic Press.

Harrison, R. J., and T. Orozco Köhler 2001 Beyond Characterisation: Polished Stone Exchange in the Western Mediterranean. Oxford Journal of Archaeology 20/2:107–27.

Helms, M. W. 1993 Crafts and the Kingly Ideal. Art, Trade and Power. Austin: University of Texas Press.

Hodder, I. 1984 Archaeology in 1984. Antiquity 58:25–32.

Kopytoff, I. 1986 The Cultural Biography of Things: Commoditization as Process. In The Social Life of Things. A. Appadurai, ed. Pp. 64–91. Cambridge: Cambridge University Press.

Kostov, R. I., O. Pelevina, and V. S. Slavchev 2003 Mineralogical and Gemmological Characteristics of the Non-Metallic Jewellery Objects from the Middle Eneolithic II Necropolis Varna II. Geologija i mineralni resursi 9(2003):23–6.

Krause, R. 2003 Studien zur kupfer- und frühbronzezeitlichen Metallurgie zwischen Karpatenbecken und Ostsee. Rahden: Marie Leidorf.

Kristiansen, K. 1987 From Stone to Bronze – The Evolution of Social Complexity in Northern Europe, 2300–1200 BC. In Specialization, Exchange and Complex Societies. Elizabeth M. Brumfiel and Timothy K. Earle, eds. Pp. 30–51. Cambridge: Cambridge University Press.

Mateiciucová, I. 2004 Mesolithic Traditions and the Origin of the Linear Pottery Culture (LPK). In LBK Dialogues. Studies in the Formation of the Linear Pottery Culture. A. Lukes and M. Zvelebil, eds. Pp. 91–107. I–1304. Oxford: Archaeopress.

Neustupny, E. 1998 Otherness in Prehistoric Times. KVHAA Konferenser 40:65–71.

Pare, C. F. E. 2000 Bronze and the Bronze Age. In Metal Makes the World Go Round. The Supply and Circulation of Metals in Bronze Age Europe. C. F. E. Pare, ed. Pp. 1–38. Oxford: Oxbow Books.

Peltenburg, E. 1991 Local Exchange in Prehistoric Cyprus: An Initial Assessment of Picrolite. BASOR 282/3:107–26.

Perlès, C. 2001 The Early Neolithic in Greece. Cambridge: Cambridge University Press.

Pernicka, E., F. Begemann, S. Schmitt-Strecker, H. Todorova, and I. Kuleff 1993 Eneolithic and Early Bronze Age Copper Artefacts from the Balkans and their Relation to Serbian Copper Ores. Prähistorische Zeitschrift 68/1:1–54.

Pernicka, E., F. Begemann, S. Schmitt-Strecker, H. Todorova, and I. Kuleff 1997 Prehistoric Copper in Bulgaria. Its Composition and Provenance. Eurasia Antiqua 3:41–180.

Primas, M. 1997 Bronze Age Economy and Ideology: Central Europe in Focus. JEA 5/1:115–30.

Renfrew, C. 1975 Trade as Action at a Distance: Questions of Integration and Communication. In Ancient Civilization and Trade. Jeremy A. Sabloff and C. C. Lamberg-Karlovsky, eds. Pp. 3–59. Albuquerque: University of New Mexico Press.

Robb, J. 2001 Island Identities: Ritual, Travel and the Creation of Difference in Neolithic Malta. European Journal of Archaeology 4/2:175–202.

Shennan, S. 1993 Commodities, Transactions and Growth in the Central-European Early Bronze Age. Journal of European Archaeology 1/2:59–72.

Shennan, S. 1995 Bronze Age Copper Producers of the Eastern Alps. Excavations at St. Veit-Klinglberg. Bonn: Rudolf Habelt.

Sherratt, A. 1993 What Would a Bronze-Age World System Look Like? Relations Between Temperate Europe and the Mediterranean in Later Prehistory. Journal of European Archaeology 1/2:1–58.

Sherratt, A. 1994 The Emergence of Elites: Earlier Bronze Age Europe, 2500–1300 BC. *In* The Oxford Illustrated Prehistory of Europe. Barry Cunliffe, ed. Pp. 244–76. Oxford: Oxford University Press.

Stos, Z. A. 2003 Origins of Metals from Sitagroi as Determined by Lead Isotope Analysis. *In* Prehistoric Sitagroi: Excavations in Northeast Greece, 1968–1970. Volume 2: The Final Report. Monumenta Archaeologica 20. E. S. Elster and C. Renfrew, eds. Pp. 325–9. Los Angeles: UCLA Cotsen Institute of Archaeology.

Thomas, J. 1996 The Cultural Context of the First Use of Domesticates in Continental Central and Northwest Europe. *In* The Origins and Spread of Agriculture and Pastoralism in Eurasia. David R. Harris, ed. Pp. 310–22. London: UCL Press.

Tilley, C. 1996 An Ethnography of the Neolithic. Early Prehistoric Societies in Southern Scandinavia. Cambridge: Cambridge University Press.

Todorova, H., ed. 2002 Durankulak Band II. Die prähistorische Gräberfelder von Durankulak. DAI. Sofia: Anubis.

Tringham, R. 2000 Southeastern Europe in the Transition to Agriculture in Europe: Bridge, Buffer or Mosaic. *In* Europe's First Farmers. T. Douglas Price, ed. Pp. 19–56. Cambridge: Cambridge University Press.

Tykot, R. H. 1996 Obsidian Procurement and Distribution in the Central and Western Mediterranean. Journal of Mediterranean Archaeology 9/1:39–82.

Zvelebil, M., and M. Lillie 2000 Transition to Agriculture in Eastern Europe. *In* Europe's First Farmers. T. Douglas Price, ed. Pp. 57–92. Cambridge: Cambridge University Press.

7 (b)
Trade and Exchange in Later Prehistory

Peter Wells

Introduction

The ways in which societies engage in trade and exchange can tell us a great deal about those societies. By focusing research and analysis on interactions between individuals and communities, rather than on characteristics of particular persons, villages or nations, we gain new insights into social, political, economic and ritual behaviour. Study of archaeological evidence for trade and exchange between communities provides understanding of the interrelated processes of change identifiable in the complex dynamics of later prehistory.

My topic is the later Bronze Age and the Iron Age, roughly 1500 BC to the Roman conquest around the time of Christ. Until recently, archaeologists studying this period focused mainly on individual sites, especially settlements and cemeteries. Only since the 1970s have many European archaeologists begun to investigate larger patterns of interaction in the cultural landscape. 'Trade' has always been a topic of attention, since foreign objects often show up clearly in the archaeological material, but only recently has much attention been devoted to trying to understand the place of trade and exchange within larger contexts of cultural behaviour.

The archaeological evidence shows that most communities were linked together to some degree in later prehistoric times. The clearest indication of the connections is the presence of bronze objects. Bronze ornaments are well represented at most settlements and cemeteries throughout Europe. Copper and tin, the constituents of most of the bronze, are restricted in their natural occurrence. In order for the great majority of communities to have obtained bronze, there must have been a web of connections that linked settlements to the places where copper and tin were mined, smelted and alloyed. Many other materials, such as amber, coral, glass, graphite, jet and lignite, and pottery circulated as well. The presence on archaeological sites of all of these substances aids us in understanding patterns of social interaction among the peoples of later prehistoric Europe.

Network theory (Barabási 2002) offers a useful approach to understanding the interconnectedness of communities and the role that that interconnectedness played in cultural change. Network theory views all entities involved in interaction as nodes linked together in a web. Any change in one part of the network necessarily results in changes in all parts. This theory provides a model for conceptualizing social, political, economic and ritual change.

Why were communities linked in networks? One reason was to provide goods not available within a community's local environment. Basic commodities such as bronze, tin and salt are restricted in their natural distributions, yet they were much procured, processed, transported and consumed by communities all over Europe. Materials favoured for ornaments and other purposes, such as amber, coral and jet, also circulated along the networks.

But there were other motivations that are not as apparent in the material evidence. People maintain networks for social reasons, as well as to obtain goods. Linkages with other communities can offer protection against natural disasters, such as floods, droughts or crop blights. Linked communities might provide assistance to others struck by catastrophes. Networks are valuable in times of military danger – information can be carried along a network to warn others of approaching enemies. Networks are means of maintaining family ties across distances, of finding spouses in other communities and for people living in different settlements to join to celebrate religious ceremonies and seasonal festivals.

In systems of trade and exchange, the objects that circulate play important roles. Studies by Appadurai (1986) and by Gosden and Marshall (1999) offer valuable ways of thinking about the objects that circulated in later prehistoric Europe (see also Diepeveen-Jansen 2001:26). Things that people make and use have a social aspect that can be very important. Objects can be active agents, mediating relations between people, and stimulating reactions. People use objects to convey meanings, but objects also act on people. The processes of fashioning and using objects create relationships between objects and people (Hingley 1997). Much has been written recently about ways that material culture is used in the construction, negotiation and altering of identity, on many different levels – personal, family, residential community, regional community, nation, and so forth (e.g. Jones 1997). People use objects to express their identities (clothing, jewellery, cars), and their identities are formed by the material culture with which they surround themselves.

The focus of this chapter is on archaeological evidence for trade and exchange that informs us about the creation and expression of identity. By identity I mean feelings of belonging and of commonality among a group of people, and of difference from members of other groups. Making, trading, exchanging, using and ultimately depositing objects was intimately linked to the formation and expression of identities. By examining the archaeological evidence for the movement and consumption of various kinds of objects, we can work to understand the social relations that were parts of the systems of circulation.

Two kinds of evidence will be of particular importance – distribution and context. Spatial distribution of objects as they are recovered archaeologically tells us where they ended up relative to the surface of the land in Europe – how far they were carried from their sources, and where they were consumed and deposited. Context can tell us what roles the objects played for the people who used and deposited them. We need to know in or with what structures the objects were found, and with what other objects, to gather information about context. The great majority of intact objects that we have for analysis – personal ornaments, tools, weapons, vessels – have been recovered from contexts in which they had been purposely deposited.

The distinction frequently made in modern research between trade and exchange – trade associated with transactions aimed at acquiring goods needed for basic physical purposes, exchange linked more to social interactions – is probably not one that people living in late prehistoric Europe would have recognized. This distinction is rather the result of modern social science wanting to divide behaviours into categories. More likely there was a continuum of transactions that were done mainly to acquire needed commodities (such as buying groceries or shoes today), to transactions that were mostly social in purpose (such as giving birthday presents and sending Christmas cards). But as is true of these modern examples, there is some degree of the social in every material transaction, and some degree of the material in every social one.

Past research on later prehistory has emphasized the most visible archaeological evidence. This evidence includes hilltop walled settlements, richly outfitted burials, hoards of bronze tools and weapons, and luxury imports from Mediterranean workshops. Research in recent decades has helped to provide a broader view of the archaeological data. As the discussion below will show, the circulation of objects was much more widespread than a focus on the larger centres would suggest. Many different systems of exchange and trade were in operation at any one time, and they were always changing. Examination of the circulation of objects, as that process is represented by things recovered archaeologically, gives us an opportunity to look at the social interactions of which they were parts.

Elites have played a disproportionate role in most studies of later prehistory. Elite contexts, such as rich burials, tend to contain more objects and more elaborate items than others, and they attract the majority of popular and scholarly attention. In this discussion, material culture associated with elites will play a part, but I hope to show that the systems of trade and exchange that had such significant roles in the formation and transformation of communities and identities were complex and varied.

Geographically I deal principally with the central regions of temperate Europe, but other parts of the continent come into the discussion as well.

Later Bronze Age (1500–800 BC)

Several trends are evident during this period that indicate processes of formation of larger regional groupings of peoples who participated in exchange networks and thus shared much of their material culture. On the basis of characteristics such as pottery forms, metal ornaments and burial practices, Kristiansen (1998:64) for example, identifies eight 'regional traditions' in Europe, that he calls Atlantic, Nordic, Lusatian, North-Alpine, Carpathian and Lower Danubian, Aegean Balkan, Italian and Iberian (Figure 7.9). Common forms of objects, ornamental motifs and ritual practices among the peoples in these regions attest to regular interaction that involved the movements of persons (such as merchants, visiting families, pilgrims) and the exchange of objects. Within the regions, material culture can be strikingly uniform, as in the pottery and bronze ornaments in the Urnfield cemeteries of the North-Alpine area.

On a smaller regional scale, we can identify the first major evidence for centralization in temperate Europe during this period, in the appearance of some larger and more complex settlements and in the emergence of what are believed to be leaders of regional groups, represented by new kinds of graves outfitted with the military equipment of warriors. Numerous settlements were established on hilltops

Figure 7.9 Map showing Late Bronze Age regional groupings of communities, as defined by Kristiansen (1998:64, fig. 26. Used with permission of Kristian Kristiansen and Cambridge University Press)

and enclosed with substantial defensive walls during the Late Bronze Age. Often these hill forts were situated along major routes of communication, especially at points where routes crossed, as at the Wittnauer Horn in Switzerland (Figure 7.10). Apparently the ever-greater quantities of bronze produced and consumed, as well as other materials accumulated, such as gold and amber, necessitated the creation of these fortresses for the protection of portable wealth. Many hill fort settlements yield indications of substantial production of bronze objects, but bronze-working is

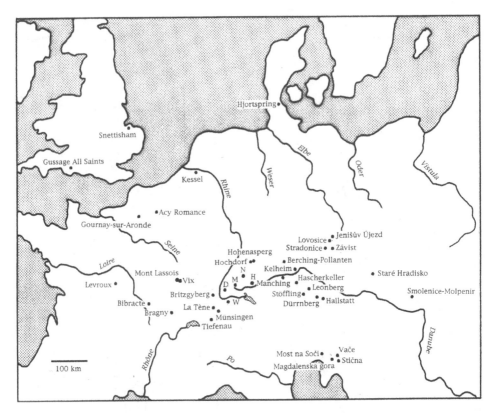

Figure 7.10 Map showing sites mentioned in the text. Abbreviations in centre: D = Dattingen, H = Heunehurg, M = Magdalenenberg, N = Nebringen, W = Wittnauer Horn

also well attested in lowland settlements as well, as at Hascherkeller in Bavaria (Wells 1996).

Weapons in the wealthy warrior graves provide important information about social connections between regional elites. Particular types of swords, helmets and shields often have Europe-wide distributions, indicating that elites in different parts of the continent maintained ties with one another (Harding 2000). For example, the same types of swords are found from Sweden to Italy, the same helmets from the Atlantic coast to Bulgaria. Besides ornate weapons, many of these richly equipped men's graves include sets of vessels associated with feasting – pails, cups, sometimes sieves, as at Hart an der Alz. Their widespread occurrence along with the weapons indicates that besides objects, rituals in which those objects played parts were also transmitted interregionally. In women's graves that are outfitted with wealth comparable to the rich men's weapon graves, we find gold ornaments of types that also occur throughout Europe. The similarity of such objects in burials hundreds of miles apart indicates that these elite groups were linked through exchange systems across Europe.

Distributions of personal ornaments that were not associated with the warrior elites provide a view into identities on a scale of much smaller regions. The distributions of particular types of decorative bronze pins, for example, suggest that in more densely populated parts of central Europe, communities within an area about

50 kilometres across participated in exchange networks along which personal ornaments circulated. In other less densely inhabited parts of the continent, those areas may have been larger, on the order of 100–200 kilometres. The receiving and wearing, and ultimately depositing, of a particular type of pin linked the user to the communities of that region, expressing and reinforcing local regional identity through a particular form of ornament.

An important subject for future research will be examination of situations at the edges of distributions of particular kinds of bronze pins, decorated pottery and other items that were exchanged within regional social networks. What do the edges of distributions of particular kinds of material culture signify with regard to patterns of social interaction?

Early Iron Age (800–400 BC)

As in the Later Bronze Age, large regional distinctions can be drawn on the basis of similarities in metal ornaments, pottery, burial practice and other material expressions. Central parts of the continent are characterized by communities with material culture known by the name Hallstatt. In northern central Europe, communities maintained a different style, known as Jastorf. In central Scandinavia and in the British Isles, other regionally distinctive material cultures can be recognized. But to a greater extent than during the Later Bronze Age, in the Early Iron Age regional distinctions on smaller levels become apparent. For example, within the broad expanse of central Europe occupied by communities using Hallstatt material culture, investigators recognize an East Hallstatt and a West Hallstatt group, each distinguished by particular decorative pins, pottery styles and other characteristics. In eastern Europe, groups that emphasize horse-riding equipment associated with peoples further east can be understood as a distinctive expression of material culture.

On an even more local level, forms of pottery and metalwork often indicate the creation of regional communities that included just a few tens of villages, as in the case of the Bylany group in Bohemia and Alb-Salem in southern Württemberg (Griesa and Weiss 1999). In this latter case, villages were producing a highly distinctive form of pottery, similar in general ways to other Hallstatt-style ceramics, but with what appear to be extreme expressions of size, incised ornament and polychromy. Apparently, this highly visually expressive form of material culture was manufactured and circulated, likely through 'exchange' rather than 'trade,' within a local area of a size that could be traversed by a person on foot in one day. This distinctive ware thus marked the identities of these closely-linked people in communities that were in daily communication.

During the Early Iron Age, the first settlements that some investigators have called 'towns' developed in parts of Europe. They are distinguished from others by larger populations and by higher levels of manufacturing and trading. Most were situated on low hills in fertile regions, enclosed by substantial walls and with burial mounds on the land below them. At the Heuneburg on the upper Danube River in Germany, recent research has identified extensive settlement remains around the fortified hilltop.

The formation of these new communities was a widespread phenomenon across Europe, from Spain in the west to Ukraine in the east. These centres are concentrated in several regions. In west-central Europe, for example, centres such as the Heuneburg, Mont Lassois, Bragny-sur-Saône, the Britzgyberg and the Hohenasperg are linked by Attic pottery and Greek wine amphorae imported from the Mediterranean, specific types of bronze fibulae and characteristic polychrome painted pottery. The richly outfitted graves in mounds surrounding the centres are important indicators of the role that trade and exchange played in the regional identities that formed. Elite persons were buried in wooden chambers covered with monumental mounds of earth. They were outfitted with neck rings of sheet gold with impressed patterns decorating them, and with gold bracelets, earrings and fibulae. Four-wheeled wagons were part of these assemblages. Most rich graves contained sets of bronze and ceramic vessels that represented feasting, a socially and politically vital activity in these societies (Arnold 1999).

The similarity of personal ornaments, feasting sets and wheeled vehicles, and the common burial practices throughout this region, indicate an intensive level of interaction between the elites at the centres. These elites are believed to have been engaged in gift exchange, between centres in temperate Europe, and with representatives of Greek trading interests in the Mediterranean world.

Links based on exchange relations between inhabitants of small villages and those of the centres are apparent in objects in village cemeteries that came from the centres. These include items acquired through long-distance trade, such as amber from the Baltic region and coral from the Mediterranean, and materials processed at the centres, such as ornate bronze fibulae and jet and lignite jewellery. Wheel-made polychrome pottery produced at the centres also was exchanged to members of the village communities. Circulation of these materials from centres to villages, and presumably circulation in the other direction of foodstuffs and raw materials, were parts of exchange relationships that existed between these communities of different scales. (Villages ordinarily had fewer than 50 inhabitants, while centres, including 'suburbs' outside the walls, probably had several hundred and perhaps as many as a couple of thousand.)

Between neighbouring villages we can also recognize signs of identities expressed through different ways of manipulating material culture. For example, in the cemetery within the massive tumulus at the Magdalenenberg in southwest Germany, men were characteristically buried with weapons, fibulae and belts with large incised buckles. At the nearby cemetery in Dattingen, men were buried without these accoutrements, though these objects were available (Wells 1998). Thus on the level of neighbouring communities, villages adopted their own practices of displaying and disposing of material culture to distinguish themselves from their neighbours.

I have drawn the examples above from southwest Germany. Similar patterns of interactions between elites at different centres, between centres and villages, and between villages, can be expected in other regions, such as the southeast Alpine area (as at Sticna, Magdalenska gora, Vace, Most na Soci), Bohemia (Závist), Slovakia (Smolenice-Molpenir) and Ukraine (Belsk).

It is likely that the principal mechanism involved in the circulation of goods between centres and outlying villages is exchange rather than trade, in the sense that it was carried out through primarily social mechanisms rather than economic ones. Although the data are not yet adequate to describe in detail about how such a system worked, the archaeological evidence indicates close connections between centres and villages, suggesting that social obligations tied them together. Like the kula exchange network (Munn 2001), the purpose behind these relationships was probably both to provide needed goods and to maintain social relationships. An indication of the importance of such social ties is the commonality of material culture in villages and at centres. Although the elites at the centres had things that villagers did not – ornate wagons, Greek painted pottery and bronze vessels, and gold rings – they also owned and displayed objects similar to those of the villagers. The woman buried in the rich grave at Vix wore fibulae of the same types that villagers around her wore, though hers were decorated with gold and coral. The man buried in the rich tomb at Hochdorf wore two gold fibulae, but they were of the same kinds as bronze fibulae worn by local villagers. At Sticna a richly outfitted woman's burial included large numbers of common bracelets, as well as special ornaments of gold and amber that distinguished her. Such sharing of objects between the elites at the centres and villagers in the countryside underscores the close social connection between these different groups.

For long-distance trade goods, the situation was different. At the salt-mining sites at Hallstatt and at the Dürrnberg, both near Salzburg in Austria, graves contain large numbers of objects from considerable distances. Well represented are amber from the Baltic region and glass beads from the southeast Alpine area. Other exotic materials include glass vessels from Italy, ivory sword handles from Africa or Asia and bronze weapons and vessels from Slovenia. There is no evidence to link either of these sites of commercial salt production in strong social bonds to other communities, in the way that villages and centres elsewhere were connected.

In the 1950s and 1960s, the discovery of Attic pottery and Greek and Etruscan bronze vessels at the Heuneburg and at Vix stimulated intensive interest in the Mediterranean connections of the elites at the centres of west-central Europe. Much discussion has revolved around the nature of the relationships between these elites and groups in the Mediterranean world who supplied the feasting equipment and wine. The publication of many new finds of Greek, Etruscan and other Mediterranean objects from sites throughout Europe has changed the picture. Although it is still apparent that the elites at the major centres in west-central Europe had special access to Mediterranean luxury products, it is now apparent that many others who did not reside at the centres acquired Attic pottery, Etruscan bronze vessels and other items from workshops in the Mediterranean world. To understand the dissemination of these materials and their significance to the communities that used and deposited them, we need an updated comprehensive catalogue and analysis of the objects and of the contexts in which they have been recovered.

During the 5th century BC, a new style of ornament was developed. Characteristic decoration on metalwork and pottery during the early phases of the Early Iron Age was geometrical, based on squares, circles and triangles. The new style, known as Early La Tène, was not geometrical, but based on floral motifs such as tendrils and blossoms (Frey 2002). Representations of humans and animals became more common than before, but now were highly stylized and consisted largely of 'monsters' – creatures that shared features of different animals. Many of the early examples of the new style have been found in wealthy burials in the Rhineland, northeastern France, Bohemia and Upper Austria. The style is especially well represented on bronze and gold jewellery, on ornamented weapons and on bronze vessels.

The style was adopted by elites in different parts of Europe as a means for distinguishing themselves from other members of their societies. Similarities between objects ornamented in this new style in richly outfitted graves from France to Bohemia and Austria indicate social linkages between the elites in these different regions. At the same time, these similarities suggest that these elites were purposely expressing through their material culture their identity with respect to that of competing elites to the north in the region characterized by materials of the Jastorf groups, and those to the south where the Early Iron Age Hallstatt style was still in vogue.

After a generation or two, the style spread through the social network, such that many more people possessed objects ornamented with it, and geographically across much of Europe. As other social groups adopted the style during the 4th century BC, it took on new meanings as means of identification.

Middle Iron Age (400–150 BC)

During the 5th century BC, the centres in some regions, notably in particularly well-researched west-central Europe, declined in activity and ceased to play their special roles as foci of manufacturing and commerce. The exchange relations between centres and outlying villages ended, and the objects that had made manifest those relations – materials such as amber, coral, jet and fine polychrome pottery – became less common. For the next two centuries, centres of any kind played a smaller role in trade and exchange relations than they had during the Early Iron Age. Interaction between communities continued, but was carried on differently. The new patterns of circulation evident in the archaeological evidence point to new kinds of social identities that emerged during these centuries.

Richly equipped burials became rarer after 400 BC. The decline of centres and the decrease in numbers of exceptionally rich graves are connected to a new phenomenon – the adoption in much of Europe of new burial practices and of the La Tène style. These changes accompanied new kinds of exchange patterns and of identity among communities.

Many hundreds of cemeteries of this period have been excavated throughout Europe, and enormous quantities of grave goods form the basis of our understanding of funerary ritual, manufacturing, trade, exchange and of the social systems of which these patterns were part. Among especially well-researched sites are Jenisuv Ujezd in Bohemia, Nebringen in southwest Germany and Münsingen-Rain in Switzerland. In contrast to the mound burials of the Early Iron Age, the dominant practice now was flat inhumation burial, with bodies laid out on their backs with arms to the sides, often in cemeteries comprised of hundreds of graves. While richly outfitted graves comparable to those at the Early Iron Age centres are rare, significant distinctions are nonetheless apparent in quantities of wealth (Waldhauser 1987). Well-outfitted men's burials are characterized by iron weapons – swords, spears and wooden shields with iron parts. Wealthier women's graves are distinguished by quantities of bronze personal ornaments, especially ring jewellery – bracelets, neck rings, leg rings, finger rings, chain belts and fibulae.

The relatively uniform burial practices across the central regions of Europe, and the common kinds of objects placed in the graves, attest to a substantial degree of interaction between communities (Lorenz 1978). Circulation of bronze metal, which remained in use for personal ornaments, is a clear reflection of these interactions. Amber, coral, jet, lignite and glass ornaments also circulated between communities and were placed in some graves.

A generation or two after the first appearances of the La Tène style on metalwork in the richest burials in the Rhineland, east-central France and Bohemia, the style was adopted by communities all across temperate Europe, even across the Alps in northern Italy. As the style became more widespread during the 4th and 3rd centuries BC, it was applied not only to gold ornaments and to highly ornate bronze objects, but also to a wide range of fibulae, bracelets, chain belts and other items, including iron fibulae and sword scabbards.

In scholarly approaches in the past, this spread of the La Tène style and of the flat grave inhumation cemeteries have been associated with migration of 'the Celts'. This perspective was based on too-literal interpretations of Greek and Roman texts from later periods and does not hold up to modern scrutiny (Fitzpatrick 1996; Wells 2001). An approach more in concert with current understandings of identity and material culture is the question: What new kinds of interactions with other groups might have stimulated these striking expressions of uniformity among peoples over such a large area of Europe?

This uniformity was not complete. While the similar burial practices, combinations of grave goods and La Tène style indicate regular interaction between communities throughout the central parts of the continent, regional groupings are nonetheless recognizable, a pattern well represented in Britain (Haselgrove 2001). Details in the application of the La Tène style, particular combinations of grave goods and characteristic orientation of burials show regionally distinctive patterns, indicating that local groups of communities still developed their own distinctive ways of expressing, through their material culture, their feelings about who they were relative to their neighbours.

During the 4th and 3rd centuries BC, we see indications of increasing interaction between communities in the central parts of the continent – where the new burial practice and the new style of ornament are most apparent – and communities to the north on the North European Plain and to the south in the Mediterranean coastal regions. In contrast to the patterns of the 6th and 5th centuries BC, the material evidence for these interactions is not concentrated in a limited number of centres, but rather diffused throughout the landscape.

There has been much discussion of mercenary service by men from temperate Europe in armies of Mediterranean societies during the 4th and 3rd centuries BC (Szabó 1991). Greek textual sources have been interpreted to indicate that thousands of men served as mercenaries in the Mediterranean world. The impact of such experience of Mediterranean state societies would have been powerful, and it could have contributed significantly to returning soldiers' senses of identity – of who they were in relation to the larger world. But little material evidence for such mercenary service has been recognized. The only indication that has been noted as possibly related to returned mercenaries is coinage. Greek gold coins of the late 4th and 3rd centuries BC recovered in temperate Europe may have been brought back by mercenaries returning to their homes. In any case, such coins seem to have served as prototypes for the first locally minted coins during the 3rd century BC.

At the same time that the common burial practices and the La Tène style were adopted throughout temperate Europe, new kinds of sites for ritual activity were established. During the 4th and 3rd centuries BC, large open places were created where objects were ceremonially deposited in locations that had been selected and designed to be viewed by crowds of people, perhaps from many communities gathered together (Fichtl, Metzler and Sievers 2000). At the site of La Tène in Switzerland, an elaborate wooden walkway was constructed out into Lake Neuchâtel, and thousands of metal objects – especially iron swords, but many other items as well, were thrown into the lake. At Gournay-sur-Aronde in northern France, a rectangular enclosure was defined by ditches, a substantial building erected inside, pits dug, and palisades set up around the perimeter. In this created space, thousands of weapons were deposited, many after being purposefully bent or broken, along with quantities of animal bones. In southeastern Denmark, a boat capable of carrying 20 warriors, and weaponry consisting of swords, spears, shields and chain mail – enough to equip a force of 80 soldiers – were deposited in a pond at Hjortspring around the middle of the 4th century BC. Common to all of these sites are locations in open outdoor spaces and practices that seem to have been planned to involve large numbers of participants. Noteworthy is the large propor-tion of special objects deposited at these sites, such as fine swords and bronze vessels, that are typically associated with elites when they occur in burial contexts. At Acy Romance in northeastern France, archaeologists have revealed extensive evidence of public ritual activity in the context of a settlement of this period.

We know from ethnographic studies that rituals are means of binding people together – making them feel that they are part of a group, that they have interests in common. The appearance in the 4th and 3rd centuries BC of large ritual sites selected to accommodate sizeable participation signals important changes in societ-ies in Europe, including the formation of larger groups of people who shared feel-ings of common purpose and identity. While earlier ritual places were of a scale that would suggest one or a few residential communities joining for performances, these new sanctuaries were of sizes that indicate participation of hundreds, if not thou-sands, of persons, drawn from tens or hundreds of communities. This development, indicative of the dynamic creation and reinforcement of identities on a scale larger than any previously in temperate Europe, was critical for the formation of the largest settlements in pre-Roman Europe, the *oppida* of the final two centuries BC (Roymans 2004).

Late Iron Age (150 BC–Roman Conquest)

During the 2nd century BC, trade with Mediterranean societies increased substan-tially. It is particularly well represented by Roman ceramic transport amphorae and Roman bronze vessels in France, Germany and Britain that are found in graves, on settlements and in other contexts. Expanded trade systems are evident in other goods as well, such as grindstones, which were produced at sources of raw material and transported to consumers in both large and small communities.

Burials of elite individuals show the sharing across Europe of particular objects of material culture and of specific practices in funerary ritual, indicating social networks, orchestrated by means of exchange, that united elite groups in widely separated regions that now included Britain and Scandinavia (Haselgrove 2001; Roymans 2004:21).

Centres developed again on the landscape of temperate Europe during the 2nd century BC, similar in some respects to those of the Early Iron Age, but usually considerably larger (Fichtl 2000). Most of the Late Iron Age *oppida* were situated on hilltops and enclosed by massive fortification walls, as at Bibracte in France and Stradonice in Bohemia. The communities at the *oppida* (Figure 7.11) were actively involved in manufacturing and trade, as has been shown especially well at the extensively studied site of Manching in Bavaria (Sievers 2003). Large-scale iron

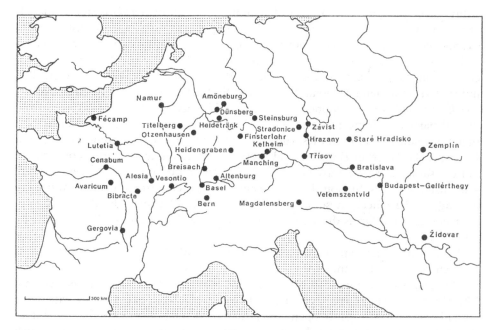

Figure 7.11 Map showing locations of some of the principal *oppida* (Source: Wells 1993:1, fig. 1.1)

production and pottery manufacture on the potter's wheel are well represented. Other specialized crafts include glass working to make bracelets and beads, bronze casting, carving of bone and antler, weaving of textiles and minting of coins. Commerce included trade relations with Roman Italy and with other regions of Europe. The clearest evidence for trade with the Mediterranean world includes ceramic wine amphorae, wooden barrels for wine transport and standardized weights and seals, the latter two being direct evidence of the transactions through which trade was managed. Other Mediterranean products, such as the bronze vessels that were arriving north of the Alps in increasing numbers during the 2nd and 1st centuries BC, may represent personal exchanges more than commercial trade.

The *oppida*, some 150 of which have been identified across Europe, display indications of both uniformity and individuality that have significant meaning for our understanding of feelings of identity among peoples of Late Iron Age Europe. Siting of the *oppida*, the character of the walls surrounding the settlements and the iron tools, pottery, bronze and glass ornaments and coins all show fundamental similarities among the *oppida* across Europe from France to Slovakia. These similarities indicate regular and intensive exchange relations, as well as trade, between the *oppida* in the different landscapes. This strong degree of similarity among the *oppida* reflects the need on the part of the peoples of these regions to express their sense of community and to differentiate themselves from the peoples to the north on the North European Plain, and from those to the south in the Mediterranean coastal lands.

At the same time, each *oppidum* was distinct from the others. The structure of the settlements in each is different, making clear that there was no central planning of multiple *oppida*, which we might expect if they had been parts of a single political entity. While the general character of ceramics at all of the *oppida* is similar, details of pottery vessels, especially those of the fine polychrome class, are distinctive of specific *oppida*. Each *oppidum* community appears to have minted its own coinage.

Understanding of the *oppida* and of their role in the Late Iron Age landscape has changed in the past few decades as the result of greater attention paid to smaller, unfortified settlements (Dobiat, Sievers and Stöllner 2002). It is now clear that the *oppida* were only one component of the cultural landscape of the final two centuries BC. Of particular importance to our revised understanding is the demonstration that many smaller communities, such as Levroux in France, Berching-Pollanten in Germany, Lovosice in Bohemia and Gussage All Saints in Britain, were carrying out the same economic functions that the communities at the major centres were – intensive iron production, bronze casting and jewellery manufacturing, pottery making on the wheel, in some cases even minting of coins. There were also, of course, individual farms during this period, but they have received little systematic attention.

As investigations explore ever-larger portions of the settlement areas, as at Bibracte in central France, Manching in central Germany and Staré Hradisko in Moravia, it is becoming apparent that the majority of the settlements were not like Mediterranean towns and cities. They did not have urban cores with large administration buildings or open spaces designed for public gathering. Nor does the evidence suggest that *oppida* generally had economically specific precincts, such as one in which craft production was concentrated. Instead, *oppidum* settlements seem to have been agglomerations of small communities, each with its own craft area, united by their situation within the enclosing walls.

Even with these changes in our understanding, it is still apparent that the *oppida* served as territorial centres. Their special siting in highly visible locations, mostly on hilltops but sometimes directly on major commercial routes, suggests their economic and political roles in their landscapes. The representational aspect of the enormous walls that enclosed the *oppidum* settlements has gained attention recently. For the larger sites, such as Manching (380 ha) and Kelheim (600 ha) both on the Danube River in Bavaria, the walls are much too extensive to have been defended by the population that inhabited the interior, or even double or triple that population, if we posit that members of local communities fled into the *oppida* in times of danger. The walls around most of the sites were faced with light-coloured stone to a height of several meters, a structure that would have made a powerful visual impression on anyone approaching the sites.

If the *oppida* were territorial 'capitals' and their walls intended to communicate information about the power of the community, then these sites were potent symbols of the identity of the communities who lived in the smaller settlements in their hinterlands, as well as of the several thousand who lived within the walls. The large *oppida* are spaced across the landscape of central temperate Europe in such a way that would not be inconsistent with this model of territorial centres or capitals.

During the 2nd century BC, coinage in silver and bronze was adopted by communities in temperate Europe, together with the gold coinage that had been developed earlier. The communities at the *oppida* used a monetary system, and coins were minted and circulated in many other locations. *Oppida* had distinctive coin faces that served as important expressions of the identity of the community at each site (Creighton 2000). In some instances, the minters even stamped the name of a people, or of a local leader, onto the coin, leaving no doubt about the role that coinage played in the political identity of the community. In other instances, where there is no proper name on the coin, the situation is not as obvious, but the fact that *oppida* maintained distinctive coinages is indication that coinage marked identity, as it does for modern countries today.

The increasing use of coinage in the Late La Tène Period was part of a larger trend towards greater material emphasis on the commonality of larger communities, with less emphasis on asserting individuality. Unlike ornate fibulae in earlier times, coins were common to everyone in a community. The fibulae produced at this time tended to be types that could be manufactured in series, without distinguishing ornament on individual pieces (Wells 2001). The same applies to other objects of personal adornment, such as bronze bracelets. The decline in the practice of individual burial and the occurrence of human bone deposits on settlements, interpreted as parts of rituals involving manipulation of the skeletal remains of the deceased, can also be understood in terms of this change in attitude about community and individual identity.

The increased emphasis on the corporate community as opposed to the individual or family unit is also apparent in the large numbers of ritual deposits that played significant roles in identity formation, negotiation and expression. The most common objects placed in deposits were iron tools, iron weapons, gold and silver coins and gold rings (Kurz 1995). Many deposits are associated directly with *oppidum* settlements. Others have been found at the rectangular enclosed farmsteads known as *Viereckschanzen* (Wieland 1999). Still others are in situations that have no apparent links to settlements, buried in pits, as at Snettisham in eastern England, or dropped into water, as at Tiefenau in Switzerland and at Kessel in the Netherlands.

We lack a basic understanding of the character of the societies of the Late Iron Age (Hill 2006). Some archaeologists base their reconstructions on assertions about the 'Celts' (or 'Gauls') in the Greek and Roman written sources, such as those by Polybius, Strabo and Caesar (Champion 1995; see Collis, this volume). But for many reasons, those accounts by outside commentators are highly problematic when applied to social and political organization of the peoples of temperate Europe (Wells 2001). The archaeological evidence of burial practices and settlement structures does not seem to correspond in any clear way to the kind of hierarchical society described by Caesar, for example. A major challenge for research in coming years is to develop an understanding of the nature of the societies that built the *oppida* and the rectangular enclosures and that deposited the tools, weapons and gold objects in ditches, pits and bodies of water.

Post-Oppidum Period and Time of Roman Conquest (50 BC–AD 50)

In the still poorly understood final half-century before Christ, when most of the *oppida* either had been abandoned or had begun to decline in importance, new archaeological evidence from many small sites shows that communities continued to thrive and to engage actively in both socially oriented exchange and in long-distance trade (Wells 2005:68–70). The evidence emerging at many sites in southern Bavaria, for example, such as Leonberg and Stöffling, is radically changing understanding of this dynamic period. Rather than the 'empty landscapes' that some investigators have posited at the time that the Roman armies invaded the region in 15 BC, the area was fully settled by small communities involved in exchange and trade. As in earlier periods, elites across Europe maintained their own linkages, evident in burials with long iron swords, openwork-decorated scabbards, spurs and bronze vessels of Roman manufacture.

Continued activity of exchange systems into the 1st century AD, both between small open settlements and between elites on both sides of the Roman Rhine–Danube frontier, indicates that social relations were maintained even during and after the textually attested Roman conquests. As this evidence continues to accumulate, and as techniques of analyzing and interpreting it improve, we shall need to develop new understandings of the Roman conquest and of the changes that those processes effected in the peoples of Europe.

Conclusion

Significant long-term trends are apparent in patterns of exchange and trade, and in the social relationships that they signify, as well as important changes over time. From at least the Middle Bronze Age, communities were linked together in networks along which goods and social relations flowed. By the Late Bronze Age, patterns of exchange indicate the formation of large regional groupings of communities that shared some level of common identity. In the Early Iron Age, a complex series of levels of community and regional identity can be recognized through similarities and differences in material culture. With the formation of larger communities, regarded as towns by some investigators, new kinds of exchange relations emerged, between industrially and commercially active centres and the villages around them.

Fundamental changes are apparent during the 4th and 3rd centuries BC, with the spread over much of Europe of common burial practices and with widespread adoption of the La Tène style of ornament. The creation of large, open places for ritual activity, at which quantities of objects were deposited in pits, ditches and water, signals the development of larger-scale social and political entities, the material manifestations of which were the *oppida* of the final two centuries BC. During and after the Roman conquests, smaller communities maintained exchange and trade relations with their neighbours and with more distant peoples in ways similar to those of pre-Roman times.

REFERENCES

Appadurai, A., ed. 1986 The Social Life of Things: Commodities in Cultural Perspective. Cambridge: Cambridge University Press.

Arnold, B. 1999 'Drinking the Feast': Alcohol and the Legitimation of Power in Celtic Europe. Cambridge Archaeological Journal 9:71–93.

Barabási, A.-L. 2002 Linked. London: Penguin.

Champion, T. C. 1985 Written Sources and the Study of the European Iron Age. *In* Settlement and Society: Aspects of West European Prehistory in the First Millennium BC. T. C. Champion and J. V. S. Megaw, eds. Pp. 9–22. Leicester: Leicester University Press.

Creighton, J. 2000 Coins and Power in Late Iron Age Britain. Cambridge: Cambridge University Press.

Diepeveen-Jansen, M. 2001 People, Ideas and Goods: New Perspectives on 'Celtic Barbarians' in Western and Central Europe (500–250 BC). Amsterdam: Amsterdam University Press.

Dobiat, C., S. Sievers, and T. Stöllner, eds. 2002 Dürrnberg und Manching: Wirtschaftsarchäologie im ostkeltischen Raum. Bonn: Rudolf Habelt.

Fichtl, S. 2000 La ville celtique (Les oppida de 150 av. J.-C. à 15 ap. J.-C.). Paris: Editions Errance.

Fichtl, S., J. Metzler, and S. Sievers 2000 Le rôle des sanctuaires dans le processus d'urbanisation. In Les processus d'urbanisation à l'âge du Fer. V. Guichard, S. Sievers, and O. H. Urban, eds. Pp. 179–86. Glux-en-Glenne: Collection Bibracte.

Fitzpatrick, A. 1996 'Celtic' Iron Age Europe: The Theoretical Basis. In Cultural Identity and Archaeology. P. Graves-Brown, S. Jones, and C. Gamble, eds. Pp. 238–55. London: Routledge.

Frey, O.-H. 2002 Frühe keltische Kunst: Dämonen und Götter. In Das Rätsel der Kelten vom Glauberg. Holger Baitinger and Bernhard Pinsker, eds. Pp. 186–205. Stuttgart: Konrad Theiss.

Gosden, C., and Y. Marshall 1999 The Cultural Biography of Objects. World Archaeology 31:169–78.

Griesa, I., and R.-M. Weiss 1999 Hallstattzeit. Mainz: Philipp von Zabern.

Harding, A. F. 2000 European Societies in the Bronze Age. Cambridge: Cambridge University Press.

Haselgrove, C. 2001 Iron Age Britain and its European Setting. In Society and Settlement in Iron Age Europe. J. Collis, ed. Pp. 37–72. Sheffield: J. R. Collis Publications.

Hill, J. D. 2006 Are We Any Closer to Understanding How Later Iron Age Societies Worked (or Did not Work)? In Les mutations de la fin de l'âge du Fer. C. Haselgrove, ed. Pp. 169–79. Glux-en-Glenne: Collection Bibracte 12/4.

Hingley, R. 1997 Iron, Ironworking and Regeneration: A Study of the Symbolic Meaning of Metalworking in Iron Age Britain. In Reconstructing Iron Age Societies. A. Gwilt and C. Haselgrove, eds. Pp. 9–18. Oxford: Oxbow.

Jones, S. 1997 The Archaeology of Ethnicity: Constructing Identities in the Past and the Present. London: Routledge.

Kristiansen, K. 1998 Europe Before History. Cambridge: Cambridge University Press.

Kurz, G. 1995 Keltische Hort- und Gewässerfunde in Mitteleuropa: Deponierungen der Latènezeit. Stuttgart: Konrad Theiss.

Lorenz, H. 1978 Brauchtum und Tracht: Untersuchungen zur regionalen Gliederung in der frühen Latènezeit. Bericht der Römisch-Germanischen Kommission 59:1–380.

Munn, N. D. 2001 Kula Ring, Anthropology of. In International Encyclopedia of the Social and Behavioral Sciences. Vol. 12. N. J. Smelser and P. B. Baltes, eds. Pp. 8176–9. Amsterdam: Elsevier.

Roymans, N. 2004 Ethnic Identity and Imperial Power: The Batavians in the Early Roman Empire. Amsterdam: Amsterdam University Press.

Sievers, S. 2003 Manching: Die Keltenstadt. Stuttgart: Konrad Theiss.

Szabó, M. 1991 Mercenary Activity. In The Celts. M. Sabatino, O.-H. Frey, V. Kruta, B. Raftery, and M. Szabó, eds. Pp. 333–6. New York: Rizzoli.

Waldhauser, J. 1987 Keltische Gräberfelder in Böhmen. Bericht der Römisch-Germanischen Kommission 68:25–179.

Wells, P. S. 1996 Location, Organization, and Specialisation of Craft Production in Late Prehistoric Central Europe. In Craft Specialization and Social Evolution. B. Wailes, ed. Pp. 85–98. Philadelphia: University Museum, University of Pennsylvania.

Wells, P. S. 1998 Identity and Material Culture in the Later Prehistory of Central Europe. Journal of Archaeological Research 6:239–98.

Wells, P. S. 2001 Beyond Celts, Germans and Scythians: Archaeology and Identity in Iron Age Europe. London: Duckworth.

Wells, P. S. 2005 Creating an Imperial Frontier: Archaeology of the Formation of Rome's Danube Borderland. Journal of Archaeological Research 13:49–88.

Wieland, G., ed. 1999 Keltische Viereckschanzen. Stuttgart: Konrad Theiss.

Index